Drawing by Dick Dodge

THE FIRESIDE BOOK OF
BASEBALL

Edited by
CHARLES EINSTEIN

With an Introduction by
FORD C. FRICK,
Commissioner of Baseball

SIMON AND SCHUSTER · NEW YORK

PUBLISHED BY SIMON AND SCHUSTER
ROCKEFELLER CENTER, 630 FIFTH AVENUE
NEW YORK, N. Y. 10020
SBN 671-25750-1
LIBRARY OF CONGRESS CATALOG CARD NUMBER: 56-9913
MANUFACTURED IN THE UNITED STATES OF AMERICA
BY THE AMERICAN BOOK-STRATFORD PRESS, INC., NEW YORK

TENTH PRINTING

ACKNOWLEDGMENTS

THE EDITOR wishes to express his gratitude to the following individuals and publishers for permission to include in this volume material from the following sources:

Franklin P. Adams for "Baseball's Sad Lexicon," from the New York *Globe*, 1908.

Nelson Algren for "The Silver-Colored Yesterday," © 1951 by The Curtis Publishing Company, © 1951 by Nelson Algren.

The American Mercury Magazine for "The Hell It Don't Curve" by Joseph F. Drury, Jr., © 1953 by American Mercury Magazine, Inc.

B. M. Atkinson, Jr., for "One for the Kid," © 1953 by The Crowell-Collier Publishing Company.

Arthur (Bugs) Baer for "The Crambury Tiger," © 1942 by The Crowell-Collier Publishing Company.

A. S. Barnes & Company for "Red, Lefty and a Few Animals," from *The Hot-Stove League* by Lee Allen, © 1955 by A. S. Barnes & Co., Inc.; "The Miracle Man," from *Baseball's Greatest Teams* by Tom Meany, © 1949 by A. S. Barnes & Co., Inc.; "Slide, Kelly, Slide," from *Sport Tales and Anecdotes*, © 1953 by Frank G. Menke; and "Cooperstown," from *Baseball's Hall of Fame*, © 1952 by Ken Smith.

Miss Ethel Blanpied for "1920: Boston Braves 1, Brooklyn Robins 1," by Ralph Blanpied, from *The New York Times*.

The Bobbs-Merrill Company, Inc., for selections from *The Southpaw*, © 1953 by Mark Harris.

Brandt & Brandt for "Finnegan and the Great American Epic," from *The Hummingbird*, © 1910, 1938 by Owen Johnson.

Warren Brown for "Mr. Gallagher and Mr. Grimm," from the Chicago *American*.

The Chicago *Daily News* for "1908: Chicago Cubs 4, New York Giants 2" by Mordecai Brown as told to Jack Ryan; "The 1934 All-Star Game" by Carl Hubbell as told to John P. Carmichael; "1942: St. Louis Cardinals 4, New York Yankees 2" by Martin Marion as told to Lyall Smith; "1912: Boston Red Sox 3, New York Giants 2" by Tris Speaker as told to Francis J. Powers; "1917: Cincinnati Reds 1, Chicago Cubs 0" by Jim Vaughn as told to Hal Totten; "1909: Pittsburgh 8, Detroit 0" by Honus Wagner as told to Chet Smith.

Lawton Carver for "1953: Wait Till Next Year."

M. W. (Bill) Corum for "1924: Washington Senators 4, New York Giants 3," from *The New York Times*.

Bob Considine and *Life* Magazine for "Mister Mack," © 1948 by Time, Inc.

Thomas Y. Crowell Company for selection from

H. G. Salsinger for "Brains in His Feet," from the Detroit *News*, 1955.

San Francisco *Examiner* for "Casey at the Bat."

Fred Schwed, Jr., for "What Happened to the Dodgers at the End of the 1953 Season?," © 1953 by Harper & Brothers.

Charles Scribner's Sons for "Polo Grounds," from *The Summer Landscape*, © 1942 by Rolfe Humphries; and for "Alibi Ike," from *How to Write Short Stories* by Ring Lardner, © 1915, 1943 by The Curtis Publishing Company.

Simon and Schuster, Inc., for "The Wild Irishman and the Gentle Indian," from *Baseball*, © 1947 by Robert Smith.

"The $64,000 Question" television program for Mrs. Myrt Power's baseball category, © 1955 by Louis G. Cowan, Inc.

Bill Slocum for "I Never Missed One in My Heart," by Bill Klem as told to Bill Slocum, from *Collier's*, © 1951 by The Crowell-Collier Publishing Company.

Collie Small for "The Man Who Hated Southpaws," from *The Saturday Evening Post*, © 1948 by The Curtis Publishing Company.

Sport Magazine for "How I Throw the Slider" by Bob Feller, "The Biggest Inning in History" by Lewis Heilbroner, and "The Pitchless Wonders" by Jack Orr, all © 1953 by Macfadden Publications, Inc.; "A Letter to My Son" by Rudy York as told to Furman Bisher, and "Sulphur Dell" by George Leonard, both © 1954 by Macfadden Publications, Inc.; "The Unbelievable Babe Her-man" by John Lardner, © 1949 by Macfadden Publications, Inc.; and for "Letters from a 'Busher'" by Tex Warfield to John C. Steadman, © 1952 by Macfadden Publications, Inc.

Sports Illustrated for "Mr. Rickey and the Game" by Gerald Holland, © 1955 by Time, Inc. All rights reserved under International and Pan-American Copyright Conventions.

Fred W. Thayer for "A Letter to A. G. Spalding," from *America's National Game*, © 1911 by A. G. Spalding.

This Week Magazine and *The Reader's Digest* for "François at the Bat" by Leslie Lieber, © 1946 by the United Newspapers Magazine Corporation.

James Thurber for "You Could Look It Up," from *The Saturday Evening Post*, © 1941 by The Curtis Publishing Company.

True, the Man's Magazine for "What Can You Believe About Series Legends?" by Milton Gross and Dan Daniel, © 1948 by Fawcett Publications, Inc.

Mrs. Virginia Van Loan Updike for "Chivalry in Carbon County," from *Score by Innings* by Charles E. Van Loan, © 1919 by George H. Doran Company.

Vanguard Press for selection from *Father and Son*, © 1940 by James T. Farrell.

P. G. Wodehouse for "The Pitcher and the Plutocrat," from *Collier's*, 1910.

Dick Young for "1947: Brooklyn Dodgers 3, New York Yankees 2," from the New York *Daily News*.

Contents

Contents

Contents

Contents

Contents

Contents

Contents

List of Illustrations

List of Illustrations

Introduction

BOTH AS *Commissioner of Baseball and as a reader of books, I recommend this book to you.*

It is a fine tribute to our nation's favorite game. It shows the fascination it has had for so many of America's fine writers and artists. It shows, further, the people and the events that have gained baseball its current stature in America.

You will laugh, you will thrill, and perhaps even shed a tear as you peruse this collection.

These stories held a particular fascination, in many cases, for me. There are some that are about my boyhood heroes, some about my contemporaries and friends, some that were written by men whom I have worked with side by side in my press-box days, and some about fascinating people from the land of make-believe that I wish I had had a chance to know.

Charlie Einstein, himself a former baseball writer, is to be congratulated on his choice of contents for this book. It's an anthology I think you'll enjoy reading and rereading. I know I will.

FORD C. FRICK

Preface

THIS BOOK is for the baseball fan, and it is a nice feeling to know, as I learned not long ago, that the word *fan* does not necessarily trace back to *fanatic*. Some etymologists believe that it goes back instead to the verb *fancy,* which is broader, gentler. To enjoy baseball, you do not need violence in your heart, and there are only one or two pieces in this entire collection where we shall encounter fans shooting players and setting fire to the ball park. That such examples are here at all reflects, I think, that baseball is a game of infinite range.

There is, indeed, no agreement at all as to what baseball's greatest single virtue may be. I have heard it argued that the game's most arresting feature is the element of speed, under which men must co-ordinate their actions in terms of a ball traveling ninety miles an hour or more. One baseball writer told me that baseball was a magnificent game chiefly for the fact that "there's something truly American about hitting one out of the park." Another pointed out that baseball alone of any sport does not discriminate against physical or regional or mental species—that it had a place for the small man, the tall man, the fat, the skinny, the fast, the slow, the brave man and the coward, Northerner and Southerner, rich and poor, idiot and sage. An ex-ball-player said he liked the game chiefly because it had no clock to regulate its duration of play. A photographer claimed the greatest sports shot he ever got was one of a catcher leaning into the stands for a foul ball, and drew from this the cogent point that baseball is not a sport limited in any total sense by boundary lines. The role of the umpire was discussed, and it was pointed out that baseball is a relatively simple sport to officiate—at the high-school level, for example, four officials are needed for football, three timers alone for track and field, two for basketball, one for baseball; and, further, it is not a game whose penalties as a rule void action that has already taken place. Baseball has been lauded as a game with a simple, wonderfully fair method of scoring—one for each run. It is a startling blend of the team and the individual (most commonly at any given moment during a game it is a question of nine men against one). It does not have any quarters or halves, no set intermissions to plague the spectator and guarantee a line at the men's room. It is a game wholly dedicated to the unexpected—for baseball, depending for action as it does on the hitting of the ball, predicates nonetheless that nobody in the park knows where, when or if the ball will be hit.

It is a game that has had no basic changes in its rules in this century, making it easy for the new generation to appreciate the glories of the old, making it possible to compare. It is an incisive, uncluttered game—your eyes can follow the play, even if on occasion the television cameraman can't—and an interesting correlative is the fact that in baseball the scoring is done by the team that doesn't have the ball! There is no grubby battling for possession; there are no interceptions. It has its elements of danger, being a sport of bodily contact both accidental and not. I know of no play in any other sport at the same time so vicious and so legal as the take-out at second base, nor of anything so vicious and so calmly premeditated as the dust-off pitch.

A nine-year-old knows baseball inside out, yet for a game that is in no wise so natively American as, say, basketball, it utterly confounds the foreigner. Bob Considine once took Fred Perry, the British tennis great, to his first baseball game, and in the course of the contest a pitcher was knocked out of the box and trudged from the field.

Perry watched him leave. "Where's he going?" he asked suspiciously.

"To have a shower," Considine replied.

Perry brightened. "He'll feel famously when he returns."

Yet the Englishman today, knowing nothing about baseball, will use *close call, screwball* and *slump* in his everyday conversation. No sport in the world has contributed so much to language. How many times in the past week have you said *batting average, here's the pitch, pinch hitter* or *rain check*? Un-

doubtedly you know somebody who's a foul ball, someone else who's out in left field, or who never got to first base, or was born with two strikes on him, or never took the bat off his shoulder, or, to reach for the *mot juste*, doesn't know his ass from third base. Reflect on the nuance: if your wife wakes you up in the middle of the night and says it's time to go to the hospital and have the baby, *it's* the ball game. If she has triplets, *that's* the ball game. We are confronted in everyday life by the man who's adjured to get in there and pitch—by the fact that the game isn't over till the last man's out in the ninth—by people who got shut out and by events that were called on account of. Everybody gets the chance sooner or later to take his last licks. And as for that miserable creature, the hit-and-run driver, he may owe his troubles to fog, whisky, or poor upbringing, but he owes his label to baseball.

The list goes on and on: *warming up, in the bull pen, touched all bases, put one over, put it across, full count, boner, hold-out, bench-warmer, Ladies' Day, squeeze play, curve ball, double play, boot* (as a verb), *assist* (as a noun), *ground rules, circus play, grandstand play, bleachers, home grounds, seventh-inning stretch, extra innings, backstop, big league, bush league, nothing- something- plenty on the ball, utility man, old pro, cleanup man, lead off, semipro, rhubarb, bobble, go to bat for, play-by-play, three strikes and out, the big time, rookie, right off the bat, play ball, caught off base, right over the plate, keep swinging, pull a fast one,* and so forth. One of the fine lines in American writing, for sheer description, was Morton Thompson's portrayal of a managing editor he once worked for. Thompson wrote, "He reached puberty but forgot to touch second."

Baseball is greatly literate, of course. Paul Fisher said that a passion for statistics is the earmark of a literate people, and baseball has the vastest statistical library of any sport in the world. If you find a great deal of sheer good writing in this collection, it is because baseball and good writing go together. Nor was it difficult to decide whether this book should be concerned first with good writing or rather with memorable moments or famous players. Time and again, the three show up together. It is no more than logical that they should. Good writers "come up" to good material. Like good ballplayers, they can hit in the clutch.

Given a variety of subject matter to match that of baseball itself, I found it of course impossible to cover everyone and everything. My mission was to try to spread-eagle the sport from Frank Merriwell to the kitchen sink, and the happy hopelessness of this task is symbolized perhaps by the fact that neither Merriwell nor the sink made it. I had never, in fact, read any Merriwell, my youth having been misspent with Baseball Joe, and on undertaking this assignment I obtained a copy of *Frank Merriwell's Sports Afield* (or, The Record Breaker at Work), and, opening to the first random page, read:

"I believe Merriwell has shown up well as a batter in practice."

"He certainly has."

"Well, I should think Old Put would use him for his hitting, if for nothing else. He is needed."

"It seems to me that there is a nigger in the woodpile."

"You think Merriwell is held back for reasons not known?"

"I do. Say, by jingoes! I am going down and talk to Putnam. If he doesn't give Merriwell a trial he's a chump."

"Hold on."

"What for? If we wait it will be too late for Merriwell to go in on the first of the seventh."

"Perhaps Merriwell may stand on his dignity and refuse to go in at all at this late stage of the game."

"He wouldn't be to blame if he did, for he can't win out."

"Something is up. Hello! Merriwell is getting out of his sweater! I believe Putnam is going to send him out!"

There was a great satisfaction in Pierson's voice. At last it seemed that he would get a chance to see Merriwell work.

"Somebody ought to go down and rap Putnam on the coco with a big heavy club!" growled Collingwood. "He should have made the change long ago. The Harvard Willies have been piling up something every inning."

In the belief that the Harvard Willies were not sole licensee, I have omitted any further Merriwell from this volume. Clearly, though, there is no intention that this preface should resemble those which—what with references to the editors' problems, the tyrannies of research, and the agonies of final selection—can only invite the conclusion that what was left out was considerably better than what was left in. The problems in editing *The Fireside Book of Baseball* were minimal. The research was fun and the final choices in no way resembled the annual Pillsbury Bake-Off at the Waldorf Astoria.

I ought to say that neither of the customary methods of arranging the table of contents seemed to fit here. To arrange by category—such as fiction, spot reporting, autobiography, history, and so forth—would be artificial; many of the pieces fit more than one category, and many of the categories have been arbitrarily assigned. To arrange by chronology would be even harder—what year, or period of years, shall we assign to Connie Mack? And so I have listed the contents alphabetically by author, with category alongside, and in most cases I have placed a brief introductory note before the contributions themselves. Also, I restricted the written works to one per author, and I did this because it made more sense than anything else. There are fourteen pieces by John Lardner that I like, eleven by Tom Meany, uncounted numbers by Bob Considine, Red Smith, Grantland Rice, and so forth. I should have liked to include the entire contents of Lee Allen's book *The Hot Stove League*, an arrangement that no doubt would have entranced my publishers, not to mention Mr. Allen's. Obviously, to complete this paragraph, there was not the need to apply a similar restriction to the illustrative material.

The considerable variety of the contents is reflected in all directions. In source, there are pieces here from out-of-print books, best sellers, court records, pamphlets, newspaper files, and so on. The numbers of magazines alone range from *Sport* and *The Sporting News* to *Harper's* and *Nation's Business*. One story, "Alibi Ike," is, I believe, one of the two most frequently anthologized short stories in this country; another has never been publicly published before. In point of time, the contents run from a probable 1774 to a known 1956. Even in choice of words, the collection ranges from an article by the Reverend Billy Sunday to a couple of epithets that ballplayers usually reserve for themselves or for umpires or, on unplanned occasion, television.

But it would be wrong if any of this implied that I was able to put this book together on my own. A great many contributors gave much more than their own material, and I want too to acknowledge the warm help of Sid C. Keener, Frank Slocum, Barney Cohan, Gene Roguski, Lurton Blassingame and the staff of his agency, John Thaxter, Peter Schwed, Ed Stein, Mike Manuche, Jim Beach, Ed Fitzgerald, Gordon Manning, John Barrington, and John Durant. I am particularly grateful as well to Dick Kaplan of *Real* magazine for the judgment and assistance he contributed to the selection of photographs.

In assembling this volume with the good help of all these people, I became more and more aware that the attempt this preface has made to state some of the things that make baseball the greatest game of them all falls dismally short of what the contributors themselves have to say, in word and picture. My own feeling is that baseball's commanding virtue, by itself and in comparison to other sports, is its sense of humor—at Yankee Stadium or at the picnic grounds for the fat men against the married men.

One other thing: baseball comes with springtime. Get the glove and the ball off the shelf. The fella up the street has a bat. Let's go out and hit a few.

Scottsdale, Arizona, 1956   CHARLES EINSTEIN

SOMEBODY should have thought to ask Franklin P. Adams, ace panelist in the halcyon radio days of "Information Please," to name three poems in which three proper names appear in a single line. I can think of four. One is "Wynken, Blinken and Nod." The other three are baseball poems, and Mr. Adams wrote one of them himself. Tom Meany believes that the following, which appeared in the New York *Globe* in 1908, "has retained a baseball immortality which is without precedent."

Baseball's Sad Lexicon

FRANKLIN P. ADAMS

These are the saddest of possible words,
   Tinker-to-Evers-to-Chance.
Trio of Bear Cubs fleeter than birds,
   Tinker-to-Evers-to-Chance.
Ruthlessly pricking our gonfalon bubble,
Making a Giant hit into a double,
Words that are weighty with nothing but
     trouble.
   Tinker-to-Evers-to-Chance.

DICK CAVALLI

Courtesy *True, The Man's Magazine.* ©

"Hey, Tompkins, there's a scout from New York wants to see you."

1

THERE ARE many viewpoints that deal with the infamous Chicago Black Sox scandal. Here is one. There can be none more vivid. Mr. Algren's piece was done in 1951.

The Silver-Colored Yesterday

———— **NELSON ALGREN** ————

ALL THAT long-ago August day the sun lay like shellac on the streets, but toward evening a weary small breeze wandered out of some saloon or other, toured Cottage Grove idly awhile, then turned, aimlessly as ever, west down Seventy-first.

The year was 1919, Shoeless Joe Jackson was outhitting Ty Cobb, God was in his Heaven, Carl Wanderer was still a war hero, John Dillinger was an Indiana farm boy and the cops were looking cautiously, in all the wrong corners, for Terrible Tommy O'Connor.

And every Saturday evening the kid called Nephew and I hauled a little red wagon load of something called the *Saturday Evening Blade*, a rag if there ever was one, down Cottage Grove to the wrought-iron Oakwoods Cemetery gate. There to hawk it past the long-moldering graves of Confederate prisoners who had died at Camp Douglas in some long-ago wrought-iron war.

When we sold out we'd just hang around the gate waiting for Nephew's Uncle Johnson to break out of the saloon directly across the way. The bartender ran us off if we came near the doors without the ironclad alibi of having a fight to watch, and Uncle J. was the white hope of that corner.

If no brawl developed of itself the barflies were certain to arrange something for poor Johnson, an oversized spastic with a puss like a forsaken moose, whose sole idea in battle was to keep his hands in front of his eyes. Some white hope.

Uncle's whole trouble, Nephew confided in me as half-owner of the little red wagon, was that he had gone to work too young.

Some uncle. We used to hear him hymning at the bar—

Oh he walks wit' me
'N he talks wit' me—

and the barflies encouraging him mockingly.

He was deeply religious, and the barflies encouraged him in everything—drinking, hymning or fighting, fornication or prayer. As though there were something wondrously comical about everything Uncle attempted.

I remember that poor hatless holy Johnson yet, lurching upon some unsaved little tough with a face shadowed by a cap and a lit cigarette on his lip—the cigarette bobbles and Uncle reels back, blood from his nose coming into his mouth. The Cap yanks him forward, feints his hands down off his eyes and raps him a smashing banneger in the teeth. "It's a case of a good little man whippin' a good big man, that's all," Nephew advised me confidentially, holding our little red wagon behind him. Then the soft shuffle-shuffle of The Cap's shoes imitating the White City professionals.

"Finish the clown off," Nephew encourages The Cap softly. That's the kind of family it was.

Uncle had never learned to fall down. He'd reel, lurch, bleed, bellow and bawl until the bartender would break the thing up at last, wiping Uncle's ashen face with a bar towel in the arc lamp's ashen light. Till the others came crowding with congratulations right out of the bottle, pouring both into Uncle right there on the street. Then a spot of color would touch his cheeks and he'd break out into that terrible lament—" 'N he tells me I am his own"— to show us all he'd won again. Uncle had some such spiritual triumph every Saturday night.

I used to hang openmouthed around that sort of thing, coming away at last feeling nothing save some sort of citywide sorrow. Like something had finally gone terribly wrong between the cross atop St. Columbanus and that wrought-iron gate, out of an old wrought-iron war, forever guarding the doubly-dead behind us.

No one could tell me just what.

The wisest thing to do was simply to go beer-cork hunting behind the saloon. With the city spreading all about. Like some great diseased toadstool under a sheltering, widespread sky. Then to haul our little red wagon slowly home, with Nephew humming all to himself, "Be my little bay-bee bum-bul bee, buzz buzz buzz."

Maybe the whole town went to work too young.

For it's still a Godforsaken spastic, a cerebral-palsy natural among cities, clutching at the unbalanced air: top-heavy, bleeding and blind. Under a toadstool-colored sky.

Maybe we all went to work too young.

* * *

Yet that was a time of several treasures: one sun-bright-yellow beer cork with a blood-red owl engraved upon it, a Louisville slugger bat autographed by Swede Risberg, and a Comiskey Park program from one hot and magic Sunday afternoon when Nephew and I hid under the cool bleachers for three hours before game time. To come out blinking at last into the roaring stands, with the striped sun on them. And Eddie Cicotte shutting out Carl Mays.

The morning we moved from the far Southside to North Troy Street I had all three treasures on me. And Troy Street led, like all Northside streets—and alleys too—directly to the alien bleachers of Wrigley Field.

"Who's yer fayvrut player?" the sports in baseball caps waiting in front of the house had to know before I could pass. I put the horn of the Edison victrola I was carrying down on the sidewalk at my feet before replying. It didn't sound like something asked lightly.

But the suddenly far-distant White Sox had had a competent sort of athlete at short and I considered myself something of a prospect in that position too. "Swede Risberg," I answered confidently, leaning on the Louisville slugger with the autograph turned too casually toward the local loyalty board.

I didn't look like such a hot prospect to North Troy Street, I could tell that much right there and then. "It got to be a National Leaguer," the chairman advised me quietly. So that's how the wind was blowing.

I spent three days leaning on that autograph, watching the other sprouts play ball. They didn't even use American League bats. "Charley Hollocher then," I finally capitulated, naming the finest fielding shortstop in the National League, "account I t'row righty too."

"Hollocher belongs to Knifey," I was informed—but I could fight Knifey for him. I had the right.

I wouldn't have fought Knifey's baby sister for Grover Cleveland Alexander and Bill Killefer thrown in. And could only think nostalgically of the good simple life of the far Southside, where kids had names like "Nephew" and "Cousin," and where a man's place among men could be established by the number of *Saturday Evening Blades* he sold. I went through the entire roster of National League shortstops before finding one unclaimed by anyone else on Troy Street—Ivan Olson, an ex-American Leaguer coming to the end of his career with the team then known as the Brooklyn Robins.

But Olson was taking a lot of booing from the Flatbush crowd that season because he had a habit of protesting a called third strike by throwing his bat in the air—and every time he did it an umpire would pick it up and toss it higher. No eleven-year-old wants to be on the side of any player who isn't a hero to the stands. "If I *got* to pick a Swede—" I stood up to The Committee at last—"I'll stick to Risberg—I seen him play once is why."

Well, you could say your old man was a millionaire if that was your mood and nobody would bother to make you take it back. You might even hint that you knew more about girls than you were telling and still get by. But there wasn't one of those Troy Street wonders who'd yet seen his "fayvrut player" actually play. You had to back that sort of statement up. I pulled out the Comiskey Park program hurriedly.

They handed it around in a circle, hand to grubby hand, examining the penciled score for fraud. When it came back to my own hand I was in.

In without selling out: I'd kept the faith with The Swede.

The reason I never got to play anything but right field the rest of that summer I attribute to National League politics pure and simple.

Right field was a coal-shed roof with an American League sun suspended directly overhead. A height from which I regarded with quiet scorn the worshipers of false gods hitting scratchy little National League bloopers far below. There wasn't one honest-to-God American League line drive all summer.

It wasn't till a single sunless morning of early Indian summer that all my own gods proved me false: Risberg, Cicotte, Jackson, Weaver, Felsch, Gandil, Lefty Williams and a utility infielder whose name escapes me—wasn't it McMillen? The Black Sox were the Reds of that October and mine was the guilt of association.

And the charge was conspiracy.

Benedict Arnolds! Betrayers of American boyhood, not to mention American Girlhood and American Womanhood and American Hoodhood. Every bleacher has-been, newspaper mediocrity and pulpit inanity seized the chance to regain his lost pride at the expense of seven of the finest athletes who ever hit into a double play. And now stood stripped to the bleacher winds in the very sight of Comiskey and God.

I was the eighth. I climbed down from right field to find The Committee waiting.

"Let's see that score card again."

I brought it forth, yellow now with a summer of sun and honest sweat, but still legible. When it came back this time I was only allowed to touch one corner, where a grubby finger indicated the date in July of 1920. Risberg had sold out in the preceding September and I was coming around Troy Street almost a year later pretending I believed Risberg to be an honest man. I'd gone out to the ball park, seen him play in person and was now insisting I'd seen nothing wrong, nothing wrong at all. The moving finger stopped on Risberg's sorrowful name: four times at bat without a hit, caught sleeping off second, and a wild peg to first. And I still pretended I hadn't suspected a *thing!*

"I wasn't there when he *really* thrun the game," I tried to hedge. "It was a different day when he played bum on purpose."

The Tobey of *that* committee was a sprout who had a paying thing going, for weekdays, in the resale of colored paper-picture strips of major-league players. He bought them ten for a penny and resold them to us for two, making himself as high as a dollar a week, of which fifty cents went to his Sunday-school collection plate. I'd once seen his lips moving at the plate, praying for a hit. "What do *you* think he was doin' tossin' wild to first?" this

one wanted to know now.

"I figure he was excited. It was a real close play."

"You mean for your all-time All-American fayvrut player you pick a guy who gets excited on the close ones?"

"I didn't know it was for all time" was all I could think to reply. "I thought it was just for this year."

"What kind of American *are* you anyhow?" he wanted to know. He had me. I didn't know what kind I was.

"No wonder you're always in right field where nothin' ever comes—nobody could trust you in center." He was really cutting me up, this crusader.

"Well, I asked for Hollocher in the first place," I recalled.

"You could still fight Knifey for him."

"I'll just take Ivan Olson."

"That's not the question."

"What *is* the question?"

"The question is who was the guy, he knock down two perfec' pegs to the plate in a World Series game, one wit' the hand 'n one wit' the glove?"

"Cicotte done *that.*"

" 'N who was Cicotte's roommate?"

Too late I saw where the trap lay: Risberg. I was dead.

"We all make mistakes, fellas," I broke at last. "We all goof off, we're all human—it's what *I* done, I goofed off too—it just goes to show you guys I'm human too. I ain't mad at you guys, you're all good guys, don't be mad at *me.*" Choked with guilt and penitence, crawling on all fours like a Hollywood matinee idol, I pleaded to be allowed, with all my grievous faults, to go along with the gang. "Can I still have Olson, fellas? Can I keep my job if I bum-rap some people for you?"

Out of the welter of accusations, half-denials and sudden silences a single fact drifted down: that Shoeless Joe Jackson couldn't play bad baseball even if he were trying to. He hit .375 that series and played errorless ball, doing everything a major-leaguer could to win. Nearing sixty today, he could probably still outhit anything now wearing a National League uniform.

Only, I hadn't picked Shoeless Joe. I'd picked the man who, with Eddie Cicotte, bore the heaviest burden of all our dirty Southside guilt. The Black Sox had played scapegoat for Rothstein and I'd played the goat for The Swede.

So I wound up that melancholy season grateful to own the fast-fading Olson. When he went back to Rochester or somewhere they started calling me "Olson" too. Meaning I ought to go back to Rochester too. I took that. But when they began calling me "Svenska" that was too much. I fought.

And got the prettiest trimming you'd ever care to see. Senator Tobey himself administered it, to ringing applause, his Sunday-school change jingling righteously with his footwork. Leaving me at last with two chipped teeth, an orchid-colored shiner and no heart left, even for right field, for days.

However do senators get so close to God? How is it that front-office men never conspire? That matinee idols feel such guilt? Or that winners never pitch in a bill toward the price of their victory?

I traded off the Risberg bat, so languid had I become, for a softball model autographed only by Klee Brothers, who were giving such bats away with every suit of boy's clothing bought on the second floor. And flipped the program from that hot and magic Sunday when Cicotte was shutting out everybody forever, and a triumphant right-hander's wind had blown all the score cards across home plate, into the Troy Street gutter.

I guess that was one way of learning what Hustlertown, sooner or later, teaches all its sandlot sprouts. "Everybody's out for The Buck. Even big-leaguers."

Even Swede Risberg.

THIS ONE's about baseball nicknames—an excerpt from Lee Allen's fascinating and great-humored book *The Hot Stove League*.

Red, Lefty and a Few Animals

LEE ALLEN

BENNY FIELDS, a talented song-and-dance man with a long memory who, with his wife, Blossom Seeley, has toured the night-club circuit for years, is an apparently incurable baseball fan whose greatest pleasure is to lounge with acquaintances in the press room of some major-league team and dissect the game from every angle. Invariably, in such company, he will propose playing a little game he enjoys. "Name for me," he will say, "an all-star team consisting of major-league players whose names or nicknames are the names of animals and insects." Then he will sit back and smile as others suggest the names he is waiting for: Rabbit Maranville, Moose McCormick, Ox Eckhardt, Flea Clifton, Spider Jorgensen, Harry (The Cat) Brecheen, Goose Goslin, Ducky Medwick and Hippo Jim Vaughn. Perhaps he will then add a few that were missed: Turkey Tyson, Mule Haas and Bullfrog Dietrich.

Most of these men were players whose nicknames reflected their size. Hippo Jim Vaughn was a Cub pitcher of enormous proportions; Ox Eckhardt's bulk made him as durable as his nickname would imply; and Rabbit Maranville was as agile as the rodent for which he was named.

But the size of a player is only one of numerous characteristics that can determine a nickname. A player can inherit such a name from his father (as Smoky Burgess of the current Phillies did), he can have it as a hangover from his childhood (as Bubba Church, now a pitcher for the Cubs, did), he can give it to himself (as Babe Herman did, patterning himself after Babe Ruth) or he can get it because of some quirk of his physical appearance, age, temperament, or from some mannerism or some buried incident in his life. Often the incident that caused the nickname is forgotten

by the player in question. Frank (Noodles) Hahn, a fine southpaw at the turn of the century, never could account for his nickname. "All I know is they always called me Noodles," he will say. But a friend of Hahn's recalls the origin quite well. "When Hahn was a boy in Nashville," the man explained, "he always had to carry his father's lunch to him. His father worked in a piano factory, and the lunch was always noodle soup. You never saw the boy without the noodle soup, so the nickname was a natural."

A few nicknames, however, are absolutely unaccountable. One day in 1924 a young pitcher with the Cubs, John Fred Blake, was sitting around in a Chicago hotel room talking with his cronies. As easily might have happened in such a place and at such a time, the talk turned to Prohibition, bootleggers and revenue officers. In the course of the fanning bee one of the men began to refer to Blake as Sheriff, though for no observable reason. The name stuck, and so well known did it become that by the time Blake retired as a pitcher in 1937 few were aware that his real first name was John. What percentage of present-day fans know that the given name of the Yankee catcher, Yogi Berra, is Lawrence, or that Brooklyn's flashy second baseman, Junior Gilliam, answers to the name of James?

A colorful nickname can endear a player to his followers, but there has been a striking lack of originality shown in selecting most of them. The two most common nicknames are the equally obvious Red and Lefty, and there are others almost as tiresome.

Cy, one of the common or garden variety of nicknames, is an abbreviation of Cyclone and usually is reserved for a pitcher gifted with extraordinary speed. The similar sounding Si is an abbreviation of Silas and, like Rube, is usually given to show that a player is of rural origin.

Players endowed with great physical strength are apt to be called Moose, Buck, Zeke (short for physique), Hack (after the great wrestler, Hackenschmidt) and Ox. Athletes who are small of stature or light of weight may be called Flea, Bitsy, Tiny, Bunny, Imp, Rabbit, Shorty, Skeeter, Peanuts and Jigger (incorrect for Chigger).

The best of nicknames are those that indicate some distinctive mannerism the player has. It was Jimmy Cannon, the New York baseball writer, who first referred to Luke Hamlin, the Dodger pitcher, as Hot Potato because of the way he juggled the ball in his glove while readying his pitch. Similarly, after watching the players in action, any fan could understand the origin of the nicknames assigned to Fidgety Phil Collins, Pretzels Pezzullo, Twitchy Dick Porter, Jumping Jack Jones and Herky Jerky Horton.

Nicknames can show a player's place of origin (Dixie Walker, Texas Jack Kraus, Rebel Oakes, Broadway Jones), they can indicate his skill (Cannonball Crane, Smoky Joe Wood, Scooter Rizzuto, Deerfoot Harry Bay, Harry the Cat Brecheen), they can commemorate his home town (Pea Ridge Day, Vinegar Bend Mizell), they can call attention to his temperament (Jittery Joe Berry, Sad Sam Jones, Sunny Jim Bottomley, Bugs Raymond, Scrappy Bill Joyce, Mysterious Walker, Smiling Mickey Welch) and they can even hint at his eating habits (Sweetbreads Bailey, Oyster Burns, Spud Krist).

A few nicknames, however, are so complicated in origin and so related to the deep past that they can be explained only in the form of anecdotes. A few samples:

Pongo Joe Cantillon was a major and minor league player and manager who was in uniform for forty-five years, from 1879 through 1924, and for all those seasons his strange nickname followed him around, though few players or fans were aware of its origin. Early in his career Cantillon played for San Francisco at a time when Charlie Dryden, later more famous as a baseball writer and wit in Chicago and Philadelphia, was with one of that city's papers. A reader wrote to Dryden one day, asking Cantillon's nationality, and the printed reply, written with the Dryden tongue in cheek, stated: "Cantillon's real name is Pelipe Pongo Cantiliono. He is an Italian no-

bleman who fled to America to escape an idle life of social ease." The Italian residents of the Bay area were delighted and immediately made the Irish Cantillon their favorite. The cry of "Pongo, Pongo" reverberated through the stands each day, but whenever rooters approached Pongo Joe and spoke to him in Italian, he would draw back fiercely and reply in tones so guttural and threatening that his listeners would hurry off in astonishment.

Honest John Kelly was another of the game's early figures whose nickname was universally applied. He was a famed National League umpire of the previous century, such a good one that he is listed on the Honor Roll of the game's immortals at the Hall of Fame in Cooperstown, New York. One bleak winter day Kelly and a friend had dinner at a roadhouse just outside of Akron, Ohio. Hurrying back to town in the darkness over bad roads, their horse lost his footing in a snowdrift and bolted, but Kelly and his companion escaped injury by jumping out. After walking three miles to a farmhouse, Kelly knocked at the door and was soon greeted by a bewhiskered old man holding a lantern.

"My name is John Kelly, and I want to hire a conveyance to get to town," the umpire said.

"I ain't never heard of ye, but ye look honest to me, John Kelly, and I'll give ye a lift," replied the farmer.

Harnessing up the farmer's mare to a buckboard, Kelly gave his benefactor two dollars and promised to return the rig the next day. He reached Akron safely, but the mare died during the night, and the following day Kelly had to return to the farmhouse with the buckboard hitched on behind his stylish buggy. The farmer's face fell when he saw the mare was missing, but Kelly explained the circumstances, paid the farmer twenty dollars and was glad to escape so easily. "You're honest, John Kelly," the farmer said with satisfaction. Thereafter he *was* Honest John Kelly, an admirable name and an appropriate one for an umpire.

Equally picturesque was the manner in which Frank Schulte, hard-hitting outfielder of the Cubs from 1904 through 1916, acquired his nickname of Wildfire. Schulte was a great admirer of that heroine of the theatrical world, Lillian Russell, an affection that she reciprocated. She thought his Pennsylvania Dutch twang was lovely and always made it a point to attend games in which he played. One spring when Lillian was touring in the play, *Wildfire*, she made an appearance in Vicksburg, Mississippi, where the Cubs were also scheduled for an exhibition game. She staged a big party for the players, and Schulte, who owned trotting horses, gratefully named his best one Wildfire, racing it successfully around Syracuse, New York. Fans followed the course of these events in the newspapers and began calling the player Wildfire Schulte.

Although it would be impossible for followers of the game, without knowing the circumstances, to figure out how Pongo Joe Cantillon, Honest John Kelly and Wildfire Schulte got their names, most such designations are more obvious. But even so there can be confusion because sometimes nicknames mean exactly the opposite of what they seem to indicate. Tiny Osborne, for instance, stood six feet four inches in height when he reported to the Cubs as a pitcher in 1922. On that same team a rookie catcher named Charles Leo Hartnett was nicknamed Gabby because he never said anything at all. Hartnett, of course, overcame that timid start to become a star, and in later years when he was positively garrulous few fans knew him as anything but Gabby, although fellow players usually called him Leo. Jumping Joe Dugan was not so named because of the way he leaped to spear line drives at third base but because, as a sensitive youngster with the Athletics, he was so troubled by the hooting of the fans that he often jumped the club. And Peach Pie Jack O'Connor, the old catcher for and later the manager of the Browns, did not receive his nickname because of an inordinate fondness for a particular pastry but because, as an amateur player, he had performed for a St. Louis street team known as the Peach Pies. By referring to him always as Peach Pie Jack O'Connor, newspapermen and fans avoided confusing him with another Jack O'Connor prominent in the game, just as Spartanburg Mike Kelly has always been called that to distinguish him from Minneapolis Mike Kelly.

Not all players are known in the dugouts as they are in the newspapers. Babe Ruth's intimates on the Yankees usually referred to him as Jidge, a nickname that never caught on with the public. Honus Lobert, called that because of his physical resemblance to that greatest of Honuses, Wagner, prefers to be called John, his correct given name.

When Dazzy Vance was blazing his fast ball past National League hitters, those who watched the Brooklyn pitcher assumed that his nickname was derived from the way he dazzled the batters. Actually, Vance was known as Dazzy by the time he was eleven. As a child in Nebraska, he knew a cowboy who used to look down at his pistol, pat it, and say affectionately, "Ain't it a dazzy?" under the impression that he was saying "daisy." Vance picked it up and later, when he began pitching, he started to refer not to his fast ball but to his change of pace as a "dazzy" because it was such a thing of tantalizing beauty.

College is usually a fertile breeding ground of nicknames, and several big league players picked up good ones in such surroundings. Charles (Spades) Wood was a southpaw who saw brief service with the Pirates in 1930 and 1931. Wood attended Wofford College in Spartanburg, South Carolina, and one Sunday morning he passed up the compulsory religious services for a friendly game of bridge. When one deal provided him with thirteen spades, a local newspaper publicized what seemed to be his good fortune, but college authorities expelled him. Thereafter he was Spades Wood. Gordon Slade, a shortstop who came up with the Dodgers at about the same time, brought with him his old University of Oregon nickname, Oskie, given to him because his Alma Mater had a cheer that went, "Oskie, Wah Wah!"

Players do not always care for their nicknames, and some are so sensitive about them that few people are rash enough to utter them in their presence. The most extreme case of this kind was John McGraw's revulsion for his nickname, Muggsy. It was originally given to him because he resembled physically a corrupt Baltimore politician who was called that. McGraw's hatred for the name was so well known that players only whispered it. Umpire Bill Klem was similarly, although not quite so acutely, sensitive about being called Catfish, and many were the players who were thrown out of games for calling him that. But George (Catfish) Metkovich, the first baseman and outfielder of the present day, never minded the nickname despite the fact that he acquired it painfully, as he was actually bitten by a catfish in one of those strange, off-the-field injuries that ballplayers are susceptible to. Johnny (Grandma) Murphy, finest of Yankee relief pitchers, was another player who never particularly cared for his nickname. It was given him by Pat Malone, his crony of the bull pen, because he was so sedate and reserved. It is understandable too that Walter (Duster) Mails never cared for his nickname, a souvenir of beaning a player named Coltrin at Seattle in 1915.

Other players with nicknames that might be interpreted as derogatory do not seem to mind them. Lynn (Line Drive) Nelson, so called because of the ringing glee with which batters greeted his delivery on certain occasions, has never objected to being called that, and Walter (Boom Boom) Beck, named for similar reasons, was always amused by the designation. A splendid fellow and one of the few players who could recite "Casey at the Bat" in its entirety, Beck acquired the nickname one day at old Baker Bowl in Philadelphia, when ball after ball boomed off his delivery and hit the tin of the right field fence. "I don't mind being called Boom Boom," Beck used to say. "Why, even my wife calls me Boom!"

Some unfortunate players, through the years, have borne real names or nicknames that were the names of girls. One of the first of these was Arthur Shafer, a pink-cheeked, quiet and respectable young man who reported to the Giants in 1909. When John McGraw introduced him to the players in the clubhouse by saying, "Men, I want you to meet Arthur Shafer, our new third baseman," one of the veterans of the team, Cy Seymour, ran over to Shafer, kissed the startled recruit on both cheeks and screamed, "Hello, Tillie! How are you?" After that it was Tillie Shafer to players and fans alike. A natural ballplayer but ridden unmercifully, Shafer became depressed and quit the game, entering the haberdashery business in Los Angeles.

Russell Blackburne, a shortstop and later manager of the White Sox, was another in the feminine brigade, picking up his nickname as a rookie at Worcester, Massachusetts. Sent there by the Athletics in 1908, he was known as Lean, Slivers and Slats because of his thin frame. On Decoration Day a morning game was scheduled with Brockton, and on that club was an outfielder named Cora Donovan. When Blackburne returned to the bench after making an inning-closing play so brilliant the fans arose to cheer, one noisy rooter, seated directly behind the Worcester dugout, yelled, "Oh, you Lena! Are you any relation of Cora Donovan?" It was Lena Blackburne after that.

Charles (Lady) Baldwin, a great southpaw of the previous century who won forty-two games for Detroit of the National League in 1886, acquired his nickname because he did not smoke or swear and never joined his fellows in the drinking bouts that were customary in that era. He would probably be known as Deacon today. The most unfortunate experience of all must have been that of Florence Sullivan, who pitched for Pittsburgh in 1884, for that was his actual name.

When the batteries were announced one day at Reading in an International League game with Rochester, tittering fans thought they heard the names of four girls. Bell and Florence were announced for the visiting team, Francis and Grace for the home club. At about the same time Pittsburgh had a battery, Meine and Susce, that was dangerously close to Minnie and Susie.

A player's nationality has often inspired his nickname. Irish Meusel, Frenchy Bordagaray, Dutch Schesler, Scotty Robb and Shanty Hogan serve as examples. But this practice can be deceiving. Dominic (Mike) Ryba was a utility player who first reported to the Cardinals when Bill McKechnie managed the team. All through spring training McKechnie called him Mike, and Ryba, frankly puzzled, asked why. "My name's not Mike," he insisted. "I'm a Pole, not an Irishman" . . . "From now on your name is Mike," McKechnie told him. "I don't go for that Dominic."

Even the comic sections of newspapers have been the source of nicknames. The Reds had a catcher in 1935, Hank Erickson, who was so good at contorting his face in imitation of the comic-strip hero, Popeye, that he was often called that by other members of the team, and Edmund (Bing) Miller, who batted in the winning run of the deciding game of the 1929 World Series for the Athletics, was given his name as a child by his brother, Eugene, because of his fondness for following the doings of a character called "Uncle George Washington Bing, the Village Story Teller," who appeared in the Vinton, Iowa, *Eagle*. Wellington Quinn, a pitcher who arrived with the Cubs in 1941, was gleefully dubbed Wimpy after the cartoon character, J. Wellington Wimpy.

Hollis (Sloppy) Thurston was the most immaculate of players. Thurston inherited his nickname from his father, who ran a high class restaurant at Tombstone, Arizona, that became known as Sloppy Thurston's place because of the proprietor's habit of feeding soup to tramps at the back door. Later, Sloppy, Jr., while a pitcher for the Dodgers, opened a bar and grill on the Pacific Coast that he called First Base. Dropping in one night for a snack and a chat, Earl Sheely, a teammate of Thurston's on the White Sox years before, said to the proprietor, "Why do you call your place First Base, Sloppy? Nobody ever stopped at first when you were pitching!" And at the same time there was in Chicago a saloon called Third Base, and in the window was a sign that read, "Always stop at Third Base on your way home."

Like Thurston, Herold (Muddy) Ruel, the battery mate of Walter Johnson at Washington, was not unkempt, but obtained his nickname after falling into a mud puddle as a child.

Two of the most appropriate nicknames of all time were Big Poison and Little Poison, as applied to Pittsburgh's famous outfield brothers, Paul and Lloyd Waner. But they were not referred to that way because they constituted a lethal dose for enemy pitchers. The name is a corruption of "person," and came into being when a baseball writer overheard an Ebbets Field fan continually say, in Brooklynese, as the Waners came to bat, "Here comes that big poison" or "Here comes that little poison."

The greatest of players acquire sobriquets in addition to nicknames. So it was that Ty Cobb was called the Georgia Peach, Tris Speaker the Gray Eagle, Honus Wagner the Flying Dutchman, Walter Johnson the Big Train and Amos Rusie the Hoosier Thunderbolt. Attempts to bestow sobriquets on lesser players usually fail. Ed Heusser, a pitcher for the Cardinals, among other teams, was called the Wild Elk of the Wasatch because he hailed from the Wasatch mountain region of Utah, and although it was a vivid designation, the fans never really picked it up.

But nicknames come inevitably to almost all players. Any performer named Collins or Rhodes or Young or O'Neill knows in advance and usually to his disgust what his baseball nickname is going to be. Because in baseball every Collins is Rip, every Rhodes is Dusty, every Young is Pep and every O'Neill is Tip. The first players in the game to bear such surnames have passed along their nicknames to their descendants.

P. BARLOW

"Aunt Claire asked you a question, dear. Are you the pitcher or the catcher?"

FREUDIANS among the readership may find themselves comparing this engaging story, which appeared in *The New Yorker* a decade ago, with "A Report to Felony Court," to be found elsewhere in this collection. Proceed at personal risk.

A Killing

ROGER ANGELL

THE YOUNG MAN with steel-rimmed glasses walked into the dark hall of the apartment house and let the door close behind him. In a moment the clicking of the lock release stopped and he heard a door being opened two flights above him. A shrill feminine voice called down, "Who's that?" He stood still and said nothing. "Who's down there?" the voice cried, more insistently. Let her call, he thought. It was what Mr. Penney had said was one of the First Points of Approach. In a walkup you rang an upstairs bell but you didn't go up. No housewife would listen to you if you made her wait while you climbed two or three flights and her expecting God knows who—the iceman, perhaps, or the delicatessen or maybe even a boy friend. A salesman would just make her sore. Silently he put down his big case and listened to his breathing in the hall until he heard the upstairs door close. When his eyes became accustomed to the darkness, he carried his case over to a door on his right. He took off his hat and smoothed down his pale hair. He felt in his right overcoat pocket for the box containing the matched English military hairbrushes ("Our quickest seller and a fine opening line," Mr. Penney had said), but he didn't take it out. You didn't show what you had to sell at the door, but you had it handy. First establish your personality, then your merchandise. He felt for his discharge button on his overcoat lapel and made sure it was right side up. That was his own best First Point of Approach. He bent over and read the smudged typewritten card beside the door: "Foltz." Mrs. Foltz. All set. He pressed the doorbell.

Smiling, not touching the door frame, he waited for almost thirty seconds. He was about to press the bell again when the door was thrown open by a woman. She wore a faded pink housecoat that bulged at the seams, and her plump face was powdered dead white. Her bleached hair was pinned in tight curls against her head. Without curiosity she leaned against the door jamb and looked at him with pale little eyes.

"Mrs. Foltz," he began hastily, "Mrs. Foltz, I trust I'm not disturbing you. I would consider myself an intruder if I were not convinced that I am here to help you. I am here because I know that you, like every American housewife, are interested in the latest and the best in modern accessories to ease work and strain in your home. My concern also is anxious to get your reaction to our line of personal accessories for the entire household. We have hairbrushes for your husband and children as well as the finest in hair and nail brushes for feminine allure." He paused for a moment. The woman hadn't moved or spoken; she was still staring at him dully, or rather at the top of his head. Damn! It was all wrong. He should have mentioned brushes right away. Maybe she was a dummy or something.

"What is it?" she said abruptly. "What have you got?"

"Brushes," he said loudly. "Brushes, Madam." He fingered the box in his pocket and wondered whether he should begin again.

Just then there was a hoarse cry from inside the apartment. "Who's 'at? Who's your pal out there?"

Mrs. Foltz suddenly bent from the waist in a loud giggle of laughter. She straightened up, her hand over her mouth, and giggled louder. "My God!" she gasped. "My good, sweet God!"

She turned from the open door and walked back into the apartment. She was still laughing. "It's the brush man," she whispered loudly. "The Fuller Brush man."

"Well, go ahead," the voice inside the apartment said. "Don't just stand there. Ask him in, give 'm a drink. I gotta see a Fuller Brush man. Don't let him stand out there in the cold hall with his brushes. Bring him in here."

Mrs. Foltz came back to the door, dabbing at her eyes with a tiny handkerchief. "C'mon in," she said, still giggling faintly. "Come in and sit down."

The young man picked up his case hastily and followed her into the apartment. This was a break, he thought, after a bad start. All the good sales were made inside; in the hall you didn't have a chance. He put his hat down on a chair inside the door and carried his case into the room. The place was small, and the air was thick with smoke and the smell of whisky. Although it was still afternoon, the shades on the two windows had been drawn and a bridge lamp in the corner was lit. A woman was sitting on a small, flowered couch between the windows, and before her was a small table crowded with two whisky bottles, a pitcher of water, an overflowing ash tray, and a huge glass bowl, almost an urn, half-filled with potato chips. There were ashes and bits of potato chips on the floor. The woman was sitting carefully erect in one corner of the couch, a glass in her hand. Her wrinkled purple dress was pulled up over her knees and she wore a black velvet hat slightly askew. She looked about forty.

"This is Mrs. Kernochan," said Mrs. Foltz. "We were having a little drink here. Honey, this is the brush man."

"Sit down," said Mrs. Kernochan hoarsely. "Sit down there where I can see you. Take off your coat, Mr. Fuller."

"No, thank you," he said, smiling. He put his case down and sat uncomfortably in a little wooden chair under the bridge lamp. "I'll just keep it on, thanks."

"Lily, give Mr. Fuller a drink," said Mrs. Kernochan, squinting her eyes at him across the room.

"I am," said Mrs. Foltz. She poured some whisky into a glass. "You like it neat or with water?"

"I don't think—"

"Oh, go ahead, go ahead," Mrs. Kernochan said. "We won't snitch on you, Mr. Fuller."

"All right, then," he said. "A small one with water."

"We haven't got no ice," said Mrs. Foltz. She walked over and handed him his drink. "We just ran out."

"So you're Mr. Fuller," Mrs. Kernochan said. "The original one and only. My God! Imagine you right here in the same room with me. How's business, Mr. Fuller?"

The young man smiled and glanced at Mrs. Foltz. "Well, you see, Madam," he said quickly, "I don't represent the Fuller people. They have their line and we have *ours*. Now, I don't like to knock a competitor, so I'll just say that **we** think we have about as fine an assortment of merchandise as you can find in the field. Now, if you'll let me show you . . ." He put his drink on the floor and knelt down to open his case.

"The original one and only," repeated Mrs. Kernochan, peering at him.

"Honey, didn't you hear him?" asked Mrs. Foltz as she sat down on the other end of the couch. "He's not Mr. Fuller. He don't even work for them. He's Mr. . . ."

"Mr. Schumacher," the young man said, from the floor. He had his case open and was arranging brushes on the floor. "Mr. Linwood P. Schumacher." He looked up and smiled at Mrs. Foltz. "Now, Madam," he began, "here you see our complete line. A brush for every imaginable need. You will notice that they are ornamental as well as useful. The modern plastic bristles are—"

"Prince Hal!" cried Mrs. Kernochan from the couch. "My Prince Hal!" Mr. Schumacher started and almost upset his drink.

"Old Prince Hal," she repeated loudly. "Ah, you were the boy. Always in trouble. Always men on the bases. But how you could bear down! Prince Hal and King Carl! What a pair! You two and Fat Freddie. Those were the days, huh, Hal?"

Mr. Schumacher looked around wildly. For a moment he seemed ready to bolt from the room. Then he saw that Mrs. Foltz was shaking with laughter.

"Ballplayers!" she gasped. "She always talks ballplayers when she gets like this. Ballplayers or babies. Today it's ballplayers. She thinks you're Hal Schumacher now. My God! Prince Hal!" She rocked back and forth on the couch, dabbing at her eyes.

"Hubbell, Schumacher, and Fitzsimmons," Mrs. Kernochan intoned, looking now at her glass. "Fitz on Saturday and you and Carl on the double-headers. Those were the days, huh?

Lou Gehrig, Babe Ruth

Wide World
New York *Herald Tribune*, Nat Fein

WHAT CAME NATURALLY...

Mr. Joe DiMaggio

United Press   International News

Mr. Ted Williams

and Mr. Ty Cobb

International News

International News

THE BIG TRAIN...

Walter Johnson

THE BIG SIX...

Christy Mathewson

International News

12D

Remember 1933? Remember 1936, Schumie?"

"I'm afraid there's a misunderstanding," said Mr. Schumacher nervously. Still on his knees, he rummaged in his pocket for a card. "I'm Linwood P. Schumacher. No relation to the ballplayer, I'm afraid." He smiled up at Mrs. Foltz, but she was still laughing too hard to see him. "Prince Hal!" she repeated, almost speechless. "Always in trouble."

"You look different, Hal," said Mrs. Kernochan anxiously. She was squinting across the room at him again. "You look thinner. How's the soupbone, Schumie?"

"Well," he said slowly, "I did lose some weight in the army, but it's coming back now."

"We've missed you, Hal," Mrs. Kernochan said, nodding her head. She downed her drink and unsteadily set the glass on the table. "We've all missed you. I remember when they said you were washed up. And what happened to the Giants then, Hal? What happened then? Who did they get? I'll tell you who. Mungo, that's who." She almost spat the name out. "Van Lingle Mungo. Just a refugee from Brooklyn."

She was silent, vaguely watching him as he began to put the brushes back in his case. Suddenly she groped on the couch beside her and found a pocketbook. Clutching it, she stood up, showering more pieces of potato chips on the floor.

"I'll take them," she said, looking into her purse. He could see the tears squeezing out of her eyes. "I'll take your dear, sweet brushes, Hal—every last one of them. You don't have to get on your knees, Schumie." She found some wadded bills and held them out to him blindly.

He had risen to his feet and stood in the middle of the room, looking from the money to Mrs. Foltz. Mrs. Foltz had stopped laughing. Now she laboriously stood up and walked over to the weeping Mrs. Kernochan.

"Now, wait a minute, Gloria," she said warningly. "This isn't Hal Schumacher and you know it. Hal Schumacher's up at the Polo Grounds with the Giants right now. And you don't need no brushes. Hal Schumacher isn't selling no brushes."

"Don't you do it!" cried Mrs. Kernochan. "Don't you stop me! Schumie was nothing in your life, Lily Foltz, but he'll always be my Prince Hal. And now look at him, with his brushes, the poor lamb!" She burst into a flood of tears, got up, pushed past Mrs. Foltz, and

pressed the money into Mr. Schumacher's hand. "Take it, Hal," she sobbed. "Take it and have that chipped elbow operated on."

Mr. Schumacher looked over her shoulder at Mrs. Foltz. She looked at the weeping woman for a minute, then shrugged and turned back to the couch. "O.K.," she said. "Maybe it'll shut her up."

Hastily, Mr. Schumacher sat down on the chair and pulled out his account book. On the printed slip he checked off the names of the brushes and added the figures up. He looked at the money in his hand and felt in his pocket for change. "There you are," he said, cheerfully. "Exactly twenty-seven fifty for the entire line." Then he ripped the receipt off, carried the case to the couch, and took out the brushes in handfuls. They made quite a pile beside Mrs. Foltz. He handed her the receipt and the change. "I'll just give it to you to hold, Mrs. Foltz," he said, talking fast. "Two dollars and a half makes thirty. And thank *you!*"

"O.K.," said Mrs. Foltz. She stood up and walked out behind him. At the door he stopped and looked back, but Mrs. Kernochan had collapsed onto the little wooden chair and was sobbing quietly.

"I'm sure she'll find it useful," he said to Mrs. Foltz as he put on his hat. "We don't often sell the complete line to one person, but I'm sure she'll be satisfied. Of course, I don't usually sell my samples, but with a big order like this at the end of the day I made an exception, just for your friend. Now with—"

"O.K., O.K.," said Mrs. Foltz quickly. "Just beat it now, Prince Hal, that's a good boy."

He went out and slammed the door behind him.

* * *

In the hall he put down his empty case—without the brushes it was very light—and lit a cigarette. Twenty-seven fifty! It was a killing, nothing less. Already he knew that Mr. Penney would mention it at the next sales meeting. Perhaps he might even be called on to give a little talk about it. As he picked up his case and started down the hall, he decided that it wouldn't do to tell about the liquor and the ballplayers. They might not understand. But no matter how you looked at it, it was a killing. "The initial resistance was high," he would say, "but once I got admittance and set up the display . . ." He began to whistle as he opened the outside door.

THIS QUATRAIN is supposed to have appeared in print in this country in 1774.

Baseball

——————————— ANONYMOUS ———————————

The ball once struck off,
Away flies the boy
To the next destined post
And then home with joy.

BECAUSE this is an unusually well-done exercise in an unusually difficult form of fiction, the short-short story, do not settle in advance merely for a surprise ending. Viewed at arm's length, this is also a horror story. Pure horror. At precisely the sixth paragraph you will *hate* Big Jim Mabry.

One for the Kid

B. M. ATKINSON, JR.

JIM MABRY was an old man who played center field for the Sox, and he had gone thirteen games without a hit. The sports page he was reading shouted the fact in an eight-column banner. And the story beneath the headline said that if the old rumor was true that Big Jim Mabry would sell his soul for a base hit, then he'd better start taking bids. Ball clubs didn't pay a man sixty-five thousand dollars a year to go thirteen games without a hit.

He put the paper down.

"They're pitching Marko today," he said to his wife and eleven-year-old son, who were sitting across the breakfast table from him. "I'll have him here at ten. You two be ready."

"Jim Mabry," his wife said, "I don't care if you never get another hit. I'm not going through that again."

Big Jim ignored her.

"She'll bandage your head," he said to the boy. "You've got two months to live."

"You want me to stick my fingers in my eyes this time?" the boy asked eagerly. "Make tears like I'm—"

Big Jim smiled. "Like you're overcome? Yeah. That'll be good."

He started for the telephone, but his wife stopped him. "Did you hear me?" she asked. "I am not going to disgrace myself again. I warn you!"

"Honey, just one hit. Just one stinking hit! That's all I ever need to break a slump."

He called the Hotel Lampton and asked for Tom Marko's room. "Tom?" he said. "Big Jim Mabry. How are you?"

Tom Marko was twenty years old. For fourteen of the twenty, Big Jim Mabry had been

his hero, and despite some of the tales Marko had been hearing, he still was.

"I'm fine, Mr. Mabry," he said, trying not to sound awed. "How are you?"

"Fine. Look, Tom, I know you're pitching today and I hate to bother you, but this lady just called me. Got an awful sick kid. Seems we're his heroes. She says that if we could just drop out and say hello, she thinks he could die happy. I'm going out. I thought, if you could, maybe—"

"Gee," Marko said, "I'd be tickled to death to!"

"I figured you would. I'll pick you up in half an hour. And, Tom, this is just between us. You know how the papers mush these things up."

"Sure, Mr. Mabry, I know."

• • •

An hour later Tom Marko was standing at the foot of the boy's bed. He'd a lump in his throat the size of a bowling ball, and he was biting his lip. It was the most heartbreaking experience he had ever been through. The little boy with the great, trusting blue eyes and the big bandage around his head was clutching Big Jim's hand, pleading.

"You'll hit a homer for me today, won't you, Big Jim? You will, won't you?"

"Sure," Big Jim said huskily, "just for you."

The boy sighed happily. "Mama says I'm going to that big diamond up in the sky soon. I'll tell the Babe you hit one just for me."

Tom Marko turned away. The best pitcher who ever lived, as the boy had called him, mustn't be seen with tears in his eyes.

Big Jim felt like weeping too. How many times would he have to warn the boy about ad-libbing? "Sure," he said softly, "you tell the Babe I hit one just for you."

The little boy's mother looked as though she was going to be ill. "I'm afraid you'll have to go now. He tires so quickly these days."

They were in the cab before Big Jim spoke. "How low can a man get, Tom?" he asked bitterly. "Thirteen days without a loud foul and I promise a poor, sick kid a homer. I'm going back there."

"You'll hit," Tom Marko said. "I promise you."

Big Jim looked at him. "No, Tom," he said gently. "Don't you go throwing me any fat balls just a little above the letters and a little on the outside the way I like 'em. Baseball's a business, Tom. A sick kid's got no place in it."

Big Jim shook his head sadly. "He did look pitiful, though, didn't he, Tom? Every time I go to the plate I'll see those big, trusting blue eyes. 'Hit one for me, Big Jim, hit one for—' " He slapped Marko on the leg. "Forget it, Tom. What's a poor sick kid compared to a pennant, hunh?"

* * *

It was not until the third inning that Big Jim faced the grieving Marko. The first pitch startled him somewhat by the whoosh it gave off, but then he relaxed. Marko was merely setting the stage. The second pitch was a mate to the first, only a little more blurred. Big Jim dug in. Now for the fat one, the Santa Claus ball.

The pitch came, but it was not fat. It looked like a moth ball and seemed to leave a vapor trail in its wake. Big Jim heard the umpire's bitter verdict and the roar of the crowd. He weaved back to the bench, staring in disbelief at Marko. The boy was pitching like he knew who and what lay behind those big, trusting blue eyes.

In the sixth Big Jim was positive of it.

Marko had an eight-one lead, but again Tom set him down on three straight pitches—hissing, corner-cutting pitches. Bile seeped into Big Jim's soul; the taste of ashes was in his mouth. If there was one thing he despised, it was a double-crosser.

Big Jim led off in the last of the ninth with the score nine-one. He was set now. There would be no waiting for the fat pitch. When the fast one came this time, so help him, he would make Marko eat the thing. Marko wound up and cut loose. Big Jim quivered and coiled, his eyes unbelieving.

It was the fat pitch, the Santa Claus ball, the ball with a heart. It was just a little above the letters and a little on the outside. He swung and saw the right fielder go racing back.

He held up at third, dusted himself off, and stared again in disbelief at Marko. The kid *hadn't* known a thing. He *had* kept the faith. He'd just been playing it safe. Or had he? Maybe his control was . . . It wasn't. The next two men fouled out and the third fanned to end the game.

It was Big Jim's finest hour. The slump was broken; the deathbed routine was still deadly. He headed for Tom Marko. The boy's heart was in the right place even if his brain was off center. But what boy could match wits with Big Jim Mabry? Then he saw Marko coming toward him.

"Here's a ball for your boy, Mr. Mabry," he said. "He's there in the box behind our dugout. Been calling me a glass-arm bum all afternoon."

Big Jim made himself look. The boy was there all right. So was his mother. He should have known from her warning that morning that she would be. He shuddered and turned to Marko. Maybe Tom still didn't know the boy in the bandage and the boy in the box were the same.

Marko fought to keep a straight face. "Tell him I'll save him a seat for the series—" he broke down and grinned—"if he lives that long!"

Ha! You don't think there *is* such a thing as fact-fiction? Read.

The fact part, as far as I can tell, includes the dilemma of L'n'h's'r, cf, in the funniest box score of all time. The Cobb incident *did* happen and Detroit, playing with a pickup team in order to retain its franchise, *did* lose to the A's 24 to 2. As for the rest . . . well, meet Mr. Baer.

The Crambury Tiger

ARTHUR (BUGS) BAER

Sure, the trouble was over a girl. What isn't? Tink was too good-looking for his own good before there were movies. He had the tickets to make the big leagues but he was as lazy as a fed cat. Tink could pitch at times.

Nippers had the general appearance of an accident looking for a lawyer and he had a profile you could saw lumber with. He couldn't field good enough to stop a water wheel in a dry spell. But he sure shook that pepper-box around the infield.

Playing semipro baseball in the summer was a softer touch than face powder. We got around like ringworms and if we weren't bums we would certainly do until bums came along.

I called myself a semipro although it might have been closer to three eighths. Too much beer in Bustleton is what stopped me in addition to other habits that would have tightened the hide on a bloodhound's jowls. John Mc-Graw once sent a scout to look me over but he decided I was too much of a grandstand player when I wasn't throwing them into the bleachers.

At the bat I couldn't hit all the leather in the world if I owned all the lumber. But both Tink and Nippers could throw their weight around at the plate. I was so round-shouldered I had to have my coats made twice as long in the back as in the front. I guess I played in more places than sunbeams in a forest. I wound up as the only left-handed shortstop in semipro baseball, but I finished better than Tink.

Fast as Nippers got a girl in the small towns Tink would take her away from him. But once he gave Nippers a girl, and it was just too bad.

It was all the fault of Ty Cobb. And a bit over like a baker's dozen.

Now, I know that Ty never heard of us cow-pasture punks who used a fence post for a bat and slid into a lot of things that weren't second base. But when he came up from Georgia to the Detroits he was gamer than a dentist pulling his own teeth and could take it like a carpet on the line. But he was as touchy as fingerprint powder and would climb a mountain to take a punch at an echo.

Ty fought everybody on the Detroits until the other Tigers realize that all he wants to do is win baseball games. Then they get in back of him as solid as wet sand and Detroit cops the berries in 1907, '08 and '09—and almost repeats in '10 and '11. But they go very bad in the spring of '12 and Cobb is sorer than ingrown hairs on a porcupine.

There's no living with Ty when he's in that mood, so when a grandstand manager in New York named Lucas or Lookis or something like that gives him the Bronx roll call from the dollar seats, Ty climbs into the stands and hands him a dry shave with his knuckles. The other Yankee fans choose up sides and Cobb is elected Queen of the May on the sixteenth of that month as I remember. The Yanks' fans were sure going to town on Ty's transportation system when the entire Detroits barge into the stands and rescue him with their baseball bats. When the cops pull everybody loose from their pet holds it turns out that the fellow Cobb popped has no fingers on his right hand.

Well, Ty didn't know that and Lucas or

Lookis has certainly used some pretty rough talk. That doesn't stop Ban Johnson from giving Cobb the indefinite works with the option of making it permanent.

The entire Detroits club their mad money in a lump and send Ban a testimonial telegram: "Feeling that Mr. Cobb is being done an injustice by your action in suspending him, we the undersigned refuse to play in another game until such action is adjusted to our satisfaction. We want him reinstated or there will be no game. If players cannot have protection we must protect ourselves." (Signed) Sam Crawford, Jim Delahanty, Davey Jones, Oscar Stanage, Oscar Vitt, George Moriarity, Jack Onslow, Ed Willett, Bill Burns, Covington, Paddy Bauman, Louden, George Mullin and all the others.

That makes it serious for the Detroit owners if they don't put a team in the field on Saturday, May 18, 1912, in Philly where their next game is. Owner Navin can lose his franchise and can be plastered with a five-grand fine.

Manager Hughey Jennings comes to Philly at the Aldine Hotel and gives out word that he is in the market for a brand-new Detroit team and no reasonable offer will be refused. Any ballplayer who can stop a grapefruit from rolling uphill or hit a bull in the pants with a bass fiddle has got a chance of going direct from the semipros to the Detroits and no questions asked.

Tink, Nippers and me are booked to play for Millville in southern Jersey the next day but we light out for the Aldine Hotel in time to run into a parade of seven hundred semipros all anxious to fill Ty Cobb's shoes. A baseball writer named Isaminger on the *North American* said that seven hundred was about the right number. The seven hundred of us semipros walk single-file past Jennings and he taps the ones he wants on the shoulder with a pool cue like we were buttons on a wire over a billiard table. He runs us fifty or no count and that's his team for tomorrow.

Out of that fifty he will pick nine players who will get fifty smackers each. Then he will pick a couple more for emergency who will get twenty-five just for sitting on the bench. That was almost a full season's salary for a semipro in Philly. Tink and me are among the fifty but Nippers can't score with the pool cue even though he has a piece of chalk in his vest pocket.

That all gets into the papers and the Georgia

folks get behind Cobb. A congressman named William Schley Howard made a speech about it in Washington and sent Ty a wire as follows: "As Georgians we commend your action in resenting uncalled-for insult in New York. We hope for complete exoneration and reinstatement in clean sport of baseball. Congratulations to you as a leader and fighter of your profession."

Howard signed the telegram and it was seconded by a famous senator from Georgia named Hoke Smith. Howard also tagged Senator Bacon's name to it. One more signature and Gordon McKay of the *Inquirer* said it would have been an amendment to the Constitution. Cobb got thousands of wires and letters and the Wall Street brokers got up a petition for him that I guess they could use themselves now.

Cobb spent that Friday night in conference with his fellow Detroits and they sent a telegram or two. The White Sox were playing the Red Sox in Boston, so Ty wired Harry Lord of the Chicagos and Smokey Joe Wood of the Bostons asking if they would join a protective association of players with short tempers. That was thirty years ago and Lord and Wood are still giving the matter their serious attention. Us ballplayers stick together like a wishbone in a pulling contest.

Philly is giving the strike of the Detroits a lot of publicity because their Athletics look like sure pennant winners even though the Red Sox finally cop and Washington winds up second. So, even if Nippers doesn't make the grade he decides to cut Millville and watch us play for the Detroits. When you're a semipro, your schedule is as loose as a skeleton on roller skates. The three of us light out for the A's park Saturday morning at eight o'clock. We swiped a bottle of milk and a loaf of bread off a porch and ate it under a bridge.

At ten, Jennings drives up with his trunks and bats. He has picked fifty ballplayers on suspicion and he wants to see if we are guilty or not. He also has two faithful Detroits with him named Sugden and McGuire and I'll tell you about them. They are so old they can sleep in a swamp without mosquito netting. At the present time Jennings was using them for coaches and scouts but he announces McGuire will catch anything that comes near him, and Sugden will play first base for everything except fast grounders and overthrows. Jennings elects himself captain, manager, coach and utility. I know my baseball and I remember Sugden was with Baltimore in 1889 and here it is 1912. He was a fatigued old gent who should have spent his summers pointing out sea shells for his grandkids to pick up.

There was a McGuire with Washington in 1892 when Washington was in the National League. I think he bobbed around a lot and finally tried umpiring but he had spots before his eyes and gives a batter his base on four of them.

That leaves seven positions for Jennings to fill and Tink and me are out. But we make the bench for twenty-five smackers and that suits us. He picks a semipro named Travers to pitch and a good lightweight fighter Billy McHarg for third. There are also a couple of old-timers from Georgetown University and a few more sand lotters who can field all right but can't hit their weight on a diet.

The fellow who got the toughest break was the semipro picked to play Ty Cobb's spot in center. His monicker was too wide for the printers and it came out in the Sunday papers this way, "L'n'h's'r." Today nobody knows whether his name was Loopenhouser or Lagenhassinger and I bet his wife stills calls him a liar when he says he once played on the Detroits.

Anyway, the fans didn't ask for their money back when they saw a lot of bums in Tigers' clothing. Here's the way the game came out in the box scores:

DETROIT

	AB	H	O	A	E
McGarr, 2b	4	0	3	0	1
McHarg, 3b	1	0	2	0	0
Irwin, 3b, c	3	2	1	2	1
Travers, p	3	0	7	0	1
McGarvey, lf	3	0	1	0	3
L'n'h's'r, cf	4	0	1	0	0
Sugden, 1b	3	1	2	1	1
McGuire, c	2	1	3	1	2
Smith, 3b	1	0	1	0	0
Meaney, ss	2	0	3	0	1
Ward, rf	2	0	0	0	0
x Jennings	1	0	0	0	0
Totals	29	4	24	4	10

x Batted for exercise.

ATHLETICS

	AB	H	O	A	E
Maggert, lf	4	3	0	0	0
Strunk, cf	6	4	0	0	0
Collins, 2b	6	5	0	1	0
Baker, 3b	5	2	0	0	0
Murphy, rf	3	2	1	0	0
McInnis, 1b	6	3	7	0	0
Barry, ss	4	2	3	1	1
Lapp, c	4	1	16	1	0
Coombs, p	1	0	0	1	0
Brown, p	3	2	0	2	0
Pennock, p	1	1	0	1	0
Totals	43	25	27	7	1

										Runs	Hits	Errors
DETROIT	0	0	0	0	2	0	0	0	0	2	4	10
ATHLETICS	3	0	3	0	8	4	4	2	x	24	25	1

SUMMARY OF THE GAME

RUNS, Sugden, McGuire, Maggert 2, Strunk 3, Collins 4, Baker 3, Murphy 4, McInnis 2, Barry 2, Lapp, Brown 2, Pennock.

TWO-BASE HITS, Maggert, Strunk, Barry, Pennock.

THREE-BASE HITS, Strunk, Baker, Murphy, Irwin 2, Brown, Maggert.

SACRIFICE HIT, Lapp.

SACRIFICE FLY, Barry.

STOLEN BASES, Collins 4, Baker, Murphy, McInnis 2, McGarvey.

STRUCK OUT, By Coombs 3, by Brown 5, by Pennock 7, by Travers 1.

DOUBLE PLAY, McGarvey and Smith.

LEFT ON BASES, Detroit 4, Athletics 4.

FIRST BASE ON ERRORS, Athletics 2.

BASES ON BALLS, Coombs 1, Pennock 1, Travers 7.

TIME OF GAME, One hour and forty minutes.

UMPIRES, Dineen and Perrine.

Outside of shooing Sugden and McGuire around the bases for old times' sake the A's bore down all the way like guards putting a strait jacket on the star pupil in a laughing academy. Eddie Collins did more yelling than Solomon's thousand wives catching him out with another dame. Eddie hustled all the way like a long-haired rabbit in a prairie fire. This was a regular baseball contest and it held the Detroit franchise. I still feel sorry for L'n'h's'r, who blew his big chance like a pyromaniac sneezing on his last match. It was just as well that I never got into the game because I raised a pompadour of goose pimples on the bench.

Jennings saved the bacon for Navin but

when Ban Johnson got the result of the game between the A's and the Pick-Ups and heard that four apostrophes were playing center field for Cobb he called himself out on that one strike.

For the first time in his life Ban copped a plea and let Cobb off with a ten-day suspension. The regular Detroits played again and got their uniforms back from the semipros. All except the one shirt that Tink wore home under his coat. It belonged to Ty.

Tink wore the Detroit shirt next Monday morning out on the sand lots in the park and word went around that he was one of the striking Detroits who refused to go back. There's a Glassboro scout there and when he hears that, he gets hotter than a one-cycle engine. He offers Tink fifteen dollars a game but Tink is stringing a couple of towns along and finally nails twenty bobbins for himself for Crambury on Decoration Day. I went with the deal and got eight dollars for playing shortstop.

Tink won for Crambury by his pitching and batting and actually lived up to the Detroit "D" on his shirt. The visiting team couldn't holler about it because they were padded like an idiot's cell themselves. The Crambury fans and the local girls thought he was the top berries and there was one pretty little girl who went for him big.

Going home on the train that night Tink told me her name was Jennie and her father was a motorman. Well, that's society for Tink. He pitches four Saturdays straight for Crambury and wins against Big Timber, Tacony, Southwark and Upper Darby. But for some reason he switches to Pennsylvania towns in August even though Crambury is offering him up to thirty-five dollars a game. I'm still playing short for short dough and I see Jennie each Saturday afternoon looking for Tink. She asked me about him and I said he had sprained his arm and gone back home to Philly. She doesn't even know his last name.

Well, the biggest day in semipro baseball in Jersey and Pennsylvania is Labor Day. Crambury is going to play its big rival North Chester for the weedbending championship and it wants Tink. But Tink is going to Bound Brook for less money and I know why. I tell the Crambury manager I can get a pretty good man named Nippers but he says the local folks want a big leaguer and I tell him that maybe I can get one. He says he will pay forty for a leaguer and raise me from eight to ten. I tell Nippers about it and he tells Tink he will split

the forty with him if he will lend Nippers his Cobb shirt for Labor Day.

That's twenty more in the bag for Tink and he grabs it. When I tell the Crambury manager that I have another Detroit pitcher who walked out with Cobb and didn't go back he snaps it up.

Nippers touched up the big D on his chest with black ink until it stood out like a frog's eyes. On Labor Day he looked like a leaguer and pitched all the way like one coming down to the ninth. North Chester is leading one to nothing mostly because they have a ringer from the Tri-State who can pitch and bat. He smacks a homer in the first half of the ninth and is a little winded, so he hits a Crambury in the ribs, passes one, and they move up on an infield out. The next bird is a soft touch and it brings Nippers up with two on, two out and a single needed to cop.

It gets down to three and two on Nippers and it's closer than beds in a charity ward. Nippers is waving his bat at the big Tri-Stater, who winds up and is about to let it go when he sees he is pitching to two men at the plate. The other fellow is a middle-aged gent and he is packing a shotgun, which is aimed at Nippers. The Crambury manager claims a balk but the umpire disallows because nobody can outpitch a shotgun. The fellow with the gun then explains himself.

"I've lived in this town for sixty years," he said, "and the population has been exactly six hundred and thirty-two from 1852 to 1912. The reason for that is every time somebody is born somebody leaves town."

Well, Nippers wants to know what that has to do with him. The old boy said, "My daughter told me to look for a fellow with a Detroit D on his shirt," so I know now it's the motorman speaking, "and you're going to marry her."

Well, we plead with the old man to let the game go on and settle the matter in a legal way. But he swings the gun around to the umpire and says, "Pridemore, you're the Justice of the Peace and you're going to marry my daughter with this Detroit fellow." He calls out, "Jennie," and Jennie walks out of the crowd with her head down and a handkerchief stuffed in her mouth to hold her sobs back. She never once looks up during the ceremony, not even when the Crambury runner on third tries to steal home when Pridemore is asking, "Do you take this man for your lawful wedded husband?"

He goes back when the shotgun swings his

way for Jennie's daddy knows his baseball. Then the ceremony is over and Jennie looks up and sees it isn't Tink and she faints. She's married to Ty Cobb's shirt all because Lucas or Lookis or something had to shoot his face off. Pridemore makes a wave of his hand that declares the couple married and starts the game again.

The fans go back to their places, everybody on the field gets set, the runners take a big lead and the Tri-Stater winds up and lets her go.

Nippers takes a toe hold on some loose dust and swings. Well, the happy bridegroom misses it farther than a dunce getting Constantinople in a spelling bee.

Nippers is now in a fine spot. He is struck out and married on a wide outshoot.

Jennie's daddy has brought her around okay and he also collects Nippers and they go down the road looking like Daniel Boone moving his family farther west. I get myself invited to the wedding supper and the motorman isn't a bad sort of apple-knocker if you let him have his way. I tell Nippers that I will take the Detroit shirt back to Tink, but I advise him to keep the whole forty buttons for himself for he has earned it. Nippers keeps the shirt.

Let me tell you something about Ty's shirt. It must be magic because the bird who wears it acts like a leaguer. It is better for nailing a job in a small town than an average of 99.9 in a civil service quiz for letter carriers. Nippers has a couple more pitching jobs that fall and wins both. He gets sixty-five dollars for the last game of the season. Along about February at the end of winter I hear the population of Crambury has finally hopped to six hundred and thirty-three. Also that Nippers is offered a trial with a Hoss and Buggy League in Carolina.

Down there he meets Tink, fights him for the shirt and hammers him to a blister. They meet a second time that season and Nippers breaks the blister. The man wearing Cobb's shirt gets to think he is Ty and when the war busts loose in 1917 Nippers enlists and wins a whole flock of decorations.

He goes over the top in his Detroit shirt and eighty-seven Germans surrender to him because they think a new nation has declared war on the Kaiser.

When he got home to Crambury, Jennie and number six hundred and thirty-three are waiting for him. He starts in pitching again and he gets offers from the Three-Eye, the International and the South Atlantic leagues. But he refuses to play in any town that doesn't fit his shirt.

And, Believe It or the Marching Chinese, before the 1919 season is half over, the population of Crambury is one less than its average for sixty years, for Jennie and six hundred and thirty-three have packed up and gone west with Nippers, who is a fine husband and loving father, but once he gets out there on that baseball field, is meaner than the man who invented uphill.

And he gives Ty Cobb his shirt back. For Nippers now has a Detroit shirt of his own.

From *Tallulah*

ATTENDING a Giant game with me, say my cronies, is an experience comparable to shooting the Snake River rapids in a canoe. When they lose I taste wormwood. When they win I want to do a tarantella on top of the dugout. A Giant rally brings out the Roman candle in me. The garments of adjoining box-holders start to smolder.

I once lured the young Viennese actor, Helmut Dantine, to a set-to between the Giants and the Pirates. Mr. Dantine had never seen a game before. My airy explanations confused the *émigré*. Rapt in his attention to my free translation of the sacrifice hit, Helmut was almost decapitated by a foul ball. Mr. Dantine looked upon the *faux pas* as a hostile act. He felt I had tricked him into a false sense of security that the hitter might have an unsuspecting target. He left before the ninth, a grayer if not a wiser man.

It's true I run a temperature when watching the Giants trying to come from behind in the late innings, either at the Polo Grounds or on my TV screen. I was hysterical for hours after Bobby Thomson belted Ralph Branca for that ninth inning homer in the final game of the Dodger-Giant playoff in '51. The Giants had to score four runs in the ninth to win. Remember? There was blood on the moon that night in Bedford Village. But I don't know nearly as much about baseball as Ethel Barrymore. Ethel is a real fan, can give you batting averages, the text of the infield fly rule, and comment on an umpire's vision.

Someone has said that Ethel Barrymore has the reticence born of assurance whereas my monologues indicate my insecurity. The point is moot. It's unlikely I'll ever submit to a psychiatrist's couch. I don't want some stranger prowling around through my psyche, monkeying with my id. I don't need an analyst to tell me that I have never had any sense of security. Who has?

My devotion to the Giants, dating back to 1939, has drawn the fire of renegades, eager to deflate me. One of these wrote that on my first visit to Ebbets Field in Brooklyn I rooted all afternoon for Dolph Camilli, the Dodger first baseman. I had been tricked into this treason, swore my enemy, because I wasn't aware that the Giants wore gray uniforms when traveling, the residents white. Though I invaded Flatbush to cheer Mel Ott, Giant right fielder, I wound up in hysterics over Camilli because both had the numeral "4" on the back of their uniform. Stuff, balderdash and rot, not to use a few other words too hot to handle in a memoir.

A daughter of the deep South, I have little time for the "Yankees." They're bleak perfectionists, insolent in their confidence, the snobs of the diamond. The Yankees are all technique, no color or juice. But they keep on winning pennants year after year. Not the Giants! They've won one flag in the last fourteen years.

I blew my first fuse over the Giants in the summer of '39, when introduced to Harry Danning and Mel Ott. Ott was so good-looking, so shy, so gentlemanly—and from Louisiana. For two weeks I got up in the middle of the night—around noon by the actor's clock—to charge up to the Polo Grounds.

I worked myself up into such a fever that I invited the team to see a performance of *The Little Foxes*. After the play I served them a buffet supper, and drinks compatible with their training rules, on the promenade which fringed the rear of the balcony. The Giants, following this soiree, dropped eight games in a row. Had I hexed them? The suspicion chilled me. I denied myself the Polo Grounds and they started to win again. . . .

Looking back on my fiascoes with wishbones and four-leaf clovers reminds me that I once put the whammy on Daddy. I went to a ball game between a team of Congressmen and the Washington's firemen's nine, played in behalf of charity. Daddy had been a great athlete at the University of Alabama. I was sure that he would distinguish himself. To my horror he fanned three times. I was crushed for days.

My heroes are not necessarily headliners. I swooned over Burgess Whitehead, Giant second baseman, because he moved like a ballet dancer. He was a Phi Beta Kappa, a brilliant fielder, but he couldn't hit his way out of a paper bag. Then there was Lou Chiozza. One of his traducers said that he weighed 170 and hit the same figure. Pursuing an outfield fly Lou collided so violently with Jo-Jo Moore that he broke his ankle. When he was carted off to the hospital, I banked his bed with flowers. Two visiting teammates were paralyzed with fright on walking into his dimly lit room. They found their white-clad comrade asleep in a profusion of lilies and came to the conclusion he was dead. Why was I fascinated with Chiozza? He was born in Tallulah, Louisiana.

"BASEBALL," wrote Gerald Beaumont shortly following the First World War, "is a peculiar profession, possibly the only one which capitalizes a boyhood pleasure, unfits the athlete for any other career, keeps him young in mind and spirit, and then rejects him as too old, before he has yet attained the prime of life." In writing baseball fiction, Mr. Beaumont said, "Some of the characters . . . portrayed are just as the writer observed them while serving as an official scorer for the Pacific Coast Baseball League; others are composites. The incidents are nearly all suggested by actual occurrences which might have turned out as narrated had only Fate been a little more indulgent." Mr. Beaumont went pretty good, Fate or no. And here is his most famous story.

The Crab

GERALD BEAUMONT

Not until the orchestra at 11:30, with a cheery flourish from the clarinets, launched into a quaint little melody, did the Crab's expression of disapproval change. Then his eyes sought a velvet curtain stretched across one end of the room. The drapery parted to admit a slip of a girl in a pink dress who came gliding down between the tables, slim white arms swaying in rhythm with her song. The Crab, obeying a sentiment he did not try to analyze, eyed her just as he had done every night for a week.

Those at the tables who had been there before nudged newcomers and whispered, "Watch her smile—it's the whole show."

It was a bright little tune—soothing as a lullaby. She sang the second chorus, looking straight at the Crab:

"Smile a-while, and I'll smile, too,
What's the good of feeling blue?
Watch my lips—I'll show you how:
That's the way—you're smiling now!"

A spotlight from the balcony darted across the room and encompassed the girl and the man to whom she was singing. Amid general laughter and applause, the Crab squirmed, reddened and achieved a sheepish grin.

The singer passed to other tables, the light playing on her yellow hair and accentuating the slimness of her figure.

"I'm the Smile Girl, so folks say—
Seems like smiles all come my way.
Want to smile? I'll show you how:
That's the way—you're smiling now."

People continued smiling and humming to the tuneful melody long after she had declined further encores. The Crab stared into the bottom of his empty glass. His face was still very red. Her fingers had brushed the Crab's sleeve as lightly as a butterfly's wing but he was exalted by the contact.

* * *

Coast League fans said of Bill Crowley that if he ever learned to moderate his crabbing, the majors would one day be bidding for the greatest third baseman in history. He was chain lightning on his feet and could hit around .290 in any company. Moreover, he had perfect baseball hands, an arm of steel, and the runner was yet to wear spikes who could scare him into exposing even a corner of the bag if the play was close.

But Bill was a crab by instinct, preference and past performances. He was hard-boiled in the dye of discontent, steeped in irritability— a consistent, chronic, quarrelsome crab, operating apparently with malice aforethought and intent to commit mischief.

Naturally the fans rode him. It is human nature to poke sticks at a crab and turn it over on its back. In time, a crustacean becomes imbued with the idea that it was born to be tormented, hence it moves around with its claws alert for pointed sticks. That was the way with Bill Crowley, third-sacker extraordinary, and kicker plenipotentiary to the court of Brick McGovern, sorrel-topped manager of the Wolves. Looking for trouble, he found it everywhere.

At that, Bill the Crab was not without a certain justification. A third baseman has enough woes without being afflicted with boils on the back of his neck. Such ailments belong by the law of retribution to the outfield. The fact that little pink protuberances appeared every now and then due south from the Crab's collar button, where the afternoon sun could conveniently find them, was further proof that even Providence had joined in the general persecution.

No infielder or outfielder ever threw the ball right to the Crab. It was either too low, or too high, or too late, or on his "meat" hand. There wasn't a scorer on the circuit who knew the definition of a base hit. The only time the umpires were ever on top of the play was when Bill was the runner, and then they had their thumbs in the air before he even hit the dirt.

Under such circumstances there was nothing for the Crab to do but register his emphatic disapproval. This he invariably accomplished by slamming his glove on the ground and advancing on the umpire stiff-legged after the manner of a terrier approaching a strange dog. Had there been hair on the back of his neck, it would have bristled.

The arbiters of the diamond took no chances with the Crab. They waved five fingers at him when he took the first step, and held up both hands when he took the second. If that didn't hold him, they promptly bestowed the Order of the Tin Can by waving the right arm in the general direction of the shower baths. This meant in all a fine of twenty dollars and the familiar line in the sporting extras:

CROWLEY THROWN OUT FOR CRABBING

In the last game of the season, the Crab distinguished himself by clouting a home run in the first inning with the bases full, but before the contest was over he was led from the park by two policemen, having planted his cleats on the sensitive toes of Umpire Bull Feeney and thereby precipitated the worst riot of the year.

McGovern, astute pilot of a club which had won two pennants, clung to the Crab in the forlorn hope that time and patience might work one of those miracles of the diamond which are within the memory of most veteran managers.

Had any one told the red-headed campaigner that he would yet live to see the day when the Crab would be a spineless thing of milk and water, pulling away from a runner's spikes, flinching under the taunts of the bleachers, accepting meekly the adverse decisions of the men in blue, he would have grinned tolerantly. The Crab might mellow a little with advancing years, but lose his fighting spirit? Not in this world!

*　　*　　*

It was in the spring of the following year when the team came straggling into camp for the annual conditioning process, and all but the Crab and one or two others had reported, that the Wolves were subjected to a severe jolt.

Rube Ferguson who had an eye for the dramatic waited until the gang was at morning batting practice. Then he broke the astounding news.

"The Crab's got himself a wife."

The Wolves laughed.

"*All* right," said Ferguson, "*all* right—you fellows know it all; I'm a liar. The Crab's been married three months. I stood up with him. What's more, you fellows know the girl."

He took advantage of the general paralysis that followed this announcement to sneak up to the plate out of turn. He was still in there swinging when they came to life and rushed him. News is news, but a man's turn at bat, especially after an idle winter, is an inalienable right. Rube clung to his club.

"Three more cuts at the old apple," he bargained, "and I tell you who she is."

They fell back grumbling. Ferguson's last drive screamed into left field and whacked against the fence. Grinning contentedly he surrendered his bat and took his place at the end of the waiting line.

"Not so bad—I could have gone into third on that baby standing up. Trouble with you fellows is you're growing old. Now I—"

Brick McGovern raised a club menacingly. "Who'd the Crab marry?"

"Keep your shirt on," advised Ferguson. "I'm coming to that. It was the blonde at Steve's place."

"Not the Smile Girl?" The quick objection sprang from a dozen lips. "Not the little queen who sings—not the entertainer?"

Ferguson beamed happily. He had his sensation.

"You said it," he told them. "The Smile Girl is now Mrs. Crab. She married Bill because the whole world was picking on him and it wasn't right. Ain't that a dame for you?"

They were inexpressibly shocked. The Smile Girl—daintiest wisp of cheer in the city—married to the Crab—surliest lump of gloom in baseball. The thing seemed incredible and yet—that was just the sort of girl she was—gravitating toward any one who was in distress. They swore in awed undertones.

"What a bonehead play," sighed Boots Purnell, "what a Joe McGee! Imagine *any* one, let alone the Smile Girl, trying to live with the Crab! Give her an error—oh, give her six!" He made his sorrowful way to the plate, moaning over the appalling blunder.

Rube Ferguson's rich tenor sounded the opening lines of the Smile Girl's own song:

"Smiling puts the blues to flight;
Smiling makes each wrong come right—"

They joined mechanically in the chorus but they did not smile.

Pee-wee Patterson, midget second baseman, expressed what was in every one's mind:

"If anyone can tame the Crab, it's Goldilocks —but I'm betting she slips him his release by June. I wonder will he bring her to camp with him?"

The Crab settled this point himself the following day by showing up—alone and unchastened. He invited no questions and they forbore to offer any. He was as truculent and peevish as ever. The food was the bunk; someone had the room that he was entitled to; the bushers were too thick for comfort; the weather was "hell," and the new trainer didn't know a "charley horse" from a last year's bunion.

"The Crab's going to have a good year," observed Pee-wee, "twenty bucks says she gives him the gate by the first of June. Who wants it?"

Rube Ferguson whistled thoughtfully.

"If Brick will advance it to me I'll see you," he hazarded. "Some Janes are bears for punishment and the Crab ain't so worse. He made

her quit her job and he staked her to a set of furniture and a flat. My wife says they're stuck on one another."

Pee-wee snorted. "Flypaper wouldn't stick to Bill after the first ten minutes." He raised his voice a little in imitation of Bull Feeney addressing the grandstand: "Batt'ries for to-day's game," he croaked, "the Smile Girl and the Crab. Bon soir, bye-bye, good night."

The Rube grinned. "Sure is a rummy battery," he agreed ruefully, "but the bet stands." He departed in search of McGovern and a piece of the bankroll.

Those of the Wolves who had not already met the Smile Girl, and they were mostly the rookies, learned to know her in the final days of the training season when the Wolves sought their home grounds for the polishing-up process.

She was enough of a child to want to accompany the Crab to the ball park for even the morning workouts and to say pretty things to each one individually. The Crab accomplished the introductions awkwardly, but it was evident that he was very proud of her and that she was very much in love with him.

"Some guys have all the luck," lamented Boots Purnell. "If she ever benches the Crab, I'll be the first one to apply for his job."

At the opening game of the season, the Smile Girl's pink dress and picture hat were conspicuous in the front row of the grandstand just back of third base. Pink for happiness, she always said.

Rube Ferguson confided an important discovery to Brick McGovern and others between innings as they sat in the Wolf dugout.

"The Crab's keeping one eye on the batter and the other on his wife. I don't think he knows there's anybody else in the park. They've got a set of signals. Every time the Crab starts to splutter, she gives him the tip to lay off the rough stuff, and he chokes it back. Pee-wee, you lose!"

The diminutive second-sacker did not reply at once. He was searching wildly for his favorite stick. At length he found it and trotted off for his turn at the plate. He was back shortly, insisting loudly that the "last one was over his head."

"Now about the Crab," he confided to Rube, "everything's coming his way, get me? Wait until we hit the road for a while and the hot weather comes and the ace-in-the-hole boys get to working on him, then we'll see."

The Wolves, always a slow team to round

to form because of the many veterans on the roster, trailed along in the second division and swung north in fifth place for their first extended road trip.

Gradually it became apparent to all that Pee-wee Patterson had called the turn on the Crab. He was plainly settling back into his old surly ways, snarling at the umpires, grumbling over the work of the pitchers, and demanding angrily that McGovern get someone behind the bat who didn't have a broken arm—this of Billy Hopper who could handcuff nine third basemen out of ten.

They were on the road four weeks and the Crab's batting average climbed steadily while his temper grew hourly worse. This was characteristic. He seemed able to vent considerable of his spite on the inoffensive leather. It was the nerves of his teammates that suffered.

"What did I tell you?" demanded Patterson, "now when we hit the home grounds next week—the Crab will get the panning of his life and the Smile Girl will break her heart over it. I tell you I'm calling the play!"

Brick McGovern and Rube Ferguson regarded their comrade-at-arms soberly. They felt that he spoke the truth.

"Well," commented Rube, "you can't bench a man that's hitting over .300 just to spare his wife's feelings." And with that understanding, the Crab was retained in the clean-up role.

* * *

Most ballplayers have a dislike for one or more cities on the circuit. The Crab's pet aversion was the St. Clair grounds. There, the huge double-decked grandstand, with its lower floor on a level with the infield itself and not forty feet from the foul lines, brought players and spectators into closer contact than was good for either. Back of the heavy screening and paralleling a well-worn path between the home plate and the dugout assigned to the home club, stretched "Sure Thing Row" where men who wagered money in downtown poolrooms before the game congregated like birds of prey to await the outcome.

"Sure Thing Row" ran to checked suits, diamonds and stacks of half dollars, the latter held lightly in one hand and riffled with the thumb and forefinger of the other. It broke no law of the land; it knew its rights and exercised every one of them.

"The Row" maintained a proprietary interest in the Crab. He was theirs by right of dis-

covery. In him they recognized not only the strongest link in the Wolf defense but likewise the weakest. He was an unconscious instrument to be used or not as the odds might require. Now that the Crab was married, the problem was simplified.

It was in the third game of the series that Rube Ferguson, sitting beside Brick McGovern in the dugout while the Wolves were at bat, reported to his leader what was going on.

"The ace-in-the-hole boys are after the Crab. When he went up to bat just now they were whispering stuff to him about his wife—get me, Brick? They're handing him the laugh about the Smile Girl. He'll blow up before the inning's over."

McGovern nodded. His gnarled and sun-scorched hands opened and shut helplessly. "I know," he groaned, "I know—they used to hand it to me like that and if it hadn't been for my wife and kids I'd have done murder twenty times. There's no law against insulting a ballplayer. That goes with the price of admission. They'll not break the Crab's nerve but they'll get him thrown out. Ah!"

The gray-clad figures in the Wolf dugout sprang to their feet. The high-pitched yelp of the timber wolf pierced the clamor, followed by cries of "tear 'em, puppy!"

The Crab had lashed a terrific drive along the right field foul line and was rounding first base in full stride.

McGovern tore for the coaching box with both arms raised, palms outward. Walker in right field had knocked the drive down. He had one of the best arms in the league.

"None out," yelled the Wolf leader, "two bags—play it safe! Back—go back!"

But the Crab had eyes or ears for no one. He was running wild, bent only on showing "Sure Thing Row" he was its master. Blind with rage and excitement he bore down on third base. The ball zipped into the hands of the waiting fielder in plenty of time. The Crab must have known he was out, but he arose from a cloud of dust, wildly denunciatory, and frantic under the jibes of the bleachers and the fox-faced gentry back of the screen.

In the old belligerent way, he stalked after Tim Cahill and grabbed the umpire by the arm.

"You—you—" he foamed.

McGovern dashed out on the diamond but the mischief was already done. Cahill knew his business and he stood for no breach of discipline. Freeing himself from the Crab's clutch, he jerked a thumb in the direction of the club-house in center field.

"You're through for the day," he snapped, "off the field or I'll nick you for a ten-spot. Beat it!"

McGovern pulled his infielder away and shoved him in the direction indicated. "Don't be a fool, Bill," he advised, "you were out a mile."

The target for a storm of derisive hoots, the Crab made his way sullenly along the fence and into the clubhouse shadows. Not until he had vanished from sight did the last sibilant hiss die out.

McGovern walked back to the Wolves' pit and shot a quick glance at the Smile Girl sitting in her usual place just back of third. All around her, men were laughing at the Crab's discomfiture. She was smiling bravely but even at that distance he was certain that her chin was quivering.

"Sure Thing Row" settled back contentedly and winked. The Crab and his bludgeon had been eliminated from the crucial game of the series.

The Wolves lost by one run.

On the last day of June, just before the club left for another long swing around the circle, Rube Ferguson encountered little Patterson in front of the clubhouse. He drew the midget aside and handed him a twenty-dollar bill.

"Much obliged," acknowledged Pee-wee, "what's the idea?"

"The Crab's wife has left him."

"No!"

"Yes. She's been gone three days. She told my wife he came home and beefed because she was sewing something, and she said she could stand his crabbing about everything else but *that*."

The second baseman looked incredulous.

"Seems like somebody's got their signals crossed, don't it? Why should that get her goat particularly? What was she sewing?"

The Rube shrugged. "What do women always sew? The money's yours."

The little infielder's eyes hardened. "I'm clean," he admitted. "I haven't got a red—but you put that twenty back in your pocket or I'll beat you to death."

Ferguson nodded his comprehension. "I feel that way about it, too. There's something likable about the Crab but I've never found out what it is. Will he be better or worse now?"

"Does a Crab ever change?" asked Pee-wee.

During the next few weeks it seemed as though Patterson's question could admit of but one answer. The Crab drew if anything a little closer into his shell. He was more morose, more savage in the clubhouse and on the diamond. He snarled his refusals when they offered him the usual hand of poker up in Boots Parnell's hotel room. When they left the clubhouse in the afternoons, he disappeared and they did not see him until the next morning. They forbore to question him. The ballplayer's code of ethics does not include discussion of domestic averages. While he continued to hit and field as he was doing, he was entitled to behave off the diamond in any way he saw fit.

Not until August when the club was in third place and going like a whirlwind, did the Crab give any indication that he missed the slim little figure in the pink dress who used to blow him kisses from the grandstand.

Then, so gradually that they had difficulty in comprehending the process, something under the Crab's shell began to disintegrate.

It was his hitting—that infallible barometer to a ballplayer's condition, that fell off first. Not that the Crab didn't connect just as frequently as ever, but his swings lacked the old driving power. Outfielders who used to back against the fence when he came up, now moved forward and had no trouble getting under the ball. From fourth place in the batting order he was dropped to sixth and then seventh without result. His huge shoulders seemed devitalized.

Next it was his fielding. He fumbled ground balls that ordinarily would have given him no trouble. He was slow on his feet and erratic in his throwing.

Jiggs Peterson, guardian of the right field pasture, called still another deficiency to the attention of the entire club one afternoon when, in a tight game with the Saints, a runner slid safely into third despite a perfect throw from deep right.

"I had that guy nailed by twenty feet," he complained to the Crab, "and you let him slide into the bag. What's the idea of taking the ball in back of the sack?"

The Crab's only reply was a mumbled, "You peg 'em right and I'll get 'em."

"Jiggs had called the turn," whispered Pee-wee, "the Crab is pulling away from the runner's spikes right along. I don't understand it."

"Nor I," Ferguson responded, "there was a time when he would have broken Jiggs in two for trying to call him like that."

The next day the Crab, seated beside his manager in the dugout, turned suddenly to McGovern.

"Brick—I can't find her—it's August and I can't find her."

McGovern masked his surprise. The Crab's eyes were bloodshot, the lines on his weather-beaten face sunk to unnatural depths. Several times McGovern opened his mouth but the right words did not occur to him.

"I can't find her," reiterated the Crab dully. "I lost her, and I can't find her."

McGovern scraped in the soft dirt with his cleats. He spoke as one man to another. "I'm sorry, Bill, I didn't know just how you felt about it."

The Crab contemplated the palm of a worn-out glove. The muscles of his face twitched.

"I thought it was doll clothes she was sewing, Brick—she's such a kid. Honest to God I thought it was doll's clothes. I never knew different until I read her note. Now you know why I *got* to find her."

The pilot of the four-time pennant winners was again bereft of speech. He nodded slowly.

"She left no address," continued the third baseman. "She thought I was crabbing at her because—" his voice cracked sharply.

The Wolves came trooping noisily in from across the diamond. Their sorrel-topped pilot threw an arm carelessly around the Crab's shoulders.

"The Smile Girl couldn't hold a grudge against anyone," he whispered, "you'll hear from her one of these days. Why, man, any one could see she was nuts about you!"

The Crab's fingers closed on his leader's arm with a grip that made McGovern wince.

"You think so, Brick—on the level?"

"On the level, Bill."

That afternoon the Crab got two hits, the first he had negotiated in a week, but as the fifteenth of August approached, he slumped again, and McGovern benched him and made three unsuccessful attempts to bolster up the one weak spot in his infield. But good third basemen are not lying around loose in the middle of August. The Crab at his worst was better than the newcomers and McGovern put him back in the fray. Two of three major league scouts who had been attracted by the Crab's hitting and who had lingered in the hope that he would emerge from his slump, packed their grips and went elsewhere. The third man was a product of the school of Mc-

Graw. He studied the Crab through half-closed eyelids and—stayed.

With seven weeks of the season still unplayed, the Wolves returned from a southern trip in second place. The fine lines of worry between McGovern's eyes deepened. He caught himself watching the apathetic figure of the Crab and praying that the third baseman would regain just a little of his old fighting spirit.

And then one afternoon just before the umpire called the Wolves and Tigers together for the opening game of the week, Rube Ferguson, idol of the right field bleachers, tossed a number of neatly folded newspapers into the pit.

"Compliments of 'Pebble Pop,' champion groundkeeper of the world," he told them, "pipe the write-up they gave the old boy."

The Crab opened his paper listlessly, glanced over the tribute to the veteran caretaker, and permitted the pages to slip to the concrete floor of the dugout. He was in the act of thrusting the paper aside with his cleats, when his eye caught a single word in black-face type up near the top of the column on the reverse side of the sporting page. It was his own name. Hypnotically, he picked up the page and stared at it. The words that followed the black-faced capitals burned themselves into his brain.

A sharp ejaculation caused McGovern to look up. The Crab's teeth were chattering.

"What's wrong?"

"N-n-nothing," stammered the Crab. The paper rustled from his nerveless hands. He straightened up, looked around wildly and then walked up and out of the pit—straight as a chalk line to the exit back of first base. With the entire team watching him, open-mouthed, the Crab wrenched savagely at the gate. A special officer drew the bolt, and the third baseman disappeared into the crowd, uniform and all.

Pee-wee Patterson broke the silence.

"I knew it was coming. He's cuckoo. Somebody better follow him."

But Brick McGovern was scanning the paper that the third baseman had dropped.

"Cuckoo, nothing," he exclaimed, "the Crab has found his wife!"

They all saw it then—two lines of agate type that began: "CROWLEY—"

The paper was eight days old.

*   *   *

A sorrel-topped Irishman with a fighting face, but rather too generous about the middle for perfect condition, plodded up the steps of St. Joseph's Hospital at dusk. One hand grasped a bouquet of pink roses.

"Ah, yes," said the little woman in the office, "second floor of the Annex—Room 41."

McGovern located the room and tapped gently on the white door.

"Come in," chirped a voice.

The pilot of the Wolves turned the knob dubiously and peered into the room.

The Smile Girl was sitting up in bed. Her eyes were bright with the look that comes to a woman who has borne her mate his first man-child. She beckoned to McGovern and then held a pink finger to her lips.

"S-sh!" she whispered, "look!"

In an armchair facing the window and away from the door, McGovern made out a familiar figure, still in uniform. It was rocking gently back and forth, cleats tapping on the linoleum-covered floor, and as it rocked it sang most unmusically to a rose-colored bundle held awkwardly over one shoulder:

"Smile awhile—and I'll smile, too,
What's the good of feeling blue?
Watch my lips—I'll show you how:
That's the way—you're smiling now!"

McGovern blew his nose. The singing stopped abruptly.

"Honey," said the Smile Girl, "bring William, Junior, to me. You've had him for most an hour and I want to show him to Mr. Mc-Govern."

The Crab's cleats click-clacked across the room. He held up the bundle for McGovern's inspection.

"I'd let you hold him, Brick," he confided, "but it's got to be done just a certain way. The nurse put me wise; see—you keep one hand back of the neck and shoulders, so you don't do no fumbling."

McGovern nodded. He deposited the roses on the bed and laid the tip of one pudgy finger ever so lightly on the cheek of the sleeping infant.

"Some kid," he marveled, "*some kid!*"

The Smile Girl emitted a cry of surprise. From an envelope attached to the roses she had extracted a hundred-dollar bill.

"What's that?" demanded the Crab crossly, "what you trying to put over, Brick? I haven't touched a bean of my salary for three months. I don't need—"

"Shut up!" admonished McGovern. "Can't I take an option on the little fellow's services if I want to? Look at those hands, Bill—ain't they made for an infielder—they're yours all over—he's got your eyes and your hair and—"

The baby squirmed and moved its hands restlessly. The lusty wail of a perfectly healthy and hungry man-cub brought a nurse hurrying into the room.

With obvious reluctance, Bill Crowley surrendered his possession. He brushed one hand hastily across his eyes.

"Darn little crab," he said huskily, "he *does* look like me just a little bit, *don't* he, Brick?"

*   *   *

Digger Grimes, base runner par excellence, flashed past first and second in an ever-widening circle and headed for third. He was well between the two bags when Pee-wee Patterson, crouched in short center, took the throw from his old and esteemed friend Rube Ferguson and with a single motion shot the ball, low and a trifle wide of the waiting figure at third.

It was the seventh inning of the last game of the season. Thirty thousand fans in bleachers and grandstand rose to their feet. The play was close, so close that men forgot to breathe. Twenty feet from the bag, the runner made his leap. Spikes flashed in the sunlight menacingly. The Digger was coming in at an angle opposite to the guardian of the bag—charging with his fangs bared!

At the same instant, a heavy-shouldered figure in the familiar uniform of the champion Wolves swept up the ball with one bare hand and flung himself headlong in the path of the plunging runner. The two figures thudded together—threshed a moment in a flurry of arms and legs and then were still.

With his cleats still six inches from the bag, Digger Grimes found himself pinned to the dirt under 180 pounds of inexorable bone and muscle.

Out from a cloud of dust, while the bleachers and grandstand rocked in a tempest of glee, came an indignant bellow:

"He's out—I tell you!—he ain't touched the bag yet—he's out!"

The Crab catapulted to his feet and advanced on Dan McLaughlin. The umpire turned mild blue eyes on the Wolf infielder.

"I called him out," he protested, "what do you want—a written notice?"

The Crab blinked a moment, and stalked back to his position. From under the visor of his cap he shot a swift glance at the crowded benches just back of third. A blur of pink and a smaller blur of blue showed up against the dark background of masculine fandom and told him all he wished to know.

The Crab's chest expanded, as is only proper when a man has got his two hits. Pounding the palm of his worn glove, he dug his cleats into the dirt and set himself for the next play.

"Come on," he called, "get the next man! Ump—it's too bad you only got one lung— can't call a play louder than a whisper, can you? Pipes all rusty, huh? Too bad!"

Over in the Wolf dugout, a red-headed manager who had seen his club climb into the lead in the closing days of the grueling struggle, smiled faintly and stared with unseeing eyes across the diamond. His fingers twisted a telegram that had come to him that morning from New York.

Ten thousand dollars cash and spring delivery is too tempting an offer for any minorleague manager to reject. But there would be a wide hole at third base next year, and Brick McGovern was already wondering how he would ever plug it.

"What do you boys think the pictures will show?"

THE Dodgers were the Robins in those days. This particular line score went:

```
BROOKLYN:  0 0 0 0 1 0 0 0 0 0 0 0 0 0 0 0 0 0 0 0 0 0 0 0 0 0—1
BOSTON:    0 0 0 0 1 0 0 0 0 0 0 0 0 0 0 0 0 0 0 0 0 0 0 0 0 0—1
```

1920:
Boston Braves 1,
Brooklyn Robins 1

RALPH D. BLANPIED

THE ROBINS and the Braves celebrated May Day in this ordinarily peaceful city by staging a prolonged, heartbreaking struggle for twenty-six innings at Braves Field and bombing to bits all major-league records for duration of hostilities. When darkness drew its mantle over the scene, both teams were still on their feet, interlocked in a death clutch and each praying for just one more inning in which to get in the knockout blow.

As far as results in the chase for the pennant go the game was without effect, for the final score was 1 to 1. In the matter of thrills, however, the oldest living man can remember nothing like it, nor can he find anything in his granddad's diary worthy of comparison. Heart disease was the mildest complaint that grasped the spectators as they watched inning after inning slip away and the row of ciphers on the scoreboard began to slide over the fence and reach out into the Fenway.

Nervous prostration threatened to engulf the stands as the twentieth inning passed away in the scoreless routine and word went out from the knowing fans to those of inferior baseball erudition that the National League record was twenty-two innings, the Robins having beaten the Pirates by 6 to 5 in a game of that length played in Brooklyn on Aug. 22, 1917.

The twenty-second inning passed in the history-making clash, and then the twenty-third, with a total result of four more ciphers on the scoreboard and a new National League record.

Now the old-timers in the stands began to whisper that the big-league record was twenty-four innings, established in an American League game in the Hub on Sept. 1, 1906, on which occasion the Athletics downed the Red Sox by 4 to 1. The Robins and the Braves didn't care. They didn't even know it. They simply went along in their sublime ignorance and tied this record, then smashed it, and by way of emphasis tacked on a twenty-sixth session.

At this stage of the proceedings Umpire McCormick yawned twice and observed that it was nearly bedtime. He remembered that he had an appointment with a succulent beefsteak and became convinced that it was too dark to play ball. Thereupon he called the game.

The fielding on both sides was brilliant in the crises. Olson saved Brooklyn in the ninth, when, with the bases filled and one out, he stopped Pick's grounder, tagged Powell on the base line and then threw out the batter.

In the seventeenth inning one of the most remarkable double plays ever seen in Boston retired Brooklyn. The bases were filled and one was out when Elliott grounded to Oeschger. Wheat was forced at the plate, but Gowdy's throw to Holke was low and was fumbled. Konetchy tried to score from second and Gowdy received Holke's throw to one side and threw himself blindly across the plate to meet Konetchy's spikes with bare fist.

Joe Oeschger and Leon Cadore were the real outstanding heroes among a score of heroes in the monumental affray of this afternoon. The two twirlers went the entire distance, each pitching practically the equivalent of three full games in this one contest, and, *mirabile dictu*, instead of showing any sign of weakening under the prolonged strain, each of them appeared to grow stronger. In the final six innings neither artist allowed even the shadow of a safe bingle.

The Braves' twirler had rather the better of the duel in some respects. Fewer hits were made from his delivery than from that of Cadore. Oeschger practically twirled three 3-hit games in a row, while Cadore pitched three 5-hit games in the afternoon's warfare. In only one inning, the seventeenth, did Oeschger allow two safe blows, and Cadore let the local batters group their hits only in the sixth and ninth.

At the receiving end of the batteries, O'Neil gave way to Gowdy for the Braves before hostilities were concluded, and Elliott took Krueger's place behind the bat for Brooklyn.

Robbie's men got their tally in the fifth inning. Krueger was walked by Oeschger, who offended in this way very seldom this afternoon. Krueger went to second while Oeschger was fielding Cadore's little pat and getting his man at first. Ivy Olson slashed a line drive over Maranville's head for a single, on which Krueger crossed home plate. Olson went to second on a wild pitch but was left there as Oeschger tightened up and fanned Neis and Johnston lined to Mann in left field.

The Braves tied the score in the succeeding inning, jamming over the final run of a game which was destined to go on for twenty scoreless innings thereafter, equaling the existing record in this respect. Cadore threw Mann out at first. Cruise came along with a mighty drive to the scoreboard for three bases. Holke popped up a short fly to left which Wheat caught. Boeckel delivered the goods with a single to center upon which Cruise tallied. Maranville followed with a double to center but Boeckel was caught at the plate in the effort to score on the Rabbit's blow, Hood, Cadore and Krueger participating in the put-out.

After this session, save for the Braves' flash in the ninth and the Robins' effort in the seventeenth, the two twirlers were entire masters of the situation.

THE OPENING sentence of the following account, which appeared in
the old New York *World*, is probably the most famous in baseball
journalism, and the piece itself won several prizes and has been exhibited as a model lead. Damon Runyon, elsewhere in this book, deals
with the preceding game of the same 1923 World Series.

1923:
New York Yankees 4,
New York Giants 2

HEYWOOD BROUN

THE RUTH is mighty and shall prevail. He
did yesterday. Babe made two home runs
and the Yankees won from the Giants at the
Polo Grounds by a score of 4 to 2. This
evens up the World Series with one game for
each contender.

It was the first game the Yankees won from
the Giants since October 10, 1921, and it
ended a string of eight successive victories for
the latter, with one tie thrown in.

Victory came to the American League champions through a change of tactics. Miller Huggins could hardly fail to have observed
Wednesday that terrible things were almost
certain to happen to his men if they paused
any place along the line from first to home.

In order to prevent blunders in base running he wisely decided to eliminate it. The
batter who hits a ball into the stands cannot
possibly be caught napping off any base.

The Yankees prevented Kelly, Frisch and the
rest from performing tricks in black magic by
consistently hammering the ball out of the
park or into sections of the stand where only
amateurs were seated.

Through simplicity itself, the system worked
like a charm. Three of the Yankees' four runs
were the product of homers, and this was
enough for the winning total. Aaron Ward was
Ruth's assistant, Irish Meusel of the Giants

also made a home run, but yesterday's show
belonged to Ruth.

For the first time since coming to New
York, Babe achieved his full brilliance in a
World Series game. Before this he has varied
between pretty good and simply awful, but
yesterday he was magnificent.

Just before the game John McGraw remarked:

"Why shouldn't we pitch to Ruth? I've said
before and I'll say again, we pitch to better
hitters than Ruth in the National League."

Ere the sun had set on McGraw's rash and
presumptuous words, the Babe had flashed
across the sky fiery portents which should have
been sufficient to strike terror and conviction
into the hearts of all infidels. But John Mc-
Graw clung to his heresy with a courage worthy of a better cause.

In the fourth inning Ruth drove the ball
completely out of the premises. McQuillan
was pitching at the time, and the count was
two balls and one strike. The strike was a fast
ball shoulder-high, at which Ruth had lunged
with almost comic ferocity and ineptitude.

Snyder peeked at the bench to get a signal
from McGraw. Catching for the Giants must
be a terrific strain on the neck muscles, for
apparently it is etiquette to take the signals
from the bench manager furtively. The catcher

is supposed to pretend he is merely glancing around to see if the girl in the red hat is anywhere in the grandstand, although all the time his eyes are intent on McGraw.

Of course the nature of the code is secret, but this time McGraw scratched his nose to indicate: "Try another of those shoulder-high fast ones on the Big Bum and let's see if we can't make him break his back again."

But Babe didn't break his back, for he had something solid to check his terrific swing. The ball started climbing from the moment it left the plate. It was a pop fly with a brand new gland and, although it flew high, it also flew far.

When last seen the ball was crossing the roof of the stand in deep right field at an altitude of 315 feet. We wonder whether new baseballs conversing in the original package ever remark: "Join Ruth and see the world."

In the fifth Ruth was up again and by this time McQuillan had left the park utterly and Jack Bentley was pitching. The count crept up to two strikes and two balls. Snyder sneaked a look at the little logician deep in the dugout. McGraw blinked twice, pulled up his trousers and thrust the forefinger of his right hand into his left eye. Snyder knew that he meant: "Try the Big Bozo on a slow curve around his knees and don't forget to throw to first if you happen to drop the third strike."

Snyder called for the delivery as directed and Ruth half-topped a line drive over the wall of the lower stand in right field. With that drive the Babe tied a record. Benny Kauff and Duffy Lewis are the only other players who ever made two home runs in a single World Series game.

But was McGraw convinced and did he rush out of the dugout and kneel before Ruth with a cry of "Maestro" as the Babe crossed the plate? He did not. He nibbled at not a single word he has ever uttered in disparagement of the prowess of the Yankee slugger. In the ninth Ruth came to bat with two out and a runner on second base. By every consideration of prudent tactics an intentional pass seemed indicated.

Snyder jerked his head around and observed that McGraw was blowing his nose. The Giant catcher was puzzled, for that was a signal he had never learned. By a process of pure reasoning he attempted to figure out just what it was that his chief was trying to convey to him.

"Maybe he means if we pitch to Ruth we'll blow the game," thought Snyder, but he looked toward the bench again just to make sure.

Now McGraw intended no signal at all when he blew his nose. That was not tactics, but only a head cold. On the second glance, Snyder observed that the little Napoleon gritted his teeth. Then he proceeded to spell out with the first three fingers of his right hand: "The Old Guard dies, but never surrenders." That was a signal Snyder recognized, although it never had passed between him and his manager before.

McGraw was saying: "Pitch to the Big Bum if he hammers every ball in the park into the North River."

And so, at Snyder's request, Bentley did pitch to Ruth and the Babe drove the ball deep into right center; so deep that Casey Stengel could feel the hot breath of the bleacherites on his back as the ball came down and he caught it. If that drive had been just a shade to the right it would have been a third home run for Ruth. As it was, the Babe had a great day, with two home runs, a terrific long fly and two bases on balls.

Neither pass was intentional. For that McGraw should receive due credit. His game deserves to be recorded along with the man who said, "Lay on, Macduff," "Sink the ship, Master Ginner, split her in twain," and "I'll fight it out on this line if it takes all summer." For John McGraw also went down eyes front and his thumb on his nose.

Some of the sportsmanship of the afternoon was not so admirable. In the sixth inning Pep Young prevented a Yankee double play by diving at the legs of Ward, who was just about to throw to first after a force-out. Tack Hardwick never took out an opposing back more neatly. Half the spectators booed Young and the other half applauded him.

It did not seem to us that there was any very good reason for booing Young, since the tradition of professional baseball always has been agreeably free of chivalry. The rule is, "Do anything you can get away with."

But Young never should have been permitted to get away with interference. The runner on first ought to have been declared out. In coming down to second Young had complete rights to the baseline and the bag, but those rights should not have permitted him the privilege of diving all the way across the bag to tackle Ward around the ankles.

It was a most palpably incompetent decision by Hart, the National League umpire on second base. Fortunately the blunder had no effect on the game, since the next Giant batter hit into a double play in which the Giant rushline was unable to reach Ward in time to do anything about it.

Ruth crushed to earth shall rise again. Herb Pennock, the assistant hero of the afternoon, did the same thing. In the fourth inning, Jack Bentley toppled the slim Yankee left-hander into a crumpled heap by hitting him in the back with a fast ball. Pennock went down with a groan which could be heard even in the dollar seats. All the players gathered around him as he writhed, and what with sympathy and some judicious massage, he was up again within three or four minutes, and his pitching efficiency seemed to be in no wise impaired. It was, of course, wholly an accident, as the kidney punch is barred in baseball.

Entirely aside from his injury, Pennock looked none too stalwart. He is a meager athlete who winds up with great deliberation, as if fearful about what the opposing batter will do with the ball. And it was mostly slow curves that he fed to the Giants, but they did nothing much in crucial moments. Every now and then Pennock switched to a fast one, and the change of pace had McGraw's men baffled throughout.

Just once Pennock was in grave danger. It looked as if his three-run lead might be swept away in the sixth inning. Groh, Frisch and Young, the three Giants to face him at that point, all singled solidly. It seemed the part of wisdom to remove Pennock immediately after Young's single had scored Groh. Here Huggins was shrewd. He guessed wisely and stuck to Pennock.

Irish Meusel forced Young, and it would have been a double play but for Young's interference with Ward's throw. Cunningham, who followed, did hit into a double play, Scott to Ward to Pipp. The Giant's rally thus was limited to one run.

Their other score came in the second inning,

when Irish Meusel drove a home run into the upper tier of the left field stands. It was a long wallop and served to tie the score at that stage of the game, as Aaron Ward had made a home run for the Yankees in the first half of the inning. Ward's homer was less lusty, but went in the same general direction.

In the fourth the Yankees broke the tie. Ruth began it with his over-the-fence smash, and another run came across on a single by Pipp, Schang's hit to right—which Young fumbled long enough to let Pipp reach third—and Scott's clean line hit to center. This is said to be Scott's last year as a regular and he seems intent on making a good exit, for, in addition to fielding spryly, he made two singles.

The defensive star of the afternoon was Joe Dugan, third baseman of the Yankees. He specialized on bunts. McQuillan caught him flat-footed with an unexpected tap, but he threw it on the dead run in time to get his man at first.

Again he made a great play against Kelly, first batter up in the last half of the ninth. Kelly just nicked the ball with a vicious swing and the result was a treacherous spinning grounder that rolled only halfway down to third. Dugan had to run and throw in conjunction this time, too, but he got his man.

For the Giants, Frisch, Young and Meusel batted hard, and Jack Bentley pitched well after relieving McQuillan in the fourth. He was hit fairly hard and he was a trifle wild, but the only run scored against him was Ruth's homer in the fifth.

As for the local color, the only bit we saw was around the neck of a spectator in a large white hat. The big handkerchief, which was spread completely over the gentleman's chest, was green and yellow, with purple spots. The rooter said his name was Tom Mix, but offered no other explanation.

ALL RIGHT, the Merkle incident. In 1908, Fred Merkle was on first base when what should have been the game-winning hit drove in a Giant teammate from third with two out in the ninth. Merkle, seeing the runner score and the crowd pour onto the field, headed directly for the clubhouse without going to second. Johnny Evers, Chicago Cubs' second baseman, called for the ball—folk differ as to whether what he finally ended up with was *the* ball—and stepped on second for the inning-ending force. Run didn't count. Game ended in a 1-1 tie, since the churning crowd on the field made further play impossible. The Giants claimed they should have won, 2-1, since the rule called by Umpire Hank O'Day had never before been enforced. The Cubs claimed *they* should have won, 9-0, the score of a forfeit, since the home team was responsible for keeping the field playable and the onpouring crowd took care of *that*. The game was ruled a tie—this was late September—and it was ruled that it would be played off the day after the season ended if necessary. It was necessary—the Cubs and Giants wound up in a tie for first!

Mordecai (Three Finger) Brown, Chicago pitching immortal, takes up from here.

1908:
Chicago Cubs 4,
New York Giants 2

—— **MORDECAI BROWN** ——
as told to JACK RYAN

WHEN Manager Frank Chance led the Chicago Cub team into New York the morning of October 8, 1908, to meet the Giants that afternoon to settle a tie for the National League pennant, I had a half-dozen "black hand" letters in my coat pocket. "We'll kill you," these letters said, "if you pitch and beat the Giants."

Those letters and other threats had been reaching me ever since we had closed our regular season two days before in Pittsburgh. We'd beaten the Pirates in that final game for our 98th win of the year and we had waited around for two days to see what the Giants would do in their last two games with Bos-

ton. They had to win 'em to tie us for the National League championship.

Well, the Giants did win those two to match our record of 98 wins and 55 losses so a play-off was in order. I always thought that John McGraw used his great influence in National League affairs to dictate that the play-off must be held on the Giants' home field, the Polo Grounds.

I'd shown the "black hand" letters to Manager Chance and to the Cub owner, Charley Murphy. "Let me pitch," I'd asked 'em, "just to show those so-and-sos they can't win with threats."

Chance picked Jack Pfiester instead. Two

weeks before, Pfiester had tangled with Christy Mathewson, McGraw's great pitcher, and had beaten him on the play where young Fred Merkle, in failing to touch second on a hit, had made himself immortal for the "boner" play. Since Mathewson had been rested through the series with Boston and would go against us in the play-off, Chance decided to follow the Pfiester-Mathewson pitching pattern of the "boner" game. I had pitched just two days before as we won our final game of the schedule from Pittsburgh.

Matter of fact, I had started or relieved in 11 of our last 14 games. Beyond that I'd been in 14 of the last 19 games as we came roaring down the stretch hot after the championship.

In our clubhouse meeting before the game, when Chance announced that Pfiester would pitch, we each picked out a New York player to work on. "Call 'em everything in the book," Chance told us. We didn't need much encouragement, either.

My pet target, you might say, was McGraw. I'd been clouding up on him ever since I had come across his sly trick of taking rival pitchers aside and sort of softening them up by hinting that he had cooked up a deal to get that fellow with the Giants. He'd taken me aside for a little chat to that effect one time, hoping, I suppose, that in a tight spot against the Giants I'd figure I might as well go easy since I'd soon be over on McGraw's side.

Sure, it was a cunning trick he had and I didn't like it. So, the day after he'd given me that line of talk I walked up to him and said, "Skipper, I'm pitching for the Cubs this afternoon and I'm going to show you just what a helluva pitcher you're trying to make a deal for." I beat his Giants good that afternoon.

But that was early in the season and I want to tell you about this play-off game. It was played before what everybody said was the biggest crowd that had ever seen a baseball game. The whole city of New York, it seemed to us, was clear crazy with disappointment because we had taken that "Merkle boner" game from the Giants. The Polo Grounds quit selling tickets about one o'clock, and thousands who held tickets couldn't force their way through the street mobs to the entrances. The umpires were an hour getting into the park. By game time there were thousands on the field in front of the bleachers, the stands were jammed with people standing and sitting in

aisles, and there were always little fights going on as ticket-holders tried to get their seats. The bluffs overhanging the Polo Grounds were black with people, as were the housetops and the telegraph poles. The elevated lines couldn't run for people who had climbed up and were sitting on the tracks.

The police couldn't move them, and so the fire department came and tried driving them off with the hose, but they'd come back. Then the fire department had other work to do, for the mob outside the park set fire to the left-field fence, and was all set to come bursting through as soon as the flames weakened the boards enough.

Just before the game started the crowd did break down another part of the fence and the mounted police had to quit trampling the mob out in front of the park and come riding in to turn back this new drive. The crowds fought the police all the time it seemed to us as we sat in our dugout. From the stands there was a steady roar of abuse. I never heard anybody or any set of men called as many foul names as the Giant fans called us that day from the time we showed up till it was over.

We had just come out onto the field and were getting settled when Tom Needham, one of our utility men, came running up with the news that, back in the clubhouse he'd overheard Muggsy McGraw laying a plot to beat us. He said the plot was for McGraw to cut our batting practice to about four minutes instead of the regular ten, and then, if we protested, to send his three toughest players, Turkey Mike Donlin, Iron Man McGinnity and Cy Seymour charging out to pick a fight. The wild-eyed fans would riot and the blame would be put on us for starting it and the game would be forfeited to the Giants.

Chance said to us, "Cross 'em up. No matter when the bell rings to end practice, come right off the field. Don't give any excuse to quarrel."

We followed orders, but McGinnity tried to pick a fight with Chance anyway, and made a pass at him, but Husk stepped back, grinned and wouldn't fall for their little game.

I can still see Christy Mathewson making his lordly entrance. He'd always wait until about ten minutes before game time, then he'd come from the clubhouse across the field in a long linen duster like auto drivers wore in those days, and at every step the crowd would yell louder and louder. This day they split the air. I watched him enter as I went out to the bull pen, where I was to keep ready. Chance still insisted on starting Pfiester.

Mathewson put us down quick in our first time at bat, but when the Giants came up with the sky splitting as the crowd screamed, Pfiester hit Fred Tenney, walked Buck Herzog, fanned Bresnahan, but Kling dropped the third strike and when Herzog broke for second, nailed him. Then Turkey Mike Donlin doubled, scoring Tenney, and out beyond center field a fireman fell off a telegraph pole and broke his neck. Pfiester walked Cy Seymour and then Chance motioned to me to come in. Two on base, two out. Our warmup pen was out in right-center field so I had to push and shove my way through the crowd on the outfield grass.

"Get the hell out of the way," I bawled at 'em as I plowed through. "Here's where you 'black hand' guys get your chance. If I'm going to get killed I sure know that I'll die before a capacity crowd."

Arthur Devlin was up—a low-average hitter, great fielder but tough in the pinches. But I fanned him, and then you should have heard the names that flew around me as I walked to the bench.

I was about as good that day as I ever was in my life. That year I had won 29 and, what with relief work, had been in 43 winning ball games.

But in a way it was Husk Chance's day.

That Chance had a stout heart in him. His first time at bat, it was in the second, the fans met him with a storm of hisses—not boos like you hear in modern baseball—but the old, vicious hiss that comes from real hatred.

Chance choked the hisses back down New York's throat by singling with a loud crack of the bat. The ball came back to Mathewson. He looked at Bresnahan behind the bat, then wheeled and threw to first, catching Chance off guard. Chance slid. Tenney came down with the ball. Umpire Bill Klem threw up his arm. Husk was out!

Chance ripped and raved around, protesting. Most of us Cubs rushed out of the dugout. Solly Hofman called Klem so many names that Bill threw him out of the game.

The stands behind us went into panic, they were so tickled and the roar was the wildest I ever heard when Matty went on to strike out Steinfeldt and Del Howard.

Chance was grim when he came up again in the third. Tinker had led off the inning by tripling over Cy Seymour's head. We heard afterward that McGraw had warned Seymour that Tinker was apt to hit Mathewson hard, and to play away back. Seymour didn't. Kling singled Tinker home. I sacrificed Johnny to second. Sheckard flied out, Evers walked, Schulte doubled. We had Matty wobbling and then up came Chance, with the crowd howling. He answered them again with a double, and made it to second with a great slide that beat a great throw by Mike Donlin.

Four runs.

The Giants made their bid in the seventh. Art Devlin singled off me, so did Moose McCormick. I tried to pitch too carefully to Bidwell and walked him. There was sure bedlam in the air as McGraw took out Mathewson and sent up the kid, Larry Doyle, to hit. Doyle hit a high foul close to the stand and as Kling went to catch it, the fans sailed derby hats to confuse him—and bottles, papers, everything. But Kling had nerve and he caught it.

Every play, as I look back on it, was crucial. In the seventh after Tenney's fly had scored Devlin, Buck Herzog rifled one on the ground to left but Joe Tinker got one hand and one shin in front of it, blocked it, picked it up and just by a flash caught Herzog who made a wicked slide into first.

In the ninth a big fight broke out in the stands and the game was held up until the police could throw in a cordon of bluecoats and stop it. It was as near a lunatic asylum as I ever saw. As a matter of fact the newspapers next day said seven men had been carted away, raving mad, from the park during the day. This was maybe exaggerated, but it doesn't sound impossible to anyone who was there that day.

As the ninth ended with the Giants going out, one-two-three, we all ran for our lives, straight for the clubhouse with the pack at our heels. Some of our boys got caught by the mob and beaten up some. Tinker, Howard and Sheckard were struck. Chance was hurt most of all. A Giant fan hit him in the throat and Husk's voice was gone for a day or two of the World Series that followed. Pfiester got slashed on the shoulder by a knife.

We made it to the dressing room and barricaded the door. Outside wild men were yelling for our blood—really. As the mob got bigger, the police came up and formed a line across the door. We read next day that the cops had to pull their revolvers to hold them back. I couldn't say as to that. We weren't sticking our heads out to see.

As we changed clothes, too excited yet to put on one of those wild clubhouse pennant celebrations, the word came in that the Giants over in their dressing room were pretty low. We heard that old Cy Seymour was lying on the floor, in there, bawling like a baby about Tinker's triple.

When it was safe we rode to our hotel in a patrol wagon, with two cops on the inside and four riding the running boards and the rear step. That night when we left for Detroit and the World Series we slipped out the back door and were escorted down the alley in back of our hotel by a swarm of policemen.

VIRGIL PARTCH

Courtesy *True, The Man's Magazine.* ©

"Apologize!"

WARREN BROWN, author of the book *The Chicago Cubs* and one of the country's finest sports writers, turned, in 1948, severest critic as well as best friend. The Cubs, under general manager James Gallagher and field manager Charley Grimm, looked lousy, and Mr. Brown, in the sporting pages of the Chicago *Herald-American,* chose the deadliest way of saying so. Remember Gallagher and Shean? Brown parodied them daily. Here are two samples:

Mr. Gallagher and Mr. Grimm

WARREN BROWN

Oh, Mr. Gallagher, Oh, Mr. Gallagher,
The schedule gives another day of rest
Which is something we don't need
To establish our clear lead
For outresting all contenders, East or West.

Oh, Mr. Grimm, Oh, Mr. Grimm,
Our stout-hearted athletes are in losing trim;
To make it very terse
Their speed's always in reverse.
Battery weakness, Mr. Gallagher?
Clutch trouble, Mr. Grimm.

Oh, Mr. Gallagher, Oh, Mr. Gallagher
In another day we'll have to leave once more
To play Pirates, then the Cards
In their very own back yards
I hope it ain't what it was like before.

Oh, Mr. Grimm, Oh, Mr. Grimm,
These contenders may well tear us limb from
    limb
We may emulate the dive
Of the Cubs of '25
We ain't *that* bad, Mr. Gallagher,
That's what you think, Mr. Grimm.

THE WORLD SERIES hero of 1954 . . . Dusty Rhodes. The World Series hero of 1955 . . . Johnny Podres. In the winter of 1955-56, this piece by Jimmy Cannon.

The Hot Hand

JIMMY CANNON

IT WAS strictly a gimmick but it busted for space. The famous petits fours, which are, of course, high-class cookies, were supposed to name the guys they'd leap at during leap year. Run down the list and you see guys such as Sinatra, Brando, DiMaggio, Ty Power. It figures and so does Johnny Podres. The kid grabbed a hot hand. They're giving him the treatment since he beat the Yanks two games in the World Series.

All guys with hot hands get the ride until the straights stop filling in the middle. The cold wind blows away the aces and deuces are in the hole. Bet the hot hand before the cold wind freezes your fingers. Some guys never run out of it. They stay lucky forever. Luck comes and holds. So, Johnny, take the plaques and deliver your talks at the banquets. Stand up there and let the television cameras inspect your kisser.

Some guys don't just get cold. They get lost and mixed up because they can't understand what happened. It was there, now it's gone. He's 1A now. So who knows? No one can measure how much a hot hand wins. It's table stakes and beyond that there's no limit at all.

You take Dusty Rhodes. He sizzled in '54. Cleveland couldn't get him out. Step down, Monte Irvin, Dusty Rhodes is hitting for you. And the Giants won in four straight. It runs the same way. They had parades in Rhodes' home town, too, back in Alabama. The mayor talked, just like the mayor of Witherbee, N. Y., when Podres went back where he came from.

It was hotter because Rhodes had Leo Durocher going for him. Two guys, Willie Mays and Dusty Rhodes, the manager spoke about that winter. He entertained a lot of people telling them what a big cut Dusty took at the bourbon. Every one laughed. You're hot, everything's funny.

They didn't sit Dusty in an open car and take him down the big street back down in Alabama this October. Next thing he was in the papers getting banged up in an auto accident. But Ed Sullivan wasn't demanding his presence. Television got along very well without Dusty Rhodes. This was the winter they took the shot with Podres who held a hot hand against the Yankees.

* * *

Where's Durocher? Did you ever think he'd get chilly? One year the pennant, the next Durocher is out of baseball. He was allowed to quit a job he didn't hold. Don't worry about him. He can come back when he wants to.

The money will be right, too. I don't know where he'll light but a lot of clubs will take a shot with him. He's a big name. But it didn't help him on that television show. Did it? You ever see a colder man?

Often when I see Pee Wee Reese I think of the kid who came up with him. It runs across my mind that Pete Reiser led the National League in batting the first year he landed. No one ever did that before, or since. But he ran into a fence the next season. That was the end of it. It didn't just stop right there. He lasted but the greatness was lost and he hurt all over. And then he was being traded. And then he was gone.

Dizzy Dean stayed warm, long after his arm lost it. But he had won 30 and that's in the book. He's a talker and a comedian and he works at broadcasting and hollers up a loud commotion. But I remember him when he should have been right, pitching for the Cubs

43

against the Yankees in a World Series. The fog was off the fast ball. The curve didn't jump. And he tried to sneak by on con but he didn't make it. But that's another tale. He didn't stick around as long as some. But while he was up, they all knew about it. He played the hot hand the way it should be handled. He's still pulling high hole cards.

* * *

Once he was a hell of a fighter and he was loaded with money. The horses took it. The broads trimmed him. The joints got a lot of it. And then the doctors told him it would be hazardous for him to fight any more. They picked up his ticket and he owed last month's room rent. I met him at the gym one afternoon.

"Help me get a license," he said.

"You're liable to be hurt," I said.

"Naw," he said. "They got it in for me. Nothing wrong with me. I'm as good as ever."

They told him how bad it could be. Punches around the head could kill him or set him crazy. He's fine now but he's willing to take a chance. That's what it means to be hot. There's one guy willing to die for it.

You do, or you don't. It's not that simple. Lew Jenkins, when he was lightweight champion of the world, never believed it at all. It was money and money was made to spend and the hell with it all. Out of the Army, originally a blacksmith, Jenkins is back in it again. He's a paratrooper now. I never heard him complain. But years afterwards he was fighting for small purses and money was money. He wanted it then.

"When you got a kid," Jenkins said, "it makes a difference."

* * *

Anyway, Nancy Berg and the other petits fours held still for this gag about leaping at Johnny Podres. The press agent didn't bother with Dusty Rhodes. He held the hot hand in '54 and that's a century ago when a guy's shooting angles to grab some space. The hot hand's Johnny's until there's a new deal.

WELCOME HOME!

Three immortal pennant-crisis homers: on this page, Hank Greenberg for the Tigers in 1934; overleaf, Gabby Hartnett's "home run in the gloaming" for the Cubs in 1938 and Bobby Thomson's "homer heard round the world" for the Giants in 1951. Mystery: Where are Greenberg's teammates?

International News

Wide World

DOUBLE PLAY! ·

In order: Oncoming runners of the old days seemed more polite in their approach to the pivot man in the double play than they are these days to Bobby Avila of Cleveland or (overleaf) to Red Schoendienst, then with the Cardinals.

Culver Service

International News

As of 1955, next year is now, but as of 1953, when this was written, the Brooklyn Dodgers had the most dispiriting record in World Series annals—seven series played, seven series lost.

1953: Wait Till Next Year

LAWTON CARVER

THE AWFUL FRUSTRATION of it all was best symbolized by Duke Snider on the final play of the game when the Dodgers lost a World Series for the seventh time in seven tries.

In a tense ball game, one that was wonderful in many ways, the Dodgers, as everybody knows by now, had tied the score in the upper half of the ninth inning on a two-run homer, on a 3-and-2 pitch by Carl Furillo, the National League batting champion hitting against old Wahoo himself, Allie Reynolds.

One was down when this occurred, and the big Indian from out yonder then struck out Billy Cox and Clem Labine to leave the score tied at 3 and 3.

In the under side of the ninth Labine walked Hank Bauer, who advanced to second on a dribbling single by Mickey Mantle, and at this point Manager Casey Stengel of the Yankees, headed for a record-cracking fifth straight world championship, turned to Phil Rizzuto in the dugout and said:

"This feller is going to break up the game."

This feller was Billy Martin, the little Yankee Clipper, who hit to center field on the next pitch after arguing with Umpire Bill Stewart on a called first strike.

Bauer was off from second and running for home on the hit, and crossed the plate without a play for him while Snider casually reached down and picked up the ball, stuffed it in his pocket and headed for the Dodger dugout of defeat.

You wanted to scream at Snider to throw the ball to the plate, where catcher Roy Campanella stood braced; you wanted to remind him that Bauer might stumble and break a leg, that he might be hit by a bolt of lightning and be delayed or prevented entirely from ever getting home.

You wanted to see the Dodgers go down fighting, knowing that they didn't have a chance to catch Bauer on a throw without a helpful accident, but you wanted that throw, even though you had picked the Yankees to win and you wanted them to win.

You even wanted Snider to pick up that ball and throw it over the center-field fence in a last dying desperate gesture of contempt if nothing else.

Presently, Campanella turned and headed for the dugout and the dressing room while Snider came on in from center field with the game-losing ball—from the Dodgers' standpoint—in his pocket.

A Yankee most likely would have thrown that ball somewhere under similar circumstances—and that is the difference between ball clubs.

Aside from all else the Dodgers could not have won this series. Even if they had won yesterday's game, the Yankees would have come back with Ed Lopat today, leaving the Dodgers to select whom—perhaps coach Jake Pitler.

In the final analysis, the Yankees won because they played cleaner baseball—one error against seven for the Dodgers—and they hit in the clutch. They also pitched in the clutch.

As is almost customary, the National League team found itself in the majors for the first time in its experience upon entering the World Series. The Yankees actually should have and nearly did make it four in a row.

HENRY CHADWICK is recognized in the Hall of Fame as "baseball's pre-eminent pioneer writer for half a century" and "inventor of the box score." Here, from the New York *Sunday Mercury* of 1869, are the opening paragraph and box score of a Chadwick report. Included in the summary that followed the box scores in those days, by the way, was a category called "Fatal Errors."

Passing though is the notice this book can give this particular game, it was worthy of inclusion, and not just as a brief sample of Chadwick's work. The winning team was the Cincinnati Red Stockings (also known in those days, as now, as the Reds). The Red Stockings, who are known as baseball's first professional team, had a pretty fair season in '69—won 57, lost 0.

1869:
Cincinnati Red Stockings 7, New York Mutuals 1

──────────── **HENRY CHADWICK** ────────────

ON OCTOBER 26th the Red Stockings returned to New York from Troy, after defeating the strong nine of the Haymakers of that village by a score of 12 to 7, and on the afternoon of that day played the first game of a new series of contests with the Mutual Club. The Saturday previous they had opened play in the east with a noteworthy triumph over the Athletics in Philadelphia by a score of 15 to 8, and therefore they entered upon this contest flushed with two victories, that at Troy being the most creditable display. The Reds, however, went into this game minus the services of Allison, their famous catcher, Deane taking his place in the nine and McVey playing in his position as catcher. The Mutuals, too, were shorthanded, they not having that useful player, Swandell, in their nine. They had a fair substitute, however, in Higham. The weather was all that could have been desired, the temperature being quite warm, and, as a close contest was anticipated, fully 3,000 persons were in attendance at the Union grounds, though the admission fee was double the usual rate. Mr. Ferguson had been agreed upon as umpire before the game, and no more impartial man could have been chosen for the position.

1869: Cincinnati Red Stockings 7, New York Mutuals 1

MUTUAL	R	1b	PO	A		CINCINNATI	R	1b	PO	A
Hatfield, ss	1	1	4	2		G. Wright, ss	2	3	3	4
Eggler, cf	0	1	2	0		Gould, 1b	0	2	14	1
Patterson, lf	0	1	3	0		Waterman, 3b	0	1	2	4
Nelson, 3b	0	1	2	1		Deane, rf	2	2	3	0
E. Mills, 1b	0	0	6	0		H. Wright, cf	1	1	1	0
Martin, rf	0	1	2	0		Leonard, lf	1	1	1	0
C. Mills, c	0	0	3	1		Brainard, p	0	2	0	2
Wolters, p	0	0	1	1		Sweasy, 2b	0	1	2	5
Higham, 2b	0	0	4	1		McVey, c	1	1	1	0
Totals	1	5	27	6		Totals	7	14	27	16

INNINGS	1st	2d	3d	4th	5th	6th	7th	8th	9th	
MUTUAL	1	0	0	0	0	0	0	0	0	—1
CINCINNATI	0	3	2	1	0	0	1	0	0	—7

THE FOLLOWING has been excerpted from a letter which hangs in the Hall of Fame at Cooperstown, written at the request of Mr. E. J. Lanigan, the Hall's historian. One of my own private delights in this letter is the fact that Cobb goes around the infield first-second-short-third, which makes sense. Baseball writers, in scoring, do it first-second-third-short. For what?

From a Letter to E. J. Lanigan

TY COBB

MENLO PARK, CALIF.
APRIL 21, 1945

DEAR MR. LANIGAN:

. . . Enclosed find selection of all-star team. Note that I do not select anyone that I have not played with or against, or seen much of.

PITCHERS: Walsh, Johnson, Alexander, Mathewson and Plank.
CATCHERS: Cochrane and Dickey.
FIRST BASE: Sisler.
SECOND BASE: Collins.
SHORTSTOP: Wagner.
THIRD BASE: Weaver.
LEFT FIELD: Joe Jackson.
CENTER " : Tris Speaker.
RIGHT " : Babe Ruth.

Note I have placed Weaver and Jackson, am only judging them on their ability.* I saw Jimmy Collins after he was through. I never saw Traynor. . . To my way of thinking no contest at second base, Hornsby couldn't catch a pop fly, much less go in the outfield after them, could not come in on a slow hit, Lajoie could not go out, nor come in, and did not cover too much ground to his right or left. Collins could do it all, besides being a great base stealer and base runner. Career average of .330-odd, I think. Also another manager on the field . . .

Sincerely
TY COBB

* Black Sox whose records have been stricken from the books . . . ED.

BOB CONSIDINE'S is one of the great journalistic names of our times. The following article appeared in *Life* magazine for July 29, 1948, and I wanted to include it here for what may be paradoxical reasons—it is a piece topical to that particular time, when the Philadelphia Athletics were still in Philadelphia; yet its subject represents all that is ageless and permanent in baseball. Needless to say, Mr. Considine was writing about the late Connie Mack. The last sentence of this article is one of particular poignancy in view of Mack's death within what was relatively so brief a period following the departure of the A's from Philadelphia.

Mr. Mack

BOB CONSIDINE

CORNELIUS MCGILLICUDDY, who was given the enduring alias of Connie Mack by an unsung newspaperman in 1884—because his full name could not fit in the small space of a newspaper box score—must be one of the oldest truly active businessmen in the U. S.

As president-treasurer-manager of the Philadelphia Athletics baseball club he works seven days a week 365 days a year and pays himself a salary comparable to that of the President of the U. S. But Mr. Mack, as his countless associates, friends and acquaintances call him religiously and with a certain awe, is not a rich man. He has, among other responsibilities, 15 great-grandchildren and a small army of personal pensioners dependent on his earning capacity. In 1946 he reported an income of $79,000, which made him perhaps the highest-paid 84-year-old employe in the country, but he was unable to buy the Buick he had on order. Minor stockholders in the Athletics, which Mister Mack has managed since 1901, chipped in, bought him the car and provided a chauffeur—one of the rare concessions made to Mr. Mack's incredible age.

Mister Mack, who will be 86 years old next December, might almost ask for patent rights to the game of baseball if he had not signed away such claims by lending himself to the pretty fable that the sport was the handiwork of the late General Abner Doubleday. He did much to fashion its rules, pioneered in developing the torturous art of catching, was a major manipulator in the rape of the National League at the turn of the century (which produced the American League and made big-league baseball big) and he introduced the modern style of pitching.

This occurred one day in Waterbury, Conn. when Mister Mack, crouching fifteen feet behind home plate and catching the ball on its first bounce with the aid of a fingerless kid glove, decided that there must be a better way for his pitcher to deliver the ball. He felt it was essentially unfair for his thrower to hop, skip and run through his cramped little 6x4 pitching box and to throw underhanded to a batter who not only was given seven balls and four strikes but could also demand that the ball be delivered to him at a favored height. So he walked out to the marked-off box in which his hurler stood and said, "Try throwing the ball overhand."

The man looked up at him as if he had gone mad, but followed his advice. The ball shot over the plate at a lively clip and the batter—as startled as a batter of today might be if Bob Feller suddenly delivered a through-the-legs pitch—missed it vaguely. It took the fans three more pitches to realize that Waterbury was being cruelly had. Then they rose and made as if to come out on the field and attack the pitcher.

But Connie reached him first. "Don't listen to those fellows," he ordered. "Just pitch your own game." The man did, and his daring new delivery produced a considerable vogue; so considerable, in fact, that the pitcher's box was moved back from 45 feet to its present 60 feet 6 inches from the plate. And pitchers have been throwing like that ever since.

Mack was one of the first catchers to move up to a position just behind the batter and catch the ball before it bounced. His proximity to the batters of that dimly distant era stimulated in him the devil which is part of his kindly nature. It occurred to him that if he was that close to a man who was bent upon bringing ruin to him and the Mack team he might as well trip him or "tip" his bat—to interfere with his swing—or in other ways militate against the man's getting a hit.

"Don't ever say I was a great catchaw," he told this reporter recently. "But," he added with a bit of glitter in his slightly watery blue eyes, "I was kinda tricky. We got away with a lot back in the days when we played with only one umpire. The only time I ever really got caught was by an old ballplayer named Weaver. I must have been with Washington. Anyway, this Weaver—a fine fellow—he got angry with me after I had tipped his bat a few times, and he used to say that he'd get even with me.

"Well, Mr. Constantine, he did. By gosh, the next time he had two strikes on him he just stepped back from the plate and instead of swinging at the ball he brought his bat down on my wrists. I dropped like a shot. Let me tell you it hurt.

"But I figured out a way to get back at him. I waited until our last game of the year against Weaver's team, and Weaver's last time at bat, and when he had two strikes on him I tipped his bat again, just to show him I could still do it."

Except that each passing decade gives him more and more the appearance of a stately and well-plucked gobbler, Mister Mack has not changed much in the last fifty years. He was born in East Brookfield, Massachusetts, either just before or just after the midnight which separated December 22, 1862, from December 23, 1862. His brother Mike, who lived to be ninety by sticking steadfastly to a daily glass of whisky (Connie gave up his own modest drinking and golf when he was seventy-six), liked to cackle that Mister Mack, who preferred the December 23 date, was a pretty smart fellow but just didn't know what day he was born on. Mike always said he saw the birth on December 22.

Whatever the date, the son of Michael Mc-Gillicuddy—who was at that moment fighting against the South with the Massachusetts Regiment—was christened Cornelius. At the end of the Civil War, Michael McGillicuddy returned to his job in an East Brookfield cotton mill, and when Cornelius was nine years old he also got a job there, working summers. He was given an hour for lunch but never used more than fifteen minutes of it to eat. The remaining forty-five were given to games involving a bat and ball, variously called one o'cat, four o'cat, roundball and baseball.

When he was fifteen Connie presented himself to the keeper of a general store in his neighborhood and asked to be measured. He blanched a bit when the man announced that he stood 6 feet 1. This confirmed his secret fear that there was something freakish about him. He began suffering claustrophobia at his cramped little desk in the local public school, and so, shortly after his sixteenth birthday, he abruptly quit. There was no furor in the Mc-Gillicuddy family. His schooling seemed adequate for the job he had in mind—that of a general hand in the Green and Twitchell shoe factory in East Brookfield.

Connie could pay more attention to his baseball now and by 1882 was the regular catcher on East Brookfield's best ball club. In 1883 his imagination was irrevocably fired by the appearance in East Brookfield for an exhibition game of the Worcester team, then in the National League. Later that year Cap Anson brought his mustached and mighty Chicago Colts to East Brookfield and Connie rubbed shoulders with these gods from another world and knew that nothing must stop him from trying to be one with them.

Early in March 1884 Connie received a telegram prompted by his East Brookfield battery mate, Billy Hogan, who had plunged onward to the comparatively lofty position of pitcher for the Meriden club of the Connecticut League. The telegram offered him a job with the club. Connie went straight to his foreman and told him he was quitting. "You'd better stay," said the foreman, a man named Morris (he is still alive today, at 100). "No, Saturday night's my last night in the boot shop," Connie insisted, a statement which he sometimes now regrets having made. "I hope Mr. Morris didn't think I was rude," he mused not long ago, as if he had been mulling it over for sixty-four years.

There was still the matter of proving to the manager of the Meriden club that he was able as well as willing. This Connie did in a game against Yale in which he handled his pitcher so well that the man struck out twenty-one Yales, including a vigorous young New Haven star named Amos Alonzo Stagg, who was later to make something of a name for himself in football. The lanky young catcher from East Brookfield was promptly offered $60 a month, held out and got $80, and became so popular with Meriden fans that at the close of the season they presented him with a gold watch.

Mister Mack was to become an almost starchy upholder of baseball ethics in the generations to come. But the game was unhampered by niceties in the '80s. With no twinge of conscience he deserted his loving fans in 1885 and jumped to the Hartford team of the same league because the Hartford management offered him $125 a month. By 1886 he was earning $200 a month, and in September of that year he and four other members of the club were sold to Washington of the National League for $3,500. It was a heady burst of good fortune, but Mister Mack was not dazzled out of his wits. He insisted on being paid $800 to catch the final month of the season at Washington. He also got a contract for $2,750 for the 1887 season and once again was so well received in a town whose ball park's grandstands then seated 1,800 (and whose White House incumbent was Grover Cleveland) that the fans presented him with a silver tea set.

Two years later, happily married to his childhood sweetheart, Margaret Hogan, and father of a growing family, Mister Mack jumped his job with Washington to join the ill-started Brotherhood, a league which the players themselves hoped to operate as a co-op in opposition to the entrenched National. He jumped for the same salary as was paid to him by the Washington team and became so warmly attached to the prospects of the new organization—especially those of his new club, Buffalo—that he invested all the money he had saved and all that he could borrow. The league folded after its first year and with it went everything the little family possessed. The gaunt young man of the house hooked on to the Pittsburgh Pirates in '91, however, and was well on his way to becoming the National League's outstanding catcher in '93 when his left ankle was fractured in a game with Boston.

His uselessness as a player, plus his keen baseball mind, prompted the Pittsburgh owners to appoint Connie manager of the club at the end of the 1894 season.

Mister Mack was 32 and considered, in those days, rather elderly for a freshman manager. But the owners, perhaps tolerant of his years, maintained their patience. When the Pirates finished sixth in 1896, however, he was discharged.

The man who was to be hailed forty-seven years later as perhaps the best manager in the American League was saved from complete obscurity by Ban Johnson, president of the Western League. Johnson, a ruthless dreamer who lived and died believing that baseball was perfected in order to serve him as a gigantic chess board on which to move his living pieces, lifted Mister Mack out of reluctant retirement and set him up as manager and one-fourth owner of the Milwaukee club. Johnson changed the name of his league to the American in 1900 and laid plans to invade the big time monopolized by the National. He ordered his friend Charles Comiskey, owner of the St. Paul franchise, to move his club to Chicago. He set up other clubs in Cleveland and Buffalo, and took over Detroit and Kansas City. He dispatched Mister Mack to Philadelphia one cold December day in 1900 to raise money for a ball park and to find a club which could successfully compete with the well-established Phillies.

Mister Mack found the needed money in the pocket of a dour and crusty baseball manufacturer named Ben Shibe, who spent enough of it to build a small park at 29th and Columbia Avenue, named Columbia Park. With $500 of a bankroll supplied by a willing but naïve Clevelander named Somers, Mister Mack persuaded the Phillies' greater star, Nap Lajoie, to jump to the new Philadelphia club. Then he talked another Phillies star, Lave Cross, into switching his allegiance. He also kept his eyes open for young men who showed promise. One of the young players he found before the curtain went up on American League baseball history in Philadelphia was a pitcher at Gettysburg College named Eddie Plank, who was later to enter baseball's Hall of Fame.

John McGraw, sharp-tongued critic of every club except his New York Giants, inadvertently gave the new Philadelphia American League team its nickname. Asked by a reporter to comment on the new club, Muggsy barked,

"Looks like the American League's got a white elephant on its hands in Philadelphia." Mack read the interview and placidly selected the name "White Elephants" for his club. They finished fourth in 1901 and were on their way to winning the pennant in 1902 when the Supreme Court of Pennsylvania ruled that Mister Mack could no longer use Lajoie and other appropriated stars. He was forced to break up his team and the experts immediately wrote off the chances of the club—which had by now been given the additional nickname of Athletics.

But Mister Mack was not defeated. He remembered an eccentric southpaw named Rube Waddell who had played in the Western League and whose major ambition in life was to become a bartender. He found Waddell pitching in a California league and had him shipped East. With the Rube's help the Athletics, or A's, won the pennant, their first of nine under Mister Mack, who also has the appalling record of finishing last in his league sixteen times.

From that time through the season of 1914 Mister Mack won five pennants and three World Series and produced in 1911 one of the two or three greatest ball clubs of all time, a team whose infield was made up of Stuffy McInnis at first, Eddie Collins at second, Jack Barry at short and Frank (Home Run) Baker at third. It was given the greatest plaudit that could be contrived in the minds of the sports writers of that uninflated day. They called it "the $100,000 infield."

When the Athletics lost the 1914 series to the somewhat talentless Braves, Mister Mack smashed the club like an expensive china vase. His players had cupped attentive ears to the offers of the newly created Federal League, a rival to the American League which Mister Mack had so successfully built up, and several of them did make the jump. With this and a general housecleaning, the greatest reversal of fortunes in the history of any city's club got under way. His 1914 team had outdistanced its competitors by winning 99 games and losing 53. The 1915 relics won only 43 games and lost 109. The 1916 A's won 36 and lost 117. They finished eighth for seven consecutive seasons.

After a decade in the environs of the cellar Mister Mack came up again. By astute outbidding of his rivals he assembled a superb combination of ballplayers. With this crew, built around Al Simmons, now his rough and adoring third-base coach, Lefty Grove, who was to win more than 300 games, Jimmy Foxx, Mickey Cochrane, George Earnshaw, Jimmy Dykes and others, the A's jumped from fifth in 1924 to second in 1925, and when the great Yankees declined after 1928 forged on to win the pennants of 1929, 1930 and 1931.

Mister Mack sometimes gets a little sentimental about that club. Recalling it recently, he remembered the seventh inning of the fourth game of the 1929 Series against the Cubs. The Cubs were leading 8 to 0.

"It was my intention at that stage of the game to send in substitutes for all the regulars at the start of the eighth inning," he said. "But when we came to bat in the seventh some odd things began happening. Al Simmons, the first man up for us, hit a home run which landed on the roof of the left-field stands, fair by just inches. If it had been foul—well, that doesn't matter now.

"Foxx then singled. So did Bing Miller. Dykes singled. It was his fourth straight hit of the day and I got the feeling that we had something special on the fire. Dykes's single scored Foxx, and now Joe Boley singled, scoring Miller. Burns batted for Rommel and flied out to English for the first out. But Bishop singled, scoring Dykes. The score was now 8 to 4.

"Joe McCarthy, a fine manager, took out Charles Root, his pitcher, and put in Artie Nehf. Mule Haas then hit a long fly to center which Hack Wilson lost and it went for a home run, making the score 8 to 7 in favor of the Cubs. When Cochrane walked, Joe McCarthy, a fine manager, replaced Nehf with Sheriff Blake. But Simmons singled to left, Foxx singled to center scoring Cochrane with the tying run. Big Malone started pitching then. He hit Miller with a pitched ball. Dykes then doubled for his fifth hit, scoring Simmons and Foxx with the ninth and tenth runs of the inning, and Burns and Boley—they struck out.

"You know, Mr. Constantine," said Mister Mack with a slight cough, "there was talk that I danced with joy during that big inning. It's not true. I just sat there, and when we won the game I walked off with hardly a word to the boys. It doesn't help any to appear to be too pleased before such an important series is won. Such an attitude might lead to overconfidence, and that's fatal."

These wondrous years of the A's lasted until 1933. Financially they represented a high tide in the fortunes of the ball club. With the possible exception of the New York Yankees, the Athletics had the fattest payroll in any league. Shibe Park had been renovated and with that and other expenses the club's overhead mounted. By 1933 the crash, which had already cut Philadelphia's ability to support a high-class ball team, hit Mister Mack: his club was $500,000 in debt. Simmons, Haas and Dykes had been sold to the White Sox for $150,000. Now, pressed to the limit by financial stringency, Mister Mack sold Grove, Foxx, Bishop and Rube Walberg, leaving himself with only tattered remnants of his former starring team. When the massacre was over he was told that if he dared come out of the dugout and show himself in the opening-day ceremonies of 1934 he would be booed as no man in the history of the city had ever been blasted. In face of the threat Mister Mack stalked gingerly off his barren bench on opening day and walked, head up, to the centerfield flagpole. The old man dared them to howl him down, and no one took the challenge. Suddenly a whole city seemed to agree with him that he had been forced to sell in order to survive.

From 1934 through 1947 Mister Mack's hapless teams never finished in the first division. But by late 1940 Mister Mack, who had bought out the shares of John Shibe, owned 58 per cent of the stock in the A's. He was now the Mr. Chips of baseball. The fans delighted in his gentle whimsy. There was the story of the Philadelphia cab driver, apparently new to the town because he did not recognize his passenger, who carried Mack to the North Philadelphia Station one night. The old gentleman, lost in thought, mechanically paid the sum recorded on the meter, picked up his bag and wandered off.

"Hey, pop," the driver snarled, "what about a tip?"

Connie stopped, lost in thought. "A tip?" he asked in a voice that sometimes spurts up an octave.

"Yeah, pop, a tip. How about one?"

"Certainly," Connie answered. "Don't bet on the A's."

By June of 1947 any outside observer might have been forgiven for assuming that Mister Mack's long career in baseball was drawing to a rather weary close. He had assembled a club of nobodies whose strength he estimated at the start of the season by telling Art Morrow of the Philadelphia *Inquirer*, "We can promise our patrons good baseball and nothing more."

But to everyone's surprise he began getting excellent pitching from the likes of Phil Marchildon, who still bore the scars of his months of captivity by the Germans; Dick Fowler, a young man seemingly crushed by family troubles; Bill McCahan, whose uncle had played in the outfield for Mister Mack in 1905 (McCahan went on to pitch a no-hitter for him before the season was over); Joe Coleman, given to Connie by his friend, the late Brother Gilbert (who had discovered an incipient young tailor named George Herman Ruth at St. Mary's Industrial School in Baltimore 33 years before); Bob Savage, first bigleaguer wounded in World War II, and a 20-year-old Pennsylvania Dutchman named Carl Scheib who had been pestering him for a job for the previous five years. He shaped these earnest young men around a resurrected second-rater named Bill Dietrich, who had been in and out of the league since 1930, and the A's began winning games.

Mister Mack decided about seventy years ago that pitching is 75 per cent of a team's worth, and nothing in the interim has changed his mind. By the end of the 1947 season he had added one or two other willing young hands, including the staff's only southpaw, Lou Brissie, a big courageous fellow who must play with a clumsy plastic guard over his shell-riddled left leg, part of which he left in Italy. He built a new infield around a revitalized veteran shortstop named Eddie Joost, put Hank Majeski, a Yankee castoff, on third base and unveiled an excellent young infielder in Ferris Fain, for whom he was subsequently offered a reported $100,000 by the Yanks. He inspired a phlegmatic young Czech named Elmer Valo with the energies of a human dynamo and breathed new life into a Detroit outfielder named Barney McCosky. In the other outfield position he placed Sam Chapman, a muscular former All-American gridman. The A's made a race of it and looked better than their fifth-place finish would indicate.

Mister Mack began to live all over agai and the undercurrent of sincere wishes that h retire melted away. This year, more than ever, he is the grand old man of baseball, and though most of the seasoned observers feel that it would be too good to be true if Mister Mack in his fantastic antiquity came home in front, players, managers and owners throughout the league like to say that if they themselves cannot win the banner they want the old man to cop it.

Prosperity has returned to the Athletics. The 1947 spurt attracted 900,000 paid admissions to Shibe Park and the A's drew a million customers on the road, sharing the money those outlanders deposited at the box offices. This year the Athletics, contenders from the opening gong, will draw more than a million clients at home—the biggest attendance in the tremendous history of the team—and perhaps a million and a half on the road, though they have one of the smallest payrolls in either big league.

The highest-paid men on the team—Marchildon and Joost—make $17,500 a year or less, and the sweatful young Valo probably does not make more than $8,500. Mister Mack just does not believe in the kind of salaries paid by the rich owners of the Yankees, Red Sox, Indians and Tigers. Nor does he believe in paying a lot of money and trying to buy a ready-made winner. Except for the cost of helping half a dozen of his players through their colleges—Mister Mack's first advice to any teen-ager who wants to play for him is, "You'd better let me send you to school first"—he paid only $20,000 for his present pitching staff.

But seldom in the history of baseball has there been a closer affinity between labor and management than there is with the 1948 Athletics—otherwise a typically soulless baseball corporation. Mister Mack is a fabulously beloved figure, as such love is measured in baseball. There is no cow-eyed infatuation for him among his players. That would be asking too much of the average big-leaguer, who is fundamentally a mercenary. But the warmth of the player for Mister Mack is readily apparent. "I love that old guy," one said recently, "but what a shrewd old goat he is!"

Except for a new and sometimes alarming trembling of his classic scorecard, with which he wigwags signals to his boys from his vantage point in the dugout, Mister Mack has shown few outward indications this year of the suffocating excitement that is in him. He still wears the high, starched collars that have been his trade-mark for half a century; when the style went out in Teddy Roosevelt's day, Mister Mack persuaded the firm to keep making them for him. His 150 pounds are smoothed out tautly over his 6-foot 1-inch frame. The story that his strongest exclamation is "Fudge!" is as hardy a fairy tale as the never-dying report that Babe Ruth was an orphan. A historic outburst of his temper will always be remembered in the dugouts of America: his chronically griping pitching ace, Lefty Grove, trudged into the dugout one day after Mister Mack had pulled him out of a game, threw down his glove in disgust, and growled, "Nuts!" Mister Mack stood up quickly and walked over to him. He pushed his face close to Grove's. "And nuts to you, too!" he shouted, then marched back to his place in his spindly way and sat down.

To Mister Mack this 1948 club is something special, and in his comparatively rare bursts of loquaciousness he likes to say it is his favorite team because it is his fightingest. It could be, too. By the July 4 turning point of the season, when it was only half a game out of first place, it had won seventeen of its games by one-run margins; had snapped back to win after the Red Sox had annihilated it in an early July game with a fourteen-run rally in one inning, and had otherwise paid dividends on his enormous affection. At the end of July the A's were still only half a game behind the Red Sox.

In his excitement these days Mister Mack sometimes makes plainly discernible mistakes in simple strategy, and if these cost him a game he is distraught as he goes home after a contest. He is beginning to shake like a great angular twig whenever the team loses, and he finds it hard to sleep those nights until he has reviewed each move of the game in his mind. When he signals for an obviously wrong move these days Al Simmons turns his back a bit sadly on the old man, as if he did not detect the signal, and calls for the right move. But this never fools Mister Mack. When Al comes back to the bench at the end of the inning Mister Mack usually speaks up.

"You used better judgment than I did, Al," he will say quietly, and then go about his timeless task of wagging his scorecard at his fielders.

It is not good taste on the Philadelphia bench to second-guess Mister Mack openly, but it has been done even in this year of dizzying success. Not long ago he ordered his leading run-producer, Majeski, to lay down a bunt. One man was out at the time and the A's were behind. Majeski reluctantly did as he was bidden and sacrificed the runner to second. But the next hitter popped up futilely and Majeski said with warm sincerity, "That was lousy baseball, Mister Mack."

Mister Mack thought for a time and said, "You're right, Mr. Majeski!"

Mister Mack calls a lot of his players

"Mister." In his relations with them he reveals many other niceties which another manager might scorn as a show of weakness. If one of his pitchers works himself out of a tight hole, or a player makes a timely hit or a fine defensive play, Mister Mack often will stand up as the player returns. He will shake hands with him and say with voice-cracking warmth, "Thank you," then sit down and go on with the business of running the game.

The A's bench is perhaps the quietest in baseball. Remarkably few obscenities are heard and the razzing of the other team is always kept above the belt. When a newcomer violates one of the unwritten laws of bench conduct he soon learns that he has blundered. Bobo Newsom, a garrulous soul who loves Mister Mack with a vociferous affection, showed up at Philadelphia a few years ago in the course of his endless march through the majors. "Hello, Connie!" he roared at their first meeting. Just before the start of his second game with the A's, Bo was called upon by six rather grim young A's. "We call him Mister Mack, see?" their spokesman growled. So did Bobo after that.

Mister Mack is handed a new scorecard before every game, and in warm weather a fresh bath towel is placed behind his back by any of a half dozen roughly adoring coaches, clubhouse attendants, players and the like. He makes impatient sounds like "stop babying me" when minor homages are being paid to him, but it is the belief of those very close to him that the old man would feel hurt if he were not thus pampered. Certainly what he gets in this line is precious little compared to the still enormous physical energies he alone must expend each day.

The old gentleman seldom sees his players after a game, unless one has made some catastrophic blunder. But, perhaps once a month, he does pop into the locker room, usually to have a concerned word with a coach or his son. Now and then it is a simple ceremonial call. Not long ago, pleased with the way in which his hard-working young team had just won another, Mister Mack poked in his head, patted his long, knuckly hands together in polite applause, looking around the room as he did. "This is for you," he said with quiet warmth.

Mister Mack doesn't go in for that newfangled nonsense of a telephone line running between the A's dugout at Shibe Park and the bull pen at the far end of the field. To call in a relief pitcher he uses a system that went out of style in most other big-league ball parks years ago. To get in Joe Coleman from the distant reaches of the pen Mister Mack orders a coach to stand out in front of the dugout—in view of the pen—and to pantomime a man shoveling coal. If the call is for Carl Scheib, the coach stands up and beats his fists against the nearest wall. Consulting briefly with himself, the bull-pen coach interprets this act as "man pounding on Shibe Park—Shibe—Scheib." But only a group well versed in the gentle wanderings of Mister Mack's mind could piece together his signal which calls in Dick Fowler. He orders the coach to stand out in front and make a stooping motion as if he were picking flowers. Mister Mack is extremely fond of Fowler and with unfailing courtliness always addresses him as "Mr. Flowers."

Mister Mack has possibly had more personal friends than any American now alive, for he has outlived several crops of them and is still enormously popular. A devout Catholic who never misses a Sunday Mass or a holyday of obligation, Mister Mack seems to attract waves of sports-minded priests at each stop along the big-league circuit. Considering the wideness of his circle of friends and those who feel friendly toward him, Mister Mack's memory is phenomenal. At Connie Mack Day in Meriden in 1947 an old fellow was helped to the microphone at home plate and recalled, "Con, you remember when we played against each other right here in '83? And remember I got a hit in the ninth and knocked in a run?"

Mister Mack took the microphone. "I certainly do!" he exclaimed, then added, "And I also remember that we won the game, 2 to 1."

Off and on since 1915 there have been reports that Mister Mack was ready to retire. He did quit once, without public knowledge. It happened a few years ago when he decided to hire Al Horwits, former Philadelphia baseball writer, as publicity man for the team. To show his sons, who hold various executive offices in the organization, that he was open-minded about the appointment he submitted it to them for approval. Two of them voted against Horwits and Mister Mack waxed indignant. "You have my resignation," he told his glum sons, and stalked out of his office. His retirement lasted for as long as it took the boys to run after him, telling him that on more sober thought they had decided that Horwits was just about the finest public-relations man obtainable—which he is. Mister Mack cocked his head like a reflective crane for a moment and relented.

The old gentleman has no thought of retiring, not even if by some dazzling and dramatic accident he wins the 1948 pennant to crown gloriously his sixty-fourth year in professional baseball. He has gone beyond the stage when a man can lay down his chores of his own volition. The sheer weight of his experience precludes a decision to call it a day. "People ask me if I'm tired of baseball," he said not long ago. "I can only give one answer. There is nothing in baseball I dislike. I'll stay in the game as long as my mind is clear. When I reach the stage when I don't know my business, or trade a .300 hitter for a .200 hitter, then you'll know I'm unfit."

But to his closest associates—his boys, his wife, his traveling secretary and chief minority stockholder, Benjamin Shibe Macfarland, and one or two others—the old man willingly gives the true reason why he'll never quit of his own accord.

"If I did," he says, and his old eyes mist up as he looks around helplessly, "I'd die in two weeks."

By permission, P. F. Collier, 1905

TWO OUT, TWO STRIKES, BASES FULL,

STRUCK OUT!

WITH MANY who are surely better qualified to judge, I believe this
is one of the best baseball pieces ever written.

1924:

Washington Senators 4,
New York Giants 3

—————————————— BILL CORUM ——————————————

Dreams came true in the twelfth—Washington's dream and Walter Johnson's—and when the red September sun dropped down behind the dome of the Capitol the Senators were the baseball champions of the world.

Washington waited twenty-five years for a World Series, but when it came it was the greatest one in history, and the king of pitchers waited eighteen years for the sweetest victory of his career.

For just long enough to beat the Giants, 4 to 3, in the seventh and deciding game the Old Master was the Johnson of old, the Kansas Cyclone, sweeping the proud champions of the National League down to their bitterest defeat.

"The team that won't be beaten, can't be beaten." Today that team was Washington. But the Giants did not deserve to lose. Chance and fate turned against the gray-clad team from the banks of the Hudson, but they went down fighting in the only way they knew and New York may still be proud of them.

Fate made a mark after the name of John McGraw in the eighth and closed the book. It was in that inning the Little Napoleon of the Diamond met his Waterloo. With the dogged, never-say-die Senators an all but beaten team and victory hovering over the Giants' bench, Bucky Harris hit a lucky bounding single over the head of young Lindstrom which scored two runs, tied the count and stemmed the tide that a moment before had been sweeping his team to defeat. It was not a hard hit, nor a clean

one, but it counted and the Giants never quite recovered from it.

When the Senators took the field it was behind the broad shoulders of Walter Johnson, and this time their hero did not fail them. In danger in every one of the four innings that he worked, he rose superbly to every emergency. In each succeeding crisis he became a little more the master, a little more the terrible blond Swede of baseball fable. Twice he struck out Long George Kelly when the game hung by a thread so fine that thousands in the tense, silent throng turned their heads away with every pitch.

Somewhere, perhaps, in that little patch of sunlight that was filtering through the shadowy stands and down in front of the pitcher's mound the once mightiest arm of all was finding the strength to do the thing that twice before had balked it. In those four innings the grand old man struck out five batters, and when his need was direst he was best. Twice he turned McGraw's team back with two runners waiting to score and two other times with one.

In the very first inning that Johnson pitched, Frisch, the second batter to face him, tripled and then stayed on third to fret and fume while the calm Kansan passed Young intentionally, struck out Kelly and then made Meusel roll to the third baseman for the final out.

Again in the tenth, Wilson, first to face him, drew a pass, stayed on first while Jackson fanned and then died in a double play, Johnson to Bluege to Judge.

But it was in the eleventh that Johnson reached his greatest heights. Here it was that McGraw made his most desperate bid for victory. He sent the crippled Heinie Groh up with his bottle bat to hit for McQuillan when the inning began, and Heinie delivered a difficult single to right. Southworth scurried down to first to run for Groh, and no sooner was he there than Lindstrom moved him on to second with a perfect sacrifice bunt. The winning run was on second, there was only one out and Frankie Frisch was at bat.

Here was a situation to make any pitcher quail. That is, any pitcher but Walter Johnson. Frisch was captain of his team, but not of his fate, as it turned out; that was in the big, broad palm of the man he was facing. Up and down went that right arm. There was a prayer on every pitch, but there was something else on them, too. Frisch will tell you that. He swung three times, missed three times and sat down.

But the danger was not over yet. Young and Kelly were still to come. Young came, and went to first on four pitched balls. Kelly came, and went to first on three strikes, but the rest of the Giants went with him, and the Senators came in to bat. Long George had paid dearly for that home run he hit off Johnson last Saturday. He knows now why they call Walter the Old Master.

Once more in the twelfth the Giants put the Big Train in the hole at the start when Irish Meusel singled to right, but this time the lower end of the batting order was up and Wilson fanned, Jackson grounded to Bluege and Gowdy flied to Goslin.

Johnson not only saved the game with his arm, he also helped to win it with his bat. In the tenth he nearly turned the trick all alone. He drove a mighty fly to deep left center, but it lacked a few feet of being long enough for a home run, which would have turned a great game into an epic.

Wilson was under the ball and Sir Walter was out, but not down. He came back in that fierce and final rally in the twelfth. With Miller out on a grounder to Frisch, Gowdy made a $50,000 muff of a foul pop off Muddy Ruel's bat when he stumbled over his mask and let the ball get away from him. It was baseball history repeating itself. McGraw and Christy Mathewson lost the 1912 championship when Fred Snodgrass dropped a fly ball in the tenth.

Granted this reprieve, little Muddy from the Big Muddy hammered a double over third base and Washington's first baseball championship was in the making. Johnson jabbed a hard grounder at Jackson and Travis made the second error of a bad afternoon. Ruel wisely clung to second while Jackson scrambled for the ball.

With first and second occupied, Earl McNeely hit another hopper over Lindstrom that was a twin brother to Harris' hit of the eighth except that it was a little harder and, therefore, a more legitimate hit. As the ball rolled into left Ruel, running as he had never run before, rounded third and charged toward the plate. Meusel, galloping from deep left, picked up the ball, but didn't even throw it. It would have been the proper gesture, but neither one of the Meusel boys are given to gestures.

Irish knew, as did the joy-mad crowd, that the game was over. He kept running on in toward the plate with the ball in his hands. The rest of the Giants stood motionless and stunned and in the next instant the crowd swirled over the field and blotted out the quiet men in gray and leaping ones in white.

Many in the roaring throng that came piling on the field like college boys after the victory of their football team thought that it was Pep Young who carried off the ball that beat the Giants. With two out and two on, in the Senators' half of the eleventh, and Bluege, a dead left-field hitter at bat, McGraw had shifted Young and Meusel to get the faster man into left, but they went back to their regular positions in the twelfth.

This jockeying about of players was typical of the entire game, for it was a battle of wits as well as bats and balls. Manager Harris tried to cross his veteran rival on the New York bench even before the game started. He announced that he would pitch Curley Ogden, a right-hander, and actually sent him to the mound, although he planned to have him pitch to only one batter. The idea was to induce McGraw to name the line-up he had been using against right-handers and then to send Mogridge, a southpaw, to the mound.

The New York manager could, of course, shift his team to meet the change, but if he did he could not change back again if Mogridge was knocked out and Marberry, another right-hander, sent in. In other words, Terry's being named in the line-up actually put him in the game and he could not be withdrawn and then sent back.

Ogden struck out Lindstrom and then started walking toward the Washington bench, but Harris showed himself to be a shrewd leader by calling him back and having him pitch to Frisch also. If Ogden was going to have a great day—and that would have been wholly possible in the face of his record—Bucky wanted to take advantage of it. He worked the same trick in Detroit near the end of the American League race, and successfully, but against the canny McGraw he derived no great benefit from it.

McGraw allowed Terry to stay in until the pinch in the sixth, when he substituted Meusel. Harris met the change by waving in Marberry to replace Mogridge, but Meusel hit the Texas right-hander for a fly that traveled long and far to right and Young scored with the tying run. So while there was no very decisive and far-reaching effect from the strategy one way or the other, what little there was came to McGraw.

Just prior to this, and in the same inning, McGraw had introduced a bit of strategy on his own part which had far more effect on the game. With Young on first, Kelly at bat and Mogridge patently nervous, McGraw called for the hit and run, with the count three balls and one strike on Kelly. The obvious play, of course, would have been to let Kelly take the next one in the hope that it would be a fourth ball. But McGraw seldom does the obvious thing. He figured that Mogridge would try for the heart of the plate, and that was just what Mogridge did. Kelly singled over second and Young easily reached third. It was from that point that he counted on Meusel's fly, and it was smart baseball that had put him there.

From the eighth on both teams were threatening each time they came to bat and any one of a hundred things might have changed the result completely.

"It might have been" were sure to be the saddest words, no matter which team lost.

Many a Washington fan who had more gray hairs in his head tonight than he had this morning could testify to the chances that the Giants had and missed. Time after time any kind of a hit or any kind of a play but the one which was forthcoming would have settled the issue for good and all. When the break came finally, it came to Washington. Washington had waited for it, watched for it, and deserved it, but all the heroes did not wear spotless white.

There was Virgil Barnes of Centerville, Kan., for instance. Virgil proved that while all the great pitchers may come from his state they do not all come to Washington. For seven and two-thirds innings Barnes was a master pitcher. Until Harris hit a long fly, which just did drop over the temporary bleachers wall for a home run in the fourth, the Senators had not got a single ball past the Giant infield. Only three batters faced Barnes in each of the first three innings, four in the fourth, three in the fifth and three in the sixth, and four in the seventh again, making only twenty-three batters to face him in seven innings.

In those seven frames he yielded only three hits, a homer and fluky single by Harris and a single by Goslin. Even in the eighth, when he was taken out, he did not break completely, but he faltered, and that was enough to let the Senators break through and cause his downfall. That blow of Harris', which a high bound and the sun in Lindstrom's eyes helped to make a hit, was the one that ruined him. Until then he had furnished the most brilliant bit of pitching seen in the series. Besides Barnes, there were Frisch, Kelly and Wilson, all three of whom made sparkling plays in the field and timely hits at bat.

But to the victor belong the spoils. When future generations are told about this game they will not hear about Barnes, or Frisch, or Kelly, or even about Harris or McNeely. But the boy with his first glove and ball crowding up to his father's knee, will beg:

"Tell me about Walter Johnson."

ALTHOUGH I have not checked the point, I assume that some time between May 1 and October 10, 1920, the Brooklyn club came to be more popularly known as the Dodgers, rather than the Robins. See the piece on page 33 and now this one, both from *The New York Times*.

Featuring the only unassisted triple play in World Series history—which, with Harry Cross's news sense working correctly as it always did, had to take second billing to the first grand-slam home run in series annals—this has to be accounted one of the most unforgettable World Series games of all time.

1920:
Cleveland Indians 8,
Brooklyn Dodgers 1

HARRY CROSS

THE UNROMANTIC name of Smith is on everybody's lips in Cleveland tonight, for Elmer Smith, the right fielder of Speaker's Indians, accomplished something in the fifth World Series clash this afternoon that is the life ambition of every big league ballplayer. Elmer crashed a home run over the right-field fence with the bases full in the first inning and sent the Indians on their merry way to an 8-to-1 victory over Brooklyn. Fate tried to conceal this lucky boy by naming him Smith, but with that tremendous slap Elmer shoved his commonplace identity up alongside the famous Smiths of history, which include Captain John, the Smith Brothers and the Village Smithy.

This home-run punch which shoved over four runs in a cluster is the first of its kind ever made in a World Series game. Cleveland now has won three games to Brooklyn's two, and an overjoyed city this evening has about come to the conclusion that the championship streamer will float over the proud fifth city of the U.S.A.

While the delirious crowd of more than 25,000 was still rejoicing over Smith's sumptuous smash, Bill Wambsganss broke into the celebration to steal some of Smithy's thunder by accomplishing the first unassisted triple play that has ever whisked a World Series populace up to the heights of happiness.

The crowd was already husky-voiced and nerve-wracked with wild excitement when Wamby started to make baseball history. It seemed as if everything that could happen to make Cleveland's joy complete had happened.

Along in the fifth inning, when Bagby, with a commanding lead behind him, was taking it easy, Kilduff and Otto Miller both made singles and were perched on second and first. Clarence Mitchell, who had succeeded the badly wrecked Burleigh Grimes on the pitching mound, was at bat, and for the first time during the afternoon it looked as if the slipping Robins were going to accomplish something.

Uncle Robbie had evidently wigwagged a sign from the bench for a hit and run play, which means that the runners were expected to gallop just as soon as Mitchell swung his bat. Mitchell connected solidly and jammed a tearing liner over second base. Wamby was quite a distance from second, but he leaped over toward the cushion and with a mighty jump speared the ball with one hand. Kilduff was on his way to third base and Miller was almost within reach of second.

Wamby's noodle began to operate faster than it ever did before. He hopped over to second and touched the bag, retired Kilduff. Then Wamby turned and saw Otto Miller standing there like a wooden Indian. Otto was evidently so surprised that he was glued to the ground, and Wamby just waltzed over and touched him for the third out.

The crowd forgot it was hoarse of voice and close to nervous exhaustion and gave Wamby just as great a reception as it had given Elmer Smith.

Those two record-breaking feats were not all that happened in today's game to make Cleveland feel proud of its baseball club and itself. Not by a long shot! Along in the fourth inning when Grimes was still trying to pitch, Jim Bagby, the Indians' big, slow, lazy boxman, became suddenly inspired and, with two fellow Indians on the bases, soaked a home run into the new bleachers which protrude far out into right center field.

No World Series pitcher has ever received such a humiliating cudgeling as Grimes did this afternoon, for the simple reason that no other pitcher has ever been kept in the box so long after he had started to slip. Uncle Robbie kept him on the mound for three and two-thirds innings and in that time he was badly plastered for nine hits, including two home runs and a triple.

With half a dozen able-bodied pitchers basking in the warm sun, Grimes was kept in the box until he was so badly battered that the game became a joke. Instead of being enormously wealthy in pitchers as Robbie was supposed to be, he became a pauper as far as pitching talent is concerned. When the Indians had the score 7 to o Grimes limped out of the game and Mitchell, who had been faithfully warming up ever since he hit Cleveland, went out to the mound and one more run was the best that the Indians could do off him.

The first inning is one which will ever linger in baseball memory. The Sunday crowd jammed every inch of the park. Strong-lunged young men went through the grandstands with megaphones and implored the fans to give the Indians their vocal and moral encouragement.

The Indians were on their toes and ran back and forth to their positions like a college baseball team. The roar of the faithful followers was like a tonic and Tris Speaker's men reveled in the wonderful reception they received. The thing that was uppermost in their minds was to show the home folks that they appre-

ciated the loyalty, and they showed 'em. It didn't matter that it was a one-sided game and that the Brooklyn club, minus good pitching, looked woefully weak and, with the absence of the injured Jimmy Johnston at third base, was inclined to be panicky. The only thing that mattered was that the more runs the Indians could make the more fun there was in it for the Cleveland fans.

Jamieson was the first Indian to face Burleigh Grimes in the opening inning. He pounded a roller down through Konetchy which was too warm for the Dodger first baseman to handle. Wamby poked another single off Grimes and Jamieson went to second. The crowd chanted a flattering chorus of cheers to Speaker when he came to the plate. The wee bit of a tap which bounded off Tris's bat dropped in the infield and Grimes ran over to pick up the manager's bunt. Grimes slipped as he was about to pick up the ball and he was reclining on his back when he made a useless throw to first. It was a hit, and the bases were loaded with no one out.

The National Boiler Works laboring overtime never made the racket that was now taking place in the ball park. The noise waves echoed all over the city of Cleveland, finally rumbling far out in Lake Erie.

Elmer Smith is at bat. You'll find Smiths here, there and everywhere, so there was nothing about the name to arouse enthusiasm. Elmer took a fond look at the high screen on top of the right-field fence and Grimes began to pitch to him. The three Indians on the bases jumped up and down on their toes impatiently.

Elmer took two healthy swings at the ball and missed, and the next one was wide and he let it waft by. Grimes looked around the bases and saw that he was entirely surrounded by Indians. He was ambushed by the Redskins. He felt that danger lurked in this Smith boy at the bat.

When Grimes hurled the next pitch over, Smith took a mighty blow at the ball and it rose like a bird, went so far up in the air that it looked like a quinine pill.

Jamieson, Wamby and Speaker all took one good look at that rapidly rising ball, then they bent their heads, dug their spikes into the dirt and started to run. Grimes was knocked dizzy. As he looked about him he could see nothing but Indians chasing themselves around in a circle.

Smith, who only a few seconds before was just plain Elmer Smith, had become Home Run

Smith before he trotted as far as second base. When he reached third, he was Hero Smith, and by the time he crossed the plate he was a candidate for a bronze statue in City Square along with General Moses Cleveland, who founded this town, and Tom L. Johnson, who decorated the park just opposite old General Mose.

Manager Speaker, still a young man, yet gray and bald from baseball worries, was waiting at the plate when Smith touched the platter. Around Smith's neck went Tris's arm. Grimes stood out in the pitcher's box stupefied. The other Brooklyn players walked about in a daze and waited for the noise riot to subside.

Grimes was still pitching when the game was resumed. The Cleveland players wondered just what had to be done to a Brooklyn pitcher before he is taken out of the game. However, Grimes became a little better, and the side was retired after Burleigh had been aided by a double play.

Big Ed Konetchy walloped a triple to left center field in the Brooklyn second, with one gone, but when Kilduff hoisted a fly to Jamieson and Koney tried to score after the catch Jamieson chucked him out at the plate with a perfect throw.

This was the first of three double plays which, with Wamby's matchless triple killing, furnished a defense for Bagby's loose flinging that would have prevented any pitcher from losing. The Dodgers got ten hits off Bagby in eight innings and couldn't put over a single run. Peerless defensive work saved him.

Brooklyn's most wasteful inning was the third, when Miller singled and Grimes hit into a double play. Olson and Sheehan both singled. Griffith hoisted a foul to Gardner, ending the inning. There were three smacking singles without a runner getting beyond second base.

Smith got a tremendous cheer when he came to bat in the third inning. There were two down at the time, and he jarred a terrific triple to left center. The smash went to seed because Kilduff tossed Gardner out at first.

The next citizen to be hailed as a hero is lazy James Bagby. No pitcher ever before was pounded for thirteen hits in a World Series and emerged a hero. Jim Bagby, big Sergeant Jim, did it. He pitched what was really a bad game of ball, but when it was over he was proud of it.

Doc Johnston opened the fourth inning with a hit off Grimes's leg. Yes, Grimes is still pitching for Brooklyn. Doc went to second on a passed ball and to third as Sheehan was retiring Sewell at first. Grimes walked O'Neill purposely to get Bagby, and that is just where Jim, the barge, has the laugh on Grimes. Bagby slammed a long drive to right center and Johnston and O'Neill both romped home ahead of Jim amid scenes of wild, barbarous disorder.

When the riot was quelled, Grimes was still pitching for Brooklyn. Does this fellow Grimes stand so strongly with Uncle Robbie that he is never taken out of a game, no time, no place, no how?

Jamieson spanked a roller down to first base, and although three Brooklyn fielders, Grimes, Koney and Kilduff, tried to retire the runner at first, Jamieson was too swift and got a hit for himself out of the confusion. It suddenly dawned upon Manager Robinson that the Indians were hitting Grimes, so he took him out and Mitchell went to the box.

Sheehan, at third, was naturally nervous in his first big game and in the fifth, when Speaker hit a roller to him, Sheehan threw the ball right over Konetchy's head, and Speaker went to second. "Home Run" Smith got a single and Speaker went to third. Gardner cracked a single to center and Speaker crossed the plate with the Indians' last run.

Brooklyn's run came in the ninth inning. Bagby fanned Griffith as a starter, and then, as he listlessly chucked the ball over, Wheat singled to right. Jim was still listless when he threw the ball at Myers, who slapped a single to center which sent Wheat to second. Konetchy hit a mean hopper down through Doc Johnston, the ball bounding out into the field as Wheat scampered home and saved the Dodgers from a shutout.

Brooklyn's stock has taken an awful drop.

BUTTER wouldn't melt in Ty Cobb's mouth—possibly not, at any rate, in 1945, when columnist Daley of *The New York Times* did this one.

A Mild-Mannered Gentleman

ARTHUR DALEY

TY COBB had the reputation of being one of the snarlingest, fightingest ballplayers that the game has ever produced. He denies it all in his present-day mild-mannered fashion. In fact, if you listen to him long enough, you leave with the inescapable conclusion that butter wouldn't melt in his mouth and that the swashbuckling Tyrus Raymond Cobb was the original Casper Milquetoast.

"I never had as many fights as they said," he protests, and then adds, "As far as spiking anyone is concerned, I doubt that I deliberately spiked more than one or two players in the entire twenty-four years I was in the big leagues." The big sissy! It's kind of late to be destroying all those illusions. But let's listen to his story for a moment.

"When I came up to Detroit," he recounts, a dreamy look in his eyes, "I was just a mild-mannered Sunday-school boy. Sam Crawford then was the big dog in the meat house and I was just a brash kid. But, as soon as they started to put my picture in the papers and give me some publicity, the old-timers began to work on me.

"They practically put a chip on my shoulder, hazed me unmercifully and every time I'd put down my hat I'd find it twisted into knots on my return. But now that I look back on it, I think that's a better system than the gentlemanly treatment the rookies get these days. If I became a snarling wildcat, they made me one.

"Another thing was that the manager didn't correct mistakes. He never had the chance. Your teammates climbed all over you first of all. I remember that famous 17-inning game with the Athletics in 1907, the very game that won the pennant for us because we used up three or four of Philadelphia's star pitchers. We should have won in the eleventh, except

that Davey Jones shied away from the crowd and let a ball fall safely for two bases. When he came back to the bench our players were so mad that they practically tore the uniform off his back. That's the way we played ball in those days."

Ty paused and glanced nostalgically out the window. "As for all those stories that I went around spiking people," he continued, "that's nonsense. I tagged a base just with my shoe tip and there are no spikes in the toe of your shoe. Did you ever hear of Cobb getting spiked? No. You just heard of Cobb spiking some of our more illustrious citizens. Look!"

Tyrus Raymond pulled up his trouser legs and displayed the most amazing collection of scars ever seen outside of a dissecting room. "Of course, I never before admitted any of these," he said. "There never was any sense in tipping off the opposition on how black and blue or damaged I was.

"I never tipped them off on anything. Wait a minute. Yes, I did. Remember Billy Sullivan? There was a truly great catcher and I never could steal a base on him. So one time I'm up at bat and I decide to try a little psychology on him because I've absolutely nothing to lose. 'Billy,' I said out of the corner of my mouth, 'if I get on base I'm going down on the second pitch.' He didn't know whether or not to believe me. At any rate, he became rattled and I stole second as promised.

"So the next time I'm at bat, I'm so tickled at the way that system worked that I told him the same thing again." Ty looked a little sheepish. He glanced around as if expecting to see Billy Sullivan peering accusingly over his shoulder and then continued his tale. "I lied to him," he said shamefacedly. "I stole on the first pitch. But, at least, I was one of the very few base runners who ever stole on Sullivan."

Cobb's record of ninety-six stolen bases in a season probably never will be broken, because modern ball has virtually eliminated the steal as a method of progression. Why risk a steal when the next guy is liable to hit one into the seats? His record of having a lifetime batting average of .367 never will be broken either, because a Cobb comes along about once every century.

"There was only one infielder who ever bothered me," he stated. "That was Bobby Wallace. He just straddled the bag and waited for me to come into him—as I had to do. With the rest of them, though, it merely was a case of waiting for the last possible moment before committing yourself. Then you had the initiative, and not he. With the fall-away slide that I worked on and developed, the infielder had nothing more than the tip of a shoe to tag. You could neither spike nor be spiked with that slide, either."

Ty was just as much a student of batting as he was of stealing bases. The great Georgia Peach practiced place hitting so intensively that he always sought the holes left open by infielders covering bases. "The secret of hitting," he explains, "is the stance at the plate, an open stance for pull hitting and a closed one for pushing the ball—just like golf. If you're a left-handed batter, never try to pull on a left-handed pitcher."

But why try to explain Cobb's method of doing things? He was so far beyond the average that what might seem simple and fundamental to him would be out of the reach of the ordinary athlete. The fiery Georgian—pardon me, he is a very meek chap—made so much baseball history that his like never will come again. It's too bad about Cobb, though. Can you picture what a ballplayer he would have been had he only a modicum of fight and spirit in his make-up? Ahem!

GARRETT PRICE

"Strike him out."

DATELINE Detroit . . . May 2, 1939 . . .

2,130

JAMES P. DAWSON

Lou GEHRIG's matchless record of uninterrupted play in American League championship games, stretched over fifteen years and through 2,130 straight contests, came to an end today.

The mighty iron man, who at his peak hit 49 home runs in a single season five years ago, took himself out of action before the Yanks marched on Briggs Stadium for their first game against the Tigers this year.

With the consent of Manager Joe McCarthy, Gehrig removed himself because he, better than anybody else perhaps, recognized his competitive decline and was frankly aware of the fact he was doing the Yankees no good defensively or on the attack. He last played Sunday in New York against the Senators.

When Gehrig will start another game is undetermined. He will not be used as a pinch hitter. The present plan is to keep him on the bench. He may swing into action in the hot weather, which should have a beneficial effect upon his tired muscles.

Meanwhile Ellsworth (Babe) Dahlgren, until today baseball's greatest figure of frustration, will continue at first base. Dahlgren had been awaiting the summons for three years.

It was coincidental that Gehrig's string was broken almost in the presence of the man he succeeded as Yankee first baseman. At that time Wally Pipp, now a business man of Grand Rapids, Mich., was benched by the late Miller Huggins to make room for the strapping youth fresh from the Hartford Eastern League club to which the Yankees had farmed him for two seasons, following his departure from Columbia University. Pipp was in the lobby of the Book Cadillac Hotel at noon when the withdrawal of Gehrig was effected.

"I don't feel equal to getting back in there," Pipp said on June 2, 1925, the day Lou replaced him at first. Lou had started his phenomenal streak the day before as a pinch hitter for Peewee Wanninger, then the Yankee shortstop.

The latest momentous development in baseball was not unexpected. There had been signs for the past two years that Gehrig was slowing up. Even when a sick man, however, he gamely stuck to his chores, not particularly in pursuit of his all-time record of consecutive play but out of a driving desire to help the Yankees, always his first consideration.

What Lou had thought was lumbago last year when he suffered pains in the back that more than once forced his early withdrawal from games was diagnosed later as a gall bladder condition for which Gehrig underwent treatment all last winter.

The signs of his approaching fade-out were unmistakable this spring at St. Petersburg, Fla., yet the announcement from Manager McCarthy was something of a shock. It came at the end of a conference Gehrig arranged immediately after McCarthy's arrival by plane from his native Buffalo.

"Lou just told me he felt it would be best for the club if he took himself out of the line-up," McCarthy said. "I asked him if he really felt that way. He told me he was serious. He feels blue. He is dejected.

"I told him it would be as he wished. Like everybody else I'm sorry to see it happen. I told him not to worry. Maybe the warm weather will bring him around.

"He's been a great ballplayer. Fellows like him come along once in a hundred years. I told him that. More than that, he's been a vital part of the Yankee club since he started with it. He's always been a perfect gentleman, a credit to baseball.

"We'll miss him. You can't escape that fact.

But I think he's doing the proper thing."

Gehrig, visibly affected, explained his decision frankly.

"I decided last Sunday night on this move," said Lou. "I haven't been a bit of good to the team since the season started. It would not be fair to the boys, to Joe or to the baseball public for me to try going on. In fact, it would not be fair to myself.

"It's tough to see your mates on base, have a chance to win a ball game, and not be able to do anything about it. McCarthy has been swell about it all the time. He'd let me go until the cows came home, he is that considerate of my feelings, but I knew in Sunday's game that I should get out of there.

"I went up there four times with men on base. Once there were two there. A hit would have won the game for the Yankees, but I missed, leaving five stranded. Maybe a rest will do me some good. Maybe it won't. Who knows? Who can tell? I'm just hoping."

Gehrig's withdrawal from today's game does not necessarily mean the end of his playing career, although that seems not far distant. When the day comes Gehrig can sit back and enjoy the fortune he has accumulated as a ballplayer. He is estimated to have saved $200,000 from his earnings, which touched a high in 1938, when he collected $39,000 as his Yankee salary.

When Gehrig performed his duties as Yankee captain today, appearing at the plate to give the batting order, announcement was made through the amplifiers of his voluntary withdrawal. A deafening cheer resounded as Lou walked to the dugout, doffed his cap and disappeared in a corner of the bench.

Open expressions of regret came from the Yankees and the Tigers. Lefty Vernon Gomez expressed the Yankees' feelings when he said:

"It's tough to see this thing happen, even though you know it must come to us all. Lou's a great guy and he's always been a great baseball figure. I hope he'll be back in there."

Hank Greenberg, who might have been playing first for the Yanks instead of the Tigers but for Gehrig, said, "Lou's doing the right thing. He's got to use his head now instead of his legs. Maybe that Yankee dynasty is beginning to crumble."

Everett Scott, the shortstop who held the record of 1,307 consecutive games until Gehrig broke it, ended his streak on May 6, 1925, while he was a member of the Yankees. Scott began his string, once considered unapproachable, with the Red Sox. By a strange coincidence, Scott gave way to Wanninger, the player for whom Gehrig batted to start his great record.

With only one run batted in this year and a batting average of .143 representing four singles in twenty-eight times at bat, Lou has fallen far below his record achievements of previous seasons, during five of which he led the league in runs driven home.

Batter's Best Friend

DUANE DECKER

As you settle down in a comfortable chair in front of your TV set for the World Series, take a good look at what the pitcher does when the umpire tosses him that shiny new baseball. Five will get you ten that you'll see exactly this:

The pitcher will take the ball and feel it all over, rub it up and down and sideways, roll it around between the cupped palms of his hands and even stare at it momentarily, like a scientist examining a new species of bug under a microscope.

He doesn't indulge in this hocus-pocus out of superstition, although ballplayers are notoriously full of that. He does it in the dim hope that he'll find some slight flaw in one of the 108 stitches which hold a baseball together. *If he can spot one, no matter how tiny, he'll have gained a secret advantage over the batter.* Even the slightest ridge or indentation resulting from an unskillful stitch in the horsehide cover can be utilized to make his curve ball curve more sharply, his slider slide more furtively, his dipsy-doodle doodle more devastatingly.

However, the odds are several thousand to one that he won't find such a helpful little gimmick in the stitching of the ball. Because, when big-league pitchers face big-league batters they are throwing baseballs put together by big-league stitchers. These last-mentioned big leaguers all happen to be women.

In a big wing of the A. G. Spalding and Brothers' factory, located in Chicopee, Mass., all the baseballs used in both the major leagues are turned out.

The fabulous salaries and careers of the Fellers and DiMaggios depend on the care and cunning of 300 New England ladies whose work is something to watch. The stitcher seats herself before a small, cup-shaped vise which comes about level with her lap. Then she picks up two horsehide panels precision-cut in the shape of crude dumbbells, fitted over the round skeleton of the baseball and stapled into place.

She then clamps the ball into the vise so that just the top third of it peeps out.

Next, she takes two sturdy needles (double-o harness needles from England) and strings them with the traditional waxed red thread of all official baseballs. She jabs both needles into and through the machine-cut holes of the panels and pulls them through by violently flinging her arms back. This arm-flinging makes the sewing circle quite a startling sight when all 300 ladies are hard at work.

When she finishes stitching the visible part of the ball, she loosens the vise with a foot pedal and turns the ball over further. (She has to turn it about eight times before the baseball is completely stitched.)

Machines never could stitch a baseball properly and they probably never will be able to because the porous horsehide is so flexible that it takes the human eye to gauge just where it needs to be pulled tight and where it needs more leeway.

A rookie stitcher goes through a ten-week apprenticeship during which she works under close supervision. Her output rises slowly. However, she is sure of a guaranteed minimum even if she doesn't turn out a perfect baseball all day. Once she produces better than 34 baseballs a day she gets a piece-work bonus. An extremely fast stitcher can turn out 75 baseballs in an eight-hour day, but 50 a day is nearer a general average. The best stitchers aren't necessarily the fastest; where a real champ gets only two per cent rejection, the average is around four per cent.

It's probably not too surprising to discover that all 300 members of the Chicopee sewing circle are rabid baseball fans, but it's curious that the vast majority are American Leaguers. Most root for the Boston Red Sox, and most of the rest root for the New York Yankees. When big-league ballplayers visit the plant, as they occasionally do, work comes almost to a dead stop.

But despite the fact that this exclusive little band of 300 ladies turn out *all* the baseballs that are belted around the big stadiums, few of them ever get to see a big-league game. "They simply haven't time to go to ball games," Foreman Doug Marcus explained. "They're too busy stitching you-know-what."

JEFF KEATE

Courtesy *Sport* Magazine. ©

"Just give him anything—he's a sucker for a thrown ball."

WHAT does the catcher tell the pitcher? Seven times out of ten, it's, "For crissakes, they're stealing our signals." Details:

Baseball's Counterspies

BOB DEINDORFER

SOME forty years ago a brash convivial personality named Dan Murphy hired himself out to the Philadelphia Athletics at prevailing big league wages, meaning not much at all. As a batter he hit the ball with occasional fervor and out in the field he caught the normal quota of tall wind-blown flies without getting brained. Nobody, not even Murphy, ever ranked him much more than a good reliable outfielder, hardly a prospect for the Hall of Fame yet hardly a prospect for baseball's lower depths either.

Old Dan Murphy never amounted to much in a lasting record book sense except by way of illustration. At the end of his playing days he shifted from the competitive to the reflective phase of the game with only minor adjustments. Instead of leasing a pool hall or a filling station or going back home to the wrong end of a plow when his reflexes started to blur and he used up the last of his legs, Murphy continued spending his summers in Philadelphia, as a coach instead of a player because of one rare and strategic skill. Through long practice he had learned how to steal the signals rival teams used for confidential communication purposes.

For the next few years Murphy stole enemy signs, literally hundreds of times, and stole them at considerable profit to the Athletics, too. In a silky, subtle specialty noted for all sorts of harebrained intrigues, his own most productive technique seemed refreshingly simple. On a good clear day there was Dan, perched on a rooftop across the street behind center field, focusing his binoculars on the rival catcher and decoding the finger exercises that pass for memoranda between catcher and pitcher.

The project worked out rather well for the Philadelphia hitters who grew stiff-necked peering out over center field to learn from Murphy precisely what the fellow right behind them just said to the pitcher, fast ball or curve? After an inning or so he cracked even the most elaborate rival batting codes and—often by slowly crossing or spreading his legs—let the hitters know what to expect. Batters just naturally have a better chance of ambushing a fast ball if they can call it by name while the pitcher is still whirling through his windup.

One of the memories old-timers relish the most concerns Dan Murphy and a particular case of attempted larceny that didn't quite pan out. At the time Dan was relaying stolen signs back to the hitters by spinning a large weather vane on the rooftop one direction or the other according to the pitch. In the fifth inning he tried to spin the weather vane to read curve when an abrupt, almost cyclonic, gale insisted it was a fast ball.

Yet what made Murphy a really unique character in a hungry hardrock big league era was the blunt fact that he had become the first known case of anyone employed as a regular team coach on the basis of his ability to pick the competition's pockets. Baseball's front office, which includes a traditionally strict accounting department, officially recognized on payday the high market value of an exceptionally talented espionage specialist.

In many ways the rare experts in the field have had a pretty good thing ever since. From time to time a few players with no known managerial talent have signed on as major league coaches or even minor league managers. Some others have hung on in the big time as players beyond their normal span while slightly heavier hitters and stronger pitchers fallowed down on the farm teams. Why? Simply because they knew how to steal enemy secrets.

Even the most attentive fans know little about what has come to be a brisk subsidiary part of the more publicized, more obvious major league communications system. The visible charms of a gymnastic double play or the arc of a long booming hit to the stadium wall mask a silent jittery undercover war out on the diamond. And baseball's counterspies, bringing an incredible amount of ingenuity into play, win games, series and even an occasional pennant for the owners who pick up their paychecks.

All season long wise and resourceful professionals have artfully studied the competition's fraternal manual alphabet patiently searching for leaks. Out of a maze of approximately 200 signs passed across the field every day by the rival team, they successfully intercept anywhere from one to a dozen. Through shrewd, revealing techniques, tight coordination and sometimes a glaring slip by an enemy signalman, these largely unsung specialists translate stolen signs into hits and runs without ever lifting a bat.

"I'd hate to guess how many hits result from coaches calling the pitches for batters ahead of time," says Fresco Thompson, general manager of the Brooklyn Dodgers. "We seldom make book on it but I can say one thing. Stolen signs win a lot of ball games."

The popularity of this seamy pickpocket practice is such that anyone who scratches his nose comes under suspicious scrutiny. Was it a good honest itch or a signal? At times some third base coach intently trying to pick up the rival catcher's signs is himself the object of wide-eyed study by other experts who wonder what he might be saying to a base runner. The tangled cross currents of big league espionage focus on every sign except the advertising poster up on the right field fence.

An occasional potluck interception ruffles even the lowliest team playing out a dreary string toward an eighth-place oblivion, but what really rubs the calloused nerves of the manager is a consistent pattern of ambush. To prevent any further diamond robberies, every team has a fateful emergency signal to be handed down from on high at critical junctures during the game. The signal serves as an SOS to all hands. In mute and urgent tones it says that the competition has broken the code and so let's try another one as of right now. Last season a superior counterspy forced a team to change signs three times in one game.

Hank Greenberg got caught in one of those switches one day and it almost cost him his head. Detroit's Del Baker had been reading Cleveland battery signs with great success most of the afternoon. Up stepped Greenberg to the plate and Baker called down to him "Hit it now" for a curve ball. Anticipating the curve, Hank spread his feet and leaned out over the plate. What neither one knew was that Cleveland, aware of too many interceptions, had just altered its code by interchanging the curve and fast ball signs. Hank sprawled in the dirt to escape a pitch whistling at his features at roughly 90 mph. After the game he politely thanked Baker for all the help and said he'd blankety-blank steal his own signs in the future.

No matter how many blokes drawing big league paychecks might mysteriously dwell on their own occult powers, only a handful of men qualify as legitimate members of the craft. Partly by instinct and partly by long patient training they consistently steal enough signs to give their teams a valuable, often critical, edge. Baker, Bob Ramazotti, Terry Moore, Bill McKechnie, Frank Crosetti, Hardrock Johnson, Casey Stengel, Paul Schreiber, Red Smith and Mike Sandlock all read enemy secrets with what amounts to a calculating nonchalance.

Yet even fellow burglars admit that the best set of tools for sign-stealing inhabit the skull of Charley Dressen, a loud, raspy, thoroughly likable man who manages the Brooklyn Dodgers. Any time Charley is ever between jobs, as they say, he can pick up a big league coaching berth for as much as $15,000 on the strength of his reputation as the most effective counterspy in the business. Charley does not quarrel with this view.

"Last year I called pitches and stole signs which accounted for nine wins," he said not so long ago. Since the Dodgers won the National League flag by only six games the inference was plain.

It is one of the most poetic ironies of the game that Dressen, for all his ability, was hoist with his own petard at the conclusion of his long and tiring season of larceny in the National League. After three games in the World Series last fall Brooklyn led the Yankees two games to one, and then look what happened! Halfway through the fourth game, one run down, Brooklyn moved Andy Pafko around to third base and Gil Hodges to second on a sacrifice. The clawing series tension mounted as Andy jiggled off the bag only 90 feet short of a tying run.

In the third base coaching box Dressen, his intellect humming smoothly, decided to let hitter Joe Black squeeze Pafko home with the big run. Here's how it's supposed to work: The moment the pitcher releases the ball the runner starts down the base path toward home while the hitter attempts to bunt the pitch somewhere—almost anywhere—to keep it out of the catcher's hands for a tagout at the plate.

Blessed with big league imaginations as well as big league arms and legs, Yankee players realized how circumstances suggested a Brooklyn squeeze. Aside from the infield playing in tight, though, there was little they could do—unless someone learned the exact pitch on which the Dodgers planned to squeeze Pafko on home. The count on Black read one ball, one strike.

Dressen nervously went through all the fiddling gestures of a coach, rubbing his hands together, pulling at the bill of his cap, slapping his thigh, kicking the dust around, hitching at his belt. Both Black and Pafko watched closely as he abruptly gave them what he had considered exclusively a Dodger sign. For only a moment he had put one hand to his throat.

Reynolds' right arm spun around and let the pitch go. Down the base path, high-tailing it for home, came Pafko. Then abruptly the antique squeeze play blew up in Brooklyn's face.

For Dodger fans the next few split seconds took on the odd, distorted aspects of a nightmare. Reynolds' one-one pitch was a blazing fast ball aimed low and outside, just beyond the normal strike zone. Black lunged for the ball, trying desperately to get his bat on it before it plunked into Yankee catcher Yogi Berra's big glove. Pafko never had a chance to score.

To sour, let-down players slumped in the Brooklyn dugout, and to a few of the more perceptive spectators in the stands, it was plainly a case of enemy sabotage. They didn't know exactly how it happened, but the pressure of the game had dimmed what is usually an acute businesslike memory. In passing the sign, Dressen had overlooked only one thing, a player named Martin; Billy, 2B, New York Yankees. Several years before, out at Oakland in the Pacific Coast League, the two had worn the same style monkeysuits, Dressen as team manager, Martin as one of the infielders.

"So when I looked over to the coaching box and saw Charley go to his throat I knew right away," Martin recalls now. "It was the same old squeeze sign he used back in Oakland. I signaled Berra and he passed it along to Reynolds. All Allie had to do was waste a pitch outside and that was that."

From the looks of things Martin may some day develop the skills of an authentic virtuoso but that one was strictly a blunder marked off against Dressen. Habitual sign-stealing calls for something more than a fortunate flicker of memory and one season as lodge brothers back in a vagabond past. To many professionals, it amounts to a genuine form of art.

For obvious security reasons the few participants maintain a tight closed-mouth policy when it comes to details. They have spent too many hours, too many seasons sharpening their own bizarre talents to say anything at all except in a vague general way. Asking one of them which rival pitchers, catchers and coaches he reads the best—and how—is something like asking a wise old detective who first tipped him off to the murderer.

Lefty O'Doul, almost a landmark in the coast league and one of the best of the species, goes to some lengths simply so he won't be misunderstood. His own ballplayers, often awed to a point of inquiry by one of his baffling interceptions, hear a rambling long-winded spiel the text of which seldom varies: "I can't tell you how I do it because these tricks are my stock in trade and it would be like taking tools away from me and besides you might be traded to some other team next year so I won't tell you a thing."

In general, though, sign-stealing comes down to the same old basic entrance requirements necessary in any other branch of cloak-and-dagger work. At the least a prospect must develop keen powers of observation, a swift photographic memory and a flexible catch-all mind. Two and two, if they happen to be the number of fingers a catcher shows his pitcher, sometimes makes a curve ball as well as four.

Sign-stealers are always on the lookout for what may abruptly show through as regular systematic patterns. After studying a rival third-base coach most of the afternoon, mentally cataloguing his mannerisms and any corresponding team strategy, the counterspy suddenly hits on a vital hit-run sign through a laborious process of elimination.

A standard trick of boiling down coaching

signs sounds like a witless loudspeaker tuneup. In the shelter of the dugout two players sit side by side coordinating four eyes in an effort to break the enemy code with a base runner on first. One watches the third base coach and delivers a running commentary while the other focuses on the base runner. Their dialogue, covering every motion the rivals make, runs something like this:

"He's looking away," says the man covering the base runner.

"He's rubbing his shirt," says the one covering the coach.

"He's still looking away."

"He's cupping his hands."

"Now he's looking toward third."

"He's hitching his belt."

"He's still looking toward third."

"He's wiping his face."

"Now he's looking away."

What they obviously try to learn is a sequence of the coach's gestures during the crucial time the base runner looked over toward him presumably for instructions. If in this particular case the runner went down on the next pitch—and less than a half dozen big league swifties are given carte blanche on the base paths—hitching the belt or wiping the face must spell out "steal."

A really good man has two possible opportunities to read pitches from a coaching box. If the catcher doesn't quite hide his signs between his knees behind the glove a spy will take the instructions right along with the pitcher and then pass them along to his batter.

Sometimes a certain grip on the ball or a muscular tightening will show an attentive coach what the pitcher plans to throw next.

But the victims have come up with an answer for that one as long as they occupy the dugout behind third base.

Utility players sitting on the bench often tune up in loud, full voices any time it looks as though the coach might yell instructions down to his batter.

This effective jamming device, drowning out standard "Let's hit one," "Come on now," or "Rally" code expressions, has cost many batters the tips they could exploit for maybe two bases off the left-field fence.

Old reliable Tom Henrich, then playing for the Yankees, credits an accurate tip with one of the longest home runs he ever hit—although he didn't bother to split his gift carton of cigarets with his collaborator after the

game. Monte Stratton was pitching for the White Sox with his usual aplomb until Art Fletcher, a coach, read the catcher's request for a fast ball.

Just before Stratton let it go Fletcher yelled in to Henrich. Tom pulled his bat around in an awful arc and the ball was last seen somewhere over Yonkers.

Much as managers may worry about intercepted signals collapsing the smooth flow of coordinated strategy during the game, they face another hazard too. The practice of using signs which team members must commit to memory presents constant dangers. The arrangement satisfies everyone except for an occasional Alibi Ike personality who, unable to recollect even his own home number, would probably write an explanatory set of crib notes on his flannel breeches if he could only write.

"If you do get my signs," one manager told a rival sign-stealer, "then you're a lot better than some of my own players."

For a long time now unpublicized counterspies has been robbing the competition blind. Only rarely do things reach a point where suggestions of the practice drift out of the clubhouse shadows onto the sports pages.

But for all the long hours of locker room espionage conferences, the study of tips and possible enemy codes, the interrogation of an expatriate outfielder bailed off another club and the specialists hired on the basis of rare talents, these fleeting references seem ridiculously sparse.

One of the last occurred in the summer of 1949 in what was otherwise a normal season. In mid-August someone hollered cops to the effect that the Cleveland Indians hid a utility infielder up in the center-field scoreboard with a pair of long-range glasses. It was a new twist to an old trick of which many men, including John McGraw, had been accused. The infielder stole signs from an enemy catcher 450 feet away and shouted to a caretaker standing under the scoreboard who relayed them to Indian hitters by crossing or spreading his legs.

Bill Veeck, a colorful type who keeps one eye on his ball club and the other on his five or six brass bands, fireworks displays, hog callers, glockenspiel artists and miscellaneous vaudeville, was stopping in Cleveland that year as the team president. In loud indignant tones he emphatically denied the whole story.

Maybe so. But Veeck overlooked a reliable source of information. Players who wear Cleveland uniforms seldom wear them forever and are sold or traded to other teams under the free enterprise system which is known as baseball's reserve clause.

The backslid Indians talked, and while they talked in whispers and not for publication by name and number, what they said added up to one thing: Cleveland had used its scoreboard peeping Tom for a long time.

Shocking? Not at all. In one way or another, so has everyone else. And as long as baseball counterspies can steal the enemy signs that account for hits and runs and plug defensive holes at the right times, winning games and pennants, the big leagues will continue listing organized larceny as simply another business expense.

VIRGIL PARTCH

Courtesy *True, The Man's Magazine.* ©

"Watch it . . . he's pretty wild."

RICHARD DONOVAN's profile of Satchel Paige appeared in *Collier's* in 1953, when Paige was with the St. Louis Browns, and the reader will want to take this time element into consideration. You may also observe that this is the longest piece in the book. That is because it is too good to cut.

The Fabulous Satchel Paige

———————— **RICHARD DONOVAN** ————————

MR. SATCHEL PAIGE, the lank and languid patriarch, raconteur and relief pitching star of the St. Louis Browns, fairly vibrated with dignity and satisfaction as he strolled around the St. Louis railroad station one recent evening. To begin with, his physical tone was splendid—no stomach gas, store teeth resting easy, plenty of whip in his pitching arm. More important, he was in a powerful moral position.

Because of an error in reading his watch, Mr. Paige had arrived almost an hour early for the train that was to take the Browns to Chicago for a series of games with the White Sox. Never before in nearly thirty years of baseball had Paige, called by many of history's greatest pitchers the greatest pitcher who ever lived, been early for a train or anything else. It gave him an uneasy, but exceedingly righteous, feeling.

As he strolled past the baggage stand, a police officer tapped his shoulder. "What's your name?" he asked, dispensing with preliminaries.

"Leroy Paige," said Paige, surprised.

"How old are you?"

Satchel pondered; it was a question he had heard many times before.

"Well, now," he said guardedly, "people says different things. I'd judge between thirty and seventy."

"Is that so?" said the policeman, his eyes narrowing. "Just get into town?"

"Oh, I'm in and out, in and out."

"What're you out of lately?" asked the officer.

"California," said Paige, referring to his re-cent participation in the Browns' spring training.

"And what were you doing in California?"

"Playing," sighed Paige.

The officer was reaching for his handcuffs when Browns catcher Les Moss arrived on the scene. "What's he done?" asked Moss.

"We're looking for a murder suspect," the officer replied triumphantly, "and I think we've got him."

"How old is this suspect?"

"Twenty-two," said the cop.

Moss grinned, and Paige swelled visibly. "Twenty-two!" the pitcher exulted. "You hear that?"

People, as Paige truthfully said, say different things about his age, but not for twenty years or more had anyone suggested that the count might be less than twenty-five. In fact, the usually forgetful Paige knew (to his sorrow, for it had cost him a $500 wager to find out) that he had been firing his hard one in the Negro Southern Association at least as early as 1926—or five years before the officer's murder suspect was born.

Apprised of these facts, the policeman retired. But from that night to the present, Paige, whose true age undoubtedly lies somewhere between forty-five and fifty-three, has belabored his teammates with accounts of the adventure. "Twenty-two," the youthful-looking Paige says on these occasions, casting up his eyes. "That's what the polices thought I was. Imagine."

Lately, however, it has been noticed that Paige's delight at being mistaken for a youth by the officer has vied with uneasiness at not being recognized by the man. "He probably thought I was passed on," he has been heard to grumble. There are many fans in the country who actually believe Paige is passed, and that irritates him. Even more aggravating are those who stubbornly accuse him of impersonating himself.

Paige recently was asked to make a round of bars in Harlem with two reporters who introduced him to patrons and recorded their reactions. Twelve of the twenty-three people approached told him to his face that he was too young to be the original Satchel. From this experience alone, it is clear that, somewhere along the line, that rarest of human conditions has crept up on Mr. Paige. He has become a legend.

That is an exasperating situation for Paige, who, before the 1953 season was a week old, had helped save three games for the Browns and who last year was probably the most valuable relief hurler in the American League (12 wins, 10 games saved, 10 losses).

Judging by his early-season performance, his fifth year in the majors may be his best.

"I'm making no predictions," his manager, Marty Marion, commented recently, "but I wouldn't be surprised if Satch crowded the 20-game-win mark this year."

Legend aside, the Browns rate Paige mostly in terms of present performance. His side positions of morale builder, historian and minstrel may have made him the most popular player on the club. But more important is his earned-run average, which was 3.07 last year—good enough to lead the Browns' regulars.

Not that the legend isn't useful. Paige is still one of the half-dozen great draws in baseball. Thousands of fans who first got wind of him in the mid-twenties now crowd parks in uneasy fascination, for who knows when he may come apart before their horrified eyes, like the one-hoss shay? It is a moving sight to see the old gentleman rise from his special canopied contour chair in the bull pen and creep out to the mound with his interminable, haste-makes-waste walk. It is even more moving to see him strike out highly advertised sluggers when he finally gets there.

Any sight of Mr. Paige is arresting, in fact. Rising six feet three and a quarter inches above size 12s, on semi-invisible legs, with scarcely 180 pounds strung between foot and crown, he sometimes seems more shadow than substance. His face mystifies many fans who peer at it to discover the secrets of time. Head on, it seems to belong to a cheerful man about thirty. From another angle, it looks melancholy and old, as though Paige had walked too long in a world made up exclusively of pickpockets. From a third angle, it seems a frontispiece for the great book of experience, with expressions of wisdom, restrained violence, cunning and easy humor crossing it in slow succession.

"We seen some sights, it and I," says Paige of his face.

Inside Paige, conditions are even more confusing. He faces batters, crowds, TV cameras or whatever, with the regal calm of a Watusi chieftain; yet his nervous stomach shows signs of long and severe emotional tension. He is a congenital AWOL, missing appointments, practice and, on a couple of occasions, games without much excuse ("My feet told me it was gonna rain," he explained after failing to show for a Red Sox game). He is one of the last surviving totally unregimented souls. Contracts box him in; off-field demands on his time make him jumpy; long stays in one place give him nervous stomach. With ballplayers, he is the soul of ease and friendliness; with reporters, people after him for public appearances, promoters of one kind and another, he is wary, abrupt or sullen.

When it is recalled that he had to pitch out most of his best years on cow pastures because of big baseball's color line, and that every time he pitched he was expected to win or else, Paige's more antic attitudes are easy to understand. Now that he's up there, it is also understandable that he should feel opposed to being called a legend. Legends are tricky. On this point, however, Paige should feel entirely at ease. For underneath all the mythology lies a fact. Paige threw, and occasionally he still throws, what was probably the fastest ball ever to leave the hand of man. That is the main and enduring reason for his having been raised to the supernatural.

There are other good reasons, of course. Although records of his career are lost, forgotten or twisted by generations of sports writers, it is reasonably certain that he pitched twenty-two years of organized sand-lot, semipro or Negro League ball (about one and a half lifetimes for the average pitcher) before he ever ascended to the majors, and he has been in that high company almost five years. Although he may be the oldest man on record to perform regularly in the big leagues, last year he was invited to play in the All-Star game. Year upon year, he has pitched summer (over most of the

NORMAN ROCKWELL

THE THREE UMPIRES: The original of this *Saturday Evening Post* cover hangs in the Hall of Fame at Cooperstown, New York.
© 1949 by The Curtis Publishing Co.

WILLARD MULLIN

THE PHANTOM DOUBLE PLAY

Everything that has made Willard Mullin of the New York *World-Telegram and Sun* one of the great illustrators of our time can be

found in the following spread which he drew for *Sport* Magazine. Here is why the typewriter, as a journalistic weapon, never quite replaced the pen.

... by Mullin

...THE RUNNER DASHES FOR SECOND....

...THE SHORTSTOP TAKES THE BALL... TOSSES TO SECOND...

...THE SECOND BASEMAN, WHO HAS CROSSED THE BAG **BEFORE** HE GOT THE BALL "COMPLETES THE **D.P.**" TO FIRST!

Y'R OUT!

THE DOUBLE PLAY IS ONE OF THE MOST EXCITING PLAYS IN THE GAME... AND WHEN TURNED IN BY SUCH MASTERS AS **JOE GORDON** AND **LOU BOUDREAU** OF THE INDIANS IT IS A THING OF REAL BEAUTY...

....LET'S NOT CHEAPEN IT WITH THE PHANTOM PHONIES...

FICTION IS STRANGER THAN TRUTH...

St. Louis Browns at bat against Detroit Tigers . . . August 19, 1951. Ten years after it was written, James Thurber's story about a midget in baseball (see page 339) comes true!

Wide World

United States and Canada) and winter (in California and Central and South America), and has pulled in more customers than Babe Ruth.

When historians meet, the matter of Paige's performance over the years is often the subject of mettlesome debate. It seems certain that Paige has worked a record total of at least 2,500 ball games in his life, often pitching 125 games a year, frequently working five to seven days a week without rest. He has won around 2,000 of those games, it is estimated, including some 250 shutouts and 45 no-hitters. In one month in 1935, he pitched 29 days in a row against smart hitters with but one loss; in four winter seasons (1932 to 1936), often playing against the best of the Negro leaguers and various off-season combinations of major-league all-stars, he lost but four games.

For some twenty years Paige was booked as a solo star, wearing a uniform with "Satchel" across the shirt, and playing with any team that could dig up $500 to $2,000 for three innings of his work. His travel average was 30,000 miles per year, and his earnings, in some years, $35,000. He was advertised as "Satchel Paige, World's Greatest Pitcher, Guaranteed to Strike Out the First Nine Men." Either he performed as advertised or he took side streets back to his hotel.

The Browns, who now have the legend as well as the man under contract, sometimes aren't sure whether it is a disadvantage or a benefit. On the disadvantage side, Paige's presence often tends to make opposing teams gun for early scores. Whenever the Yankees start to take the Browns too lightly, for example, Yankee manager Casey Stengel begins to pace up and down in front of the bench, pointing toward Paige warming up, and intoning: "Get the runs now! Father Time is coming!"

On the benefit side, rookie hitters, their little heads stuffed with stories of Paige's fast ball, are often retired flailing when they get nothing but floaters, slow curves and bloopers from the old gentleman. Many seasoned hitters are even more delightful to Paige because they are convinced he has lost his blinding speed and are laying for the soft one. These fellows seem perpetually outraged when the ball, delivered with the same motion Paige uses for his cute stuff, blazes across the sound barrier.

Once last season, Walt Dropo, Detroit's giant first baseman, swung embarrassingly wide of two Paige pitches, lost his head and loudly accused him of showboating. For reply, Paige threw a vicious fast ball.

Dropo swung so hard that he whirled around, ending in an odd, stooped position with the seat of his pants pointing toward the stands.

"My, my," clucked Paige, reproachfully. "Talk about showboatin'."

The anxious desire of most hitters, old and new, to drive him from the mound is regarded by Paige with fatherly amusement. Hitters have been trying it for approximately thirty years. As his legend grew, he became an individual target, like an old Western gun fighter whose reputation had gone out before him. Every hot-eyed bush kid, burning for immortality around the feed store, was fired up to knock him off as he rode through.

"Bangin' around the way I was, playing for guarantees on one team after another that I never heard of, in towns I never seen before, with players I didn't know and never saw again, I got lonesome," says Paige. "People didn't come to see the ball game. They came to see me strike out everybody, all the time. Occasionally I didn't."

One such breakdown took place in Union Springs, Alabama, one steaming Sunday in 1939. Paige had ridden all night in a bus, and had holed up at a hotel for a few hours' sleep before game time. He overslept, but it made little difference since the game was a social occasion and it was considered gross to arrive much before the third inning.

When Paige appeared, red-eyed and dragged out, in the middle of the fourth, the folks were just settling themselves, waving to friends, talking, sweating, looking everywhere but at the field.

"Then," says Paige, "I went in and it got quiet."

He went to work as usual and retired the first five men in order. Then, with the nonchalance of a seasoned barnstormer, he turned and waved the outfielders off the field. The crowd rose with a roar.

"I laughed to see it," Paige says. "I was still laughing when a little, no-account-looking fella come up, took that big, greasy swing and put my fast ball where my left fielder formerly was."

Paige sighed heavily at the memory. "The polices escorted me from the place as the little man crossed home," he said. "Without my guarantee."

Country boys were not the only ones seized with intimations of immortality after hitting Paige. In 1935, Joe DiMaggio, who was to go up to the Yankees the next year, got a single off Satchel and immediately lost all doubts about how he would fare in the majors.

Paige has forgotten this game, along with a couple of thousand others, but Oakland, California sports writers have not. At the time, DiMaggio was playing around the Bay Area with an off-season team of major-league all-stars. Yankee scouts, who wished to see how their new find reacted to serious fire, finally got hold of Paige, who was taking the sun in Los Angeles. Paige was willing, after hearing about the guarantee, and started north with his team, composed entirely of Ebel Brooks, catcher for the New York Black Yankees of the Negro National League.

In Oakland, Paige found three local semipro players, filled out the roster with high-school boys and gazed solemnly at the terrifying line-up of major-league talent. Then he proceeded with the business of the day, which was to fan fifteen, allow three hits in ten innings and lose the game, two to one, when his youths, possibly rendered hysterical by the reputation of the opposition, threw to the winds the three balls that came their way. With a man on third in the tenth inning, DiMaggio, who had struck out twice and fouled out once in his previous official times at bat, finally hit a hopper which Paige lost in the shadows of dusk. One ex-Yankee scout remembers sending a telegram east: DIMAGGIO ALL WE HOPED HE'D BE. HIT SATCH ONE FOR FOUR.

Paige, whose memories of names, dates and faces tend to blend in the haze of time, is always interested to learn of such past feats from archivists in the various towns he visits. But he is essentially a forward-looking man, besides being a seasoned raconteur, sage, wit and student of the human race.

As a guest of the Second International Gerontological Congress, held in St. Louis in 1951, Paige was almost as interested in the gerontologists as they were in him. The doctors had gathered to report on their studies of the effects of age upon the human body. "They heard there was a man ninety years old playing major-league baseball in the United States," says Paige, "so, naturally, we had to meet."

The doctors interested Paige because he had the impression that only one of them spoke English. "They was all from Venice [Vienna]," he explains. Everything about Paige interested the doctors—his legs, which resemble golf-club shafts, his great feet, his stringy chest and neck muscles. When they got to his right arm,

there was acclaim and astonishment.

"Most of you could be between thirty-five and fifty-five," translated the English-speaking doctor, tensely, "but your arm—" the doctor hesitated—"your arm doesn't seem to be a day over nineteen."

"I just explained to the gentlemen," Paige says, "that the bones running up from my wrist, the fibius, which is the upper bone, and the tiberon, which is the lower bone, was bent out, making more room for my throwing muscles to move around in there. I attributed most of my long life, and so on and so forth, to them two bones. The gentlemen was amazed to hear about that."

The doctors did not examine Paige's head, which is a pity, for there is enough in it to go around the average infield. He is a mountain of information on hunting dogs, expensive cars, jazz, Central American dictators, quartet singing, cameras, Kansas City real estate, Missouri River catfish, Indian maidens, stomach powders, mules and other matters. Whenever the Browns gather in a railroad club car, Paige is generally in the middle, spreading light on such matters as the futility of spring training under men like Rogers (Rajah) Hornsby, the Browns' manager the first part of last season.

"With Mr. Hawnsby, it's all runnin'," Paige told some listeners recently. "Now, I don't generally run at all, except for the showers, because of the harmful effects. I believe in training by rising gently up and down from the bench. But old Mahjong had me flyin' around, shakin' my legs and carryin' on until I very near passed. Now, what did all that do for my arm?"

Despite his sharp observance of many things, Paige's coaches complain that he does not look closely enough at the faces of the men batting against him. According to St. Louis sports announcer Bud Blattner, for example, switch-hitter Mickey Mantle hit a left-hand home run off Paige his first time up in one Yankee-Browns contest last year, then changed over and batted right-handed from there on. All the rest of the game, Paige kept asking: "Where is that boy done me the injury?"

Chicago first baseman Ferris Fain has an explanation for the confusion Mantle created. "Paige always seems to be looking at my knees. I think he recognizes batters by their stance."

Besides his difficulty in identifying his opponents, Paige is said to suffer from a couple of delusions—that he is swift on the base paths and that he is a powerful hitter. Paige runs like an unjointed turkey, except when covering a bunt, at which time he runs like a jointed turkey. (When last checked, his major-league fielding average was 1.000.) As for his hits, he bunches them. He got five hits in 1952, three fifths of them in one 17-inning game against the Senators. Paige came on in the eleventh with the score 2-2 and, besides holding Washington hitless for five and two-thirds innings, got three singles, the last of which drove Joe DeMaestri home with the winning run. In gratitude and astonishment, owner Bill Veeck bought him a new suit.

Paige's uncertainty about names, while confusing to his audiences, rarely bothers him; he invents reasonable approximations of the original handles. Sitting in the trophy room of one of his two large brick houses in Kansas City a while ago, he recalled the tension Mark Griffin (Clark Griffith, owner of the Senators) must have felt in that 17-inning game. Reminiscence took him back a piece and he called up some of the great pitchers he had known. Bob Rapid (Feller) and ol' Homer Bean (Dizzy Dean) were among the best, he said. His memories of Grover (Big Train) Cleveland (a composite of Grover Cleveland Alexander and Walter Johnson) were vague, but he was positive about the hurling characteristics of Tom Lemons (Cleveland's Bob Lemon) and The Actor (ex-Brownie Gene Bearden of Chicago, who has been in two movies).

Hitters loom larger in Paige's mind, naturally. Josh Gibson, late home-run king of the Negro leagues, is the best batsman he ever faced, he says, with Detroit's Charley Gehringer next, and Larry Doby, Cleveland's stylish and cultivated outfielder, third. DiMaggio, with whom Paige never had much trouble, is also well remembered, probably as a social gesture. So is Boston's Ted Williams, now of the U. S. Marines.

Now that Paige is getting on toward evening, reporters are constantly prying into him for treasures of the past. Paige is discomfited by this curiosity, for he claims to be only forty-five and the questions hint at retirement.

"Who's gonna straighten out 2,500 ball games in my head?" he inquired indignantly a few weeks ago. "How many cow pastures you played on, Satchel? they wanta know. How many bus rides you took? Who put the spike scars on your shinbone? Why is your feet flat? Who was it offered you $50 to pitch a triple-header that time?" Satchel screwed up his face, which indicated that the concentration was giv-

ing him indigestion. "Man," he said, "the past is a long and twisty road."

Leroy Robert Paige started down the road during the Teddy Roosevelt administration from a small frame house in the Negro section of Mobile, Alabama. His father was a gardener. His mother, Tula Paige, who is now eighty-three and for whom Satchel bought a house in Mobile recently, said he was the sixth of eight children when questioned by Bill Veeck a while ago. She also put his birth year at 1903.

"What mama knows when her little child was bawn?" Paige said patiently when he got this news. "My draft card says 1906. I say 1908. Take your pick."

Food and living room were permanent problems for the family, but for Leroy, who was almost six feet tall at age twelve, the big problems apparently lay on the outside. One problem—where to find money to buy baseball equipment—he solved by becoming a redcap at a Mobile railroad station. After a couple of days' labor, the headwork for which he is now revered manifested itself and he rigged a "totin' device" of sticks and ropes on which he could hang as many as ten bags for one trip. Staggering along one day, looking like a tree of satchels, he caught the eye of someone who gave him the name he has carried down the road.

The predatory warfare between Mobile's boy gangs was a much bigger problem for Paige. Several times he was beaten; just as often, he participated in the gang-beating of others. He rarely went to school. Reasoning that continuous battle against odds was the staff of life, he turned sniper, breaking windows and lumping heads with deadly, accurate rocks from his hand. The truant officer became a weekly caller; the police called, too, with complaints from parents of winged children. Finally, a juvenile judge sentenced him to the Alabama Reform School for Boys, at Mount Meigs. He was approximately twelve when he went in, sixteen when he got out.

"One thing they told me in the refawm school," Paige says, "they told me that all that wild-a'-loose feelin' I put in rock throwin', I ought to put in throwin' baseballs. Well, I listened to that. Many men have watched my fast ball all these years without thinkin' what put that mean little hop on it. That's the wild-a'-loose."

Paige was six feet three inches tall and weighed 140 pounds when he rejoined society; he was reedy, solemn and taciturn in conversation but highly expressive on the mound. His mother kept him home nights but most afternoons he spent in sand-lot games, one of which happened to be witnessed by a Pullman porter in from Chattanooga. This man spoke to Alex Herman, owner of the Chattanooga Black Lookouts, and forthwith Mr. Herman appeared at the Paige house with offers. Mrs. Paige, who smelled sin in the footloose baseball life, refused to let Satchel go until Herman promised to watch him like a father and send his $50-a-month salary home. Full of reform-school warnings and memories at seventeen years of age, Satchel took the next train into the outer world.

When he appeared on the Lookouts' field for the first time, the legend-to-be was an arresting sight. His uniform flapped about him, his neck, arms and legs indicated severe emaciation, spikes had to be nailed to his street shoes until some size-12, triple-A baseball shoes could be found, his walk was labored, he cranked up like the Tin Woodman of Oz and he appeared to be speechless. Looking at him, veteran players expressed the gravest fears for owner Herman's judgment. The first man to face him in a practice session held his bat in one hand, for charity's sake.

Then Satchel threw his fast ball.

That evening, as the newly established most valuable player on the Lookouts, he was invited to dinner by several veterans. But he informed them that he had to eat at Mr. Herman's house and go to bed at nine-thirty.

When the team went on the road, Herman's watchfulness trebled. Crowds were wild about Satchel, female eyes followed him relentlessly, and scented notes, addressed to Mr. Paige, appeared at every hotel desk. This was heady stuff to Mrs. Paige's child; sometimes, after Herman had locked him in his hotel room, Paige felt the strain was too much for flesh to bear. In the warm Southern dusk, Satchel, gazing down from high hotel windows, could see the older players talking to the girls down below. When he chanced to hear soft voices inquiring as to the whereabouts of the tall pitcher, there were times he felt he'd have to jump.

Although Alex Herman delivered Satchel to his mother, as was, at the end of his first season, it was obvious that this arrangement could not go on. By the time he was twenty-one, Satchel Paige was a seasoned traveler and an apprentice philosopher, to say the least. He had run through two roadsters. He had sat in with Louis Armstrong and his band ("I played my own chords on the Spanish guitar"); he had had ham and whisky with ol' Jelly Roll Morton at a wake in Memphis ("I didn't know the dead man but Jelly thought he'd want me to be there"); he had gone across the river from New Orleans to have his palm read by the seers of Algiers, who found a short life line; he had been a running story in the Negro press, and from Savannah to Abilene and Mobile to St. Joe, he had heard of dozens of young ladies he had never seen who were letting it be known that they might shortly become Mrs. Paige.

"It was an education," Paige recalls now. "I was tired all the time."

As he put on a little more meat, Paige's fast ball got faster. This phenomenon has been explained by Biz Mackey, a memorable catcher for the Baltimore Elite Giants, of the late Negro National League.

"A lot of pitchers have a fast ball," says Mackey, "but a very, very few—Feller, Grove, Johnson, a couple of others besides Satchel—have had that little extra juice that makes the difference between the good and the great man. When it's that fast, it will hop a little at the end of the line. Beyond that, it tends to disappear.

"Yes, disappear. I've heard about Satchel throwing pitches that wasn't hit but that never showed up in the catcher's mitt, nevertheless. They say the catcher, the umpire and the bat boys looked all over for that ball, but it was gone. Now how do you account for that?"

Word of such disappearances got around the Negro leagues quickly, it seems, for competition for Satchel's services was intense. Since clubs issued loosely worded agreements in lieu of contracts, players could switch to the highest bidder.

Paige, a man of sound fiscal policies except in the savings department, jumped often, playing for such teams as the Birmingham Black Barons, the Nashville Elite Giants and the New Orleans Black Pelicans. But always he had in mind the goal of most Negro players of the time, Gus Greenlee's Pittsburgh Crawfords, a team that at one time might have won pennants in either major league. For the late Mr. Greenlee, who once managed light heavyweight champion John Henry Lewis, Paige was also a goal. In 1930, he sent Satchel an offhand note: "The Crawfords might possibly be interested in having you pitch for them next season." Paige replied: "I might possibly be interested in pitching for the Crawfords sometime."

When Paige joined Pittsburgh in 1931, his receiver was Josh Gibson, a better-than-average catcher, and one of the great right-hand hitters. With the Paige-Gibson battery in action, the Crawfords could afford to be big.

At one time, for example, they were playing an exhibition game against a champion team from the U.S. Marine Corps. In the last of the ninth with the Marines up, two out, and the score 12 to 0 in favor of the Crawfords, Satchel and Gibson had a worried consultation.

"The United States Marines have got to have at least one run," said Paige.

Back behind the plate, Gibson asked who was the captain of the Marine team. It was the man at bat. "You're gonna be the hero," Gibson said.

Thereupon, Satchel pitched one so fat the surprised Marine chopped it into the ground a few feet in front of home. Gibson grabbed it and threw it thirty feet over the first baseman's head. While the Marine rounded the bases and dug for the plate, the astonished right fielder retrieved the ball and threw it home for the putout. The ball hit Gibson's chest protector and bounded high in the air. "I had a feeling you were gonna be the hero," Gibson informed the Marine captain later.

With the Crawfords, Satchel's pitching bag grew. He threw overhand, sidearm and underhand; he served up the "two-hump blooper," a queer-acting slow ball; "the barber," an upshoot that grazed the batter's chin; "Little Tom," a medium fast ball; "Long Tom," *the* fast ball, and the "hesitation pitch," a bewildering delivery in which Paige stops in mid-throw before following through.

Paige's reputation, by this time, had traveled afar. Toward the end of the 1931 season, he got a pleasing offer from a Señor Linares, owner of the Santa Clara, Cuba club, to play winter ball. He accepted with every expectation of adding to his education. He did.

As a pitcher in the United States, Paige had been expected to win most of the time, but it was also realized that he might lose someday. In Cuba, this realization never came to the fans. When he got behind in a game, a terrible hush settled over the barefoot señors in the low, rudely constructed stands; if he got further behind, he could see the sun glinting on machetes all around him. And then there was the language barrier. While Satchel toiled, his teammates would hop around, chattering in Spanish.

"Speak English, brothers!" Paige would cry helplessly. "I is with you!"

After twenty-four straight wins for the Santa Clara club, Paige finally did lose.

"I didn't wait," he says. "I started yellin' Polices! Polices! and then I begin flyin' around the infield with the fans flyin' behind. They caught up with me at second base but the polices was a couple of jumps in the lead and we stood 'em off, knockin' some heads here and there.

"They wrote me up in the paper the next day," Paige said sourly. "Said I threwed the game."

2

An air of uneasiness hung over the home stadium of the last-place St. Louis Browns one day last August. Local fans, accustomed to great suffering, had the feeling that their team was about to throw away another ball game. Over six innings, the Browns had compiled a 2-0 edge over the league-leading Yankees. But now, with two out in the last of the seventh, pitcher Gene Bearden was beginning to wobble. One Yankee run scored. Then, while St. Louis supporters cringed, Bearden loaded the bases.

Among those shrinking into themselves at this critical moment was the Browns' shortstop-manager, Marty Marion. He glanced guiltily at his relief pitchers warming up in the bull pen. Then, stifling an impulse to call for volunteers, he made what seemed to be the only possible decision. He nominated Leroy (Satchel) Paige to douse the fire.

Languorous and serene, Mr. Paige, the eminent traveler, linguist, sage and relief-pitching mainstay of the Browns, rose and began his usual interminable stroll toward the mound.

In his thirty-or-so years in professional baseball, he had been in worse spots. If he failed here, at least he would not have to sprint from the field before enraged masses of machete-wielding fans, as he had so often had to do in the twenty years he played winter ball in Latin America. Nor would his outfielders stroll off the diamond without his knowing it, as had happened in North Dakota in 1934. There was positively no danger of politicos threatening him with the firing squad, as they had done in the Dominican Republic in 1936.

Humming a little tune, Paige took his regular half-dozen warmup pitches on the mound, sighted on pinch hitter Irv Noren, and fed him a fast curve. He smiled pleasantly as Marion gathered in a short pop-up, retiring the side.

Later, still humming contentedly, Mr. Paige did away with Phil Rizzuto, Joe Collins and

Hank Bauer in the eighth, and Yogi Berra, Gil McDougald and Gene Woodling in the ninth, to save the game.

Afterward, despite the satisfactory outcome, there was some discussion among local fans over the soundness of manager Marion's strategy in selecting the aging Paige at a time of such crisis.

When these comments reached the sensitive ears of Browns owner Bill Veeck, he seemed astonished. "Well, what else was there to do?" he inquired of one doubter. "Marion needed the greatest baseball brains, experience, speed, control and coolness he could find in one man. So he put in the world's greatest relief pitcher. No particular strategy about that!"

Veeck's was a generous, but not a wildly extravagant, statement. By any yardstick, the venerable Paige, whose age is thought to lie somewhere between forty-five and fifty-three, is one of the two or three best relief men in baseball. In the first eleven games the Browns played this season, he was called upon four times. He helped save three of the games, and was compelled to retire from the fourth when a line drive struck his foot. In 1952, he pitched in almost one third of the St. Louis Browns' contests, struck out 91 batters, won twelve games, lost ten, saved ten, and ended up by making the American League All-Star team and becoming—in the opinion of most experts—the most valuable relief hurler in that circuit.

In his approximately thirty years of baseball, two lifetimes for the average pitcher, Paige has broken all records for number of games pitched and won (some 2,000 out of 2,500). Working winter and summer in many lands, often as an itinerant solo star, for some 250 different sand-lot, semipro and Negro-league teams —not to mention the Cleveland Indians and St. Louis Browns—he has also very probably broken all records for travel and number of customers drawn by any individual ballplayer.

Barred by the color line from rewriting big baseball's record book in his prime, Paige contented himself with striking out most of the traveling major-league all-stars who came his way over the years in exhibition games. Those feats not only caused Paige to be called the greatest pitcher who ever lived by such recognized authorities as Dizzy Dean and Charley Gehringer, among many others, but they did a great deal to lay the groundwork for the entry of Negro players into the major leagues in 1947.

"They was tall times, tall times," Paige says of those years. "But let whosomever wishes sit around recollecting. I'm looking up the line."

Up the line looms a busy season. Last year, Paige worked in a staggering 46 games; this year he may wind up working even more often. "If we don't have to use him in relief every other game," said Marion early in the season, "he'll get plenty of starting assignments."

That prospect does not dampen Paige's celebrated self-confidence. Now, as always, Satchel is so certain of his powers, both physical and mental, that sometimes he makes himself uneasy.

In the Browns' shower room after a recent game, for example, several players were tossing a slippery cake of soap at a wall dish, trying without success to make it stick there. Paige entered, picked up the soap casually, and tossed it. It stuck. There was a general raising of eyebrows, none higher than Satchel's. He tossed another bar, even more slippery. It stuck, too. Paige looked thoughtfully at the sober faces around him.

"Boys," he said, "there is apparently things that even I don't know I can do."

Paige's powers have raised him to a patriarchal position among the Browns. Such recognition is not easily won, but when a man can explain to a club car full of ballplayers not only what the hull and superstructure of Noah's ark were made of, but the composition of its doors and hinges as well, respect must be paid where it is due.

The elderly pitcher's abilities as a graduate student of the human race also have had frequent workouts. During spring training this year, it was noticed that one of the Browns' promising rookies was mooning around the ball field instead of trying to make the team. When management failed to diagnose the trouble, Paige cast an eye on the spaniel droop of the young man's features.

"The child is down with love," he announced flatly.

After Paige's analysis proved correct, his observations on love were naturally sought by other Browns players. For a man who has made lifelong researches into the subject, it turned out that he had a rather low opinion of it.

"Love," said Paige, "is a proposition I wouldn't advise you to mess with, as regards the general run of women. You restrict yourself to one or two lady friends and you're gonna be all right. But you expand to include the field and you're bound to get cut up. Myself," he added dismally, "I'm a passel of scars. Oh, I seen some terrible times, terrible times. . . ."

One such time overtook Paige when he was approximately twenty-three and playing for the town of Santa Clara, Cuba, in his first winter season in the banana leagues. When love came, Paige was sitting in a Santa Clara park on a hot evening, eating peanuts and listening to the palms clacking. Then a lovely, huge-eyed creature, who spoke a little English, walked by.

"She dropped some Sen-Sen in my hand," he recalls sadly. "That was the signal."

Eventually, Paige called at the girl's mud-walled home and found he had to stand out in the street among snoring pigs, talking to her through a barred window because he had not known her long enough to enter. Some weeks later, when her family let him in, he was dismayed to learn that his admission was a sign he and the girl were officially engaged, and that the authorities would be so informed.

"I quit callin' immediately," Paige says, "but pretty soon the owner of the ball club comes to my hotel and says the polices is lookin' for me. So I started goin' back to her house."

Ultimately, says Paige, the strain told and he began to lose ball games. The club owner bowed to the inevitable.

"One night he phones my hotel and says it's all fixed," Paige recalls. "He's gonna get me out in a car to the mountains. Then I'll get on a horse and go on over the top and get another car. This car will take me to a place where I can catch a motorboat and go on out to a ship to take me back to the U.S.A. That's how it was gonna be."

Paige, who suffers from a nervous stomach, winced as memories of that night came back to plague him.

"The hotel telephone operator was the girl's cousin," he said miserably. "Them polices was after me when I was in the car, and on a jackass runnin' up the mountain, and on foot runnin' down the mountain, and right on out to the motorboat.

"Man," he concluded, his voice heavy with strain, "when I finally come flyin' up that gang-plank, I was through with love."

When Paige made this retreat across the wilds of Cuba, he was the summer property of one of the most formidable teams then in existence, the all-Negro Pittsburgh Crawfords. The late Gus Greenlee, owner of the Crawfords, had been vaguely aware of Paige from the year 1923, when Paige's two pitches, hard and harder, had begun to terrorize semipro teams

in his home town of Mobile. Greenlee had followed Paige's career from the time he joined the Chattanooga Black Lookouts in 1926 through various subsequent jumps to other teams in the Negro Southern Association. By 1930, when Greenlee offered Paige $200 a month to join the Crawfords, Satchel was winning up to 60 games a year, striking out from 10 to 18 men in every game.

In three years at Pittsburgh, he won an estimated 105 games while losing 37.

Paige's battery mate on the Crawfords was the late Josh Gibson, the *aficionado's* choice for the long-ball hitter of all time. Paige has the greatest reverence for Gibson, and it shocks him to run into people who have not heard of the great man.

Not long ago, a sassy young reporter, fuddled with the doings of the Musials, the Mantles and so on, tried Paige severely by yawning while he was recounting some of Gibson's prodigies. To fix him, Paige recalled one game.

"We was playin' the Homestead Grays in the city of Pitchburgh," he said quietly. "Josh comes up in the last of the ninth with a man on and us a run behind. Well, he hit one. The Grays waited around and waited around, but finally the empire rules it ain't comin' down. So we win.

"The next day," Paige went on, eying the youth coldly, "we was disputin' the Grays in Philadelphia when here come a ball outta the sky right in the glove of the Grays' center fielder. The empire made the only possible call.

"'You're out, boy!' he says to Josh. 'Yesterday, in Pitchburgh.'"

Paige was quite a sight around Pittsburgh at this time—six foot three and a quarter inches tall, slow-moving, meatless and loose-limbed, with a wide-roving eye. The calm, dry, sadly comic air, the sly humor and itchy foot, the unwillingness to be pinned down by statistics, appointments or contracts were all there in embryo. So was the now famous Paige self-confidence.

Satchel thought—and still thinks—of himself as a great hitter and base runner. There is some evidence that he may once have been pretty fair in those departments, and additional evidence that he could be still. Perhaps the best measurement of his current capacity at the plate, however, is his last season's batting record—five hits in thirty-nine tries. As to his speed, there is much debate among observers. Some question that he could beat Casey Stengel to first base. Others note that he moves quickly enough afield to have handled all chances in his first four years in the majors without a single error.

"In my opinion," says White Sox manager Paul Richards, a Paige fan, "he could play short-stop."

The fact is, he has, in his time, been an in-fielder and a pretty good one. Catcher Roy Campanella of the Brooklyn Dodgers tells of playing against Paige in Puerto Rico during the winter of 1939-'40. "In Sunday double-headers," says Campanella, "Satch would pitch the first game and strike out maybe seventeen batters, and then play first base in the second game. Did all right, too."

Although there may have been some basis for Paige's belief while at Pittsburgh that he could run and hit with the best of them, there was less justification for another view he held at the time—that he was a dangerous man in the ring. When Gus Greenlee had Paige under contract he was also managing the light heavy-weight champion of the world, John Henry Lewis. Watching Lewis work out, Paige became overpowered with manly urges and challenged him.

Greenlee visited the gym one day and was horrified to see his two most expensive com-modities in the ring, the one weaving and laughing, the other stilting fiercely about in many-colored shorts like an enraged flamingo. Before Greenlee could get to them, Paige man-aged to hit Lewis on top of the head, where-upon Lewis feinted, stood off and rapped the pitcher on the chin. Some time later, while Lewis, Greenlee and the trainers worked fev-erishly with ammonia and massage, Paige opened his eyes.

"I stang him," he was saying happily. "Git me a shot at Joe Louis."

As a man already on the way toward becom-ing a legend in fields other than boxing, Paige was generally believed in Pittsburgh to have size 15 feet and to be wealthy, a wild dresser, the owner of several fiery-red cars, and a very frying pan of romance. Actually, he walked on mere size twelves and was flat broke, modestly clad except for ties and shoes, the owner of a piece of a roadster he was buying from Gus Greenlee, and a lover too winded from constant flight to be impressive when cornered.

It was the opinion of most of the local young ladies at the time that Satchel was just too ornery to settle down. Miss Janet Howard, a bright and resourceful waitress at Gus Green-lee's Crawford Grill, thought otherwise, how-ever.

"From the minute she first set a plate of as-paragus down in front of me," Satch Paige re-calls, "I began to feel paralyzed."

Marriage to Janet brought responsibilities undreamed of by Paige. He had saved no money at all. When he had to bring his salary home, only to find it wasn't enough, and when Greenlee balked at giving him a raise, he be-gan looking around. One offer of $250 a month came in, but it made Paige uncomforta-ble.

"It was from a car dealer named Neil Churchill away out in a place called Bismarck, North Dakota," Paige recalls. "Churchill had a semipro team of mostly white boys, but he needed pitchin' so he calls Abe Saperstein, who owns the Harlem Globetrotters, and asks who he should get. Abe says me. Well, now," said Paige, "I wasn't exactly sure that North Dakota belonged to Sam (the U.S.A.) at the time, and I didn't want to go. But Janet says jump, so we jumped."

In Bismarck, a city that contained few Ne-groes, Paige and his wife looked fruitlessly for housing and finally settled in a boxcar that had housed section hands. Still broke, Satchel rus-tled up early meals with a shotgun in the sur-rounding jackrabbit country.

At the time, 1934, Paige was just rounding into his prime, which is to say that he was prob-ably the greatest pitcher then alive. When some of the other Bismarck players seemed inclined to doubt the Paige prowess, he quickly set them right. He placed a small matchbox on an upright stick beside home plate and knocked it off with thirteen of twenty pitches from the mound. That established the control. Then he pitched a fast ball which took a nasty hop near the plate, skipping off the catcher's mitt to graze his temple. The catcher called for a chest protector and mask. He needed them, for he was unable to hold the next eight pitches out of ten. That established the speed. (Satch's present receiver, the Browns' Clint Courtney, reported nine years later that Paige's fast ball was still hard to follow. "It has a hop on the end," complained Courtney, "and it keeps tick-ing off the top of my mitt.")

For a couple of years, the Bismarck team had been humiliated regularly by the neighboring Jamestown Red Sox. In his first game against Jamestown, Paige allowed no runs and fanned fifteen, using only Little Tom, his medium fast ball, and leaving Long Tom, his real fast ball, for future use. Paige beat Jamestown four more times that season, in addition to winning 37 other games for Bismarck, but the season was not a success. Jamestown beat Bismarck once.

The one Jamestown victory came about in a strange way. During the season, Paige had occasionally electrified the prairie fans by signaling his outfield to walk off the field, thus leaving himself with nothing but an infield for defense. The signal was easy to see. Paige stood on the mound, wiping his brow elaborately with his pitching hand.

On the night of the final game against Jamestown, Paige was off form. The opposition batters hit everything—floaters, curves, the "two-hump blooper," the chin-grazing "barber pitch," the "hesitation pitch" and even Long Tom. Luckily, Bismarck was also hitting, so Paige was able to keep a shaky lead as the score mounted.

In the last of the ninth, with the score 15 to 14 in Bismarck's favor and Jamestown's murderers' row coming up, Paige began to perspire freely. Curves got the first man. The second man singled and Paige's blood pressure rose. Long Tom dispatched the third batter, but as the cleanup man walked to the plate, Paige was seized by a premonition of evil. He mopped his brow nervously.

Paige is still outraged by the memory of that night game.

"While my outfield was strollin' off the field behind my back," he says, "I fed the cleanup man a little outcurve which I intended him to hit on the fly to right field. He did. It was some time," says Paige grumpily, "before I again visited the city of Bismarck." (Actually, he rejoined the team the next summer.)

In the autumn of 1934, Paige and his wife headed for Denver, where he had been invited to pitch for the House of David in the *Denver Post* semipro tournament. The House had a talented organization, but what impressed Paige most was the amazing growth of whiskers on all the players. Paige had never been able to grow any whiskers himself, and he felt naked and alone. Although he won his first three tournament games for the House without facial hair, he complained bitterly. Finally, his teammates presented him with a lengthy false beard of reddish hue.

Thoroughly pleased, Paige wore the red whiskers in his final appearance. While he was winding up to deliver a hesitation pitch in the fourth inning, however, the beard became entwined with his pitching arm and was torn from his jaws with the delivery.

Finding himself denuded again, Paige became so unsettled that he very nearly lost the game. He squeaked through, however, and the House went on to win the tournament.

"It was the tamperin' with nature that rattled me," Satchel says.

In California that winter, Paige commanded the Satchel Paige All-Stars, an impressive pickup team of Negro-league players. This team included catcher Josh Gibson, third baseman Judy (Sweet Juice) Johnson, the catlike Harry Williams at second base, and Cool Papa Bell, whose speed and daring in the outfield and on the bases may have surpassed that of Willie Mays. In three previous years wintering on the West Coast, the Paige Stars, with or without the members named, had won some 128 games —at least 40 of them against teams of major-league all-stars—while losing 23.

The games against big-leaguers were of tremendous importance to Paige and the others. They knew, the sports writers knew, and many of the fans knew that many of the Negro stars were better ballplayers than some of the high-salaried, internationally famous men they faced. Yet they were denied a shot at the big fame, big money, big records and big company. Paige burned with a quiet resentment at this denial. He felt that someday the color line would be broken. But his great fear, he says, was that he would be too old, his prime wasted in cow pastures, when the great day came.

The bigger the major-league stars, the more Paige bore down. According to accounts passed down by witnesses, he struck out Rogers Hornsby five times in one game, Charley Gehringer three times in another, Jimmy Foxx three times in a third. In 1934 in Hollywood, Paige pitched what Bill Veeck says is the greatest game he ever saw. In that game, which lasted 13 innings, Paige was opposed by Dizzy Dean, a 30-game winner for the Cardinals. Dean was superlative, holding the Paige Stars to one run and fanning 15. But Paige shut out the Dean Stars and fanned 17. After the game, Dean informed the press that Paige was the best pitcher in the business.

Later that winter, Paige made his usual leisurely barnstorming trip through the tropics. After a series of games in Mexico City, he and a couple of his American All-Stars were invited to the ranch of a local ball-club owner, whose side line was raising bulls for the ring. Standing behind a stone wall in a ranch pasture one day, one of the stars saw Paige gazing over into another pasture where some local *toreros* were tempting the horns of the terrible black bulls. His natural bravery seemingly aroused by the spectacle, Paige expressed to a bullfighter who was resting nearby his burning desire to defy the bulls himself someday.

"I got a way with animals," Paige is supposed to have said fiercely.

Absorbed by the violence over the wall, Paige failed to observe some animals grazing behind him. Satchel was just repeating his defiance of the bulls, according to the story, when a shape loomed at his elbow. Annoyed, Paige turned to see what it was. It was all looming bulk, black hair and horns.

Slowly, almost wearily, says the witness, Paige turned back to the bullfighter on the wall.

"Toreador," he called in a small strained voice. "Oh, toreador."

But the bullfighter was watching his fellow *toreros* work.

"Toreador!" Paige yelled suddenly. "Polices! Polices! Help!"

While the bullfighter jerked around to see what was the matter, the visiting bull, apparently alarmed by the noises issuing from Paige, turned and trotted back to the grazing herd.

"Scared?" Paige now says, in recalling the incident. "That bull was jelly. I turned the cold eye on him. The chances are, that bull never was any good when he got to the ring in Mexico City. Fear ruins 'em."

Back from Mexico in the summer of 1935, Paige rejoined Bismarck while his wife stayed in Pittsburgh. The team's problem that year was to find competition. Of the 102 games played, it lost five. In midseason, Paige pitched 29 days in a row with one loss; his total for the summer was 43 wins and two losses. As Bismarck's renown grew, the inevitable team of major-league all-stars appeared, this one boasting Earl Averill, Heinie Manush and Jimmy Foxx, among others. Bismarck beat the big-leaguers 7-4 at Grand Forks, North Dakota, 10-0 at Valley City and 16-2 at Bismarck before they could get out of the bush country.

Among the customers who sat fascinated by the sight of Paige at his peak were many Sioux Indians from nearby reservations. They named him the Long Rifle and worked him into at least one tribal legend, in which he uses the bean ball on a cantankerous local Indian commissioner. One Sioux in particular, a Dorothy Running-Deer, as Paige recalls, often hung about the grounds after game time. Paige took little notice of her; he was a married man, and also she was short and rather plain. Nevertheless, she did him a great service.

"One day," Paige recalls, "this Dorothy Deer invited me out in the hills to meet her papa who raised rattlesnakes in a deep pit in back of his hut. I looked at the snakes and said good-by. Before leavin', however, I ask the old man if he'd ever been bit, and he said lots of times, but he had an ointment that took out the harm. When he gave me a great big jug of it, I ask him if the ointment might be good for rubbin' my arm. He said he wouldn't advise it."

After heeding the warning for a couple of days, Paige finally dabbed a finger into the snake oil and cautiously rubbed a few drops on his tired biceps. Forthwith, he declares, energies and sensations of a kind he had never known vibrated from shoulder to fingers.

"My mistake was I didn't dilute it," Paige says reflectively. "Man, it's a wonder my arm didn't fly outta the room."

For many years since then, ballplayers in hundreds of locker rooms, including those of the Cleveland Indians and the St. Louis Browns, have speculated endlessly about the ingredients of the secret preparation which the Long Rifle uses to revitalize his arm. Some say it's kerosene and olive oil and some say it's wolfbane and wild cherry stems. Paige doesn't say. He just calls it Deer oil.

As the terror of the northern Midwest, the 1935 Bismarck team was invited to play in the national semipro tournament at Wichita, Kansas. En route, in McPherson, Kansas, they encountered a problem. Local citizens, apparently rendered unsteady by a winning team of their own, openly referred to the Bismarcks as hayshakers.

A six-inning challenge game was promptly arranged and the Bismarcks took an early two-run lead. In the final inning, the disgruntled McPherson fans began to hoot at Paige.

That was a mistake. Paige fanned the first man. Then, repeating his Jamestown gesture, he called in his outfield and struck out the next man. Then, outdoing the Jamestown gesture, he called in his infield. With nobody representing Bismarck but Paige and catcher Quincy Troupe, he struck out the third man. He used nine fast balls in all.

Bismarck won the Wichita tournament in seven games, and barnstormed west for new fields to conquer. In Denver, Paige confronted the House of David, which he had pitched to victory in the *Post* tournament the year before. The beards still fascinated him. One unusually lush growth so attracted him, indeed, that he fired a pitch into it, thus raising a technical baseball point so fine that no one has yet been able to settle it.

The argument took place in the seventh inning. Paige had two strikes on the owner of the great beard when he was seized by an overpowering desire to part the man's whiskers with a Long Tom. When he did, the umpire promptly ruled that the man had been hit by a pitched ball and waved him on to first.

According to an impartial witness, Paige then raised an arm to halt the game. Striding up to the struck man, he asked permission to exhibit his beard to the umpire.

"Empire," said Paige, combing the luxuriant growth with long fingers, "if you will kindly observe here, you will see that these whiskers can't rightly be called no part of a man. They is air."

The umpire, seeing the logic, began to hem and haw. After about five minutes, however, he got mad and returned to his former ground. Paige was defeated, but the crowd was with him and the question is still considered wide open.

After his second appearance in Denver, Paige's fame as a pitching phenomenon began to spread across the nation, and beyond. One Denver wire-service story, translated into Spanish, reached the eyes of Dr. José Enrique Aybar, dean of the University of Santo Domingo, deputy of the Dominican Republic's national congress, and a man with a mission. Some days before, Dr. Aybar had been given $30,000 by President Rafael L. Trujillo, absolute dictator of the country and by all odds the fiercest strong man in Central America, and told to go out and get a ball club. An election was coming up and Trujillo's opponent was showing surprising strength—due almost entirely to the fact that he had imported ballplayers who were beating everything in sight and thus ballyhooing his name.

After reading the stuff on Paige, Dr. Aybar got in touch with him at once, asking him to round up as many American Negro players as he could find and fly to Ciudad Trujillo, the capital. Thinking he'd like to spend a restful winter in the tropics, Paige recruited Josh Gibson, Cool Papa Bell, Harry Williams and some others and took off.

At Ciudad Trujillo, Paige and his teammates were met by barefoot soldiers with ammunition belts over their chests and long, bayoneted rifles in their hands. Paige thought them very distinguished. The soldiers convoyed the players to a hotel and took up posts outside their rooms. Thereafter, every place Paige and his friends went, the soldiers went with them. When Paige met Dr. Aybar, the doctor explained that the situation was very serious and that Trujillo's team must win an upcoming series of seven games against the Estrellas de Oriente, the opponent's team, at whatever cost.

When the day of the great series arrived, the city was decorated with flags and the streets were jammed with people. Gaiety and laughter, machetes and shooting irons were everywhere. At the ball park, the heavily armed followers of Trujillo bulked threateningly along the third-base line; and the heavily armed followers of Trujillo's opponent bulked just as threateningly along the first-base line.

"I knew then that whichever way the series went, I lost," says Paige.

The series went as badly as possible. With the strain giving Paige nervous stomach, the Trujillo forces dropped two straight. The reaction from the president's office was very bad. Then they lost one more, and all Dr. Aybar could do was wring his hands when Paige asked how his chances were for getting back to the States. In desperation, Paige and his mates played as never before, taking the next three in a row while tension mounted throughout the country. On the last day, with the score in games three and three, Paige might have been excused had he been unable to walk to the mound. Instead, he strode out confidently, his stomach gas all gone.

"I had it fixed with Mr. Trujillo's polices," Paige says. "If we win, their whole army is gonna run out and escort us from the place. If we lose . . ." Paige hesitated. "If we lose, there is nothin' to do but consider myself and my boys as passed over Jordan."

Paige did not lose.

Back with the all-forgiving Crawfords the next summer, Paige found that his hectic, itinerant past was beginning to catch up with him. Word-of-mouth advertising of his exploits had made his name magical in many cities and backwoods of the Western Hemisphere.

Communities he had never heard of suddenly wanted to see him pitch. Offers ranging from $100 to $500 for three innings' work began to come in. Paige began traveling around the country as a solo star, making guest appearances with one club after another, week after week. With every appearance, the pressure mounted, his fame grew and his nervous stomach got worse. He was billed as "Satchel Paige, the World's Greatest Pitcher, Guaranteed to Strike Out the First Nine Men!" The trick word was "guaranteed." Crowds jammed ball parks to see him win—all the time. He was not supposed to lose any more than Bojangles Robinson was supposed to fall down while executing a buck-and-wing. People said that Satchel Paige was not only extra-human, but that he was just rounding into his greatest years at thirty-one, or thirty-three, or thirty-seven, or whatever.

"Everything is still in front of him," they said.

In Venezuela at the height of this clamor, Paige pitched two innings of a three-inning guest shot without incident, which is to say he struck everybody out. In the third inning, throwing a routine sidearm fast ball, however, he felt a small, sharp pain in his pitching shoulder.

That evening he caught a plane for his next guest appearance in Mexico City. With the first ball he pitched in that rarefied atmosphere, his shoulder joint snapped audibly and he sat down on the mound, in the midst of a rising storm of catcalls, bewildered by the pain.

Back in Kansas City, unable to lift his right arm, Paige thought he had better see a doctor. The examination took only a couple of minutes.

"Satchel," said the doctor, briskly, "you're through."

3

Mr. Leroy (Satchel) Paige, the tall, urbane and seemingly imperishable relief-pitching star of the St. Louis Browns, cast a startled glance at Joe DiMaggio during an all-star charity game in Hollywood a while ago. Before his eyes, the thirty-seven-year-old Clipper, who had come out of retirement to make one last appearance at bat, took a couple of swings in an elderly fashion, then popped out feebly to short. The sight absolutely dismayed Mr. Paige.

Back in 1926, when Paige was pitching for the Chattanooga Black Lookouts, in the Negro Southern Association, DiMaggio was a San Francisco schoolboy of eleven. In 1935, when Paige was a 10-year semipro veteran and already a legend in the land, DiMaggio was still a year away from the Yankees. Thirteen years later, when Paige was just breaking into the majors as a Cleveland rookie, sports writers were calling DiMaggio the Yankees' grand old man. Now, when Paige was being hailed as one of the best relief prospects in baseball, DiMaggio was bowing out of the game.

With time jumping around like that, no wonder Paige was confused.

Mr. Paige, whose own age is believed to fall somewhere between forty-five and fifty-three, is unalterably opposed to time. As soon as he learns the hitting weaknesses of one generation of sluggers, for example, time does away with them. Time also makes off with pitchers—a circumstance Paige feels is not only an inexcusable affront to his profession, but harmful to society in general.

"All this comin' and goin'," he says indignantly. "Rookies flyin' up the road and old-timers flyin' down, and nobody in between but me and ol' John Mize, standin' pat, watchin' 'em go by.

"And I ain't even sure about ol' John," says Paige. "Maybe he's flyin' on, too. If he is," Paige adds, accusingly, "I can always watch 'em go by myself. Time ain't gonna mess with me!"

This last seems to be indisputable fact. Paige currently is enjoying what is probably his thirtieth year as a professional pitcher. In that span, he has not only set athletic longevity records, but has pitched and won more ball games (some 2,000 out of 2,500), traveled more miles (nearly a million), drawn more customers (an estimated 10,000,000), seen more astonishing sights and thrown a faster fast ball than any other moundsman known to man.

"I've never seen anything quite like Lee-roy," says Browns owner Bill Veeck, who also was a schoolboy of eleven when Paige was with Chattanooga. "He's been my hero since 1934 when I saw him beat a Dizzy Dean All-Star team 1-0 in thirteen innings in California. Last year, when the wise men were saying he'd come apart if he pitched more than three innings once a week, he worked in almost a third of all our games and won twelve and saved ten for us. He was easily the best relief man in the league, in my opinion, and the only Brownie to make the All-Star team."

Veeck pondered. "If this keeps up," he added reflectively, "what will he be like five years from now?"

Paige is too busy with the here and now to consider such questions. Age or no age, he is the Browns' highest-paid player, at $25,000 a year. To hold this exalted status, he is obliged to keep pace with the other Browns, some of whom were born after he started pitching for pay.

The sight of Paige keeping pace can be deceptive, of course. Before games, when other players are prancing around, swinging four bats, doing knee-bends and so on, Paige may be seen reclining gracefully in his canopied contour chair by the Browns' bull pen, throwing gently to a catcher, counting the house or possibly playing "skidoodle."

"Skidoodle is a game I invented some years ago to exercise without doin' myself permanent harm," Paige says. "I throw the ball on one bounce to another man, he bounces it back at me. We jangle around. Nobody falls down exhausted."

Paige has conditioned himself so long and so well that on a hot day he can warm up his celebrated right arm with five or six pitches. Par for most pitchers is about fifteen minutes of steady throwing. Browns manager Marty Marion never tells the old gentleman how to live or what to throw. Even Clint Courtney, the Browns' combative catcher, has given up trying to get him to follow pitching signals, since Paige will throw what he wants to, anyhow.

Courtney's restraint is doubtless wise, for what Paige wants to throw has impressed many of the American League's most formidable hitters. Mickey Mantle, who up until recently had hit Paige one for ten, says flatly that he would "rather face any other pitcher in the league in a pinch situation." Detroit's Johnny Pesky, who at last count also had just one hit off Paige in many tries, says he hesitates to think what might have happened had Paige come to the majors while in his youth. "He used to average fifteen strike-outs a game, five days a week," Pesky says wonderingly. Outfielder Bob Nieman, also of Detroit, adds that he saw Paige load the bases with none out against Cleveland last year, and then retire the next three men on twelve pitches. "That stayed with me," Nieman says.

Paige's battery mate, Courtney, gives three reasons why the elderly pitcher is a present danger instead of a disturbing memory to hitters. "You hear about pinpoint control," Courtney says, "but Paige is the only man I've ever seen who really has it. He threw me six strikes out of ten pitches over a chewing-gum wrapper one time. Also," says Courtney, "his fast ball still burns my mitt when he lets it go, which is whenever he needs it. Finally, he just thinks faster than most hitters. Satchel is a very smart man."

What Paige thinks about various hitters can usually be heard by fans some distance from the Browns' bull pen during games. Sitting in his chair, Paige keeps a running commentary going, most of it seemingly for his own benefit.

"Don't ever feed that man low outside," he cautioned himself recently, as Mantle came to bat. "He will harm you." Ferris Fain, the 1952 American League batting champion, once caused Paige to cry a rhymed warning to the man pitching to him. "Throw it high, the skin will fly," hollered Paige. When Larry Doby of the Indians is up, Paige usually suggests using "the barber." (The barber is Paige's name for a high, inside pitch that shaves the batter's chin.)

Mickey Vernon, of the Senators, is the only man who leaves Paige speechless. For some mysterious reason, Vernon hits Paige almost at will.

Because Paige is the oldest established one-man traveling baseball spectacle now active, the Browns' management feels squeamish about cramping him with rules. He is on the honor system, which is to say that he does not have to stay in hotels with the team on road trips if he wishes to stay with friends, as he does in about half the towns the Browns play. Nobody orders him to bed by midnight. He is presumed to have outlived most of the ballplayer vices and so escapes spiritual lectures. All he is expected to do, besides win, is to appear on time for trains, practice or games.

That requirement, unhappily, is the very one Paige has to struggle hardest to meet. Punctuality undermines him, somehow. When he is late nowadays, guilt sits so heavily upon him that he usually assumes some other character, completely foreign to his normal self, to help bear it.

On such occasions, Paige often comes into the dressing room in the character of a hurt or outraged man and makes some immediate and inscrutable statement, such as, "They oughta bust the clocks down there" or "The taxi drivers is in cahoots!" or "He was bound to send me air mail!" Translated, these comments mean that Paige was late because the clocks in some hotel were wrong, or that the taxi drivers were in league with the opposing team to delay him, or that some friend kept him so long he had to take a plane to catch up with the team.

Paige's real character, as opposed to his character when tardy, is an arresting blend of warmth and reserve, humor, cunning, dignity, slapstick and competitive drive—all governed by one of the most penetrating, though unschooled, intelligences in or outside baseball. Whether he appears as the soul of assurance in a desperate situation on a ball field, or as a lean, expensively dressed, rather regal, languid and melancholy-looking man on the street, the rare but unmistakable stamp of originality is upon Paige.

"I'm Satchel," he sometimes explains simply, when people try to fit him into various molds. "I do as I do."

Doing as he does, Paige communicates his personality to whole ball parks full of fans with theatrical ease. Every time he rises from his bull-pen seat, even to get a drink, an excited murmur runs through the stands. When he starts his slow, slightly bent, sadly comic amble to the mound to save a game, fans get the impression from him that the whole situation is too simple for concern. The unconcern is the essence of Paige and always causes the crowd to explode in appreciation.

Even opposing fans are for Paige. In Boston last year, for example, he went in to put down a Red Sox uprising and was promptly shelled for an unbelievable six runs before he could get the side out. Throughout this disaster, the Red Sox stands sat in stony, embarrassed silence. When he finally wobbled off the diamond, the cheers could be heard in Cambridge. Paige has never been booed in the majors.

Because he has pitched so long, and has disappeared so many times into backwoods baseball in this and other countries, many fans have lost track of Paige and have come to the conclusion that he is deceased. During spring training this year, he says, he was riding in a Los Angeles cab when he noticed the driver scrutinizing him in the rear-vision mirror. Finally the driver shook his head and exclaimed: "No, it ain't possible. He's passed."

"Who's passed?" Paige inquired guardedly.

The driver explained that for a minute he could have sworn his passenger was a famous, long-gone pitcher named Satchel Paige.

"I knew Ol' Satch well," the driver sighed. "Even though I was only a little child of eight when he was in his prime."

"When was that?" asked Ol' Satch, gloomily.

"About 1913," said the driver.

Paige's mother, Mrs. Tula Paige, who is eighty-three and has never seen Satchel play, also has certain delusions about him. She thinks of him as a child who has wandered into a shiftless, sinful life. For thirty years, she has remained inexorably opposed to his playing baseball, writing him regular instructions about attending Mass and avoiding gambling, late hours, wild women and other evils.

"I sure wish she'd change her mind about baseball," Paige complains. "It's a big strain when your mama ain't with you."

Other Browns players do not share his mother's view that Paige requires protection from the hazards of life. They have heard stories about how he once made his way on foot across tropical jungles to escape romance, and how he was later feted by Venezuelan savages. They have heard how he personally intimidated a brave bull in Mexico, and how he was canonized in 1935 by the North Dakota Sioux. These stories, among dozens of others, have given Paige an aura of wisdom, experience and mystery impressive to many veteran ballplayers and practically all rookies.

Occasionally, when reminiscent moods overpower him, Paige himself gives his clubhouse admirers, and a select few others, a glimpse or two into his adventurous past. These reviews are never complete without discussion of the fans. Fans have always fascinated Paige. In South America, where he played winter ball off and on for twenty years, they were always running him around, trying either to carry him on their shoulders or decapitate him with machetes.

The fans Paige remembers best lived in the wild country of northwestern Venezuela. These fans were short, dark, fierce fellows who ran about the forest in G strings, shooting poisoned arrows at birds and occasional oil-line workers. Every so often, some of them sneaked into the Maracaibo ball park and had to be run out to keep them from scaring the customers and stealing baseballs.

"The only time I seen these fans," Paige recently recalled for some teammates, "I was on a jackass ridin' around in the jungle sightseein'. I was wearin' some cream-colored pants, a sport shirt and two-tone shoes, as I recollect. When I come to a clearin' in the forest I thought I'd get off and rest. But the clearin' was jammed with these fans, sittin' around in front of a big grass house and eatin' pig and roots and bugs and all that mess they eat. When they seen me," Paige said, "they grabbed up their blowguns and aimed right at my new Stetson hat."

For a long time, Paige gazed silently at the

fans and the fans gazed silently at Paige. Then, he said, one of them ran into a hut, returned with a baseball and stood pointing from the ball to Paige and jabbering excitedly. The blowguns came down at once, Paige said, and he was thereupon obliged to dismount and join the fans in a meal of pig, roots and bugs. They gave him a blowgun of his own, and wouldn't let him leave until the day was almost gone.

"I could of been a big man in that outfit if I'd stayed on," Paige concluded offhandedly. "But I had to get on back to the States, where I also had some fans."

Paige has grown so used to autograph hunters among his stateside fans that he often fails to observe them closely. In Phoenix last spring, a slight, partially bald, agitated-looking man came bounding into the Browns' dressing room after an exhibition game. Paige was reclining in a whirl bath at the time, but he borrowed a pen from the man and signed his program obligingly. When the man suddenly began firing ad-lib witticisms, however, twitching his eyebrows and sidling around bent-kneed, Paige, who is the official humorist on the Browns, began to regard him so coolly that he finally crept away.

"Who was that character?" Paige asked Browns trainer Bob Bauman as he emerged from the bath.

"Groucho Marx," Bauman said.

Paige, who mourns this unfortunate meeting, blames it almost entirely on the fact that Marx was not wearing his stage eyebrows at the time, not on his own failure to scrutinize Marx properly. Usually, of course, Paige does not have to peer at anyone in particular, since he deals with fans mostly in groups.

On train trips, for example, other players usually arrive at stations singly, or in pairs. Paige almost inevitably appears at the center of a large and enthusiastic delegation. Friendly and relaxed, he nevertheless maintains a certain reserve toward his admirers, as befits a man who has been one of the authentic folk heroes of America's Negroes, not to mention thousands of others, for many years.

When Paige takes to the road, he usually carries one enormous bag containing four conservative suits, several pairs of shoes, bottles of pills, ointments and philters to combat anticipated ailments, and a great miscellany of other items. One of the twenty cameras he owns inevitably dangles from a shoulder strap. Redcaps compete desperately to carry his luggage. As Paige strolls regally along the train platforms

on his way to the Browns' car, all the cooks and porters hang out of car windows on both sides to salute him.

"All right, brothers," Paige exclaims, waving and grinning broadly as he passes. "Let us ramble."

In the club car, Paige is inevitably surrounded by other Browns players, who consider him a library of general information and probably the most authoritative train-window commentator in the land.

Paige thinks creatively in almost any field, which is to say that even though he may not know what he is talking about on some subject, what he says nevertheless sounds more factual than the facts. Recently, for example, Paige told one teammate how to make straw hats. This man, who had once worked in a straw-hat factory, came away convinced that he had spent years laboring in error. In a conversation on the theory of engineering stresses with ex-Brownie outfielder Frank Saucier, an honor student in engineering who is now in the Navy, Paige waxed so eloquent that Saucier had to retreat to his books to reassure himself.

One subject Paige rarely discusses is his home life. The main reason is that his pretty second wife, Lahoma, does not approve of mixing his public and private affairs.

At home in one of the two large, dark-brick houses he owns in Kansas City, Missouri, Paige usually moves with the patriarchal gravity of a settled landholder. (He lives in one house, rents the other.) A restless man, he constantly prowls about the trophy room, the Chinese antique room and the twelve other rooms, including his roost on the second floor.

Paige's home activity tends to dampen the natural ebullience of the many relatives and friends always to be found in the household, several of them on a semipermanent basis. But it has little effect on Mrs. Paige, who has a strong character, or on his four children: Pamella, five; Caroline, two and a half; Linda, one and a half; and Leroy, Jr., six months. Mrs. Paige, who first caught her husband's eye as a clerk in a Kansas City camera store when he wandered in to buy film six years ago, keeps him on rather short tether, which he seems to find agreeable, since he grumbles about it all the time. Paige's first wife, Janet, a vivacious Pittsburgh waitress whom he married in 1934 and from whom he was divorced some years ago, also kept him on short rein. Too short, he says.

Outside his home life, no field of conversational inquiry is too remote for Paige to venture into. If other players have problems with love, finances, batting averages, falling hair or whatever, Paige may be counted on for remedies. Occasionally, of course, he comes upon something that ruffles his composure.

In the club car of a Chicago-bound train this year, some players presented Paige a book called *How to Pitch,* by Cleveland's wealthy squire, Bob Feller, Paige's junior by perhaps fifteen years. Retiring to a window seat with this volume, Paige, who has beaten Feller a staggering number of times in exhibition games, at once began snorting and shifting about.

"Here, now!" he exclaimed, starting up in astonishment at one point. "Is that how you do it?"

A few pages later, he leaped up and began to execute one of the illustrated techniques. But he couldn't seem to get the hang of it.

"That's a good book," he informed one of his teammates later. "Only thing is, if I start pitchin' the correct way now, I'll probably break my arm. I just about broke it once," he said, darkly, "and I can't risk it again."

When Paige just about broke his arm, he was in Mexico City, in 1938, at the peak of his fame and pitching power. Throwing a simple sidearm curve one day, he snapped his arm so badly that he couldn't lift it. Back in Kansas City, the doctor who examined him said flatly that he was through.

No news could have been more inconceivable to Paige. His arm had lifted him from poverty and childhood delinquency in Mobile. It had survived Canadian cold, 117-degree desert heat, thousands of all-night bus rides and greasy hamburger joints and cheap boardinghouses. It had stood up to every trial to which Paige could subject it, including four Negro World Series and East-West all-star games before crowds of 50,000 and up. Had it been of a different hue, major-league club owners might have paid up to $150,000 cash for it at 1938 prices.

All this notwithstanding, Satch Paige couldn't lift it. Within a month, the only job he could get was a coach for the Kansas City Monarchs. For the next year, he traveled with the Monarchs' second team, growing more and more obscure and irascible. "Man," Paige says, "it was a long year."

It was an interminable year, hard on the young players trying to expand under the brooding shadow of the former "greatest pitcher in the world," and impossible for Paige, who seemed to grow taller, thinner and grimmer-looking every day. By 1940, when he was thirty-four, or thereabouts, and hadn't pitched for fourteen months, Paige was ready to quit.

Then, just before a Monarchs game one afternoon, a queer thing happened. Someone overthrew first in a pre-game warmup and Paige ambled over, picked up the ball and threw it back to the pitcher. It was the most unobtrusive of acts, but just about every player on the field seemed to see it and to stop stock-still.

Walking thoughtfully toward the dugout, Paige picked up a glove and called for a ball. Without a word, the Monarchs' catcher left the plate and stationed himself about pitching distance from Paige. Then Paige began to throw, easily at first, then harder and harder. Nobody moved, the stands were silent, the game waiting. The catcher called, "Easy, Satchel, easy!" But Paige leaned into his pitches until the ball seemed to diminish in space. Then, abruptly, he stopped, and gazed around at all the eyes upon him.

"Well," he said, "I'm back."

The news traveled fast. Semipro club owners flocked around with contracts as soon as they heard, and the fans began to roar. Life once again became a pleasure for Paige. He traveled far and wide, showing new generations of hitters a whole new assortment of curves, floaters and so on, to go with his fast ball, which he now used only in the pinches. His fan mail was staggering. His income as a solo performer ranged up to $35,000 a year.

"It was all so nice," Paige recalls, "that I almost forgot time was passin' and I hadn't begun to do what I'd always wanted."

What Paige had always wanted was to play for a major-league club. By 1946, when every hot stove buzzed with rumors that the big-league color line was about to be broken, Paige lived at a high pitch of excitement.

"Maybe I was too eager," Paige says. "But then I figured that with all those writin' men sayin' I'm due for the Hall of Fame and all that ruckus—well, I figured I'd be the first one under the wire."

When Jackie Robinson became the first one, Paige went on pitching for semipro teams without comment. When Larry Doby and others followed Robinson, Paige spoke less and less.

"When 1948 come around," Paige says, "and I still got my nose to the window, I realized what the club owners was thinkin'. They was thinkin' that when I was with Chattanooga, Larry Doby wasn't bawn."

However, Bill Veeck, then owner of the Cleveland Indians, was not thinking just that way.

"Abe Saperstein, who owns the Harlem Globetrotters basketball team, and who always seems to turn up when Satch needs him, had been after me for a long time to sign him up," Veeck says. "But Lou Boudreau, who was managing Cleveland, didn't think it was there any more. Still, he was desperate for relief men so he put on a catcher's mitt at the stadium one day and says to Satch: 'All right, here's the plate. See if you can get it up here.' Well," Veeck says, "Lee-roy threw fifty pitches. Forty-six of them were strikes. That was that."

If the Indians management was convinced, some sports writers were not. J. G. Taylor Spink, publisher of the influential St. Louis *Sporting News,* let go as follows:

"Many well-wishers of baseball emphatically fail to see eye to eye with the signing of Satchel Paige, superannuated Negro pitcher. . . . To bring in a pitching rookie of Paige's age . . . is to demean the standards of baseball in the big circuits."

"I demeaned the big circuits considerable that year," Paige says. "I win six an' lose one."

The night that Paige walked out of a quarter century of circus baseball into the rarefied atmosphere of the big leagues, some 20,000 fans at Cleveland Stadium rose for ten minutes of unbroken roaring. Paige obliged by blanking the Browns for two innings in relief.

By the end of the season, Paige, besides his six-and-one record, had an earned-run average of 2.47, had struck out 45, made no errors afield and got himself two hits. Sports writers were so amazed that several of them voted to name him Rookie of the Year.

"I declined the position," Paige says calmly. "I wasn't sure which year the gentlemen had in mind."

When Paige joined the Indians, the news penetrated instantly to the remotest backwoods; all over the American League, crowds poured out to watch the legend in the flesh. The climax was reached on August 20th, when Paige started against eighth-place Chicago at Cleveland, and the all-time record night crowd of 78,382 paid to see him win.

Toward the end of the 1948 season, to Paige's vast surprise, certain creaks in his physical mechanism had begun to appear. "Ol' No. 1," which is what Paige calls his back muscles and diaphragm, remained in good shape. So did "Ol' No. 2," his pitching arm. But he was having a time with his nervous stomach—the product of too many years of barnstorming as "The World's Greatest Pitcher—Guaranteed to Strike Out the First Nine Men." His flat feet hurt and the emaciated calves attached to them seemed weighted with stone. On top of all this, the dentist had a message for him.

"The dentist says to me that all my teeth will have to come out," Paige recalls, with horror. "I says, doctor, I will not abide with store teeth, and he says, then you will not abide."

If emotion was on Paige's side, fact seemed to be on the dentist's. Paige felt worse and worse as the 1948 season closed, and he was full of miseries when he reported to the Indians in Arizona for the 1949 season. However, in mid-season, when the hot weather began, he felt better and began to expand and advise the young pitchers in the devious ways of the game.

During one grindingly tight game with Boston, Paige was advising Mike Garcia, a young Cleveland pitcher of great promise. It was the last of the eighth, Cleveland led by one run, the Red Sox were up with nobody out and Garcia was squirming with nervousness in the Indian bull pen. He had just been told that he might have to go in for relief.

"Boy," said Paige, lounging back on the bullpen bench and exuding vast confidence, "I wouldn't worry about them Red Sox. There ain't a hitter among 'em."

As Paige spoke, a pinch hitter singled sharply, and lead-off man Dom DiMaggio came to bat. "Now, this fella," Paige drawled, "there is a mess." DiMaggio singled to center and Johnny Pesky came up.

"Pesky!" Paige snorted, disdainfully. "Why they say that man can hit, I don't know. You just feed him in close on his knees . . ."

Pesky hit the first pitch for a single, loading the bases. While the dreaded Ted Williams strode to the plate, Paige clapped the quaking Garcia on the shoulder and declared jovially: "Now we're gonna be all right."

As Satchel made this announcement, manager Lou Boudreau beckoned to the bull pen—not for Garcia, but for Paige. There was a moment of deep silence in the dugout. Then, as though in a trance, Paige rose from the bench.

"Son," he said, huskily, concluding his message to Garcia, "just remember, when you're disputin' the Red Sox, put your trust in the power of prayer."

Prayer got Paige out of the hole with the loss of but one run.

During the long August pull in 1949, all of Paige's miseries came back and the batters started injuring him repeatedly. Of the thirty-one games he appeared in that year, he won four and lost seven. The next winter, when Bill Veeck sold out as principal owner of the Indians, Satchel Paige's contract went up for sale. There were no takers.

"That winter, I went back to that dentist," Paige recalled with annoyance, a while ago. "Well, he come at me with them pliers, and I reared back, and then we got to rasslin' and I give him a few knocks in the excitement. But he win," said Paige, taking out his uppers and gazing at them with grudging admiration. "Couple days and the misery was gone."

The end of Paige's miseries seemed to interest nobody in the majors in 1950, however, so he started back over the old itinerant trail, pitching any- and everywhere, and nearly doubling the $20,000 a year he had made in the majors. When the Giants and Braves offered him contracts in the pennant drive, Paige had to turn them down. "I couldn't afford to lose money pitchin' for nobody but Bill Veeck," he says. "With Burrhead, I didn't feel it so much."

When Veeck bought control of the St. Louis Browns in mid-1951, one of his first acts was to sign Paige.

"Lee-roy was a must," says Veeck. "Everybody kept telling me he was through, but that was understandable. They thought he was only human.

"Later on in the season," Veeck added reflectively, "I began to think so myself. Satch won three and lost four for us. When he announced at the end of the season that it might be his last year, the wire services carried the story mostly for sentimental reasons."

When the juices of spring began to rise in Mr. Paige in early 1952, however, he set out for the Browns' training camp at Burbank, California, with no thought for last year's statements to the press. The California weather filled him with such energies that he could hardly wait for the season to begin.

When it did begin, however, the other Browns were also so steamed up that they were astonished to find themselves in first place.

"I was just a bull-pen pitcher," Paige recalls, with dismay. "Every man we put in the first four games went the route. The buck fever was among us. But I says to myself, look here, Satchel, them old-time ballplayers on them other clubs ain't loosened up yet. Wait 'til the hot weather hits them and they'll all be stompin' around up there on top, fightin' each other for that third of a game, that little piece of a game to put them in the lead. Then you'll be pitchin', I says to myself. Oh, my, yes."

By June, it seemed to Paige that he was pitching every other day. The fast-slipping Browns would get a slim lead, watch it begin to vanish and call loudly for Paige. If the opposition had managed to tie the score before Paige went in, games would go on endlessly, because Paige would yield no runs and his teammates could never get any when they were most needed.

By July 4th, Paige had appeared in 25 games. He had pitched 10 innings of an 18-inning game at Washington, holding the Senators to a 5-5 tie until the game was called at 1:00 A.M. Against the Indians, he had gone 11 innings of an incredible 19-inning game, finally losing it when he and the fans could hardly keep their eyes open. Time and again, he had gone in to protect one-run leads for the Browns and retired the best hitters of the American League, one, two, three. Watching him do just that to the Yankees one night, Casey Stengel, manager of both the Bombers and the 1952 American League All-Star team, picked Paige as one of his pitchers for the July dream game.

"That took care of the third one of my big ambitions," Paige says. "Before I'd hardly got started in my career, I'd played for a big-league club, pitched in a World Series" (two thirds of an inning with Cleveland in 1948) "and made the All-Star team. That did my stomach gas a lot of good."

The rest of the season did his digestion little good, however. As the Browns went down and down to seventh place, Paige rose more and more often to pitch. By season's end, he had worked a staggering total of 46 games, struck out 91, and won 12 games, lost 10 and saved 10.

In the long grind, he had even worked against railroad timetables. At 9:30 one evening, with the Browns leading Washington by one run and due to catch a 10:30 train, Paige had come ambling in to stem a ninth-inning Washington rally. He retired three Senator hitters on nine called strikes and one ball. On the train later on, he had apologized for the ball.

"When the shootin' finally stopped," says Paige, "I found out I was tired. I figured a few hot baths and a few days layin' around the house would take care of that, and it did, as far as my frame was concerned. But I had another kind of tired. I was kinda tired of baseball."

This new fatigue took a long time to show up. Most of the winter, Paige took it easy around his house, doing a little carpentry and plumbing here and there, thinking he ought to fix up the back yard, and worrying about his 35 per cent income tax. Time and inaction were great problems. Winter, itself, was a problem. Satchel hated the cold—it had always driven him to the tropics in other years. In winter, time seemed to drag, leaving nothing to do but shoot some pool, or do a little after-dinner speaking around Kansas City, or answer his fan mail, or hunt, or regard the television, which wasn't much good for his pitching eye.

By early February of this year, the new fatigue really began to work on Paige. He descended the long staircase in his house like a remote chieftain, scattering relatives and friends right and left with a cold eye. He got out his Spanish guitar and sang gloomy tunes up in his room.

Then, one gray day, things came to a head. The first thought Paige had on awakening was of a talk he was supposed to give at a luncheon in his honor that noon. The thought wearied and depressed him. He put it out of his mind until midday, when some civic leaders called for him in a limousine. On the way downtown, he sat silent and somber. At a loss to explain Paige's mood, the leaders talked around it, finally inquiring, heartily, what he intended to say at the banquet.

Paige took his time answering. He roused himself slowly from a slouched position. He stared at the gentlemen.

"I'm gonna say that they got the wrong man for this speech," he said finally. "I'm gonna say I'm through with baseball! Worn out runnin' around! Sick and tired!"

That stopped all conversation. Many blocks farther on, the limousine approached a vacant lot where some piping, stick-legged boys were rushing the season with a pickup ball game. Paige began to stir restlessly at the sight. He looked away but his eyes seemed to be drawn back. He coughed nervously. When the limousine was passing the lot, Paige suddenly sat up and ordered the driver to stop. Despite the heated protests of the civic gentlemen, he got out.

"You run on along to the lunch," he said. "I'll just set here a while."

After the lunch, says one witness, the gentlemen satisfied their curiosity by driving back past the lot. They arrived in the middle of a hot ball game. The battery was Paige, six feet three and a quarter inches tall, weight 180, age indefinite, pitching; Slattery, four feet two inches tall, weight 85, age nine, catching. The up team, the Jackson Street White Sox, was hitting Satchel Paige unmercifully. Also, the umpire, Yogi Olzewschki, wasn't giving him the corners.

After watching the game for a moment, the dignitaries looked at one another with visible dismay and told the driver to move on.

"Empire," Paige was protesting happily as they vanished down the street, "are you by any chance in need of spectacles?"

"I see fine!" Olzewschki was shouting authoritatively. "Play ball, or I'll throw you out of the game!"

HOW TO STAY YOUNG

1. Avoid fried meats which angry up the blood.
2. If your stomach disputes you, lie down and pacify it with cool thoughts.
3. Keep the juices flowing by jangling around gently as you move.
4. Go very light on the vices, such as carrying on in society. The social ramble ain't restful.
5. Avoid running at all times.
6. Don't look back. Something might be gaining on you.

(Signed) LEROY SATCHEL PAIGE

THIS STREAK of Joe D.'s was probably the greatest hitting record of major league history. This story was datelined Cleveland, July 17, 1941. The Jim Bagby was the son of another pitching Jim Bagby— see Harry Cross's story on page 61.

1941:
New York Yankees 4,
Cleveland Indians 3

JOHN DREBINGER

IN A BRILLIANT SETTING of lights and before 67,468 fans, the largest crowd ever to see a game of night baseball in the major leagues, the Yankees tonight vanquished the Indians, 4 to 3, but the famous hitting streak of Joe DiMaggio finally came to an end.

Officially it will go into the records as fifty-six consecutive games, the total he reached yesterday. Tonight in Cleveland's municipal stadium the great DiMag was held hitless for the first time in more than two months.

Al Smith, veteran Cleveland left-hander and a Giant castoff, and Jim Bagby, a young right-hander, collaborated in bringing the DiMaggio string to a close.

Jolting Joe faced Smith three times. Twice he smashed the ball down the third-base line, but each time Ken Keltner, Tribe third sacker, collared the ball and hurled it across the diamond for a put-out at first. In between these two tries, DiMaggio drew a pass from Smith.

Then, in the eighth, amid a deafening uproar, the streak dramatically ended, though the Yanks routed Smith with a flurry of four hits and two runs that eventually won the game.

With the bases full and only one out, Bagby faced DiMaggio and, with the count at one ball and one strike, induced the renowned slugger to crash into a double play. It was a grounder to the shortstop, and as the ball flitted from Lou Boudreau to Ray Mack to Oscar Grimes,

who played first base for the Tribe, the crowd knew the streak was over.

However, there were still a few thrills to come, for in the ninth, with the Yanks leading, 4 to 1, the Indians suddenly broke loose with an attack that for a few moments threatened to send the game into extra innings and thus give DiMaggio another chance.

Gerald Walker and Grimes singled, and though Johnny Murphy here replaced Gomez, Larry Rosenthal tripled to score his two colleagues. But with the tying run on third and nobody out the Cleveland attack bogged down in a mess of bad base running and the Yanks' remaining one-run lead held.

It was on May 15 against the White Sox at the Yankee Stadium that DiMaggio began his string. As the great DiMag kept clicking in game after game, he became the central figure of the baseball world.

On June 29, in a double-header with the Senators in Washington, he tied, then surpassed the American League and modern record of forty-one games, set by George Sisler of the Browns in 1922. The target was the all-time major league high of forty-four contests set by Willie Keeler, famous Oriole star, forty-four years ago under conditions much easier for a batsman than they are today. Then there was no foul-strike rule hampering the batter.

But nothing hampered DiMaggio as he kept

getting his daily hits, and on July 1 he tied the Keeler mark. The following day he soared past it for game No. 45, and he kept on soaring until tonight, in seeking his fifty-seventh game, he finally was brought to a halt.

Actually, DiMaggio hit in fifty-seven consecutive games, for on July 8 he connected safely in the All-Star game in Detroit. But that con-

test did not count in the official league records.

DiMaggio's mark ends five short of his own Pacific Coast League record of sixty-one consecutive games, which he set while with San Francisco in 1933. The all-time minor league high is sixty-seven, set by Joe Wilhoit of Wichita in the Western League in 1919.

GEORGE PRICE

"Grab a mitt. The world situation won't deteriorate any faster because you get in a little one o' cat."

ELSEWHERE in this book, H. Allen Smith wonders how the first curve-ball pitcher knew he was throwing a curve. Others, Mr. Smith points out, have wondered whether a ball curves at all, and among these was the world-famous aerodynamics wizard Igor Sikorsky. Mr. Sikorsky happened to have a wind tunnel, so tests were undertaken. His findings are reported in the following article.

The Sikorsky test found that a curve ball does curve, which accounts for Mr. Drury's title to his article, "The Hell It Don't Curve." The Sikorsky test also found that while a curve ball does curve in the sense that it follows a steady arc, it does not travel in a straight line and then "break." To which, I can only add, as editor of this anthology and a .240 hitter, the hell it don't.

The Hell It Don't Curve

JOSEPH F. DRURY, JR.

IN THE early 1870's, two major controversies stormed in the world of sports. One of these arguments ended in a generally accepted decision just five years later. But the other still rages spasmodically today, after more than eighty years of scientific rhubarb.

It was California's Governor Leland Stanford who, in 1878, collected a $50,000 bet by proving that all four feet of a galloping horse are off the ground at the same time. And it was Igor Sikorsky, internationally famous expert on aerodynamics, who not long ago used a wind tunnel to show that a human being *can* make a baseball curve.

Before Sikorsky approached the thesis, it had been argued and refuted, proved and exploded, sworn to and Bronx-cheered-at by scientists, photographers, and fans in general. Even the philosophers got into the act, one of them observing that "it would be at variance with every principle of philosophy" to contend that the ball does not curve.

Two of the most recent tests of the curve ball controversy were made by two national picture magazines. Each of them used an elaborate photographic technique, and the conclusions of both were regarded as more or less au-

thoritative. But while one magazine (*Life*) claimed that its studies "raise once more the possibility that this stand-by of baseball is, after all, only an optical illusion," the other (*Look*) insisted that its own photographs proved "that a curve ball actually does curve." The high-speed cameras merely added fuel to the fires of both camps.

The pictures which purported to indicate that a baseball does *not* curve were themselves branded optical illusions by traditionalists. And when he studied pictures made to show that the ball *does* curve, Ernest Lowry, an outspoken member of the optical illusion school, called them "a most convincing demonstration of the complete *collapse* of the entire curve ball theory."

Incidentally, Mr. Lowry, who says the optical illusion is caused by "persistence of retinal impressions," also entertains some rather bitter convictions about what baseball men are doing to the country's juveniles. "The great injustice of the much publicized 'curve pitch,'" he contends, "is that of the manner in which millions of American boys have been misled on the question. They have been forced to delude themselves into thinking that their pitches do curve, or else be cruelly frustrated when they sense that their heroic efforts failed to achieve that which is now proved an impossibility."

* * *

Thus it was with righteous zeal that Sikorsky took up the scientific gauntlet. If American youth was being outrageously deceived by an unscrupulous combine of club owners and sports writers, if the curve ball religion was nothing but an opiate for the mustard-smeared masses, then he would explode the myth and rock baseballdom with his sock-dolager exposé.

At the time Sikorsky turned to the wind tunnel, major league baseball men openly propagandized the curve ball doctrine. A survey to measure their reactions to the "optical illusion" photographs brought in some interesting comments. Some were subtle. Others carried the impact of a hard-swung fungo bat.

"I am not positive whether a ball curves or not," said Eddie Sawyer, former manager of the Phillies, "but there is a pitch in baseball much different from the fast ball that 'separates the men from the boys.' If this pitch does not curve, it would be well to notify a lot of baseball players who were forced to quit the game they loved because of this certain pitch, and may be reached now at numerous gas stations, river docks, and mental institutions."

Ex-Cincinnati pilot Luke Sewell asked a very pertinent question. "Isn't it strange," he said, "that the optical illusion only happens when someone tries to throw a curve ball, and never when a fast or straight ball is attempted?" And Earl Mack, of the Athletics, followed up with this: "Is the magazine author crediting pitchers with the power of turning on optical illusions at will?"

And so the reactions went. Obviously, you would wire-tap a lot of locker rooms and subpoena many a ton of baseball records before you'd find a modern major-leaguer to support Mr. Lowry's suspicions. But he might have found a useful witness in Colonel J. B. Joyce, who, in 1877, was a ruling spirit in the old Cincinnati Red Stockings. It was to convince Joyce that the first publicized test of the curve ball issue was made. According to A. G. Spalding, who describes the test in his volume, *Baseball, America's National Game*, Colonel Joyce insisted that it was "absurd to say that any man could throw a ball other than in a straight line."

The test was made in Cincinnati in the presence of a large crowd. A surveyor set three posts in a row, twenty feet apart. Then two high fences were built, extending beyond each end post and in a direct line with all three posts. Will White, one of the league's best right-hand pitchers, stood to the left of the fence at one end of the course. When he made his throw, the fence prevented his hand from crossing the straight line between the posts.

"White pitched the ball," says Spalding, "so that it passed to the right of the middle post. This it did by three or four inches, but curved so much that it passed the third post a half foot to the left. The test was a success in everything but the conversion. Colonel Joyce would not be convinced."

Shortly after the 1877 experiment, the *Cincinnati Enquirer* printed the views of three college professors on the possibility of a pitched curve ball. Professor Stoddard, of Worcester University, wrote: "It is not only theoretically but practically impossible for any such impetus to be conveyed to a moving body as would be required . . . to control the movement of what is termed a curved ball."

But Professor Lewis Swift, of Rochester University, disagreed. "It is true that some time ago, when the subject was first broached to me," he said, "I denied that it was possible to do it. But I began to investigate the matter and soon saw that, instead of being impossible, it was in accordance with the *plainest principles of philosophy*."

It is doubtful that principles of philosophy were in the mind of Ralph Lightfoot while he was test-flying in a helicopter over Bridgeport, Conn., some time ago. Lightfoot is chief of flight research at United Aircraft Corporation's Sikorsky plant. When he landed, he was given a message to report immediately to Mr. Sikorsky for discussion of an "important project."

Sikorsky had just received a telephone call from New York, where United Aircraft's Lauren (Deac) Lyman had been lunching with Walter H. Neff of United Air Lines. During their luncheon conversation, the topic had turned to the opening of the baseball season and the curve ball talents of leading pitchers.

"Doesn't it strike you as strange," asked Neff, "that science counts the wing-beats of insects and controls planes at supersonic speeds—but it can't seem to prove what happens when a man throws a baseball sixty feet?"

"The problem should be simple enough," said Lyman. "Just a combination of human factors and pure aerodynamics."

"Then why couldn't one of your company's engineers do it, Deac?"

Lyman smiled thoughtfully. "I wonder . . ." he said. "By gosh, why don't we phone Igor?"

When Lightfoot entered his office, Sikorsky greeted him in his soft, continental accent. "Look, Mr. Lightfoot," the helicopter genius began, gesturing with cupped hands. "Here we have a solid sphere, moving rapidly in space and rotating on a vertical axis. You see?"

Lightfoot nodded. His mind raced ahead of Sikorsky's words. It sounded alarmingly like flying saucers. But as his boss continued, the engineer grinned broadly. "The object," said Sikorsky, "is to elude the man with the stick."

Whatever he lacked in baseball lingo Sikorsky made up for in scientific lore. For instance, he knew that a pitched ball, traveling in a curved path, is an example of aerodynamic action in everyday life. He realized, too, that the force which causes a ball to curve in flight is the same force known to engineers as "the Magnus effect," because it was explained by Professor G. Magnus, of Berlin, way back in 1851. Needless to say, Magnus wasn't interested in baseballs. His subject was *cannon* balls, and he was trying to find out why German artillery couldn't throw more "strikes."

But 25 years later, a British physicist named Lord John Rayleigh applied the Magnus findings to a report on the flight of a tennis ball. Briefly, what Rayleigh found was this: That when a ball is in flight but not spinning, it is exposed to a uniform air flow in one direction. So it follows a straight line. But when the ball is made to rotate sideways, friction between the ball and the air around it forms a sort of whirlpool. When this happens, the air flow is no longer in one direction. The whirlpool brings another force into play. And this double force on only one side of the ball produces a *lateral* force which drives it in the direction toward which it is spinning.

The picture magazine which favored the optical illusion explanation of the curve ball theory accepted, of course, the more obvious fact that a tennis or Ping-pong ball curves. In fact, the author wrote: "If a baseball could be spun with the same amount of power relative to its weight that a tennis ball is spun, then its path, it is agreed, would also be curved to the same extent. But," he added, "no pitcher, it seems, has a strong enough finger and wrist motion to put the necessary spin onto the ball which would materially affect its sidewise motion."

It was Sikorsky's first problem, then, to determine how much "stuff" or spin a pitcher can put on the ball in the regulation sixty-foot,

six-inch distance from the mound to the plate.

To learn this, baseball fans among the plant's engineers were glad to contribute some of their off-duty time. Careful studies were made of rapid-fire flash photographs showing the progress of a single pitch. Aircraft technicians, experienced in observing the behavior of whirling propellers, examined the change in the position of the ball's stitches from picture to picture. They figured that the ball was spinning at the rate of one-third of a revolution during each one-thirtieth of a second between exposures. Since the entire pitch took less than a half second, the rate of rotation was seen to be about five revolutions for the pitch, or about 600 per minute.

So far, the engineers knew how much spin a human could put on a pitched baseball. But they still had to find out whether that was enough to make it curve. For the wind tunnel, that job was literally "a breeze."

Using official National and American League balls—identical except for their markings—Sikorsky and Lightfoot impaled them on a slender spike connected to the shaft of a small motor. During the next "stand-by time" between aircraft tests, the baseballs were inserted into the tunnel and rotated by the motor at speeds from zero to 1,200 revolutions per minute. Since official army devices had clocked Bob Feller's fast ball at 98.6 miles per hour, the forward speeds of the air moving through the tunnel were varied between 80 and 110 miles per hour. The motor was mounted on a delicately-balanced scale which measured the direction and force of all pressures brought on the balls.

To observe maximum and minimum effects, the baseballs were spiked and rotated at two different angles. In one position, four seams met the wind during each revolution. This produced the greatest amount of side force on the ball. In the other position, only two seams met the wind, producing less friction and less side force.

When the wind tunnel results were plotted on conventional engineering graph sheets, Sikorsky knew he had "something for the books." The results have so much significance that they could even cause changes in pitching and batting techniques. Here, in the order of their importance, are the findings.

1. *It can be definitely concluded that a pitched baseball does actually curve, in addition to any optical illusion which may exist.*

2. A pitched baseball travels in a *uniformly*

curved path from the time it leaves the pitcher's hand until it reaches the catcher's glove. There's no such thing as a "sharp-breaking curve" in the sense that a ball can be thrown so that it flies first in a straight line and then suddenly veers off. That kind of "remote control" is strictly from *fiction,* not friction.

3. To an observer at or behind the plate, it *appears* that the ball travels fairly straight most of the way and then breaks suddenly and sharply near the plate. Actually, the curve ball *arcs* toward or away from the plate *throughout* its flight; but the batter, because he views the flight at an angle, cannot discern the gradual arc and believes the ball "breaks" at an angle.

4. Here's one for the coaches. The pitcher who learns to release the ball so that *all four* seams meet the wind each time it rotates will have the nearest thing possible to a "jug-handle" curve. If he has Feller's speed of over 80 miles per hour, and Carl Hubbell's spin of 600 revolutions per minute, his curve will "break" as much as 19 inches. With the same speed and rotation, but with only two seams meeting the wind, the amount of curve will drop to about 7½ inches.

If you're an average fan, you'll be content to measure a curve by how well it fools the batter. But for those with technical minds, here's a Sikorsky formula that will tell you how much a baseball will curve:

$$d \text{ equals } \frac{^cL \, P \, V^2 \, t^2 \, g \, C^2}{7230 \, W} \text{ feet}$$

Where: *d* equals displacement from a straight line; cL equals circulation of air generated by friction when ball is spinning; P

equals the density of the air (normal at .002-378); V equals the speed of the ball; *t* equals the time for delivery; g equals the acceleration of gravity (32.2 feet per second²); C equals the circumference of the ball (9 inches); and W equals the ball's weight (.3125 pounds); while the number 7230 relates other values of pounds, inches, feet, seconds, etc., to arrive at an answer in feet.

Sikorsky and his co-workers may well have produced the most convincing evidence yet that a pitcher can throw curves. Happily enough, their findings offer both the curve ball *and* the optical illusion squads their inning of vindication. The fact of the matter, stated simply, is that the curve ball *does* curve, but the batter—because of his angular view of the pitch—experiences the *optical illusion* that the ball curves more radically than it does.

Al Schacht, the "Clown Prince of Baseball," now runs one of the world's swankiest "cracker barrel leagues" at his New York restaurant. And to illustrate how seriously the world of baseball takes its curves, Al revives this favorite story:

A farm-belt ballplayer, locally famous for his hitting powers, won a major league tryout during spring training. Each week, as his batting average and confidence soared, he wired his mother. The first week, he said: "Dear Mom. Leading all batters. These pitchers not so tough." A week later, he boasted: "Looks like I will be regular outfielder. Now hitting .433." Early in the third week of training, the yokel's mother got a wire that led her to dismiss the new farmhand and get out her son's work clothes. "Dear Mom," it said. "They started throwing curves. Will be home Friday."

CHARLES DRYDEN, the prototype of baseball reporting with wit and imagination, was, among other things, inventor of the phrase "Washington—first in war, first in peace, last in the American League." Washington won this particular game, but, happening then even as happens today, the losing team backed into the pennant. Dryden dispatched this story from Washington to his paper in Philadelphia.

1905:
Washington Senators 10,
Philadelphia Athletics 4

CHARLES DRYDEN

ALL THE FRET and worry have been wiped from the schedule, and the fanatics may seek some needed repose. The pennant is ours.

Mr. Mack's tired toilers lost today, 10 to 4, but they can do the shouting, since St. Louis cleaned up Chicago. The double-header here tomorrow carries no terrors. If necessary, we can drop both games while the White Sox pound away at the Browns until they are blue in the face. Nothing more doing until the post-mortem series to decide which is the dead one —Giants or Athletics. Let us all emit three cheers, anyhow, for luck.

The Rube broke into the busy whirl today, but he was too rusty to rescue like he once did. Coakley needed help, and Rusty Rube gave the best he had, and which gives promise of the best there is later on.

The weary but willing Coakley again mounted the hill, only to be knocked off in the second round by a fusillade of five queer hits that scored four runs. One Falkenberg, the human whisper, went to the woods in one round. We reached him for three counts in the first, and tied in the third with Wolfe pitching.

At this time the Browns were pouring hot shot into the Sox far away, so Mr. Mack took a chance on Waddell. The giant won much applause and a few grunts and hisses as the old Stain-of-Guilt stride carried him to the slab.

He had the new snap ball, the whiffer and the smoke, but little control. Beyond spasms of wildness, Rusty Rube was as good as ever. The steam was there, the shoulder joint worked freely, and the Senators made but five hits. One of the five passes, a bunt hit and errors by Rube and Davis gave the enemy the game in the sixth round.

Plenty of work will put Rube in trim. He also pitched his head off to save the day for Andy and Mr. Mack. All the great flinger needs to put him right is a little dash of oil in his steering gear.

Wolfe was in excellent shape, holding the Athletics to four swats in eight rounds. But that made no difference while St. Louis was hitting the ball. The pennant winners tore off enough yesterday to entitle them to one day of restful ease. Forget the weak poling of today.

A jubilee in honor of hard-earned and well-deserved victory broke out in the eighth inning. Sam Erwin, who is Uncle Ben's fishing pard at Phillie and elsewhere, had built here yesterday a number of flags and banners. One large pennant bore the inscription, "Champions of 1905." The smaller ones were labeled "Athletics," done in white on a blue ground.

Erwin smuggled these emblems into the boxes occupied by the wives of the Athletic players, back of the visitors' bench. The flags remained under cover until the eighth round, when the Browns had the Sox, 6 to 1. Then Erwin and the women turned on the jubilee, full blast. Mr. Schreck's mother, who is an ardent fanatic, flapped the big flag and the little ones over the rail. Poor Rube was getting his bumps in that round. Four of the five hits came off in close order, and a wild pitch added to the tumult.

Another big crowd filled the stand, it being "Ladies' Day." The good-natured howls of the home rooters, the bumps and the frantic flags had Reuben guessing some. He didn't know just what it all meant, being too busy to watch the scoreboard while the Senators were scoring on him.

It certainly was an odd proposition to see a losing team win the pennant on alien soil, in the midst of rival demonstrations of joy on both sides. But that is the way the banner of 1905 came to Connie Mack.

Among the distinguished arrivals today was Mr. J. Schroeder, the talented groundkeeper for Columbia Park. He rode in a parlor car, and gave no thought to train sandwiches and sour mustard, for Joe was on pennant pleasures bent. In his face he carried a fine cigar, and under his arm a casket of little white metal elephants, attached to blue and white ribbons. These emblems of prowess were passed out to the players and Phillie rooters for breastplates.

Think of the contrast in groundkeepers, and how fate toys with them. Here was Joe, riding on the top wave of glory, while his rival, S. Payne, lingered at home alone with his dead and dying dandelions. Let us draw a veil over this harrowing picture. All hands are wearing lapel elephants tonight and floating the flag of the championship Athletics.

This historical old town, the home of more heroes, dead and living, than any spot on earth, still sounds the tall praises of Mr. Bender. Even though he canned the Senators twice in one day, the fanatics are proud to grasp the hand of Charles Albert and shake his splendid hurling stem. By noon today he wore a moist and feverish palm, caused by too much adulation at short range.

Charles got his picture and large strings of words about himself in all the papers. He is the talk of the town, and deserves to be.

In the morning, Charles Albert took a steam lift to the top of the monument, which is more than five hundred feet high. He wanted to enjoy a calm and comprehensive view of the great city which he held under his brown thumb the day before. Mr. Bender said the general vista looked good to him, even at that altitude.

In the afternoon some tokens of esteem were lavished upon Charles Albert. A gentleman from Norfolk purchased a 25-cent cigar at the Riggs House and handed the same to Mr. Bender in the presence of a large throng. Then Gene Demont rushed in with a couple of pointer pups. Gene had more dogs than he needed and was just looking for a good place to unload a few.

Keeper Newhouse took charge of the live stock, which will be trained to hunt buffaloes at Devil's Lake, Dakota. Once a hero, and all sorts of rare and costly tokens roll in to the foot of the throne. The Indian is having a new card engraved "C. Albert Bender," for use in high society. He is a pennant winner.

I take it as a compliment all around that when this novel first appeared in serial form in *Collier's*, a man who lives in upstate New York wrote me that he had identified my mythical city of Conway, New York, as Utica. I wrote him back it wasn't Utica. This may, though, be somewhat typical as an atmospheric setting for the minors.

From *The Only Game in Town*

CHARLES EINSTEIN

FAIRCHILD PARK, home of the Conway Bears, was situated along the main-line tracks of the Delaware and Hudson Railroad a mile or so south of the Conway depot. Nobody knows how many young boys, yearning to become professional ballplayers, have gazed out of the windows of D & H trains, viewed Fairchild Park, and decided then and there upon medicine, plumbing, or the law. The site of the park, which was named for Leland Fairchild, United States senator from Conway 1892–98, was used, a good number of years ago, as a coaling station for the D & H. In time, the coaling station was moved some three city blocks north, leaving enough uncontested acreage for the construction of a ball field. Thus Fairchild Park grew up without a glorious past, a rosy future, or, for that matter, a discernible present. In common with many other sooty, ramshackle, and splinter-fenced ball yards in towns across the country, it rapidly took on that not wholly describable quality of appearing vacant and discarded even when in use.

The grandstand, which had these many years withstood the unwritten law that all minor-league ball parks at one time or another burn down, was uncovered and could, conceivably, seat nearly four thousand fans. The stands, which biennially were painted a hideous and fast-decaying green, were fronted by a sagging wire screen some thirty-five feet back of home plate; underneath on the first-base side was a long wooden hutch which served as dressing quarters for the contestants; and, starting where the stands ended shortly beyond first and third bases, a seven-foot wooden fence—also painted green, but only in election years—circled the field.

The trains ran on an embankment back of the fence from right to center field, and it was possible to see over the fence from the windows of passing railroad cars. But these days the Conway Bears played only at night, and the lighting system was such that the free view was hardly worth it.

Still, it was a way of life for the fifteen men —four infielders, one utility man, five pitchers, two catchers, and three outfielders—who made up the roster of the Conway Bears of the Class C Empire League. As human beings went, they were no less ambitious, articulate, bigoted, or clanish than the men who worked in the railroad yards up the street; nor noticeably more so. Some of them, the young ones, still were uncertain of their craft; others, the old-timers, who had been up for a trial with the majors or the fast minors, now went through the motions with the mechanical imperfection of an unaccomplished physician treating the free patients at a clinic.

One of them—his name was Andrew Hunter —had spent sixteen years in the major leagues. Now he managed the Bears and played center field for them. He was a good hitter, though he seldom hit the long ball, and his legs were all right even as he neared his thirty-seventh birthday. It was the arm that had gone on him. In consequence, he had accepted almost gratefully the opportunity to manage the Conway Bears in behalf of the Philadelphia Bears, the major-league team whose farm system, cut to the bone because of the financial inroads made

104

by television, consisted now of just six teams, only one of them—Conway—classified as low as Class C.

All six teams in the Philadelphia farm system were called the Bears, a handy system that effected a considerable saving in home uniforms. By the time the uniforms filtered down as far as Conway, their residual advantages were neglegible, but this was the least of the local worries. Next year there might be no baseball at all in Conway, and for Stat Hunter —he had earned the nickname "Stat," short for "Statutory," from rival bench jockeys at the very start of his big-league career after having had several dates with the seventeen-year-old daughter of an umpire—for Stat Hunter, at any rate, there might next year be nothing but memories and the hope of finding another baseball job somewhere. That was why it was important to him to do a workmanlike job as manager of the Bears in Conway. It was incumbent upon him to develop at least one good young player, as well as to win enough games to stay the Conway Bears from utter bankruptcy, though nowadays bankruptcy seemed inevitable for bush-league clubs, and Philadelphia was interested first of all in Joe Whittier, the coming star. All this Hunter knew.

"Ol' Stat heah," George Crimeau, the first-string catcher for the Bears, would say upon occasion, "he goin' be back in th' *big* league one of these days not too far from now, managin' one of them *ball* clubs. You listen to ol' George when he tells you about ol' Stat. Ol' George and ol' Stat used to *play* together up in th' *big* league. I know ol' Stat from way back."

In actuality, ol' George had never advanced beyond a season and a half with Syracuse of the International League, but Stat Hunter never challenged his catcher's reminiscence. Were it not for the record book, Stat Hunter could easily have come to be persuaded that he and George did indeed play in the majors together at one time or another. A ballplayer—a ballplayer who cares for his job—remembers what happened. He remembers the enemy baserunner he doubled off first after a belly catch in right-center field, and the pitcher who threw a waster too close so he hit it down the left-field line for a double, and the umpire who blew the call when he had the plate with his foot ahead of the tag. He remembers games rather than years, and innings rather than games, and situations rather than innings, and individual mo-

ments best of all. And his remembrance of associated subjects is not nearly so keen, so that if a catcher like George Crimeau said he played with you, well, by God, maybe he did. You didn't really remember him *not* playing with you, and besides, a man like George Crimeau was fortified with song and fable.

"Ol' Stat and I was playing for Chicago— when was that, Stat, you recollect? Back in 'thirty-*six*, I think it was, and ol' Magerkurth was umpirin', and *Jurges* was playin' short— you remember that now, Stat? That real *hot* day in St. Louis? Well, Paul Dean's pitchin' for *them* . . ."

"I remember it," Andrew Hunter would say. "Vaguely."

Not everyone on the team exhibited Hunter's brand of patience. "You son of a bitch," Monk Gladstone, the third baseman, said one day to George Crimeau, "the closest you ever got to St. Louis was a Memorial Day doubleheader in Peoria. I was playing for Davenport. You give it to me coming into third. I remember you real good."

"Sure," the catcher replied acquiescently. "I remember *you*. You was playin' for Davenport and I was on th' way *up*. Next season, ol' Stat and I was playin' together for *Chicago*. That's th' way it was, ain't it, Stat?"

Later, Andrew Hunter would take someone like Gladstone to one side and say, "Come on, now, Monk, leave George alone. Lay off him."

"Well, he boils my crabs," Gladstone would reply. "He never got up in the big league and he knows it."

"He's not harming anybody," the manager would say.

"I'm going to tell you something, Stat, a guy like that browns me off. I'm the ballplayer he is any day in the week and two times on holidays, and I don't go around claiming I was in the big league."

"All right," Hunter would say. "All right, Monk, all right. The hell with it."

They were little antagonisms, but over a summer of hot, sticky nights, of dismal bus rides from town to town, of second-class food and third-class hotels, they would build their own angry pyramids. Andrew Hunter knew what he was doing when he decided to set no fixed time for the players to show up before a game. That way, only the youngsters were likely to appear much ahead of practice time. The old ones, like George Crimeau and Monk

Gladstone and Vagrancy Williams, the pitcher, would take their time, and there would be that much less chance for them to be sitting around together, nursing their petty hurts and irritations.

No night was a typical night in the Empire League, and yet every night was the same. No ballplayer was a typical ballplayer, and yet they too were all alike. Good nights were the nights you won, bad nights were the nights you lost, and when you were the manager you played the games all over again when you got home—the winning games as well as the losing games. If you worried only about the losing games, you were not a good manager.

In a way, you did more thinking in Class C than the managers did in the big league. You worried about the other team stealing your signals, not, as in the majors, because signal-stealing was an art, but because of necesssity your signals were so simple. You had to be sure not to pitch Bo Walsh, the left-hander, on a night when Cross-Eyed Collins, the umpire, was scheduled to work balls and strikes. You would not use Phil Gold, your second catcher, as a pinch-hitter in an early inning unless you absolutely had to, because then you could not use him to pinch-hit later on in the game, and besides, you wanted to have him to warm up your relief pitchers and to be ready to spell George Crimeau in case ol' George came down suddenly with that mysteriously private ailment which he called "th' heats," an affliction that occurred in greatest frequency late in the game when it seemed unlikely ol' George would get another turn at bat.

There was always something. This was only the first season as manager of the Bears for Andrew Hunter, but now, as early as the month of June, he felt he had become a somewhat unrealistic combination of tutor, teammate, and turnkey—not to mention his role as camp counselor, seeing to it that the youngsters wrote home twice a week.

June can be hot in Conway. The city lies in the lake valley, a valley some eight miles in width between twin ridges of the Adirondacks, and in the summer sun it becomes becalmed. Someone had put a small electric fan up on the wall of the Bears' clubhouse, and tonight, when Hunter got there, the fan was whining angrily.

Old Jack Merced, who served as caretaker for Fairchild Park and took tickets at the gate, came in the room behind him and said, "Hey, Stat, we gonna win tonight?"

"Try," Hunter said.

"That scout's coming in town tomorrow or the next day," Merced said. "What's his name? Marcus or something? Gonna have to see young Joe Whittier in action."

"That's right," Hunter said. "His name's Marcus." The manager was undressing at his locker. When he was down to his shorts, he took a safety razor down off the locker shelf, together with a tube of brushless shaving cream, and walked through the door to the combination shower and lavatory room that connected to both the home and visiting clubhouses.

Merced followed him. The two of them made up an uncommon picture—the one in front tall and black-haired, his body perhaps too slender, his face not handsome but pronounced, the eyes deep and alive, the nose and chin a trifle outsize; and the man behind, dressed in old Army pants and open-collared white shirt, white-haired, wizened, and small of stature. Old Jack Merced's face was set in a perpetual smart, like that of a man who has applied an overdose of after-shave lotion.

"There was a letter for you, Stat. You get it?"

Hunter shook his head, looking into the mirror.

"I left it in the box," the old man said.

"Didn't look in the box."

"I'll get it for you now." Merced went out of the room. Andrew Hunter debated calling after him, to tell him to hold the letter till he got back to his locker, but it was too hot to shout. Besides, the old man was back immediately. Hunter wiped his hand on his shorts and took the letter, and when he saw who had written it, he went back into the other room with the soap still on his face and sat down on the bench in front of his locker and read the letter there.

DEAR DADDY,
We went and saw the cows, and I held open the gate they went into. Mommy said I could have a surprise. Not a kitten or a dog but a real live . . . GUESS?? The kids next door have the chiken pox. I am fine.

x x x x x x x x

x x x

JANET

Sitting there, reading the letter with the soap on his face, Andrew Hunter looked not unlike an old-time circus clown between acts. Outside the window, a window that looked out on the underside of the grandstand where it sloped down toward the field past the roof of the clubhouse, he could hear the sound of small boys running on the planking of the stands. The gate would be open now, but there still remained two hours before game time, and the only fans that would be coming this early would be the small boys.

But the sound from the window was a distant sound. Sitting there alone, Stat Hunter found his mind, like an old, old man's, retracing the past. The past was a pyramid. It built itself into the day that Marian, his wife, took their daughter and left him, and from there it sloped down and away, at an angle so steep that a man must stumble and fall.

"You're not a father," she had said. "You're a center fielder."

It was a line a comedian might have worked to get a laugh, but it was not funny. When he came home at night, he brought the game of baseball with him, and there was nothing else for him to see or know.

"You're a stranger in your own house," Marian had said to him.

He looked at her, still without seeing. "Let me alone. Lay off me for a while."

"No," she said, and he saw then that she was crying. "I'm not going to do it any more. There's not going to be any more."

He had nodded, silently. She had said this before.

But this time she went away and did not come back to him.

He had seen once, long, long ago, that she was beautiful—beautiful to him: small, and brown-haired, and made up of a soft fire that he could not describe and would not want to.

And that was always the way he remembered her now.

The old man, Merced, had gone out to his place at the gate. Now when the door to the clubhouse opened, it was two of Hunter's players, two of the young ones, who came in. As a minor league manager, Andrew Hunter caught himself thinking from time to time within the framework of the player roster as it was printed in the four-page program, the program that sold for a dime and contained a lucky number that would be flashed on the scoreboard during the seventh inning. The lucky number was sponsored alternately by some half a dozen Fairchild Street merchants, and entitled the fortunate holder to anything from free gas, oil, and grease at Peconi's Service Station to a ten-dollar merchandise certificate at the Ludlow-Berg department store.

Always, the roster, with the starting players listed in batting order, hung on a wall in Hunter's mind, just like (he once told himself) an eye chart in a doctor's office. It looked like this:

5 Whittier, 2b
2 Gladstone, 3b
1 Hunter (mgr), cf
8 Crimeau   9 Gold, c
10 Maracz'ki, rf
6 Aloya, 1b
3 Rosch, lf
4 Johnson   14 O'Brien, ss
7 Vincent   11 Williams
        16 Walsh
12 North   15 Masick, p

And when a player came into the room or walked through a hotel lobby or boarded the bus, the quiet process of recognition on the part of Andrew Hunter would be not that this was Joe Whittier, but, instead, 5 Whittier, 2b; not that it was Bill O'Brien, but 14 O'Brien, ss. He was aware of this mental custom he had; it amused him, in fact, that he would think of 14 O'Brien, ss, when in truth O'Brien was his utility man and had played practically everywhere except shortstop. It was the custom of the printer who made up the programs to put the utility man on the same line with the eighth man in the batting order, so that automatically whatever was the position that the eighth man played, that also would be the position listed for the utility man. This was done not so much to save space as to accommodate the fans, some of whom had indicated some years before that they did not know the meaning of "ut" after a player's name. It was not too important a point. There seldom was more than one utility man on the squad anyway, and toward the end of the season, when clubs higher in the chain started moving for the pennant and the roster limits were off, Conway would be lucky if it finished out the season without having to recruit players off factory teams or the campus of Conway State Teachers College, which had a baseball team of sorts.

The program that sold for a dime had other special fascinations for Andrew Hunter. He did not know why this was so. It bemused him, for example, to observe that Chet Maraczewski's name was apostrophized to Maracz'ki even though there was ample room for spelling it out. He did not quite know why Bo Walsh should have his name centered among the five pitchers, or why, once the printer had set out obviously to list the pitchers in the order of the numbers on their uniforms, he should put 16 Walsh behind 7 Vincent and 11 Williams, but ahead of 12 North and 15 Masick.

Nor did it escape the manager that there was no number 13 on the Bears. That was understandable, inasmuch as the uniforms originated with the parent Philadelphia Bears, whose front office gleaned a small amount of publicity each year by pointing out that 13 was an unlucky number. The Philadelphia press agent had even won a degree of attention the day Bobby Thomson won the '51 pennant for the Giants with his ninth-inning home run against the Dodgers. The story from Philadelphia quoted the Bears' manager as saying that this could never have happened to his club, because it had no number 13—the number of Ralph Branca, who threw the pitch to Thomson.

It was proper, however, for the program to list all five of the Conway pitchers as starters, because they were. When you played four-game series—and, with postponements, they could quickly stretch to five and six games—and you only had five pitchers, you started them all. There were six teams in the Empire League, each of which played a 120-game schedule, meeting each other team twelve times at home and twelve times on the road. That meant the league as a whole would play a total of 360 games in the season, exclusive of playoff games. The schedule was drawn up by Dr. T. T. Yates, a dentist in Conway who was a nut on baseball and statistics. He had explained to Andrew Hunter, before the season began, that you could find out how many games would have to be played in any given league in order for each team to meet each other team once. "You multiply the number of teams by one-less-that-number," he said, "and divide by two." He reached for a piece of paper—he was working on Hunter's teeth at the time—and wrote:

$$S = \frac{n\,(n-1)}{2}.$$

"Now," he continued cheerily, "you take the Empire League. Six teams, so n is 6. Six times n-minus-one, which is 5, is 30, and you divide by two and get 15. So there have to be fifteen games for each team to meet each other team once. But each team plays each other team 24 times, twelve at home and twelve away, so you multiply 15 by 24 and you come out with 360." He beamed. "Here, you can take this with you." And he gave Hunter the piece of paper that possessed the magic formula.

Later that night, Andrew Hunter had asked Ed Rosch, his eighteen-year-old left fielder, if he could guess how many games the Empire League as a whole played.

Rosch pondered it briefly. Then he said, "Three hundred and sixty."

"How'd you guess?"

Rosch shrugged. "Each team plays 120 games. Six teams in the league. Six times 120 is 720. Divide by two—360. Simple."

Hunter looked at him. "Why'd you divide by two?"

His fellow outfielder regarded him pityingly. "Because each game is played by two teams."

Next time he had his teeth done, Hunter told himself, he would instruct Dr. Yates as to what he could do with his formula.

All this formed the train of thought that ambled through Stat Hunter's mind—an intelligent but a cluttered mind—as he sat on the bench before his locker, soap on his face, and in his hand the letter from his daughter. All this, just because two of his ballplayers had walked in the door.

They were Luis Aloya, the first baseman, and Simon North, one of the pitchers.

"Hey, there, Stat," Aloya said. "Jee-sus, it's hot in here. What's a-matter with that goddam fan?"

"Watch the language," Hunter said. "Simon, how's the foot?"

"All right," North said. He was the only local boy on the Conway team. "I can pitch tonight."

"Vagrancy's going to pitch," Hunter said. "I want to use you day after tomorrow when Batavia comes in."

"Well, I didn't work since Sunday," North said.

"And you cut the foot Monday," Hunter said. "You can do some running out there tonight before the game. Practice starting and stopping. Go through your motion and then pretend there's a bunted ball to either side and see how you break down off the rubber going for it."

North nodded and went to his locker, across from Hunter's. The lockers were numbered in the order of the uniforms the players wore. Andrew Hunter was at the end of the row nearest the door, and Monk Gladstone was next to him.

Hunter stood up now and opened his locker. He put the letter in the inside pocket of his suit coat and then, leaving the locker door open, went back inside to finish shaving. There was activity around him. The visiting Rome Senators had arrived in the dressing room to

ARGUING WITH THE UMPIRE...

Wide World

Mr. Durocher . . .

Wide World

Mr. Stengel . . .

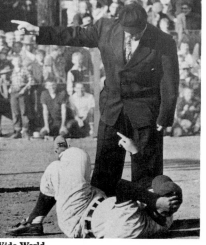

Wide World

Mr. Bragan . . .

and occasionally a fan desires to register a protest **direct**. The umpire is
George Magerkirth.

New York *Daily News*

International News

International News

BOTH ARE SURROUNDED...

but the ball in this unique fair-or-foul shot (top) seems to have a better chance than Andy Cohen (bottom, white cap), trapped in history's most defensively populated rundown.

United Press

THEY ALSO SERVE...

Coach at work.

his right. A couple of them came in to use the bathroom and said, "Hey, Stat," and "Goes-a-boy, Stat?" Hunter nodded at them in the mirror and went on shaving, and in his mind now he began to plot tonight's game in advance. It was a necessary thing to do, and besides, it was a way to avoid thinking about the letter from his daughter, Janet, and about his wife, Marian, who had left him two years ago. *No,* his mind amended, *not quite two years. It was in August . . .*

There would be no need to go over the Rome hitters with his players. They had done this two nights before, Tuesday night, before the four-game series with the Senators began.

Now it was Thursday night, and Conway had taken two straight from Rome. The Bears were in second place, four games back of Auburn, which had a club that hit well but which already had dropped two series to the Bears. Stat Hunter liked that. If your club beat the front-runner with any kind of consistency, then your club had to be sound. He liked that, Hunter did, and he liked the fact that the Bears only once so far this season had lost as many as four games in a row. They were good signs—good signs in the majors, good signs in Class C.

He finished shaving and went back into the locker room.

MARC SIMONT

From *Views of Sport* by Red Smith, © 1954 by Walter W. Smith.
Courtesy Alfred A. Knopf, Inc.

THREE PORTRAITS

CASEY STENGEL

TED WILLIAMS

DON NEWCOMBE

MR. ELLARD helped organize the undefeated Cincinnati Red Stockings of 1869 as baseball's first professional club.

The Red Stockings

GEORGE ELLARD

We used no mattress on our hands,
No cage upon our face;
We stood right up and caught the ball
With courage and with grace.

From *Constitution and By-laws*, 1860

EXCELSIOR BASEBALL CLUB, BROOKLYN

9. Members, when assembled for field exercise, or for any meeting of the club, who shall use profane and improper language, shall be fined ten cents for each offense.

10. A member disputing the decisions of the umpire shall be fined twenty-five cents for each offense.

11. A member who shall audibly express his opinion on a doubtful play before the decision of the umpire (unless called upon to do so) shall be fined twenty-five cents for each offense.

13. A member wearing or using the apparel of a fellow-member, without his *written* permission, shall be fined one dollar.

14. All fines incurred for violation of Sections 9, 10, and 11 must be paid to the umpire, before leaving the field.

GEORGE PRICE

HERE is Danny O'Neill, in early adolescence, faced with a decision: shall he be a priest, or shall he be a ballplayer? How many boys have faced moments of similar crisis? How many have written the same letter to Mr. Connie Mack that appears in this excerpt from James T. Farrell's tetralogy on Danny O'Neill? The date in the story is 1919.

From *Father and Son*

JAMES T. FARRELL

DANNY WAS TERRIFIED. He sat alone in his bedroom, thinking about what had happened. Perhaps this man was a temptation of the Devil, and God had sent this temptation as a way of telling him that he really had the call. God had often sent the Devil to saints to tempt them. But, of course, God had given the saints the strength and grace to resist temptation. But he wasn't a saint and he had never been strong enough to resist temptation.

Could he ever be a saint?

Anybody would laugh at him if they knew he even asked himself such a question.

He couldn't be too sure that this old man had been put in his path as a way of letting him know that he was really called. He had no right to think that God was going out of His way for anybody like Danny O'Neill, did he? Of course he didn't.

Danny wandered restlessly to the parlor. He began to wonder if baseball scouts went to Washington Park. If they did, maybe one of them might see him on one of his good days. They might see how promising he was. If they did, would they get in touch with him?

But he had to give up that idea. He had to recognize that this question of the call had been on his mind for months. If it stuck in his mind so much, now mustn't it mean that it was the sign? If it kept coming back to him at so many different times, when he had so many different things in his mind or he was doing so many different things, why, didn't that mean something?

Sometimes it was like a voice inside of him talking to him, and the voice would say to him:

You know you have the call! You know you have the call! You know you got the call!

Did he? Now, there was that voice again, right now, this minute.

You know it! You know you have the call!

Suppose he did. He could first be a baseball player, and never marry, and then, when his playing days were over, he could be ordained. But if he really had the call, he wouldn't always be fighting with himself this way. If he had the call, and God had poured grace into his soul, he would want to be a priest. He wouldn't love Roslyn. He wouldn't be dreaming of being a baseball player the way he always did. Yes, he was convinced. He didn't have the call.

He jumped to his feet, happy, feeling a sudden lightness of mood.

But how could he tell Sister?

As soon as one worry left your mind, another took its place. Here was one. But then, Sister couldn't say that he had to be a priest when he didn't have the call. A person who didn't have a vocation shouldn't be a priest. That stood to reason.

* * *

Danny sat at his desk with his bedroom door closed. He was elated. Just after he had made up his mind that he didn't have the call, the idea had come to him like an inspiration. And now he had gotten the letter finished, written carefully and legibly so that it looked as if a man had written it. It ought to work, too. Connie Mack was known above all other managers as the man to pick promising players off the sand lots and develop them into stars. Well, after receiving this letter, why shouldn't Connie send a scout out to Washington Park to look him over? And maybe the scout would see him on a good day and sign him up for a tryout with the Athletics a couple of years from now when he was old enough. Players had been signed up at fifteen before. There was the case of that pitcher, Hoyt. Proud of himself, he read the letter he'd just composed.

Mr. Connie Mack
Shibe Park
The Philadelphia Athletics
Philadelphia, Pennsylvania.
Dear Mr. Mack:

I am writing you this letter to tip you off about a kid named O'Neill who is to be seen playing ball in Washington Park in Chicago all of the time. He isn't ripe just yet because he is only fifteen or sixteen

That was a smart idea, to make out that the man who was supposed to be writing this letter didn't know too much about him, so it was best not to give his exact age.

but he is coming along fast for his age, *and he will be ripe soon enough and he looks like a real comer. If you look him over you can pick up a promising youngster now for nothing and he seems destined for the big show. I am a baseball fan and like to see kids get a chance, and take pride in picking them. I picked some before and was a good picker. Years ago when George Moriarity was playing on the sand lots of Chicago I picked him, and I think you must admit I picked a big leaguer then because Moriarity is a big leaguer. You can pick this kid up now for nothing and you will never regret it. He plays out in Washington Park all the time, and you can send a scout out there to look at him and easily find out who he is.*

I know you will not be sorry for this tip.
A baseball fan, a real one
T. J. Walker

He was pleased and satisfied with his letter. All year he'd really felt that 1919 was going to be an important year for him. Maybe this letter might begin to prove that it was. He was smart to have thought up this idea.

THIS is the only real self-help piece in this book—but fascinating if, like me, you've had only a vague notion as to what a slider is. The writer, may I say, is something of an authority.

How I Throw the Slider

BOB FELLER

PROBABLY the best thing about the slider is that it looks like a fast ball. A good batter usually can spot a curve coming in by the early arc it describes, by its spin or by the delivery motion of the pitcher. But he has trouble detecting a slider because it looks and spins and moves like a fast ball—except, of course, that it breaks just at the last moment. In fact, I throw my slider almost the same way as my fast ball. I grip the ball the same, except that my forefinger and index finger, instead of being placed directly over the center of the ball, are moved out a bit, just off center. I throw my slider faster and harder than I do a curve ball, and as it comes into the plate I don't think many batters can tell that it isn't going to be a fast ball. Then, as it crosses the plate, it breaks a bit and the batter doesn't meet the ball quite where he expected to. Remember that most of the time the batter swings on a slider still thinking it's a fast ball.

When I throw the slider sidearm, it hooks; when I give it the overhand delivery, it tends to break and drop. But either way you throw it, the slider is a good extra pitch, a valuable addition to your assortment of stuff. However, I don't think it is good to use as your main delivery. Personally, I don't use it too often. I have found that it tends to be hard on my arm and it takes something off my fast ball. Your arm must be strong and finely developed in the pitching motions and strains before you can make much use of it. I do use it a lot in Boston against the Red Sox' right-hand hitters, but that's because of that short left-field fence. It is a tough pitch for the batter to pull because it breaks away from a right-hand batter (if you're a right-hand pitcher like I am). Against left-hand batters, I throw it when I want them to pull the ball foul. I let up on it and make sure it's a bad pitch. The slider then comes in a little closer than it looks and they usually pull slightly ahead of the ball, enough to make it go foul. The reason I do this is to try to get them off balance so that when I throw my fast ball they will hold up just a bit and hit it straight away instead of pulling it.

I've noticed that most low-ball hitters are able to bang the slider pretty good for some reason, but it's the type of pitch you can throw at anyone once in a while. Of all the pitches I tried to get past Joe DiMaggio, the slider worked best. Joe had more trouble with it than with my fast ball or curve. He just couldn't hit it consistently.

A lot of people seem to think that the slider is a new pitch; others claim it's nothing more than a nickel curve with a new name. As far as I know, George Blaeholder, who pitched for the St. Louis Browns in the late twenties and early thirties, was the originator of the slider as we know it. Johnny Allen used it a lot, too. Now, of course, it appears that every pitcher has included it in his repertoire. Allie Reynolds, Early Wynn and Bob Lemon have very good sliders. So do a lot of other pitchers. Lemon's breaks more than mine does but I think that's because Bob has a natural break in every pitch he throws. His fast ball, for instance, is really a sinker; I think even if he tried to throw the ball straight it would sink. My slider, like my curve, doesn't have a deep break but, for the same reason, it doesn't break big, either.

I really developed my slider in the service although I did use it as early as 1941. It takes time to learn and it wasn't until I came back to baseball in 1945 that I had the pitch working properly. Now I almost never have a bad day with it. I don't know why this is but on those days when my fast ball lacks zip or my curve isn't breaking, the slider still goes good. Once you've learned how to throw it properly, it seems to work all the time. That's another reason why it is a valuable asset. Quite a few times I've been able to stick in there without much of my stuff because I was able to fall back on my slider for the important pitches.

Any young fellow who wants to throw a slider should remember these points: it takes a lot of practice and training, and it's hard on your arm, so don't be in a hurry learning to throw it. I would suggest that you just get your fast ball and curve and control down pat. Then you'll find that your arm is strong enough and disciplined enough to handle the slider—and you'll have a good, dependable extra pitch to get them out with.

F. S. PEARSON II AND R. TAYLOR

From *Butchered Baseball*, © 1952 by Frederick S. Pearson II

Tom Meany has written that the "saucer-eyed dames" drawn by cartoonist Richard Taylor "all look like somebody's sister—but not yours, thank God." Some years ago, Taylor and caption writer F. S. Pearson II combined to produce *Fractured French*, in which I believe Helmut Dantine was portrayed as a man who had gum in his hat. Then, in 1952, the Taylor-Pearson combine came up with *Butchered Baseball*.

RAP A BOUNDER

BLEACHERITE

INTENTIONAL PASS

SINGLE

FIFTEEN MINUTES before midnight on June 14, 1949, first baseman
Eddie Waitkus, then with the Philadelphia Phillies, was shot and criti-
cally wounded by a young woman whom he did not know, but who
had insisted on seeing him at his hotel because of "something important." The assailant was arrested and the following is excerpted from
the report prepared by the chief of the county behavior clinic pursuant
to an order from the felony court. The young woman was adjudged
insane and spent three years in a state hospital after which she was
found to have recovered her sanity and was freed of a pending charge
of assault with intent to kill. Following surgery, Waitkus accomplished a full recovery and went on to play in the 1950 World Series.

From "A Report to Felony Court"

FILE NO. ---, THE BEHAVIOR CLINIC

As A CHILD she was gay and happy. As
she reached adolescence she changed in
many ways. She did not want people to look at
her. She became apprehensive and self-conscious when riding in street cars. If in crowds
she became fearful that she would be the
center of attention. She was overly careful
about her personal appearance, especially her
hair and nails, but was not concerned about
her shoes. She would buy new clothes, but preferred to wear old ones. She was very interested
in music, and at one time had a "crush" on
Liszt and played his *Hungarian Rhapsodies* over
and over. Then she got a craze about Andy
Russell and had to have his records. Two years
ago she changed to boogy-woogy music and
would play these records until the family felt
they would go "crazy."

At the age of sixteen she went with a girl
friend and this girl's brother to a ball game.
Following this she attended the games
often. This boy was very interested in her, but
she never really cared for him. He was
slow and easygoing. At times she would
make a date with him and then purposely not
be home when he called. She is methodical
and exact about many things, especially in
relation to money. She is careful about
keeping promises. As a child she attended the
Lutheran Church. Of late she has attended
church with her girl friends. Her parents

have been told that during some emotional
services she would sit staring and trembling
all over.

She was never interested in baseball until
she attended with her girl friend and
brother. She then attended several times and
began to know the different players. She
became especially interested in Eddie Waitkus, who was playing first base with the Cubs
at the time. She became more and more sentimental in her talk, but no one in the family
took her seriously. She started to collect his
pictures and press notices. Her friends in turn
would send her what they could obtain. As
time went on it became more than an ordinary teen-age infatuation. It continued in the
winter as well as the summer. She talked constantly about this man. She stated that her father, her boss, other men characters in the
movies, etc., reminded her of Eddie. His number was 36 and she became extremely sensitive
to that number. She bought all the records
she could obtain that were produced in
1936 and she would play them over and
over again. Because he came from Boston she
began to eat baked beans and wanted them
all the time. The family had a hard time talking about any other subject except Eddie. If
they intentionally diverted the subject she
would say, "Let's talk about Eddie." If her
father became irritated she told him to be

quiet, adding, "You just don't care about me." She persuaded her father, who cared nothing about baseball, to attend a game one day, and another time her mother. After the game she would stand with the other "bobby-soxers" who rushed up for autographs and would watch for Waitkus to pass. She would get close to him, but never spoke a word. She would get pale and tremble, and one time almost fainted when he went by.

She became nervous at work and extremely miserable because she thought that her boss looked like Eddie Waitkus. In the middle of November 1948 she suddenly walked out of the office with no explanation. She wandered around town where she thought she might see Eddie, finally coming home at seven o'clock. She told her parents she would not return to work, so they made arrangements for her to have a six-weeks' leave of absence. At this time she was referred to a psychiatrist who saw her for a period of ten days and, as he was leaving town, she was referred to another psychiatrist whom she saw only once. She did not like to appear in crowds, and refused to see another doctor. She stayed home and rested until Christmas time, when she returned to her job in a new department where the work was not so hard. There was less excitement and she got along better. At work she talked constantly of ending her life and stated that she was very miserable. She had mentioned this to her parents, but they did not take it seriously. In January 1949 the work in the office speeded up and she began to have less interest in her affairs at home. She wanted a room of her own, stating that she needed more rest. Because of her continued references to Eddie Waitkus the family agreed to this arrangement.

Because of his nationality she became interested in Lithuanian. She bought books and lessons on that language; she listened to all the Lithuanian programs she could. She secured a room a few blocks away from home and came home almost every night for dinner, which she insisted on paying for. The patient had seen the picture *The Snake Pit*. She liked it and kept going to see it over and over. She said one of the players reminded her of Eddie Waitkus. She felt that it was sure evidence that those considered insane were the normal ones, but the keepers were crazy. She developed a complex about bugs which flew in the house at night, that they must not be killed but should be caught and carried out of the house and released. At night she would spread pictures and press notices of Eddie Waitkus on her bed and make a shrine out of it. She slept with his picture under her pillow at night. In 1948 after his transfer to Philadelphia she cried for a day and a night, stating that she could not live if he went away. She wanted him for her boy friend. When he was in Boston she talked endlessly of going to Boston to have dates with him. When she learned that he would be in town in June she decided she was going to see him and ask him for a date. During that week she cried a great deal and appeared depressed, according to her parents.

Both parents appeared genuinely interested in the patient and are greatly upset over the circumstances.

Her closest girl friend revealed that she and patient had been friends since the fourth grade. She knew all about the "crush" on Eddie and stated that prior to this the patient had a crush on Alan Ladd, and then on "Peanuts" Lowery. At that time they would joke, saying, "You trip him and I will drag him to a cab, take him to Crown Point and marry him." The informant at the same time had crushes on ballplayers, particularly one pitcher named Johnny. When the two attended games each one would discuss the merits of her favorite player. The informant remembers distinctly that the first time the patient noticed Eddie was April 27, 1947. At that time some girl spectators yelled "Hello, funny-face!" and from that time on the patient became very interested in him. They saw every game in which Eddie played, and if, while waiting in the crowd for the players to appear, Eddie should pass close to her, she shrank and hid herself so she would not be seen by him.

She liked movies, especially in regard to prisons and in which psychiatrists were portrayed, liking especially *Parole, Inc.* and *The Snake Pit*. Sex was never discussed. She would tell the informant that Eddie was always near her. She had his picture with her at all times. She would sometimes place his picture against some object and talk to it, saying, "You're so cute. You made such a good play today," etc. She discussed suicide several times with the informant. She was always on time, and furious if she kept people waiting. She never wanted to draw attention to herself and was always shy and self-conscious. The first week in May informant went with patient to buy the gun. At first patient wanted a revolver, but learned that she would have to have a permit, so she looked up pawnshops in the Red Book and finally went to a pawnshop where they bought a .22 rifle for $21. The man showed them how to take it apart and put it together again, and gave her two boxes of shells. She seemed pleased with it and handled it as though it were a new toy. She never said exactly what she wanted it for. On the Monday before the alleged offense the patient and informant got the gun and wrapped it up in heavy paper. She was not suspicious about it at the time, as it appeared to her as just a lark. They called a cab and went to the hotel, where patient had reserved a room. The following day they saw a baseball game and both girls were happy. Nothing unusual occurred. They planned to leave the game together and she was to go to the patient's room because she had stated that she did not like to pass all the wealthy women in the hotel lobby, because they looked at her. Then as the game progressed she appeared nervous and asked what if she should meet Eddie in the lobby. She knew she could not stand it, so she left the game early. The informant did not want to miss seeing Johnny walk out, so did not leave with her. She told the informant she was going to send a note to Eddie that night and ask him to meet her. The informant laughed, because she did not believe she would have nerve enough.

The sister, when interviewed, stated that they got along very well as children. They shared their toys, and the sister added that she was very much surprised when she discovered that when patient moved out she took with her a suitcase full of dolls, Teddy bears, and such toys as she had as a child. They had both objected to the neighborhood. They were reared as gentle, quiet, well-mannered youngsters and did not get along with the rather impolite playmates. They did not know how to fight back.

The sister was extremely bored by ball games, which the patient induced her to attend. She especially hated waiting afterward in the hot sun for as much as an hour for the players to come out. When Eddie would appear the patient would shrink back and never have the courage to ask him for an autograph. For a long time the patient has talked of suicide. When the patient left home they were all glad because they had been getting on each other's nerves. Each Thursday she ate with her sister, who objected if anyone looked at her and would always arrange the chairs so that

there was an empty chair facing hers. She stated that Eddie was in this chair. She frequently told her sister that she was sorry for Eddie, because his mother was dead and she wanted to take care of him. Sex was never discussed.

Patient was especially interested in astrology and bought many books on the subject. Informant feels that her sister is enjoying all the publicity and attention she is getting, particularly because she is trying to get revenge for everything that has ever happened to her, all the unhappiness in school, and all the unhappiness she has had because she could not have Eddie.

She was given several psychological tests. On the Bellevue-Wechsler test she had a full-scale I.Q. of 99. She had a brief attention span and it was necessary to call her back to test items. There is a noted lack of social intelligence. On the Rorschach test, a summary reveals that there are indications of a childlike emotional status, incapable of meeting personality conflicts. Her pseudo-solution has been to use reality selectively. It is felt that this investigation indicates an incipient schizophrenic psychosis.

The mental examination was performed in the County Jail. She was seen on numerous occasions. At all times she was cooperative, neat, cheerful, at ease, and volunteered information. She apparently enjoyed talking, and at no time appeared bored with the interview. There were only two occasions in which there were emotional outbursts: One was after an examination by the jail doctor, and the other was when she was discussing what she thought of the people of Philadelphia for buying Waitkus. When discussing the shooting of Waitkus there was no change of emotion whatsoever. At no time were there any tears, but frequently she laughed when discussing the shooting and other serious problems. She gave personal identification and stated that she had eight years of grammar school and four years of high school. She went into detail to tell of difficulties she had with other children while in the grades. At times she would return to difficulties in the first few grades to give minor details such as, "One girl always picked on me. When she said 'Come here' I would do it. I was always afraid of her . . . Boys used to yell at me." She feels that she was unpopular in high school because she knew very little about sex and for this reason the other students made fun of her.

When she was interviewed for her first position she says she was told that she needed a psychiatric examination. She feels that she is sick mentally, but not insane, adding, "There must be something the matter with me if I go around shooting people . . . My first idea was that I would shoot him because I liked him a great deal and I knew I never could have him, and if I couldn't have him neither could anybody else. Secondly, I had the idea that if I shot him I would have to shoot myself. In the third place I wanted publicity and attention for once." She has dreamt about killing Waitkus and found herself sitting with him in her arms. She adds, "All my dreams have come true."

She attributes many of her nervous features after first knowing Eddie. First of all, April 27, 1947 was the big day in her life. "The first year I was crazy about him. The second year, when I went out I became self-conscious. I thought people were looking at me. I thought my head was shaking. I pretended he was along with me and talked to me—not out loud—it was in a mental sense, not physical. We walked down the street together. I was not afraid to leave my parents' home. The neighborhood was not so good. I wouldn't take a street car because Eddie was with me. I didn't tell my mother because she would have laughed at me. If I told my dad he would have sent me to a psychiatrist right away . . . I told my girl friends. At no time did I actually feel him—I did mentally, not in body. Mentally I can recall him any time I want to. He has been with me in jail . . . The whole thing sounds so silly. I asked him, 'What are you going to do about me now? You wanted me to do this.' At the present time he evades me. He says, 'Don't you think it would be better if you went to some hospital?' . . . I kept asking him over and over again how he felt about the whole thing, but he keeps evading me, so I got mad and didn't talk to him the rest of the night. . . . One thing I'll say for him, he has always paid a lot of attention to me. Finally I got so far I got this gun. I made plans for going to him. I wanted to get away from here and planned on going to Boston. He got awfully mad about that."

She tells in detail about the registration at the hotel and her infatuation with Eddie Waitkus. "I had my first good look at him on April 27, 1947. I used to go to all the ball games just to watch him. We used to wait for them to come out of the clubhouse after the game, and all the time I was watching him I was building in my mind the idea of killing him.

As time went on I just became nuttier and nuttier about the guy and I knew I would never get to know him in a normal way, so I kept thinking I will never get him and if I can't have him nobody else can. And then I decided I would kill him. I didn't know how or when, but I knew I would kill him . . . After a year went by and I was still crazy about him I decided to do something about it. Then I decided to kill him with a gun it would be the easiest way. I actually got the gun in May. I didn't think I would have the courage to get a gun, because I am afraid of one. I knew I couldn't get a small gun like I wanted because you have to go through the trouble of getting a permit, so I went to the pawnshop and got this second-hand rifle. My girl friend was with me at the time. After that I looked up the schedule to see when the Phillies would be here. I knew they were staying at this hotel, so I put my reservation in for the time when they would be there. I got the reservation and it was just a question of waiting. During that time I learned how to put it together and take it apart. Then I just waited until it was time to go. . . . The whole thing seemed so funny. After I registered we went back to the house and picked up the gun." She then tells in detail of the events of the next two days, adding, "I had no more than got to sleep when I was awakened by the telephone ringing. It was Waitkus. Well, he wanted to know what the note was all about and why I wanted to see him. He said 'What's so darn important?' and that shocked me. I hadn't figured a guy like him. I didn't expect that from a guy like him. I thought he would ask me what it was all about, but he was so informal. I said, 'I can't discuss it over the 'phone with you.' I said, 'Can you come up tonight for a few minutes?' and he said, 'Yes.' I said, 'Give me half an hour to get dressed . . .' Then I got dressed and waited for him. I remember when he knocked on the door. I was scared stiff, but I thought to myself I will settle this once and for all and really kill him. At that time I had a knife in my skirt pocket and was going to use it on him. When I opened the door he came rushing in right past me. I expected him to stand there and wait until I asked him to come in and during that time I was going to stab him with the knife. I was kind of mad that he came right in and sat down and didn't give me a chance to stab him. He looked at me surprised and said, 'What do you want to see me about?' I said, 'Wait a minute. I have a surprise for you.' I went to the closet and got out the gun. I took it out and pointed it at him and he had such a silly look on his face. He looked so surprised. I was pretty mad at him, so I told him to get out of the chair and move over by the window. He got up right away and said, 'Baby, what's this all about?' That made me mad. He just stood there stuttering and stammering and he asked me again, 'What is this all about? What have I done?' I said, 'For two years you have been bothering me, and now you are going to die'— and then I shot him. For a minute I didn't think I shot him, because he just stood there, and then he crashed against the wall. For a minute I just looked at him. I didn't believe he was shot. He kept saying, 'Baby, why did you do that?' and then I said, 'I don't believe I shot you,' because I was still smiling. Then I knelt down next to him. He had his hand stretched out. I put my hand over his. He said something to the effect, 'You like that, don't you?' I took my hand away from his when he said that. I asked him where he had been shot—I couldn't see a bullet hole or blood or anything. He said I shot him in the guts, and I was convinced he was shot. I don't know why. I thought, well now's the time to shoot myself, and I told him. Then I tried to find the bullets, but I couldn't find them, and I lost my nerve. I was frantic by that time and I called the operator to call the doctor. He kept moaning, 'Oh, baby, why did you do it? Why did you do it?' He was groaning and I didn't like to hear it, so I went out in the hall. The doctor and house detective came. It was so silly. Nobody came out of their rooms. You would think they would all come rushing out. I got mad. I kept telling them I shot Eddie Waitkus, but they didn't know who Eddie Waitkus was. I thought they were just plain dumb if they didn't know who Eddie Waitkus was. After that the police came, but I was burning because nobody was coming out of those other rooms. Nobody seemed to want me much. I could have walked right out of the place and nobody would have come after me."

She denies excessive alcoholism and states that she had three drinks that night in order to bolster her courage. She states she was sober at the time of the shooting. She has read several books on psychiatry. She has had frequent messages from Waitkus, such as seeing his name on a bar of soap, or seeing the number 36 on the screen, etc. She does not feel that she wants to kill anyone else, but should she get out she would want to kill Eddie because he is the only one worth killing. She feels that she should be sent to Dwight, but not to any mental institution. She has read books on American penal and prison systems, so knows what life would be in a prison. She is oriented in all spheres. Questions of general information and calculation are adequately answered.

DIAGNOSIS: Schizophrenia in an immature individual. She is committable to an institution for the mentally ill. At no time does she show concern, nor appear to realize the seriousness of her behavior. She discusses suicide freely and has thought of many methods that she would try. She should be under constant surveillance.

THE THRILL THAT COMES ONCE IN A LIFETIME

HERE is a classic story. It has never before been publicly printed. The author, a former Kansas City reporter and now an executive for a large aircraft corporation, submitted the story to a leading magazine. There was an immediate enthusiasm to publish it, but two or three changes in wording were requested. The author refused, and I don't blame him. Later a few hundred copies were printed privately for friends— Charles Lindbergh, Admiral Duke Ramsey, Phil Rizzuto, the late General Hoyt Vandenberg, Don Gutteridge, Phil Reed, Mike Berger, General Rosy O'Donnell. Mickey Cochrane has called this "the funniest and truest baseball piece" he ever read.

The Spitter

PAUL FISHER

I SAID at supper you was the first baseball writer I seen since I left the Giants. That's not strictly so. Right after the war got good and started, another baseball writer was down here to see me. I reckon I never knowed what the war was going to do to the country till then. Wimmern welders, wimmern hack drivers, wimmern rasslers, wimmern boilermakers —we was bound to have them when the young fellers marched off. But dogged if I ever expected to see a womern baseball writer.

She was on one of the St. Louie papers, and she come all the way down here to see me special. If you was out in the Pacific with the troops most of the war for your paper, then you prolly seen what she was working on. It was a book called *My Greatest Day in Baseball.* After they run it off regular style, they put it out with a paper back for the fighting boys. Real life stories. They would look up some ol' big league ballplayer like me, and he would recollect a good day he had up there, and then the writer would doll up his language and dig out the box score for that pertickler day, and that would be his greatest day in baseball.

Different writers done different players. That was because of geography. Ballplayers come from purt near every place, and they usually hit back home when they wind up, like me. This here womern baseball writer drawed me to write up, I reckon, because St. Louie is the closest big league town to the hills down here in Arkansas.

She aint a gal, but she aint a ol' womern either. I judge she was twenty-four-twenty-five, age most wimmern round here got three-four young uns. Real thin with specs. She aint going to win no prizes on her face or on her shape, but still and all I took to her right off. Intellectual grounds I reckon you'd called it. Fur four years I figger she's smartest womern I ever spent a day talking to.

She was shore well read in baseball. She knowed my record from a to izzard. She knowed what I hit all the twelve years I was up there. She knowed about the time I got three for four agin Carl Mays in the fourth series game in '21, and about the time in the '23 series I taken a three-bagger away from Bob Meusel and doubled the Babe off first from deep left center. She even knowed I murdered a titty-high pitch, except she called it letter-high. That was her big difference from most of you baseball writers. She used real refined language.

She had picked out them two games to choose from as my greatest day for this here book. She says not only was them good days for me, but they was historic games and us Giants win 'em both.

It was a rule for this here book, she says, that the player's good days had to be a day his club wins. She had a real nice smile and she turned it on then. She says I could choose any of them days, of course, but like a womern, she says, smiling, she wants to guide me and help herself a wee bit. As my Buzzwell, she says, she perferred my day when I made the great throw to get the Babe because that showed me, not for my great nacheral physical gifts, but for what characterized me most—I was always out there thinking.

Up to that point we was getting along like a well-broke team. She was setting here in the parlor. right in the rocker you're in, and she'd fetched out a notebook and a pin and was all braced to take down my every word. I was setting right here. I was thinking. The more I figgered, the more I knowed in my own heart I ort not to be so muley, but I couldn't go along with her. That day agin the Yanks wasn't my greatest—least not in the thinking line. Finally I says so.

"Well," she says, and she aint smiling now, "certainly you have the choice. If you perfer to select another day and another game, why, then, most certainly that's within your perview."

"It's a game that aint never been writ up," I says. "But lots of games down in these here hills never is. We aint like New York. Here everybody comes to a game, so they aint no need to write 'em up."

"You mean," she says, "you are selecting a game that isn't even recorded in organized baseball?"

"Why, yes, ma'am," I says. "In this here book you say you want my greatest day in baseball, and you perfer me thinking. This time I'm going to tell you about, I done some of the tallest thinking I ever done in all my life."

"Perceed," she says, and I done so.

*　　*　　*

After I left the Giants in '24, crops down here wasn't so good, so for a couple of summers I got together a nine called the Gray Travelers, and we went around playing the country and town teams with us always as the visiting club. They was good money in it—if you win. Mostly we played winner-take-all, with a side bet I seen run as high as nine-ten hunnert dollars. Crops was bad, but they was lots of money loose in them days and people had real pride and dug deep for their local nines.

All through this country—not only here in Arkansas, but in Missouri, Kansas and Oklahomy—they was sending up some great young ballplayers. Fellers like Bill Dickey, Arky Vaughan, the Waner boys, Glenn Wright, the Deans, Schoolboy Rowe. Purt near every town and pea patch had three-four young fellers so good they made the rest of their club look real solid.

Traveling, batting agin home town empires, playing on diamonds that was mostly on the sides of mountings, we had a lot of strikes on us. The crowds was no pleasure. They wasn't above flashing mirrors in your eyes or flinging them giant firecrackers under your feet or running you lickety-split out of town if you done a little hard sliding into their favor-ites.

So my nine had to be a whole lot better. The first year we win about seven out of every ten games, and when I totted up the season's figgers, we done jist a little better than even. Then the second year I got ol' Heinie Aunfeldt who use to catch for the Cubs, Cornbread Jones who had been up, too, three real good young infielders, and a big farmer from Pea Ridge who was good enough finally to go up to Brooklyn. Day, this Pea Ridge feller was named. You recollect him. I heerd he always gave a hog call in Ebbets Field when he was slated to pitch and scared them Dodger fans most to death. My legs was too fur gone to play the outfield, so I took over third base.

They's things you do in the big leagues, natcher'ly, that's way past town ball, and up there they expect you to do things a certain way. That's why they's called the big leagues, I reckon. But after being up twelve years, I had to re-learn myself some ol' town ball tricks with my Travelers. I had to learn Pea Ridge to pull his cap right down over the bridge of his nose so the home-town rooters can't blind him with mirrors. I had to learn my outfielders how to run down the side of the mountings spraddle-legged to take low liners. Me and ole Heinie and the first baseman got to learn ourselves how to climb like mounting goats up on the hoods of the autos parked all along the field to catch them foul balls. In fact, by '26, I done away with spiked shoes. We played in tennis slippers. You could climb up on Fords and Dorts and Chevvies purty good in spikes, but for Marmons and Hupmobiles and Franklins in them days, tennis slippers was best.

Anyways, by the time July rolled around in my second year with the Travelers, we was going real good. We was up through Missouri and over through Kansas and we got clear down into Oklahomy before we lost a game. We was way ahead financially. We win twenty-three before we lost that game in Oklahomy. Pea Ridge Day had pitched most every other day, so we took two weeks off, and decided for me to work up a schedule in Arkansas where things was a-booming.

When I got back home here, all the people in the hills was talking about a nine over at Simmons Run, not too fur from the Oklahomy line. They was putting a railroad through there, and some oil had been sighted, so they was a kinda boom on. Folks said this Simmons Run nine was made up entirely of local fellers except for pitchers. They brung in pitchers from outside, most of the time one of three left-handed Indians which had made life so mizzible for us Travelers in '25. They was three Indians in three separate hearses, two black and one pearl gray. . . .

You never *heerd* of them three left-handed Indians?

No, they wasn't dead Indians. I shore wished many a time that they was. They owned them hearses personally. They was three things them three Indians liked to do that I knowed of. They liked to drive them hearses. They liked to carry their whole famblies and most of their tribe everywhere in the hearses with 'em. And they shore liked to pitch. I expect the thing they liked to do most was sit back in the hearse with a little mounting water, because when they pitched agin you, they made return trips to the closed end of the hearse. They would go back in them hearses in the third, fifth, sixth, seventh, eighth and ninth innings, and a thing I allus noticed was that all three, after the sixth inning, pitched with one eye closed, sump'n a man only does when he's shooting a fararm or drinking stimulates.

The folks said this Simmons Run nine had got both Little Rock and Fort Smith's perfessional teams to come up fur games and beat 'em both. I was told that the Indian in the gray hearse, Willie Wildflower his name was, the one who allus wore the miller's cap and the striped overhalls when he pitched, had shut both of 'em out. I knowed these Indians had oil wells over by Miami, Oklahomy, so I got in my car and went over there.

They was home all right. I seen a million Indian wimmern and young uns out in the backyards of the three big stone houses the three left-handed Indians had built, but I was real formal and went to the door of the middle house. It had a pure big silver knocker and I purt near tore that door off, knocking. Nobody

answered. Finally I went around to the back, and down in a grove, maybe fifty yards away, there was the three hearses and the three Indian wrongarms. They had put up tents in the grove of trees. They wasn't living in them big stone houses at all. They had jist built them houses fur show.

They knowed me all right. We talked about how good they was the year before and they says they was even better this year. Then I done a thing that wasn't real ethical. I says I heerd the big distilleries up at Peory, Illinois, was hiring left-handed pitchers, paying regular money and a bonus of gov'ment spirits for every win. I says it was a real fast league, but having seen the three of 'em pitch, I figgered they could win. Jist by chance I had a road map and if they wanted I'd be glad to pencil out the best route. I never seen three more excited Indians. They didn't give a dang about salaries, but that bonus shore whetted 'em. Even before I walked back up to my car, they was slinging their wimmern and kids in the hearses, the hulabaloo was deaf'ning, and I knowed they was off, fur three weeks or a month, anyways.

So I clumb in my auto and drove lickety-split over to Simmons Run. The town barber was running the Simmons Run nine—funny how often in country ball you find a barber who thinks he's a Connie Mack, John McGraw, and Colonel Ruppert all rolled into one. Before we talked two minutes, I seen he thought they was going to really clean out plow. So I ast him about the very next Sunday and he says they'd have to cancel out on the Watts, Oklahomy, club, but if they did, they would have to have a tolable big side bet. I says we might scrape up five hunnert, but, no, he figgers that was purty small. Twelve hunnert dollars, he says, and winner take all the gate. He near choked on that figger, so I knowed it was the biggest bet in the history of Simmons Run.

"I reckon you'll pitch the Indians?" I says to him.

"I reckon we will," he says, real chipper. "And to win, we'll rotate 'em, three innings a-piece, if we think it need be. But it won't. You fellers never beat 'em onct last year."

"They're mighty good," I says. "But it's worth a try. You figger to have much of a gate with this little notice?"

"We shore do," he says. "This is the Sunday we plan to unveil our nine in the new sateen uniforms we bought 'em fur beating Fort Smith and Little Rock. Folks have heerd so much about the nine and now about these sateen uniforms that they's coming all the way from Siloam Springs and Gravette and Fayetteville, jist to see us."

"Well," I says, "we'll be in Sunday morning, and I'll meet you here with the twelve hunnert. We know a good base empire—"

"Don't you worry about empires," he says. "Home club furnishes the empires. We allus use one on the bases, too; we wasn't born yestidday."

I lost there, but still and all, I feels purty keen. I never knowed a left-hander to leave a forrarding address, and I was purty certain left-handed Indians was no exception. But keen as I feels then, I feels keener Sunday morning as young Pea Ridge Day and me was driving toward Simmons Run. Thirty miles away, even early in the morning, the road was lined with buckboards and buggies and even ol' hayricks, with people hanging on from every which side. And I never seen so many autos out in Arkansas in my life. The traffic was all one-way to Simmons Run.

* * *

It's peculiar thing about this here hill country. You can stand up on a mounting and look fur miles and maybe you won't see more'n three-four houses. Country seems real empty. But have a fox hunt or a square dance or a fight or a ball game where the home nine is going to play some perfessionals like Cornbread and ole Heinie and I used to be, and the folks just seem to spring from the hills and the hollers. They come pouring out of every cranny, packing their young uns and their wimmern folks and follered by their hounds. Every auto and every buggy has a market basket filled plumb up with cold-fried chicken and smoked ham and 'tater salad and piccalilli, and they's stone jugs full of spring-cold buttermilk or sweet cider, and all the folks is grinning and real neighbor-like, willing to feed you till you bust. They's quick to fight, but down deep, these here folks is as good a friends as you'll find.

I drapped young Pea Ridge at the railroad commissary where our nine was dressing and picked up five hunnert dollars from both ole Heinie and Cornbread to fill out the bet. Then I went to the barber shop. Simmons Run is only two roads intersecting, you might say, but I was about tuckered out fighting my way through the crowd. They was firecrackers going off right and left and hounds baying and dozens of young uns already lost and howling fur their folks. The barber had pervailed on Judge Damon to hold the stakes. We counted out the money and when I seen we wasn't being shortchanged none, I says to the barber,

"You starting Dryshell or Willie Wildflower?"

"Here at Simmons Run," he says, swelling up and looking real smart-alecky, "we make it a practice never to reveal our plans. Aint that right, judge?"

The judge looked sour at such high-falutin manners, but he didn't say nothing.

"Fact is," says the barber, "we may start John Bearpaw."

"Well," I says, "I didn't see their hearses. Most usually them Indians get right in the middle of all the firecracker shooting."

"Don't let it worry you none at all," this here barber says, and he winks knowing like at Judge Damon. "Whoever we pitch will purely dazzle you fellers. And we'll dazzle you some more when you see our brand new uniforms. Slickest in three states."

Going back to the commissary to get in my own monkey suit, I seen quite a few fellers I knowed personal and ast if they had seen the three Indians or even the three hearses. Nobody had. I reckon I was like every feller that's laid out a slick plan. I feared I'd missed some place. But purty soon I got to listening to our shortstop, Tommy Ringle, who says he's seen this Simmons Run nine a couple of times and played agin' 'em onct. He was briefing Pea Ridge on how to pitch to 'em.

Tommy says they can hit but he figgers Pea Ridge is too fast for 'em—they won't get around quick enough theirselves to pull the ball fur distance. They's one exception, Tommy says—the catcher.

"He's bigger'n a horse and jist as strong," Tommy says. "His name's Ory. He's got the stutters, but it shore don't hurt his hitting none. I aint never seen a man who could hit a ball so fur. He hits 'em off his ears and off his shoe tops. You'll jist have to figger him out yourselves."

"Them kind," says ole Heinie, who's lacing up his tennis slippers, "sometimes can't hit a change-up. We'll tippy up a couple to him, Pea Ridge, and see how he likes the slow stuff."

* * *

We was the first nine on the diamond. Ball fields down here is a lot more uniform than in the big leagues, if that surprises you. They's no place with enough level ground fur a complete field, so they mostly set on the side of the mounting with home plate at the foot and the infield sloping upwards. I never seen a diamond in all these hills with home plate at the top of the mounting. Onct I figgered out why. These boys hit fur distance in these here hills, and if they was swinging down hill, it would take a mint to keep 'em in baseballs. They's another advantage. The autos and buggies and wagons can park along the foul lines, and being as one is parked a little higher than the other, right on out to the top of the mounting, it makes seeing easier fur all concerned.

I never seen a crowd in Arkansas like they had there that day at Simmons Run. The furthest auto on the left field line looked like a speck. A stand had been built back of home plate to seat eight-nine hunnert, but they musta been a full thousand packed on the seats. The Simmons Run nine was charging admission fur everything except hounds and suckling young, fifty cents each fur the grownups and a quarter fur the walking young. The gate come to eighteen hunnert and ten dollars. So I figger a good five thousand had paid to get in.

We was warming up along the third base line when I seen everybody craning their necks looking into the crowd back of first. My heart shore sunk then. Usually that's where the three left-handed Indians pulled up in their hearses and slid open the back doors fur a million Indians to fly out, most of 'em carrying greenbacks in big wads to buy sarsparilly and popcorn and hot dogs. But it turned out diff'runt. Thirty-forty Simmons Run folks was clearing a path through the crowd. Purty soon they had a big hole. A covered wagon was backed up to the hole, and all at once someone inside the wagon slung up the canvas and out jumped the Simmons Run nine, one after the other, and come running out into the middle of the field.

I never heerd sich a roar, not even at the Polo Grounds when the Babe hit one agin us in the '21 series. The noise jist growed and growed. Man, they was never a sight or sound like it in the history of baseball. They had stole a leaf from them big football colleges like Illinois U. and Michigan U. and Pennsylvania U. One by one they'd drap out of the covered wagon and run all alone over to the pitcher's mound where they squatted in a perfect line.

It was stupendjous. The folks was standing up shouting, the hounds was baying and the young uns, scared by all the hulabaloo, was screaming. Firecrackers was going off every which way, and every horn in every auto was sounding. It wasn't that they was jist the undefeated Simmons Run nine. It wasn't that they was jist local boys who wasn't afeerd to cross bats with any club, amateur or perfessional. Mostly it was them new uniforms the barber had bragged up.

They was sateen, jist as he said, and while I never seen sateen ball suits before, that didn't stun me near so much as the color. They was purely black. When the sun struck that black sateen, it purt near blinded you. I seen ball suits with lots of red and lots of green and lots of yaller, and onct when I was with Telsy on my way up to the big leagues, we had powder blue road uniforms till the fans near hooted us out of the league. But fur a real eye-catching ball suit, them black sateen outfits the Simmons Run nine had beat anything I ever hope to lay eyes on.

They was country boys so they couldn't hold on to the pose in the center of the field long. As they begun to go back to the first base line, I seen one more player crawling out of that covered wagon. He was in a gray road suit, well made, too, and when he turned around, he made two quick tugs at his cap brim and then quick wets his right finger tips with his tongue. Fur me, that was as much as if he had wrote his name. I knowed him before he follered up by tugging twice at his belt.

Yes sir, you're right, it was ol' Tug Monahan. And onct he had got onto the field, he done jist like he allus did at Forbes Field in Pittsburgh—he begin lookin all 'round, counting the house.

In country and town ball, you're expected to do a little social visiting before a game so I went right over. Ol' Tug looked at me as if it had only been yestidday since I seen him, but leastways he shook hands.

"I thought you was still with the Pirates?" I says.

"I got waived out the same year you did," he says. "And you should know it."

"Where'd these fellers find you?" I says.

"You know and they know I live in K.C.," he says, "and that's where you can always find me."

"I reckon, Tug," I says, "that it's no fun pitching without your spitter—" but I didn't get in a word more.

"They outlawed the spitter only in organized ball," he says. "This is a hell of a long ways from organized ball."

"These are jist kids, Tug," I says, "and they might walk right into that spitter."

"Some kids, Muley," Tug says. "Ole Heinie must have grandsons up there, and Cornbread Jones and you both broke in before I did."

Right about then I had a feeling I was standing in the shade. I was, too. The big Simmons Run catcher, Ory he was called, has moseyed up and he was standing on the sunny side of me. He was six foot six-seven inches and built to fit. I never seen a uniform fit a man so snug. But the thing I seen about his uniform that struck me as strange was his sweat shirt. Most wrist bands on sweat shirts don't have a long bunch of ridges running from halfway up to the elbow, but his did. Then it come to me that was no sweat shirt he had on—that was the top part of long underwear sich as they was selling down in these hills fur several years. And when I looked down at his legs, I seen the legs of his long drawers had been folded under his baseball stockings. Glancing here and there, I noticed all the Simmons Run nine was wearing long underwear, and I reckoned the answer was that never having had sweat shirts, and seeing pitchers of full baseball outfits, they had reasoned that even in the big leagues, the players wore long underwear right through the heat of the summer.

I must have missed some of the talk between Ory and Tug, because when I come to, Tug was saying,

"Speak up, man, I won't bite you."

"I-I-I-I fou-fou-fou-fought we sh-sh-should t-t-talk over the s--s--s--s--signals," Ory says. You see, he stuttered some.

"Signals?" Tug says. "What signals?"

"He means your signs," I says. "This here is your catcher, Tug."

Ory laid a hand on my shoulder and I purt near was pushed through the ground.

"I-I-I'll d-do my own t-t-t-talking," he says to me. "I-I-I'm b-big enough to s--sp-speak my own m-m-mind."

"You shore are," I says and I wandered over by the water keg at the end of the Simmons Run bench. I aint planning to listen in, but you couldn't help yourself, what with that high squeaky voice of Ory and that deep cellar voice of ol' Tug.

Well, it was a long conversation without much said for several minutes. I heerd Tug say he'd sign for pitchouts, and then I missed a few lines and purty soon both their voices rose up stronger than ever.

"You mean," Tug says real loud, "that you won't catch a spitter?"

"N-n-n-no, sir-e-ee," Ory screams, and hurls his little two-bit kid's catching glove on the ground. "A s-s-s-spitter t-t-takes off every wh-wh-which way. A-a-and th-there's g-g-g-germs on sp-s-spit."

"What?" Tug hollers.

"G-g-g-germs," screams Ory. "S-s-s-spit is un-un-un-s-s-unsanitary."

"Gaddlemighty," Tug hollers. "You afraid of a little old germ? Don't you know my spitter is my best pitch?"

"C-c-can't help it," Ory says. "D-d-don't th-th-th-throw that g-g-g-gol-goldanged spitter."

"Listen, you big ape," Tug screams, "you know who's hitting agin us? Take a look. Muley hit in the five spot for McGraw for years. Cornbread Jones was as good a hitter as I ever hope to see in the big leagues. Ol' Aunfeldt won more games in the clutch for the Cubs than any hitter they had. You think I came 250 miles to have my ears pinned back?"

"I-I-I w-w-won't catch n-n-n-no sp-spitters," Ory says coldly.

Well, finally it ended up in a compromise, you might say. Tug would throw his spitter only if he got in a bad hole and only if Ory gave him the sign. They used the oldest set of signs in baseball, as it worked out. One finger was for Tug's fast ball, two for his hook, the fist for his change-up, and they decided that if Ory put down three fingers, that was for the spitter. I slaunched off about then, and went back to my bench.

* * *

Tug begin warming up, and he looked as loose and easy as he ever looked up there. But he aint what took my eye. This Ory was a ballplayer if I ever seen one. He drapped in a natural crouch on the first warmup toss, and you could see every muscle in his body as he set there on his toes. Fact is, so tight was his black sateen suit and his long drawers that I could count the four buttons on the trap door of the underdrawers—the buttons that hold up the flap. If you could forget the clo'es and the little toy mitt he wore, you'da swore he was the purtiest catcher you ever seen in all your born days.

And one thing I knowed. Watching him, I knowed simple as their signs was, we wasn't going to steal them signs. He was one of them natcheral catchers that hide their signing hand from everyone except the pitcher and even the pitcher's got to look sharp to see how many fingers are down for the called pitch.

Well, in a ways it was a dull game the first seven innings. But purty. Ol' Tug Monahan was pulling the ball up to his mouth purty near every pitch, faking saliver on it, but he never throwed a spitter onct. He was pitchin me and Cornbread low, half-speed hooks, and he kept his stuff high and tight on ole Heinie, so none of us was getting any wood on the ball. His control was perfect and he was sneaky fast. Pea Ridge was slinging his high hard one till it jist whistled. Except to this big Ory. First time Ory came up Pea Ridge slang two fast balls way wide, then jist ante-ed a soft one up, and Ory like to broke his back sending a little toy fly down to me near the third sack. He did it again in the fifth and we went into the last of the eighth without either them or us getting a man as fur as second, much less scoring.

The sun was bearing down, and when Ory come up with one out and nobody on in the eighth, he was something to see. His black britches was so soaked with sweat that they seem glued to him and every time he took a practice swipe with his war club, the sweat jist flew all round him. Pea Ridge throwed him a couple way wide, and then, like young pitchers jist natcherally seem to do, he let one go right down the alley but Ory jist stood there and watched her sail by for a strike.

Heinie came out from behind the plate and he was sore.

"You young fool," he shouts to Pea Ridge, "pitch like I tell you to. No more of that."

So Pea Ridge wastes another, and I reckon he was smarter'n ol' Heinie. He ra'red back and slang another right in the gut.

Ory swang and before I could even duck, the ball shot past my ear, climbing fast. I turned and seen Cornbread beginning to spin to go back on his ol' legs, but it was no use. That ball was still lifting when it went over the mounting top. In all my born days, I never seen a ball hit so fast or so fur. And as I turned back, I knowed without a piece of stupendijous luck we're gone gooses.

Ory was halfway between first and second when the real roar went up from all that mob of hill folks. He was one of them big fellers that run with all their arms and legs spraddled and their head down. All he knowed was that he had hit one on the nose, the crowd was yelling their lungs loose, and so he was put-

ting on all his horses to run till someone tole him to stop.

Right then I figgered out two of the things in a thinking way that won that ball game.

I knowed if we could get Ory out of there, Simmons Run prolly didn't have no one to hold Tug Monahan and maybe we could push a run or two across. I knowed, too, that outside Ory, none of them is going to hit Pea Ridge, if we play a week of Sundays. Sitting here now —jist as I did seven-eight years ago when that womern baseball writer came to write up my greatest day in baseball—I can recollect jist as clear how my mind was churning and I was reaching for a solution to win by.

One thing I gave up immejiately as Ory rounded second. I knowed I couldn't give him the hip as he swang around third. He'da knocked me stem-winding, and all of us woulda got rid out of Simmons Run on a rail to boot. So to keep away from that devil idey, I begun backing toward home plate, acting as if I was going to take a relay throw and whip it home.

Ory swang round third and he was still going hell-bent with his head down. So I eased over toward the line and when he was about twenty-five feet from the plate and the panjemonium was so stupendijous I couldn't hardly think, I drawed in all the air I could and hollered as I never hollered before,

"SLIDE, ORY, SLIDE!"

He heerd me. He slud. He musta weighed 270-280 pounds and he was no Ty Cobb or Max Carey fur sliding grace. He flang hisse'f up in the air and came down square on his hine-end, with his feet up off the ground. A reg'lar explosion of dust blew in the air. He slud fifteen-twenty feet before he hit the plate and he slud right on for another ten feet. Before I got choked up on the dust, I smelled the burnt sateen he had skidded off from the friction, you might say, of all that meat hitting on that sun-baked ground.

I never expect to hear a crowd like that agin. They purely blowed that huge cloud of dust away they made so much racket. You couldn't have made a body hear you if you'da clumb right in their ear. It was that deaf'ning. And Ory was up to the occasion. He clumb to his feet after sitting there about two minutes. First he bowed to the thousand folks crammed into the stands back of home. Then he decided to dust hisse'f off with his cap and that took a couple of minutes. Presently he marched over to home plate and bows to all the folks stretched out along third base to the mounting top. After he figgered they should be satisfied, he executes a right-about-face, and makes a big long bow to the folks stretched out along the right field line.

When he made the turn-about, I seen his backside fur the first time. I knowed then why people not only was cheering but was laughing fit to kill and nudging at each others ribs and p'inting. Ory's whole hine-end was out. When he slud, he not only burned up the seat of them black sateen britches, but he created so much heat he burned the flap off his long drawers. One of the buttons was hanging by a thread, and the light brown piece of cloth—a kinda reinforcement they had on them models of underdrawers—was all that was left of the whole flap. An it was ready to break loose and fall down between his legs like a ribbon with the first strain he put on it.

*   *   *

You ever notice what happens when a man gits in a fix like Ory was in? Not only down here in this country—everywhere. Like the saying—not even their best friends will tell him. Ory figgered, I reckon, that the p'inting and the mixed laughing and cheering was for his homer. They was no breeze stirring to give him a idey of his raw state, and before he was done bowing, one of their men had made the last out and his own nine, pleased to be winning and maybe jist a little bit willing for Ory to look as much fool as hero, had tooken to the field.

Ory quit bowing long enough to put on his two-bit mask and his two-bit glove and get behind the plate. They was still so much noise you couldn't hear nothing. I was trying to far up our nine on the bench, but they couldn't hear me and most of 'em, anyways, was craning around, trying to get a glance at Ory's backside to see if the button still held up that brown ribbon.

With two out, Ringle worked Tug fur a free pass—the only one he given us that day. Ol' Cornbread laid into the first pitched and lined a hard single into left field. He hit a hook, I seen, which hung and I knowed Tug was tiring. Ol' Heinie come up and he didn't waste a second. He cracked one a mile a minute down the third base line. Their third-sacker knocked it down deep behind third, but it was a hit and the bases was full and I was up.

I allus had a superstition about crossing to the plate in front of the catcher, specially with men on. I wasn't thinking about Ory's bare hiney but when I went around him, I seen that there last button had bit the dust and the brown reinforcement ribbon was flapping around between his legs with his action. Om'-nous as things was for Simmons Run and noisy as the crowd was, people was making half the noise, jist enjoying Ory's delicate condition. Only he never knowed it.

The first pitch Tug throwed me was around my ankles and the Simmons Run empire called it a strike. Tug faked a spitter and come in with a curve ball that was way wide. He faked twice more and they was too wide even for the Simmons Run empire to call anything but balls. Then Tug put one in there, and run the count to three and two.

You recollect how Tug allus rested his left hand on his left knee and leaned way forrard to get his signs? Well, I was watching him like a hawk and I seen his whole face light up sudden-like. He scrooched forrard to take still another look and a kinda grin comes over his face and then he r'ars back in his holding stance and puts the ball up to his mouth. He done this maybe twenty-five - thirty times through the game, faking his spitter. But this time I suspicioned from his grin and his action that it was the real spitter coming, a pitch that allus troubled me up there and I knowed would trouble me here.

I got cocked, and the second he came around, I knowed it was a spitter. All told I got maybe a fifth of a second to figger what to do. This pitch is coming right down the middle fast as a bullet, titty-high, right where I like 'em. But when it was no more than twenty feet out of Tug's hand, you could feel it getting ready to sail. I knowed when the saliver on it took a real hold, it would jump at least two feet and would be so fur outside that I'd draw me a free pass and force in the tying run.

Same time, churning through my head, was the fact Ory didn't like them there spitters. If I swang wild and lit fur first, chances was Ory would miss the ball complete, and we'd be free to take all the bases we could on a passed third strike. Maybe we'd score two-three runs and win.

All this passed through my brain in the blink of the eye. I made the most desperate swing a man ever made and knowed the minute the ball jumped by me I done the right thing. Ory was still squatting. He jist let that spitter sail by.

Everybody, natcherally, was running with the count full and two out. As I rounded first I seen

Ringle and Cornbread high-tailing it in, and right behind 'em ole Heinie was chuffing. My legs was killing me time I got to second, so I slowed up to look. Ory was standing straight up, his face purple behind the little toy mask an his Adam's apple jumping up and down. The whole Simmons Run nine was standing jist friz in their tracks. The ball was way back by the backstop, so I lit out for third, and it wasn't till I was heading into home that their first-sacker woken up and started for the ball. So I scored and that made four runs for us on my strikeout.

Ory was standing about three feet in front of home plate when I crossed. Sudden-like he took off his toy mask and slang it on the ground and then he slang his toy mitt on the ground and jumped up and down on it. Then real puppusful he started marching out toward ol' Tug. Tug kin take care of hisse'f agin most people, but with this big baboon Ory I figgered I better go out to give him a hand.

When Ory gets about ten feet from Tug, he stops and screams,

"I-I-I-I f-f-f-f-f-fought I t-t-t-tole you to n-n-never to th-th-throw that sp-sp-spitter!"

"Gaddlemighty, boy!" Tug says. "You give me the spitter sign, didn't you? You showed me three fingers, didn't you?"

"S-s-s-sign?" Ory shouts. "Three f-f-f-fingers? I-I-I-I g-g-give you the s-s-s-sign for a curve b-b-ball. Two f-f-f-fingers. L-l-l-like this."

He scrooched down and wagged two fingers. But hanging right down beside his middle finger so it looked like a third finger was the brown reinforcement piece of his long drawers. Tug and me studied it for maybe a minute before the whole thing lighted up for us and then we fell down right there on the pitcher's mound and laughed till we near died.

* * *

I tole the story of that game to this here womern baseball writer, jist about word for word as I tole you. I tole her how it all ended up regulation. They had their last bats and Pea Ridge fanned the side and it ended 4-1, our favor. Shore, I got no hits and didn't do nothing mechanical to rave about. But fur pure puppusful thinking, that was my greatest day in baseball.

When she left here that afternoon, that womern baseball writer said she'd write it all up, jist as I given the facts. That was in '42. As I said, fur four years I figgered she was the smartest womern I ever talked to. Then, in '46, Hod Eaton's boy who lives down the road a piece come home from fighting all over Europe, and he brang back a paper back copy of that there book, *My Greatest Day in Baseball*. He give me the loan of it and I spent one whole winter reading it forrards and backwards.

I aint in it, so they's no use for you to put out good money for a copy. Oh, they's a couple of times I show up in box scores—Waite Hoyt's greatest day, when he beat us Giants in '21 and I went nothing fur four agin him, and Muddy Ruel's greatest day when ol' Walt Johnson comes in to stop us Giants cold in the '24 series and I only git one scratch hit that don't mean nothing in the final result. But there aint a line about me out there allus thinking.

I brooded on it some and now I figgered it out. Wimmern aint got the background fur baseball writing. This womern, I'd say, had learned herse'f the game outta books or from watching a college nine play. It was past her to see that maybe they's ten thousand games played every year in town ball and country ball that's jist as bristling with real playing and real thinking as anything you'll see up there.

So when we et, maybe it was my unconscious mind, you might say, that made me declare you was the first baseball writer I seen since I left the Giants. Come to think of it, all I had was her word for it that she was a baseball writer and wimmern aint above claiming something they really aint. Leastways, some wimmern.

Well, after us talking so long as this, how 'bout wetting your whistle with a drap of cider?

THE ARTICLE "How to Pitch" appeared in a booklet called *History of Colored Baseball*, printed in Philadelphia in 1907.

From "How to Pitch"

ANDREW FOSTER

THE REAL TEST comes when you are pitching with men on bases. Do not worry. Try to appear jolly and unconcerned. I have smiled often with the bases full with two strikes and three balls on the batter. This seems to unnerve. In other instances, where the batter appears anxious to hit, waste a little time on him and when you think he realizes his position and everybody yelling at him to hit it out, waste a few balls and try his nerve; the majority of times you will win out by drawing him into hitting at a wide one.

JOHN GALLAGHER

Courtesy *Sport* Magazine. ©

"But I didn't signal for a slow ball—this guy murders a slow ball!"

WHEN this short story appeared in the *Saturday Evening Post* in 1942, it created a noticeable stir. Mr. Frank, long at the forefront of big-time magazine writers in the field of articles, brought his true-to-life touch to fiction here, to the point where at least one baseball man doubted grimly that it was fiction at all. Of all modern short stories about baseball, this has to be counted among the very best.

The Name of the Game

STANLEY FRANK

MESSLIN was in the clubhouse the day they found the Big Guy's World Series watch in Gaban's spare glove. Pinning the rap on Gaban as the sneak thief who had been raiding the team's lockers since spring training should have been a relief to Messlin. He was a new man, a rookie punk like Gaban; the nervous finger of suspicion had brushed him before it transfixed Gaban. But Messlin, who derived a sense of personal dignity from baseball, flinched in an agony of embarrassment when the Big Guy slashed Gaban's mouth with the back of his hand.

The blow sent Gaban reeling across the room like a cornered rat and the rasp of his spikes was harsh in the clubhouse The Big Guy, emboldened by the righteous indignation of the team and conscious that he represented it, advanced upon Gaban to scramble his unhandsome features. Gaban was a rat, all right, but he did not cringe. He lashed out and punched the Big Guy's pulpy nose into his face. They always said Gaban had the guts of a burglar.

Gaban had a wonderful pair of hands and he knew how to use them. He might have cut the Big Guy down to his inconsiderable size in a formal fight, but this was a pleasure fight and the Big Guy weighed two hundred and twenty pounds, and not all of it was blubber.

He grabbed the collar of Gaban's uniform, twisted it in his huge paw and brought up his free arm under Gaban's chin. The smack of Gaban's skull against the wall was loud and distinct above their muffled explosions of breathing. The Big Guy, lusting with purposeful pleasure, was about to let Gaban have it again when the Old Man, the manager, rescued the locker-room thief and flung him away as if he were an obscene thing.

"Get out of here!" the Old Man snarled. "Don't stop to take a shower! You've polluted the place enough already!"

Gaban went back to the minors that night and Messlin was among the half-dozen rookies who went with him. Madden, the team secretary, phoned the boys and gave them their marching orders.

"The Old Man would've told you this himself," Madden said, "but he's pretty cut up by what happened this afternoon. That dirty bum, that Gaban! It's not the first time. You'll be back, kid. You're young. By the way, keep that rumpus in the clubhouse under your hat. You understand?"

Messlin said he understood. He was young and he had pride of ambition, but he understood a phony could not be tolerated in baseball. Sure, they had to release him and a few others at the same time to make a splash story and not make it too pointed that a ballplayer was a crook. For the game's sake, not for Gaban's.

Anyway, Messlin figured, he would have been sent back to the minors three weeks later, in the middle of May, when the rosters were cut. He needed work on his curve ball, and his change of pace was no bargain. Going out three weeks earlier meant a difference of only a couple of hundred bucks in salary. It was a small sacrifice for Messlin when he was twenty to keep the shame of baseball that was Gaban under his hat.

It was different with Gaban, though. Gaban was a fine ballplayer with possibilities of greatness; he was ready for the big league. The team needed him, couldn't win the pennant without him. Fesler, the veteran second baseman, was a cinch to fold up when the sun baked the diamond and the heat drained a man's vitality and his willingness to punish himself.

The Old Man had planned to break in Gaban gradually at second base, then make him the fulltime regular when Fesler wilted, but the Old Man unhesitantly kissed off the pennant when Gaban turned out to be a wrong guy. The private assurance that baseball was clean sustained Messlin through the disappointment and drudgery of the minor leagues, served as a cushion against disillusion when the boys spoke, as ballplayers will, of the Black Sox and the soulless baseball corporations.

Messlin knew he was strictly a sucker for baseball and Gaban alone disturbed the illusion he kept deep within himself. Gaban was back in the majors a year later—the other league, but still the big league. Gaban presently had a World Series watch he could show in public, and two years later he had another memento to go with it, a diamond ring in proof of his membership on the best ball club in America. Gaban was a great star, a hero.

Sometimes, when he thought of it, Messlin liked to believe Gaban was a reformed character, but he guessed from behind-the-hand whispers he heard in the dugouts that Gaban still was a poolroom bum at heart. Messlin felt someone had pulled a bad boner somewhere along the line.

And now Messlin and Gaban were on the same ball club. Gaban's ball club. Gaban was manager of the Drakes, the team that was bringing Messlin back to the big leagues after twelve years of semi-anonymity in the minors. Twelve years of pretty good pitching had gone for Sweeney because a few men wanted to forget they had been in the clubhouse the day the Big Guy's watch was found in Gaban's glove and all the others remembered that he had failed once. They weren't kidding Messlin. They didn't have to tell him he was getting another shot at the big leagues because the war suddenly invested old-timers, who knew the racket and were unlikely to be drafted, with a brief measure of value.

Now they were asking him to win games for the one man in baseball he despised. His boss was the one guy in the business who resented him as a man resents the reminder of a half-forgotten indiscretion more than the stigma itself. The Old Man was dead; the Big Guy was living on his annuities; only two or three of those who had been in the clubhouse that day still were in baseball, and they were in the other league.

There were four hundred major leaguers and they picked the one wrong guy Messlin had ever known, to be a manager. Messlin guessed what Gaban was thinking: *Five thousand bush leaguers in America and I draw the one jerk who knows where the body is buried.* Messlin, a simple man who had neither the talent nor the temperament for philosophy, laughed out of the wrong side of his mouth and tried to forget the one day neither cared to remember.

Messlin made a good try the first time he saw Gaban in training camp. He gave the boss a big hello and said, "Hi, Froggy, you look ready." That was bad; that was a mistake.

Unconsciously, automatically, Messlin used the nickname by which Gaban had been known when he was breaking in. They called him Froggy in the old days for his funny half hop in pouncing on ground balls, for the green and garish, they're-off-and-running clothes he affected, and for his grating, irritating voice, which he used incessantly. The nickname struck a clamorous gong across the years, vibrating memories both preferred to forget.

Messlin should have known the hop had gone out of Gaban's legs and he should have seen that Gaban now dressed like the successful, publicity-hungry actors and businessmen who fawned upon him. Gaban's voice had not changed, though. It still was a penetrating, brassy bellow and it had inspired the nickname which he now was called with affection by ten million fans. Gaban had put the nickname and the affection to work by talking himself into the managership of the Drakes, and it was no surprise to Messlin. Anyone, he reflected, who could talk himself off the commissioner's blacklist and out of jail was a cinch to talk himself into a job.

The man they called Gabby gave Messlin a furtive once-over. He studiously ignored Messlin's proffered hand and pulled his five-buck tie deeper into the billowing collar of his silk initialed shirt. Gaban looked sharp, like money in the bank. His snappy sports jacket and doeskin slacks made Messlin uncomfortably conscious of his own wrinkled, dark gray suit. His other suit.

"You look older than the pictures make you out," Gaban was saying. The inference was plain and Messlin got it on the first bounce. Gaban didn't want him, wouldn't have had him if he had not been bought before the Drakes appointed a new manager.

"Maybe you can pitch. I'll find out soon enough. The draft hasn't taken all the good ballplayers yet. Hey, Dog Face!" Gaban raised his voice to greet the hotel golf pro and startled three aged ladies in a far corner of the lobby. "I'll buy you a drink! A Mickey."

Gaban went off and left Messlin feeling as unnecessary as another neck. The brush-off told him another guy remembered a certain day in a certain clubhouse. The knowledge that he had Gaban on the hip gave Messlin a fleeting surge of superiority, but it didn't stay with him long. He could take refuge in his virtue and his morality, but he would be taking it in the minors while Gaban would be taking the bows and the big money in the majors.

It could have been worse though. During the first weeks of training, Messlin perceived that Gaban was vain enough to want the pennant more than he wanted an undisturbed conscience. Gaban would keep him on the ball club as long as he pitched and kept his mouth shut. It was a running gag among the Drakes that Gaban would haul his mother out of bed and give her a shot in the arm if he thought she could steal a base and win a ball game for him.

Pitching for the Drakes and winning games for Gaban gave Messlin no lift of stimulation, even after the squad was cut to twenty-five men and he was safe for the season. Messlin had thought it would be different. When he learned the Drakes were bringing him back to the big league, he dusted off the shining hope locked in a pigeonhole of his brain for twelve years and he thrilled privately to the prospect of playing on a proud pennant winner.

But the Drakes were all arrogance and no pride. Playing with the Drakes was a degrading experience for Messlin, because the Drakes had to debase themselves to play Gaban's way. Taking their cue from the manager, they were vicious and ruthless and overbearing. They argued excessively with the umpires, they antagonized unduly the other clubs and, goaded by Gaban, they made unnecessary muscles.

In Messlin's book, they were a shrill neighborhood gang imitating the local loafer and trying to be very tough indeed about the whole thing. He was ashamed to find himself hoping they, his own club, would get their ears knocked off.

It could have been different. The Drakes were a good club and they were winning ball games. Messlin might have been animated by the discovery that he was a better pitcher in the big league than he was in the minors. His infield cut off and turned into double plays ground balls which sifted through the humpty-dumpties in the minors for base hits. Wild-swinging kids in the bushes took a cut at everything they could reach and hit stuff that was supposed to fool them, but the big leaguers tried to guess with the pitcher, and Messlin, who knew the racket, did all right in the strategy department.

In midseason it was obvious that the Drakes had only the Kings, the co-favorites, to beat for the pennant, and Messlin was forced to admit Gaban might do it. By dint of great hammering, one becomes a blacksmith. Gaban told them they could win, and his voice, a raucous needle playing a cracked record, pounded at the players until the idea obsessed them and drove them wild. Every ball game was a crusade, and Messlin, who could distinguish between spirit and hysteria, wondered how long it would be before the relentless pressure Gaban was piling on them blew the team apart at the seams.

Gaban, always a great ballplayer, was playing the game of his life and the inspirational impact on the team was making him a winning manager. That was the hell of it for Messlin.

One Gaban in baseball was bad enough; a team of Gabans was infinitely worse. All the players were aping Gaban's bombastic mannerism and his selfish, cynical attitude toward the game. Messlin really didn't blame the other guys. Gaban was the big noise, the most magnetic personality of the year. His success and his recklessness were contagious. Messlin could even see himself falling in line with the others, except for the superimposed picture which gave him perspective and depth every time he looked at Gaban.

Messlin was an alien in his own clubhouse, and that's how he wanted it to be when Clemons, the rookie catcher, was victimized by Gaban's maniacal greed for victory. They were playing the Phillies, and Gaban, maneuvering the staff to have his regular starters ready for a series with the Kings opening the next day, tried to get away with a second-string pitcher. The Drakes powdered the ball and had the game safely in the bag until the Phillies put on a storm in the eighth. Gaban called Messlin from the bull pen to put out the fire. Clemons, who had been in the game all the way to rest Payne, the No. 1 catcher, gave him the old pep-and-vinegar chatter, and Messlin, after a few warm-up throws, went to work.

A couple of outfield flies scored a run for the Phils, but the Drakes still were three to the good. Messlin, pitching carefully, operated on the batter who represented the third out. With the count three and two, Messlin tried to break off his big jug, the slow curve. The batter expected a fast ball and was fooled by the pitch, but he got a small piece of the ball and lifted a high foul which climbed lazily toward the stands between first and home.

Clemons ripped off his mask and chased the ball. Messlin relaxed when he saw the foul would drop into the stands, but Clemons kept going with his head up, digging furiously.

"No! No!" Messlin yelled. "Can't get it! No, Clem! No!"

Messlin hollered as loudly as he could, but he might have been whispering for all the good it did. Gaban opened his wonderful set of pipes and his voice drowned Messlin's, rose above the crowd's roar.

"Lots of room!" Gaban bawled. "Yah, go get it! Lots of room!"

Clemons heard Gaban and he kept going. Now the ball was dropping swiftly and Messlin, going tight with fear, saw it would fall three or four rows behind the low railing separating the field from the stands. Messlin recoiled violently when Clemons, still listening to Gaban and going all out, collided heaviy with the stand.

He hung grotesquely over the railing for a moment, like a sack of flour, then slumped back on the field. The ball bounced crazily on the concrete and the fans chased it, but Clemons lay where he fell.

Messlin was the first to reach Clemons. The kid wasn't out, but he was pretty woozy and he moaned softly while he was coming out of the ether. They carried him off, and Messlin, seeing his jaws twitch spasmodically, guessed it hurt like hell.

There were one strike and one inning to go. Payne climbed into his harness and caught the third strike Messlin threw past the batter in a cold rage. Messlin got rid of the Phillies

in the ninth just in time to get the team back to the clubhouse as Clemons was going out on a stretcher.

The kid tried to whip up a smile when Messlin squeezed his arm, but it was a feeble effort. Gaban looked at him casually, almost impersonally. His interest in ballplayers ceased at that precise instant when they no longer were able to help him win games.

The intern from the ambulance waited for the Great Man to ask him the obvious question. He finally tapped Gaban on the shoulder. "I suppose you want to know about this man."

"Yeh, what goes, doc?" Gaban was as offhand as if he were asking the clubhouse boy to get his shoes shined.

"He has a cracked rib, for one thing."

Gaban snorted. "Gehrig won pennants for the Yankees with busted bones sticking out through his skin. We'll strap him up and he'll be catching in three weeks."

"Maybe," the intern said wryly, "but you can't fix that torn cartilage in his knee with a strip of adhesive. He'll be lucky if he's walking in three months. It may be longer if he needs an operation."

Gaban sailed his glove across the room and hitched up his pants. He sensed the sobering thought which suddenly tempered the team's exhilaration: *It could have been me. So the club wins the pennant and I wind up in the hospital with a stiff leg. Where do I come off?* Gaban was fast on the upbeat. His face was flushed and his eyes were bright with invention.

"You got to take it to win in this league!" he screamed at the players. "You don't win by waving how-do-you-do to the tough ones and playing 'em safe! They don't give that World Series dough to the nice, careful guys! Yah, you got to knock yourself out trying or you'll get knocked off! You, Payne! Tear up them dames' phone numbers! You got to catch every day from here in!"

Payne, a swaggering youth who was wearing out the seat of his pants sitting in Gaban's lap, went into his hardboiled act.

"That World Series dough won't be as hard to take as the work," he sneered, blowing hard on his cigarette. "I'll make new gates in the stands surroundin' those fouls."

The clubhouse was a babble of bravado. The Drakes assured one another they would murder the Kings, and a piece of Messlin's heart went dead inside him.

He was shocked by the brutality and he was

outraged by the stupidity which had cost them a valuable player for the sake of an out in a game they were in no danger of losing. Ballplayers had to stick together and protect themselves from the wolves waiting to stick them. Gaban was willing to sacrifice the entire career of Clemons, a good kid, for one lousy ball game, and nobody cried out in protest.

Messlin had to get out of there before the band constricting his throat choked him. Walking under the deserted, clammy stands toward the exit, Messlin abruptly decided to get good and stiff for the first time in three years. He went out on the street, and he was heading for a little joint where a ballplayer could get a load without everybody in the world knowing about it when he heard his name called from a cab parked at the curb. He looked and saw Harren, the King coach, waving.

Messlin knew all about the rule against fraternizing with opposing ballplayers. He also knew Harren from way back, and he said nuts to the rule. Harren was his catcher in the minors eight years ago and had taught him everything he knew about pitching.

Harren was a good guy, his kind of guy. He appreciated the worth of a ballplayer and he prized his self-respect above a pennant. Messlin got into the cab.

Harren gave the driver the address of a restaurant downtown, but he didn't know it was around the corner from Gaban's apartment. Messlin knew, but he didn't care. Harren started to say he had taken advantage of an off day to scout the Drakes, but Messlin was in no mood to make small talk and they drove to the restaurant in silence. Harren ordered a beer, and Messlin said he wanted bourbon, straight. Harren started to say something when he heard the order, but he glanced at Messlin's face and shrugged.

"How's the kid?" Harren asked after they had taken a belt from their drinks. "It looked like he gave himself a bad jolt."

"He's out for the season," Messlin said grimly. "Gaban ran him in to the hospital."

Harren cursed Gaban, softly, savagely and fluently. He called him seventeen different species of low, no-good animal life, and Messlin punctuated each blast against his manager with short nods.

"You go into the game for the money," Harren raved, "but it doesn't last long. Then you play for peanuts and you have no home life, but you want to hang on because you get a bang just being part of the game. Then you see a dirty, contemptible skunk like Gaban hit the jackpot. It's enough to make you cut your throat. There'll be no living with that cheap phony if he wins, but he won't make it."

"Why not?" Messlin demanded. After all, the pennant meant five or six grand to him and you can't eat illusions.

"Everybody in the league hates Gaban's guts and they'll break a leg to stop him. It's not enough that he beats you. He must humiliate you and rub it in. You guys have the best team, but you won't win, because the percentages must catch up with Gaban."

Harren said he wanted another drink, and Messlin had more of the same. The drinks cooled the hot anger gnawing at them and they began, as ballplayers will, to trade stories of people they knew and things they had seen. Harren told of the time Lefty Gomez delayed a World Series game to stare at a plane overhead, and then Messlin told the one about the bushleague umpire who was quick to pull a watch on the boys when the peace was disturbed. The umpire got into a jam one day, and he tried to work the watch gag when the boys began to push him around. In the confusion, though, somebody lifted his watch, and the umpire almost went out of his mind when a dog ran up to the plate with the watch in its mouth.

To illustrate the story, Messlin took out his own watch and held it aloft. He was coming to the punch line when the chuckle died in his throat and his grin froze into a grimace.

Gaban was standing at the bar glaring at him, too far to hear what he was saying, too close to the guilty suspicion lurking in his mind to escape the significance of the watch. Gaban's eyes shifted to the eager anticipation on Harren's face, darted back to Messlin and singed him with hatred before he walked out.

"Uh-uh," Harren breathed. "There goes trouble. We better get out of here. No, that's no good. He may be hanging around outside, and it'll look worse if we leave together. I'll go first, and if I see him I'll try to square you. Sorry this happened, kid. See you."

Messlin settled down to do some serious drinking. He figured he might as well be stiff as the way he was. Gaban could fine him a couple of hundred for giving hard liquor a play, and Messlin decided to get his money's worth. He sat there belting the stuff until the bartender, who was wise in these things, took the money out of his wallet, replaced it with a note to that effect, and gave a reliable cabbie two bucks to take him to the hotel.

Messlin was not a drinking man and he could not persuade the cat to crawl out of his mouth until noon. He looked terrible and he felt worse, and it was only by strenuous exercise of his will power that he got to the ball park no more than a half hour late. He pulled himself together a little when he found Gaban was late himself. Gaban, in fact, did not show up until it was almost time to go out for batting practice.

The Great Man was not quite himself, and it was a vast improvement. He went over the Kings' batting order quietly and methodically, telling his pitchers what he wanted them to throw, but he warmed up as he went along. At the end he was screaming and slobbering, and the Drakes broke down the door in their zeal to beat the Kings' brains out, in keeping with their manager's parting exhortation.

The mob was large and devoted in its allegiance to the home team, and the Drakes, already full of fire and fury, reacted splendidly. They put on a show for the people. They peppered the customers in the cheap seats with line drives, and even Messlin, shagging flies in the outfield, began to get the fever.

A swelling chorus of catcalls greeted the Kings as they straggled on the field, and the faithful told them, with virtuosity and vehemence, to take a flying jump for themselves. Messlin presently sensed something was cooking. The Kings were not tossing the ball around or taking prodigious swipes at the atmosphere with their bats. They were lined up in silence along the steps of their dugout, as though they were waiting for something to happen.

It happened when Gaban went up for his last round of batting practice. The Kings suddenly came to life. They began to yell at Gaban, and Messlin, in the outfield, could tell by the volume and intensity of their voices that this was an extra-special dose the jockeys were giving Gaban. And then Messlin's ear, trained to pick up only what he wanted to hear, began to distinguish the taunting words, and his knees sagged under him.

"Hey, Gabby, what time is it?" the Kings roared in unison. "Pardon me, sir! Have you a watch?" they shrieked in a shrill falsetto. "Who stole the watch, Gabby? Is that number on your uniform from the program or the warden's office? Who stole the watch? Where are your stripes, Gabby? Who stole the watch?"

Gaban turned livid, then white. He tried to foul off the ball into the Kings' dugout, and when that failed, he let his bat fly when he swung at a pitch, and he scattered his tormenters on the bench. The Kings poured it to him and Gaban went crazy.

Someone had blown the whistle on the secret a handful of men had kept for twelve years. Messlin wondered wildly who it could be. And then another thought hit him between the eyes and staggered him.

He remembered the silly story he had told Harren the night before in the bar. Again he saw Gaban's contorted face and his own dangling watch turning back time in the archives of Gaban's memory.

Gaban had seen him laughing and showing the watch to Harren. Harren was a King coach. The Kings were jabbing him with the bones of an exhumed skeleton. Messlin knew that was how it had to add up for Gaban. Messlin wanted to drop into a hole in the ground and pull the lid over him.

The umpires tried to pipe down the rumpus when the game started, but the Kings had too much on Gaban to let him get away and, besides, the umpires never counted Gaban among their favorite people. Gaban had Hovey, his ace pitcher, dust off the King hitters, but they got up screaming vile abuse, and their spikes reflected the sunlight when they slid into second base.

Gaban, who had the guts of a burglar, challenged the Kings to meet him under the stands after the game, then stepped up to the plate and knocked in two runs with a double. The Kings got a run back when Krindle, the league's leading hitter, teed off and belted one out of sight and mind. It was a ball game and Gaban was winning it with his double and the small miracles he was working in the field with the wonderful pair of hands which had been known to dip into teammates' pockets.

The eighth, with the meat of the King's batting order coming up, figured to be Hovey's tough inning and it was launched with the promise of a storm when the lead-off man singled. Krindle, who could hit a ball farther than it could be shot from a gun, strode toward the plate hefting three pieces of lumber. Hovey dusted his hands on the resin bag and nodded when Gaban raised both hands and brought them down with a sweeping motion. It was no secret; everybody in the ball park knew Krindle was going to be knocked down by the next pitch.

Hovey wound up and let the thing go. Krindle stood there motionless and Messlin, sitting on the bench, stopped breathing. He had seen it happen before and it was going to happen again. Krindle was frozen at the plate. He couldn't duck the pitch. He didn't.

Krindle swayed slightly, then collapsed in sections. The King bench erupted in a stream of players going for Gaban and Hovey, and the Drakes went out to meet them, but the umpires and the cops were on the alert and they broke it up. A doctor ran on the field, pushed back Krindle's eyelids and told them to call an ambulance. A concussion.

The field was cleared and King runners perched on first and second with none out. Hovey went back to the mound, but Hovey, who really wasn't a bad guy, was through. The beaning had unnerved him completely and his first two pitches sent Payne diving into the dirt.

Gaban called time, looked at the men in the bull pen, then wheeled and barked at the bench, "Messlin! Get on your horse! Come on! Yah, you! Messlin!"

The men on the bench were accustomed to Gaban's giddy hunches, but this one floored them. Messlin had worked the day before; he wasn't warmed up. A helluva situation to throw a guy into, cold.

But Messlin knew the score. He knew Gaban was putting him on the spot deliberately. If they lost the game, the rap would be on him. The customers had no truck with technical explanations.

Gaban took charge of the infield conference while Messlin was trying to get the hinges out of his arm.

"Two balls and no strikes on this bum," he snapped. "We can't afford to work on him. He wants to bunt. Lay it in there for him. The rest play it tight. Throw to first. I'll cover."

They squared away and Messlin bowled a good bunting ball, low and outside, down the alley. The guy laid it down nicely and Messlin bounced off the rubber fast to intercept the ball. He slapped it to the ground with his glove, wheeled and threw a strike to first.

It was a perfect throw. Gaban could have caught it in his teeth. But Gaban's teeth were buried in the dirt. Gaban had taken off in a desperate dive and the ball sailed over his head into right field. Before it was returned to Messlin, the Kings had two runs, the batter was on second base and the park was clamorous with despair.

For an agonized moment, Messlin thought Gaban had fallen in hustling to cover the bag. He actually felt sorry for the guy, lying there and beating the ground with his fists in a paroxysm of impotent rage. It was a tough break, a rotten way to blow a big ball game. But Gaban's act for the crowd was too exaggerated. He betrayed himself to Messlin, and the pitcher went limp when the shock of realization broke over him.

Gaban got up and tossed his glove in the air in a gesture of disgust. He waved to the bull pen and Messlin felt a wordless cry coming up from his belly. Gaban had been slow in covering the bag and now he was telling the people the fault wasn't his. He was telling them the throw had been wild, that Messlin had choked in the clutch and lost the game.

The people rose on their hind legs and booed Messlin out of the ball park. A lemon thrown from the upper tier bounced against his leg. Messlin went to the clubhouse, heaved a chair through the glass door of Gaban's office and went home. He heard the score over the radio and he saw the Kings win the next two games to sweep the series and go away in first place.

The Drakes were licked. There was a month to go, but the Drakes were cooked because the hypodermic of confidence Gaban had been giving them all season no longer was taking. The Kings had stripped them of their arrogance and Gaban never had fortified it with the essential core of pride.

They lost three more in a row before they came out of the swoon, and the Kings, smelling the World Series money, went on winning. Gaban raged at them, but his needles had been blunted by the Kings and they quit cold on him.

Only Gaban refused to give up. Gaban was thirty-five years old and he was playing on his nerve, but his nerve was such that he was playing the best second base in the business. Gaban picked them up and carried them on his back, and presently, when their slump scraped bottom, the Drakes got off and pulled their own weight.

Their wheels meshed again, and then the Kings started to come back to them. The hopped-up youth who had replaced Krindle in the King line-up developed a blind spot which was thoroughly exploited by the pitchers, and the teams wheeled into the stretch locked in a head-to-head struggle all over again.

They came down to the pay-off, a four-game series, with the Kings leading by two games and needing only an even break in their own park for the clincher. The Drakes had to win three out of four to keep alive, and Hovey won the first in the grand manner, with a shutout. Gaban wrapped up the second game with three base hits, but the manager of the Kings also knew the tricks of rabble-rousing and his ballplayers did not have tin ears. The Kings wore their hitting clothes in the third game and the pennant was on the line for either team to take.

Gaban had no choice for the big blowoff. He sent Hovey back to the trenches with one day of rest, and Hovey, a dead-game guy, frustrated the Kings for seven innings by sheer power of will. He had a two-run lead going into the eighth and he came out of it with only one. Nobody in the crowded bull pen had to tell Messlin to heat up for the ninth. Hovey was dying on his feet.

Hovey was brave and tenacious, but he died and Messlin went in there with the score tied, one out and a man on second base. Messlin held the hopes of twenty-five men in his right hand, and he lifted them by getting the batter on a ground ball to Gaban. The runner moved to third, but Messlin felt good. He slapped the ball into his glove impatiently when the next batter, who could be the third out, walked back to the dugout.

The round little man who was the announcer waddled out of the King dugout and picked up the microphone of the p.a. system. A big, familiar figure got off the bench and stooped over the bat rack. Krindle, the best hitter in the league, was going to be the pinch hitter. Krindle found his stick, dug his holes at the plate and the crowd tore down the joint.

Gaban called for time and Payne went out to meet him on the mound.

"Down he goes," Gaban said tersely. "This guy hasn't seen a pitch since Hovey skulled him. Throw one at his head and he'll faint. He'll be a setup for that big jug outside. You got it? Throw it down his throat, but good, with the first one."

Messlin nodded and took his stretch. He drew a bead on Krindle's ear, his target. He went into his motion and then his arm was locked in a vise.

He saw a high-speed mental movie of Krindle freezing at the plate and falling to the ground. He saw Krindle, a good ballplayer, ruined for a pennant, and Messlin knew he couldn't throw at the man's head. He had gone into his pitching motion and it was too late to change his grip on the ball for the big jug. He had to go through with the fast ball no thirty-three-year-old pitcher could throw past Krindle.

He let it go and Krindle whipped his bat. There was a one-two crack, like two pistol shots, and the second exploded against Messlin's knee. Messlin's reflexes were sharper, more urgent, than the pain which surged through him. He saw two white blurs, the man from third running home with the winning run and the ball rolling away.

Messlin started for the ball, but he had no legs to support him. He fell on his face. He crawled on his belly for the little white ball and he was reaching and grabbing the air when the other white blur roared across the plate. He still was reaching when two men helped him to his feet. Messlin didn't know the men, but their gray uniforms and brass buttons were vaguely familiar.

The park cops left him at the door of the clubhouse and Messlin went into the sullen silence broken by Gaban's choked cursing. Messlin hobbled to the nearest bench and, although his leg was sending messages of misery to his brain, Messlin laughed. His laughter soared above Gaban's raving and they looked at him in shocked disbelief.

"You're through with this club!" Gaban shouted, and his voice cracked. "You gutless, double-crossing bum! What are you laughing at?"

"Froggy, I'm laughing at you," Messlin said, but he no longer was laughing. "Imagine a louse like you winning the pennant."

BASEBALL is the greatest of outdoor sports, and plagiarism is the greatest of indoor. I was tempted toward the latter while doing the preface for this book, because Mr. Gallico's piece says so much so well. It is from his famous book *Farewell to Sport*.

Inside the Inside

PAUL GALLICO

BASEBALL CAN BE the most fascinating game in the world to watch and also the dullest, depending very often upon circumstances —that is to say, the quality of the play, the caliber and situation of the competing teams, and also what you yourself bring into the park. All games are alike in form and intent. One man tries to beat another man, or one group of men try to worst another group through skill, courage, and physical condition. It is merely the materials with which they are provided for this purpose, the rules, and the playing grounds that differ. The more intricate the game and tangled the rules and complicated the materials, the more difficult it is to understand, but the more fascinating it becomes when you do understand it.

When two men face each other in a boxing ring with gloves on their hands and begin to fight when the bell rings, and stop fighting when it rings again after three minutes, it is reasonably obvious to anyone what is going on and what they are trying to do to each other and the means they are employing. The struggle is a simple hand-to-hand trial for complete mastery within certain time limits, and because the struggle sometimes gets atavistic, abysmal, and terrifying, with show of blood, it is arresting and arousing. The novice spectator becomes an expert after witnessing his first prizefight or boxing match because everything is plain and simple and easy to see. It takes rather longer to know what is going on on a baseball field, what the trials and the problems of the various players are, what can be done and what cannot be done; and even so, many people who have been going to games for years do not know exactly what it is all about because they

have never taken the trouble to find out. They love it, though, because they do realize that there is a fine balance struck between offense and defense and that, by a lucky accident in the laying out of the playing field and the development of the game, you may sit by and witness the development of real drama and the working of keen wits in fast bodies.

Baseball talk is a great bore, baseball players are not exactly intellectual giants, and baseball figures, box scores and averages even duller. But the things that take place on the field in a tight game played to the hilt by a couple of major-league clubs can be completely captivating.

If games as a whole bore you, you will never like baseball. But if you can take pleasure in the story of conflict unfolded before your eyes, it is only necessary to become a little more familiar with the materials used by baseball players and the rules under which they operate to find something that can be quite as fascinating, for instance, as the theater. In one afternoon at the ball yard you may, if you know where and how to look for it, come upon half a dozen split-second races between a running man and a thrown ball, in which the hundredth part of a second is all the difference between success and failure, dozens of examples of skill triumphant, skill defeated, traps baited and snapped shut upon victims, human courage, human folly, and human cowardice, narrow escapes, heroes, villains, individual deeds that verge upon the miraculous, bits of co-operation between two men or among three or four that are really beautiful to see in their rhythm and perfection, heroes turned suddenly into clowns and goats, clowns becoming heroes, speed, grace, and sometimes even a curious beauty, the beauty of the perfection of a well pitched, well defended game.

The patterns of the game are of themselves interesting and pleasing to the eye. The rich chocolate-brown or pale tan of the infield is contrasted with the fine soothing green of the outfield. The base paths are neatly geometrical, and the white foul lines on either side of the home plate start their diverging roads toward infinity. There is a place for everyone and every place is neatly marked off with white lime. There is a base at each corner of the square, and a player stationed at, or close to, each base. The outfield is divided into three sections, right, center, and left field, and each field has a patrolman stationed in his appointed place. Pitcher and catcher stand on a line that is the hypotenuse of the right-angle triangle made by the three bases, home, first, and second. And pleasingly anti-geometrical is the shortstop, who is placed with no heed to design at all, midway between second and third base, upsetting the whole scheme of regularity like a tiny beauty mark on the cheek of a pretty girl.

One team dresses in white, the other in gray. And the action is static rather than fluid, with sharp, refreshing changes from tension and immobility to quick, brilliant bursts of motion. You may see this curiously exaggerated in newsreel photographs of ball games, because the camera cuts in usually just a second before the flashes of action on the diamond. You catch a glimpse of them stock-still first, and then suddenly men are streaking around the bases, heads down, legs twinkling, while fielders glide in to make their quick, graceful defensive moves.

But the plot behind the patterns is even more exciting. Let us take a simple example: the score is tied, there is one out, a runner is on first base, and a heavy hitter is at bat, crouched a little over the plate, waving his mace back and forth gently but menacingly. And, incidentally, he doesn't do this in hopes of frightening the pitcher. He is merely keeping his bat moving because the action he is to be called upon to meet is so fast that he will be hopelessly beaten if he hasn't begun to move a little in advance of it.

There they are, then, the eleven men involved at the moment in what from the point of view of the eventual outcome of the game may be definitely the crisis. The first baseman is dividing his attention between keeping the runner at his base from gaining too much of a lead, and still covering his territory defensively. If the ball is hit, the runner on first will come charging at full clip into second base. Depending upon where the ball is hit to, either the second baseman or the shortstop will have to get there to take the throw and the shock. Or he may not even wait for a hit, but try to steal in the little bit of time between the start of the pitcher's delivery and the passage of the ball to catcher and thence to second baseman. The shortstop is intent upon the delicate problem of starting a successful double play and retiring the side. The third baseman has moved in a little to speed up the fielding of a possible bunt or roller in the infield, and yet he must not leave the space around his base unprotected through which a sharply driven ball may scoot for two or three bases and disaster.

The outfielders have shifted their positions to suit the known batting habits of the hitter. The burly, powerful figure squatting behind the bat, the catcher, is the man in control of the entire situation, and the pitcher is his tool, obeying his brain and his strategy, telegraphed to him by means of finger signals. Or perhaps the catcher is merely an intermediary who transmits the signals and will of an even better strategic mind in the person of the manager sitting on the bench. And the batter is one lone man playing the other nine men, their speed and skill, the intelligence of the catcher in playing his weaknesses, and the control of the pitcher and his ability to obey the orders of the catcher, combined against him. Every move that follows will have a direct bearing upon the outcome of the game. Nothing is unimportant. A double play will badly hurt the morale of the side thus retired with victory in its grasp. A hit or an error or a stolen base may equally upset the equilibrium of the defending team. But still more fascinating and exciting is the fact that all of the men involved are playing a match against time and distance and dealing with the smallest fragments of seconds that can be split on the dial of a delicate stop watch.

The baseball diamond is no diamond at all, but actually a square set up on one of its points, and the bases, home to first, first to second, second to third, and third to home, are each exactly 90 feet apart. The pitcher's box is 60½ feet from home plate. The distance from home plate to second base, which is the line on which the catcher throws in the attempt to catch a man out who is stealing, is a fraction over 127 feet. And the entire science and thrill of the American game of baseball, developed from an old English game called rounders, lie tucked away in those measurements. They are very rarely examined, and still more rarely thought of, even by the players. Most of the men who play the game haven't the vaguest notion of the miracles of timing and precision that they perform.

The infielders, for instance, have a fraction under three seconds in which to field a batted ball and get it over to first base ahead of the runner, because the batter only has to run a distance of thirty yards to reach first. From a standing start a fast man can do it in three and two tenths seconds, and a left-handed batter perhaps one or two tenths of a second faster, because he is on the right-hand side of the plate and a yard closer to his goal. If the fielder can get that ball to first base in just under three seconds, the runner is out. A few tenths of a second over the three seconds and he is safe and a potential run is menacing the defense.

Now, look at the second hand of your watch and note the time it takes for three seconds to tick off—one . . . two . . . three and gone. In this time, the infielder judges the speed and direction of a ball hit with all the weight and force behind the body of a man, moves in to meet it, figuring the hop as he does so, and the number of steps he must take to reach it, catches it and throws it again all in one motion while still moving forward. There is nothing prettier for timing and rhythm in any sport than to watch a shortstop or third baseman (whose problems are greater because, of the infielders, they are farthest removed from first base and have a greater distance to throw) come in fast for a slow roller, and as he is moving, swoop on the ball like a gull dropping for a fish, and with a continuation of the same movement with which he picked it up, get it away on a line for first base with an underhand throw across his forward-bending body. So precious and vital are those tenths of seconds that if he tries to straighten up, or draw his arm back to gain more speed and accuracy, the play is over. The runner has crossed first base.

How much faster, then, and more beautiful in speed and execution is the double play when three men handle the ball in the same length of time and retire two runners on the one play, the man speeding to second (and he has a good head start) and the batter heading

for first. Three seconds flat or better, and yet the shortstop fields the batted ball, or rather scoops it over to the second baseman, who sends it on to first. It would take a delicate timing instrument to measure the fraction of a second that the shortstop actually has possession of the ball. Crack! goes the bat. Step, and flip, goes the shortstop! The second baseman in that time has run from his position perhaps five or six yards from the bag as the ball is started toward him by the shortstop. Ball and man meet on the base, and likewise with the same motion, in which there is no check or hesitation, the second baseman whirls and lines the ball down to first. He can whip that ball the ninety feet from second to first in three fifths of a second. And he is lucky to have that much time left.

The catcher has a pretty problem to throw out a man who is trying to steal. A good baserunner will take a lead of from two to three or four yards from first base before he suddenly ducks his head and breaks for second with every ounce of speed he can muster. He can make it in something around three seconds flat, or even a tenth or two under. Unlike a force-out, where it is merely necessary to touch the bag once the ball is in the fielder's possession, the second baseman or shortstop, who receives the throw at second, must touch the runner with the ball before his spikes cut into the bag or he hooks it with his leg. Here is a fine, brisk bit of juggling with time. The runner starts his dash with the wind-up of the pitcher or, as he rarely winds up with a man on base, with his first move to pitch the ball to the batter, usually the first tension or drawing back of the arm. From that time on, the hurler is committed and must go through with the pitch.

The ball travels the sixty feet to the plate, and, just to be mother's little helping hand, the batter takes a cut at it to make it more difficult for the catcher and throw him off if he can. The catcher must receive the ball perfectly, straighten up, whip off his heavy mask, draw back his arm, and fire the ball on a line, not in the general direction of second base, but to the foot of the bag, about ankle-high, so that the receiver is spared that precious tenth of a second or more in getting it onto the sliding runner. If the maneuver is completed inside of three seconds and the throw is accurate, the runner is out. Anything over that and he is safe. It takes a ten-second man to steal a base successfully these days—that is, a man who can run a hundred yards in ten seconds. And every inch of ground that he can chisel by increasing his lead off first without getting caught at it and thrown out at first, is important and vital to the success of this maneuver and has a direct bearing upon the eventual outcome of the game. Those seemingly endless throws that the pitcher makes over to first base to hold the runner close to the bag are not made for exercise or to annoy the customers. The purpose is to reduce those inches. The inches otherwise will be translated into hundredths of a second around second base and spell the difference between safe and out. A man can score from second on a single. Runs depend upon those tiny measurements.

As a matter of fact, no game in the world is as tidy and dramatically neat as baseball, with cause and effect, crime and punishment, motive and result, so cleanly defined. The consequences of a single error or failure pyramid inexorably as the game goes on and finally prove to be the events that have won or lost the day, exactly as the minor, unnoticed incidents unfolded at the beginning of a well-constructed play suddenly loom up as prime and all-important to the climax.

Pretty, too, is the personal duel between pitcher and batter, or rather between the pitcher and his alter or commanding ego, the catcher, and the man who is trying to hit. The problem of the batter seems tremendously magnified when one considers what might be termed the ballistics and forces under which he operates.

The distance between the pitcher's box and home plate, as has been noted, is 60½ feet. And a fast ball will make the trip from the hand of the thrower to the mitt of the catcher somewhere between three and four tenths of a second. That doesn't exactly give a batter much time to turn the matter over in his head and make up his mind whether he will take a cut at it or let it pass for a ball, though it is true the average pitch is somewhat slower and the ball takes four to five tenths of a second for its flight. The average baseball bat is only about three feet long, and the batter's arm permits it to extend for another foot or so. Actually, out of that entire distance of 60½ feet that is traversed by the ball in less than half a second, it is in position to be hit safely by the batter for only three feet of the journey. This brings the time element in which a ball remains in a position where it may be met with the bat close to an absurdity, an impossibility;

something around two one-hundredths of a second, which is cutting it rather fine. And still the batsmen manage, on an average, to hit safely one third of the baseballs thrown at them.

To assist the batter and to strike a better balance between him and the pitcher, the latter is forced, if he wishes to register a called strike, to throw the ball to the hitter down a groove a little more than a foot wide, the width of the home plate. And if the pitcher throws more than four of them outside this groove, the batter, as everyone knows, is entitled to the equivalent of a hit, a free passage to first base. The batter is further permitted two misses without penalty. If he misses the third time he is out.

Thus, the activity centered on home plate is really very simple to understand; three strikes out, four balls a walk. But the drama that is packed into that simple arrangement of figures, the swift changes of fortune and situation whereby first one and then the other finds himself in difficulties which with stunning suddenness are liable to mushroom into the loss of the game, explain a good deal of the fascination of the sport.

For instance, the so-called three strikes allotted the batter are a great snare and delusion. In point of fact it is only two strikes, for he is allowed to miss the ball only twice, but nobody but the batter ever thinks of that. The third time he misses it he is out. And yet there is magic in that number "three" and he strides to the plate with great confidence in his allotment of three strikes, a confidence that is only slightly dented upon the calling or taking of the first one, because, after all, there are still two more chances left. Two strikes and he is in for it. Now he *must* hit. The margin of possible failure has been wiped out. The pressure has suddenly become almost unbearable. And three chances had seemed such a safe margin when he first stepped up to the plate!

But note how the balance of power seesaws between pitcher and hitter. Batter up! The first one comes over—a ball. The batter smirks and pounds the plate with satisfaction. The advantage lies with him now. If the pitcher throws another wide one it means that three out of his next four pitches must be in that groove or the batter walks. Very nice. And so the next throw will bear looking at very closely, because the chances are it will be a strike. There is a little pressure on the pitcher and none whatsoever on the batter. He can afford to relax a little and let the pitcher commit himself on the next ball. He does. Ball two! Ha! Two balls and no strikes. Lovely. The batsman begins to preen himself a little and the pitcher to perspire. That man serving 'em up from the little mound is in for it now. Strike one! Oh, oh! Now the batter is doing a little more thinking. The next one will be more of a problem. Shall he let it pass and hope it will be a third ball, putting the pitcher definitely on the spot, or should he reason that the latter will try to burn it over and get *him* in the hole? Ugh! Strike two! Swung at it and missed it by a foot. Guessed wrong. The pitcher fooled him (or rather the catcher). He should have let it go. Outguessed. Now the batter begins to sweat. The advantage lies with the enemy now. Two balls and two strikes and the pitcher has another ball to waste and can tease him with a bad one, or take a chance of breaking a fast one over the corner of the plate and getting him out. Hardly a moment ago the batter had the situation well in hand. Now he is in a mess. That confounded pitcher is just playing with him. Look at him grinning up there on the mound. All the confidence has oozed out of the hitter and into the hurler. Here it comes—zip! Has the umpire's right arm flashed up? No! A ball! Three and two! Switch again. Now the pitcher is in deep trouble, although the batter is not feeling any too good about the situation. But the odds have passed to the batter because the pitcher must commit himself first. Once that ball leaves his fingers it is irrevocable. There is no calling it back or changing his mind. True, the hitter has only that tenth of a second in which to make his decision as to what he will do with the next pitch, but in a game of such delicate fractions of time it is a decided advantage. He knows that the pitcher cannot afford to walk him, especially if there is only one out, or none, or another man on base already. And if the bases are full the corresponding pressure upon the pitcher is all the greater. No, he must throw the ball down that nice, one-foot groove in which the bat may work to deadliest advantage. His only chance is to put so much spin, or "stuff," on the ball that when it meets the bat instead of rifling off into the outfield for a clean hit, it will deflect to the ground and give the fielders a chance to scoop it up, or glance off high into the air to be caught on the fly. But he might decide to risk it and make the eager hitter bite on one and strike out.

This goes on every minute of the game, and

never seems to be twice the same, as the individual duels go on, inning after inning, changing in their nature and intensity according to the situation of the game. Pitching to batters with runners on base increases the pitcher's worries and problems a hundredfold. Batting in pinches piles pressure upon the batsmen. The situation is always different, and they drive on relentlessly, piling up and piling up to a certain climax as the final innings of the game are reached, increasing in intensity as the pitcher begins to tire and it is a question how long he can respond with accuracy and control to the dictates of the brain behind the bat.

The game is as full of surprises as a mystery play. The plot and its ending may be perfectly apparent up to the ninth inning and the last man at bat, and then with stunning suddenness change entirely and go on to a new ending. A pitcher will often be the hero of a closely fought battle in which his side leads 1-0 for eight innings and the rival batsmen have been looking sillier and sillier as they fanned the air, clawing at curves and drops, or standing with their bats on their shoulders while the ball broke across the plate for perfect called strikes. A batter in the hands of a masterful pitcher is a pitiful sight, anyway. He releases enough energy with each swing to cave in the side of a building and it does nothing but create a mild breeze as bat fails to meet ball. He swings himself clear off his feet and sits awkwardly in the dust from the force of his useless blow. Or he stands looking like a big zany, with his ears turning a beautiful shade of cerise, while a perfect third strike burns past his bosom and the umpire calls him out and the catcher laughs sardonically and makes unpleasant remarks out of the side of his mouth.

These are moments of pure glory and unadulterated satisfaction for the pitcher and his battery mate and their adherents in the grandstands. Or the batter actually connects with the ball with a mighty swipe destined to rip the hide from it, but all that happens is that the ball takes one hop into the hands of the second baseman, who, to show his contempt for the puny effort, tosses the ball underhand to the first baseman.

Even in the ninth inning when an obviously astigmatic umpire, with two out and none on base, calls what was obviously a third strike a fourth ball, and a man reaches first base, there is no cause for alarm. The batters that day are lugging useless timber to the plate and have had no more than three safe hits the entire game. They might just as well have matchsticks in their fingers. And the next man up, the final hitter, is a weak sister, relegated to the lower half of the batting order because he has no reputation or record as a dangerous slugger. The crowd is already beginning to head for the exits, chuckling to themselves at the helplessness of the batters, admiring the skill and control of the pitcher. The catcher calls for a sizzler over the plate, loaded with spin. The weak hitter will ground it to a fielder and the game will be over. In anticipation the pitcher is already standing beneath a cooling shower, listening to the laudatory words of his comrades, and reading the "SHUTOUT" headlines in the morning papers. Next year he must ask for a raise. He winds up—let the man on base go down to second if he wants to. Now he is in a knot. Now he unwinds. Now he pitches. And now, too, it happens. For, working silently and without warning, the poisons of fatigue in that arm that seemed to be made of steel and whipcord have worked their changes. The pitcher has given the same twist, the same flip of his wrist, the same leverage and follow-through with his body, only instead of slanting towards the batter with blinding speed, the ball comes floating down the groove, all stitches showing, and looking just a shade smaller than a full moon. The batter doesn't have to be a Babe Ruth to nudge that one. He says: "Oh, baby, come to Papa!" laces it into the grandstand for a home run, and that is that.

The game is over. The pitcher has lost 2-1. All he could do was stand there with his hands on his hips, feeling his ears growing long and furry, watching the ball sail over the whisky advertisement affixed to the top balcony. The fielders cannot even make a play for it. The right fielder dutifully has his rump pressed up against the right-field wall, but he would have to be a hundred feet tall to get his hands on that ball and he can do little more than wave it a regretful farewell as it disappears into the crowd.

There you have it. One tiny, uncontrollable slip and the hero has become the dunce, the goat, and the villain. All the failures of the batters that day are forgotten and forgiven, wiped out by that one blow. The sportswriters, some of them, angrily tear sheets of paper from their typewriters, on which they have already begun to write: "In one of the most masterful exhibitions of plain and fancy hurling ever seen at the Polo Grounds, Joie

Dokes, diminutive southpaw of the New York Giants, shut out the St. Louis Cardinals 1-0 here yesterday afternoon, letting them down with three hits," etc., etc., insert a fresh piece of paper, and start all over again: "Elmer Crabtree, veteran shortstop of the Cards, hasn't been hitting the length of his cap all year, but yesterday afternoon in the ninth inning of a brilliant pitchers' duel, he stepped to the plate with two out, the score 1-0 against him, and a comrade on base due to walk, and with the count two and two on him," etc., etc., etc.

There are hundreds of these situations brought on during the course of the game, and one could write endlessly of them. I don't mean to do so. But that is why I have liked baseball and always will. It is endlessly intriguing, and when the human element is added to the weird mechanics of the sport, the wise, foxy veterans, the brash, cocky young kids, the eccentric and screwy characters who play the game, it becomes truly a part of the national scene.

But I like, too, the freedom of baseball and the physical and emotional simplicity of the relationship between player and spectator. It is the only game in the world where the onlooker is permitted to heckle, hoot, cheer, and advise the player to his heart's content. I am not particularly concerned whether it is sportsmanlike for an individual concealed beyond hope of detection in some section of the crowd, to howl, purple-faced, as a batter retires from the plate with his tail between his legs after having fanned in a clutch: "Oh, you bum! Go lay down, you bum, yah yeller. Oh, you bum!" but I know that it makes the abusive individual feel wonderful, because I have sat next to him and watched him wipe the sweat off his brow with a damp handkerchief after his tirade, tilt a bottle of pop to his lips, and then look around him to take in the admiring glances of some of the less daring and articulate fans. He has established himself as an expert and a critic. He has hoisted something off his chest. I know him, the poor little man; not man, but mouse. In the office he sits under the thumb of his niggling superior and at home under both thumbs of his wife. Taxi-drivers curse him as he scuttles out from beneath their wheels, waiters ignore him, policemen bawl him out, nobody loves him, nobody pays any attention to him. But in the ball park he can rise up on his hind legs and abuse a player. It's good for him, and it doesn't hurt the player any.

So, too, the crowd as a whole plays the role

of Greek chorus to the actors on the field below. It reflects every action, every movement, every changing phase of the game. It keens. It rejoices. It moans. It jeers. It applauds and gives great swelling murmurs of surprise and appreciation, or finds relief in huge, Gargantuan laughs. I can stand outside of a ball park and listen to the crowd and come close to telling exactly what is happening on the diamond inside. That quick, sharp explosive roar that rises in crescendo and is suddenly shut off sharply as though someone had laid a collective thumb on the windpipe of the crowd, followed by a gentle pattering of applause, tells its own story, of a briskly hit ball, a fielder racing for it, a runner dashing for the base. The throw nips the runner and the noise too. That steady "Clap-clap-clap-clap-clap. . . ." Tight spot. Men on base, crowd trying to rattle the pitcher. A great roar turning into a groan that dies away to nothing—a potential home run, with too much slice on it, that just went foul. The crowd lives the actions of the players more than in any other game. It is a release and something of a purge. It is the next best thing to participation.

JOHN GALLAGHER

Courtesy *Sport* Magazine. ©

"Could you tell me where I can find the Philadelphia Athletics?"

THIS CHAPTER from Frank Graham's immensely successful book *The New York Yankees* is a study in unsuccess. It is 1925—the year of "the world's most important stomach-ache."

With a Resounding Crash

FRANK GRAHAM

HUGGINS was so keenly aware of the part played by overconfidence in the defeat of his team in 1924 that he overlooked something even more important. Some of his key players had aged almost overnight. Neither did Barrow realize it, nor Ruppert. All three had been blinded by the rush of the Yankees through September, so well sustained that it would have overcome a less resolute crew than the Senators.

The time had come to tear the team apart and rebuild it, but no one realized it. Huggins made only two moves during the off season. He acquired Howard Shanks, an infielder, from the Red Sox and brought Urban Shocker back from St. Louis.

"Changed your mind about Shocker as a pitcher, eh?" one of the newspapermen asked him the day the deal was announced.

Huggins shook his head. "No," he said. "I didn't have to. I knew all along he was a good pitcher."

"Then why did you get rid of him in 1918?"

"Because I was foolish. I asked advice of too many people, took most of it, and learned later that some of it was bad. Remember, I was a stranger in this league. There were a lot of things I had to find out, even about my own players. So I poked around and found out as much as I could about them before the training season started. One of the things I was told was that I would do well to get rid of Shocker as quickly as possible because he was a trouble-maker. Naturally, I had reason to believe that the fellow who told me that knew what he was talking about; and to protect myself I did as he had suggested. I later discovered that my informant had done Shocker a very grave injus-

tice. Urban never has made trouble for anybody."

"Who told you he was a trouble-maker?"

Huggins shook his head. "I can't tell you that," he said. "It seems he simply heard it from somebody else. He still feels badly about it."

Whoever it was should have felt badly. He cost Shocker, who had his best years in St. Louis, thousands of dollars. In the first place, the pitcher would have been paid a better salary in New York than he drew in St. Louis. And, in the second place, there were those World Series checks he missed.

At any rate, those were the only notable additions made to the roster before the team went south to train for the first time at St. Petersburg, Fla. Among the younger men in the camp were three whom Huggins kept. Gehrig, back from another successful season in Hartford, where he had hit .369 and made thirty-seven home runs, was held; but Pipp still was the regular first baseman. Peewee Wanninger, up from St. Paul, was retained; but Scott remained as shortstop. Benny Bengough, who had sat on the bench for two years, got more attention than usual.

There were, of course, the usual number of rookies in on trial; but most of them didn't count, then or later.

There was a feeling that, once the season began, the Yankees would deal harshly with the upstart Senators and regain their rightful place at the top of the league. This feeling was not confined to Huggins and his players. Baseball experts around the league generally believed that they would win the pennant.

Once the crash had come, it was easy to see

that signs of its coming had not been lacking. The first intimation that all was not well came when the Babe was stricken with acute indigestion when the team reached Asheville, N. C., in the course of its annual exhibition tour with the Dodgers.

"The world's most important stomach-ache," W. O. McGeehan called it.

It was. The Babe's moans figuratively were heard around the world. He had collapsed on the platform of the railroad station and, as it was obvious that he was seriously ill, he was placed on a litter and put aboard the next train for New York. Half the correspondents accompanying the team climbed on the train after him and put off bulletins reporting his condition at every stop.

On his arrival in New York, an ambulance waited to rush him to St. Vincent's Hospital.

"RUTH GRAVELY ILL!" the headlines said.

There was the almost inevitable rumor, quickly coursing through the city, that the Babe had died shortly after reaching the hospital. Newspapers, news agencies, radio stations, and the hospital staff spent hours denying it.

There was no doubt, however, that he was a sick man. The possessor of a prodigious appetite, he had given it full swing. The immediate cause of the attack was an outlandish early-morning indulgence in hot dogs and soda pop, but behind it were weeks, even months, of free-style eating and drinking. He had absorbed enough punishment off plates and out of bottles to have killed an ordinary man. Only his tremendous vitality enabled him to survive it.

Starting the season without him, the Yankees started badly. They won the opening game, but immediately after it went into a tail spin. On the face of it, there was no cause for alarm that they were in fourth place at the end of the first week. But, unbelievable as it would have sounded if anyone had said so at the time, they were never that high again for the rest of the season.

When the Babe returned to the line-up after a couple of weeks in the hospital, he was pale, unsteady on his legs, and had so little reserve strength that several times he almost fell down. That night he returned to the hospital. He was back the next day, however, gamely trying to play, seeking, if he could, to pull the team out of the slump by hitting a few into the bleachers. But he was not himself and, even if he had

been, he alone could not have done much with the team.

Huggins, watching anxiously, saw that the supposed slump went deeper than a mere temporary lapse, that some changes would have to be made. On May 6 he benched Scott and sent Wanninger in to play shortstop. He didn't make the move lightly. Scott had played in 1,307 consecutive games, and the veteran's removal from the line-up meant the snapping of the longest record of its kind that baseball ever had known. But Scott had slipped so badly that, as even he realized, the change was imperative.

Curiously enough, as Scott, for the first time since June 20, 1916, sat in the dugout while a game was being played, he could have reached out and touched the man who would shatter his record. Just a few feet from him sat Gehrig.

Less than a month later, on June 1, Lou started his streak, going to bat as a pinch hitter for Wanninger. He failed to hit safely, and there was no mention of it in the stories in the papers that day or the next, except, of course, in the box score.

The following day, Pipp, who suffered recurrent headaches as a result of having been hit in the head with a pitched ball some time before, asked Huggins if he might remain out of the game. Huggins readily gave assent. As a matter of fact, Pipp hadn't been doing very well and Huggins had contemplated benching him for a week or so.

"You're playing first base today," he told Gehrig in the clubhouse a few minutes later.

Years would elapse and pennants and World Series be won, and Gehrig would become one of the great ballplayers of all time before he left the post he took up that afternoon. But no one could know that then. He was just another rookie going in to take the place of a faded regular as the Yankees stumbled on their uncertain way.

Huggins had to make another change. Schang had slowed down woefully back of the bat, and he wasn't hitting. Bengough was moved up to first-string catcher. And still the team stumbled, and there was trouble brewing. Huggins coaxed, threatened, cajoled. Barrow sent his scouts through the sticks looking for help. Huggins began to get rid of some of the older players. He asked for waivers on Scott, and Washington claimed him. Witt was released unconditionally. Walter Beall, a pitcher with a lot of stuff but no control, over whom Hug had worked patiently, was farmed out to Hartford. Barrow, on the advice of his scouts, bought two young infielders—Leo Durocher from Hartford and Tony Lazzeri from Salt Lake—for spring delivery.

Ruth, having started as robustly as his health would permit, had slipped. His health was better. Indeed, he was as well, or almost as well, as ever. But he had become affected by his environment. He wasn't used to playing with a team that bobbed up and down in the second division without ever seeing daylight. In his time in Boston the Red Sox had been pennant winners or stout contenders. Since his coming to New York the Yankees had won three pennants and never had been worse than third. This was something new for him. Some of his old pals had departed and others were marked, and he knew it as well as they did. There were strangers in Yankee uniforms, and the team was bewildered. His batting average dropped to .246, a new low for him.

The Babe, probably reasoning that a fellow must have fun somewhere if he couldn't have it on the ball field, extended his operations by candlelight. He never had been very careful of the training rules, but as long as he was hitting and the Yanks were rolling, Hug wisely had given him plenty of elbow room. Now the situation was different. He wasn't hitting, the team had tumbled into seventh place, and Huggins lost patience with him.

Quarrels between them became daily occurrences. They usually began with Huggins wanting to know, out loud, how anybody expected the team to get anywhere when the players didn't bother to keep in shape. Ruth, of course, knew whom he was talking about and would counter with criticisms of Huggins' changes in the line-up, choice of pitchers, and strategy in general. After a while the exchanges fitted into a regular pattern, which went something like this:

"Never mind me. How about some of these other fellows?"

"I'm talking about them, too."

"No, you ain't. You're talking about me. I could talk about you, too, if I wanted to. I been around a long time, but I never saw a club run as lousy as this one."

"If you don't like the way I'm running the club, you can pack up and go home."

"Why don't you send me home?"

"Why don't you send me home, you big stiff?"

"Why don't you send me, you shrimp?"

"Go home, if that's what you want."

"Send me. You haven't got guts enough."

It would end with Hug stalking from the room, muttering, and the Babe saying:

"Can you imagine that guy! Talking to me like that!"

It got so the other players didn't take it seriously. They heard it so often and didn't have a true understanding of the clash. Ruth felt that, as the biggest figure in baseball's playing ranks, he had a position to maintain. In a heavy-handed way, he was trying to do just that. Huggins felt that he had his position to maintain and that if the team ever were to get out of the doldrums, discipline must be restored and that the most certain way to restore it was to put pressure on the chief offender.

One day, as the argument waxed fiercer than ever, the Babe advanced, glowering, on the little manager.

"I wish you weighed fifty pounds more!" he roared.

Huggins glared up at him.

"It's a good thing for you I don't," he said.

The showdown came in St. Louis. The Babe had been out very late the night before, had slept late, and was late reaching the clubhouse. The team was at batting practice when he arrived, and the only ones in the clubhouse were Huggins and Hoyt, who was to pitch that afternoon. His coat was on his arm, and he was unbuttoning his shirt as he came in.

"Sorry, Hug," he said blithely. "I had some business to attend to."

He tossed his coat and cap into the locker and ripped off his shirt.

"Don't bother to uniform today," Huggins said. His voice was cold, his face expressionless.

The Babe wheeled on him. "What did you say?" he demanded.

"I said for you not to bother," Hug said.

The Babe looked as though he couldn't believe what he had heard. "Now what's the matter?"

"You know very well what's the matter," Hug said. "And I'll tell you something else."

He was speaking with difficulty now. His voice shook and he gripped his belt tightly.

"I'm sorry," he went on, "but this is the finish. You're fined $5,000 and suspended indefinitely."

Ruth raged at him. "You'll never get away with this! I'll never play another game of ball for you, you little—! I'll go to New York and see Jake! You don't think he'll stand for this do you? Why . . ."

Huggins shrugged.

"Do as you please," he said, and walked from the room.

Within an hour the Babe was on his way to New York. Across the country typewriters pounded, telegraph wires hummed, presses rolled, radio stations seethed. Miller Huggins had fined Ruth $5,000 and suspended him indefinitely! It was the biggest news of the day.

Ruth, still raging in his drawing room on the train, didn't know that before Huggins had delivered the sentence he had told Barrow, over the telephone, what he was going to do and that Barrow had said:

"You're right. Something has to be done, and you'll have the support of the Colonel and myself. But on one condition."

"What's that?" Huggins had asked.

"That you don't weaken. You've got to make it stick," Barrow had said.

And Huggins had replied, "Don't worry. I won't weaken."

A crowd of reporters and cameramen met the Babe at the Grand Central. He paused long enough to pose for the cameramen as he got off the train. To the reporters he said:

"Come up to my hotel. I'll talk to you there."

A cab whisked him away. The reporters climbed into other cabs in the line and followed him. At the hotel he held court.

"I'll never play for the Yankees again as long as Huggins is the manager," he said. "He's trying to alibi himself at my expense, and I'm not going to let him get away with it. It's either me or him. If Jake still wants him to run his club, he can get somebody else to play right field."

A telephone at his elbow rang.

"Hello!" he said. "Who? Oh, yes. Tell him I'll be right down."

He reached for his cap.

"That was Jake's office," he said. "He wants to see me right away. There isn't anything else I have to say, fellows. From now on, Jake will do the talking."

He seemed pleased at the prospect.

With the reporters trailing him, he sped to the brewery. There he was ushered at once into Ruppert's dark paneled office where the Colonel and Barrow waited. The door closed behind him and the reporters made themselves comfortable in an outer room while they discussed the case and speculated on the outcome of the conversation going on within. Five minutes

passed . . . ten . . . fifteen. No sound came from behind the closed door. And then suddenly the door was opened by Barrow.

"Come in, gentlemen," he said.

The Colonel and the Babe sat at a desk. The Colonel's expression was grim. The Babe looked defeated.

"Ruth has changed his mind," Ruppert said. "He will continue to play for Mr. Huggins. Is that right, Ruth?"

"Yes," the Babe said.

"Ruth is sorry about the whole thing," Ruppert said. "We are all sorry. But it had to be."

"When will the Babe be allowed to play again?" one of the reporters asked.

"That's up to Huggins," Ruppert said. "Ruth will report to him at the Stadium when the team returns."

"How about the fine?"

"The fine goes. I think that is all, gentlemen."

The one-man rebellion was over. The rebel was, in a manner of speaking, in chains. Huggins' authority was stronger than ever before, and never again was it to be questioned.

The Babe accepted defeat gracefully. His attitude had been that of a spoiled boy. Now it was that of a man. With the return of the team to New York, he apologized to Huggins and promised that, in future, the little manager would not have the slightest trouble with him. Huggins immediately lifted his suspension, although he did not remit the fine. Ruth, as though trying to work it off, went on a hitting rampage so that in the remaining month of the season he raised his average from .246 to .290.

But try as hard as he would, he couldn't improve the position of the Yankees. Nor, try as hard as he would, could Huggins. He brought Mark Koenig up from St. Paul to play shortstop, and Koenig was an improvement over Wanninger and the others who had sought to fill that spot; but the team tottered on, winding up in seventh place. Almost the only one who could look back with pleasure on the season was Gehrig, who had established himself as the regular first baseman, had hit .295, and made twenty-one home runs.

That winter Christy Walsh, who syndicated the Babe's ghost-written baseball articles and generally managed his affairs for him, gave a dinner for him at which James J. Walker, then the Mayor of New York, made his famous speech about the Babe's duties to the fans, including the dirty-faced little boy in the bleachers or on the sidewalk. With tears in his eyes, the contrite Babe reiterated the promise he had made to Huggins in early September, assuring those present and all those to whom he knew his words would be relayed, including the dirty-faced little boy, that he was a completely reformed character.

H. T. WEBSTER

THE THRILL THAT COMES ONCE IN A LIFETIME

In 1916, with Europe at war and the United States soon to follow, the Associated Press set up an unprecedented telegraph network for the play-by-play of the World Series. Telegraph operators in the offices of every paper subscribing to the AP service received the play-by-play. Of course, the same operators could send as well as receive. One did.

From *AP, the Story of News*

━━━━━━━━━━━━━ **OLIVER GRAMLING** ━━━━━━━━━━━━━

AFTER A SUMMER of war news, political oratory, preparedness speeches, bombings and explosions, readers turned with genuine relief to the approach of the World Series. Debating the relative merits of the Brooklyn Nationals and Carrigan's Boston Red Sox was one way to escape talk of bloodshed and violence. Sports Editor Moss headed the five-man staff assigned to report the series, but it was a Traffic Department triumph which made coverage of the 1916 World's Championship games a sensation in the newspaper world.

Ordinarily the leased wire circuits were broken at strategic points in order that the report might be readjusted for regional needs and relay. Even when the play-by-play story of the World Series took precedence over all other news, this transmission method had been followed. As preparations began for the 1916 edition of the baseball classic, Cooper conceived the ambitious idea of delivering the play-by-play story direct from the baseball park to every point on the main leased wire system without any intervening relay or delay.

Nothing of the kind had ever been attempted before in either news or commercial transmission. Cooper's Traffic Department, however, set out to make telegraphic history by arranging for an unprecedented single circuit, 26,000 miles in length, to operate from the ball parks in Boston and Brooklyn into the office of every leased wire member newspaper. The plan worked flawlessly. When John A. Bates, the chief operator assigned to the World Series staff, tapped out the play-by-play story dictated by Moss, operators in member offices across the country received the Morse code signals simultaneously.

Members were impressed by the feat, but one of the greatest expressions of praise came from an inventor:

KENT COOPER
TRAFFIC AGT AP NY

THE ASSOCIATED PRESS MUST BE WONDERFULLY WELL ORGANIZED TO BE ABLE TO ACCOMPLISH WHAT WAS DONE IN THE BALL GAMES. UNCLE SAM HAS NOW A REAL ARTERIAL SYSTEM AND IT IS NEVER GOING TO HARDEN.
    EDISON

The World Series opened in Boston on a Saturday and hundreds of operators began copying the play-by-play account. The first inning and a half had been played and Bates in the press box at Braves Field was sending evenly:

BOSTON, OCT. 7—SECOND INNING, SECOND HALF: LEWIS UP. BALL ONE. FOUL. STRIKE ONE. BALL TWO. BALL THREE. LEWIS WALKED. GARDNER UP. GARDNER BUNTED SAFELY—

Just as Gardner bunted safely the smooth flow of signals was interrupted. Then:

F-L-A-S-H
NEWPORT, R.I., OCT. 7—A GERMAN SUBMARINE HAS ARRIVED HERE.

Frank M. Wheeler, string correspondent at Newport, had tried vainly to reach the Boston

Bureau by telephone with news that the U-53, flying a German man-of-war ensign, had just put into Newport harbor. In desperation he ordered the operator at the Newport *Herald* to break in on the play-by-play with a flash and bulletin. . . . Once he had crowded all the information he had onto the special World Series wire, he put out in a motorboat to the U-boat's anchorage, exhibited his credentials and was the first person permitted on board.

ZANE GREY wrote more than fifty western novels, as you may well be aware. Are you aware also that he was a college and professional baseball player? Or that his story, "The Redheaded Outfield," written some forty years ago, is one of the most famous and widely-read boys' baseball stories ever done?

The Redheaded Outfield

ZANE GREY

THERE WAS Delaney's red-haired trio—Red Gilbat, left fielder; Reddy Clammer, right fielder, and Reddie Ray, center fielder, composing the most remarkable outfield ever developed in minor league baseball. It was Delaney's pride, as it was also his trouble.

Red Gilbat was nutty—and his batting average was .371. Any student of baseball could weigh these two facts against each other and understand something of Delaney's trouble. It was not possible to camp on Red Gilbat's trail. The man was a jack-o'-lantern, a will-o'-the-wisp, a weird, long-legged, long-armed, red-haired illusive phantom. When the gong rang at the ball grounds there were ten chances to one that Red would not be present. He had been discovered with small boys peeping through knotholes at the vacant left field he was supposed to inhabit during play.

Of course, what Red did off the ball grounds was not so important as what he did on. And there was absolutely no telling what under the sun he might do then except once out of every three times at bat he could be counted on to knock the cover off the ball.

Reddy Clammer was a grandstand player—the kind all managers hated—and he was hitting .305. He made circus catches, circus stops, circus throws, circus steals—but particularly circus catches. That is to say, he made easy plays appear difficult. He was always strutting, posing, talking, arguing, quarreling—when he was not engaged in making a grandstand play. Reddy Clammer used every possible incident and artifice to bring himself into the limelight.

Reddie Ray had been the intercollegiate champion in the sprints and a famous college ballplayer. After a few months of professional

ball he was hitting over .400 and leading the league both at bat and on the bases. It was a beautiful and a thrilling sight to see him run. He was so quick to start, so marvelously swift, so keen of judgment, that neither Delaney nor any player could ever tell the hit that he was not going to get. That was why Reddie Ray was a whole game in himself.

Delaney's Rochester Stars and the Providence Grays were tied for first place. Of the present series each team had won a game. Rivalry had always been keen, and as the teams were about to enter the long homestretch for the pennant there was battle in the New England air.

The September day was perfect. The stands were half full and the bleachers packed with a white-sleeved mass. And the field was beautifully level and green. The Grays were practicing and the Stars were on their bench.

"We're up against it," Delaney was saying. "This new umpire, Fuller, hasn't got it in for us. Oh, no, not at all! Believe me, he's a robber. But Scott is pitchin' well. Won his last three games. He'll bother 'em. And the three Reds have broken loose. They're on the rampage. They'll burn up this place today."

Somebody noticed the absence of Gilbat.

Delaney gave a sudden start. "Why, Gil was here," he said slowly. "Lord!—he's about due for a nutty stunt."

Whereupon Delaney sent boys and players scurrying about to find Gilbat, and Delaney went himself to ask the Providence manager to hold back the gong for a few minutes.

Presently somebody brought Delaney a telephone message that Red Gilbat was playing ball with some boys in a lot four blocks down

156

the street. When at length a couple of players marched up to the bench with Red in tow Delaney uttered an immense sigh of relief and then, after a close scrutiny of Red's face, he whispered, "Lock the gates!"

Then the gong rang. The Grays trooped in. The Stars ran out, except Gilbat, who ambled like a giraffe. The hum of conversation in the grandstand quickened for a moment with the scraping of chairs, and then grew quiet. The bleachers sent up the rollicking cry of expectancy. The umpire threw out a white ball with his stentorian "Play!" and Blake of the Grays strode to the plate.

Hitting safely, he started the game with a rush. With Dorr up, the Star infield played for a bunt. Like clockwork Dorr dumped the first ball as Blake got his flying start for second base. Morrissey tore in for the ball, got it on the run and snapped it underhand to Healy, beating the runner by an inch. The fast Blake, with a long slide, made third base. The stands stamped. The bleachers howled. White, next man up, batted a high fly to left field. This was a sun field and the hardest to play in the league. Red Gilbat was the only man who ever played it well. He judged the fly, waited under it, took a step back, then forward, and deliberately caught the ball in his gloved hand. A throw-in to catch the runner scoring from third base would have been futile, but it was not like Red Gilbat to fail to try. He tossed the ball to O'Brien. And Blake scored amid applause.

"What do you know about that?" ejaculated Delaney, wiping his moist face. "I never before saw our nutty Redhead pull off a play like that."

Some of the players yelled at Red, "This is a two-handed league, you bat!"

The first five players on the list for the Grays were left-handed batters, and against a right-handed pitcher whose most effective ball for them was a high fast one over the outer corner they would naturally hit toward left field. It was no surprise to see Hanley bat a skyscraper out to left. Red had to run to get under it. He braced himself rather unusually for a fielder. He tried to catch the ball in his bare right hand and muffed it. Hanley got to second on the play while the audience roared. When they got through there was some roaring among the Rochester players. Scott and Captain Healy roared at Red, and Red roared back at them.

"It's all off. Red never did that before," cried Delaney in despair. "He's gone clean bughouse now."

Babcock was the next man up and he likewise hit to left. It was a low, twisting ball— half fly, half liner—and a difficult one to field. Gilbat ran with great bounds, and though he might have got two hands on the ball he did not try, but this time caught it in his right, retiring the side.

The Stars trotted in, Scott and Healy and Kane, all veterans, looking like thunderclouds. Red ambled in the last and he seemed very nonchalant.

"By Gosh, I'd 'a' ketched that one I muffed if I'd had time to change hands," he said with a grin, and he exposed a handful of peanuts. He had refused to drop the peanuts to make the catch with two hands. That explained the mystery. It was funny, yet nobody laughed. There was that run chalked up against the Stars, and this game had to be won.

"Red, I—I want to take the team home in the lead," said Delaney, and it was plain that he suppressed strong feeling. "You didn't play the game, you know."

Red appeared mightily ashamed.

"Del, I'll git that run back," he said.

Then he strode to the plate, swinging his wagon-tongue bat. For all his awkward position in the box he looked what he was—a formidable hitter. He seemed to tower over the pitcher —Red was six feet one—and he scowled and shook his bat at Wehying and called, "Put one over—you wienerwurst!" Wehying was anything but redheaded, and he wasted so many balls on Red that it looked as if he might pass him. He would have passed him, too, if Red had not stepped over on the fourth ball and swung on it. White at second base leaped high for the stinging hit, and failed to reach it. The ball struck and bounded for the fence. When Babcock fielded it in, Red was standing on third base, and the bleachers groaned.

Whereupon Chesty Reddy Clammer proceeded to draw attention to himself, and incidentally delay the game, by assorting the bats as if the audience and the game might gladly wait years to see him make a choice.

"Git in the game!" yelled Delaney.

"Aw, take my bat, Duke of the Abrubsky!" sarcastically said Dump Kane. When the grouchy Kane offered to lend his bat matters were critical in the Star camp.

Other retorts followed, which Reddy Clammer deigned not to notice. At last he got a bat that suited him—and then, importantly, dramatically, with his cap jauntily riding his red locks, he marched to the plate.

Some wag in the bleachers yelled into the silence, "Oh, Maggie, your lover has come!"

Not improbably Clammer was thinking first of his presence before the multitude, secondly of his batting average and thirdly of the run to be scored. In this instance he waited and feinted at balls and fouled strikes at length to work his base. When he got to first base suddenly he bolted for second, and in the surprise of the unlooked-for play he made it by a spread-eagle slide. It was a circus steal.

Delaney snorted. Then the look of profound disgust vanished in a flash of light. His huge face beamed.

Reddie Ray was striding to the plate.

There was something about Reddie Ray that pleased all the senses. His lithe form seemed instinct with life; any sudden movement was suggestive of stored lightning. His position at the plate was on the left side, and he stood perfectly motionless, with just a hint of tense waiting alertness. Dorr, Blake and Babcock, the outfielders for the Grays, trotted round to the right of their usual position. Delaney smiled derisively, as if he knew how futile it was to tell what field Reddie Ray might hit into. Wehying, the old fox, warily eyed the youngster, and threw him a high curve, close in. It grazed Reddie's shirt, but he never moved a hair. Then Wehying, after the manner of many veteran pitchers when trying out a new and menacing batter, drove a straight fast ball at Reddie's head. Reddie ducked, neither too slow nor too quick, just right to show what an eye he had, how hard it was to pitch to. The next was a strike. And on the next he appeared to step and swing in one action. There was a ringing rap, and the ball shot toward right, curving down, a vicious, headed hit. Mallory, at first base, snatched at it and found only the air. Babcock had only time to take a few sharp steps, and then he plunged down, blocked the hit and fought the twisting ball. Reddie turned first base, flitted on toward second, went headlong in the dust, and shot to the base before White got the throw-in from Babcock. Then, as White wheeled and lined the ball home to catch the scoring Clammer, Reddie Ray leaped up, got his sprinter's start and, like a rocket, was off for third. This time he dove behind the base, sliding in a half circle, and as Hanley caught Strickland's perfect throw and whirled with the ball, Reddie's hand slid to the bag.

Reddie got to his feet amid a rather breathless silence. Even the coachers were quiet. There was a moment of relaxation, then Wehying received the ball from Hanley and faced the batter.

This was Dump Kane. There was a sign of some kind, almost imperceptible, between Kane and Reddie. As Wehying half turned in his swing to pitch, Reddie Ray bounded homeward. It was not so much the boldness of his action as the amazing swiftness of it that held the audience spellbound. Like a thunderbolt Reddie came down the line, almost beating Wehying's pitch to the plate. But Kane's bat intercepted the ball, laying it down, and Reddie scored without sliding. Dorr, by sharp work, just managed to throw Kane out.

Three runs so quick it was hard to tell how they had come. Not in the major league could there have been faster work. And the ball had been fielded perfectly and thrown perfectly.

"There you are," said Delaney hoarsely. "Can you beat it? If you've been wonderin' how the crippled Stars won so many games just put what you've seen in your pipe and smoke it. Red Gilbat gets on—Reddy Clammer gets on—and then Reddie Ray drives them home or chases them home."

The game went on, and though it did not exactly drag it slowed down considerably. Morrissey and Healy were retired on infield plays. And the sides changed. For the Grays, O'Brien made a scratch hit, went to second on Strickland's sacrifice, stole third and scored on Mallory's infield out. Wehying missed three strikes. In the Stars' turn the three end players on the batting list were easily disposed of. In the third inning the clever Blake, aided by a base on balls and a hit following, tied the score, and once more struck fire and brimstone from the impatient bleachers. Providence was a town that had to have its team win.

"Git at 'em, Reds!" said Delaney gruffly.

"Batter up!" called Umpire Fuller, sharply.

"Where's Red? Where's the bug? Where's the nut? Delaney, did you lock the gates? Look under the bench!" These and other remarks, not exactly elegant, attested to the mental processes of some of the Stars. Red Gilbat did not appear to be forthcoming. There was an anxious delay. Capt. Healy searched for the missing player. Delaney did not say any more. Suddenly a door under the grandstand opened and Red Gilbat appeared. He hurried for his bat and then up to the plate. And he never offered to hit one of the balls Wehying shot over. When Fuller had called the third strike Red hurried back to the door and disappeared.

"Somethin' doin'," whispered Delaney.

Lord Chesterfield Clammer paraded to the batter's box and, after gradually surveying the field, as if picking out the exact place he meant to drive the ball, he stepped to the plate. Then a roar from the bleachers surprised him.

"Well, I'll be doggoned!" exclaimed Delaney. "Red stole that sure as shootin'."

Red Gilbat was pushing a brand-new baby carriage toward the batter's box. There was a tittering in the grandstand; another roar from the bleachers. Clammer's face turned as red as his hair. Gilbat shoved the baby carriage upon the plate, spread wide his long arms, made a short presentation speech and an elaborate bow, then backed away.

All eyes were centered on Clammer. If he had taken it right the incident might have passed without undue hilarity. But Clammer became absolutely wild with rage. It was well known that he was unmarried. Equally well was it seen that Gilbat had executed one of his famous tricks. Ballplayers were inclined to be dignified about the presentation of gifts upon the field, and Clammer, the dude, the swell, the lady's man, the favorite of the baseball gods—in his own estimation—so far lost control of himself that he threw his bat at his retreating tormentor. Red jumped high and the bat skipped along the ground toward the bench. The players sidestepped and leaped and, of course, the bat cracked one of Delaney's big shins. His eyes popped with pain, but he could not stop laughing. One by one the players lay down and rolled over and yelled. The superior Clammer was not overliked by his co-players.

From the grandstand floated the laughter of ladies and gentlemen. And from the bleachers —that throne of the biting, ironic, scornful fans—pealed up a howl of delight. It lasted for a full minute. Then, as quiet ensued, some boy blew a blast of one of those infernal little instruments of pipe and rubber balloon, and over the field wailed out a shrill, high-keyed cry, an excellent imitation of a baby. Whereupon the whole audience roared, and in discomfiture Reddy Clammer went in search of his bat.

To make his chagrin all the worse he ingloriously struck out. And then he strode away under the lea of the grandstand wall toward right field.

Reddie Ray went to bat and, with the infield playing deep and the outfield swung still farther round to the right, he bunted a little teasing ball down the third-base line. Like a flash of light he had crossed first base before Hanley got his hands on the ball. Then Kane hit into second base, forcing Reddie out.

Again the game assumed less spectacular and more ordinary play. Both Scott and Wehying held the batters safely and allowed no runs. But in the fifth inning, with the Stars at bat and two out, Red Gilbat again electrified the field. He sprang up from somewhere and walked to the plate, his long shape enfolded in a full-length linen duster. The color and style of this garment might not have been especially striking, but upon Red it had a weird and wonderful effect. Evidently Red intended to bat while arrayed in his long coat, for he stepped into the box and faced the pitcher. Capt. Healy yelled for him to take the duster off. Likewise did the Grays yell.

The bleachers shrieked their disapproval. To say the least, Red Gilbat's crazy assurance was dampening to the ardor of the most blindly confident fans. At length Umpire Fuller waved his hand, enjoining silence and calling time.

"Take it off or I'll fine you."

From his lofty height Gilbat gazed down upon the little umpire, and it was plain what he thought.

"What do I care for money!" replied Red.

"That costs you twenty-five," said Fuller.

"Cigarette change!" yelled Red.

"Costs you fifty."

"Bah! Go to an eye doctor," roared Red.

"Seventy-five," added Fuller, imperturbably.

"Make it a hundred!"

"It's two hundred."

"*Rob-b-ber!*" bawled Red.

Fuller showed willingness to overlook Red's back talk as well as costume, and he called, "Play!"

There was a mounting sensation of prophetic certainty. Old fox Wehying appeared nervous. He wasted two balls on Red; then he put one over the plate, and then he wasted another. Three balls and one strike! That was a bad place for a pitcher, and with Red Gilbat up it was worse. Wehying swung longer and harder to get all his left behind the throw and let drive. Red lunged and cracked the ball. It went up and up and kept going up and farther out, and as the murmuring audience was slowly transfixed into late realization the ball soared to its height and dropped beyond the left-field fence. A home run!

Red Gilbat gathered up the tails of his duster, after the manner of a neat woman crossing a muddy street, and ambled down to first base and on to second, making prodigious jumps upon the bags, and round third, to come down the homestretch wagging his red head. Then he stood on the plate, and, as if to exact revenge from the audience for the fun they made of him, he threw back his shoulders and bellowed: *"Haw! Haw! Haw!"*

Not a handclap greeted him, but some mindless, exceedingly adventurous fan yelled: "Redhead! Redhead! Redhead!"

That was the one thing calculated to rouse Red Gilbat. He seemed to flare, to bristle, and he paced for the bleachers.

Delaney looked as if he might have a stroke. "Grab him! Soak him with a bat! Somebody grab him!"

But none of the Stars was risking so much, and Gilbat, to the howling derision of the gleeful fans, reached the bleachers. He stretched his long arms up to the fence and prepared to vault over. "Where's the guy who called me redhead?" he yelled.

That was heaping fuel on the fire. From all over the bleachers, from everywhere, came the obnoxious word. Red heaved himself over the fence and piled into the fans. Then followed the roar of many voices, the tramping of many feet, the pressing forward of line after line of shirt-sleeved men and boys. That bleacher stand suddenly assumed the maelstrom appearance of a surging mob round an agitated center. In a moment all the players rushed down the field, and confusion reigned.

"Oh! Oh! Oh!" moaned Delaney.

However, the game had to go on. Delaney, no doubt, felt all was over. Nevertheless there were games occasionally that seemed an unending series of unprecedented events. This one had begun admirably to break a record. And the Providence fans, like all other fans, had cultivated an appetite as the game proceeded. They were wild to put the other redheads out of the field or at least out for the inning, wild to tie the score, wild to win and wilder than all for more excitement. Clammer hit safely. But when Reddie Ray lined to the second baseman, Clammer, having taken a lead, was doubled up in the play.

Of course, the sixth inning opened with the Stars playing only eight men. There was another delay. Probably everybody except Delaney and perhaps Healy had forgotten the Stars were short a man. Fuller called time. The impatient bleachers barked for action.

Capt. White came over to Delaney and cour-teously offered to lend a player for the remaining innings. Then a pompous individual came out of the door leading from the press boxes—he was a director Delaney disliked.

"Guess you'd better let Fuller call the game," he said brusquely.

"If you want to—as the score stands now in our favor," replied Delaney.

"Not on your life! It'll be ours or else we'll play it out and beat you to death."

He departed in high dudgeon.

"Tell Reddie to swing over a little toward left," was Delaney's order to Healy. Fire gleamed in the manager's eye.

Fuller called play then, with Reddy Clammer and Reddie Ray composing the Star outfield. And the Grays evidently prepared to do great execution through the wide lanes thus opened up. At that stage it would not have been like matured ballplayers to try to crop hits down into the infield.

White sent a long fly back of Clammer. Reddy had no time to loaf on this hit. It was all he could do to reach it and he made a splendid catch, for which the crowd roundly applauded him. That applause was wine to Reddy Clammer. He began to prance on his toes and sing out to Scott, "Make 'em hit to me, old man! Make 'em hit to me!" Whether Scott desired that or not was scarcely possible to say; at any rate, Hanley pounded a hit through the infield. And Clammer, prancing high in the air like a check-reined horse, ran to intercept the ball. He could have received it in his hands, but that would never have served Reddy Clammer. He timed the hit to a nicety, went down with his old grandstand play and blocked the ball with his anatomy. Delaney swore. And the bleachers, now warm toward the gallant outfielder, lustily cheered him. Bab-cock hit down the right-field foul line, giving Clammer a long run. Hanley was scoring and Babcock was sprinting for third base when Reddy got the ball. He had a fine arm and he made a hard and accurate throw, catching his man in a close play.

Perhaps even Delaney could not have found any fault with that play. But the aftermath spoiled the thing. Clammer now rode the air; he soared; he was in the clouds; it was his inning and he had utterly forgotten his teammates, except inasmuch as they were performing mere little automatic movements to direct the great machinery in his direction for his sole achievement and glory.

There is fate in baseball as well as in other

walks of life. O'Brien was a strapping fellow and he lifted another ball into Clammer's wide territory. The hit was of the high and far-away variety. Clammer started to run with it, not like a grim outfielder, but like one thinking of himself, his style, his opportunity, his inevitable success. Certain it was that in thinking of himself the outfielder forgot his surroundings. He ran across the foul line, head up, hair flying, unheeding the warning cry from Healy. And, reaching up to make his crowning circus play, he smashed face forward into the bleachers' fence. Then, limp as a rag, he dropped. The audience sent forth a long groan of sympathy.

"That wasn't one of his stage falls," said Delaney. "I'll bet he's dead. . . . Poor Reddy! And I want him to bust his face!"

Clammer was carried off the field into the dressing room and a physician was summoned out of the audience.

"Cap, what'd it—do to him?" asked Delaney.

"Aw, spoiled his pretty mug, that's all," replied Healy, scornfully. "Mebee he'll listen to me now."

Delaney's change was characteristic of the man. "Well, if it didn't kill him, I'm blamed glad he got it. . . . Cap, we can trim 'em yet. Reddie Ray'll play the whole outfield. Give Reddie a chance to run! Tell the boy to cut loose. And all of you git in the game. Win or lose, I won't forget it. I've got a hunch. Once in a while I can tell what's comin' off. Some queer game this! And we're goin' to win. Gilbat lost the game; Clammer throwed it away again, and now Reddie Ray's due to win it. . . . I'm all in, but I wouldn't miss the finish to save my life."

Delaney's deep presaging sense of baseball events was never put to a greater test. And the seven Stars, with the score tied, exhibited the temper and timber of a championship team in the last ditch. It was so splendid that almost instantly it caught the antagonistic bleachers.

Wherever the tired Scott found renewed strength and speed was a mystery. But he struck out the hard-hitting Providence catcher and that made the third out. The Stars could not score in their half of the inning. Likewise the seventh inning passed without a run for either side; only the infield work of the Stars was something superb. When the eighth inning ended, without a tally for either team, the excitement grew tense. There was Reddie Ray playing outfield alone, and the Grays with all their desperate endeavors had not lifted the ball out of the infield.

But in the ninth, Blake, the first man up, lined low toward right center. The hit was safe and looked good for three bases. No one looking, however, had calculated on Reddie Ray's fleetness. He covered ground and dove for the bounding ball and knocked it down. Blake did not get beyond first base. The crowd cheered the play equally with the prospect of a run. Dorr bunted and beat the throw. White hit one of the high fast balls Scott was serving and sent it close to the left-field foul line. The running Reddie Ray made on that play held White at second base. But two runs had scored with no one out.

Hanley, the fourth left-handed hitter, came up and Scott pitched to him as he had to the others—high fast balls over the inside corner of the plate. Reddie Ray's position was some fifty yards behind deep short, and a little toward center field. He stood sideways, facing two-thirds of that vacant outfield. In spite of Scott's skill, Hanley swung the ball far round into right field, but he hit it high, and almost before he actually hit it the great sprinter was speeding across the green.

The suspense grew almost unbearable as the ball soared in its parabolic flight and the red-haired runner streaked dark across the green. The ball seemed never to be coming down. And when it began to descend and reached a point perhaps fifty feet above the ground there appeared more distance between where it would alight and where Reddie was than anything human could cover. It dropped and dropped, and then dropped into Reddie Ray's outstretched hands. He had made the catch look easy. But the fact that White scored from second base on the play showed what the catch really was.

There was no movement or restlessness of the audience such as usually indicated the beginning of the exodus. Scott struck Babcock out. The game still had fire. The Grays never let up a moment on their coaching. And the hoarse voices of the Stars were grimmer than ever. Reddie Ray was the only one of the seven who kept silent. And he crouched like a tiger.

The teams changed sides with the Grays three runs in the lead. Morrissey, for the Stars, opened with a clean drive to right. Then Healy slashed a ground ball to Hanley and nearly knocked him down. When old Burns, by a hard rap to short, advanced the runners a base and made a desperate, though unsuccessful, effort to reach first the Providence crowd awoke to a strange and inspiring appreciation. They began that most rare feature in baseball audiences—a strong and trenchant call for the visiting team to win.

The play had gone fast and furious. Wehying, sweaty and disheveled, worked violently. All the Grays were on uneasy tiptoes. And the Stars were seven Indians on the warpath. Halloran fouled down the right-field line; then he fouled over the left-field fence. Wehying tried to make him too anxious, but it was in vain. Halloran was implacable. With two strikes and three balls he hit straight down to White, and was out. The ball had been so sharp that neither runner on base had a chance to advance.

Two men out, two on base, Stars wanting three runs to tie, Scott, a weak batter, at the plate! The situation was disheartening. Yet there sat Delaney, shot through and through with some vital compelling force. He saw only victory. And when the very first ball pitched to Scott hit him on the leg, giving him his base, Delaney got to his feet, unsteady and hoarse.

Bases full, Reddie Ray up, three runs to tie.

Delaney looked at Reddie. And Reddie looked at Delaney. The manager's face was pale, intent, with a little smile. The player had eyes of fire, a lean, bulging jaw and the hands he reached for his bat clutched like talons.

"Reddie, I knew it was waitin' for you," said Delaney, his voice ringing. "Break up the game!"

After all this was only a baseball game, and perhaps from the fans' viewpoint a poor game at that. But the moment when that lithe, red-haired athlete toed the plate was a beautiful one. The long crash from the bleachers, the steady cheer from the grandstand, proved that it was not so much the game that mattered.

Wehying had shot his bolt; he was tired. Yet he made ready for a final effort. It seemed that passing Reddie Ray on balls would have been a wise play at that juncture. But no pitcher, probably, would have done it with the bases crowded and chances, of course, against the batter.

Clean and swift, Reddie leaped at the first pitched ball. Ping! For a second no one saw the hit. Then it gleamed, a terrific drive, low along the ground, like a bounding bullet, straight at Babcock in right field. It struck his hands and glanced viciously away to roll toward the fence.

Thunder broke loose from the stands. Reddie Ray was turning first base. Beyond first base he got into his wonderful stride. Some runners run with a consistent speed, the best they can make for a given distance. But this trained sprinter gathered speed as he ran. He was no short-stepping runner. His strides were long. They gave an impression of strength combined with fleetness. He had the speed of a race horse, but the trimness, the raciness, the delicate legs were not characteristic of him. Like the wind he turned second, so powerful that his turn was short. All at once there came a difference in his running. It was no longer beautiful. The grace was gone. It was now fierce, violent. His momentum was running him off his legs. He whirled around third base and came hurtling down the home stretch. His face was convulsed, his eyes were wild. His arms and legs worked in a marvelous muscular velocity. He seemed a demon—a flying streak. He overtook and ran down the laboring Scott, who had almost reached the plate.

The park seemed full of shrill, piercing strife. It swelled, reached a highest pitch, sustained that for a long moment, and then declined.

"My Gawd!" exclaimed Delaney, as he fell back. "Wasn't that a finish? Didn't I tell you to watch them redheads?"

Hugh Fullerton of the Associated Press did a take-off on *Gunga Din* in 1917 to celebrate "Heinie Zim, Heinie Zim, chasing Collins home." Its clincher line was "I'm a faster man than you are, Heinie Zim!" Zimmerman always claimed nobody was covering the plate: "Who was I supposed to throw the ball to—Klem?" ("I was afraid he would," Klem said.) In the following piece you will read another version of the same episode. You will read a description of Babe Ruth's "called shot" home run wholly at odds with the classical and more picturesque account of that event. The answer is that there is nothing wrong with the following story. There is nothing wrong with the classical account. There is nothing wrong with Mr. Zimmerman's wonderful question. There's nothing wrong with Snodgrass-with-the-bottle in this story or Snodgrass-without-the-bottle in Tris Speaker's account on page 327. You love baseball, or you wouldn't be reading this book. And love, Mr. Shakespeare tells us, looks not with the eyes.

From *What Can You Believe about Series Legends?*

MILTON GROSS *and* DAN DANIEL

It's your money. You can't be blamed for thinking you saw what you paid to see at the World Series. But why mislead your neighbors with World Series myopia?

These fall feuds between the winners in the American and National Leagues are exciting enough without imaginative embroiderings. Nevertheless, from the beginning and no doubt until the end, Series history has been and will continue to be shrouded like a mummy in Munchausen memories. Too often fact has taken a back seat to fancy in the Series post-mortems.

Certainly Babe Ruth needed no fictional hand to embellish his amazing record of Series accomplishments, unmatched in forty-five years of interleague competition.

Ruth is said to have dedicated home runs to everybody from his favorite bartender to ailing children in hospitals, which may be true because Babe was an irrepressible character with an unmatched sense for the dramatic. But Babe did not dedicate a homer to his vanity despite a legend of monstrous proportions which was born in the 1932 Series at Wrigley Field, Chicago.

It was the fourth inning of the third game. The Cubs already had been beaten twice, and the Yankees were to sweep through four straight games, just as they had demolished two other National League opponents in the years immediately preceding.

Ruth had taken two strikes thrown by Pitcher Charley Root. Before Root stepped back on the mound to stretch for his next pitch, the Babe gestured in the pitcher's direction with the index finger of his right hand.

Those of fertile imagination interpreted Ruth's gesture as a warning that the next ball was going to be batted into the center-field bleachers. The mind being quicker than the eye and ear—particularly during the Series when the spectator will be damned if he'll accept a commonplace interpretation of events which lend themselves to sentimental reverie —the fable of Babe's "called" home run was born.

Once having concluded that they had seen

Ruth indicating to Root that he was going to hit the next pitch into the center-field bleachers, the customers readily believed the fantasy when he did. It was an extreme case of wishful thinking, which conveniently ignored the facts.

Actually, the Series was a violent one, with bad feeling and considerable jockeying on both sides. The Babe and Root exchanged words as the home-run king stepped into the batter's box. Few seem to recall this. Nor do they recall that Babe also gestured after the first strike.

Root finally decided a few years ago to reveal what really happened that afternoon.

"Sure, Babe gestured to me," Root told an audience at a Los Angeles high school assembly.

"We had been riding him, calling him 'Grandpop' and kidding him about not getting to be manager of the Yankees. We wanted to get him mad, and he was when he came to bat," Root recalled.

"As he stepped up, he challenged me to lay the ball in. After I had gotten the first strike over, Babe pointed to me again and yelled, 'That's only one strike.'

"Maybe I had a smug grin on my face after he took the second strike. Babe stepped out of the box again, pointed his finger in my direction and yelled, 'You still need one more, kid.'

"I guess I should have wasted the next pitch, and I thought Ruth figured I would, too. I decided to try to cross him and came in with it. The ball was gone as soon as Ruth swung. It never occurred to me then that the people in the stands would think he had been pointing to the bleachers. But that's the way it was." . . .

Though time has somewhat healed injured feelings, Mickey Owen remains *persona non grata* in Brooklyn because of his error on Tommy Henrich's third strike in the 1941 Yankee-Dodger World Series. This was considered a capital offense rating comparable punishment.

Henrich swung at and missed what appeared to be a low-breaking, inside curve thrown by Hugh Casey in the ninth inning of the fourth game. The ball caromed off Owen's glove and before he could retrieve it, Henrich was on first.

Joe DiMaggio followed with a single. Before the deluge could be dammed, the Yankees had scored four runs. Had Owen handled the third strike properly, it would have been the

third out of the final inning and the game would have been recorded in Series records as a 4-to-3 win for the Dodgers. Instead it went as a 7-to-4 Yankee victory, and, to all intents and purposes, the Series was over instead of being tied at two wins apiece.

Owen wept, Manager Leo Durocher ranted, Casey raved and the fans prepared to hang Mickey in effigy, or points worse. The spectators hardly could have been blamed for believing Owen had been guilty of a passed ball. The umpires, four of them, thought so too.

But was Owen truly guilty of an error, or was Casey more culpable for having thrown an illegal pitch which fooled Owen as well as Henrich?

That illusive curve was a spitter, banned in 1920. The prohibition is more apparent than real, however. The pitch is kept in escrow for tough spots. The ball takes just as unpredictable a break when moistened with perspiration, as it did when the pitcher's tongue was applied to it. With the game hanging on one pitch, the time was ripe for the spitter.

Two Octobers earlier, in 1939, big, earnest Ernie Lombardi had been flayed by customers and press for his dying-swan act which resulted in the Yankees scoring three runs in the tenth inning to win the decisive Series contest, 7 to 4, and sweep the four-game set with the Reds.

The inning had opened with Frank Crosetti drawing a pass and moving up a base on Red Rolfe's sacrifice. Billy Myers fumbled Charley Keller's roller, and there were men on first and third. Joe DiMaggio singled sharply to right, scoring Crosetti. When Ival Goodman let the ball get away from him, Keller broke for the plate.

The return throw apparently had Keller beaten. Charley bumped Lombardi, who dropped the ball as he fell to the ground. The ball rolled four feet from Lombardi's outstretched hand, and the catcher lay there as if in a coma, staring at it with unseeing eyes.

DiMaggio, sensing an unexpected opening, continued around third and slid home untouched. Lombardi, by this time, was making a feeble effort to recover the ball.

Reporters, seeking the angle for their stories, offered Ernie several outs for his lapse. They asked if Keller had accidentally kicked the catcher in the groin. No, Lombardi said, Keller hadn't kicked him. Yes, he saw DiMaggio speeding around the bases.

As Ernie spoke, he was removing his dirty uniform and sweat shirt, exposing his body swathed in a fantastic pattern of adhesive tape. The newsmen stared in amazement at the big backstop whose aching joints virtually were held together by the tape.

Only because of his raw courage had Lombardi been able to carry through ten innings before figuratively falling apart after being bumped by Keller.

Lombardi's bruised, unhinged frame just refused to summon the energy necessary to retrieve the ball. As he groped for it, his dazed mind wondered why Pitcher Bucky Walters had not made a dash for the loose ball and tried for a play at the plate.

Fred Snodgrass likely was the first player to receive an unmerciful and unmerited ragging for a World Series misplay, because even in 1912 the tongue was quicker than the eye. But how many people know that, just as the Giants' outfielder started to play Clyde Engle's fly ball, a bottle was thrown at him from the stands and distracted his eye?

Five years later, the Giants' Heinie Zimmerman chased Eddie Collins of the White Sox across the plate to present to the American Leaguers the winning run in the sixth and final game of the Series.

A reverse-English trend developed shortly thereafter to acquit Zimmerman of the boner. It was argued that Heinie had to make an individual sally after Collins because Catcher Bill Rariden had left the plate uncovered.

Clarence (Pants) Rowland, Pacific Coast League president, begs to disagree. He should know. He was there, coaching at third base, as the White Sox manager.

"I was racing alongside Collins all the way from the coaching box to the plate," Rowland recalls. "I know Zimmerman could have made a play at the plate, because Rariden called for the ball. But Zimmerman shouted, 'Get out of the way. I'll get this monkey myself.'"

JOHN GALLAGHER

Courtesy *True, The Man's Magazine.* ©

"This sure is a tough town! All he said so far is 'Play ball.'"

Spot reporting? General? Autobiography? Even History? Arnold Hano's rich book, *A Day in the Bleachers,* defies easy classification. Mr. Hano's day in the bleachers was the day of the first game of the 1954 World Series between the Giants and the favored Cleveland Indians at the Polo Grounds. Arnold saw one of baseball's most memorable plays—it is already known, simply and universally, as The Catch —better than anyone in the press box. This is *real* spot reporting— direct from center field. It is the top of the eighth, score 2-2, none out, Indians on first and second.

From *A Day in the Bleachers*

ARNOLD HANO

AND LIKE WOLVES drawn to our fresh prey, we had already forgotten him (Maglie), eyes riveted on Liddle, while off to the side of the plate Vic Wertz studied the new Giant pitcher and made whatever estimations he had to make.

Wertz had hit three times already; nobody expected more of him. He had hit one of Maglie's fast balls in the first inning, a pitch that was headed for the outside corner but Wertz's bat was too swift and he had pulled the ball for a triple. Then he hit a little curve, a dinky affair that was either Maglie's slider or a curve that didn't break too well, and drove it into left field for a single. Finally, he had pulled another outside pitch that—by all rights—he shouldn't have been able to pull, so far from the right-field side of the plate was it. But he had pulled it, as great sluggers will pull any ball because that is how home runs are made. Wertz hadn't hit a home run on that waist-high pitch on the outside; he had rifled it to right field for another single.

But that was all off Maglie, forgotten behind a door over five hundred feet from the plate. Now it was Liddle, jerking into motion as Wertz poised at the plate, and then the motion smoothed out and the ball came sweeping in to Wertz, a shoulder-high pitch, a fast ball that probably would have been a fast curve, except that Wertz was coming around and hitting it, hitting it about as hard as I have ever seen a ball hit, on a high line to dead center field.

For whatever it is worth, I have seen such hitters as Babe Ruth, Lou Gehrig, Ted Williams, Jimmy Foxx, Ralph Kiner, Hack Wilson, Johnny Mize, and lesser-known but equally long hitters as Wally Berger and Bob Seeds send the batted ball tremendous distances. None, that I recall, ever hit a ball any harder than this one by Wertz in my presence.

And yet I was not immediately perturbed. I have been a Giant fan for years, twenty-eight years to be exact, and I have seen balls hit with violence to extreme center field which were caught easily by Mays, or Thomson before him, or Lockman or Ripple or Hank Leiber or George Kiddo Davis, that most marvelous fly catcher.

I did not—then—feel alarm, though the crack was loud and clear, and the crowd's roar rumbled behind it like growing thunder. It may be that I did not believe the ball would carry as far as it did, hard hit as it was. I have seen hard-hit balls go a hundred feet into an infielder's waiting glove, and all that one remembers is crack, blur, spank. This ball did not alarm me because it was hit to dead center field—Mays' territory—and not between the fielders, into those dread alleys in left-center and right-center which lead to the bull pens.

And this was not a terribly high drive. It was a long low fly or a high liner, whichever you wish. This ball was hit not nearly so high as the triple Wertz struck earlier in the day, so I may have assumed that it would soon start to break and dip and come down to Mays, not too far from his normal position.

Then I looked at Willie, and alarm raced through me, peril flaring against my heart. To my utter astonishment, the young Giant center fielder—the inimitable Mays, most skilled of outfielders, unique for his ability to scent the length and direction of any drive and then turn and move to the final destination of the ball—Mays was turned full around, head down, running as hard as he could, straight toward the runway between the two bleacher sections.

I knew then that I had underestimated—badly underestimated—the length of Wertz's blow.

I wrenched my eyes from Mays and took another look at the ball, winging its way along, undipping, unbreaking, forty feet higher than Mays' head, rushing along like a locomotive, nearing Mays, and I thought then: it will beat him to the wall.

Through the years I have tried to do what Red Barber has cautioned me and millions of admiring fans to do: take your eye from the ball after it's been hit and look at the outfielder and the runners. This is a terribly difficult thing to learn; for twenty-five years I was unable to do it. Then I started to take stabs at the fielder and the ball, alternately. Now I do it pretty well. Barber's advice pays off a thousand times in appreciation of what is unfolding, of what takes some six or seven seconds—that's all, six or seven seconds—and of what I can see in several takes, like a jerking motion picture, until I have enough pieces to make nearly a whole.

There is no perfect whole, of course, to a play in baseball. If there was, it would require a God to take it all in. For instance, on such a play, I would like to know what Manager Durocher is doing—leaping to the outer lip of the sunken dugout, bent forward, frozen in anxious fear? And Lopez—is he also frozen, hope high but too anxious to let it swarm through him? The coaches—have they started to wave their arms in joy, getting the runners moving, or are they half-waiting, in fear of the impossible catch and the mad scramble that might ensue on the base paths? The players—what have they done? The fans—are they standing, or half-crouched, yelling (I hear them, but since I do not see them, I do not know who makes that noise, which of them yells and which is silent)? Has activity stopped in the Giant bull pen where

Grissom still had been toiling? Was he now turned to watch the flight of the ball, the churning dash of Mays?

No man can get the entire picture; I did what I could, and it was painful to rip my sight from one scene frozen forever on my mind, to the next, and then to the next.

I had seen the ball hit; its rise; I had seen Mays' first backward sprint; I had again seen the ball and Mays at the same time, Mays still leading. Now I turned to the diamond—how long does it take the eyes to sweep and focus and telegraph to the brain?—and there was the vacant spot on the hill (how often we see what is not there before we see what is there) where Liddle had been and I saw him at the third base line, between home and third (the wrong place for a pitcher on such a play; he should be behind third to cover a play there, or behind home to back up a play there, but not in between).

I saw Doby, too, hesitating, the only man, I think, on the diamond who now conceded that Mays might catch the ball. Doby is a center fielder and a fine one and very fast himself, so he knows what a center fielder can do. He must have gone nearly halfway to third, now he was coming back to second base a bit. Of course, he may have known that he could jog home if the ball landed over Mays' head, so there was no need to get too far down the line.

Rosen was as near to second as Doby, it seemed. He had come down from first, and for a second—no, not that long, nowhere near that long, for a hundred-thousandth of a second, more likely—I thought Doby and Rosen were Dark and Williams hovering around second, making some foolish double play on this ball that had been hit three hundred and thirty feet past them. Then my mind cleared; they were in Cleveland uniforms, not Giant, they were Doby and Rosen.

And that is all I allowed my eyes on the inner diamond. Back now to Mays—had three seconds elapsed from the first ominous connection of bat and ball?—and I saw Mays do something that he seldom does and that is so often fatal to outfielders. For the briefest piece of time—I cannot shatter and compute fractions of seconds like some atom gun—Mays started to raise his head and turn it to his left, as though he were about to look behind him.

Then he thought better of it, and continued the swift race with the ball that hovered quite close to him now, thirty feet high and coming down (yes, finally coming down) and again—for the second time—I knew Mays would make the catch.

In the Polo Grounds, there are two square-ish green screens, flanking the runway between the two bleacher sections, one to the left-field side of the runway, the other to the right. The screens are intended to provide a solid dark background for the pitched ball as it comes in to the batter. Otherwise he would be trying to pick out the ball from the far-off sea of shirts of many colors, jackets, balloons, and banners.

Wertz's drive, I could see now, was not going to end up in the runway on the fly; it was headed for the screen on the right-field side.

The fly, therefore, was not the longest ball ever hit in the Polo Grounds, not by a comfortable margin. Wally Berger had hit a ball over the left-field roof around the four-hundred foot marker. Joe Adcock had hit a ball into the center-field bleachers. A Giant pitcher, Hal Schumacher, had once hit a ball over the left-field roof, about as far out as Berger's. Nor—if Mays caught it—would it be the longest ball ever caught in the Polo Grounds. In either the 1936 or 1937 World Series—I do not recall which—Joe DiMaggio and Hank Leiber traded gigantic smashes to the foot of the stairs within that runway; each man had caught the other's. When DiMaggio caught Leiber's, in fact, it meant the third out of the game. DiMaggio caught the ball and barely broke step to go up the stairs and out of sight before the crowd was fully aware of what had happened.

So Mays' catch—if he made it—would not necessarily be in the realm of the improbable. Others had done feats that bore some resemblance to this.

Yet Mays' catch—if, indeed, he was to make it—would dwarf all the others for the simple reason that he, too, could have caught Leiber's or DiMaggio's fly, whereas neither could have caught Wertz's. Those balls had been towering drives, hit so high the outfielder could run forever before the ball came down. Wertz had hit his ball harder and on a lower trajectory. Leiber—not a fast man—was nearing second base when DiMaggio caught his ball; Wertz—also not fast—was at first when . . .

When Mays simply slowed down to avoid running into the wall, put his hands up in cup-like fashion over his left shoulder, and caught the ball much like a football player catching leading passes in the end zone.

He had turned so quickly, and run so fast and truly that he made this impossible catch look—to us in the bleachers—quite ordinary. To those reporters in the press box, nearly six hundred feet from the bleacher wall, it must have appeared far more astonishing, watching Mays run and run until he had become the size of a pigmy and then he had to run some more, while the ball diminished to a mote of white dust and finally disappeared in the dark blob that was Mays' mitt.

The play was not finished, with the catch.

Now another pet theory of mine could be put to the test. For years I have criticized base runners who advance from second base while a long fly ball is in the air, then return to the base once the catch has been made and proceed to third after tagging up. I have wondered why these men have not held their base; if the ball is not caught, they can score from second. If it is, surely they will reach third. And—if they are swift—should they not be able to score from second on enormously long flies to dead center field?

Here was such a fly; here was Doby so close to second before the catch that he must have practically been touching the bag when Mays was first touching the drive, his back to the diamond. Now Doby could—if he dared—test the theory.

And immediately I saw how foolish my theory was when the thrower was Mays.

It is here that Mays outshines all others. I do not think the catch made was as sensational as some others I have seen, although no one else could have made it. I recall a catch made by Fred Lindstrom, a converted third baseman who had had legs, against Pittsburgh. Lindstrom ran to the right-center field wall beyond the Giants' bull pen and leaped high to snare the ball with his gloved hand. Then his body smashed into the wall and he fell on his back, his gloved hand held over his body, the speck of white still showing. After a few seconds, he got to his feet, quite groggy, but still holding the ball. That was the finest catch I can recall, and the account of the game in next day's New York *Herald Tribune* indicated it might have been the greatest catch ever made in the Polo Grounds.

Yet Lindstrom could not have reached the ball Mays hit and Mays would have been standing at the wall, ready to leap and catch the ball Lindstrom grabbed.

Mays never left his feet for the ball Wertz hit; all he did was outrun the ball. I do not diminish the feat; no other center fielder that

I have ever seen (Joe and Dom DiMaggio, Terry Moore, Sammy West, Eddie Roush, Earle Combs, and Duke Snider are but a few that stand out) could have done it for no one else was as fast in getting to the ball. But I am of the opinion that had not Mays made that slight movement with his head as though he were going to look back in the middle of flight, he would have caught the ball standing still.

The throw to second base was something else again.

Mays caught the ball, and then whirled and threw, like some olden statue of a Greek javelin hurler, his head twisted away to the left as his right arm swept out and around. But Mays is no classic study for the simple reason that at the peak of his activity, his baseball cap flies off. And as he turned, or as he threw—I could not tell which, the two motions were welded into one—off came the cap, and then Mays himself continued to spin around after the gigantic effort of returning the ball whence it came, and he went down flat on his belly, and out of sight.

But the throw! What an astonishing throw, to make all other throws ever before it, even those four Mays himself had made during fielding practice, appear the flings of teen-age girls. This was the throw of a giant, the throw of a howitzer made human, arriving at second base —to Williams or Dark, I don't know which, but probably Williams, my memory says Dark was at the edge of the outfield grass, in deep shortstop position—just as Doby was pulling into third, and as Rosen was scampering back to first.

I wonder what will happen to Mays in the next few years. He may gain in finesse and batting wisdom, but he cannot really improve much because his finest talent lies in his reflex action. He is so swift in his reflexes, the way young Joe Louis was with his hands when, cobra-like, they would flash through the thinnest slit in a foe's defense; Louis, lashing Paulino Uzcudun with the first hard punch he threw, drilling into the tiniest opening and crushing the man who had never before been knocked out. That is Mays, too. Making a great catch and whirling and throwing, before another man would have been twenty feet from the ball.

And until those reflexes slow down, Mays must be regarded as off by himself, not merely *a* great ballplayer, but *the* great ballplayer of our time.

(I am not discussing his hitting here; for some strange reason—National League-itis, I guess—when I discuss the native ability of a ballplayer, I invariably narrow my gaze to his defensive ability. DiMaggio was a better hitter in his prime than Mays is now, maybe than Mays ever will be, although no hitter was ever as good as Mays at the same stage of their respective careers—check Ruth, Wagner, Cobb, Hornsby in their second full year of play and you will see what I mean.)

Still, Willie's 1954 season at the plate may have been some freak occurence. It happens sometimes that a ballplayer hits all season far above his norm. I am thinking of Ferris Fain who led the league a few years ago, though he had never been an impressive hitter before. My wife inquired about this man Fain, of whom she was suddenly hearing so much. I told her that he was a pretty good ballplayer, an excellent defensive first baseman, and a fair hitter. She said, "Fair? He's leading the league, isn't he?"

I said, "Yes, but that's a fluke. He's hitting way over his head. Watch what happens next year."*

Or take Carl Furillo hitting over .340 in 1953. Furillo is a fine hitter, a solid .300 hitter who can drive in nearly a hundred runs a season, but .340 is not his normal average. Possibly .345 is nowhere near Mays' norm; nothing in the past had indicated he could hit that high.

I do not list Mays among the great hitters, though I concede that one day we all may. As a fielder, he is already supreme.

So much for Mays and the catch.

* The following year Fain led the league again. . . . (AUTHOR'S NOTE)

GENE MACK

Courtesy Gene Mack Cartoon Co. Here are six examples of major-league ball park "portraits" done by Gene Mack of the Boston Globe—a series so popular with fans that both the Hall of Fame and *The Sporting News* have since issued the complete set in booklet form.

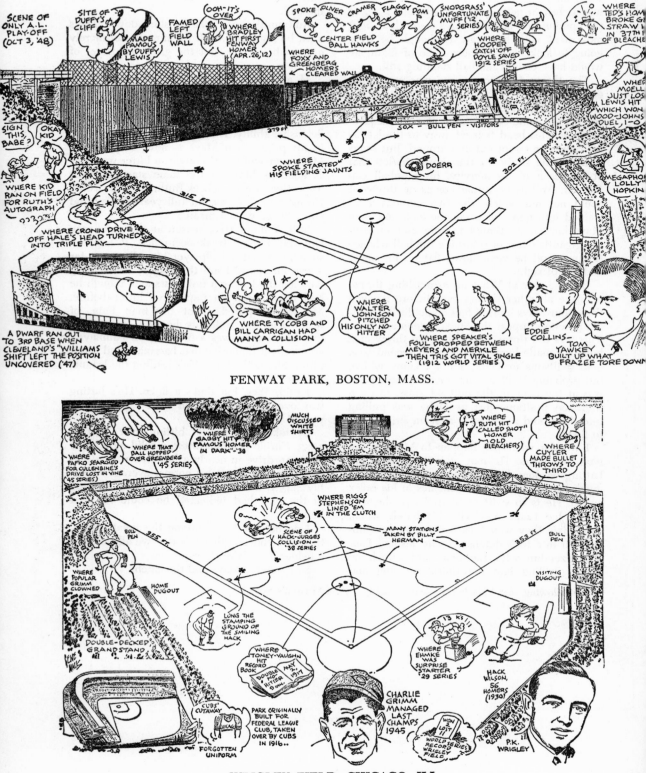

FENWAY PARK, BOSTON, MASS.

WRIGLEY FIELD, CHICAGO, ILL.

CROSLEY FIELD, CINCINNATI, OHIO

BRIGGS STADIUM, DETROIT, MICH.

171

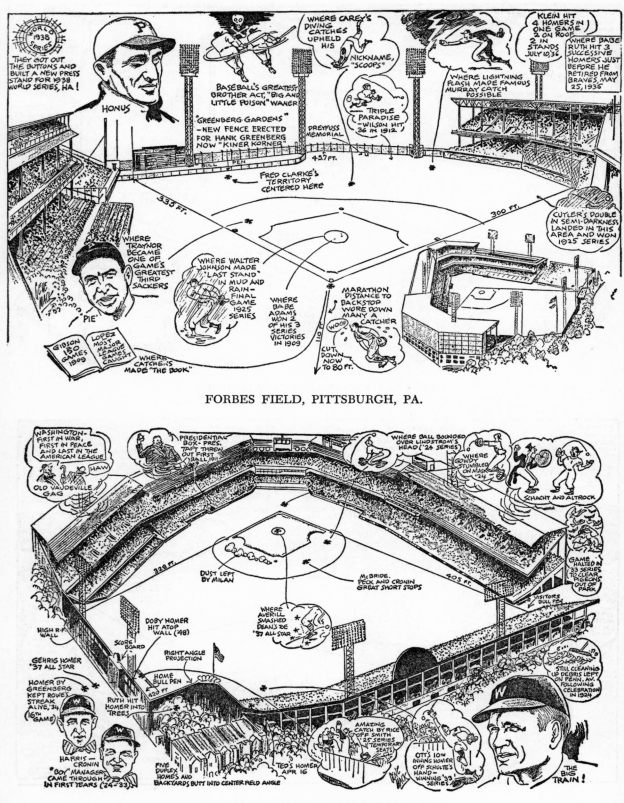

FORBES FIELD, PITTSBURGH, PA.

GRIFFITH STADIUM, WASHINGTON, D. C.

172

HERE's Henry Wiggen—a left-hander in a right-handed world—making his first major league pitching start; and opening day, at that. If I was stuck on a desert island with a choice of maybe three baseball books, *The Southpaw* would be one.

From *The Southpaw*

MARK HARRIS

I WATCHED hitting practice from the dugout. You could hear folks "oooh" and "aaah." Sid and Squarehead blasted a couple long ones. Finally I got up and took my swipes, and I could feel folks quieten down a bit and studying this punk that would be working instead of Sad Sam Yale. I hit a couple puny fouls and bunted 3.

After awhile I moved down to the first base side to the warm-up slab. Over on the other side I seen Fred Nance warming for Boston. Fred is an older man, 32 or 3, and he was already at work, the day being cool.

I felt good, although I might of liked it 5 degrees warmer, and my teeth chatted, and I was nervous. But the more I throwed the more I warmed, and after a time I could feel that folks was not looking at me so much. Goose caught me in the beginning, and then Red took over, and when I had enough we went in. I sat on the can awhile, and then I washed up and changed my shirt. Mick give her a few rubs to keep her loose, and the clock on the wall inched nearer and nearer the time, and the nearer it got the more my teeth chatted and the more I wished I had went in some other business besides this.

Sam was whistling and gay, and he stripped down and laid on the rubbing table in his jock. "Rub me slow, Mick," said he. He hummed and whistled and joked with Mick. Yet though he was whistling and humming and joking and gay and making remarks at everyone, kidding them along and all, his face was nonetheless sad. It was like a man was to be whistling whilst carrying a coffin.

Soon the place quietened down, and Dutch begun to speak, and there wasn't a sound but Dutch, and dim in the background you could hear the noise of the crowd, and you could hear Red taking whatever Dutch said and putting it in Spanish for George, and the only other sound was Sam laying on the table, whistling.

"Okay, boys," said Dutch. "There is a kid name of Heinz. We looked him over. He hits everything. He hits at bad balls, too, so be on your toes.

"I do not wish to be a gymnasium teacher, but I am going to carp again on this matter of calling fly balls loud enough for all to hear and then everybody else get out of the way. Ugly will call as usual, plus Lucky in the outfield, plus Red around and about home on both pops and bunts and such, and the first man that f - - - s up in this respect is going to get hit in the pocketbook and hit hard. Sam, stop that goddam whistling." Sam stopped.

"I got my rotation f - - - ed up in Baltimore which is partly why Sam is resting today and Henry working. If I can possibly do it every pitcher will get a full 3 days of rest and possibly 4 to begin with. Then we will not be so hard put when double-headers and such pile up. They give you 154 f - - - ing ball games and set the schedule up like it is never going to rain and wash you out and pile up your double-headers. You are supposed to do everything except shit ginger snaps and win a pennant besides. Well, I ain't complaining.

"I have not got the faintest f - - - ing idea why Fred Nance always gives us so much trouble. Make him work. Unless there is a different sign I do not want anybody to hit until at least 1 strike is called. Is that clear? Red, tell it to George.

"That reminds me. Red, there is this goddam Porto Rican with Boston so you will have to keep George up on the signs and not be shouting them out loud.

"We might manage to tire Nance. We are going to bunt some and keep him moving so keep your eyes peeled careful for your sign. To start with George will bunt, and if he gets on Lucky will swing bunt. I think we can jump off to a fast lead.

"Henry, we have got 7 minutes yet if you wish to warm some more."

"I am ready," said I to Dutch.

"I want to hear plenty of music. Henry is a first-class big-time pitcher. We all know that. Yet nobody is not shaky the first time, so I wish to hear plenty of chatter out there, and on the bench as well, and I do not aim to take him out the first little bit of trouble he might get in so you better figure on keeping tight and seeing things through if it gets rough.

"It is a little cloudy. That should hurt them more than us," meaning that I was fast and Nance more of a curve-ball pitcher.

My hands was all a-sweat, and my teeth chatted. I kept my jaws clenched.

Dutch rubbed his chin, trying to think if there was anything more to say. He paced up and down. "Sam, stop your whistling," he said, "for I am trying to think. Yet that is all I got on my mind. Is there anybody else got anything else to say?

"Oh yes, 1 other thing that has got nothing to do with baseball. After the Saturday game in Philly I get a call from some goddam gymnasium teacher wants to know why in hell you boys cannot stand still and give your attention to the anthem. I meant to tell you and forgot. I watched you Sunday. Up and down the dugout here is what I seen. Lucky is standing there scratching his ass. Ugly is fiddling with the lace of his glove. Gene is picking his goddam nose. Some is leaning against the wall and some got 1 foot up on the bench. Now I do not think it is too much to ask to stand up with your hat over your heart for 2 minutes and not give no gymnasium teachers something to squawk about. Is that clear?"

"My lace was loose," said Ugly.

George spoke in Spanish and Red put it back in English. "George says tell Ugly lay more over closer towards second on left-handed hitters. George says he goes to his own left like a shooting star. George says he feels fine and hopes the rest is the same. He says he loves everybody and wishes them good luck."

The boys fired back "Good luck" and "Adios" and "Hasta la vista" and "Manyana" and all such. George gets the drift by the tone. I wished they would stop their fussing and get out of there. "Okay," said Dutch at last, "leave us go," and out we went through the door and down the little tunnel to the dugout, and some of the boys patted me on the shoulder and elsewhere and said the things you say to give a fellow courage. I guess I know how a poor beggar feels when he walks the last mile.

We sat on the benches in the dugout. The big clock in center field showed 3 minutes to go, and they seemed like 3 weeks at least. The scoreboard showed Washington and Brooklyn 0-0 after 1 inning of play. The groundsmen pulled their smoother 1 last time across the infield, and the umpires come out and was booed, as is the custom, and the band played "Three Blind Mice" in their honor, and just when it seemed like all was set the loud-speaker called out the license of some cluck that parked his car on the sidewalk and was told to move it or get tagged.

Then Dutch said it was time and out they went on the double, starting in a bunch and then fanning out to their positions, Sid and George to first and third, Ugly and Gene down around second, Vince and Pasquale and Lucky off on the long jog to the outfield, and the crowd stood up and give them plenty of reception, and me and Red strolled out together, and the rest of the boys stood in the dugout, and the loud-speaker said, "Ladies and gentlemen, our national anthem." I took off my cap and held it over my heart and stood facing the flag like we was told, and Red done the same, standing like a knight in his gear, his cap and his mask in 1 hand, and the anthem was played and a lady sung.

Red jabbered all the way through, and when it was done a mighty shout went up, and he said, "Land of the free and the home of the brave. There ain't a 1 of them free, and there ain't 200 of them brave. 25,000 sheep."

"My old man is up there," I said. "Also my girl."

"Ain't a 1 of the whole 25,000 brave enough to sit it through with their hat on," he said.

"I notice you took yours off," I said.

"By God, I did," he said. "That is the last time. Hereafter I will never stand for the anthem. I will wait in the alley betwixt the dugout and the clubhouse," and he done it ever after as you will notice when you see the Mammoths play.

"Throw anything you want the first pitch and after that listen to your old redheaded papa," said Red. "Good luck, Henry, this is for the money."

I throwed about 6 to loosen. Then the Mayor of New York throwed out the first ball. Sid copped it and run over and got the autograph and rolled it down to the dugout. Morty Zinke was behind the plate, and he give Red another, and around it went, Red to George to Ugly to Gene to Sid, and then to me. My hand sweated, and I picked up the resin bag, and then I tossed it down, and Black stepped in, and I throwed the first pitch, wide, and Red whipped it back to me, and I was set.

Black went after the second pitch. He lifted it up behind second, and Ugly called "Gene" and Gene gathered it in.

Now I begun to hear the music. It was sweet, believe me. You hear the crowd, but they ain't really with you. They are just a lot of people and a lot of noise, and they shout things at you but you never hear much. What you hear is your own boys. You hear the dugout, and you see their face, and now and then Dutch will raise his voice above the rest and tell you something. I heard Perry and Coker and Canada and Lindon, and I heard Squarehead loud and clear, and out behind me I heard the music, and in front of me, from Red.

Red says, "To me, Henry, to me, this is my sign, to me, to me."

George says a flood of words in Spanish, and then he says your name.

Ugly says, "Baby boy, Hank is my baby boy, baby boy, baby boy, Hank is my baby boy, baby boy," over and over.

Gene says, "All you got to do is throw, that is all. All you got to do is throw. Just throw, Hank. Just throw. All you got to do is throw."

Sid sings a song. He sings different songs, but the words is always the same. He sings, "Oh they cannot hit my Henry boy oh they cannot hit my Hank oh my Henry oh my Hank my Henry Hank Hank Hank." He might sing the same song 1 inning or a whole game or a week.

You know they are there. You have got to know. When you are a kid you think you don't need nobody behind you, for when you are a kid you think you will strike out whoever comes along. You will gobble up the whole blooming world and you do not need no help. But in the big time it is different, and you have got to know they are there. You have got to know that if you make a mistake there is some-

one behind you to cover for you and help pull you out. You are always going to make mistakes. The idea is to not make too many.

I made a mistake on Granby and threwed 1 too fat, and back it come like a rocket, about ankle-high, right at me. I could not of stopped it if I tried, and it burned past me with "1 base" wrote all over it. Gene was moving fast behind me. He took it backhand behind the base, and still off balance he whipped it down to Sid. Perry or Lucky or George might of beat the throw, but Granby stays longer in 1 place and he was out by half a step. Gene got a great hand. He deserved it.

Now I heard the music clear from the outfield. I never hear Lucky much, but I hear Vincent and Pasquale, and their voice floats in, saying, "Nuttin to worry, nuttin to worry, no hitter boy, no hitter boy, never worry, nuttin to worry," and I stopped worrying right then and there, with 2 down and none on, knowing from then forwards that it was my ball game to win. I had the old confidence, and I never lost it, not then nor any other day. Give me a baseball in my hand and I know where I am at. Give me a piece of machinery and I may be more or less in the dark. Give me a book and I am lost. Give me a map and I cannot make heads nor tails, nor I could no more learn another language then pitch with my nose. But give me a baseball and I know where I am at, and I fired down to Fielding twice, 2 blazing fast balls, and then I changed up and throwed him a jughandle curve that he went for like a fool and bounced down to Sid. I raced over to cover. Sid waved me away and beat Fielding to the bag in plenty of time.

Fielding rounded the bag and went over for his glove. "Say boy," said he to me, "I hear that they have got you rooming with a nigger."

"That is right," said I to him, and I dropped my glove along the line, and the kid run up with my jacket and held it while I slipped it on, and I went in towards the dugout. I got a good hand on the way, and I touched my cap.

Then the running begun. George was on first quicker then you could tell it. He bunted down third on the second pitch, and Nance went over and fielded it and never even bothered to make the throw.

They figured Lucky for the sacrifice. Lucky swung around for the bunt and Blodgett tore in from third, but Lucky chopped at it, the swinging bunt, and it popped down the third base line where Blodgett was but wasn't no more, and Granby chased over from short and

Blodgett turned and started out after it, too. That was where he put the knife in his own back, for George rounded second never busting his stride and come barreling down for third. Nance come over to cover as soon as he seen what was happening, and Joe Jaros give George the slide sign, and George hit the dirt. Nance took the throw from Granby from short left, and George brung him to earth with the slide, and Nance was still trying to get up off his back while Lucky went streaking to second.

Vince Carucci worked the count to 3-and-2 and then lifted 1 about 410 feet into left center that Black took, and now we was running again, George tagging up and scoring easy enough from third, which was what everybody expected. The only thing they did not expect was what Lucky done. Lucky tagged, too, and he broke for third on the catch, which neither Black nor all of Boston expected, and he made it in a very close play with a neat slide. That is how ball games are won, doing the unexpected.

We wasn't through yet. Dutch ordered the squeeze, shoving his right foot up on the dugout step. That's the bunt sign, not bunt and run but run and bunt. The suicide squeeze. It means get moving and not worry about getting doubled up or trapped. All or nothing. It means the batter has got to bunt no matter what.

Thinking back on it it all sounds simple. But Dutch figured it all in a flash. They would be throwing low to keep Sid from hitting in the air where Lucky could score after the catch. The infield would lay in a little close for the possible play at the plate, though not *too* close. It would never expect the bunt from Sid, for his specialty is the long drive. Joe Jaros flashed the sign to Sid and Lucky, shouting, "Okay, Sid, leave us drive 1 about 650 feet." You will notice that the name "Sid" is the second word. So between the bunt sign from Dutch and the word from Joe both Lucky and Sid knowed that Sid was to bunt the second pitch.

The second pitch was low, the best kind to bunt, and Sid pushed it along first, neat enough for a man that don't do it much. Fielding took it, but he seen he had no chance in the world to make the play at the plate, for by now Lucky was across. Chickering covered first, and Sid was out. But we had 2.

That was how it stood when we batted in the last of the third. I come up first. I got a good hand, partly because I done well up to then and partly because I was a rookie and folks always like to see a rookie make good. I touched my hat.

"Well, well, well," said Toomy Richardson, the Boston catcher, "if it ain't Henry Wiggen that rooms with the nigger." He crouched and give his sign.

"That is me," said I, "and it will not be many weeks before you will be dizzy trying to throw that nigger out stealing."

Nance sailed 1 past me for a called strike.

"Is that so?" said Toomy. "Well, niggers was always fast runners. They ain't honest so they got to know how to run."

"That is so," said I.

Nance breezed another by, and Zinke bawled out, "Stee-rike!"

All of a sudden I got a notion maybe I could get on base. I figured Nance would waste 1 and then fog 1 through. He figured I would never take the bat off my shoulder. He throwed wide. "What in the world is the sense in wasting pitches on me?" said I to Toomy. "I wish you would throw it through good so I can go back and sit down."

"Oh," said Toomy, "we always play around a little bit with punks before we strike them out."

"Well, hurry it up," said I, "for I would like to get back and put my jacket on and keep my flipper warm," and Nance reared and throwed. I swang. When I have a mind to do it I can cut pretty good at a ball. I caught that 1 nice, with the fat of the bat, and I drove it down the line in right, and Casey Sharpe loped over. I seen him waiting to play it off the wall, and I thought, "Well, Casey old boy, how is your arm this fine day?" and I rounded first, and I dug, and I churned down the line and got them legs moving about as fast as they ever went before, and I went on down towards second like there was the flag itself resting on the outcome, and Granby come over to cover, and I hit the dirt about the instant he took the throw, and I went under him, and my foot hooked the bag just as snug as could be, and Neininger called me safe.

I think this must of upset Fred Nance's ideas of what was proper. He walked George. Lucky moved us along with the sacrifice. Vince Carucci popped out, but then they walked Sid to load the bases and have a play at every bag, figuring they had a little better chance with Pasquale then with Sid. But Pasquale lined 1 into right center that was still on the rise when it left the infield. We was all running, of course, with 2 down, and the drive hit the Gem sign about 10 feet off the ground. I jogged in, and George was right behind, and Sid was rounding third when Heinz begun his throw. Nance cut the throw off, seeing there was no chance on Sid, and that kept Pasquale from taking third. It did not matter, for Ugly singled him home anyways, and that was all for Nance. Nippy Lewis come on to relieve. Gene almost kept the rally going with a smash down third, but Blodgett took it backhand on the bag, and that was the end of the inning. 6-0.

That was how things stood through 6. In the top of the seventh Dutch lifted Sid Goldman and sent Canada in at first. Sid is a fair enough fielding first baseman, but he tends to weight, and the weight slows him down. He says if he lived in the hotel with the boys he might keep his weight down better, but he lives with his mother on Riverside Drive when the club is home and she feeds him too much. I ate up there 1 Friday night and must of put on 2 pounds betwixt the time we sat down and the time we tried to get up. So Dutch lifted Sid and played Canada at first so as to bolster the defense. It was a good hunch, like all Dutch's hunches that day, like pitching me in the first place and then again jumping off to a fast lead by bunting. Everything was working. I do believe if we sent the bat boy up to hit he would of rapped a triple.

I been going good up to the seventh. I was really enjoying myself. The boys was singing behind me and threatening at bat almost every inning, and the sun come out bright and strong about the fifth, and the crowd was with us all the way, for next to beating Brooklyn they love best to beat Boston.

I felt a little sorry for Squarehead. I guess when Dutch sent Canada in poor Squarehead knowed for sure what was in the cards. Yet he kept booming out from the dugout like he never thought a thing about it. Soon I was too busy to worry about Squarehead. I was up to my eyeballs in trouble.

Fielding opened the inning with a single. Canada sung to me over from first, "It does not mean a thing, Hank, does not mean a thing," and I throwed down to first a couple times, not half so much trying to pick Fielding off as give Canada a chance to loosen and get over being nervous. I knowed he was nervous. Casey Sharpe followed with a Texas League single

that Lucky and Ugly and Gene all raced for, yet it fell between them in short center. Canada went down to cover second, and I shot over to first. Fielding took third.

Heinz was up. We had got him out twice before, mixing curves and the fast 1. Red give me the sign for the curve, and I shook him off. Okay, he signals, throw the screw, which was what I wanted to throw. Red don't like me to, though. He says I'm too young and will ruin my arm. I throwed it, and Heinz popped it foul down by the Mayor of New York's box, and Canada streaked over. Sid would of never made it. I did not think Canada would neither, but over he went, and about 5 feet from the barrier he left this earth and took off. I caught a glimpse of Kellogg racing over to call it. Then I lost sight of Canada, for down he went behind the rail, and Kellogg jerked back his thumb, meaning that Canada made the catch, and the next thing I seen the ball was flying back out of there. It was a pretty good throw, considering that the poor boy was laying on his back all tangled up with the seats and the spectators, and I took the throw about halfway between the line and the stands, and I wheeled and whipped it to Red, figuring that Fielding would of tagged by now and been headed for home. That was what he done, never expecting Canada to get the ball back in play like that, and now he was trapped betwixt third and home. Red run him back towards third and flipped to George. George run him back towards home and flipped to me, for I was backing up Red by now. I run Fielding back towards third and flipped to Ugly, for Ugly come over from short to back up George. Ugly run Fielding down towards home. Red was waiting, and he stuck up his hands like he was expecting the throw, and Fielding seen the hands go up and naturally reversed again and started back towards third. Only Ugly never throwed a-tall, and Fielding tried to reverse still again, but Ugly was roaring fast down the line, and he tagged Fielding and turned and wheeled and fired back to George at third and damn near caught Casey Sharpe besides.

I was out of it now. Chickering drove Casey home with a single, but I got Blodgett on strikes.

In the top of the ninth, with 2 gone and none on and the crowd moving towards the exits, Casey Sharpe hammered a homer into the upper stands in right. Then Heinz rolled to Ugly, and that was it. That was my first.

* * *

We had dinner together that night in the hotel, me and Holly and Pop and Perry and Aaron and Red and Rosemary Traphagen and George. I suppose I might of hogged the conversation somewhat, hashing over the afternoon about 5 times. Nobody else got much of a word in edgewise until towards the end I noticed I was talking and nobody was listening. Pop and Perry was gassing together, and Aaron and Red was discussing I do not know what and now and then turning it in Spanish for George, and Rosemary was telling Holly about some of the problems of a ballplayer's wife. It used to be that when I won a game I spent hours and hours jawing it over again for the benefit of anybody that cared to listen, though I got over the habit as time wore on. When I lost I never considered it worth discussing and still don't.

Finally we broke it up, and me and Holly went walking, and after a time I said, "Well, Holly, I hope Rosemary has filled you in on some of the fine points of marrying a ballplayer."

"She told me of the problems," said Holly.

"You are putting me off again," said I, for I could tell she was stalling like she done that night in February just before I shoved off south. "What problems? There is 20,000 girls that would give their right arm to be married to such problems."

"I am not of the 20,000," she said. "It takes thought."

"To hell with thought," said I. "I must have the answer, yes or no."

"Now is not the time for big decisions," she said. "You are sitting on top of the world, and it is too easy to be in love when you are sitting on top of the world. How about on afternoons when the chips are flying all wrong? How about on afternoons when all does not go so smooth as it went today? Will you then be in love with me and all the world? Rosemary Traphagen has told me about such afternoons."

"Why so gloomy?" said I, but she went on being gloomy nonetheless, and after about 6 blocks we turned around and went back, hardly saying a word the whole time. Later her and Pop and Aaron grabbed the 11 o'clock. I seen them off, and I walked clear back to the hotel. I felt sore.

But walking cooled me off some, and I kept thinking about the dinner that night and what a fool I probably was. At least that's what I *think* I was thinking. Yet maybe it wasn't until some time later in the summer that I begun to wise up to myself, for I soon seen where it is easy enough to be in love with all the world on a fine spring night after you have just throwed a 6-hit win but maybe not so easy come steaming August and the September stretch. A lot of things Holly ever said begun to sink in, and I learned a lot about such things as love, and actually, when you think about it, it is a wonder that she didn't cut me loose then and there, for I was so stupid, and so green, that it makes me sick to mention it.

The box score:

BOSTON

	AB	R	H	PO	A
Black, cf	4	0	0	1	0
Granby, ss	4	0	1	2	1
Fielding, 1b	4	0	1	7	2
Sharpe, rf	4	2	2	2	0
Heinz, lf	4	0	0	2	0
Chickering, 2b	3	0	2	2	3
Blodgett, 3b	2	0	0	3	1
Richardson, c	3	0	0	5	2
Nance, p	1	0	0	0	1
Lewis, p	1	0	0	0	2
aHampden	1	0	0	0	0
Tawney, p	0	0	0	0	0
	—	—	—	—	—
Totals	31	2	6	24	12

aHit into force play for Lewis in eighth.

Boston .... 0 0 0 0 0 0 1 0 1 —2
New York .... 2 0 4 0 0 0 0 0 - —6

NEW YORK

	AB	R	H	PO	A
Gonzalez, 3b	4	2	1	1	2
Judkins, cf	3	1	1	2	0
V. Carucci, lf	4	0	1	2	0
Goldman, 1b	1	1	1	7	0
Smith, 1b	1	0	0	3	1
P. Carucci, rf	4	1	2	1	0
Jones, ss	4	0	2	2	3
Park, 2b	3	0	0	3	3
Traphagen, c	4	0	1	5	1
Wiggen, p	4	1	1	1	2
	—	—	—	—	—
Totals	32	6	10	27	12

Error—Chickering.

Runs batted in—V. Carucci, Goldman, P. Carucci 3, Jones, Chickering, Sharpe.

Two-base hits—Wiggen, P. Carucci, Goldman, Granby.

Home run—Sharpe.

Double plays—Jones, Park and Goldman; Chickering, Granby and Fielding; Smith, Wiggen, Traphagen, Gonzalez and Jones; Gonzalez, Park and Smith.

Left on bases—Boston 3, New York 7.

Bases on balls—Off Wiggen 2, Nance 2, Lewis 2.

Struck out—By Wiggen 5, Nance 1, Lewis 2.

Hits—Off Nance 5 in 2⅔ innings, Lewis 4 in 4⅓ innings, Tawney 1 in 1 inning.

Winning pitcher—Wiggen. Losing pitcher—Nance.

Umpires—Zinke, Kellogg, Neininger and Bowron.

Time of game—2:32.

Attendance—29,812.

Mr. Harrison, of *The New York Times,* calls this one "the best and worst game of baseball ever played in this country." Of course, the game he covered here took place twenty years before the sixth game of the 1945 World Series, which I nominate as the worst game of baseball ever played in this country. Now, to details:

1925:
Pittsburgh Pirates 9,
Washington Senators 7

JAMES R. HARRISON

In the wettest, weirdest and wildest game that fifty years of baseball have ever seen, the Pirates today proved their right to the mud-horse, twilight and all other championships of the national game. In mire and rain and fog they beat the Senators, 9 to 7, and won back the title which went away from here fifteen years ago.

Water, mud, fog, mist, sawdust, fumbles, muffs, wild throws, wild pitches, one near fist fight, impossible rallies—these were mixed up to make the best and the worst game of baseball ever played in this country. Players wallowing ankle-deep in mud, pitchers slipping as they delivered the ball to the plate, athletes skidding and sloshing, falling full length, dropping soaked baseballs—there you have part of the picture that was unveiled on Forbes Field this dripping afternoon.

It was a great day for water polo. Johnny Weissmuller would have been in his element. The web-footed amphibians would have had a field day. But it was the last possible afternoon that you would pick out for a game of baseball on which hung the championship of the country.

And still the game was packed with more thrills to the square inch than any other game possibly could be. This is a broad statement, but it was a broad game—a game painted on a great canvas, ranging from the errors of Roger Peckinpaugh and the bad pitching of Vic Aldridge and Walter Johnson to the inspired hitting of the garlanded Pittsburgh heroes, Kiki Cuyler, Max Carey, Carson Bigbee and Pie Traynor.

It was Bigbee's two-bagger when he was sent up to pinch-hit for Kremer in the eighth that tied the score. It was Cuyler's double with the bases full that brought the flag to Pittsburgh in the same round. And it was the errors of Peckinpaugh—a muffed fly and a bad throw—which sent Washington back into the shadows of oblivion.

In a grave of mud was buried Walter Johnson's ambition to join that select panel of pitchers who have won three victories in one World Series. With mud shackling his ankles and water running down his neck, the grand old man of baseball succumbed to weariness, a sore leg, wretched support and the most miserable weather conditions that ever confronted a pitcher.

Probably the old veteran would have liked to have gone home and gone to bed, but he stuck it out with a great heart and a wise head against a team of youngsters who were just beginning to unleash the strongest batting attack in the game.

From one angle the game was a ghastly joke,

a travesty on the national sport. Looking at it one way, the game proved nothing except that Pittsburgh won in the rain and the twilight. And from the other point of view, the Pirates proved their superb courage, their hitting power and their fielding steadiness on a terrain where to make a hit was record-breaking and where to handle a ball cleanly was a distinct moral triumph.

It was no disgrace for the Senators to lose, and they can say with some justice that the Pirates have not a sound title to the championship. Still, it was the Pirates who made fifteen hits and the Pirates who did not make the fatal errors and the Pirates who won under conditions that were as fair for one team as the other.

After all, rain may slow up the legs and trick the batting eye, but it has no effect on courage. And it seemed to this historian that Pittsburgh won as much by courage as by physical achievements. The team that can see the enemy score four runs in the first inning and can still surge through to the misty heights is a real team.

Washington, getting the jump on the Pirates, getting the first advantage of bad conditions, can scarcely moan loudly if the Buccaneers came from behind and turned those same bad conditions to their own advantage. What was sauce for the goose in the first inning was sauce for the gander in the eighth.

Besides which the Senators need to have no sympathy wasted on them. They won the golden laurels last October because of the freakish vagaries of two badly bouncing balls, by pure luck, as Bucky Harris himself admitted. If Fate chooses to turn her face from Washington it is tough luck for Washington, but otherwise not very deplorable. Things have a way of squaring up in this world. Retribution sometimes is a long time coming, but it generally gets there.

Next to winning the championship the best thing Pittsburgh did in this series was to lay the ghost of faintheartedness. The chap who says next year that the Pirates have no grit will have 46,000 eyewitnesses and several million radio witnesses to fight.

For pure, raw nerve, look at the first inning and then at what the Pirates did thereafter. This was the maddest first inning ever played. It comprised three bases on balls, two wild pitches, a fumble, a catcher's interference, a near brawl between McInnis and Ruel, four

runs and 46,000 or more broken hearts.

With the Senators four to the good and Johnson serving, the experts said, "Well, the Pirates were good fellows when they had it."

Much sympathy and honest sentiment was spilled on the head of Vic Aldridge, for Vic, after winning two games in this man's series, lasted long enough in the initial frame to undo everything he had done before. He was yanked abruptly with two runs in, the bases full and only one out, Morrison carrying on.

But in the third those Pirates took up the business of rebutting. A single, a double and another single put two runs in and Carey on second. Max stole third without drawing a throw—great baseball in or out of the mud. Barnhart's single scored him, and Pittsburgh was only one in arrears.

Joe Harris knocked in a couple of Washington runs in the fourth, and everybody inquired what was the use, or words to that effect.

Still, it's a game fish that swims upstream, and that was the direction in which the Pirates were headed. They combed Mr. Johnson for one more in the fifth on Carey's double and Cuyler's ditto. Carey made four hits, three of them doubles, and if this didn't win him his varsity letter, there is no justice.

In the seventh Peckinpaugh proved that he is also the most valuable player in the National League by making a two-base muff of Moore's high fly to start the inning. This was no great shakes as a start. Carey slapped a double down the left-field line and Moore scored, and then Carey fetched in the tying run when Traynor tripled to right center. Pie tried for a homer and was out.

Peckinpaugh did his best to make amends. He whipped a home run over the left-field fence in the eighth, putting Washington ahead again, but this did not square accounts. By no means. For in the eighth, with the first two men retired, Smith doubled, and so did Bigbee, tying the score.

Now Johnson walked Moore, and when Carey grounded to Peckinpaugh the shortstop made his eighth error of the series by tossing high to Stanley Harris at second. The play crammed the bases and gave Cuyler the chance to become all kinds of a hero by doubling down the first-base line.

What looked like a thousand Pittsburgh runners dashed around the bases, and as the crowd gave itself over to delirious idiocy while Bucky Harris watched the happy procession and saw the referee count ten, you could almost see in fancy's eye those two bounding balls that decided another great game a year ago. You could almost hear the Fates giving vent to a loud chuckle.

In the ninth Oldham followed Kremer to the mound and fanned Rice and Goslin and had no trouble with Bucky Harris, either. Oldham was the fourth Pittsburgh twirler. Morrison succored poor Aldridge in the first frame and lasted until a pinch hitter forced him out in the fourth. Kremer carried the load from

the fifth through to the eighth and gets official credit for the victory.

Possibly it was not a conclusive test of championship fitness. Perhaps it decided the baseball title as much as a three-legged race would prove whether Charley Paddock is faster than Loren Murchison. Certainly there was no dishonor in losing such a game. But the horse that can win in the mud as well as in the dust is quite a horse. The heavy going is generally the toughest. As said before, it takes a game fish to swim upstream.

THE FOLLOWING is excerpted from an editorial in *The Sporting News.* My copy came from an advertising executive who keeps it in his desk drawer at the office. There are many like him.

From "The Game for All America"

ERNIE HARWELL

BASEBALL is President Eisenhower tossing out the first ball of the season. And a pudgy schoolboy playing catch with his dad on a Mississippi farm.

A tall, thin old man waving a scorecard from the corner of his dugout—that's baseball. So is the big fat guy with a bulbous nose running out one of his 714 home runs.

There's a man in Mobile who remembers a triple that Honus Wagner hit in Pittsburgh 46 years ago—that's baseball. And so is the scout reporting that a 16-year-old sand-lot pitcher in Cheyenne is the new Walter Johnson.

Baseball is a spirited race of man against man, reflex against reflex. A game of inches. Every skill is measured. Every heroic, every failing is seen and cheered—or booed. And then becomes a statistic.

In baseball democracy shines its clearest. The only race that matters is the race to the bag. The creed is the rule book. And color is merely something to distinguish one team's uniform from another's.

Baseball is a rookie (his experience no bigger than the lump in his throat) trying to begin fulfillment of his dream. It's a veteran too —a tired old man of 35 hoping his aching muscles can pull him through another sweltering August and September.

Nicknames are baseball. Names like Zeke and Pie and Kiki and Home Run and Cracker and Dizzy and Dazzy.

Baseball is the clear, cool eyes of Rogers Hornsby; the flashing spikes of Ty Cobb; and an over-aged pixie named Rabbit Maranville.

Baseball? It's just a game—as simple as a ball and bat. Yet, as complex as the American spirit it symbolizes. It's a sport, business and sometimes even religion.

The fairy tale of Willie Mays making a brilliant World Series catch and then dashing off to Harlem to play stick-ball in the streets with his teen-age pals—that's baseball. So is the husky voice of a doomed Lou Gehrig saying, "I consider myself the luckiest man on the face of the earth."

Baseball is cigar smoke, hot-roasted peanuts, *The Sporting News*, Ladies' Day, Down in Front, Take Me Out to the Ball Game, the Seventh-Inning Stretch and the Star-Spangled Banner.

Baseball is a highly-paid Brooklyn catcher telling the nation's business leaders: "You have to be a man to be a big leaguer, but you have to have a lot of little boy in you too."

This is a game for America—this baseball. A game for boys and for men.

The Biggest Inning in Baseball

LEWIS HEILBRONER

THE SEASON of 1951 was an unhappy one for the baseball fans of Tarboro, North Carolina. Having just had two bad seasons in a row, the Tarboro club—a Coastal Plain League farm club (Class D) of the Philadelphia Athletics—had enjoyed a wonderfully successful spring training exhibition schedule, only to sink right back into the cellar when the regular season began. The A's decided it was time for them to get out—and they announced they were giving up Tarboro. Aroused fans, promising to buy up a given number of season-tickets, prevailed upon the A's to keep the team going—but it was too late. The league directors, eager to have an even number of teams, voted Tarboro out. But before the club disbanded, the fans were treated—exposed, is a better word—to a sight that made the 1951 baseball season permanently imprinted on their minds.

It happened the night of June 2, with Tarboro playing a home game against Wilson. Joe Antolick, the visiting team's manager, had previously managed Tarboro, and there was a friendly but hot rivalry between the clubs. Tarboro fans always cherished a win over Antolick.

The two clubs played on fairly even terms until the fifth inning, when Tarboro came to bat. Bill Carr, the first man up, lined a double. Milburn Felton reached first on an error and Carr went to third. Manager Joe Rullo came through with a single; Carr scored the first Tarboro run. Manager Antolick of Wilson brought in a new pitcher but Johnny Wolfe of Tarboro hit a grounder which the second-baseman booted, and Felton scored, with Rullo going to third. Jim Stevens walked and the hitting vendetta continued when Ray Shiffner doubled. Again, Antolick produced a new pitcher. By this time, with four runs in and nobody out, the local fans could smell blood. The league doormat was getting some sweet re-venge and the home folks were enjoying every bit of it.

The new pitcher walked the first man to face him, Bob Brown. Russ Hand, Tarboro's catcher, also walked. There were only 400 fans in the stands but when Tom Davis, the Tarboro pitcher, smacked a solid single to score runs six and seven, they could be heard for miles. Bill Carr, who had started it all off, loaded the bases by walking. Antolick waved in another pitcher, his fourth. By this time, the Tarboro fans were really having themselves a ball, but what had gone before was nothing compared with what was to come. Felton slammed a base-clearing double to make the score 10-0 and manager Rullo scored run no. 11 with another double. Johnny Wolfe, swinging from his heels, blasted a home run to make it 13-0. And still nobody out! But at least, manager Antolick reflected as he surveyed the carnage, nobody was on base. However, that condition was soon remedied. Stevens tripled, Shiffner singled and Brown walked. Antolick, desperate, put himself in to pitch. The hapless manager couldn't find the plate at first and when he did, Bill Carr knocked his pitch over the fence for a grand-slam homer. Moments later, run 21 scored and not an out had been recorded. In fact, 25 batters came to the plate before Wilson retired a man. The inning dragged on and so did Wilson's agony. Before the third out, 24 runs were scored by Tarboro, seven pitchers were used by Wilson and the fans were all dizzy. A number of records for organized baseball were set. Among them were the run total for one inning, number of batters in one inning (29), number of batters before an out was made (25). Bill Carr set three records by scoring four runs himself, getting three hits and driving in seven runs. The final score of that unforgettable evening of baseball (?) was 31-4.

SHORTLY before his death, Damon Runyon was asked who he thought was the best young sports writer in New York. Runyon, unable to use his voice, took pad and pencil and vigorously jabbed one word: "Heinz." Here is something of what Runyon meant—one of W. C. Heinz's columns from The New York Sun of 1949. It touches on a facet of baseball not dealt with elsewhere in this collection.

A Tale of Two Pitchers

W. C. HEINZ

THE BROOKLYN DODGERS, on the long way home from their training camp at Vero Beach, Florida, are now moving through the Southwest. A couple of days ago they played a game at Fort Worth, Texas, and well down in the stories about that game there was reference to the fact that two pitchers, Carl Erskine and Willie Ramsdell, combined to finish a game that Rex Barney had started.

There was no reason for anyone writing about the game to get excited about that, and no excitement is felt here, either. It merely set someone to remembering a night last July when the Dodgers were pulling out of Chicago on their way to Pittsburgh. Johnny Schmitz had defeated them again, and it was going on midnight and they were tired from the day and from the effects of the long Western trip.

The way it is with a ball team, the players and the baseball writers traveling with them leave their bags in the lobby of the hotel about two hours before train time. Then someone— in the case of the Dodgers it is Senator Griffin —sees that the bags get to the station, and when the players and the writers get there they start pawing through the luggage on the track platform or on the cars, trying to find what belongs to them.

Thus it is that there is always a little confusion when a ball team leaves one town for the next. On this night there was this confusion when one of the writers, hurrying along the platform, spread the word that the Dodgers were bringing Erskine up from Fort Worth.

When the word came down it was about fifteen minutes before train time. It was no great story, but if you worked for a newspaper you had to feel that your paper should get it, and so the writers broke out their typewriters and went to work.

There was one writer working right on the track platform. He had his typewriter set up on a baggage truck and, standing there, he was banging away like that. The rest were in one of the cars, working with their suitcases as desks, and they were working quickly, not only because they had only a few minutes to file their stories before the train left but because they were familiar with the story and it was easy to write.

First Branch Rickey and then Burt Shotton had been lauding this Erskine for about a week. They had scouted him at Fort Worth and had described him as a right-hander with some speed, and so the writers wrote it quickly like that.

"Hey!" one of those in the car said suddenly, stopping his typing and looking up. "Who goes down to Fort Worth to take Erskine's place?"

"Ramsdell," another shouted back, and they went back to working at it.

As it was, they all finished their little stories and, running with their copy to the telegraph desk in the station, they all managed to get back before the train left. Then they settled back in one of the bedrooms, and they started to relax.

"Say," one of them said as a thought seemed to come to him, "has anyone told Ramsdell about this?"

"They're telling him now," another said.

"Well, he must have heard it anyway," the first said, "while we were running back and forth shouting it."

Then they started talking about something else. They were not talking about baseball and, as a matter of fact, they were talking about Hubert Heever, which is what one of them calls Herbert Hoover, when they looked up and saw Ramsdell standing in the doorway. The train was moving now, and he was leaning against the doorway. He had his coat off, and he was just looking at them in the little bedroom.

"Oh," the first to see him said. "Hello, Willie."

"A fine bunch of ———," Ramsdell said.

For a moment they didn't say anything. There seemed to be kind of a small, cynical smile on Ramsdell's face, but then he didn't seem to be smiling, so they just looked back at him.

"What's the matter, Willie?" one of them said finally. "It's not our fault. We didn't do it."

"A fine bunch of ———," Ramsdell said, and then he left.

They knew what he meant. He is a nice little guy and intelligent. Once they had written that—what with his knuckle ball and his fine record in the minors—he looked like the man to take Hugh Casey's place as king of the Dodger bull pen, and now he was going back. When a major leaguer goes back to the minors they seldom do more than mention his name, because they are writing about the kid coming up.

The next day Erskine joined the Dodgers in Pittsburgh. When he pitched his first game for the Dodgers his father was in the stands at Forbes Field, and they wrote about that. The night the team left for New York several of them sat with Erskine, asking him about his minor league past and hearing him tell of his hopes for a major league future, and that is all there was to that. That is all, except not long ago the one writing this met one of the other writers who was on that trip.

"Say," the other said. "Do you remember that night Ramsdell was sent down to Fort Worth?"

"Yes," this one said.

"I can't forget it," the other said. "I've written a fiction piece about it. I keep thinking about him standing there, and I had to find someplace to write about it, if I could."

There was no reason, as said above, to get excited about this. It was just something that happens with a ball team when one guy is going down so another may come up.

THE TITLE to the ensuing article, which appeared in *Sports Illustrated*
magazine, is most apt. Mr. Rickey and The Game go together.

Mr. Rickey and The Game

GERALD HOLLAND

I AM ASKED to speak of the game," said Branch Rickey, restating a question that had been put to him, "I am asked to reflect upon my own part in it. At the age of 73, on the eve of a new baseball season, I am importuned to muse aloud, to touch upon those things that come first to mind."

Seated in his office at Forbes Field, the home of the Pittsburgh Pirates, Branch Rickey nibbled at an unlighted cigarette and sniffed the proposition like a man suddenly come upon a beef stew simmering on a kitchen stove.

Abruptly he threw himself back in his chair and clasped his hands over his head and stared up at the ceiling. He looked ten years younger than his actual age. Thanks to a high-protein, hamburger-for-breakfast diet, he was thirty pounds lighter than he had been three months before. His complexion was ruddy and his thick brown hair showed only a little gray at the temples. Now his great bushy eyebrows shot up and he prayed aloud:

"Lord make me humble, make me grateful . . . make me *tolerant!*"

Slowly he came down from the ceiling and put his elbows on the desk. Unconsciously, perhaps, a hand strayed across the desk to a copy of *Bartlett's Familiar Quotations*. The hand was that of an old-time catcher, big, strong and gnarled. He turned slowly in his chair and swept his eyes over the little gallery of framed photographs on the wall. Among them were George Sisler, Rickey's first great discovery, one of the greatest of the left-handed hitters, now at work down the hall as chief of Pittsburgh scouts; Rogers Hornsby, the game's greatest right-handed hitter, a betting man for whom Rickey once dared the wrath of baseball's high commissioner, Kenesaw Mountain Landis; Jackie Robinson, chosen by Rickey as the man to break down baseball's color line; Honus Wagner, the immortal Pittsburgh shortstop, now past eighty, at this moment growing weaker by the day at his sister's house across town; Charley Barrett, the old Cardinal scout, Rickey's right arm in the days when St. Louis was too poor to make a Southern training trip.

Turning back to his desk, Rickey grimaced and then spoke rapidly, almost harshly:

"Of my career in baseball, let us say first of all that there have been the appearances of hypocrisy. Here we have the Sunday school mollycoddle, apparently professing a sort of public virtue in refraining from playing or watching a game of baseball on Sunday. And yet at the same time he is not above accepting money from a till replenished by Sunday baseball."

He paused and bit the unlighted cigarette in two. He dropped his voice:

"A deeply personal thing. Something not to be exploited, not to be put forward protestingly at every whisper of criticism. No, a deeply personal thing. A man's promise, a promise to his mother. Not involving a condemnation of baseball on Sunday, nor of others who might desire to play it or watch it on Sunday. Simply one man's promise—and it might as well have been a promise not to attend the theater or band concerts in the park."

His eyes went around the room and were held for a moment by the blackboard that lists the players on the fifteen ball clubs in the Pittsburgh farm system. His lips moved and the words sounded like, "But is the boy *ready* for New Orleans?" Then, with a quick movement, he leaned across the desk and waggled an accusing finger.

"Hell's fire!" he exploded. "The Sunday school mollycoddle, the bluenose, the prohibitionist has been a *liberal!* No, no, no—this has nothing to do with Jackie Robinson, I contend that there was no element of liberalism there. I will say something about that perhaps, but now the plain everyday things—the gambling, the drinking, the . . . other things. I submit that I have been a liberal about *them!*"

He was silent. He did not mention or even hint at the names of managers who won major league pennants after everyone but Branch Rickey had quit on them; nor the men who gladly acknowledge that they are still in baseball because of the confidence Rickey placed in them.

The telephone with the private number rang. Branch Rickey picked it up and traded southpaw Paul La Palme to the St. Louis Cardinals for Ben Wade, a relief pitcher. "You announce it," he said into the phone, "and just say La Palme for Wade and an unannounced amount of cash. We'll talk about a Class A ballplayer later. Anybody but a catcher. I don't need a catcher at that level." He put down the phone and his eyes twinkled. "Later in the day I may make a deal with Brooklyn," he said, "if I can get up the nerve." As things turned out, either he did not get up the nerve or he was unable to interest the Flatbush authorities.

He whirled around in his chair and stared out the window. He could see, if he was noticing, the end of a little street that runs down from Hotel Schenley to the ball park. It is called Pennant Place, a reminder of happier days for the Pittsburgh fans, now so ashamed of their eighth-place Pirates that only a few of them show up at the ball park—even for double-headers.

Rickey ran both hands furiously through his thick hair.

"A man trained for the law," he said, "devotes his entire life and all his energies to something so cosmically unimportant as a game."

He examined minutely what was left of his cigarette. Carefully, he extracted a single strand of tobacco and looked at it closely before letting it fall to the floor. Usually he chews unlighted cigars, but this day it was a cigarette.

He began to laugh.

"The law," he chuckled, "I might have stayed in the law. I do not laugh at the great profession itself. I am laughing at a case I had one time—the only case I ever had as a full-time practicing attorney. I had gone to Boise, Idaho from Saranac to try to gain back my strength

after recovering from tuberculosis. I got an office and hung out a shingle and waited for the clients. None came. Finally, I was in court one day and the judge appointed me attorney for a man who was being held on a charge the newspapers used to describe as white slavery.

"I was apprehensive, but at last I summoned enough courage to go over to the jail and see my client. Oh, he was a horrible creature. I can see him now, walking slowly up to the bars and looking me up and down with contempt. He terrified me. I began to shake like a leaf. After a minute he said, 'Who the hell are you?'

"I tried to draw myself up a little and then I said, 'Sir, my name is Branch Rickey. The court has appointed me your attorney and I would like to talk to you.' He looked me up and down again and then spat at my feet. Then he delivered what turned out to be the final words of our association. He said, 'Get the hell out of here!'"

Rickey threw back his head.

"I not only got out of there," he said, "I got out of the state of Idaho and went to St. Louis and took a job with the St. Louis Browns. I intended to stay in baseball for just one year. But when the year was up, Mr. Robert Lee Hedges, the owner, offered me a raise. There was a new baby at our house. And not much money, new or old. So I was a moral coward. I chose to stay with the game."

Rickey thought a moment.

"I might have gone into politics," he said. "As recently as fourteen years ago, there was the offer of a nomination for a political office. A governorship. The governorship, in fact, of Missouri. I was tempted, flattered. But then, as I ventured a little into the political arena, I was appalled by my own ignorance of politics. But the party leaders were persuasive. They pledged me the full support of the regular party organization. They said they could not prevent any Billy Jumpup from filing, but no Billy Jumpup would have the organization's backing. It is an overwhelming thing to be offered such prospects of reaching high office. I thought it over carefully and then tentatively agreed to run, on condition that another man —a seasoned campaigner—run on the ticket with me. He said that was utterly impossible. He invited me to go with him to New York and talk to Mr. Herbert Hoover about the situation in Missouri. But afterward I still was unable to persuade my friend to run. He was

Arthur Hyde, Secretary of Agriculture under Mr. Hoover. Later I learned to my sorrow the reason for Mr. Hyde's decision. He was even then mortally ill. So, regretfully, I asked that my name be withdrawn. The man who ran in my place was elected and then went on to the United States Senate.

"So, conceivably, I might have been a governor. Instead, I chose to stay with the game."

Rickey made elaborate gestures of straightening the papers on his desk.

"A life of public service," he said, peering over his glasses, "versus a life devoted to a game that boys play with a ball and bat."

He turned and picked up a baseball from a bookcase shelf.

"This ball," he said, holding it up.

"This symbol. Is it worth a man's whole life?"

There was just time for another mussing of the hair before the phone rang again.

"Pooh," said Rickey into the phone after a moment. "Three poohs. Poohbah." He hung up.

"I was listening last night to one of the television interview programs," he said. "Senator Knowland was being interrogated. It was a discussion on a high level and the questions involved matters affecting all of us and all the world. I was listening intently and then I heard the senator say, 'Well, I think the Administration has a pretty good batting average.' "

Rickey blew out his cheeks and plucked a shred of tobacco from his lips.

"It must have been a full minute later," he went on, "and the questions had gone on to other things when I sat straight up. Suddenly I realized that to answer a somewhat difficult question this United States senator had turned naturally to the language of the game. And this language, this phrase 'a pretty good batting average,' had said exactly what he wanted to say. He had not intended to be frivolous. The reporters did not smile as though he had made a joke. They accepted the answer in the language of the game as perfectly proper. It was instantly recognizable to them. I dare say it was recognizable even in London."

He frowned, thinking hard. Then his face lit up again.

"The game invades our language!" he exclaimed. "Now, the editorial page of *The New York Times* is a serious forum, not ordinarily given to levity. Yet at the height of the controversy between the Army and Senator McCarthy, there was the line on this dignified editorial page, 'Senator McCarthy—a good fast ball, but no control.' "

Rickey slapped his thigh and leaned over the desk.

"Now, didn't that tell the whole story in a sentence?"

He waved an arm, granting himself the point.

He cherished his remnant of a cigarette.

"A man was telling me the other day," he went on, "he said he was walking through Times Square in New York one blistering day last summer. The temperature stood at 100° and the humidity made it almost unbearable. This man happened to fall in behind three postmen walking together. Their shirts were wringing wet and their mailbags were heavily laden. It struck this man that these postmen might well be irritable on such a day and, since he saw that they were talking animatedly, he drew closer so that he might hear what they were saying. He expected, of course, that they would be complaining bitterly of their dull drab jobs on this abominable day. But when he had come close enough to hear them, what were they talking about with such spirit and relish?"

He paused for effect, then with a toss of his head, he exploded:

"Leo Durocher and the New York Giants!"

Carefully, he put down his cigarette butt. Then he leaned back and rubbed his eyes with the back of his fists. He tore furiously at his hair and half swallowed a yawn.

"Mrs. Rickey and I," he said, "sat up until two o'clock this morning playing hearts."

He straightened the papers on his desk and said as an aside: "I contend it is the most scientific card game in the world."

He searched the ceiling for the point he was developing, found it and came down again.

"The three postmen, heavily laden on a hot, miserable day, yet able to find a happy, common ground in their discussion of this game of baseball. And in their free time, in their hours of leisure, if they had no other interest to turn to, still there was the game to bring color and excitement and good wholesome interest into their lives."

He took up the fragment of paper and tobacco that was left of the cigarette as though it were a precious jewel.

"Leisure," he said, sending his eyebrows aloft, "is a hazardous thing. Here in America we do not yet have a leisure class that knows what to do with it. Leisure can produce something fine. It may also produce something evil. Hell's fire! Leisure can produce a great symphony, a great painting, a great book."

He whirled around to the window and peered out at Pennant Place. Then, turning back like a pitcher who has just cased the situation at second base, he let go hard.

"Gee!" he cried. "Leisure can also produce a great dissipation! Leisure can be idleness and idleness can drive a man to his lowest!"

He recoiled, as from a low man standing at the side of his desk.

"Idleness is the worst thing in this world. Idleness is doing nothing and thinking of wrong things to do. Idleness is the evil that lies behind the juvenile delinquency that alarms us all. It's the most damnable thing that can happen to a kid—to have nothing to do."

He put the tattered cigarette butt in his mouth and spoke around it.

"The game that gives challenge to our youth points the way to our salvation. The competitive spirit, that's the all-important thing. The stultifying thing in this country is the downpressure on competition, the something-for-nothing philosophy, the do-as-little-as-you-can creed—these are the most devastating influences today. This thinking is the kind that undermines a man's character and can undermine the national character as well."

He studied his shreds of cigarette with the deliberation of a diamond cutter.

"Labor and toil," he intoned, "by the sweat of thy brow shalt thou earn thy bread. Labor and toil—and something else. A joy in work, a zest. Zest, that is the word. Who are the great ballplayers of all time? The ones with zest. Ty Cobb. Willie Mays. The man down the hall, one of the very greatest, George Sisler. Dizzy Dean. Pepper Martin. We have one coming back to us this year here at Pittsburgh. Dick Groat. He has it. Highly intelligent, another Lou Boudreau, the same kind of hitter. He has it. Zest."

Rickey smiled. "Dick Groat will be one of the great ones. There will be others this year. We have 110 boys coming out of service, 475 players under contract on all our clubs. A total of $496,000 invested in player bonuses. There will be other good prospects for the Pirates among these boys. This ball club of ours will come in time. No promises for this year, but in '56, I think, yes."

He turned to look down the street to Pennant Place, then added: "A *contending* team in '56—at least that."

(At the barbershop in Hotel Schenley it is related that Rickey's defense of his eighth-place ball club is considerably less detailed. "Patience!" he cries, anticipating the hecklers as he enters the shop.)

The door opened and Harold Roettger, Rickey's assistant, entered the room. A round-faced, studious-looking man, Roettger has been with Rickey since the old St. Louis Cardinal days. He was in the grip of a heavy cold.

"Do you remember a boy named Febbraro?" he asked, sniffling, "in the Provincial League?"

"Febbraro, Febbraro," said Rickey, frowning. "A pitcher. I saw him work in a night game."

"That's the boy," said Roettger, wiping his eyes. "He's been released."

"Aha," said Rickey, "yes, I remember the boy well. Shall we sign him?"

"We ought to talk about it," said Roettger, fighting a sneeze.

"Harold," said Rickey, "Richardson [Tommy Richardson, president of the Eastern League] is coming down for a meeting tomorrow. I wish you could be there. I devoutly wish you were not ill."

"I, too, devoutly wish I were not ill," said Roettger. "I'll go home now and maybe I'll be ready for the meeting."

"Please try not to be ill tomorrow," said Rickey. "I desperately need you at the meeting."

"I will try very hard," said Roettger, "and will you think about Febbraro?"

"I will," said Rickey. "Go home now, Harold, and take care of yourself."

(Later, Roettger recovered from his cold and signed Febbraro for Williamsport in the Eastern League.)

As Roettger left, Rickey searched for the thread of his soliloquy.

"Hornsby," he said suddenly, "Rogers Hornsby, a man with zest for the game. And Leo, of course.

"Leo Durocher has come a long way, off the field as well as on. A quick mind, a brilliant mind, an indomitable spirit. A rugged ballplayer—and I like rugged ballplayers. But when he came to St. Louis, Leo was in trouble. No fewer than 32 creditors were breathing down his neck, suing or threatening to sue. An impossible situation. I proposed that I go to his creditors and arrange for weekly payments on his debts. This meant a modest allowance of spending money for Leo himself. But he agreed.

"There were other matters to be straightened out. Leo's associates at the time were hardly desirable ones. But he was not the kind of man to take kindly to any criticism of his friends. I thought a lot about Leo's associations, but I didn't see what I could do about them.

"Then one day during the winter I received a call from the United States Naval Academy at Annapolis. The Academy needed a baseball coach and they asked if I could recommend a man. I said I thought I could and would let them know.

"I knew my man. But I didn't dare tell him right away. Instead, I called his wife [Durocher was then married to Grace Dozier, a St. Louis fashion designer] and asked her to drop in at the office. When she arrived, I told her that I intended to recommend Leo as baseball coach at the Naval Academy.

"She looked at me a moment. Then she said, 'Would they take Leo?' I said they would if I recommended him. Then I told her I proposed to get a copy of the Naval Academy manual. I said I knew that if I handed it to Leo myself, he was quite likely to throw it back in my face. But if she were to put it in his hands, he might agree to look it over. Mrs. Durocher thought again. Then she said, 'Get the manual.'"

(Rickey has a habit of presenting ballplayers with what he considers to be worth-while reading. When Pee Wee Reese was made captain of the Dodgers, Rickey sent him Eisenhower's *Crusade in Europe*.)

"When I told Leo," Rickey continued, "he was stunned and unbelieving, then enormously but quietly pleased. I told him that I would arrange for him to report late for spring training. I made it clear that he was to decline any payment for his services. Treading softly, I mentioned that the boys he would be coaching were the finest our country had to offer. I suggested gently that any leader of such boys would, of course, have to be letter perfect in his conduct. Leo didn't blow up. He just nodded his head.

"When he reported to spring training camp, he was bursting with pride. He showed me a wrist watch the midshipmen had given him. He said, 'Mr. Rickey, I did it, I did it!'

"I said, 'You did half of it, Leo.'

"'What do you mean, half!' he demanded.

"'To be a complete success in this undertaking, Leo, you must be invited back. If they ask you back for next season, then you may be sure you have done the job well.'"

Rickey smiled.

"They did invite him back," he said. "And this time the midshipmen gave him a silver service. He had done the job—the whole job—and I rather think that this experience was a big turning point for Leo. It lifted him into associations he had never known before and he came away with increased confidence and self-assurance and, I am quite sure, a greater measure of self-respect."

(Years later, just before Leo Durocher was suspended from baseball for a year by Commissioner A. B. Chandler, Rickey called his staff together in the Brooklyn Dodgers' offices to say of his manager: "Leo is down. But we are going to stick by Leo. We are going to stick by Leo until hell freezes over!" Today, in a manner of speaking, it is Rickey who is down—in eighth place—and Leo who is up, riding high as manager of the world champions.)

Rickey straightened his tie. He was wearing a four-in-hand. Ordinarily, he wears a bow tie, but once a month he puts on a four-in-hand as a gesture of neckwear independence.

"More than a half-century spent in the game," Rickey mused, "and now it is suggested that I give thought to some of the ideas and innovations with which I have been associated. The question arises, 'Which of these can be said to have contributed most to making baseball truly our national game?'

"First, I should say, there was the mass production of ballplayers. The Cardinals were three years ahead of all the other clubs in establishing tryout camps. We looked at 4,000 boys a year. Then, of course, we had to have teams on which to place boys with varying degrees of ability and experience. That brought into being the farm system.

"There were other ideas not ordinarily remembered. With the St. Louis Browns, under Mr. Hedges, we originated the idea of Ladies' Day, a very important step forward. Probably no other innovation did so much to give baseball respectability, as well as thousands of new fans.

"With the Cardinals, we developed the idea of the Knot Hole Gang. We were the first major league team to admit boys free to the ball park and again the idea was soon copied."

(In the beginning, boys joining the Cardinal Knot Hole Gang were required to sign a pledge to refrain from smoking and profanity —clearly the hand of Rickey.)

"These were ideas," Rickey went on, "and baseball was a vehicle in which such ideas might comfortably ride."

Rickey's eyes strayed to a framed motto hanging on the wall. It read: "He that will not reason is a bigot; he that cannot reason is a fool and he that dares not reason is a slave."

Rickey bent down and went rummaging through the lower drawers of his desk. In a moment he came up holding a slender book. The jacket read: *Slave and Citizen: the Negro in the Americas.* By Frank Tannenbaum."

"This book," said Rickey, "is by a Columbia University professor. Let me read now just the concluding paragraph. It says, 'Physical proximity, slow cultural intertwining, the growth of a middle group that stands in experience and equipment between the lower and upper class; and the slow process of moral identification work their way against all seemingly absolute systems of values and prejudices. Society is essentially dynamic, and while the mills of God grind slow, they grind exceeding sure. Time will draw a veil over the white and black in this hemisphere, and future generations will look back upon the record of strife as it stands revealed in the history of the people of this New World of ours with wonder and incredulity. For they will not understand the issues that the quarrel was about.' "

Rickey reached for a pencil, wrote on the flyleaf of the book and pushed it across the desk. He leaned back in his chair and thought a moment. Then he sat straight up.

"Some honors have been tendered," he said, "some honorary degrees offered because of my part in bringing Jackie Robinson into the major leagues."

He frowned and shook his head vigorously.

"No, no, no. I have declined them all. To accept honors, public applause for signing a superlative ballplayer to a contract? I would be *ashamed!*"

He turned to look out the window and turned back.

"Suppose," he demanded, "I hear that Billy Jones down the street has attained the age of 21. Suppose I go to Billy and say, 'You come with me to the polling place.' And then at the polling place I take Billy by the arm and march up to the clerks and say, 'This is Billy Jones, native American, 21 years of age,' and I demand that he be given the right to cast a ballot!"

Rickey leaned over the desk, his eyes flashing.

"Would anyone but a lunatic expect to be applauded for that?"

It immediately became clear that although Rickey deprecated his right to applause, he had never minimized the difficulties of bringing the first Negro into organized baseball.

"I talked to sociologists," he said, "and to Negro leaders. With their counsel, I worked out what I considered to be the six essential points to be considered."

He started to count on his fingers.

"Number one," he said, "the man we finally chose had to be right off the field. *Off* the field.

"Number two, he had to be right *on* the field. If he turned out to be a lemon, our efforts would fail for that reason alone.

"Number three, the reaction of his own race had to be right.

"Number four, the reaction of press and public had to be right.

"Number five, we had to have a place to put him.

"Number six, the reaction of his fellow players had to be right.

"In Jackie Robinson, we found the man to take care of points one and two. He was eminently right off and on the field. We did not settle on Robinson until after we had invested $25,000 in scouting for a man whose name we did not then know.

"Having found Robinson, we proceeded to point five. We had to have a place to put him. Luckily, in the Brooklyn organization, we had exactly the spot at Montreal where the racial issue would not be given undue emphasis.

"To take care of point three, the reaction of Robinson's own race, I went again to the Negro leaders. I explained that in order to give this boy his chance, there must be no demonstrations in his behalf, no excursions from one city to another, no presentations or testimonials. He was to be left alone to do this thing without any more hazards than were already present. For two years the men I talked to respected the reasoning behind my requests. My admiration for these men is limitless. In the best possible way, they saw to it that Jackie Robinson had his chance to make it on his own.

"Point four, the reaction of press and public, resolved itself in the course of things, and point six, the reaction of his fellow players, finally—if painfully—worked itself out."

Rickey reached across the desk and tapped the Tannenbaum book.

"Time," he said, "time."

He despaired of his cigarette now and tossed it into the wastebasket. His eyes moved around the room and he murmured half to himself: "We are not going to let anything spoil sports in this country. Some of the things I read about boxing worry me, but things that are wrong will be made right . . . in time."

He laughed.

"I don't think anyone is worried about wrestling. Isn't it a rather good-natured sort of entertainment?"

He chuckled a little more, then frowned again.

"I am asked about the minor leagues. The cry is heard, 'The minors are dying!' I don't think so. The minors are in trouble but new ways will be found to meet new situations and new problems. Up to now, I confess, the major leagues have been unable to implement any effort to protect the minor leagues from the encroachment of major league broadcasts."

(A baseball man once said that Branch Rickey is constitutionally unable to tell a falsehood. "However," this man said, "sometimes he pours over the facts of a given case such a torrent of eloquence that the truth is all but drowned.")

The door opened and Rickey jumped to his feet. His eyes lit up as he cried: "Mother!"

In the doorway stood Mrs. Rickey, carrying a box of paints the size of a brief case.

"Well, Mother!" cried Rickey, coming around from behind the desk. "How did it go? Did you get good marks?"

Mrs. Rickey, a small, smiling woman, stood looking at her husband. Childhood sweethearts in Ohio, they have been married for 49 years.

Rickey pointed dramatically to the paintbox.

"Mother has joined a painting class!" he exclaimed. "At 73 years of age, Mother has gone back to school! Well, Mother? Did you recite or what? Do they give marks? What is the teacher like?"

Mrs. Rickey walked to a chair and sat down. It was plain that she was accustomed to pursuing a policy of containment toward her husband.

"They don't give marks," she said quietly. "The teacher is very nice. He was telling us

that painting opens up a whole new world. You see things and colors you never saw before."

Rickey was aghast.

"Wonderful!" he cried. "Isn't that just wonderful! Mother, we must celebrate. I'll take you to lunch!"

"All right," said Mrs. Rickey. "Where will we go?"

"The Duquesne Club," said Rickey.

"That'll be fine," said Mrs. Rickey.

(In sharply stratified Pittsburgh society, there are two standards by which to measure a man who stands at the very top: one is membership in the Duquesne Club, the other is a residence at Fox Chapel, the ultra-exclusive Pittsburgh suburb. Rickey has both; the residence is an 18-room house set down on 100 acres.)

Rickey was the first to reach the sidewalk. He paced up and down waiting for Mrs. Rickey, flapping his arms against the cold, for he had forgotten to wear an overcoat that morning. Guido Roman, a tall, handsome Cuban who is Rickey's chauffeur, opened the car door.

"You want to get inside, Mr. Rickey?" he asked.

"No, Guido," said Rickey, blowing on his fingers, "I'm not cold."

A car drew up and stopped across the street. A tall, muscular young man got out.

Rickey peered sharply and ducked his head. "A thousand dollars this lad is a ballplayer," he muttered out of the side of his mouth. "But who is he, who is he?"

The young man came directly to Rickey.

"Mr. Rickey, you don't remember me," he said. "My name is George—!"

"Sure, I remember you, George!" Rickey exploded, thrusting out his hand. "You're a first baseman, right?"

"Yes, sir," said George, blushing with pleasure.

"Go right in the office and make yourself at home, George," Rickey said, beaming. "There's another first baseman in there named George— George Sisler. Say hello to him!"

"Say, thanks, Mr. Rickey," George said, hurrying to the office door.

In a moment Mrs. Rickey came out and the ride downtown in Rickey's Lincoln began. As the car pulled away from the curb, Rickey, a notorious back-seat driver, began a series of barked directions: "Right here, Guido! Left at the next corner, Guido! Red light, Guido!"

Guido, smiling and unperturbed, drove smoothly along. As the car reached the downtown business district, Rickey, peering this way and that, shouted, "Slow down, Guido!"

Guido slowed down and then Rickey whispered hoarsely: "There it is, Mother! Look!"

"What?" smiled Mrs. Rickey.

"The largest lamp store in the world! Right there! I inquired about the best place to buy a lamp and I was told that this place is the largest in the whole wide world! Right there!"

"We only want a two-way bed lamp," said Mrs. Rickey.

"I know," said Rickey. "But there's the place to get it. You could go all over the world and not find a bigger lamp store. Right turn here, Guido!"

"One way, Mr. Rickey," said Guido, cheerfully.

That was the signal for a whole comedy of errors, with Rickey directing and traffic cops vetoing a series of attempts to penetrate one-way streets and to execute left turns. Rickey grew more excited, Mrs. Rickey more calm, Guido more desperate as the Duquesne Club loomed and faded as a seemingly unattainable goal.

"Judas Priest!" Rickey finally exclaimed. "It's a perfectly simple problem! We want to go to the Duquesne Club!"

"I know how!" Guido protested, "I know the way!"

"Then turn, man, turn!"

"Get out of here!" yelled a traffic cop.

"For crying out loud!" roared Rickey. "Let's get out and walk."

"I'm not going to walk," said Mrs. Rickey, mildly. "We have a car. Let Guido go his way."

"Oh, all right," Rickey pouted. "But you'd think I'd never been downtown before!"

In a moment the car pulled up at the Duquesne Club and Rickey, serene again, jumped out and helped Mrs. Rickey from the car.

"Take the car home, Guido," he said pleasantly. "We'll call you later."

"Yes, Mr. Rickey," said Guido, mopping his brow.

A group of women came out of the Duquesne Club as the Rickeys entered. The women nodded and smiled at Mrs. Rickey. Raising his hat, Rickey bowed low, then crouched to whisper hoarsely behind his hand:

"Classmates of yours, Mother?"

He stamped his foot and slapped his thigh, choking with laughter.

"One of them is in the painting class," said Mrs. Rickey placidly. "The others are in the garden club."

At the luncheon table on the second floor, Rickey ordered whitefish for Mrs. Rickey and roast beef for himself. There were no cocktails, of course; Rickey is a teetotaler.

("I shudder to think what might have happened if Branch had taken up drinking," a former associate has said. "He does nothing in moderation and I can see him facing a bottle of whiskey and shouting: 'Men, we're going to hit that bottle and hit it *hard!*'")

The luncheon order given, Rickey excused himself and made a brief telephone call at the headwaiter's desk. Returning to the table, he sat down and began to speak of pitchers.

"The greatest pitchers I have ever seen," he said, "were Christy Mathewson and Jerome Dean."

(Rickey likes to address a man by his proper given name. He is especially fond of referring to Dizzy Dean as "Jerome.")

"Mathewson," Rickey continued, "could throw every pitch in the book. But he was economical. If he saw that he could win a game with three kinds of pitches, he would use only three. Jerome, on the other hand, had a tendency to run in the direction of experimentation. Murry Dickson (formerly of the Pirates, now of the Phillies) has a fine assortment of pitches, but he feels an obligation to run through his entire repertory in every game."

The food had arrived and Rickey picked up knife and fork and, eying Mrs. Rickey closely, began to speak more rapidly.

"Yes," he said loudly, "Murry is the sort of pitcher who will go along splendidly until the eighth inning and then apparently say to himself: 'Oh, dear me, I have forgotten to throw my half-speed ball!' And then and there he will throw it."

Abruptly, Rickey made a lightning thrust with his fork in the direction of a pan-browned potato on the platter. Mrs. Rickey, alert for just such a stratagem, met the thrust with her own fork and they fenced for a few seconds in mid-air.

"*Jane!*" pleaded Rickey, abandoning the duel.

Mrs. Rickey deposited the potato on her own plate and passed over a small dish of broccoli.

"This will be better for you," she said quietly. "You know you're not to have potatoes."

Rickey grumbled: "I am weary of this diet. It is a cruel and inhuman thing."

"Eat the broccoli," Mrs. Rickey said.

"Jane," said Rickey, "there are times in a man's life when he wants above everything else in the world to have a potato."

"You get plenty to eat," said Mrs. Rickey. "Didn't you enjoy the meat patty at breakfast?"

Rickey shrugged his shoulders, conceding the point, and attacked his roast beef and broccoli with gusto.

"That subject of my retirement comes up from time to time," he said. "And to the direct question, 'When will you retire from baseball?' my answer is, 'Never!' But I qualify that. Now, I do foresee the day, likely next year, when I shall spend less time at my desk, at my office. I shall spend more time in the field, scouting, looking at prospects, and leave the arduous responsibilities of the general manager's position to other hands."

He looked admiringly at the baked apple before him. He put his hand on the pitcher of rich cream beside it and glanced inquiringly across the table. This time the veto was not invoked and, happily, Rickey drained the pitcher over his dessert.

After he had dropped a saccharin tablet in his coffee, he leaned back and smiled at Mrs. Rickey. Then he leaned forward again and rubbed his chin, seeming to debate something with himself. He grasped the sides of the table and spoke with the air of a conspirator.

"Here is something I intend to do," he said. "My *next* thing. A completely new idea in spring training."

He arranged the silverware to illustrate the story.

"A permanent training camp, designed and built for that purpose. Twin motels—not hotels, *motels*—with four playing fields in between as a sort of quadrangle. A public address system. Especially designed press accommodations. *Now.* One motel would be occupied by the Pittsburgh club, the other by an *American League* club. They would play a series of exhibition games and would draw better than two teams from the same league. Everything that went into the camp would be the re-

sult of our experience with training camps all through the years. It would be foolproof. And it would pay for itself because it would be operated for tourists after spring training. I *have* the land. At Fort Myers, Florida, the finest training site in the country for my money. I *have* an American League Club ready to go along with me. I *have* two thirds of the financial backing necessary."

Rickey leaned back in triumph, then came forward quickly again.

"Everybody concerned is ready to put up the cash now," he whispered, "*except me!*"

He paused for effect, then suddenly realized he had not said exactly what he intended. He burst into laughter.

"Sh-h-h," said Mrs. Rickey.

"What I mean," he said, sobering, "is that I can't go along with the plan until we have a contending ball club. But we'll get there. We'll put over this thing. It will revolutionize spring training."

It was time to get back to the office. Rickey was for sprinting down the stairs to the first floor, but Mrs. Rickey reminded him of his trick knee.

"Ah, yes, Mother," he said. "We will take the elevator."

On the street outside, Rickey remembered he had sent his car home.

"We'll get a cab down at the corner," he said. "I've got a meeting at the office. Where can I drop you, Mother?"

"Well," said Mrs. Rickey, "I thought I'd go look at some lamps."

"Oh, yes," Rickey exclaimed. "Go to that store I showed you. Mother, I understand they have the largest selection of lamps in town."

Mrs. Rickey looked at him and shook her head and smiled.

Rickey, already thinking of something else, studied the sidewalk. He raised his head and spoke firmly over the traffic.

"The game of baseball," he said, "has given me a life of joy. I would not have exchanged it for any other."

He took Mrs. Rickey by the arm. They turned and walked down the street together and vanished into the crowd.

THE GREATEST right-handed hitter of all time, Rogers Hornsby, had six different managerial jobs in the majors. In 1953, while managing the Cincinnati Reds, Hornsby did the following piece for *Look* magazine which includes a graphic picture of the 1926 World Series game in which Grover Cleveland Alexander struck out Tony Lazzeri. As titles go, Hornsby's article was prophetic. He no longer manages the Reds.

How to Get Fired

———————— ROGERS HORNSBY ————————
as told to J. ROY STOCKTON

As I LOOK BACK to my youngest days, I can't remember anything that happened before I had a baseball in my hand. I guess I started playing as soon as I could close a fist around a ball. I know I was playing team ball when I was nine and ten years old.

One of my brothers, Everett, pitched in the Texas League, so I guess that's how I happened to have a ball in my hand as the first plaything I can remember. My brother got me a tryout with the Dallas club. It was Class B at that time, I believe, in 1914. I was a shortstop, a little young and a little small, I guess, because I didn't make it. After about two weeks, I was sent to Hugo, Oklahoma, in the Class D Texas-Oklahoma League. The club blew up after about six weeks, and I was sold to Denison for $125.

Bob Connery, a scout for the Cardinals, and one of the greatest scouts and one of the best friends I ever had, was in charge of the St. Louis Cardinals' second team, playing exhibition games. The squad played in Denison, and Connery saw me. He didn't say anything, and I didn't think anything about it, but, in midseason, he came back to Denison on a scouting expedition and bought me for the Cardinals for $400.

There wasn't any bonus for me when I signed to play with Dallas or Hugo or Denison or with the Cardinals. I was glad to get a chance to play ball. Today, tremendous bonuses are being paid to boys who have never had a professional uniform on. But I don't believe the big bonuses have helped baseball or the boys, either. Rewards in any line of work should be given for doing things. It's silly to give a boy a tremendous bonus when you don't know, and he doesn't know, whether he'll ever get near the major leagues.

I joined the Cardinals in Cincinnati on September 1, 1915. In eighteen games during the remainder of the 1915 season, I hit only .246. When that season closed, Miller Huggins was not very optimistic about my future.

"You're too little, kid," he told me. "Those strong-armed pitchers in the big leagues will handcuff you. You ought to be farmed out, till you put on some weight."

I was just a green country kid from Texas, and to me farming out meant just that. I didn't know about any farm system in baseball. In fact, we didn't have anything like that in those days. It was just a way of expressing himself that Huggins used. So I literally did what I thought he meant. I arranged to spend the winter on a farm with an aunt and an uncle. I drank all the milk I could hold and consumed great piles of fried chicken and dozens of homemade biscuits every day.

Even if I was a green pea about being farmed out, I did get the job done. When the Cardinals gathered in the spring, I reported to Manager Huggins weighing 160 pounds. I told him that I had done just what he recommended —I had farmed myself out. I was on my way then. It took several years for the Cardinals to discover I wasn't too hot as a shortstop but could do fairly well at second base, after whirls at third and first as well as shortstop.

The story of my own activities at the plate and around second base in the ten years before I was called into the managing end of baseball I'll leave to the record books. They were great years for me. When a man is climbing to the top in the game he loves above all, every year is a great one. Under managers like Huggins and, later, Branch Rickey, that skinny Texas kid traveled a long way from the diamond at Hugo, Oklahoma.

* * *

Branch Rickey, a great builder of ball clubs, a great judge of talent and one of the smartest men baseball has ever known in any capacity, really believed the Cardinals had a chance to win the pennant in 1925. Rickey knew all there was to be known about baseball, but he had one fault. He was too smart, I believe, for the ballplayers. He talked over their heads. He was one of the greatest percentage players in baseball, one of the first to utilize each individual's special skill. But his language in the clubhouse was not the language of the ballplayers. They were a little confused by it all, a little tight trying to think of all the things he outlined to them in speeches and in blackboard sessions.

When the club got off to a bad start, Sam Breadon, the club president, got to mulling over what Rickey had been telling him all winter—that the club was good enough to win a pennant. Then Breadon looked at the standings, saw we were in last place and decided to do something about it.

Breadon told me he was going to make a change and asked me if I would accept the job as manager of the ball club. I told him I thought Rickey was doing all that anybody could do with the club, to give him a little more time. But Sam had made up his mind. If I didn't take it, he'd have to give the job to somebody else.

Naturally, Rickey was broken up about the change, but he knew that I hadn't sought or wanted the job. Breadon told him in front of me that I had been loyal to him, had urged that he be given more time. But it was a blow, and Rickey insisted that, if he surrendered the management of the club on the field, he would dispose of his stock holdings in the Cardinals.

This was a break for me. Breadon insisted that I buy the stock and arranged to help finance the deal.

While the Cardinals were in last place that Memorial Day, they were a better ball club than that. One of the first things I did was to recall Tommy Thevenow from our International League farm club. Tommy was a good shortstop. We also bolstered the catching by getting Bob O'Farrell from the Cubs. Another thing I did quickly was to change the mental attitude of the pitchers. They had become a little panicky. I made them understand that I expected the other ball club to get a few base hits and score a few runs, but that I would give a pitcher a chance to work out of trouble.

I had the pitchers ease up on the idea that their control had to be pinpoint perfect. If a pitcher has good stuff, with speed and a fair assortment of curves, or just a good fast ball, a curve, and knows how to change up, he can do all right if he can get the ball through the strike zone often enough to avoid those bases on balls. Go over any club's pitching records for a season and you'll find that the bases on balls are what get you into trouble and beat you.

The pitching improved, and pitchers didn't try to hit the corners of the plate while watching the bull pen at the same time. The Cardinals moved from the bottom of the league, and we finished fourth that season, despite the bad start.

In 1926, we trained at San Antonio, Texas, and I believe the fine start we made that year was because of the hard work we did. I made up my mind everybody would be ready when the bell rang.

"We're going to win the pennant," I told my Cardinals. "Don't go around telling everybody we're going to win, but we are. And if there's anybody here who doesn't believe we're going to win, there's a train leaving for the North tonight."

Then, in June, we got a good break when Joe McCarthy of the Cubs decided he didn't want Grover Cleveland Alexander any more. We got Alexander for the waiver price, which in those days was only $4,000. That was one of the best bargains in the history of the Cardinals.

Alexander may have been a problem for the Cubs and Joe McCarthy, but he wasn't for us. I didn't do any preaching to him or anybody else on the ball club about not doing any drinking.

What they did after baseball hours was their own business. All I ever asked was that every man on the squad be in condition to give me a full day of his best work on the baseball field. Alexander did all of that. So did everybody else who stayed on the ball club.

It was a close race all the way. It was late in September, with only a couple of days of the season still to go, before we finally clinched the pennant by beating the Giants at the Polo Grounds. That pennant and our victory over the Yankees in the World Series combined to give me the greatest thrill of my baseball career.

Nobody figured the Cardinals had a chance in the 1926 World Series. The Yankees were regarded as a super team. Miller Huggins had two of the greatest sluggers the game has ever known in Babe Ruth and Lou Gehrig, and it was that kind of a ball club all the way down the line.

But the Cardinals weren't scared by the big names. We figured the Yankees were only human and that we wouldn't be playing the series if we didn't have a chance to win.

We lost the first game, 2 to 1. The second game marked the 39-year-old Alexander's first World Series appearance since 1915, and Old Pete pulled us even with a 6-2 victory.

At Yankee Stadium in those days, there used to be a groove between the right-field boxes and the old wooden bleachers, now torn down; New York writers called it the "bloody angle." In that second game, Thevenow, our hitting star, lined a ball into that groove for what was generally figured to be a two-base hit. There were more than 60,000 people in the park, and most of them could see the ball, but Ruth, playing right field, couldn't find it and Thevenow ran around the bases for an inside-the-park homer.

The Babe, they say, stormed back into the Yankee dugout raving: "I kept yelling out there, 'Where's that blankety-blank ball?' but not one of those stupid so-and-sos in the stands would tell me."

Everybody figured the series was going about as they had expected when we left St. Louis, trailing three victories to two, with the Yankees playing the last two on their home grounds. Alexander pitched for us in that sixth game. We won by 10 to 2, and so we had the series all squared again. After the game I told him to take it easy that night.

"You're the best we've got if we get into trouble, so get to bed as early as you can," I told him. "You've got a long winter ahead when you can do whatever you please."

"I'll be ready if you need me, Rog," was all he said, and I didn't worry about him.

We got into the jam, all right. We got out in front, scoring three runs after Ruth produced the first run with a homer off Jess Haines in the third inning. The Yankees made it 3 to 2 in the fifth, and in the seventh the Yankees filled the bases with two out.

Haines had a great knuckle ball, but he had been throwing it so much that a blister had developed on the gripping finger. When he walked Gehrig, filling the bases, I knew we had to do something.

People have asked me many times about what happened that day, in that seventh-inning clutch, when Alexander was called from the bull pen to relieve Haines. They wanted to know what I said and what Alex said, and whether he had a gin bottle out there in the bull pen.

Well, I left my position at second base and walked out to meet him. Naturally, I wanted to get a close look at him, to see what shape he was in. And I wanted to tell him what the situation was, in case he'd been dozing.

"We're still ahead, three to two," I told Alex. "It's the seventh inning, two out, but the bases are filled and Lazzeri's up."

Alex didn't say much. "Bases filled, eh? Well, don't worry about me. I'm all right. And I guess there's nothing much to do except give Tony a lot of hell."

Alexander took care of Lazzeri, all right, striking him out. On the second strike, Tony hit a tremendous line drive that crashed into the left-field seats, foul. Then Alex fooled Tony with a low curve, outside, and we were out of the jam. Alex protected that 3-2 lead, and emerged as the popular hero of the series.

There was a great celebration on the way home. Alexander drank enough black coffee to float a battleship as we tried to have him in condition for the reception we knew was ahead. But the old boy stayed in character.

"They're calling me a hero, eh?" he said quietly. "Well, do you know what? If that line drive Lazzeri hit had been fair, Tony would be the hero and I'd be just an old bum."

They say that no New York celebration over a Lindbergh or a returning army ever was a greater demonstration than the one they held in St. Louis when the city finally had a winner after such a long famine. But you never know what's going to happen in baseball. I certainly had no idea, returning to the city where I started my major-league career, that I'd be wearing a different uniform the next season.

* * *

In those days, the Cardinals were a poor club, compared to some controlled by wealthy men in larger cities. The only big crowds were on Sundays and during the deciding days of a pennant race. So the Cardinals booked exhibition games on every available day. The club picked up a few thousand dollars extra that way. It was an exhibition game that caused my trouble with Sam Breadon.

When the 1926 season started, I believed we had a chance and was proved right, as I have related. We had a small squad, with no reserves to play those exhibitions. So I asked Breadon if he wouldn't write to the promoters of some of those exhibitions and try to cancel the games.

Breadon saw our side of it, all right. It so happened that the timing was bad when he finally brought us the bad news that we'd have to go through with all those exhibition games. We had just lost a tough game to the Pirates. It was a typical clubhouse scene of a pennant contender that had just lost one that might have been won.

It might have been different if Breadon had waited until we all cooled off. I suppose I spoke more bluntly than usual. I told him what I thought of exhibition games and people who would book them to take away the days of rest that ballplayers needed. He was flushed and angry when he left the clubhouse. I believe he made up his mind then and there that, come pennant or last place, Hornsby wouldn't be with the Cardinals the next season.

Breadon went through the motions of trying to sign me to a contract for the 1927 season. But I wanted two years at least. It was pretty much of a surprise to me when I was informed that I had been traded to the New York Giants for Frankie Frisch and pitcher Jimmy Ring a few short months after that pennant celebration in the streets of St. Louis.

I thought I got along pretty well with John McGraw, the Giant manager. He wanted to win and I wanted to win, and that was all we had to have in common. His health wasn't very good that year and, on several occasions, he turned over the active management to me.

It was on one of those trips, filling in for McGraw, that there was an incident that resulted in my leaving the club, I believe. We were playing in Chicago, and we lost a tough one to the Cubs. Travis Jackson missed what looked like an easy grounder. Cub runners scored from second and third on the error, to turn what promised to be a victory into a defeat.

The traveling secretary with the club was named Jim Tierney. There was a story that he had done some great favor for the owner of the Giants, Charles Stoneham. He was waiting for me after that game. Tierney started blasting Jackson for making that error. What Tierney said certainly burned me. I told him all he had to do was get the train tickets and arrange the hotel rooms, and not to be blasting Jackson because he happened to make an error.

Nobody ever bothered to give me an explanation of why I was traded to the Boston Braves after that season. I'm certain in my own mind that when I bawled out Tierney I was writing out my transfer from the Giants.

McGraw had talked Judge Emil Fuchs into buying the Braves. Jack Slattery was the new manager. I guess I was getting three or four times as much money, as second baseman, as Slattery was as manager. I was afraid people might think I wanted Slattery's job. When Fuchs broached the subject of making a change, after the club got off to a bad start, I objected strenuously. Slattery resigned, however, and there was nothing for me to do but to accept the job.

The Boston Braves' ball park is supposed to be a poor place for hitters, but it didn't bother me any. I got enough hits to lead the league with .387. About the end of the 1928 season, the pennant bee had begun to buzz in Chicago. William Wrigley, Jr., Bill Veeck, Sr., general manager for the Cubs, and Manager Joe McCarthy decided that if they could just add a little to their batting power they could win in 1929.

It was a new experience for me, after being fired at St. Louis and traded without warning by the Giants, to have a club owner tell me he didn't want to get rid of me.

Judge Fuchs told me the Cubs had offered a lot of dough and several players. The judge was a soft-spoken man, and I always felt like it wasn't right to swear in his presence. But I forgot myself and told him he'd be a goddamn fool if he didn't take the offer.

The judge surprised me when he decided to become manager in 1929, my first year at Chicago. Some of the stories told about the judge's career are hard to believe. One day, with the bases loaded and nobody out, he is supposed to have turned to the bench and asked, "What shall we try now, boys?"

"What about a squeeze play?" someone said.

"A squeeze? Oh, no," protested the judge. "Let us score our runs in an honorable way."

The deal that sent me to Chicago turned out all right for a club that paid a lot of money to fill one spot. The Cubs won the pennant my first year in Chicago, and I helped a little by hitting .380. Hack Wilson had a great season, driving in 159 runs. He was a great hitter. But while he had a couple of outstanding years, he ruined his health by not taking care of himself.

I didn't do so good in the World Series that fall, striking out eight times. All the Cubs had trouble. Thirteen of us fanned in each of the first two games. We lost four out of five to the Philadelphia Athletics, including one game none of us will ever forget—the time we had an 8-0 lead as late as the seventh inning.

Hack Wilson had his biggest year in 1930, but everybody was still moaning about our sorry showing in the World Series. Before the season ended, McCarthy was informed that the job of managing the Yankees was open to him. William Wrigley and Bill Veeck asked if I would take charge of the ball club.

We finished third in 1931. But we were getting along all right, and I figured we'd make it in 1932. The Cubs had bought a young outfielder named Frank Demaree on a look-see basis. Now, you can look over a ballplayer in batting and fielding practice and not know too much about him. We couldn't afford to experiment or test out any rookies during our fight for first place, but the only way you can judge a ballplayer accurately is to see what he can do when the chips are down.

One afternoon, we needed a pinch hitter. I sent in Demaree. It was a perfect setting for a trial. Well, Demaree didn't get a hit that particular time at bat. Bill Veeck asked me why the hell I had sent in Demaree in a clutch like that. He said I should have hit myself.

Once more, I spoke too bluntly to the front office. I didn't like anybody in the front office telling me, who happened to be the manager, how to run the club. If he didn't like the way I was running the ball club, he could get himself another manager.

Veeck got himself another manager. He fired me and appointed Charlie Grimm.

They always said the Cubs didn't like me and were happy when Grimm was made manager. Well, that's all right. I never asked ballplayers to like me. All I asked was for them to give a good day's work and play to win.

I was nearly 37 years old, but Sam Breadon was persuaded by Branch Rickey that I still might be able to help the Cardinals with my hitting. The old story that I had been fired from Chicago for betting on the horses was going the rounds. Judge Landis had called me to his office one time and asked if it was true I bet on the horses. I told him I certainly did. He said that wasn't a thing for a ballplayer to do, and I told him I didn't think it was anybody's business what I did with my money. He never did tell me I was behind the eight ball or would be barred. But I understand Landis got pretty mad when Rickey insisted I ought to have a chance in my profession. But Rickey outtalked the judge. So I joined the Cardinals.

Past the middle of July, Rickey told me that Phil Ball, owner of the Browns, was interested in having me take over the job of managing the St. Louis American League club. I could have the job if Ball and I could hit it off together. Mr. Ball was a blunt man who said what he had to say without any fancy words. That's the way I like it. The Cardinals gave me my unconditional release July 25, and the next day I took over as manager of the Browns. Mr. Ball and I had a perfect understanding. He never bothered me about the running of the baseball side. Money didn't make any difference to him.

What happened on a rainy afternoon will illustrate what I mean. The umpires figured we'd call the game and schedule a double-header some other day. Mr. Ball was told there weren't any people in the stands, and it would be bad business to start the game.

"I'm here, ain't I?" Mr. Ball said. "I don't care how many people are here. I came out to see a ball game. Go ahead and play it if I'm the only one here."

I believe Mr. Ball and I would have got along great. But before another season opened, he died, and the ball club passed into the hands of the estate, which isn't a good situation for a baseball business.

It was just four days short of four years after I took over the job as manager for Mr. Ball that I was fired. Bobo Newsom figures in that story.

I never promised anybody anything about what I would do with my private life. It was this belief that my private life is my own business, and that I have a right to invest my money the way I please, on horses, if I wish, that figured in my leaving the Browns in 1937.

One day in St. Louis, I got a telegram from my handicapper giving me three horses for a round-robin bet. I phoned to a bookmaker in St. Louis and made a long-distance call to Chicago and placed a bet. As I was leaving the booth, a group of Red Sox players passed. Bobo Newsom grabbed the telegram. Then Newsom and another player or two went across the street where a guy was running a handbook and bet on the three horses, round robin, just like I did.

Well, the three horses won. I collected a good chunk of dough. It so happened that in the handbook saloon they had a good lunch counter, and Bill DeWitt, general manager for Don Barnes, new owner of the club, ate there. Naturally, there was a lot of talk about the bets.

At the time, I was buying some stock in the investment company that Barnes headed, a small loan company. I still owed him $4,000. When I gave Barnes the check for $4,000, he asked me where I got that money.

"I won it," I told him honestly. "How the hell do you think I'd get it?"

The next day, Barnes told me that the cashier's check had been traced to a bookmaker, and he didn't want to take that kind of money for his stock.

"I won that fair and square," I countered. "It's as good as the money you take from people in your small-loan business."

That was it. Barnes and DeWitt fired me. I hadn't made any promises not to bet on the races. This is a free country.

Between the time I left the major leagues in 1937 and returned in 1952, I bounced around from job to job, getting too old to play, but not too old still to love the game that had been my life.

Baseball men showed considerable interest in acquiring my services as manager after the Beaumont club won the pennant in the Texas League in 1950, but the interest was still strictly in the minor-league field. I got an offer to manage Seattle. Maybe they thought it was an accident that the Beaumont club did all right. But when the Seattle club won in the Coast League, the situation changed. At long last, major-league clubs began to show an interest in Hornsby, and I received several offers. I picked the Browns because they were

down, and I believed there was a greater opportunity to get results. I was to be complete boss on the field. Bill Veeck, who had just bought the Browns, had been close to baseball most of his life. I figured he'd be easier to work with.

I contend that the spirit of the Browns squad was good. Nobody complained about working too hard. Unfortunately, some of the players didn't show consistent major-league ability immediately. I guess it was the old, old story. You have to win in this business—win or else. Apparently there were some grousers, and apparently Veeck took their complaints seriously. When he came to Boston and fired me, he obviously was doing something he had decided on doing some time before. There wasn't any haggling over our contract settlement. It was just another firing of Hornsby, until the newspapers of the country carried photographs of the players presenting a trophy to Veeck as a token of their pleasure at my being fired. The trophy was inscribed as a reward for "the greatest play since the Emancipation Proclamation." The story the Browns gave out was that the players chipped in dough and that it was the players' idea. However, I got many telephone calls and messages from players, assuring me they had nothing to do with the trophy.

The fact that a ball club fires you or several give you the gate doesn't put you behind the eight ball, like I imagine you'd be if you were canned by several banks or industrial concerns. I wasn't out of work very long. Before some of the Brownie ballplayers had time to learn what the Emancipation Proclamation really was, I was signed to manage the Reds.

When you are fired from a big-league club, it stays with you, mornings, afternoons, evenings and nights, for a long time. But I couldn't find that I had done anything that I would want to change.

I figured the players on the Cincinnati ball club probably would expect to see a fellow with horns. I tried to straighten out the players in the first clubhouse meeting.

"Some of you guys may have heard that I was tough," I told the squad. "If wanting to win is being tough, I guess I am tough. I've always done my best, as a player, an instructor, and as a manager. That's all I will ask of you."

A DECADE or so ago, the Chicago *Daily News,* under the supervision of its gifted sports editor, John P. Carmichael, ran an utterly fascinating series called "My Biggest Baseball Day." The series later was put into book form, then appeared as a pocket edition. Here is one of half a dozen from that collection that you will find in this book (there were 47 in all, I believe). To the speaker's rostrum, Mr. Carl Hubbell. Even grandmothers (see page 270) remember *his* greatest day.

The 1934 All-Star Game

CARL HUBBELL
as told to JOHN P. CARMICHAEL

I CAN REMEMBER Frankie Frisch coming off the field behind me at the end of the third inning, grunting to Bill Terry: "I could play second base fifteen more years behind that guy. He doesn't need any help. He does it all by himself." Then we hit the bench, and Terry slapped me on the arm and said: "That's pitching, boy!" and Gabby Hartnett let his mask fall down and yelled at the American League dugout: "We gotta look at that all season," and I was pretty happy.

As far as control and "stuff" is concerned, I never had any more in my life than for that All-Star game in 1934. But I never was a strikeout pitcher like Bob Feller or "Dizzy" Dean or "Dazzy" Vance. My style of pitching was to make the other team hit the ball, but on the ground. It was as big a surprise to me to strike out all those fellows as it probably was to them. Before the game, Hartnett and I went down the lineup—Gehringer, Manush, Ruth, Gehrig, Foxx, Simmons, Cronin, Dickey and Gomez. There wasn't a pitcher they'd ever faced that they hadn't belted one off him somewhere, sometime.

We couldn't discuss weaknesses . . . they didn't have any, except Gomez. Finally Gabby said: "We'll waste everything except the screwball. Get that over, but keep your fast ball and hook outside. We can't let 'em hit in the air." So that's the way we started. I knew I had only three innings to work and could bear down on every pitch.

They talk about those All-Star games being exhibition affairs and maybe they are, but I've seen very few players in my life who didn't want to win, no matter whom they were playing or what for. If I'm playing cards for pennies, I want to win. How can you feel any other way? Besides, there were 50,000 fans or more there, and they wanted to see the best you've got. There was an obligation to the people, as well as to ourselves, to go all out. I can recall walking out to the hill in the Polo Grounds that day and looking around the stands and thinking to myself: "Hub, they want to see what you've got."

Gehringer was first up and Hartnett called for a waste ball just so I'd get the feel of the first pitch. It was a little too close, and Charley singled. Down from one of the stands came a yell: "Take him out!"

I had to laugh.

Terry took a couple of steps off first and hollered: "That's all right," and there was Manush at the plate. If I recollect rightly, I got two strikes on him, but then he refused to swing any more, and I lost him. He walked. This time Terry and Frisch and Pie Traynor and Travis Jackson all came over to the mound and began worrying. "Are you all right?" Bill asked me. I assured him I was. I could hear more than one voice now from the stands: "Take him out before it's too late."

Well, I could imagine how they felt with two on, nobody out and Ruth at bat. To strike him out was the last thought in my mind. The thing was to make him hit on the ground. He wasn't too fast, as you know, and he'd be a cinch to double. He never took the bat off his shoulder. You could have pushed me over with your little finger. I fed him three straight screwballs, all over the plate, after wasting a fast ball, and he stood there. I can see him looking at the umpire on "You're out," and he wasn't mad. He just didn't believe it, and Hartnett was laughing when he threw the ball back.

So up came Gehrig. He was a sharp hitter. You could double him, too, now and then, if the ball was hit hard and straight at an infielder. That's what we hoped he'd do, at best. Striking out Ruth and Gehrig in succession was too big an order. By golly, he fanned . . . and on four pitches. He swung at the last screwball, and you should have heard that crowd. I felt a lot easier then, and even when Gehringer and Manush pulled a double steal and got to third and second, with Foxx up, I looked down at Hartnett and caught the screwball sign, and Jimmy missed. We were really trying to strike Foxx out, with two already gone, and Gabby didn't bother to waste any pitches. I threw three more screwballs, and he went down swinging. We had set down the side on twelve pitches, and then Frisch hit a homer in our half of the first, and we were ahead.

It was funny, when I thought of it afterwards, how Ruth and Gehrig looked as they stood there. The Babe must have been waiting for me to get the ball up a little so he could get his bat under it. He always was trying for that one big shot at the stands, and anything around his knees, especially a twisting ball, didn't let him get any leverage. Gehrig apparently decided to take one swing at least and

he beat down at the pitch, figuring to take a chance on being doubled if he could get a piece of the ball. He whispered something to Foxx as Jim got up from the batter's circle and while I didn't hear it, I found out later he said: "You might as well cut . . . it won't get any higher." At least Foxx wasted no time.

Of course the second inning was easier because Simmons and Cronin both struck out with nobody on base and then I got too close to Dickey and he singled. Simmons and Foxx, incidentally, both went down swinging and I know every pitch to them was good enough to hit at and those they missed had a big hunk of the plate. Once Hartnett kinda shook his head at me as if to say I was getting too good. After Dickey came Gomez and as he walked into the box he looked down at Gabby and said: "You are now looking at a man whose batting average is .104. What the hell am I doing up here?" He was easy after all those other guys and we were back on the bench again.

We were all feeling pretty good by this time and Traynor began counting on his fingers: "Ruth, Gehrig, Foxx, Simmons, Cronin! Hey, Hub, do you put anything on the ball?" Terry came over to see how my arm was, but it never was stronger. I walked one man in the third . . . don't remember who it was . . . but this time Ruth hit one on the ground and we were still all right. You could hear him puff when he swung. That was all for me. Afterward, they got six runs in the fifth and licked us, but for three innings I had the greatest day in my life. One of the writers who kept track told me that I'd pitched 27 strikes and 21 balls to 13 men and only 5 pitches were hit in fair territory.

ONE OF America's foremost poets, Rolfe Humphries, was awarded the 1956 Fellowship of the Academy of American Poets, largest award of its kind, for outstanding achievement.

Polo Grounds

ROLFE HUMPHRIES

Time is of the essence. This is a highly skilled
And beautiful mystery. Three or four seconds only
From the time that Riggs connects till he reaches first,
And in those seconds Jurges goes to his right,
Comes up with the ball, tosses to Witek at second
For the force on Reese, Witek to Mize at first,
In time for the out—a double play.

(Red Barber crescendo. Crowd noises, obbligato;
Scattered staccatos from the peanut boys,
Loud in the lull, as the teams are changing sides . . .)

Hubbell takes the sign, nods, pumps, delivers—
A foul into the stands. Dunn takes a new ball out,
Hands it to Danning, who throws it down to Werber;
Werber takes off his glove, rubs the ball briefly,
Tosses it over to Hub, who goes to the rosin bag,
Takes the sign from Danning, pumps, delivers—
Low, outside, ball three. Danning goes to the mound,
Says something to Hub, Dunn brushes off the plate,
Adams starts throwing in the Giant bull pen,
Hub takes the sign from Danning, pumps, delivers,
Camilli gets ahold of it, a *long* fly to the outfield,
Ott goes back, back, back, against the wall, gets under it,
Pounds his glove, and takes it for the out.
That's all for the Dodgers. . . .

Time is of the essence. The rhythms break,
More varied and subtle than any kind of dance;
Movement speeds up or lags. The ball goes out
In sharp and angular drives, or long, slow arcs,
Comes in again controlled and under aim;
The players wheel or spurt, race, stoop, slide, halt,
Shift imperceptibly to new positions,
Watching the signs, according to the batter,
The score, the inning. Time is of the essence.

Time is of the essence. Remember Terry?
Remember Stonewall Jackson, Lindstrom, Frisch,
When they were good? Remember Long George Kelly?
Remember John McGraw and Benny Kauff?

Polo Grounds

Remember Bridwell, Tenney, Merkle, Youngs,
Chief Meyers, Big Jeff Tesreau, Shufflin' Phil?
Remember Mathewson, and Ames, and Donlin,
Buck Ewing, Rusie, Smiling Mickey Welch?
Remember a left-handed catcher named Jack Humphries,
Who sometimes played the outfield, in '83?

Time is of the essence. The shadow moves
From the plate to the box, from the box to second base,
From second to the outfield, to the bleachers.

Time is of the essence. The crowd and players
Are the same age always, but the man in the crowd
Is older every season. Come on, play ball!

The Hummingbird, by Owen Johnson, is out of print now, but it may have been the very best of the Lawrenceville stories that made their author, a Lawrenceville graduate, as famous as such of his schoolboy characters as Hungry Smeed and Dink Stover. Of *The Hummingbird,* Thomas L. Stix wrote that it was, "Perhaps as good a kid's baseball story as was ever written. . . . If you can find a copy of that classic of the early years of this century—read it and weep." Here is an excerpt from Johnson's book-length classic. Read it, but not necessarily to weep. Here we have Dennis de Brian de Boru Finnegan, age twelve, turned baseball writer for *The Lawrence,* the school paper.

Finnegan and the Great American Epic

——————— OWEN JOHNSON ———————

The Lawrence usually is languidly circulated on a Saturday. On the present occasion, twenty minutes after it was put on sale the faculty telephones were buzzing with excited inquiries, while Bingham, standing at his receiver, gazed in horror at a copy of *The Lawrence* and sought in a dazed way to explain to each rapidly succeeding inquirer just how it had happened. Meanwhile a crowd of delirious non-subscribers was storming *The Lawrence* editor and offering twenty-five cents each for the remaining copies of the following picturesque account, which Bingham still gazed at in classic horror:

SPINKED!

LAWRENCEVILLE SPANKS THE PIPPIN
ON THE NOSE!

LAWRENCEVILLE, 6; PRINCETON, 1

Barrett, the peerless one, the nifty ten-thousand-dollar beauty from Walla Walla, was in form—that's all. His delivery would have kept a cryptograph specialist figuring through the night. His outdrop had the Princeton scrub carving arabesques on the ozone in mad, frantic, muscle-racking lunges for the elusive horsehide. He had 'em digging trenches with his drops and climbing for cherries with his high ones. He had 'em reaching for the wide ones, like July tomcats sitting on the edge of a fountain and striking for goldfish.

Ross, the scrub pitcher, was very much appreciated by our favorite sons. They bumped him for five ordinaries, soaked a couple of repeats, spanked a three-sacker and smeared the bun for one smoking, sizzling homer.

SCORE BY INNINGS

Smith, the first to lift the locust for the Jungle Puppies, pushed a hoist to Wallader, who swallowed it without blinking. Hanson frisked the daisy-tops with a whistler that Hicks gobbled up and posted to Stevens. Branch stung a broiler that DeSoto stonewalled and wafted to first.

For Lawrenceville, Charlie DeSoto lounged until he drew four misfits, burglared the second story, and whisked to third when Hickey spilled a Texas Leaguer to right. Wallader jolted a fast bounder to second, which Hanson congealed in time to slaughter Hickey at the midway, DeSoto sneaking up the home boulevard with the first brass ring. Butcher Stevens pushed a blue-domer to center. Hastings slapped a screamer over first and, when the footrace was over, Wallader was carving his initials on the doormat and our Bill was dusting third. Billy Barnes held up two strikes and three balls to draw for fours, but got three of a kind instead. Hard luck, Bill!

SECOND INNING

Oberfield miscued twice and then shot a safe one over second pocket. Maguire was out on a floater to Hickey. Ross died in his tracks on three fractures, and Hickson chopped a playful one to DeSoto, who jabbed it into Oberfield, making the third demise.

Flash Condit worked out a pass. Cap Keefer, our cerise specialist, could do no better than a gentle winger to center, Barrett nicked one to the chicken coop, which Maguire annexed, while De-Soto raised a steeplechaser which scratched the nebulae.

THIRD INNING

Our peerless one's assorted strikes continued as deceptive as the green spectacles the farmer put on the cow who wouldn't eat straw.

Wright was sent up for three murderous assaults, Rogers diverted one to the poultry yard, Cap Keefer hugged it, and Smith popped up to Wallader.

Hickey refused to bite on a wild one and splashed a rippler over third. Wallader expired to send him to Second Avenue with a slow chugger to third; Butcher Stevens caught a sweeper on the solar plexus and hammered it where the nightingale warbles its plaintive lays. Hickey ambled home, and Butcher Stevens roosted on third. Billy Barnes went after a fadeaway and died on a zephyr to the curve-box. Flash Condit received the courtesy of the house and toddled, but Keefer was slaughtered on a twister that beat him to first by the Ross-Smith route.

FOURTH INNING

Things looked as squally as an actors' boarding-house when the invited guest takes two charlotte russes on the first pass. Hanson reached the initial hassock on a butterfinger specialty of Wallader's. Branch dropped a hot one in left field, Maguire poached another on the same order, Hanson dusting the pan. Ross showed himself a cute little waiter and strolled as a deadhead, filling the bases. Hickson smote a broncho-buster to Hickey, who massacred it and nailed Branch to the rubber; Hickson bit the dust on Keefer's quick flip to first. Wright ended the suspense by boosting a ladybird to short.

At this point, Mr. Bingham's self-possession completely deserted him. He fell into an easy chair, ran his lank fingers wildly through his hair and stared at *The Lawrence* in awe, amazement and consternation.

At this moment, who should come in smiling but Dennis de Brian de Boru Finnegan in the flesh. A smile of perfect content was on the young revolutionist, while his right hand held proudly secure his next installment.

"Finnegan," said Bingham, waving *The Law-rence* toward him. "Did you—? Is this your work?"

"Why, yes, sir," said Finnegan brightly. "How did you like it?"

Mr. Bingham slowly collected his wits, and his feelings turned from awe to admiration. What he wanted to say was: "Good Heavens, you extraordinary youngster, how did you ever concoct it?" But it is not always wise for a master to say what he thinks. There was the English of Spenser and Addison to be protected. So he simply stared.

"It was a bit rough, sir," said Finnegan apologetically, "but I've done better with this. I think it will please you."

"You have done another, Finnegan?"

"Why, yes, sir—yesterday's game. Would you like to hear it, sir?"

The expounder of the Elizabethan line drew his hand across his forehead, steadied himself and said: "You may begin, Finnegan."

Finnegan curled up on the sofa, flattened his manuscript over his knee, gazed at it fondly a moment and began as preface:

"I thought I'd tell the story by innings, sir. It makes it more dramatic, I think, than to give a résumé first."

"Is that a criticism on modern journalism, Finnegan?"

"Well, sir," said Finnegan with unusual modesty, "I think this is an improvement. It holds you in suspense—gives you the feeling of being there, you know."

"Go on, Finnegan."

" 'Lawrenceville, 5; Pennington, 4,' " said Finnegan. " 'In the breakaway Tyrell, the first to dust the rubber for the Chaperons—' "

"Chaperons?" said Bingham, puzzled.

"It's co-ed, you know, sir. 'Chaperons' gives rather a touch of humor, don't you think?"

"I see."

" 'In the breakaway Tyrell, the first to dust the rubber for the Chaperons, selected a hole in the circumambient and poked a buzzer over short . . .' "

"Go slow, Finnegan."

"Yes, sir—'Minds soaked a clover-kisser to the far station, which Wallader kittened to and whipped to first . . .' "

"I don't get that, Finnegan."

"What is it, sir?"

"Well, the whole episode is a trifle hazy. What is a clover-kisser?"

"Why, a daisy-scorcher, sir."

"You mean a grounder?"

"A certain kind of grounder, sir, very low—

one that doesn't rise from the grass. Quite difdrent from a broncho-buster or a dewdrop, sir."

"I'm afraid I have specialized too much in medieval English; what is this thing you call 'a broncho-buster'?"

"A broncho-buster is a grounder, a rather tabasco grounder, that bucks and kicks."

"Very lucid, Finnegan, and a 'dewdrop'?"

"Why, that's a weakling—a toddler—all luck, you know."

"Ah, yes. Now let me think. Wallader stopped the daisy-scorcher—"

"Clover-kisser, sir."

"Exactly. So Wallader stopped it and retired the man at first?"

"Why, yes, sir."

"Proceed, Finnegan, proceed."

" 'Tyrell, who had purloined the second perch, started to ramble to Walladersburg when Jackson stung the planet DeSoto-wise for a safety, but our iridescent little body-snatcher lassoed it and slaughtered the rally with a staccato lunge to the midway that completed the double demise.' "

"Ah yes, that is simpler," said the master gravely. "Now for Lawrenceville."

" 'DeSoto streaked the empyrean blue with a white winger that was strangled in center.' "

"A fly, Finnegan?"

"Yes, sir."

"Just an ordinary fly?"

"Oh no, sir, a rather high one."

"Continue."

" 'Hickey ticked off a slow freight to the pretzel counter and cannon-balled to first just ahead of Tyrell's slap.' "

"Let us go back."

"Why, what's wrong, sir?"

"Ticked off a slow freight?"

"Bunted a slow one."

"Naturally—but pretzel counter?"

"The curve-box—the pitcher."

"Of course!"

" 'Stevens frisked the lozenge once to the backwoods and then unmuzzled a hummingbird to the prairies which nested in Jackson's twigs—' "

"Repeat that."

" 'Stevens unmuzzled a humming bird which—' "

"I don't like unmuzzled."

"I could say uncorked, sir."

"No, I don't fancy uncorked, either."

"Unhitched, then."

"Never unhitched. The fact is, the use of the word hummingbird in this connection does not seem to me appropriate at all."

Finnegan looked very solemn and said with difficulty: "Please, sir, I would like to keep that expression, sir. I'm rather proud of that. A hummingbird is a liner, you know, that hums. Please, sir, I hope you'll let me leave that in?"

"Finnegan," said Mr. Bingham with difficult gravity, "you may as well know the truth now. We have decided to adhere to the English of our fathers."

"I beg pardon."

"I mean that I shall have to edit your copy in future down to the comprehension of the most ignorant college graduate."

"Isn't the grammar right, sir?"

"The grammar is irreproachable."

"What are you going to do, sir?"

"I'm going to translate, Finnegan."

"Translate!"

"And you're going to help me, Finnegan," said Bingham, taking up paper and pencil. "From what I gather the first inning should begin like this: 'Tyrell singled. Minds was out on a grounder to Wallader, Tyrell, who had started for third, was caught off second on DeSoto's brilliant catch of Jackson's liner.' "

Finnegan sat silent, staring at his thumbs.

"Is that the way it's got to be done?" he said at last.

"I'm afraid so, Finnegan."

"You're not going to leave in the hummingbird, sir?"

"I'm afraid not, Finnegan. 'Unmuzzled' or 'uncorked' or 'unchained' a 'hummingbird' is daring, enthusiastic and undoubtedly expressive, but at the present moment the English Department of the Lawrenceville School does not feel strong enough to offer it to the nation."

"What are you going to do with it?" said Finnegan abruptly.

"We'll say: 'Stevens' sizzling liner went straight into the mitt of—' "

"I won't sign it," said Finnegan hoarsely.

"No, Finnegan, you shall not be subjected to that humiliation."

"You won't let it stand, sir?" said Finnegan, with a last hope.

"No, Finnegan."

"Then I *resign!*" said Finnegan, walking out of the room with trembling lips.

The shock was terrific. Nobody could console him, not even the Tennessee Shad, who told him for his consolation how Keats and Shelley, English poets, had been cut off in the flower of youth by just such savage critics. For two whole days Irish remained dumb, to the great alarm of the entire house.

Then suddenly, as though nothing had happened, he turned up as voluble as ever. But if outwardly he seemed to have forgotten, inwardly he cherished a mighty scheme of revenge. The Woodhull must taste the bitter dregs of defeat—Bingham was the master of the Woodhull.

JOHN KIERAN ran this poem in his *New York Times* column **twice** in 1927. The second time was the day after Babe Ruth hit his sixtieth home run of the season.

A Query

JOHN KIERAN

You may sing your song of the good old days
    till the phantom cows come home;
You may dig up glorious deeds of yore from
    many a dusty tome;
You may rise to tell of Rube Waddell and the
    way he buzzed them through,
And top it all with the great fast ball that
    Rusie's rooters knew.
You may rant of Brouthers, Keefe and Ward
    and half a dozen more;
You may quote by rote from the record book in
    a way that I deplore;
You may rave, I say, till the break of day, but
    the truth remains the truth:
From "One Old Cat" to the last "At Bat," was
    there ever a guy like Ruth?

He can start and go, he can catch and throw,
    he can field with the very best.
He's the Prince of Ash and the King of Crash,
    and that's not an idle jest.
He can hit that ball o'er the garden wall, high
    up and far away,
Beyond the aftermost picket lines where the
    fleetfoot fielders stray.
He's the Bogey Man of the pitching clan and
    he clubs 'em soon and late;
He has manned his guns and and hit home
    runs from here to the Golden Gate;
With vim and verve he has walloped the curve
    from Texas to Duluth,
Which is no small task, and I beg to ask: Was
    there ever a guy like Ruth?

A BOOK at least as big as this one would be needed to define, assay, and delineate the function of the ghost writer. Here is one of a number of ghosted pieces in this anthology, this one handled by the brilliant Bill Slocum. The "and/with/as-told-to" craft is tough work for the writer. People like to hear from famous men. High among the famous in baseball is the late, great umpire Bill Klem. As you read his fascinating story, from *Collier's* of March 1951, note for what it is worth—and it is worth more than a little—Klem's choice for the best player of all time—Honus Wagner, the Flying Dutchman.

"I Never Missed One in My Heart"

—————— **BILL KLEM,** *with* **BILL SLOCUM** ——————

WHEN the Miami sun is hot and bright, and I'm up to it, I rest outdoors and listen to the waters of Biscayne Bay lap against my sea wall. My wife, Marie, reads me the baseball news in the morning, and in the evening the radio tells me what the boys have been doing. My eyes have gone so bad I cannot read and no man living has enough guts to be completely philosophical about that. But there is one consolation. It seems, as the years go on and the light grows dimmer, that the faces and deeds of great men I have known grow clearer. I relive a half-century of laughter and battle, victory and defeat, and wonderful friendships. I enjoy it and perhaps you will enjoy sharing some of these memories with me.

I can still see a wild-eyed Philadelphia fan poised on the edge of a box preparing to jump on me after I had forfeited a game to Pittsburgh because the Phillies were stalling for darkness. As he coiled for the spring a ballplayer, bat in hand, stepped beside me and yelled, "If you jump, mister, I'll knock your head off with this bat." The man didn't jump and the ballplayer cleared a path for me with his bat through the milling mob.

My protector was Hans Wagner, as great a man as he was a ballplayer. He was the best I ever saw—and I saw them all in the last sixty years.

And I can remember going to bed at seven-thirty one night in St. Louis because I was to work behind the plate the next day in a World Series game. About midnight I was unable to sleep because I was hungry, so I went out for a sandwich. As I left the hotel I saw three sports writers, all feeling no pain, get out of a taxicab. They tried to convince a fourth man to join them, but he roared, "Go on, you sissies, I'm going back." And back he went. He stayed out until 4:00 A.M. And the next afternoon at the ball park he looked like what he was—a ballplayer who hadn't been to bed. He looked that way until I yelled, "Play ball!" and before the afternoon was done he had belted three tremendous home runs. It was Babe Ruth, of course.

They insist upon making a plaster hero of the Babe in death. I don't know why, because he was a decent man who loved and lived the full life but did no harm as he passed this way, and he did an awful lot of good. It was risky business to set Babe loose in a room filled with sheltered ladies. You could bet he would let slip a word or tell a story within fifteen minutes that would make the ladies, and some of the gentlemen, long for that shelter. But you could turn Babe loose in a hospital room filled with sick kids and watch miracles unfold before your eyes.

Babe's appetites were his only concern, except children. This devotion to children was as genuine as his talent for playing baseball. One of his ghost writers, who knew him as well as any man in the world, once told me, "For every picture you see of Babe with kids in one hospital or another, he visits ten without fanfare, publicity or even the slightest idea of the name of the hospital.

"When we're on the road," the writer continued, "the Babe will pass me in the lobby about ten o'clock. He's going out to paint the town red; I'm going to bed. Babe will say, 'I told some guy I'd go to a hospital tomorrow morning at eight. Named Saint something-or-other. Meet me at seven-thirty tomorrow morning and we'll go together.' Next morning the Babe is on hand, whether he's been to sleep or not. And sometimes he hasn't."

Lou Gehrig was a kindly man and my friend of many a pleasant evening. Lou once asked me a favor which I couldn't perform. I was umpiring in a World Series at second base when Lou came to bat. He motioned to me to move, and I stepped a few feet closer to first base. He waved again and I moved no more, so he stepped out of the box and beckoned to Yankee coach Art Fletcher. Fletcher and Lou talked, and then Fletch came over with a message.

"Lou wants you to move behind the third-base side of second, Bill," Fletcher said.

"Tell him I wouldn't move to the other side of second base for my own mother. I'd be out of position. And what difference does it make to him, anyhow?"

"Aw, I'll tell you the truth, Bill. He's superstitious about where the umpire stands."

I stood my ground and the mighty Gehrig unloaded one of his patented power drives that would have taken my head out to center field had I not ducked. To his last day Gehrig could summon up the strength to laugh about that. "When I tell you to move, Wilyum, you better move," he'd say. "Remember how I 'moved' you in a Series game?"

I call men like Ruth, Gehrig and Wagner "champions." To me a "champion" is a man who is a full cut above most of us in class and courage and charm. Dizzy Dean is one of my champions. The first time I saw him he was a fresh busher blazing third strikes past the batters. He struck out the third man in an inning and, strutting by me, he said, "What did you think of that?"

"You're going to be great," I answered. I think my gentle reply surprised Dizzy because he stopped and said, "You think that's good pitching? Wait'll you see my brother Paul. He's even better."

The man who brought Dizzy to the National League, Branch Rickey, is a "champion," too. In my opinion Branch Rickey, and his farm systems, saved the National League. The American League was spending all the money and getting all the great young players. Had it not been for the stars developed in the St. Louis Cardinal chain, I shudder to think of the massacres that would have occurred in All-Star games and World Series. What *has* happened to the National League in those contests is nothing to be happy about, but had it not been for Rickey they would have been no-contests.

I remember umpiring a game for the Cardinals at their spring base in Bradenton, Florida, in the early twenties and driving up to Sarasota later to dine with John McGraw. When I entered his room I said, "John, I saw the greatest thing in my life today over at the Cardinals' park. They had 78 young ballplayers working out."

"Yeah, I know about it," McGraw answered. "It's the stupidest idea in baseball. What Rickey's trying to do can't be done."

"If they get two or three ballplayers out of that farm, it will be worth while," I argued.

"They'll go broke," John predicted. So we had another argument. But today we are at the point where a big-league club is only as good as its farm system.

And no roll of the champions can be compiled without including Uncle Robbie—Wilbert Robinson, of the old Orioles, manager of the Brooklyn Dodgers, and a gentleman in triumph and disaster. The only thing that would make Robbie mad at me was my refusal to play golf with him when his club was in the pennant race. Robbie had too much class to expect a favor from an umpire who was his golfing partner so he was always completely unimpressed when I pointed out that some of his rivals were not blessed with such gifts.

I remember Casey Stengel when he was playing for Robbie topping a roller down the first-base line. It went foul and I yelled, "Foul!" but it trickled back into fair territory. The first baseman grabbed it and tagged Casey, and I had to chirp, "You're out!" Casey was furious and Uncle Robbie came waddling out from the dugout to get in the battle.

I explained what had happened; the rule is quite clear. Robbie listened, then turned to Casey and said, "If Bill says you're out, you're out! Stop making so much noise and get back to the dugout."

How I enjoyed listening to the radio the last two years as Casey maneuvered his Yankees to the pennant. It was good to see a fine manager at last come into his own. I've always been both elated and irritated watching the great New York Yankees win pennant after pennant under the guidance of National Leaguers—Miller Huggins, Joe McCarthy and Casey Stengel. It was nice to know our league produced smart ballplayers. It was sad to realize we kept letting them get away.

The American League has come a long way since it first challenged the National in 1901. The junior circuit owes its success, first, to the driving, tenacious man who founded it, Ban Johnson. Then, the drawing power of Babe Ruth helped all the American League owners make money and most of them plowed some of it back for expensive young ballplayers. But I believe the current superiority of the American League will rapidly lessen under the influence of the freewheeling men who in recent years have bought teams in the National League. Six of the eight senior circuit teams are now under fairly new management and the other two, Chicago and New York, are in sound hands.

I remember, when I was in the American Association, I refused Johnson's offer to go to work for him, and signed with the National League instead. It was typical of Johnson that he took ten years to forgive me for exercising my right not to do his bidding. Everybody did Johnson's bidding as he set about welding together a powerhouse of a league. His owners finally had to curb his arrogance by discharging him. But his work had been well done.

Johnson's domineering personality made a mockery of the National Commission, the body that governed baseball before Landis. This commission consisted of three men—the president of each league and a chairman. But no chairman ever was a match for Johnson.

This anecdote is typical of Johnson's domineering tactics. Umpires had been getting $400 for umpiring a World Series and I led a revolt for more money. Garry Herrmann, chairman of the National Commission, agreed that it should be at least $1,000, but Johnson realized that I, the man who had turned him down, would benefit by the raise. So when we were paid off, we got only $650 each.

I refused to umpire another Series unless I got $1,000. Johnson was adamant. So was I. Johnson set $650 as the limit. So the National League paid the extra $350 out of its own funds. Thus a World Series was umpired with three umpires getting $650 each and the fourth, me, getting $1,000. In addition, I

signed a three-year umpiring contract, the first in baseball history.

The hiring of Landis was the thing that turned Johnson into a screaming harridan. And had Ban been just a little less arrogant he might have saved himself the crushing burden of dealing with the equally arrogant Landis. When the 1919 World Series began there were rumors that the White Sox had been fixed. After the first two games it was common talk, and John Heydler, at the time president of the National League, went secretly to Johnson to ask him to do something about the obvious larceny of the American League team.

Johnson's answer was typical. "You run your league," he told Heydler, "and I'll run mine."

The scandal that followed forced the panic-stricken magnates to hire Judge Landis to clean up baseball.

That phase of the famous "Black Sox" scandal has been told before, but while I'm about it, I would like to explore a theory of mine anent that mess. When I umpire for a player, I think I learn whether he's a man or not. I had umpired at one time or another for all the Black Sox and I say that the Chicago White Sox management must share the responsibility for the scandal with the fixers. The Chicago ballplayers with the exception of one man (Chick Gandil, the first baseman) were honest. But they were embittered weaklings. And they had every right to be embittered.

Charley Comiskey, who owned the White Sox, was a fine man. But he made a mistake in hiring his aide, Tip O'Neill. Tip signed the ballplayers for Comiskey and he took full and ruthless advantage of the reserve clause in the contract. The reserve clause, in effect, says that a ballplayer must accept whatever he is offered or stay out of baseball. It sounds inequitable and I suppose it is, although I think it is essential to the further growth of baseball. The rule today limits a club owner's authority to cut salaries to a maximum of 25 per cent. In the old days he could cut at will.

The White Sox players were superb. But they were working for peanuts. O'Neill fell back on his right to say to them, "Work for what I choose to pay or don't work." Baseball was their profession and they had to accept the chiseling terms. They were obviously a setup for the first gambler who could get to them. Gandil carried the message to White Sox players and it was roughly this: "Look, you're as good as anybody in baseball. You're hitting .340 and getting $3,500. Smith, with

New York or Detroit, can't carry your glove and he gets $7,000. You're being cheated."

So it was with several White Sox stars. Some players were smart enough or honest enough to shun the bribes. Others were not. Crooks are crooks and must be punished. But Tip O'Neill served his master too well. Better, I'm convinced, than his master wanted to be served.

I wonder what Judge Landis would have done had I reported the colorful Cuban pitcher, Adolfo Luque, for twice attempting to "tip" me. Barry McCormack and I were scheduled to work one day when Luque walked into our dressing room. "Beell, you gonna work behind the plate?" Luque asked.

"No, Barry is."

"Beell, I give you ten dollars you work behind plate, today."

"Why?"

"I'm gonna peetch. Ten dollars you ump."

"What's the matter with Barry?" I asked.

Luque nodded wisely. "Barry, heez all right. But you ump and I know how to peetch to them boms."

I told Luque he would get into trouble for that kind of nonsense and to get out. Two months later, in another park, he was back. "Beell, you ump today I geeve you $25." I gave the Cuban quite a tongue-lashing and he left.

Technically, I suppose, I was being bribed. But Luque didn't mean it that way. He just wanted to win a ball game and he was willing to pay for what he, in his great wisdom, considered superior umpiring. It means a lot to a pitcher to know a curve that nicks a corner of the plate will be called a strike and Luque simply thought I would not only call 'em as I saw 'em, but also see 'em correctly.

That wasn't always easy. I remember particularly, in a game between Chicago and St. Louis in 1934, a heavy wind was blowing. With the bases filled, a Chicago batter hit a towering fly that was buffeted about in the wind so much that the St. Louis infielders were lucky they weren't collectively skulled when it finally landed about twenty feet from home plate on the first-base side.

I ruled the ball was not an infield fly—and so an automatic out—because the infield fly is defined as a "ball that can reasonably be handled by the infielders, pitcher or catcher." Nobody in the St. Louis infield was ever in a position to claim he could handle that ball. But Frank Frisch protested the game on the spot. That night Sam Breadon, the Cardinals' owner,

sent in instructions to overrule me in the form of a protest.

I was not very worried for two reasons. In the first place I had made the same decision on the same grounds against Pittsburgh in 1921 and Barney Dreyfuss' protest had been tossed in the wastebasket. And, luckily for me, John Heydler, the man who would rule on Breadon's protest, was at the game and saw the disputed play. In my dressing room he assured me I had called it correctly.

But Breadon's pressure became severe and Heydler asked me to admit the ball was an infield fly and I was wrong. After my fifth refusal he agreed officially that Breadon was correct and my decision was reversed. When next I met Breadon he gloated, "Well, Bill, you missed one at last."

I answered, "I didn't miss it. You should know, Mr. Breadon, that I am not on the field to help out your club—or any club."

It was my opinion that the Cards were attempting to take advantage of the notoriously badly written rules of baseball. As I have said, they were written by gentlemen for gentlemen rather than by lawyers for lawyers. Therefore, they were frequently ambiguous. (They have been rewritten at long last and the new set went into effect with the start of the 1950 season.) A typical example is the batter who hits a home run and fails to touch second.

In my lifetime I have seen many runners fail to touch second as they trotted around the bases after clouting the ball out of the park. When the opposing team raised the point and demanded the home run hitter be called out for failing to touch a base I always said, "To me he touched second." And to me he did, the minute he hit the ball out of the park. The next time I saw the man who forgot to touch the bag I would say to him, "You know they put those bases out there to be tagged."

I have answered hundreds of knotty baseball problems in my life but I have no use for the hypothetical ones like, "Batter hits ball fairly over fence and breaks his leg going to first base." That, to me, is easy. When the fine gentlemen who wrote the rules phrased them, they assumed that in such a case it would be a home run. I always assumed the same thing.

The same goes for that old barroom chestnut: "Batter hits ball over the fence and drops dead." I have answered that one several hundred times thusly: "Send me a clipping of story of this odd occurrence and I'll send you the proper decision." Of course a runner who fails to touch second on an *inside*-the-park homer is out, if he gets caught. And play continues if a man is injured playing the ball or running the bases. However, for humanitarian reasons I refused to call an out on a player who, safe at third, snapped his leg in the slide and rolled off the base unconscious. I didn't think the original rule makers had broken legs in mind when they wrote the regulations about overslides.

Clark Griffith, the Old Fox, won a protest on one of my decisions in 1909 when he was managing Cincinnati. With men on bases and the great Honus Wagner at bat Griff wisely ordered Wagner purposely passed. With the count 3-0 and the fourth wide pitch en route, Wagner made a derisive gesture at the Cincinnati pitcher and crossed the plate on his way to first. Griff immediately protested that Wagner was out. "He stepped across the plate and interfered with the pitcher. Rule 44, Section 5," Griff complained in that high-pitched voice.

"You got just what you bargained for, Mr. Manager. A walk. Play ball."

The Old Fox smiled gleefully and said, "I'm continuing this game under protest." A few days later I was notified by John Heydler that Griffith's protest had been received and denied. Heydler told all umpires to do as I had done if the occasion arose again. But Griffith appealed to the league directors, George Dovey, Boston owner, Charles Ebbets, Brooklyn owner, and Charles Murphy, Chicago president. Dovey was disgusted by the protest and voted against Griffith. But Ebbets and Murphy voted for Griffith because, I surmised, they could thus hurt Barney Dreyfuss, owner of the Pittsburgh club and a man with whom they were feuding.

More than 39 years later a benighted manager attempted to pull a Griffith on umpire George Barr when Eddie Stanky did exactly what Hans Wagner had done. Barr laughed at the manager, who was too smart to file a protest with league president Ford Frick, the best brain in the game today.

In 1938, Frick asked me if I had given any thought to the pension due me when I retired. I was a mere sixty-four and I sent the president on his way. In 1939 he asked me again,

In 1940, I went out and umpired better than I had in 1939. Or 1909. But late in the season of 1940, I was hit by a ground ball at the Polo Grounds. It was the first time in my career that such an embarrassing catastrophe had occurred.

It worried me for the remainder of the game and as I limped off the field a lady said to me, "Oh, Pop, I'm so sorry you were hit with that ball." I had been called "Uncle" in my day; "Pop" was something to think about. But I umpired my eighteenth World Series in 1940.

When Frick again offered me the superintendent's job, I said, "Okay, but I won't be superintendent. That's too political." Frick chose "Chief" as a better word. I was made "Chief" of National League umpires.

In 1941, I worked a few games. Toward the season's end, St. Louis and Brooklyn were in a crucial series and I joined the three-man umpiring team as a fourth man. I was working at second base and I played a little deep as an experiment. I was out of position and I knew it. And I was uncomfortable.

A St. Louis man attempted to steal second. Billy Herman took the throw and put the ball on the runner. I called him out. The runner jumped up and protested. "He didn't touch me. He never tagged me," he yelled. I walked away from the beefing ballplayer, saying to myself, "I'm almost certain Herman tagged him." Then it came to me and I almost wept. For the first time in all my career I only "thought" a man was tagged.

Frick came in the dressing room after the game. I said to him, "I started umpiring in 1902. This is 1941. I can say I've umpired forty years, can't I, Ford?"

Frick said, "Of course you can, Bill."

"Well, then, that's the last, Ford," I said. "I'm through." And I never again umpired a big-league game.

But I didn't stop umpiring. I could only see with one eye, but I could still walk. In 1944, Branch Rickey demanded my services for some spring exhibition games and I got by fine. I wasn't surprised because I never thought eyesight was the most important thing in umpiring. The most important things are guts, honesty, common sense, a desire for fair play and an understanding of human nature.

SELECTING one article by John Lardner for inclusion in a collection such as this is like deciding, as Lefty Gomez once had to, what kind of pitch to throw Jimmy Foxx. Lardner, like Foxx, is good for extra bases any time, but my choice was considerably more pleasant and less hazardous than the one confronting Gomez, who finally told catcher Bill Dickey he preferred not to throw the ball at all. The following Lardner, which appeared in *Sport,* is a personal favorite of mine.

The Unbelievable Babe Herman

—————————— JOHN LARDNER ——————————

FLOYD CAVES HERMAN, known as Babe, did not always catch fly balls on the top of his head, but he could do it in a pinch. He never tripled into a triple play, but he once doubled into a double play, which is the next best thing. For seven long years, from 1926 through 1932, he was the spirit of Brooklyn baseball. He spent the best part of his life upholding the mighty tradition that anything can happen at Ebbets Field, the mother temple of daffiness in the national game.

Then he went away from there. He rolled and bounced from town to town and ball club to ball club. Thirteen years went by before he appeared in a Brooklyn uniform again. That was in the wartime summer of 1945, when manpower was so sparse that the desperate Dodger scouts were snatching beardless shortstops from the cradle and dropping their butterfly nets over Spanish War veterans who had played the outfield alongside Willie Keeler. In the course of the great famine, Branch Rickey and Leo Durocher lured Babe Herman, then 42, from his turkey farm in Glendale, California, to hit a few more for the honor of Flatbush. A fine crowd turned out to watch the ancient hero on the first day of his reincarnation.

"It looks like they haven't forgotten you here, Babe," said one of the players, glancing around the grandstand.

Mr. Herman shook his head. "How could they?" he said with simple dignity.

And he went on to show what he meant. In his first time at bat he was almost thrown out at first base on a single to right field. The Babe rounded the bag at a high, senile prance, fell flat on his face on the baseline, and barely scrambled back to safety ahead of the throw from the outfield. The crowd roared with approval. Fifteen years earlier they would have booed themselves into a state of apoplexy, for that was a civic ritual at Ebbets Field—booing Herman. But this was 1945. You don't boo a legend from out of the past, a man who made history.

Before he went home to California to stay, a few weeks later, the Babe gathered the younger players around his knee and filled them with blood-curdling stories about his terrible past.

"You know that screen on top of the right-field fence," he said. "They put that there on account of me. I was breaking all the windows on the other side of Bedford Avenue."

Looking around to see if this had sunk in, he added: "There used to be a traffic tower on Bedford Avenue there. Once I hit one over the wall that broke a window in the tower and cut a cop's hand all to pieces. Wasn't my fault," said the Babe philosophically. "When I busted 'em, there was no telling where they'd go."

* * *

It's beyond question that Mr. Herman could bust them. He always admitted it. He used to be irritated, though, by the rumor that he was the world's worst outfielder, and a constant danger to his own life. He was also sensitive about his base-running.

"Don't write fresh cracks about my running," he once told an interviewer, "or I won't give you no story. I'm a great runner."

He proceeded to tell why he stole no bases in 1926, his first year with Brooklyn, until the very end of the season. It seems that the late Uncle Wilbert Robinson, then managing the Dodgers, came up to Mr. Herman one day and said, sourly: "What's the matter, can't you steal?"

"Steal?" said the Babe. "Why, hell, you never asked me to."

So then he stole a couple of bases, to prove he could do everything.

One talent for which Babe never gave himself enough public credit was making money. He was one of the highest-salaried players of his time, year after year. He got these salaries by holding out all through the training season. Other players, starving slowly on the ball club's regular bill of fare in Southern hotels, used to go down the street to the restaurants where Herman, the holdout, ate, and press their noses against the window like small boys, watching the Babe cut huge sirloin steaks to ribbons. It wasn't just the food that kept Babe from signing early. Holding out is a common practice with good-hit-no-field men, like Herman, Zeke Bonura, and Rudy York, in his outfielding days. The reason is obvious. The longer they postpone playing ball in the spring (for nothing), the less chance there is of getting killed by a fly ball.

Mr. Herman had such ambitious ideas about money that one year, returning his first contract to the Brooklyn office unsigned, he enclosed an unpaid bill from his dentist for treatment during the winter. The ball club ignored the bill. After all, Herman didn't hit with his teeth.

The Babe, as a player, was a gangling fellow with spacious ears who walked with a slouch that made him look less than his true height, six feet, four inches. He was born in Buffalo in 1903. Leaving there for the professional baseball wars in 1921, Mr. Herman worked for eighteen different managers before he met up with Uncle Robbie, and for nine more after that. It is said that he broke the hearts of 45 per cent of these gentlemen. The rest avoided cardiac trouble by getting rid of the Babe as fast as they could.

He came up from Edmonton, in the Western Canada League, to Detroit, in the year 1922, and was promptly fired by Ty Cobb, the Tigers' idealistic manager.

"The Detroit club," said the Babe, his feelings wounded, "has undoubtedly made some bad mistakes in its time, but this is the worst they ever made."

He was fired from the Omaha club later in the same year while batting .416. A pop fly hit him on the head one day, and the Omaha owner lost his temper. The owner and the manager began to argue.

"Much as I would like to," said the manager, "I can't send away a man who is hitting .416."

"I don't care if he's hitting 4,000!" yelled the owner. "I am not going to have players who field the ball with their skulls. Fire him!"

The Babe explained later that the incident was greatly exaggerated.

"It was a foul ball," he said, "that started to go into the stands. The minute I turned my back, though, the wind caught the ball and blew it out again, and it conked me. It could happen to anybody."

Just the same, Mr. Herman was fired.

The Babe tried baseball in Boston briefly, when Lee Fohl managed the Red Sox. He never played an inning there. Studying his form on the bench, Mr. Fohl fired him. The Babe was just as well pleased. He said the Boston climate did not suit him. He went to Atlanta, where Otto Miller, later a Brooklyn coach, managed the team. Every morning for five days in a row, Mr. Miller resolved to fire Mr. Herman. Every afternoon of those five days, Mr. Herman got a hit that drove in runs and changed Mr. Miller's mind for the night. On the fifth day, playing against Nashville, he had four hits in his first four times at bat. He was robbed of a fifth hit by a sensational catch by Kiki Cuyler. After the game, Mr. Miller told the Babe that they might have won the game but for Cuyler's catch. He meant it kindly, but Mr. Herman took it as a personal criticism of himself. He was hurt. He began a loud quarrel with Otto, and was traded to Memphis on one bounce.

The Brooklyn club bought the Babe for $15,000 a couple of years later, while he was causing nervous breakdowns and busting up ball games in Seattle. Then Brooklyn tried to get rid of him for nothing, and failed. This gross insult to the name of Herman occurred as follows: The Dodgers wanted a Minneapolis player of no subsequent consequence, named Johnny Butler. They traded Herman and eight other men to Minneapolis for Butler. Minneapolis took the eight other men, but refused to take Herman. Brooklyn was stuck with the Babe, and history began to be made.

Jacques Fournier, the Dodger first baseman, hurt his leg one day in the summer of 1926. Herman replaced him. He had a good season at bat that year and the Brooklyn fans began to take to the Babe, wide ears, chewing tobacco, and all. Uncle Robbie took to him some days. Other days gave him pause—like the day famous in ballad and prose when Mr. Herman smote a two-base hit that ended in a double play.

The bases were full of Brooklyns, with one out, when the Babe strode to the plate on that occasion, swinging his bat like a cane in his right hand. He was a phenomenon physically, a left-handed hitter with most of his power in his right arm. Scattered around the landscape before him were Hank DeBerry, the Brooklyn catcher, on third base; Dazzy Vance, the immortal Dodger fireball pitcher, on second; and Chick Fewster, an outfielder, on first. Mr. Herman swung ferociously and the ball hit the right-field wall on a line. DeBerry scored. Vance, however, being a man who did not care to use his large dogs unnecessarily, hovered between second and third for a moment on the theory that the ball might be caught. When it rebounded off the wall, he set sail again, lumbered to third base, and made a tentative turn toward home. Then, deciding he couldn't score, he stepped back to third. This move confounded Fewster, who was hard on Vance's heels. Fewster started back toward second base. At that moment, a new character, with blond hair and flapping ears, came into their lives.

Mr. Herman has described himself as a great runner. What he meant was, he was a hard runner. He forgot to mention that he ran with blinkers on, as they say at the race track. He concentrated on running and ignored the human and animal life around and ahead of him. Passing Fewster like the Limited passing a whistle stop, the Babe slid into third just as Vance returned there from the opposite direction. Herman was automatically out for passing Fewster on the baseline, though nobody realized it at once but the umpire, who made an "out" sign. The third baseman, not knowing who was out, began frantically to tag Herman, who was already dead, and Vance, who stood perfectly safe on third base.

"What a spectacle!" observed Vance nonchalantly to Herman, as the third baseman looked in vain to the umpire for the sign of another out. Fewster, confused, stood a little distance away. His proper move was to go back to second and stay there, but Herman's slide had destroyed his powers of thought. Finally, the third baseman caught on. He began to chase Fewster, who ran in a panic and did not even stop at second, where he would have

been safe. He was tagged in the outfield for the third out of the inning.

Cheap detractors may say what they like about Herman merely doubling into a double play. It's obvious that what he really did—the rule-book to the contrary—was triple into a double play.

It's also obvious that Vance and Fewster were as much at fault as Herman. That is the old, true spirit of Brooklyn co-operation. But Vance regarded Herman as the star of the act. A few years afterward, when Chicago officials announced that they expected a Chicago pennant in 1933 to make things complete for the Century of Progress exposition, Vance announced his counter-plan for that year in Brooklyn. Instead of a Century of Progress, said Dazzy, they would feature "A Cavalcade of Chaos; or, the Headless Horsemen of Ebbets Field." Herman was to be the star. Unfortunately, by the time the year 1933 rolled into Brooklyn, Herman had rolled out of there, to quieter pastures.

Uncle Robbie's comment on the celebrated double play of 1926 was "#$&%$%!!" However, that was Robbie's comment on practically everything, and he meant it in a friendly way. He was tolerant of Herman, for he understood that criticism or scolding drove the Babe crazy. When 30,000 people booed him in unison—and that happened often enough in 1927, when his batting average slipped to .272, and 1929, when he led the league's outfielders in errors—the Babe would sulk for days. It took Robbie a little while, at that, to learn patience with Herman. He asked waivers on him in 1927, but changed his mind and kept the Babe when John McGraw, of the New York Giants, refused to waive.

"If that crafty blank-blank McGraw wants him," reasoned Mr. Robinson, "there must be something in him."

As time went on, the Brooklyn crowds became more sympathetic, too. That's understandable. After 1927, Herman hit for averages of .340, .381, .393, .313, and .326. In 1930, he had 241 hits for a total of 426 bases, including 35 home runs. He scored 143 runs and batted in 130. The fans barbecued him one moment and cheered him the next.

"Not only is that fellow a funny-looking blank-blank-blank," said the manager, "but he is blankety-blank unlucky. Other men, when they're on third base, can sometimes beat the outfielder's catch when they start home on a fly ball. But not this blankety-blank Herman. He always gets called for it."

The wailing and the keening were great in Brooklyn when the Babe, called by Rogers Hornsby, "the perfect free swinger," was traded to Cincinnati in December 1932, in a six-player deal. It was not a bad deal for Brooklyn, in a strictly practical way. Herman never hit in high figures again after that year, while some of the players from Cincinnati helped the Dodgers into the first division. But the fans, in the main, never forgave Max Carey, who had replaced Uncle Robbie as manager, for sending Herman away. They didn't care about being practical. They wanted salt in their stew.

Removed from the choice Brooklyn atmosphere, where he flourished, the Babe began to bounce from place to place again as he had in the days of his youth. Managers resumed the practice of firing him to save their health. He went from Cincinnati to Chicago to Pittsburgh to Cincinnati to Detroit to Toledo to Syracuse to Jersey City, and finally, with a strong tail wind, clear out to the Pacific Coast. The slower he got as a player, the more money he asked, and the more loudly he asked for it. However, the Babe did not like the word "holdout." Once, in the early spring of 1934, he denounced the press of Los Angeles, near his home, for using that term to describe him.

"You got the wrong idea entirely," he told the reporters sternly. "I am not holding out. I just don't want to sign this ———— contract the Cubs have sent me, because the dough ain't big enough."

*   *   *

On his second time around in Cincinnati, in 1936, Mr. Herman came into contact with baseball's leading genius, Leland Stanford MacPhail, who was the Reds' general manager. They were bound to get together sometime, even though the Babe left Brooklyn before MacPhail was ripe for that city. It was also inevitable that MacPhail should some day fine Herman, and some day fire him. They were not made to be soulmates. MacPhail fined him, and Paul Derringer, the pitcher, $200 each, one day in July. It was a true Herman episode. With hostile runners on first and third, Derringer made a balk. The runner on third went home, and the runner on first went to second. Herman, communing with nature in the outfield, missed the play completely. He thought there were still men on first and third. When the next hitter singled to the Babe on one bounce, he studied the stitches on the ball and lobbed it back to the infield. The runner on second scored standing up. MacPhail turned purple, and levied his fines on both the pitcher and the Babe.

It's a matter of record that Derringer got his fine canceled, by throwing an inkwell at MacPhail, which impressed the great man. Mr. Herman was less direct, and therefore less successful. He waited a few weeks after being fined. Then he demanded from MacPhail a cash bonus over and above his salary. It was an ill-timed request.

"A bonus!" yelled the genius. "Why, you're not even good enough to play on the team!" He added that Herman was fired. And he was.

Right to the end of his playing days, the Babe retained his fresh young affection for cash money. He was farming turkeys at his home in Glendale by the time he landed with the Hollywood club of the Pacific Coast League in the twilight of his career. One day in 1942— just a short while before that final, nostalgic, wartime bow in Brooklyn—he arranged to have his turkeys advertised on the scorecards in the Hollywood ball park. He then announced that he was holding out. The holdout kept him home in comfort among the turkeys, but not so far away from Hollywood that he couldn't drive over from time to time to negotiate. When he finally got his price and signed up to play ball, the Babe was fat and his reflexes were slow. So he made his season's debut at a disadvantage.

Hollywood was playing a game with Seattle. The score was tied going into the tenth inning. Seattle's young pitcher, a kid named Soriano, had already struck out ten men. Hollywood filled the bases on him, with two out, in the last of the 10th, but the boy was still strong and fast. The manager asked Mr. Herman if he was in shape to go in and pinch-hit.

"I may not be sharp," said the Babe, reaching for a bat, "and maybe I can't hit him. But I won't have to. I'll paralyze him."

He walked to the plate. He glowered at the pitcher, and held his bat at a menacing angle. He never swung it. Five pitches went by— three of them balls, two of them strikes. Then Mr. Herman pounded the plate, assumed a fearful scowl, and made as though his next move would tear a hole in the outfield wall. The last pitch from the nervous Soriano hit the ground in front of the Babe's feet for ball four. A run was forced in, and the ball game was over.

"That's a boy with an education," said the Babe, as he threw away his bat. "I see he's heard of Herman."

HERE's the big baby right here.

Alibi Ike

RING W. LARDNER

HIS RIGHT NAME was Frank X. Farrell, and I guess the X stood for "Excuse me." Because he never pulled a play, good or bad, on or off the field, without apologizin' for it.

"Alibi Ike" was the name Carey wished on him the first day he reported down South. O' course we all cut out the "Alibi" part of it right away for the fear he would overhear it and bust somebody. But we called him "Ike" right to his face and the rest of it was understood by everybody on the club except Ike himself.

He ast me one time, he says:

"What do you all call me Ike for? I ain't no Yid."

"Carey give you the name," I says. "It's his nickname for everybody he takes a likin' to."

"He mustn't have only a few friends then," says Ike. "I never heard him say 'Ike' to nobody else."

But I was goin' to tell you about Carey namin' him. We'd been workin' out two weeks and the pitchers was showin' somethin' when this bird joined us. His first day out there he stood up so good and took such a reef at the old pill that he had everyone lookin'. Then him and Carey was together in left field, catchin' fungoes, and it was after we was through for the day that Carey told me about him.

"What do you think of Alibi Ike?" ast Carey.

"Who's that?" I says.

"This here Farrell in the outfield," says Carey.

"He looks like he could hit," I says.

"Yes," says Carey, "but he can't hit near as good as he can apologize."

Then Carey went on to tell me what Ike had been pullin' out there. He'd dropped the first fly ball that was hit to him and told Carey his glove wasn't broke in good yet, and Carey says the glove could easy of been Kid Glea-

son's gran'father. He made a whale of a catch out o' the next one and Carey says "Nice work!" or somethin' like that, but Ike says he could of caught the ball with his back turned only he slipped when he started after it and, besides that, the air currents fooled him.

"I thought you done well to get to the ball," says Carey.

"I ought to been settin' under it," says Ike.

"What did you hit last year?" Carey ast him.

"I had malaria most o' the season," says Ike. "I wound up with .356."

"Where would I have to go to get malaria?" says Carey, but Ike didn't wise up.

I and Carey and him set at the same table together for supper. It took him half an hour longer'n us to eat because he had to excuse himself every time he lifted his fork.

"Doctor told me I needed starch," he'd say, and then toss a shovelful o' potatoes into him. Or, "They ain't much meat on one o' these chops," he'd tell us, and grab another one. Or he'd say: "Nothin' like onions for a cold," and then he'd dip into the perfumery.

"Better try that apple sauce," says Carey. "It'll help your malaria."

"Whose malaria?" says Ike. He'd forgot already why he didn't only hit .356 last year.

I and Carey begin to lead him on.

"Whereabouts did you say your home was?" I ast him.

"I live with my folks," he says. "We live in Kansas City—not right down in the business part—outside a ways."

"How's that come?" says Carey. "I should think you'd get rooms in the post office."

But Ike was too busy curin' his cold to get that one.

"Are you married?" I ast him.

"No," he says. "I never run round much with

girls, except to shows onct in a wile and parties and dances and roller skatin'."

"Never take 'em to the prize fights, eh?" says Carey.

"We don't have no real good bouts," says Ike. "Just bush stuff. And I never figured a boxin' match was a place for the ladies."

Well, after supper he pulled a cigar out and lit it. I was just goin' to ask him what he done it for, but he beat me to it.

"Kind o' rests a man to smoke after a good workout," he says. "Kind o' settles a man's supper, too."

"Looks like a pretty good cigar," says Carey.

"Yes," says Ike. "A friend o' mine give it to me—a fella in Kansas City that runs a billiard room."

"Do you play billiards?" I ast him.

"I used to play a fair game," he says. "I'm all out o' practice now—can't hardly make a shot."

We coaxed him into a four-handed battle, him and Carey against Jack Mack and I. Say, he couldn't play billiards as good as Willie Hoppe; not quite. But to hear him tell it, he didn't make a good shot all evenin'. I'd leave him an awful-lookin' layout and he'd gather 'em up in one try and then run a couple o' hundred, and between every carom he'd say he put too much stuff on the ball, or the English didn't take, or the table wasn't true, or his stick was crooked, or somethin'. And all the time he had the balls actin' like they was Dutch soldiers and him Kaiser William. We started out to play fifty points, but we had to make it a thousand so as I and Jack and Carey could try the table.

The four of us set round the lobby a wile after we was through playin', and when it got along toward bedtime Carey whispered to me and says:

"Ike'd like to go to bed, but he can't think up no excuse."

Carey hadn't hardly finished whisperin' when Ike got up and pulled it.

"Well, good night, boys," he says. "I ain't sleepy, but I got some gravel in my shoes and it's killin' my feet."

We knowed he hadn't never left the hotel since we'd came in from the grounds and changed our clo'es. So Carey says:

"I should think they'd take them gravel pits out o' the billiard room."

But Ike was already on his way to the elevator, limpin'.

"He's got the world beat," says Carey to Jack and I. "I've knew lots o' guys that had an alibi for every mistake they made; I've heard pitchers say that the ball slipped when somebody cracked one off'n 'em; I've heard infielders complain of a sore arm after heavin' one into the stand, and I've saw outfielders tooken sick with a dizzy spell when they've misjudged a fly ball. But this baby can't even go to bed without apologizin', and I bet he excuses himself to the razor when he gets ready to shave."

"And at that," says Jack, "he's goin' to make us a good man."

"Yes," says Carey, "Unless rheumatism keeps his battin' average down to .400."

Well, sir, Ike kept whalin' away at the ball all through the trip till everybody knowed he'd won a job. Cap had him in there regular the last few exhibition games and told the newspaper boys a week before the season opened that he was goin' to start him in Kane's place.

"You're there, kid," says Carey to Ike, the night Cap made the 'nnouncement. "They ain't many boys that wins a big league berth their third year out."

"I'd of been up here a year ago," says Ike, "only I was bent over all season with lumbago."

II

It rained down in Cincinnati one day and somebody organized a little game o' cards. They was shy two men to make six and ast I and Carey to play.

"I'm with you if you get Ike and make it seven-handed," says Carey.

So they got a hold of Ike and we went up to Smitty's room.

"I pretty near forgot how many you deal," says Ike. "It's been a long wile since I played."

I and Carey give each other the wink, and sure enough, he was just as ig'orant about poker as billiards. About the second hand, the pot was opened two or three ahead of him, and they was three in when it come his turn. It cost a buck, and he throwed in two.

"It's raised, boys," somebody says.

"Gosh, that's right, I did raise it," says Ike.

"Take out a buck if you didn't mean to tilt her," says Carey.

"No," says Ike, "I'll leave it go."

Well, it was raised back at him, and then he made another mistake and raised again. They was only three left in when the draw come. Smitty'd opened with a pair o' kings and he didn't help 'em. Ike stood pat. The guy that'd raised him back was flushin' and he didn't fill.

So Smitty checked and Ike bet and didn't get no call. He tossed his hand away, but I grabbed it and give it a look. He had king, queen, jack and two tens. Alibi Ike he must have seen me peekin', for he leaned over and whispered to me.

"I overlooked my hand," he says. "I thought all the wile it was a straight."

"Yes," I says, "that's why you raised twice by mistake."

They was another pot that he come into with tens and fours. It was tilted a couple o' times and two o' the strong fellas drawed ahead of Ike. They each drawed one. So Ike throwed away his little pair and come out with four tens. And they was four treys against him. Carey'd looked at Ike's discards and then he says:

"This lucky bum busted two pair."

"No, no, I didn't," says Ike.

"Yes, yes, you did," says Carey, and showed us the two fours.

"What do you know about that?" says Ike. "I'd of swore one was a five spot."

Well, we hadn't had no pay day yet, and after a wile everybody except Ike was goin' shy. I could see him gettin' restless and I was wonderin' how he'd make the get-away. He tried two or three times. "I got to buy some collars before supper," he says.

"No hurry," says Smitty. "The stores here keeps open all night in April."

After a minute he opened up again.

"My uncle out in Nebraska ain't expected to live," he says. "I ought to send a telegram."

"Would that save him?" says Carey.

"No, it sure wouldn't," says Ike, "but I ought to leave my old man know where I'm at."

"When did you hear about your uncle?" says Carey.

"Just this mornin'," says Ike.

"Who told you?" ast Carey.

"I got a wire from my old man," says Ike.

"Well," says Carey, "your old man knows you're still here yet this afternoon if you was here this mornin'. Trains leavin' Cincinnati in the middle o' the day don't carry no ball clubs."

"Yes," says Ike, "that's true. But he don't know where I'm goin' to be next week."

"Ain't he got no schedule?" ast Carey.

"I sent him one openin' day," says Ike, "but it takes mail a long time to get to Idaho."

"I thought your old man lived in Kansas City," says Carey.

"He does when he's home," says Ike.

"But now," says Carey, "I s'pose he's went to Idaho so as he can be near your sick uncle in Nebraska."

"He's visitin' my other uncle in Idaho."

"Then how does he keep posted about your sick uncle?" ast Carey.

"He don't," says Ike. "He don't even know my other uncle's sick. That's why I ought to wire and tell him."

"Good night!" says Carey.

"What town in Idaho is your old man at?" I says.

Ike thought it over.

"No town at all," he says. "But he's near a town."

"Near what town?" I says.

"Yuma," says Ike.

Well, by this time he'd lost two or three pots and he was desperate. We was playin' just as fast as we could, because we seen we couldn't hold him much longer. But he was tryin' so hard to frame an escape that he couldn't pay no attention to the cards, and it looked like we'd get his whole pile away from him if we could make him stick.

The telephone saved him. The minute it begun to ring, five of us jumped for it. But Ike was there first.

"Yes," he says, answerin' it. "This is him. I'll come right down."

And he slammed up the receiver and beat it out o' the door without even sayin' good-by.

"Smitty'd ought to locked the door," says Carey.

"What did he win?" ast Carey.

We figured it up—sixty-odd bucks.

"And the next time we ask him to play," says Carey, "his fingers will be so stiff he can't hold the cards."

Well, we set round a wile talkin' it over, and pretty soon the telephone rung again. Smitty answered it. It was a friend of his'n from Hamilton and he wanted to know why Smitty didn't hurry down. He was the one that had called before and Ike had told him he was Smitty.

"Ike'd ought to split with Smitty's friend," says Carey.

"No," I says, "he'll need all he won. It costs money to buy collars and to send telegrams from Cincinnati to your old man in Texas and keep him posted on the health o' your uncle in Cedar Rapids, D.C."

III

And you ought to heard him out there on that field! They wasn't a day when he didn't pull six or seven, and it didn't make no difference whether he was goin' good or bad. If he popped up in the pinch he should of made a base hit and the reason he didn't was so-and-so. And if he cracked one for three bases he ought to had a home run, only the ball wasn't lively, or the wind brought it back, or he tripped on a lump o' dirt, roundin' first base.

They was one afternoon in New York when he beat all records. Big Marquard was workin' against us and he was good.

In the first innin' Ike hit one clear over that right field stand, but it was a few feet foul. Then he got another foul and then the count come to two and two. Then Rube slipped one acrost on him and he was called out.

"What do you know about that!" he says afterward on the bench. "I lost count. I thought it was three and one, and I took a strike."

"You took a strike all right," says Carey. "Even the umps knowed it was a strike."

"Yes," says Ike, "but you can bet I wouldn't of took it if I'd knew it was the third one. The scoreboard had it wrong."

"That scoreboard ain't for you to look at," says Cap. "It's for you to hit that old pill against."

"Well," says Ike, "I could of hit that one over the scoreboard if I'd knew it was the third."

"Was it a good ball?" I says.

"Well, no, it wasn't," says Ike. "It was inside."

"How far inside?" says Carey.

"Oh, two or three inches or half a foot," says Ike.

"I guess you wouldn't of threatened the scoreboard with it then," says Cap.

"I'd of pulled it down the right foul line if I hadn't thought he'd call it a ball," says Ike.

Well, in New York's part o' the innin' Doyle cracked one and Ike run back a mile and a half and caught it with one hand. We was all sayin' what a whale of a play it was, but he had to apologize just the same as for gettin' struck out.

"That stand's so high," he says, "that a man don't never see a ball till it's right on top o' you."

"Didn't you see that one?" ast Cap.

"Not at first," says Ike; "not till it raised up above the roof o' the stand."

"Then why did you start back as soon as the ball was hit?" says Cap.

"I knowed by the sound that he'd got a good hold of it," says Ike.

"Yes," says Cap, "but how'd you know what direction to run in?"

"Doyle usually hits 'em that way, the way I run," says Ike.

"Why don't you play blindfolded?" says Carey.

"Might as well, with that big high stand to bother a man," says Ike. "If I could of saw the ball all the time I'd of got it in my hip pocket."

Along in the fifth we was one run to the bad and Ike got on with one out. On the first ball throwed to Smitty, Ike went down. The ball was outside and Meyers throwed Ike out by ten feet.

You could see Ike's lips movin' all the way to the bench and when he got there he had his piece learned.

"Why didn't he swing?" he says.

"Why didn't you wait for his sign?" says Cap.

"He give me his sign," says Ike.

"What's his sign with you?" says Cap.

"Pickin' up some dirt with his right hand," says Ike.

"Well, I didn't see him do it," Cap says.

"He done it all right," says Ike.

Well, Smitty went out and they wasn't no more argument till they come in for the next innin'. Then Cap opened it up.

"You fellas better get your signs straight," he says.

"Do you mean me?" says Smitty.

"Yes," Cap says. "What's your sign with Ike?"

"Slidin' my left hand up to the end o' the bat and back," says Smitty.

"Do you hear that, Ike?" ast Cap.

"What of it?" says Ike.

"You says his sign was pickin' up dirt and he says it's slidin' his hand. Which is right?"

"I'm right," says Smitty. "But if you're arguin' about him goin' last innin', I didn't give him no sign."

"You pulled your cap down with your right hand, didn't you?" ast Ike.

"Well, s'pose I did," says Smitty. "That don't mean nothin'. I never told you to take that for a sign, did I?"

"I thought maybe you meant to tell me and forgot," says Ike.

They couldn't none of us answer that and they wouldn't of been no more said if Ike had of shut up. But wile we was settin' there Carey got on with two out and stole second clean.

"There!" says Ike. "That's what I was tryin'

to do and I'd of got away with it if Smitty'd swang and bothered the Indian."

"Oh!" says Smitty. "You was tryin' to steal then, was you? I thought you claimed I give you the hit and run."

"I didn't claim no such a thing," says Ike. "I thought maybe you might of gave me a sign, but I was goin' anyway because I thought I had a good start."

Cap prob'ly would of hit him with a bat, only just about that time Doyle booted one on Hayes and Carey come acrost with the run that tied.

Well, we go into the ninth finally, one and one, and Marquard walks McDonald with nobody out.

"Lay it down," says Cap to Ike.

And Ike goes up there with orders to bunt and cracks the first ball into that right-field stand! It was fair this time, and we're two ahead, but I didn't think about that at the time. I was too busy watchin' Cap's face. First he turned pale and then he got red as fire and then he got blue and purple, and finally he just laid back and busted out laughin'. So we wasn't afraid to laugh ourselfs when we seen him doin' it, and when Ike come in everybody on the bench was in hysterics.

But instead o' takin' advantage, Ike had to try and excuse himself. His play was to shut up and he didn't know how to make it.

"Well," he says, "if I hadn't hit quite so quick at that one I bet it'd of cleared the center-field fence."

Cap stopped laughin'.

"It'll cost you plain fifty," he says.

"What for?" says Ike.

"When I say 'bunt' I mean 'bunt,'" says Cap.

"You didn't say 'bunt,'" says Ike.

"I says 'Lay it down,'" says Cap. "If that don't mean 'bunt,' what does it mean?"

"'Lay it down' means 'bunt' all right," says Ike, "but I understood you to say 'Lay on it.'"

"All right," says Cap, "and the little misunderstandin' will cost you fifty."

Ike didn't say nothin' for a few minutes. Then he had another bright idear.

"I was just kiddin' about misunderstandin' you," he says. "I knowed you wanted me to bunt."

"Well, then, why didn't you bunt?" ast Cap.

"I was goin' to on the next ball," says Ike. "But I thought if I took a good wallop I'd have 'em all fooled. So I walloped at the first one

to fool 'em, and I didn't have no intention o' hittin' it."

"You tried to miss it, did you?" says Cap.

"Yes," says Ike.

"How'd you happen to hit it?" ast Cap.

"Well," Ike says, "I was lookin' for him to throw me a fast one and I was goin' to swing under it. But he come with a hook and I met it right square where I was swingin' to go under the fast one."

"Great!" says Cap. "Boys," he says, "Ike's learned how to hit Marquard's curve. Pretend a fast one's comin' and then try to miss it. It's a good thing to know and Ike'd ought to be willin' to pay for the lesson. So I'm goin' to make it a hundred instead o' fifty."

The game wound up 3 to 1. The fine didn't go, because Ike hit like a wild man all through that trip and we made pretty near a clean-up. The night we went to Philly I got him cornered in the car and I says to him:

"Forget them alibis for a wile and tell me somethin'. What'd you do that for, swing that time against Marquard when you was told to bunt?"

"I'll tell you," he says. "That ball he throwed me looked just like the one I struck out on in the first innin' and I wanted to show Cap what I could of done to that other one if I'd knew it was the third strike."

"But," I says, "the one you struck out on in the first innin' was a fast ball."

"So was the one I cracked in the ninth," says Ike.

IV

You've saw Cap's wife, o' course. Well, her sister's about twict as good-lookin' as her, and that's goin' some.

Cap took his missus down to St. Louis the second trip and the other one come down from St. Joe to visit her. Her name is Dolly, and some doll is right.

Well, Cap was goin' to take the two sisters to a show and he wanted a beau for Dolly. He left it to her and she picked Ike. He'd hit three on the nose that afternoon—of'n Sallee, too.

They fell for each other that first evenin'. Cap told us how it come off. She begin flatterin' Ike for the star game he'd played and o' course he begin excusin' himself for not doin' better. So she thought he was modest and it went strong with her. And she believed everything he said and that made her solid with him —that and her make-up. They was together every mornin' and evenin' for the five days we was there. In the afternoons Ike played the grandest ball you ever see, hittin' and runnin' the bases like a fool and catchin' everything that stayed in the park.

I told Cap, I says: "You'd ought to keep the doll with us and he'd make Cobb's figures look sick."

But Dolly had to go back to St. Joe and we come home for a long serious.

Well, for the next three weeks Ike had a letter to read every day and he'd set in the clubhouse readin' it till mornin' practice was half over. Cap didn't say nothin' to him, because he was goin' so good. But I and Carey wasted a lot of our time tryin' to get him to own up who the letters was from. Fine chanct!

"What are you readin'?" Carey'd say. "A bill?"

"No," Ike'd say, "not exactly a bill. It's a letter from a fella I used to go to school with."

"High school or college?" I'd ask him.

"College," he'd say.

"What college?" I'd say.

Then he'd stall a wile and then he'd say:

"I didn't go to the college myself, but my friend went there."

"How did it happen you didn't go?" Carey'd ask him.

"Well," he'd say, "they wasn't no colleges near where I lived."

"Didn't you live in Kansas City?" I'd say to him.

One time he'd say he did and another time he didn't. One time he says he lived in Michigan.

"Where at?" says Carey.

"Near Detroit," he says.

"Well," I says, "Detroit's near Ann Arbor and that's where they got the university."

"Yes," says Ike, "they got it there now, but they didn't have it there then."

"I come pretty near goin' to Syracuse," I says, "only they wasn't no railroads runnin' through there in them days."

"Where'd this friend o' yours go to college?" says Carey.

"I forget now," says Ike.

"Was it Carlisle?" ast Carey.

"No," says Ike, "his folks wasn't very well off."

"That's what barred me from Smith," I says.

"I was goin' to tackle Cornell's," says Carey, "but the doctor told me I'd have hay fever if I didn't stay up North."

"Your friend writes long letters," I says.

"Yes," says Ike; "he's tellin' me about a ballplayer."

"Where does he play?" ast Carey.

"Down in the Texas League—Fort Wayne," says Ike.

"It looks like a girl's writin'," Carey says.

"A girl wrote it," says Ike. "That's my friend's sister, writin' for him."

"Didn't they teach writin' at this here college where he went?" says Carey.

"Sure," Ike says, "they taught writin', but he got his hand cut off in a railroad wreck."

"How long ago?" I says.

"Right after he got out o' college," says Ike.

"Well," I says, "I should think he'd of learned to write with his left hand by this time."

"It's his left hand that was cut off," says Ike; "and he was left-handed."

"You get a letter every day," says Carey. "They're all the same writin'. Is he tellin' you about a different ballplayer every time he writes?"

"No," Ike says. "It's the same ballplayer. He just tells me what he does every day."

"From the size o' the letters, they don't play nothin' but double-headers down there," says Carey.

We figured that Ike spent most of his evenins answerin' the letters from his "friend's sister," so we kept tryin' to date him up for shows and parties to see how he'd duck out of 'em. He was bugs over spaghetti, so we told him one day that they was goin' to be a big feed of it over to Joe's that night and he was invited.

"How long'll it last?" he says.

"Well," we says, "we're goin' right over there after the game and stay till they close up."

"I can't go," he says, "unless they leave me come home at eight bells."

"Nothin' doin'," says Carey. "Joe'd get sore."

"I can't go then," says Ike.

"Why not?" I ast him.

"Well," he says, "my landlady locks up the house at eight and I left my key home."

"You can come and stay with me," says Carey.

"No," he says, "I can't sleep in a strange bed."

"How do you get along when we're on the road?" says I.

"I don't never sleep the first night anywheres," he says. "After that I'm all right."

"You'll have time to chase home and get

your key right after the game," I told him.

"The key ain't home," says Ike. "I lent it to one o' the other fellas and he's went out o' town and took it with him."

"Couldn't you borry another key off'n the landlady?" Carey ast him.

"No," he says, "that's the only one they is."

Well, the day before we started East again, Ike come into the clubhouse all smiles.

"Your birthday?" I ast him.

"No," he says.

"What do you feel so good about?" I says.

"Got a letter from my old man," he says. "My uncle's goin' to get well."

"Is that the one in Nebraska?" says I.

"Not right in Nebraska," says Ike. "Near there."

But afterwards we got the right dope from Cap. Dolly'd blew in from Missouri and was going to make the trip with her sister.

V

Well, I want to alibi Carey and I for what come off in Boston. If we'd of had any idear what we was doin', we'd never did it. They wasn't nobody outside o' maybe Ike and the dame that felt worse over it than I and Carey.

The first two days we didn't see nothin' of Ike and her except out to the park. The rest o' the time they was sight-seein' over to Cambridge and down to Revere and out to Brook-a-line and all the other places where the rubes go.

But when we come into the beanery after the third game Cap's wife called us over.

"If you want to see somethin' pretty," she says, "look at the third finger on Sis's left hand."

Well, o' course we knowed before we looked that it wasn't goin' to be no hangnail. Nobody was su'prised when Dolly blew into the dinin' room with it—a rock that Ike'd bought off'n Diamond Joe the first trip to New York. Only o' course it'd been set into a lady's-size ring instead o' the automobile tire he'd been wearin'.

Cap and his missus and Ike and Dolly ett supper together, only Ike didn't eat nothin', but just set there blushin' and spillin' things on the tablecloth. I heard him excusin' himself for not havin' no appetite. He says he couldn't never eat when he was clost to the ocean. He'd forgot about them sixty-five oysters he destroyed the first night o' the trip before.

He was goin' to take her to a show, so after supper he went upstairs to change his collar.

She had to doll up, too, and o' course Ike was through long before her.

If you remember the hotel in Boston, they's a little parlor where the piano's at and then they's another little parlor openin' off o' that. Well, when Ike come down Smitty was playin' a few chords and I and Carey was harmonizin'. We seen Ike go up to the desk to leave his key and we called him in. He tried to duck away, but we wouldn't stand for it.

We ast him what he was all duded up for and he says he was goin' to the theayter.

"Goin' alone?" says Carey.

"No," he says, "a friend o' mine's goin' with me."

"What do you say if we go along?" says Carey.

"I ain't only got two tickets," he says.

"Well," says Carey, "we can go down there with you and buy our own seats; maybe we can all get together."

"No," says Ike. "They ain't no more seats. They're all sold out."

"We can buy some off'n the scalpers," says Carey.

"I wouldn't if I was you," says Ike. "They say the show's rotten."

"What are you goin' for, then?" I ast.

"I didn't hear about it bein' rotten till I got the tickets," he says.

"Well," I says, "if you don't want to go I'll buy the tickets from you."

"No," says Ike, "I wouldn't want to cheat you. I'm stung and I'll just have to stand for it."

"What are you goin' to do with the girl, leave her here at the hotel?" I says.

"What girl?" says Ike.

"The girl you ett supper with," I says.

"Oh," he says, "we just happened to go into the dinin' room together, that's all. Cap wanted I should set down with 'em."

"I noticed," says Carey, "that she happened to be wearin' that rock you bought off'n Diamond Joe."

"Yes," says Ike. "I lent it to her for a wile."

"Did you lend her the new ring that goes with it?" I says.

"She had that already," says Ike. "She lost the set out of it."

"I wouldn't trust no strange girl with a rock o' mine," says Carey.

"Oh, I guess she's all right," Ike says. "Besides, I was tired o' the stone. When a girl asks you for somethin', what are you goin' to do?"

He started out toward the desk, but we flagged him.

"Wait a minute!" Carey says. "I got a bet with Sam here, and it's up to you to settle it."

"Well," says Ike, "make it snappy. My friend'll be here any minute."

"I bet," says Carey, "that you and that girl was engaged to be married."

"Nothin' to it," says Ike.

"Now look here," says Carey, "this is goin' to cost me real money if I lose. Cut out the alibi stuff and give it to us straight. Cap's wife just as good as told us you was roped."

Ike blushed like a kid.

"Well, boys," he says, "I may as well own up. You win, Carey."

"Yatta boy!" says Carey. "Congratulations!"

"You got a swell girl, Ike," I says.

"She's a peach," says Smitty.

"Well, I guess she's O. K.," says Ike. "I don't know much about girls."

"Didn't you never run round with 'em?" I says.

"Oh, yes, plenty of 'em," says Ike. "But I never seen none I'd fall for."

"That is, till you seen this one," says Carey.

"Well," says Ike, "this one's O. K., but I wasn't thinkin' about gettin' married yet a wile."

"Who done the askin', her?" says Carey.

"Oh, no," says Ike, "but sometimes a man don't know what he's gettin' into. Take a good-lookin' girl, and a man gen'ally almost always does about what she wants him to."

"They couldn't no girl lasso me unless I wanted to be lassoed," says Smitty.

"Oh, I don't know," says Ike. "When a fella gets to feelin' sorry for one of 'em it's all off."

Well, we left him go after shakin' hands all round. But he didn't take Dolly to no show that night. Some time wile we was talkin' she'd came into that other parlor and she'd stood there and heard us. I don't know how much she heard. But it was enough. Dolly and Cap's missus took the midnight train for New York. And from there Cap's wife sent her on her way back to Missouri.

She'd left the ring and note for Ike with the clerk. But we didn't ask Ike if the note was from his friend in Fort Wayne, Texas.

VI

When we'd came to Boston Ike was hittin' plain .397. When we got back home he'd fell off to pretty near nothin'. He hadn't drove one out o' the infield in any o' them other Eastern

parks, and he didn't even give no excuse for it.

To show you how bad he was, he struck out three times in Brooklyn one day and never opened his trap when Cap ast him what was the matter. Before, if he'd whiffed oncet in a game he'd of wrote a book tellin' why.

Well, we dropped from first place to fifth in four weeks and we was still goin' down. I and Carey was about the only ones in the club that spoke to each other, and all as we did was to remind ourself o' what a boner we'd pulled.

"It's goin' to beat us out o' the big money," says Carey.

"Yes," I says. "I don't want to knock my own ball club, but it looks like a one-man team, and when that one man's dauber's down we couldn't trim our whiskers."

"We ought to knew better," says Carey.

"Yes," I says, "but why should a man pull an alibi for bein' engaged to such a bearcat as she was?"

"He shouldn't," says Carey. "But I and you knowed he would or we'd never started talkin' to him about it. He wasn't no more ashamed o' the girl than I am of a regular base hit. But he just can't come clean on no subjec'."

Cap had the whole story, and I and Carey was as pop'lar with him as an umpire.

"What do you want me to do, Cap?" Carey'd say to him before goin' up to hit.

"Use your own judgment," Cap'd tell him. "We want to lose another game."

But finally, one night in Pittsburgh, Cap had a letter from his missus and he come to us with it.

"You fellas," he says, "is the ones that put us on the bum, and if you're sorry I think they's a chancet for you to make good. The old lady's out to St. Joe and she's been tryin' her hardest to fix things up. She's explained that Ike don't mean nothin' with his talk; I've wrote and explained that to Dolly, too. But the old lady says that Dolly says that she can't believe it. But Dolly's still stuck on this baby, and she's pinin' away just the same as Ike. And the old lady says she thinks if you two fellas would write to the girl and explain how you was always kiddin' with Ike and leadin' him on, and how the ball club was all shot to pieces since Ike quit hittin', and how he acted like he was goin' to kill himself, and this and that, she'd fall for it and maybe soften down. Dolly, the old lady says, would believe you before she'd believe I and the old lady, because she thinks it's her we're sorry for, and not him."

Well, I and Carey was only too glad to try

and see what we could do. But it wasn't no snap. We wrote about eight letters before we got one that looked good. Then we give it to the stenographer and had it wrote out on a typewriter and both of us signed it.

It was Carey's idear that made the letter good. He stuck in somethin' about the world's serious money that our wives wasn't goin' to spend unless she took pity on a "boy who was so shy and modest that he was afraid to come right out and say that he had asked such a beautiful and handsome girl to become his bride."

That's prob'ly what got her, or maybe she couldn't of held out much longer anyway. It was four days after we sent the letter that Cap heard from his missus again. We was in Cincinnati.

"We've won," he says to us. "The old lady says that Dolly says she'll give him another chance. But the old lady says it won't do no good for Ike to write a letter. He'll have to go out there."

"Send him tonight," says Carey.

"I'll pay half his fare," I says.

"I'll pay the other half," says Carey.

"No," says Cap, "the club'll pay his expenses. I'll send him scoutin'."

"Are you goin' to send him tonight?"

"Sure," says Cap. "But I'm goin' to break the news to him right now. It's time we win a ball game."

So in the clubhouse, just before the game, Cap told him. And I certainly felt sorry for Rube Benton and Red Ames that afternoon! I and Carey was standin' in front o' the hotel that night when Ike come out with his suitcase.

"Sent home?" I says to him.

"No," he says, "I'm goin' scoutin'."

"Where to?" I says. "Fort Wayne?"

"No, not exactly," he says.

"Well," says Carey, "have a good time."

"I ain't lookin' for no good time," says Ike. "I says I was goin' scoutin'."

"Well, then," says Carey, "I hope you see somebody you like."

"And you better have a drink before you go," I says.

"Well," says Ike, "they claim it helps a cold."

Sulphur Dell

GEORGE LEONARD

THERE IS only one ball park in the world where the right fielder plays on a steep bank only 235 feet from home plate, where a catcher once dived into a flooded dugout after a foul pop-up and came to the surface with the ball, where a major-league club once trained in the spring and went north to win the pennant with the highest won-and-lost percentage recorded in 60 years, and where the normal way of playing baseball is best forgotten.

It was the consensus of the Yankees, Dodgers, Giants, Braves and Indians, after making spring stop-overs in Nashville, Tennessee, this year, that Sulphur Dell is the world's craziest ball park. "I've waited ten years to see this, but I still don't believe it," Vic Raschi said, looking out of the dugout over the pancake diamond surrounded by irregular outfield hills on which fielders were perched like mountain-climbers minus alpenstocks. (At Sulphur Dell they refer to outfielders as "mountain goats.")

The field, which is the home of the Nashville Vols in the Southern Association, got its name from Grantland Rice, the dean of American sports writers. Rice didn't like the sound of the original name, Sulphur Springs Bottom, so he called it Sulphur Dell.

High embankments rim the outfield. Right fielders usually play on a well-worn, narrow ledge, about one-third of the way up the ridge. The rapid decline offers a good running start on short flies or liners to the base of the embankment, the eroded shelf is an excellent running track for drives to right center and it is only a short mountain climb up the bank for long flies. The right fielder's only danger is that, with a false step, he can tumble into one of the many alpine recesses. When the old Yankees used to stop in Nashville for exhibition games, Babe Ruth would shift from right to left field, slightly less dangerous for inexperienced mountain climbers, and would leave the "dump" to Bob Meusel.

The pop fly, or "Chinese" homer, may have originated in Nashville. Ordinary fly balls skim off the screen or ricochet off the fence for doubles and triples, or drift over the friendly barrier for homers. Yankee manager Casey Stengel tells about the time, in 1912, when he was an outfielder for Montgomery and was ordered, one afternoon in the Dell, to bunt. "I dragged the ball and guess what? It went over the right-field fence."

Not only are the fences nearby, but the grandstands maintain a constant intimacy with the baselines in "suffer hell," as some call it. Baseball rules prescribe that the distance from the plate back to the stands shall be 60 feet. At Sulphur Dell it's a cozy 40 feet. The first-base boxes are only 42 feet away at the closest point. Third-base stands are 26 feet from the bag.

Back in 1885 Cap Anson brought his Chicago Cubs to the Dell for three weeks of spring training. The sulphur water they drank at the park must have given them extraordinary energy, for that summer the Cubs lost fewer games than any team in history.

No baseball park has been flooded as often as the Dell. A quarter of a mile from the Cumberland River, it submerges every time the estuary goes on a rampage. One night the Vols were playing New Orleans after heavy rains had raised the river. The visitors couldn't sit in their dugout. It was filled with water. Going after a pop foul, Del Ballinger, the Pelican catcher, tripped over a bat near the dugout. Just as he caught the ball, he plunged headlong into several feet of water. He sank, still clutching the ball. When he came to the surface, the umpire called the batter out. Ballinger later admitted he dropped the ball in the water but grabbed it again just as he reached the surface.

Anything is likely to happen in Sulphur Dell.

THIS PIECE appeared in *This Week* magazine. The date was 1946, if it matters.

François at the Bat

LESLIE LIEBER

FOR ALMOST a quarter of a century, a Parisian sports writer named Georges Bruni has engaged in a singlehanded campaign to sell the strange game of baseball to 40,000,000 Frenchmen.

Although after twenty-two years he's only gotten halfway to first base, M. Bruni's zeal for America's national pastime has netted him election to the French Legion of Honor, has taught 5,000 splenetic French fans how to say *"tuez l'arbitre"* (kill the ump) and has won a subsidy of $500 a year from the French Minister of Sports, who is reported to have no idea whether "le baseball" resembles bullfighting or tiddlywinks.

He has also produced at least one Gallic nine capable of making mincemeat—or maybe in France it's pâté de foie gras—out of one of the best GI teams overseas.

The *Fédération Française de Baseball*, of which 65-year-old, rubicund Georges Bruni is president, director of propaganda and erstwhile second-string third baseman, was founded back in 1924. Americans never even remotely suspected its existence until the day shortly after the Liberation when France's challengers trotted out on a makeshift diamond in a climax to one of the most picturesque and comic chapters in the history of the game.

For two decades baseball in France had gone its merry Gallic way, cut off from its roots in the New World, orphaned and out of touch with its origins. When the Americans finally hove into sight, the orphan was unrecognizable. Papa Bruni had raised a soda-pop sport on a diet of Chanel No. 5 and sparkling burgundy.

The French "baseballeurs" who took the field in this long-awaited game against the American GIs on a warm August day in 1945 looked like a collection of men from Mars, Barbary Coast pirates, Rip Van Winkle and fugitives from a masquerade ball. French baseball styles were founded on those exhibited by the White Sox and Giants on a barnstorming tour in Paris twenty-two years ago. It was this game that kindled a latent sand-lot flame in Georges Bruni as he sat entranced along what he later learned was the third-base line. But Georges hadn't paid much attention to what the players wore and it never seemed very important to him.

As a result, the GIs were ill prepared for what they saw when the doughty Frenchmen began limbering up with their one ball and one bat—all that remained of the large stock of baseball equipment left behind by doughboys of World War I.

The second and third basemen were attired in blue baseball shorts, aviation goggles and coal miners' caps. The pitcher wore the costume of an ice-hockey goalie, complete with heavily-padded shin guards. Two men, the shortstop and left fielder, donned steel helmets before assuming their positions.

But conviction that the filming of a new Marx Brothers film was in the offing reached its height when an apparition in a tight one-piece bathing suit and straw hat pranced out to occupy right field.

It was the umpire behind the plate who strayed farthest from orthodox tailoring. His face was buried behind the hideous masquerade of a 1917 gas mask. And the wire mask meant for the face was strapped across the umpire's groin.

At first glance the Americans wanted to call off the game. Mutterings of revolt against so grotesque a contest spread to the whole team. But there were 800 eager spectators in the stands. Those onlookers and the signs of tears in the eyes of Georges Bruni, who had devoted his life to the consummation of this day, softened the GI team. The game went on as scheduled.

It was wild and fast and comic, and sometimes it seemed that the Frenchmen's three best "batteurs" came up with surprising frequency. But these men who dressed like scarecrows and clowns proved they could play ball. Years of culling and weaning had produced nine men who could stand up against competition from the New World. The Frenchmen won the game, five to three, turning what might have been the pathetic end of two decades of comic-opera baseball history into a vindicating triumph for Papa Bruni.

Perhaps the zaniest episode in the annals of the crêpes-suzette circuit was the time one of the rich backers of the Fédération Française de Baseball decided to import some African dust to make an infield worthy of the Third Republic.

Until that moment, all of France's ball diamonds had been in the rough. Her moist climate made excellent mud, but fell down miserably in the manufacture of de luxe dust good enough for French shortstops to scoop hot grounders out of.

There was only one solution: Morocco, the backer said, had wonderful dust. Yes, lots of sand—but plenty of honest-to-goodness, dirty old dust, too. So the vice president in charge of dust for the Fédération ordered four carloads of it from Morocco. How many Arab heads were scratched in consternation, how many African acres were combed in bewilderment will never be known.

But it *is* known that the sun-baked African soil landed at the port of Marseille and was loaded on four freight cars.

From there on the fate of one of the noblest experiments in sports becomes muddy. It never arrived in Paris and nothing was ever heard from it again. It may have roamed the French rails for years, embroiled in red tape and wrong bills of lading, a lost infield in search of second base.

One theory is that railroad men dumped it out along the right of way near Lyons—where it would have been wafted ironically back to North Africa by the mistral which blows southward over the Mediterranean every winter. Others think the infield was used by an ammunition factory in the manufacture of explosives, and that the Germans attacking the Maginot Line got some of the second-base humus in the face.

Outside of this unsuccessful dabble in dust, the two hardest jobs facing Bruni's Fédération were explaining the rules of the sport and molding players out of a people who for centuries had kicked—but had never thrown—balls. In a prospectus written by the Fédération's R. H. Goulka, the act of throwing a ball was described in awesome terms. In a warning to novices, Goulka writes:

"It is very difficult to become a good player after the age of twenty because of our total ignorance of a rather important action known as 'throwing the ball,' an athletic gesture not practiced in other sports. Certain players," he continues, "may have an inclination to throw with both arms."

Then, in a wise bid to the French preference for mental rather than bodily exertions, the manual goes on to describe the new sport as a "prodigious developer of intellectual promptitude, where the player's brain is in continual action. It is a game of speed and skill which never produces rough contact between contestants."

While Bruni publicized baseball in his sports columns and recruited adventurers willing to stand up to the plate, other members of the Fédération spent long hours formulating the rules and regulations of the game in French for the enlightenment of the new fans. They succeeded in reducing everything to one tightly crammed sheet of printed matter. Requiring about an hour's close study, and guaranteeing nothing, this baseball primer was distributed before every game. Newcomers were advised to come early and bone up while waiting for the first pitch.

Using the terms finally arrived at by the Fédération, the game of baseball, as the Frenchman sees it, shapes up approximately as follows: the "attrapeur" (catcher) has eight partners scattered over the "petit champs" (little field) and the "grand champs" (big field or outfield). Their main object in life is to "run, jump and catch." The "batteur" is "eliminated and returns to null-and-void territory" (in other words, he's out) when the "lanceur" (pitcher) throws three "bonnes" (goods—strikes), but may go to "premiere" base after watching four "mauvaises" (bads—balls) go by.

Once the "batteur" succeeds in his object of hitting the ball in front of him, he must launch himself (s'élancer) "towards the right," to attain the bases. This admonition to turn towards the right is one of the mysteries of the instruction sheet. In America, at least, a batter darting headlong off to the right would end up in his own dugout.

After nine "reprises"—which the dictionary translates as "retakings" or "reproductions" but which we may assume means "innings"—the Frenchman is free to get up and go home.

Incidentally, overseas fans have never heard of the traditional stretch for good luck in the seventh "reprise." But Bruni has made a note of it for the next edition of the rules.

One of the worst misinterpretations of the one-page baseball primer occurred in southern France, where teachers naturally assumed that left-handed hitters were supposed to do everything backwards. This meant running to third base first and thence upstream back to home plate. This supposition caused so many collisions of runners speeding in opposite directions that the tutors had to ask Paris headquarters for clarification by long-distance telephone.

Another snafu resulted from the strange warning printed at the top of the instruction sheet for the benefit of uninitiated rooters. It says:

"Spectator! Whether you are close or far away from the game, never let the ball get out of sight because it may come at you. If it does, *keep your hands off*—unless a player asks you to retrieve it."

This thoughtless counsel has caused innumerable good-hearted and literal burghers to be conked on the head by batted balls. Several spectators, after being knocked unconscious and carried from the field, with the rules and regulations still clutched in their hands, have been known to lose all subsequent interest in the sport.

Despite all odds, Bruni's efforts have produced three or four passable teams. The Paris Police Department, although not of championship caliber, has always been one of the most colorful and crafty aggregations. They specialize in the hidden-ball trick, base stealing and browbeating the umpire. The rights of umpires in home-plate litigation with overwrought gendarmes have never been made clear.

For many years both the autobus and subway systems of Paris also had their own baseball teams. Recently, when underground and surface transportation were merged into one company, cynics interpreted it as a clever move by the subway people to get their mitts on a man named Dubois—the best fielder and clean-up hitter who ever stripped the gears of a Paris bus.

* * *

The Babe Ruth of France is frail, 35-year-old pitcher and first baseman Emile Riviere, who learned the game in New York, where his father was a chef. Today Emile's reputation is so widespread that foreign countries have resorted to skulduggery to keep him out of international games.

It was probably not just an accident that Spain misplaced his passport just before a big game in Barcelona. While Riviere languished at the border, his teammates were guillotined in the Catalonian capital.

With Bruni growing old the future of French baseball now rests with a priest, the Abbé Le Meur, assistant to the General Chaplain of the French Army. Ever since he learned the game from American students at Saint Sulpice in Paris, Father Le Meur's love of baseball has provided a real-life parallel to Bing Crosby in *Going My Way*. He has preached and encouraged baseball among hundreds of his young parishioners all over France.

During the Occupation, the pitching priest took baseball underground—but not far enough. Suspected of taking part in an army officers' plot against the Nazis, his case was further complicated when the Gestapo found him at Alfort teaching young boys how to throw a roundhouse curve. He was bundled into a freight car headed for a concentration camp in the Reich. With the train going 40 miles an hour, Abbé Le Meur jumped off, landed unhurt in a ditch and escaped.

"The jump would never have been possible," he declared, "if it hadn't been for the many times I had applied similar tactics—sliding into home plate."

I NEVER SAW Wagner. I saw Boudreau, Rizzuto, Jurges, Eddie Miller
and Martin Marion, and I think that last fella played short best of all.

1942:
St. Louis Cardinals 4,
New York Yankees 2

MARTIN MARION
as told to LYALL SMITH

IT WAS a cocky bunch of Cardinals that went
into that big barn of a Yankee Stadium on
October 7 in the 1942 World Series. We'd
found out by this time that we could whip the
Yanks. We were on the long end of a 3-1
score in series games by now, but we wanted
to do one thing. And that was to beat big Red
Ruffing.

We knew we could lick him even though
he'd won the opener down in St. Louis. He
had us nibbbling out of his hands for eight innings before we finally got over our chills and
teed off on him to knock him out in the last
of the ninth. But even though we chased him,
Red won that game 7 to 4 and we still wanted
to whip him all the way.

We knew he was going to face us in the
fifth game when we went out to the park and
even though we were anxious to pick on him
we still had a few misgivings. For the day was
one of those dark, dreary ones in New York
with low misty clouds sailing in off the ocean.

Captain Terry Moore was standing at the
window when I went into the locker room under the stands to dress for the game. He was
staring out at the dull skies. "That Ruffing will
be hard to hit today," he murmured. "If that
fast one is working he'll be tough."

There's no fooling about our being chesty
when we went out that day.

None of us was superstitious except Moore
and he was really worried. I remember I walked
into the dugout with Kurowski and we started

talking about what we were going to do with
the $6,000 that went to the winners.

"Holy smokes," moaned Terry. "Don't talk
like that, you guys. We haven't won it yet." He
really was fretting.

Well, we started the game. Jimmy Brown
opened with a walk but Ruffing fooled Moore
on a third strike and Slaughter banged into a
double play. That was the first one we had hit
into all through the series and Enos was really
talking to himself when he went into the outfield.

It didn't take the Yanks long to score, for
Phil Rizzuto, their little shortstop, slammed
one of Johnny's fast balls into the stands the
first time up and boom . . . just like that we
were behind 1 to 0.

We pecked away at Ruffing in the second
when Walker Cooper got a single, and then
picked up another hit in the third on a linei
by Jimmy Brown.

Came the fourth and Slaughter put us back
in the game with a homer off Ruffing that tied
it up. We felt better but didn't have long to
feel that way for Rolfe opened up the last half
of the same inning with a bunt down to
Beazley.

Johnny was too anxious and after fielding
the ball badly he threw wild to first and Red
went on down to second. He got around to
third on a long fly by Roy Cullenbine and Joe
DiMaggio then socked a single to left on the
first pitch to put the Yanks in front again

2-1. It looked bad for a while when powerful Charlie Keller, toughest looking player I ever saw at the plate, hit another one of Beazley's slow curves for another single to put DiMag on third. But Gordon fanned and I threw out Bill Dickey.

We got our fourth hit in the fifth when Beazley broke his bat on a single but nothing came of it and we still trailed as the Yanks came up in their half. Gerry Priddy opened with a smash through the box but I was playing him in the right spot and threw him out on a close play. But Ruffing beat out a tap to Beazley and when Johnny Hopp made a low throw to me on a grounder by Rizzuto I couldn't hold the ball and they had men on second and first with one out. We got jittery for a minute and Jimmy Brown kicked Rolfe's roller to load the bases.

Then Beazley really bore down. He made Cullenbine pop out to me and Kurowski came up with DiMaggio's hot grounder to step on third for the out.

Up we came again. Moore hit Ruffing's first pitch for a single and Slaughter, who really was hungry that day, got another hit on the first pitch. We started whooping it up then and Ruffing looked a little rattled. He got Musial on an infield pop but Walker Cooper socked a fly down the foul line and although Cullenbine caught it, Terry came ripping in from third to score and tie it all up again.

That made it 2-2 and it stayed that way through the next two innings. Up came the ninth inning. Cooper was the first batter and he brought us off the bench when he reached out those long arms of his and poked a slow curve into right center. Southworth gave Johnny Hopp the bunt sign and he laid down a beauty to put Walker on second. That brought up Kurowski.

Ruffing stood out there for a few short seconds that seemed like ages while he looked down at Whitey in the batter's box. He'd

fanned him three times in that first game of the series, probably was trying to figure what he threw him those times. He got one strike and one ball on Kurowski and then served him another one. Whitey swung and he really hit it.

"There it goes," screamed Moore. "There it goes." Right into the stands and we had two more runs. We nearly killed Whitey when he crossed the plate. I remember tackling him and we mobbed him until he begged for us to let him go.

Then we sobered down in a hurry for we still knew the Yanks had a punch in those bats of theirs. And they proved it. Joe Gordon led off with a single and we started to worry. Dickey up. He hit a bouncer down to Brown at second, the kind that Jimmy had gobbled up all year easy-like. But he muffed this one and Bill was safe at first and Gordon was on second. We stopped to talk things over again with Cooper walking slowly out to the mound to talk to us.

He talked to Beazley for a while and then looked at me. "Watch it, Marty," he said. "We might try something."

That's all he said but I nodded. I knew. Priddy was at bat and we knew he was going to try to bunt those runners along. Walker called for a high fast one and Beazley sent one down a mile a minute that was right across Priddy's eyes. Quick as I could I cut behind Gordon who had about a 10-foot lead off second base. I dove for the bag and just as I hit it the ball got there too.

Cooper had reared back and thrown it with all the power he had in his big wide shoulders. And that was plenty. It came to me waist high just as I hit the bag. Gordon was on his way back to second and crashed into me. But I held the ball. He rolled over and I went at Umpire George Barr.

I just about jumped out of my shoes. "You're out," he bellowed. We'd picked him off!

BILL McGEEHAN, Stanley Frank has written, "was the founder of the " 'Aw nuts' school" of sports writing. The following piece was done during the 1925 World Series.

Where the Infield Wasn't

W. O. McGEEHAN

AFTER MATURE DELIBERATION I have come to the conclusion that only those who know little or nothing about the national pastime really enjoy a World Series. The experts are interested only in the games that put the non-experts into a state of somnolence, while they suffer great mental anguish at the games that produce thrills for those who know little or nothing about the intricacies of inside baseball.

For instance, after the opening game of the current series Mr. Wilbert Robinson, president of the Brooklyn Baseball Club, approached me beaming with enthusiasm. "Now there," said Mr. Robinson, "was a great game of baseball." "Why?" I demanded. Mr. Robinson withered me with a look of scorn. "And they send saps like you to report baseball games," he said, bitterly.

Following the second game Mr. Robinson held me with his glittering eye. "You saw it?" he asked. "Surely," I replied evasively and tried to hurry on. "You got the big story of the game?" he demanded. "Oh, yes," I replied airily. "Peck fumbled one and then Cuyler drove out a home run, and it was all over."

The World Series guest here beat his breast and emitted a loud raspberry. "Do you mean to tell me," demanded Mr. Robinson, "that you did not notice the big feature of the game? Didn't you see the Pittsburgh infield come in during the ninth inning? Anybody who knows anything about baseball would have noticed that. I asked Fred Clarke about it after the game and all he said was, 'You go to hell!' and here you are going to write a piece about the baseball game and you didn't even see that."

"If the infield did come in, what of it?" I demanded, a trifle nettled. "If the infield

wanted to play in why shouldn't it? This is a free country, including Pittsburgh, even if every hotel-keeper in the place is named Jesse James."

"Everybody noticed it," continued Mr. Robinson, ignoring the flippancy of your correspondent. "John McGraw nearly tore out of the ball park. Even Colonel Huston, who has been sleeping through the series, woke up and said, 'Somebody tell that Pittsburgh infield to deploy as skirmishers, double time.' Of course he went right back to sleep again, but he noticed it.

"Then there was Jim Tierney, of the Giants. Why even he noticed it, and Judge McQuade was hollering for somebody to get an injunction or an alibi or a habeas corpus or something to get that Pittsburgh infield where it belonged! I heard Barney Dreyfuss yelling, 'Tell that infield to play looser! Tell Bill McKechnie to tie the infield loose!' "

"But," I insisted, "nobody hit where the infield wasn't. Also Pittsburgh won the game. So once more I ask, what of it?"

"What of it?" demanded the indignant Mr. Robinson. "It wasn't right, that's all! It wasn't baseball!"

"But Pittsburgh won the game!" I persisted.

"Oh, what is the use of talking to a sap?" said Mr. Robinson. As a parting shot he added, "When you talk to Ma Robinson about the ball game do not admit that you did not notice that Pittsburgh infield. She thinks that you are intelligent. So, for heaven's sake, do not tip your mitt and your secret will be safe with me. I never will tell anybody that you did not notice the Pittsburgh infield."

Mr. Robinson merely strengthened a conviction which I have held concerning the national pastime for these many years. This conviction is that the great majority of the cash customers never get a thrill out of inside baseball, and that the perfect baseball game, if it could be ballyhooed in advance, would not draw a corporal's guard.

In support of this conviction I would offer in evidence the almost perfect Athletics owned by Mr. Cornelius McGillicuddy. They won ball games with such monotonous regularity that the customers became so wearied of seeing them win baseball games that they did not come to the ball park. When the customers do not come to baseball parks the enthusiasm of the owner for a perfect ball club and perfect baseball begins to die a very painful death. Mr. McGillicuddy scattered his perfect ball club all over the open ivory market and started fresh.

In the first game of the current World Series they staged some perfect baseball and set all of the cash customers to yawning. Mr. Mc-Graw, Mr. Jennings, Mr. Cobb and Mr. Babe Ruth were thrilled by it, but the non-experts were not. As the experts do not contribute to the support of the national pastime to any marked extent, it looks as though the magnates should strive for imperfection by all legal and reasonable means.

Baseball is a circus, and as is the case with many a circus, the clowns and the side shows frequently are more interesting than the big stuff in the main tent.

Mr. Pie Traynor, who broke out into a rash of boils, base hits and fancy fielding at the start of the current series, once posed in the role of opportunity knocking at the gates of Fenway Park, the home grounds of the Boston Red Sox.

Young Mr. Traynor is from the rock-ribbed, rock-headed coast of Massachusetts. He wanted to play baseball; consequently he used to haunt Fenway Park at practice time. He would worm himself into the practice infield and work himself into large gobs of perspiration.

The Red Sox manager (it may or may not have been Cousin Edward Barrow, who is now filling the post of secretary to the Yankees with ease, grace and abandon) noticed him one day. Said the manager of the Red Sox to Mr. Pie Traynor, "I wish you would get to hell out of here and stay out! I am tired of watching you cut our nice infield to pieces with your spikes."

Stung to the quick, young Pie Traynor left the park abruptly and in a fit of despondency moved south, where he obtained employment, as they say, with a minor league club. It was not long before Mr. Traynor was annexed by a Pirate scout.

The Red Sox could use a young man of Traynor's size, weight and general make-up at the current writing. It is very unwise to discourage earnest young men. They return later bearing wreaths of raspberries.

The downpour that stopped the game today caused some of the veteran World Series followers to reminisce in a spirit of brooding melancholy about the series of 1911, when the inmates of the traveling madhouse were held seven days in Philadelphia by the rain.

There is something to be merry about in the thought that if the rain had to come it came in Washington instead of Pittsburgh. A week in Pittsburgh at World Series rates would bankrupt organized baseball.

The conversation with a Pittsburgh hotel clerk during this series runs to this effect:

"How much for a room?"

"How much have you got with you? That's what it costs and it has to be paid in advance."

THE MOST EXCITING PLAY...

The steal of home, from Honus Wagner (top) to Jackie Robinson (bottom).

International News

Wide World

Sports Illustrated

THE MOST UNKINDEST CUT OF ALL...

Henry Thompson of the New York Giants has hit a grand-slam homer against
the Dodgers at the September height of the 1954 pennant race. He has just
this minute hit it. Look at everybody!

THE
SADDEST
OF
POSSIBLE
WORDS...

Tinker, Evers

International News

International News   Chance

BASEBALL has had two "miracle" pennant drives. In 1951, the New York Giants, in second place 13½ games off the lead on August 11, caught up to a Brooklyn team which itself was playing better than .500 ball and won the pennant on the last day of a three-day post-season playoff. In 1914, the Boston Braves, in last place 11 games off the lead on July 19, passed not one but all seven other teams in their stretch run. The relative merits of these two finishes make for happy arguments, but few people know that those Braves, starting out in the cellar on July 19, were in first place by September 2! They creamed the mighty A's in the World Series, too. Tom Meany, one of the very best, supplies the details here in a section excerpted from his fine book, *Baseball's Greatest Teams.*

The Miracle Man

TOM MEANY

GEORGE TWEEDY STALLINGS was a man of infinite impatience. One of baseball's greatest legends, Stallings may also have been baseball's first bona fide split personality. Away from the ball park, he was a dignified, fastidious man, meticulous in dress, Chesterfieldian in his manners. Nobody ever would take him for a baseball manager. Swarthy, moon-faced, bright-eyed, he would have been a cinch for today's men-of-distinction ads.

On the bench during a ball game, Stallings was another person. No man, not even John McGraw or Leo Durocher, ever reached the heights of invective stormed by George. He could fly into a schizophrenic rage at the drop of a pop fly. Sputtering with a fury which invited apoplexy, Stallings told off ballplayers as they haven't been told off since.

And, curiously enough, nobody minded the tongue lashings of Stallings. "It was an art with him," Hank Gowdy remarked with awesome reverence over three decades later.

In 1915, a year after his baseball miracle, Stallings walked home from the ball game with Owner Jim Gaffney. All the Braves rode home, for they all had purchased cars out of their series shares, all but Johnny Evers, who had won a Chalmers car as the National League's most valuable player for 1914. Stallings knew the make of every car owned by his players and

in that 1915 season, he prefaced his derogatory remarks to his men by inserting the name of the automobile. Thus Rabbit Maranville became an "Aperson Jack-rabbit bonehead," others were "Packard dunces," "Stanley Steamer clowns" and "White simpletons."

Only once did Stallings forget the name of a car owned by one of his players. Seeking to call attention to the mental shortcomings of Gowdy, who missed a sign one day, the Braves' manager turned to the rest of the bench.

"Look at him up there," he sputtered derisively, "the—the—" And there was a pause as Stallings tried in vain to recall the name of the car driven by Gowdy. He was stumped, but not for long.

"Look at him," yelled Stallings, "the bicycle-riding so-and-so."

It was Stallings' habit to sit on the same spot on the bench day after day, his knees and his feet close together. As he grew agitated—and he did so every day, win, lose or draw—he would slide his feet, still close together, back and forth over the floor of the dugout. And sometimes he would slide his body, too. He wore the seat of a pair of trousers clean through during the second game of the 1914 World Series.

Not only was Stallings superstitious but he encouraged his ballplayers in superstition. He couldn't abide scraps of paper anywhere within range of his vision, an idiosyncrasy rival ball-players exploited to the hilt when they learned of it.

Years after Stallings had left the Braves, when he managed and owned the Rochester Club in the International League, his legend persisted. Even today, two stories of the Stallings repartee are still part of baseball folklore.

One deals of his trials with two collegians, **twin** brothers who were infielders. Sometimes they're identified as the Shannon twins from Seton Hall, often they're not from Seton Hall at all, neither twins nor brothers and not even infielders. Through all versions of the story, however, they remain collegians.

The story goes that one day the twins were on second and third, with one out. The Rochester batter hit to the shortstop, who threw home to cut off the run. The twin on third was caught in a run-down and eventually tagged out. And the twin on second chose that particular moment to try and make third where he, too, was exterminated and the inning was over.

The enormity of what he had just witnessed left Stallings speechless. But only briefly. The inning over, the twins returned to their defensive positions in the field. George darted off the bench and beckoned the two tyros to him.

Paternally draping an arm on the shoulder of each, Stallings inquired, "You boys are both college graduates, aren't you?"

"Yes, Mr. Stallings," they chorused in assent.

"Well, then," said Stallings briskly and, changing his voice to imitate the staccato bark of a cheer leader, he roared: "Rah, rah, rah! Rah! rah! rah! Rah! rah! rah!"

Perhaps the most hallowed of all the Stallings legends concerns itself with the time when he retired to his plantation at Haddock, Georgia, The Meadows, broken in health and through with baseball. He was suffering from a serious cardiac disturbance.

"Mr. Stallings," said the specialist at the completion of the examination, "you have an unusually bad heart. Is there any way you can account for it?"

"Bases on balls, you so-and-so, bases on balls," cursed Stallings softly, turning his face to the wall.

Stallings managed before it became the baseball style to address managers as "Skipper" but his position with his players may be judged from the fact that they usually called him "Chief." Some of the more intimate called him "George" but none ever took any liberties with

him. Baseball, to Stallings, was too serious to permit of any levity.

There were, of course, "meetings" before Stallings' day, as those baseball skull sessions are called, but the Chief intensified these daily conclaves at which strategy was mapped. He was as careful in detail of play as he was in detail of dress, a precise, methodical planner.

Stallings is generally given the credit for being the first to use different outfield combinations for left- and right-handed pitchers. The "percentage" of having a left-hander bat against a right-handed pitcher and vice versa was recognized long before 1914, particularly in the selection of pinch hitters and relief pitchers but Stallings was the first to play the percentage wholesale. He almost was forced into it, because the Braves did not have a strong outfield that season, but Stallings made the best of it, by having Herbie Moran, Larry Gilbert and Joe Connolly as one set of outfielders, against right-handed pitching, and Leslie Mann, Ted Cather and George Whitted against southpaws.

There were others who broke into these combinations, of course—Stallings used nearly a dozen different outfielders during the year—and Connolly, the only member of the team to hit .300 for the season, frequently was used against both right- and left-handed pitchers. It was, nevertheless, the first full outfield switch in history and Stallings stuck to it during the World Series.

One thing Stallings must get credit for introducing into baseball is the "tooth" sign. The Chief would call a certain play by baring his teeth. Dark-complexioned and with teeth of pearly white, Stallings could give his sign from the shadows of the dugout and have it picked up by his coaches or players every time. When the Chief bared his fangs his men knew it was time to run—but literally, since the Braves used it as a steal sign.

      *   *   *

Every story of the Boston Braves of 1914 deals so heavily with the three-man pitching staff of Lefty Tyler, Bill James and Dick Rudolph that latter-day fans may be pardoned for assuming that these three were the only hurlers the Braves had. They were the only ones to appear in the World Series and among them they won sixty-nine of the ninety-four games the Braves won that season. There were other pitchers, droves of them in fact, including Hub Perdue who had been counted on as a regular until he was traded to St. Louis in mid-season for outfielders Whitted and Cather.

Stallings' Big Three had stamina and skill in equal proportions. Tyler was a left-hander who could really wheel the ball in, a big man as was James. Tyler was a power pitcher with a blazing fast ball, while James had one of the most difficult spitters in the league.

While Tyler and James were strong-arm boys, tiny Dick Rudolph was a pitching cutie, gifted with a great curve and superhuman control. He could get a piece of the plate with almost every pitch. Rudolph, for all of his diminutiveness, didn't lag behind the others when it came to staying power. He won twenty-seven games for the Braves that season, had a twelve-game streak going at one time and pitched a half-dozen shutouts right where they did the most good, when the Braves were moving from the cellar to the penthouse.

Rudolph, one of the earliest of the many Fordham graduates to make major league history, also threw a spitball but this was merely to be stylish. His curve and his control were the major weapons of the Bald Eagle. His spitball itself wasn't much but the fact that he faked throwing one most of the time helped throw the batters off.

"As for Dick's spitter," recollects Gowdy, "about the best you could say for it was that it was wet."

Gowdy, who did most of the catching for the Braves that year, still talks with reverence of the Big Three. "They had guts," he says simply, "and they got the ball over in the pinch." Incidentally, Hank once spoke glowingly over the radio of the relief work of a pitcher from Rochester, Tom Hughes, and expressed surprise that he isn't listed among the members of the historic team.

Hank's usually reliable memory tricked him on Hughes. In 1915, Tom did some fine pitching for the Braves but he didn't join the 1914 club until near the close of the season and as a consequence wasn't eligible for the series. He did win one game for the Braves, on September 29, beating the Cubs to clinch the pennant. It undoubtedly was the importance of that game which stuck in Gowdy's mind. Hughes, as a matter of fact, only was in two games for the '14 Braves and Otto Hess had to relieve Tom to win the second one for the Braves.

There were many remarkable things about Rudolph, Tyler and James, over and above their durability. One, and most important, was their talent for winning low-score games. The Braves were not a good hitting team and the pitchers had to make the most of what runs they got. This the Big Three was able to do, particularly from mid-July on, when the chips were down. James won nineteen of his last twenty decisions, Rudolph had his twelve-game winning streak already mentioned and Tyler was untouchable when he had to be, which was most of the time.

No surviving member of the 1914 Braves will consider a report on the pitching staff either complete or authentic unless credit is given to Fred Mitchell, an old catcher who was Stallings' first lieutenant. Fred started in baseball as a pitcher, injured his arm and had become a catcher. He caught for Stallings four years before when George had managed the Yankees.

Mitchell, who also coached at third base, conducted quiet sessions of his own with the pitchers, private confabs superimposed on the general meetings held by Stallings. Not content with this, Fred also used to go over opposing hitters with Gowdy, both before and after a game.

"Fred would ask what sort of pitch So-and-so had hit," recalls Hank, "and suggest that we might have better luck pitching low to some players. He knew pitching as few men ever have known it. Maybe it was because having begun his career as a pitcher and finished it as a catcher, he knew both ends of the business."

* * *

Stallings set a high value on morale. He was away ahead of Bill Roper, Princeton's football coach, with the-team-that-won't-be-beat-can't-be-beat theory. He believed that if his players believed that they could win, they would win. It was as simple as that with the Chief.

It is unlikely that any manager ever had a better team for his own pet theories than Stallings did in 1914. The abuse which the Chief might heap on a player who pulled a boner was equaled by that which the hapless Brave drew from his own mates. Johnny Evers, a veteran of the rowdy-dow Cubs of Frank Chance, was the second baseman and team captain and no captain ever took his duties more seriously. He ran his players ragged and considered it a personal insult when anybody on the squad let him down.

"He'd make you want to punch him," grinned Maranville one day years later, "but you knew Johnny was thinking only of the team."

That remark of Rabbit's explains the 1914 Braves better than an entire book could. Everybody, like Evers, was thinking only of the team. The Rab himself was a source of inspiration to the club, with his amazingly agile scampering around short, his quick, fliplike throws and his happy-go-lucky disposition.

Butch Schmidt, the burly first baseman, was a great jollier. He dealt only in superlatives. When Maranville ran to the outfield to make one of those vest-pocket catches of a pop fly which delighted National League fans for more than a score of years, Schmidt would roar out, "Rab, old boy, you're the best shortstop in the world." When Rudolph cut the plate with a third strike, Butch would yell, "Dick, old man, you're the best pitcher in the world." And so on, down the line.

This penchant of Schmidt's for extravagant praise was so marked that to this day Butch annually receives a Christmas card from Hank Gowdy, addressed to "Butch Schmidt, The Best First Baseman in the World, Baltimore, Md."

Whether it was Stallings or Evers who planted this fire in the 1914 Braves it would be hard to say. Perhaps it was the Chief who kindled it and the peppery Trojan who fanned it. At any rate, the fire was there and any player who came to the 1914 Braves during the season, as many did, caught fire along with them or else he didn't linger long.

No better example of the 1914 Braves' spirit could be offered than the retort of little Herbie Moran to Harry Davis, when the captain of the Athletics visited the Polo Grounds after the Braves had clinched the pennant to congratulate Moran and, incidentally, to look over the club which would meet the A's in the World Series.

"You fellows did a great job, Herbie," said Davis, "and I expect we'll have a great series."

"Harry," answered little Herbie earnestly, "I don't think you fellows will win a single game."

This pride the Braves had in themselves was present even when the club was in last place. Maybe nobody connected with the team, even Stallings, was clairvoyant enough to see a pennant at the end of the trail but they knew they weren't a cellar club. And they never played like one, either, for the Braves had good spirit in the first part of the season as well as in the last. Stallings never abandoned morning practice nor the daily meetings.

Sometime in July, while the Braves were still last, they paused on the eve of a Western trip for an exhibition game in Buffalo. Johnny Evers always claimed it was against "a soap company team" in later years but Gowdy insists it was against the International League club. Both agreed that the Braves had their ears pinned back.

"No matter what the fans think," explained Gowdy, "no big league club likes to lose to a minor league club, even if it is only an exhibition game. Maybe we were last but we were still big leaguers and the pasting we took was galling to our pride. We knew we weren't that bad.

"Western trips in those days were longer than they are now because there were only three such trips a year, instead of four, so you usually played four days in each city. It was a long trip and it was the one which got us out of the cellar and started us toward the pennant I'll always believe it was that trouncing we received from the minor leaguers which provided the spark."

* * *

The pennant race in the National League in 1914 was strange in many ways, aside from the rags-to-riches climb of the Braves. On a Sunday morning in Cincinnati, the fateful nineteenth of July, the Braves awoke to find themselves still in the cellar, eleven games behind the first-place Giants and with a doubleheader scheduled against the Reds that day. The distance from first place to eighth is usually much more than eleven games in mid-July.

Boston, however, had been moving ever since the debacle in Buffalo on the eve of this Western invasion. They had won nine games out of twelve, while the front-running Giants had been able to win only six of fourteen. On the night of July 4, the Braves were fifteen games behind the leaders but on the morning of the nineteenth, they were only eleven games back.

After winning the first game at Redland Field that Sunday, the Braves were trailing 2 to 0 in the ninth inning of the second game but rallied to score three runs and win, moving over Pittsburgh to seventh place. And once having passed the Pirates, the Braves protected their rear by moving in to Pittsburgh and winning four out of five, getting four shutouts from their great staff. Rudolph, Tyler and James each pitched a shutout and Tyler and

James pitched in to collaborate on the fourth. The great pitching was beginning to assert itself.

Once started, there was no halting the Braves. Due to the closeness of the pennant race, the Braves were fourth on July 21, two days after they had been in the cellar. Then they reeled a string of nine straight and in three weeks were in second place.

It was a brawling race by now, as tight races always were in those days. Opposing pitchers paid Boston hitters the sincere, if embarrassing, compliment of pitching under their chins and forcing them to hit the dirt. Rabbit Maranville, the midget with the arms and shoulders of a weight-lifter, flattened Heinie Zimmerman during a ruckus with the Cubs but for years afterward der Zim refused to believe that the Rab had cooled him off. He always insisted that the *coup de grâce* had been administered by one of the larger Braves, Butch Schmidt or Moose Whaling, a reserve catcher. He just couldn't see himself kayoed by the little tyke.

Boston went into first place on September 2 by winning a double-header in Philadelphia, while the Dodgers were beating the Giants. The next day the Braves tumbled to second when Grover Cleveland Alexander outpitched Tyler. Although the Braves beat the Phils three straight, to make it five out of six for the series, they were tied for the lead with the Giants as they returned to Boston for the big Labor Day series with the men of McGraw.

The present Braves Field had not yet been built but was in the process of construction in 1914 and the team of destiny played its home games at the South End Grounds. Now, however, Joe Lannin, the owner of the Red Sox, offered President Gaffney the use of the more spacious Fenway Park for the remainder of the season and the Braves took possession on Labor Day to play morning and afternoon games against the Giants.

It is doubtful if any single day of baseball in Boston ever will attract more paid admissions than were collected for the pre- and post-luncheon games with New York that Labor Day, September 7, 1914. The morning game drew more than 35,000 and the afternoon game approached 40,000. Gaffney announced a total of 74,163 paid admissions for the two games.

Cecil B. De Mille couldn't have improved on the script for the morning game, when the Braves, with Rudolph pitching, beat the great Christy Mathewson by scoring twice with one

out in the ninth. The final score was 5 to 4.

Josh Devore, a fleet-footed outfielder who was obtained from New York after the season opened, started the ninth inning rally with one out by beating out a "squib" to Merkle. Herbie Moran, who was knocked cold when beaned by Alexander in Philly three days before, hit into the overflow crowd for a ground-rule double, Devore being forced to stop at third.

Up came Johnny Evers, quite possibly the most hated member of the tough, dynamic Braves as far as the opposition was concerned. Matty worked on him but the Trojan laced a low, sinking liner to left. George Burns charged the ball but couldn't get up to it in time and it went for a two-bagger, breaking up the ball game and putting the Braves in first place.

Surrounded by a milling, ecstatic and delirious mob, the Braves had to fight their way from the playing field of Fenway Park. McGraw's club fought back in the afternoon game, behind sturdy pitching by Jeff Tesreau and won 10 to 1 to tie up the pennant race again. As the Giants, no amateurs themselves at the art of invective, taunted the Braves, feelings ran so high that James M. Curley, even then mayor of Boston, came onto the playing field in an effort to have Fred Snodgrass chased on charges of attempting to incite a riot. The Mayor appealed first to Umpire Bob Emslie and then to a police lieutenant but both refused to assist His Honor in ousting Snodgrass.

McGraw, however, did remove Snodgrass, not to placate his fellow Celt, Curley, but to keep Fred intact. The Boston fans treated Snodgrass to a shower of pop bottles, the predecessor to the barrage rained at Joe Medwick by the Detroit fans twenty years later.

Came the morrow, however, and McGraw, Snodgrass and even Mayor Curley were quickly forgotten as the Braves, behind three-hit pitching by James, went into first place to stay. Rube Marquard, who had lost eight straight, was McGraw's choice, quite possibly on a hunch, but he got nowhere, the Braves eventually winning by 8 to 3. From that point on it was a breeze, the Braves turning a dog-fight into a romp, winning the pennant by ten and one-half games.

A sample of what was to come in the closing weeks was offered the next day when George A. Davis, Jr., a student at Harvard Law School, pitched a no-hitter in the nightcap as Boston took a double-header from the Phils. Seven Philadelphia players reached first base against Davis, five on passes, two on errors.

The no-hitter pitched by this comparative unknown was typical of the '14 Braves. It was the only no-hit game pitched in the National League that season, despite the great mound feats of Rudolph, Tyler and James. And the reader will remember the previously mentioned Tom Hughes, who joined the Braves just in time to beat the Cubs in his first start on September 29 and clinch the pennant for Boston.

The Braves of 1914 were like that. It was, more than anything else, a team, a unit. If one of the name players wasn't up to it, Stallings always found somebody who was. It was perhaps for this reason that the miracle man wasn't at all upset when J. Carlisle (Red) Smith, his regular third baseman, broke his leg on the last day of the season in Brooklyn.

Smith had started the 1914 season with Brooklyn but was purchased by the Braves when the Dodgers put him on the block. A squatty slugger, Red was one of the few Braves who could be counted on for the long ball and when he was injured it should have been a crushing blow.

Stallings promptly announced that the Braves were no one-man team and that Charley Deal would play third in the World Series. Deal, a good fielder but weak hitter, had opened the season for the Braves at third but it was because of his lightness with the wood that Stallings had grabbed Smith from Brooklyn. Deal batted only .154 in the series, making two two-baggers, but he fielded perfectly and the Braves, as Stallings predicted, never missed the hard-hitting Smith.

It was felt by this time that Stallings and the Braves had run out of miracles. The injury to Smith on the eve of the series was regarded by many as an omen of things to come. The Athletics had won four pennants out of five and the three last World Series in which they had played, beating the Giants four out of five in 1913. Connie Mack's team was a topheavy favorite to cool off the Boston upstarts.

Stallings opened a war of nerves. He accused Mack of closing Shibe Park to the Braves for pre-series practice and he warned his players not to speak to the Athletics, under penalty of a fine, unless it was to insult them. He refused to use the visitors' dressing room in the Shibe Park clubhouse but dressed instead a few blocks away at National League Park, the home of the Phillies. He refused to give the Shibe Park announcer his lineup and chased him from the bench.

Now the A's were no babies at this stuff. They had been in World Series against the Giants and they knew all about bench jockeys because they had been ridden by experts. Or so they thought. But this was different. It was contempt, rather than abuse, and it was puzzling. The series was over before the Athletics ever learned the answer.

A weak hitting team throughout the National League season, the Braves exploded against Chief Bender in the opening game in Philadelphia, knocking him out in the sixth, the first time in all World Series history an Athletics' pitcher had been forced to take cover from enemy bats. And the Braves stole three bases, including a double steal by Hank Gowdy and Butch Schmidt, two of the slowest of the miracle men.

With this sort of batting support, which he rarely enjoyed during the season, Dick Rudolph had no difficulty with the American Leaguers. The only run the A's scored against him was unearned.

Hank Gowdy had a perfect day at bat with a single, double and triple. He was to hit .545 during the series, after batting .243 during the regular season. Gowdy always claimed that he should have hit .300 during the season.

"I hit just as hard during the season as I did during the series," insists Hank, "except that during the season they were going right at somebody while in the series they were going safe."

If the first game was a romp the next three were squeakers but the Braves took them all, just as they had taken the one-sided opener. Bill James had his spitter working for the Braves and the left-handed Eddie Plank was equally untouchable for the Athletics. They came to the top of the ninth locked in a scoreless tie.

It was then that the opportunism of the Braves came to the fore. It was a ball club which might well have had *carpe diem* on its coat of arms, for it never overlooked a bet. Charley Deal, the weak-hitting replacement for Red Smith, got a double with one out when Amos Strunk misjudged his drive to right. As James fanned, Deal was caught off second but, seeing he had no chance to get back, broke for third and just did beat Jack Barry's relay of Wally Schang's throw. It was a close decision and the A's squawked at Umpire Bill Byron but to no avail.

Leslie Mann, leadoff hitter for the Braves, who could pepper southpaws as good as any batter who ever lived, rifled a single to right, just out of Eddie Collins' reach at second, and Deal came in with the only run of the ball game.

Up to this point, James had spitballed his way through a remarkable game. He had held the A's hitless until Wally Schang doubled in the sixth and the second and last Philadelphia hit was a scratch single by Collins in the seventh. Bill had walked only one man, remarkable for a spitballer pitcher.

James's control wavered in the ninth and he passed Barry with one out and then wild-pitched Jack to second. He also walked Jim Walsh, who batted for Plank. Up came Eddie Murphy, the Athletics' leadoff hitter. He smashed one through the box but Maranville was behind second to field the ball almost on the bag, step on the base and flip it to Butch Schmidt at first for a game-ending double play.

As the Braves returned to Boston to resume the series, they were beginning to believe that Stallings was right when he told them they would sweep the series in four straight. And, what's more, there is reason to believe that maybe the A's thought Stallings was right, too.

Identical crowds of 20,562 had seen the first two games at Shibe Park but there were 35,520 at Fenway Park to greet the miracle men and the somewhat bewildered Athletics. Even the repose of an open date on Sunday hadn't allowed the A's to regain their equilibrium.

Stallings trotted out his third ace, Lefty Tyler, and Mack used young Bullet Joe Bush, who already was showing signs of pitching greatness. And Bush three times was given a lead by his mates, the only times in the series in which the A's enjoyed a lead.

Twice the A's were off in front and twice the Braves came back to tie up. All seemed lost in the tenth, however, when Philadelphia scored twice while Evers was kicking Home Run Baker's grounder around with the bases filled. It was one of the few times, perhaps the only time, that the Trojan was guilty of mental aberration in his career.

Hank Gowdy, who continued to plague the Philadelphia pitchers, opened the home half with a home run into the seats in center. Moran walked and raced to third on a single by Evers, scoring on Joe Connolly's fly to tie up the ball game.

Tyler had been removed for a pinch hitter and James, the pitching hero of the second game, took over in the eleventh. He needed to pitch only two innings to gain his second series victory, for in the gathering dusk of the twelfth, the obstreperous Gowdy delivered his third hit and second two-bagger of the day, a shot to the left field bleachers. Leslie Mann ran for him and Larry Gilbert, batting for James, was intentionally passed. With none out, Moran attempted to bunt the runners along and bunted right at Bush. The youngster scooped up the ball to make a play at third but threw wildly and Mann came home with the run which gave the Braves a 5-4 victory and made it three straight.

For the fourth game, Stallings called upon Rudolph, who had become a proud papa since the series had opened. Dick, opposed by Bob Shawkey, another Athletics youngster who was to become a pitching star, won by 3 to 1 and the series was over in four games for the first time in history. During the series, the Chief had called upon no pitchers save his Big Three and Rudolph and James each won two games.

It was a fitting climax to a miraculous season. The Braves of 1914 occupy a unique spot, not merely in baseball, but in American athletic tradition. They have become a symbol for the downtrodden, recorded proof that nothing is ever impossible. One by one, they overcame the seven teams which were ahead of them in the National League race, just as they overcame, one by one, the obstacles which cropped up in the course of the season. And then came the glorious sweep of the World Series against the Athletics. It is truly a great chapter in the history of the underdog, a miraculous page in baseball, fashioned by the miracle man himself, George Tweedy Stallings, aided and abetted by as spirited a group of athletes as ever banded together in any sport.

From *The American Language,*
Supplement II

H. L. MENCKEN

Charley horse. Muscular soreness in a player's leg.

Traced by Nichols to 1891. Dr. H. H. Bender, chief etymologist of Webster, 1934, sent an agent to Bill Clarke, first baseman of the Baltimore Orioles, who said that it came from the name of *Charley* Esper, a left-handed pitcher, who walked like a lame horse. Lawrence C. Salter (private communication, January 14, 1944) sent another agent to Billy Earle, an old-time catcher in the Western League, who said that it was suggested by a horse worked by one *Charley*, ground-keeper at Sioux City. The late Dr. Logan Clendening wrote to me on November 20, 1943: "*Charley horse* is a ruptured muscle. It has exactly the same pathology as string-halt in a horse." In *Treatment of Charley Horse, Journal of the American Medical Association*, November 30, 1946, p. 821, it is described as "injury to a muscle, usually the *quadriceps femoris*." This injury "consists first in a contusion, which results in a *hematoma*. Later the *hematoma* may organize into a *myositis ossificans*, forming soft bone in the muscle."

JOHN GALLAGHER

Courtesy *Sport* Magazine. ©

"Now listen—don't get homer happy!"

THE CAREER of a ballplayer named Mike Kelly began in 1873 when he joined the Troy, New York, Haymakers. He was quite a fellow. So was the late Frank G. Menke, whose *Encyclopedia of Sports* is a monument.

From *Slide, Kelly, Slide*

FRANK G. MENKE

THE INSPIRATION of the immortal poem, "Slide, Kelly, Slide," was that most idolized ballplayer, Mike Kelly, one of the most fascinating figures ever to dig a cleated shoe into the diamond.

He was a slashing, dashing, devil-may-care athlete, good-natured, big-hearted, sincere. He had perhaps the keenest brain that baseball ever knew. He devised new plays in the twinkling of an eye. His strategy was superb, and wherever he went, during his baseball years, he was the beloved titan of the game. He fought for victory every inch of the way, through every game that he played, yet never had an enemy. No umpire ever found it necessary to discipline him. Millions of words were written about him in prose. The song, or poem, "Slide, Kelly, Slide," was written to honor him for his base-running skill.

Kelly was not a fast man. Hovey, Hamilton and Sunday, and the speed marvels who came in the later days, could have given him an eight-yard start and beaten him in the one hundred. Yet he was a superb base-runner because he created the "Fadeaway Slide" and timed his thefts so accurately that he was rarely caught. Before "King Kel's" day, thievery on the sacks was almost an unknown art. Kelly saw the worth of base-stealing. For many weeks, he practiced in private. Then he startled the baseball world with his wild dashes and swift slides to the next bag. He was balldom's pioneer base burglar.

When "Slide, Kelly, Slide" was written, the fans memorized it and chanted it wherever he went. When he reached first, the crowd would begin to yell "Slide, Kelly, Slide" and "King Kel" always tried to oblige. Home-town rooters and rival fans of Kelly's era went to see him and encourage him to attempt the play which, then, was a superb thriller.

Kelly originated the trick of "cutting the bases." Before then, all base-runners religiously touched each bag en route to home. Kelly decided there wasn't any use in doing it—if he could get away with it. On every occasion, when the lone umpire wasn't looking, Kelly would take advantage of the situation and would scamper across the diamond in a direct line from first to third. Once Kelly was on first and the batter hit to right. Kelly ran for second. As he reached there, he noticed that the umpire was absorbed in watching the progress of the ball. Kelly deliberately ignored the existence of third and ran from second, through the pitcher's box, to home plate.

Of course, the opposition team protested, but the game's only umpire had not seen the act. The run stood and won the game.

THIS ARTICLE appeared in 1951 shortly before the New York Giants started their miracle drive for the pennant.

Durocher on Durocher *et al.*

GILBERT MILLSTEIN

WHEN a man gets to be 45, which Leo Durocher, the manager of the New York Giants, will get to be next Friday, the chances are that life will have worked him over assiduously, chipping small, significant pieces off his ego, fettering him with odd, inhibitory reflexes and leaving him, in the hands of fate, as tremulous as a hamster in a box of wood-shavings. On the basis of a recent pre-birthday visit, it can be reported that none of these things has happened to Durocher, although in his twenty-seven years in organized baseball he has fought spectacularly with fans, umpires and teammates (including the late Babe Ruth, whom he once gave a black eye), been suspended for a full year, and moved in mid-season from the managership of the Brooklyn Dodgers to that of their bitterest opponents, the Giants. Nevertheless, his ego still bulks as large as other men's ulcers and throbs with about the same intensity.

Direct testimony on the state of mind that has left Durocher ulcer-free after all these nervous years was taken from him in the Giants' clubhouse at the Polo Grounds on a clear, sunny morning after the team had lost three straight to the Dodgers. His bald brow was unfurrowed, his pale blue eye unhooded, his handshake firm, his smile that of a man who plainly gets along with everybody. He said that baseball was a tough business, that he tried to leave it in the clubhouse with his temper, but that he worked at it twenty-four hours a day and would be lost without it.

"You can't be too thin-skinned," he went on. "That's about the right word for it—you can't take it to heart and let it get you down in baseball. You got to keep fighting, keep coming back. What you like to see more than anything else is to see guys come from behind, guys who make great plays, bear down, like to play the game every minute, run the bases hard, play hard, play to win. Everything else is completely foreign and secondary. Temper? Everybody's got a temper. It just shows different ways.

"You take, say, Bill McKechnie, they called him 'Deacon' he was so mild. Whenever anything happened out on the field, McKechnie just used to amble out and talk to the umpire. I'm not put together that way. It isn't that I want to lose my temper. It's just my physical make-up. I can't get out there quick enough. I got to run. What makes it lucky for me, I guess, is that I never carry a grudge. I don't take it off the field. I fight every way I know how—nothing illegal, of course—but I forget it after the game. I got nothing against umpires or anybody else."

Durocher said his fights with umpires were, more or less, simply a part of his technique for winning. "That's why I admire players who are always scheming up something to beat you. Remember how Stanky used to wave his arms around out there last year until they made him cut it out? What was wrong with that? It distracted the batters, didn't it? There's a lot of talk about sportsmanship. That's always been a funny kind of word to me. Maybe I don't understand it. What're we out for, except to win? This is professional, not amateur. If I'm losing, I'll be bleeding in my heart; inside, I'll be dying. I'll congratulate you, but did I like losing? Hell, no.

"Look, I'm playing third base. My mother's on second. The ball's hit out to short center. As she goes by me on the way to third, I'll accidentally trip her up. I'll help her up, brush her off, tell her I'm sorry. But she doesn't get to third. That's just an exaggeration. But it's an illustration of what I mean. I want to win all the time. If we're spitting at a crack in the wall in this office for pennies, I want to beat you at it. Anybody can finish second. I want to finish first if I can. After that, I've done my job. Otherwise I haven't. When I bring home a pennant to this club, then I'll have had it all."

He broke off for a moment to listen to the sounds of baseball outside and his hands drifted abstractedly over a group of objects ranged on the base of a pen-and-pencil set on his desk. They were all good-luck tokens, some secular, some religious. He said Giant fans had sent them in at the time the team was losing eleven straight games. "Oh, I keep 'em naturally," he said, "but they don't influence me too much. They won't get you base hits. They won't make your pitchers pitch."

"Of course," he admitted, "I am superstitious to *some* extent. If the club is going good, I'll wear the same clothes, drive over the same route in the car. If it's going bad, I'll change —change to anything." The year he won a pennant for the Brooklyn Dodgers, he spent three and a half weeks in the same black shoes, gray slacks, blue coat and blue knitted tie. He did not shave. "Naturally," he added, "I changed my shirt, socks and shorts." This year he not only has changed his clothes with monotonous regularity, but has seen no necessity to drive over any fixed route.

* * *

Durocher, who has been divorced twice, is now married to Laraine Day, the movie actress who also does a daily baseball television show. The couple have two adopted children, Chris, 5, and Michele, 7. They live in a five-room apartment on Park Avenue during the season and in a big house in Santa Monica, California, in the wintertime. Miss Day took to baseball with the passion and accuracy of an actuary for mean average probabilities.

Durocher confessed freely that his wife had brought to fruition in him a love of the finer things, like square dancing, antique silver, china and pictures. "I don't go in for anything specific," he admitted, "but when I buy a painting I want it to fit the house. I remember once I saw a pair of lamps made out of wine buckets. Very fine silver buckets. I said if I ever saw a pair like them they would be perfect for a couple of French provincial tables we've got out at Santa Monica. I'll be damned if I didn't pick up a pair at an auction in Beverly Hills one night. Old as hell. From around 1640 or somewhere in there. I got them for eighty bucks. I had them made into lamps. And you want to know what else I did with them?" Triumph overspread his features: "I planted philodendrons all around the lamp bases. They're simply gorgeous."

He concluded on a lyrical note. "Ah, my life's been wonderful," said Durocher. He looked very much as though it had been. At 45, he weighs around 175 pounds, all well distributed over a frame 5 feet and 9 inches high. "Now, I look back, though," he conceded, "there are some things I'd do differently. I'm not the only one's that way. There are some things I wouldn't have done or said if I had them to do over. Nothing specific—just things in the heat of anger that would have been better unsaid or undone, but being the kind of guy I am, I did say or do them. It just came to me that way. I'm still the same way in baseball, but outside I think a little more now. I'm a little more careful in what I say or do. I mean, I think I am."

THERE was a wild rhyming to the lyrics of Cole Porter's *Kiss Me, Kate* that delighted Mr. Wolcott Gibbs, drama critic of *The New Yorker* magazine. Mr. Gibbs was particularly taken with Porter's rhyming "ambassador" with "Cressida." About the same time, however, the master himself, Ogden Nash, was not only rhyming "Memphis" with "overemphis . . ." he also was blandly asserting that U stands for Hubbell, something not even Cole Porter had previously insisted. Baseball was Mr. Nash's subject, of course.

Line-up for Yesterday
an ABC of Baseball Immortals

OGDEN NASH

A is for Alex
The great Alexander;
More goose eggs he pitched
Than a popular gander.

B is for Bresnahan
Back of the plate;
The Cubs were his love,
And McGraw was his hate.

C is for Cobb,
Who grew spikes and not corn,
And made all the basemen
Wish they weren't born.

D is for Dean.
The grammatical Diz,
When they asked, Who's the tops?
Said correctly, I is.

E is for Evers,
His jaw in advance;
Never afraid
To Tinker with Chance.

F is for Fordham
And Frankie and Frisch;
I wish he were back
With the Giants, I wish.

G is for Gehrig,
The Pride of the Stadium;
His record pure gold,
His courage, pure radium.

H is for Hornsby;
When pitching to Rog,
The pitcher would pitch,
Then the pitcher would dodge.

I is for Me,
Not a hard-sitting man,
But an outstanding all-time
Incurable fan.

J is for Johnson
The Big Train in his prime
Was so fast he could throw
Three strikes at a time.

K is for Keeler,
As fresh as green paint,
The fustest and mostest
To hit where they ain't.

L is Lajoie
Whom Clevelanders love,
Napoleon himself,
With glue in his glove.

M is for Matty,
Who carried a charm
In the form of an extra
Brain in his arm.

N is for Newsom,
Bobo's favorite kin.
If you ask how he's here,
He talked himself in.

Line-up for Yesterday

O is for Ott
Of the restless right foot.
When he leaned on the pellet,
The pellet stayed put.

P is for Plank,
The arm of the A's;
When he tangled with Matty
Games lasted for days.

Q is Don Quixote
Cornelius Mack;
Neither Yankees nor years
Can halt his attack.

R is for Ruth.
To tell you the truth,
There's no more to be said,
Just R is for Ruth.

S is for Speaker,
Swift center-field tender;
When the ball saw him coming,
It yelled, "I surrender."

T is for Terry
The Giant from Memphis
Whose 400 average
You can't overemphis.

U would be 'Ubbell
If Carl were a cockney;
We say Hubbell and baseball
Like football and Rockne.

V is for Vance
The Dodgers' own Dazzy;
None of his rivals
Could throw as fast as he.

W, Wagner,
The bowlegged beauty;
Short was closed to all traffic
With Honus on duty.

X is the first
Of two x's in Foxx
Who was right behind Ruth
With his powerful soxx.

Y is for Young
The magnificent Cy;
People batted against him,
But I never knew why.

Z is for Zenith,
The summit of fame.
These men are up there,
These men are the game.

THIS ACCOUNT appears in the book, *The Greatest Sports Stories from The New York Times,* but no authorship for the piece is listed. A footnote says, "Where credit is not given, the stories were written by anonymous staff members or special correspondents. . . ." Here, nonetheless, are the old Orioles.

1894:
New York Giants 4,
Baltimore Orioles 1

THE NEW YORK TIMES

NEW YORK'S baseball team added to the discomfort of the Baltimore Orioles yesterday and the chances are that the Temple Cup, offered by a Pittsburgh enthusiast for a contest between the first and second clubs in the league race, will be captured this year by the New York Giants. Only one more victory is necessary in order to bring about this result. The New Yorks have captured all three of the games played thus far and have handled the champions as though the team was composed of an aggregation of castoff minor leaguers. Yesterday's score was 4 to 1.

Since the opening of the season the Baltimores have gained a reputation for their skillful fielding, daring base running, heavy hitting, and marvelous team work, but, strange to say, in the present series they have failed to put up even an ordinary game. Their batting is weak, their field work commonplace, their base running slow, and the team work was missing altogether.

The game yesterday was a repetition of the contests in Baltimore. Rusie was the stumbling block, and when men were on bases he sent the ball over the plate with the speed of a rifle shot. After a few innings it was easily to be seen that the Baltimores would lower their colors again. They could not do any batting, and, judging from their feeble efforts both in the field and at the bat, they appeared to regard defeat as a certainty, and when it finally came along they accepted it with rare grace. Instead of the lively Orioles who met and defeated the Giants this summer, the team played like a lot of cripples.

With the Giants it was different. Early in the season their work was suggestive of the good old "has beens," but, as the contests wore on, they appeared to improve and today they are playing a wonderfully strong game of ball, and could defeat any club in the country as easily as they have the Baltimores. The had just warmed up to their work, and if the league season opened next week, they would be big favorites for first honors. The strong point in the work of the Giants is the great pitching of both Rusie and Meekin. Both are in the best possible condition and are today head and shoulders above any pair of pitchers in the profession.

The poor Baltimores are handicapped by the absence of McMahon, their best pitcher. He is suffering from a sore arm.

Every baseball enthusiast in town was at the Polo Grounds yesterday afternoon and watched the slaughter of the Orioles with feelings of pleasure. It was estimated that 20,000 persons saw the game.

"Who's going to pitch?"

The query was put to the scorecard boys a thousand times, and when it was learned that the great and only Amos Rusie would occupy the box, there was a grin of satisfaction and inward chuckle, and the average crank waited to witness the big fellow's hypnotic influence over the Baltimore batters. The wait was not a long one. Big Dan Brouthers was the only man to make two hits, and one of these was a scratch of the most pronounced order. Rusie did a good afternoon's work. Only one run was charged against him, and he retired six men on strikes.

The game was replete with incidents. The wild shouts of the onlookers, the strains of the Catholic Protectory Band, the discordant toots of hundreds of fish horns, and the general outbreak that follows the gathering of thousands of cranks caused a stampede in the horseshed. There were two runaways. One horse upset his carriage, broke the harness, and for a few moments was master of the field. He stopped the game, but was finally captured in left field.

One of the side rails of the free seats gave way, and a dozen persons fell to the ground below, but luckily none was injured. Umpire Emslie and third baseman McGraw had a tilt, and for a time a fight was imminent. Just when the umpire was about to show what he knows about Marquis of Queensberry rules, Catcher Farrell prevented them from spoiling each other's appearance.

Throughout the contest the spectators kept jeering at McGraw, whose rowdyism in the games played at Baltimore was the topic of conversation among the spectators. But McGraw was apparently undisturbed and appeared to rather like the distinction given him. Umpire Hurst was knocked unconscious by a foul tip. After he recovered he rubbed a lump as big as a walnut on his forehead, and, re-

marking that Rusie had his speed with him resumed his duties.

The Giants began to score in the opening inning. After Burke had gone out on a grounder to Jennings, Tiernan hit to Brouthers, who tossed the ball to Hemming. The latter dropped it, and the batter was safe. Then Davis hit to left field. Kelley failed to check the ball and before Brodie returned it Tiernan had scored. Davis, however, was put out while trying to make third on the play. Doyle followed with a hit, but he was disposed of trying to steal to second.

In the fourth inning Brouthers tallied the single run that saved Baltimore from the stigma of a "Chicago." Brouthers made his scratch hit, got to second on a passed ball, was advanced to third on a base on balls and a batter being hit, and came home when Ward fumbled Jennings' grounder.

Fuller, in the fifth, started by getting his base on balls, but he was forced out on Farrell's grounder to Jennings. While trying to execute a double play, Reitz threw past Brouthers, and Farrell got to third. He came in on Rusie's sacrifice and the Giants once more were in front. McGraw failed to stop Davis' grounder in the sixth, and Doyle made a two-base hit, sending in a run. Ward's sacrifice advanced Doyle, and he tallied on Robinson's poor throw to third.

In every inning but the first the Baltimores had men on bases, but sharp field work and the clever pitching of Rusie could not be overcome, nine men being left on bases. As the Baltimores left the field with measured tread, the picture of gloom and despair, a mighty shout went up from the assemblage, cheer after cheer was given for the victors, and the band played "Carry the News to Mary."

Mr. Lawton Carver once gave the all-time description of Britain's Grand National Steeplechase. "They get to a place named Tucker's Corner," he said. "Then they make a left turn and everybody falls off." The beauty of this capsule is reflected in the fact that Tom O'Reilly wrote a whole column about it. Spinning gossamer with the typewriter is columnist (N.Y. *Morning Telegraph*) O'Reilly's delightful *forte*. *Vide* the following.

Barber Knows His Weather Inside Out

TOM O'REILLY

Some people are disappointed when it rains at a ball game. Not me. Every time it looks like rain and I know the Yanks are playing at the Stadium, I quickly turn on Red Barber to get his breathtaking, thrilling rundown of the work of the grounds-keepers. Red never allows a little rain to change the pace of his coverage. Of course, he gives it that old "catbird seat" drawl, but the words come out just the same. Let me give you an example:

"It's getting a little dark out here now. It looks like rain. We had some rain last night you know. Yes, it definitely looks like rain now. In fact it's raining. There it goes. Plate Umpire Rommel has just ordered the game halted and now the Yankees must put that big canvas covering on the infield. It's really coming down now. Although not as hard as last night.

"The grounds-keepers must bring out that old canvas and they are working like beavers. Now they're going to cover first and second. There goes first. There goes second. Yes, they've definitely got the right side of the infield covered. That's first and second. Now they're working on third and home. That's on the left side. There goes third. There goes home. Now they've got third and home covered. Now they've got the entire infield covered. And even though it's raining pretty hard that infield is nice and dry.

"When the rain first started to come down, of course, fans sitting out in the unprotected seats all moved back to drier quarters. Y'know, fans, the reason for covering the infield is that it isn't all grass. Y'see, those base paths are mighty wide. They can get mighty muddy in a li'l, ole downpour like this. Although you must admit it isn't raining as hard today as it did last night. No siree.

"Now, as I explained, those infield base paths would be mighty muddy without that covering. Especially in a downpour like this. Now the outfield is all grass. So it won't get muddy and doesn't have to be covered. Moreover, the whole field forms a sort of dome and the water runs off it toward the stands.

"It's getting lighter in the sky now. But the rain's still comin' down. The weather man said we could expect light showers today. It's coming down hard for the moment but it is really just a light shower. It's nothin' like the way it came down last night. Boy, that was really somethin'! It rained drops as big as li'l ole cranberries. Yes siree. It was just as though somebody had a lake up there and just let it fall. That was a much heavier rain than this one. Although I must admit that nobody is sitting in the uncovered seats for this one, either.

"Now, while we're waitin', let's have a look at the old Suds-Side Scoreboard across the nation. Looks like those li'l ole Red Sox are beating Detroit. Boston's leading the Tigers, 9 to 6, in the sixth. Down at Baltimore, the Orioles play Cleveland tonight. And at Washington, the Senators meet Chicago tonight.

"Now over in the National League, the Dodgers are leading the Cubs, two to one, in the fifth. Out in Cincinnati the Giants play the

Reds tonight. In Milwaukee the Braves meet Pittsburgh tonight. And way out west in St. Louis the Cardinals play the little old Phillies tonight. Well, that's the old Suds-Side Scoreboard and, as you know, the score here just as the rain stopped the game, is 2 to 0 favor the Yankees. We got our two runs when Mickey Mantle blasted that homer into the stands with Whitey Ford on base, in the third inning.

"There's a little thunder to be heard now, but no lightning. However, where there's thun-der, there's bound to be lightning. Or so they tell me. The only lightning seen around here though was that homer li'l ole Mickey blasted in the second. Well, with the way things stand at the present moment, how about returning to the studio for a little music until the game starts again?"

There is a long silence and then music rends the air.

Ah luvs baseball!

CHON DAY

The Pitchless Wonders

JACK ORR

THIS IS THE STORY of a big-league ball club which had eight men with averages of .313 or better (there were only three such hitters in the whole National League last year); a club which rattled out 1,783 hits (the Cubs led the league last year with 1,408); a club which had three men who drove in a total of 389 runs (the whole Dodger roster in 1952 drove in only 725 to lead the league)—and which, nevertheless, finished last, 40 games behind the pennant-winners.

The club is the almost legendary Philadelphia Phillies of 1930, an organization symbolic of an era of bloodthirsty hitting and of a ball so lively that pitchers used to hate to get up in the morning. Even fine pitchers such as Carl Hubbell, Burleigh Grimes, Wild Bill Hallahan and Dazzy Vance had their troubles. Not one of them managed to get 20 victories.

No, it was strictly a hitter's year and the Phillies had hitters, if nothing else. Chuck Klein led the team with a .386 average, including 40 homers and 170 runs driven in. Lefty O'Doul had to be consoled because he had a bad year, slipping from .398 in '29 to .383. Third baseman Pinky Whitney hit .342 and all-around-man Benny Friberg, .341. Don Hurst, at first, hit .327, outfielder Monk Sherlock, .324, and the two catchers, Harry McCurdy and Spud Davis, .331 and .313, respectively. Shortstop Tommy Thevenow was embarrassed by a .286 average, while second baseman Fresco Thompson, the captain of the team, had a lowly .282.

"I could have hit .300, though," Thompson complained recently. "I was going along fine, hitting around .320, but the other guys were so ashamed of my average that they wouldn't let me take batting practice. I wasn't allowed even to speak to O'Doul and Klein. Yeah, I was captain, but it was like being foreman of a WPA gang. Who'd pay attention to a hitter like me?"

Unfortunately for the Phillies and their manager, Burt Shotton, then a snappy 46, they had to take the field every now and then. Immediately there would be noises resembling artillery fire as the opposition raked Philly pitchers. The Phils played in old Baker Bowl with its famous right-field fence. Often, the story went, young infielders would pick up grounders and throw to Klein in right instead of Hurst at first. And though the Philly murderers were rocking the opposition pitching at a remarkable clip of 6.8 runs and 11.4 hit a game, Philly pitchers set a record which probably never will be broken: they gave up 1,199 runs, a breathtaking 7.7 a game.

"Those pitchers were really awful," Thompson said. "Once I took the lineup to home plate. I had written in the pitcher's spot, 'Willoughby—and others.' Bill Klem didn't think it was funny and made me cross it out. I was right, though, and in the first inning, when we were changing pitchers, I yelled, 'See, Bill, what'd I tell you?'"

That would have been Claude Willoughby, who won 4 and lost 17 that year. Some of the others were better. Les Sweetland won 7 and lost 15 and the ace, Fidgety Phil Collins, won 16 and lost 11. Then there were Ray Benge (11-15), Ace Elliott (6-11), Hap Collard (6-12), Roy Hansen (0-7), Bill Smythe (0-3) and 43-year-old Grover Cleveland Alexander (0-3).

There was no help from the fielders, either. The club made 236 errors, exactly 130 more than the Dodgers made last year in setting a new National League record. Opposing hitters smacked the right-field wall as if it were a gong and Klein, who had his work cut out for him, set a record that still stands, 44 assists by an outfielder.

"These Phillies," wrote the baseball expert of *The New York Times* before the season started, "are the dark horses. Here is a team which has been lifted . . . from nowhere to a position of considerable eminence." The eminence was hard to detect. By June 1 the club was seventh and sinking fast and it hit bottom that month and never got up, even though Klein, O'Doul, Whitney and the rest continued to endanger the lives of rival infielders. Of course, they weren't alone in the dynamiting department. That year 25 hitters in the league did better than .335.

Baseball men, sitting around in gab sessions, still talk about that 1930 Philly club. As they talk, you can almost hear the rattle of base hits off the tin wall at Baker Bowl.

JOHN GALLAGHER

Courtesy *True, The Man's Magazine.* ©

"It's a hit! . . .
"A long one! . . .

". . . It may be an inside-the-park
home run! . . .

". . . Foster rounds second and
races to third! . . .

". . . He's streaking for home! Here comes
the throw! He slides! . . .

". . . He's out!"

LIKE all really good sports columnists, Dan Parker of the New York *Mirror* is a good reporter. The following piece appeared in the *Saturday Evening Post* in 1945, shortly after Senator A. B. Chandler of Kentucky had been elected commissioner of baseball. Note the last line of Parker's story. Chandler did not quit as baseball commissioner in 1951; he was, as Red Smith wrote, "publicly divested of (his) pants." In 1955, Chandler was elected governor of Kentucky.

Comes the Baseball Revolution

DAN PARKER

WHEN the sports pages announced last winter that Loud Larry MacPhail was bidding for the New York Yankees, Ed Barrow, stern, septuagenarian dictator of this vast baseball empire, snorted, "Only over my dead body will MacPhail buy the Yankees."

The tides of eight or nine moons have stirred the turgid Harlem since Barrow told Loud Larry where to get off, and Ed is still on this side of the Styx. But somewhere along the route his prediction went sour. MacPhail not only bought the Yankees for the syndicate he represented—magnanimously retaining Barrow as his assistant—but, a few months later—in a brilliantly executed coup that caught most of the other major-league-club owners fast asleep —brought about the election of Sen. Albert B. Chandler as baseball commissioner to succeed the late Kenesaw Mountain Landis.

MacPhail's double-barreled triumph is symbolic of the sudden rise to power of the Young Turks in their revolution against the Old Guard in baseball. What this bodes for the future of America's national game now will be revealed in this bright, new peacetime world, where baseball will have to fight for its existence against the growing competition of race tracks, radio, television and more luxurious means of transportation, opening up vast new fields of recreation. An important factor in shaping the game's destiny will be the reaction of the magnates and fans to Commissioner Chandler as a successor to stanch old Judge Landis, who, in death, has been consecrated as baseball's Rock of Ages.

Some of the Young Turks' accomplishments to date call for pointing with pride and some of their handiwork is being widely viewed with alarm. MacPhail, who introduced night baseball in the major leagues, has seen his favorite elixir resuscitate two moribund big-league clubs, the Cincinnati Reds and the Brooklyn Dodgers. On the other hand, he has watched it develop into a poisonous potion that has blighted at least one major-league city, St. Louis. Other big-league cities which have succumbed to the lure of this fan philter may suffer the same fate.

The astonishing contrast between strait-laced, stern Judge Landis and his ebullient, sophomoric successor, Senator Chandler, has been as productive of goose pimples to baseball as a midnight sprint through a graveyard. Some of the major-league-club owners who voted Happy Chandler into office a few hours after they met in Cleveland last April twenty-fourth to hear a report from the committee of four on eligible candidates—and with no intention whatsoever of naming a commissioner —have been wondering ever since whether they acted hastily. Fans, accustomed to looking up to the baseball commissioner with reverence second only to that reserved for the Deity, have listened to Chandler with growing bewilderment. Employing the same technique with which he was wont to charm the mountain voters back home, Chandler has spouted platitudes, written dripping essays about his love of the game, sung sentimental ballads and made snap judgments on matters with which he obviously wasn't too familiar. His behavior has been in curious contrast to his white-maned predecessor's, who spoke only when he had something to say, and then in a voice of thunder.

Hardly had the applause with which well-wishers greeted Chandler's election died down when garrulous Happy had involved baseball in a controversy with racing—a sport everybody always thought he loved. With each pop-off since, Chandler has managed to wedge his foot—if not, indeed, both of them—deeper into his larynx, embarrassing even his sympathetic sponsor, Colonel MacPhail, if that feat is possible. Tom Meany, a New York writer, got off a neat bon mot recently when he said that Commissioner Chandler should be more considerate in his remarks about horse racing, because at least two race horses, Senator C. and Happy C., and possibly a third, Foot in Mouth, had been named for him.

The contrast between Senator Chandler and the late Judge Landis is no more startling than that between the other Young Turks and their Old Guard predecessors. Colonel MacPhail is the direct antithesis of Ed Barrow, who, rockbound conservative though he is, has been connected with more championship major-league-baseball clubs than anyone else in the game—fifteen, to be specific. Ed succeeded by providing his patrons with the best brand of baseball possible, and no fancy trimmings. He was one of the last holdouts against night baseball.

Barrow believed that a club president's place was in the front office and a manager's in the clubhouse. Once the late Col. Jacob Ruppert, millionaire owner of the Yankees, invaded the clubhouse after his ball team had lost another Saturday game, and petulantly asked, "Huggins, why can't we win a few Saturday games, so we'll have some good Sunday crowds?"

"Get out of here!" roared mild-mannered Miller Huggins.

Deeply hurt, Colonel Ruppert went to Ed Barrow, his business manager, and protested.

"Good enough for you," said Barrow. "That'll teach you to keep out of the clubhouse."

The colonel never again interfered with the management of his ball club.

There are more ways of invading a clubhouse than by walking into it, as Colonel Ruppert had done. Another colonel, named MacPhail, chose one of them in mid-July of this season when he gave Will Wedge, of the New York *Sun*, a brutally frank interview in which he ripped his ball club apart. Some of

the players weren't giving their best, said MacPhail. He bluntly said that Nick Etten wasn't earning his salary and that two of his pitchers were of no use to the club.

Those who know their Joe McCarthy sat back and prepared for developments. They didn't have to wait long. Three days later, the baseball writers found out that Joe hadn't shown up for several days and that Art Fletcher, his assistant, had been handling the club. MacPhail, with no seeming provocation for such an admission, told the press that Joe had been talking of quitting since last fall. This defensive statement by Larry was enough to convince the press and public that there was trouble between him and Joe. McCarthy went to his farm near Buffalo and for three weeks wouldn't let MacPhail know whether he'd return to the club or not. The colonel, as if publicly atoning for his intrusion into his manager's province, made it clear that he was figuratively on his knees, begging Joe to come back. Finally, on August ninth, Joe returned. He brushed off questions about a clash with MacPhail with the statement that his nerves had been acting up.

McCarthy's midseason vacation, startling as it was to the fans, was soon overshadowed by MacPhail's announcement that Hank Borowy, one of the Yankees' star pitchers, had been sold to the Cubs for $100,000, to be paid for either in cash or players. The Yanks were four games out of the lead the day Borowy was sold, and badly in need of pitchers. MacPhail tried to justify the amazing transaction by producing statistics which tended to show that Borowy couldn't win in the last half of the season. With the Cubs, Borowy promptly made MacPhail's statistics look pathetically silly by winning eight of the first ten games he pitched.

The deal made baseball's waiver rule look even sillier than MacPhail's figures. With the first seven clubs in the American League still having a chance to win the pennant in the closest race that circuit has ever had, the fans couldn't figure out why Borowy had been waived out of the league. Six other teams needed him. Yet, in one of those baffling deals which bob up every so often to try the faith of fandom, Borowy was allowed to go to the National League as pennant insurance for the Cubs. Clark Griffith squawked loudly. There was a demand for an investigation of the transaction by Commissioner Chandler. Those who were aware of the Damon-and-Pythias relation between Chandler and MacPhail laughed this off as extra-naïve. Chandler announced shortly that there would be no investigation. Actually, there was no reason for one by him, unless it was to find out what had possessed the six American League club owners.

Yankee fans recalled three significant facts in connection with the Borowy deal. The first was that in 1941, when MacPhail needed a second baseman to round out his championship Dodger club, the Cubs had sold him Billy Herman. The second was that, due to a series of terrible weather breaks for week-end games at the Stadium, the Yankees were off about $100,000 at the gate. Also, at that time the prospects for a World Series were dark, as the war was still going on, with no signs of any early finish. The deal didn't grow any more popular as Borowy helped the Cubs to extend their lead in the National, while the Yanks dropped farther and farther behind the pace in the American because of deficient pitching. Thus it was that for a time the leader of the Young Turks became the Terrible Turk as far as the Yankee fans were concerned.

The Young Turk movement suffered another setback when Donald Barnes, after giving St. Louis Browns' fans their first pennant in 1944, disposed of his controlling interest last August to Richard C. Muckerman, vice-president of the club. Barnes, a man after Grand Vizier MacPhail's heart, floated a stock-selling scheme after buying the Browns in 1936 and giving the other club owners the impression he was putting up his own money. Baseball virtually became a side line at Sportsman's Park under the Barnes regime as loud-speaker plugs for the park-owned fried-fish concession and a brand of cigarettes filled in the quiet moments between cracks of the bat. Like the horse, day baseball became practically extinct in St. Louis, as the town was educated to night baseball and Sunday double-headers. Although the Browns had won their first pennant in 1944—with players sold at cut-rate prices to Barnes by the other clubs—the situation had become so bad in 1945 that Barnes peddled his stock. Muckerman's first statement upon taking office was to announce that it was up to the fans to decide whether the Browns would remain in St. Louis—a tacit admission of failure for the new style of baseball promotion, at least in so far as St. Louis was concerned.

Despite the revolutionary methods of the Young Turks, there is ample evidence that the game still has enough appeal to sell itself without trimmings. In Brooklyn this year, Branch Rickey, with a ball club that was unanimously condemned by the experts in their pre-season estimates, produced a contender that played to 1,000,000 fans. Rickey scheduled only seven night games at home—the last one on July sixth—didn't resort to any of the high-pressure promotion, spent almost nothing for ballplayers, yet virtually matched MacPhail's best figures for Brooklyn. An unexpected disciple of the Young Turks is that Old Turk, Clark Griffith. Once the most violent opponent of baseball after dark, Griffith now can't get enough night games for Washington. Twilight games and Sunday double-headers are also grist for his mill. He goes whole-hog for the revolution started by the flame-thatched torchbearer, MacPhail, in Cincinnati back in 1934, when Larry introduced the night game to the majors.

Despite MacPhail's immediate success, baseball then regarded him with misgivings, if not open hostility. He antagonized politicians, picked fights with newspapermen and, as a result, found stumbling blocks placed in his path. Although MacPhail's exit from Cincinnati was ingloriously accompanied by a left hook planted on his chin by a city detective in the town's leading hotel, fair-minded critics concede that he deserved a major share of the credit for the pennants the Reds won in 1939 and 1940, because he had built the foundation on which these successes were based.

By that time, MacPhail was well on his way to new triumphs in Brooklyn, where he had arrived in 1938. Loud Larry made America Brooklyn-Dodger conscious during his five-year stay in Flatbush. Installing a $100,000 lighting system, he took a bankrupt ball club and converted it into a gold mine. Although he spent $1,000,000 for ballplayers, he wiped out a mortgage of $1,250,000 and redeemed notes for $520,000. Each baseball season was one long brawl in Brooklyn, and hardly a nerve was left unfrayed during his high-blood-pressure regime. Beauty contests, track meets, riots, fashion shows, tableaux, automobile raffles and even ball games served to keep Brooklyn in a high state of delirium. MacPhail filled in the dull moments by quarreling with Manager Leo Durocher, sports writers and politicians. The red one gave Brooklyn a pennant in 1941, and, having reached his goal, seemed to lose interest.

He surprised the baseball world in August, 1942, when the Dodgers had a lead of about ten games, by predicting they would lose the pennant. They did, when the Cardinals won out by two games.

A vast sigh of relief went up when Mac-Phail, late that season, announced he was quitting baseball to take a commission in the Army of the United States. Larry went to Washington as a member of the staff of Robert Patterson, Under Secretary of War, with the rank of lieutenant colonel, later becoming a full-fledged colonel. It was inevitable, however, that his baseball destiny should overtake Larry again. This time it took the form of a senator and another colonel.

There are two versions of how Senator Chandler became baseball commissioner. The first is that Colonel MacPhail put him over. This the colonel of the first part denies, although few believe him. The other is that Col. John Gottlieb, a trucking magnate from Chicago, who served in the Army Transportation Corps during the war and is now on terminal leave, originated, developed and brought to fruition the Chandler boom. The colonel of the second part doesn't merely admit this, he claims it. Not many believe him, either.

Up to the day of the Cleveland meeting, last April twenty-fourth, at which Chandler was elected, Colonel MacPhail, by then out of the Army and head of the Yankees, had been ostensibly a supporter of Ford Frick, president of the National League. He didn't mention Chandler's name. In fact, when asked to comment on a Washington report that he was sponsoring Senator Chandler two days before the Cleveland meeting, Colonel MacPhail issued an unqualified denial. Yet that very day it developed he had dined with Senator Chandler and discussed the commissionership with him.

In accepting the post, the night he was elected, Senator Chandler embarrassed Mac-Phail by stating, "Until I had dinner with Larry MacPhail two days ago, I had no idea I was going to be the new commissioner."

Vincent X. Flaherty, Washington sports columnist who broke bread with Colonel Mac-Phail and Senator Chandler on that night of destiny, mentioned it in awed tones in his column after Chandler had been elected, further embarrassing Colonel MacPhail. Flaherty wrote: "MacPhail and I left Chandler at the Statler. As we walked down K Street, MacPhail said, 'He's the man for the Landis job. We need him.'"

It can be readily seen that Colonel MacPhail had nothing whatsoever to do with the Chandler boom. Well, not much, anyway. The fiery colonel's sponsoring of Chandler at the Cleveland meeting without giving his fellow club owners any tip-off as to what was cooking was a fine example of MacPhail's culinary masterpiece, diplomat pudding. The magnates had assembled that day, convinced that it was to be just another gabfest at which the nominating committee of four would present the names of suitable candidates, whom they would consider at their leisure later.

Therefore, Colonel MacPhail's innocent-sounding suggestion they they play a little game of voting for the three men they would consider for the commissionership caught them bemused. Like so many trusting housewives signing on the dotted line for the handsome salesman without knowing they were obligating themselves to buy an entire set of the books he was peddling for only twice the regular cost, they jotted down the first three names that came into their heads. It may have been just a coincidence that MacPhail had noted, with a show of surprise, the absence of Senator Chandler's name from the list of "possibilities" just before the poll was taken. A tabulation of the informal vote showed that on eleven of the sixteen ballots, Senator Chandler's name had done an Abou ben Adhem. He was 1-2 on thirteen and 1-2-3 on all sixteen. Not bad for an added starter whose name wasn't on the list of six submitted by the committee of four an hour before this. It would seem that, unless autosuggestion was being practiced, someone had been mentioning the name of Senator Chandler.

Colonel MacPhail, visibly pleased with the result of his first innocent suggestion, now made an even more naïve one. "If that's the way we feel, what are we waiting for?" he demanded, with what seemed like sound logic.

Then, on motion of Sam Breadon, they started voting for keeps. The first ballot gave Senator Chandler eleven votes and Bob Hannegan, chairman of the National Democratic Committee—since then appointed Postmaster General—five votes. On the second poll, Chandler picked up one vote and on the third, he was elected unanimously.

Colonel Gottlieb's name wasn't linked with Chandler's in connection with the commissionership until a few days after Happy had been elected. Then *Sporting News* published a story in which Colonel Gottlieb was pictured as the man who engineered the Chandler boom behind the scenes.

In Washington, Colonel Gottlieb is regarded

as a man of many and varied accomplishments. He's seen almost everywhere important people should be seen, and he's usually with Senator Chandler. Like the senator, he is a handshaker and backslapper. They spend much time together in the lobby of the Mayflower Hotel, greeting friends, and on these occasions it looks like Election Day in Kentucky. Colonel Gottlieb enjoys dancing attendance on the senator in many public places. The colonel made a fortune in the trucking business and other interests in Chicago, Moline and Rock Island, and believes in spreading it around. When no one else can get tickets for a hit show, a championship fight or a World Series game, Colonel Gottlieb can produce them, if he's a friend of yours. Mike Todd, the theatrical producer, is one of his pals. Gottlieb likes to show off his important friends before hometown acquaintances. On the way to Iowa City for an Illinois-Iowa football game a few years ago, the colonel stopped off at Rock Island, his home town, to introduce his companions, Mayor Ed Kelly and Pat Nash, rulers of Cook County and Chicago, to his flabbergasted fellow townsmen.

Otto John Gottlieb—he has since dropped the "Otto"—arrived in Chicago during the rough-and-tumble 20s, by way of Rock Island High School, Marion, Alabama, Institute and West Point. His stay at the United States Military Academy had been brief. He entered on November 4, 1918, one week before the first World War Armistice was signed, and was discharged on April 18, 1919, for deficiency in mathematics. There was big money to be made in Chicago when Gottlieb landed there, and the slim young fellow managed to meet the right people. Soon he became interested in the trucking business with his brothers, organizing the Pioneer Motor Service, Inc., which plies between Moline, Rock Island and Chicago. He also promoted fights in Rock Island, bringing such stars as Max Schmeling, Barney Ross and Young Jack Thompson to his home town, at the cost of a red-ink bath. In Chicago's trucking business, Gottlieb became a power. On January 6, 1942, during a trucking war there, Gottlieb had his jaw fractured by four goons.

Six months later, his fractured jaw mended, the affable Mr. Gottlieb was commissioned a lieutenant colonel in the army. Within a year, he had been promoted to the rank of colonel and sent to the Burma Road to help untangle the transportation mess there. After Chicago, Burma was a pushover for Colonel Gottlieb.

He was able to get things done, as usual. This assignment successfully completed, the colonel returned to Washington and has since divided his time between the Pentagon Building, where he learned all the angles he hadn't known about up to then, and the Mayflower, where he lobby-gowed with Senator Chandler. He met Colonel MacPhail, and the Chandler boom was hatched.

A feature of Chandler's election that rankled some club owners was the representation by Colonel MacPhail that baseball needed a commissioner in a hurry. After the brethren had been stampeded into a hasty betrothal, they soon found themselves with plenty of leisure to think things over. Elected on April twenty-fourth, Senator Chandler declined to quit his Senate job. In fact, he loudly announced that he would retain both posts. Several months dragged by, and baseball, which Colonel MacPhail said needed a commissioner so badly, had to struggle along with a part-time senator.

Mid-August arrived and Chandler's seven-year contract with baseball still remained unsigned by both sides. Not until the magnates had reluctantly agreed to insert in his contract the paragraph the late Commissioner Landis had insisted upon would Happy sign. In this important paragraph, the magnates pledged themselves "loyally to support the commissioner in his important and difficult task and we assure him that each of us will acquiesce in his decisions, even when we believe them mistaken, and that we will not discredit the sport by public criticism of him or of one another."

Then the magnates really had Happy, for better or for worse.

Meantime, Manager Leo Durocher, of the Brooklyn Dodgers, was arrested on the charge of feloniously assaulting a fan who claimed Leo fractured his jaw. Baseball took no action in the matter, although later Leo was indicted by the Grand Jury. The Browns and White Sox put on a Donnybrook in Sportsman's Park, St. Louis, that would have brought the wrath of Landis down on their heads. Senator Chandler was too busy issuing statements about the impropriety of ballplayers' frequenting race tracks to take notice of these shenanigans. The day after one of his blasts at racing, Senator Chandler's wife and one of their daughters, Mrs. J. K. Cabell, were photographed in a box at the Churchill Downs track, enjoying the races, but not half as much as the newspapers seemed to enjoy printing the embarrassing picture.

When Senator Chandler spoke of the danger of exposing ballplayers to contact with gambling at race tracks, Lexington, Kentucky, sports writers, who love horse racing more than they do Senator Chandler, recalled that while the University of Kentucky basketball team was competing in the Madison Square Garden invitation tournament in 1944, they had seen Senator Chandler, seated in the front row, shaking hands with Ed Curd, Lexington's leading bookmaker.

Joe Estes, of the *Blood-Horse*, in an open letter addressed to "Dear Happy" in the issue of May twelfth, took him to task for "knifing racing in the back," and added: "Now, old Judge Landis could get away with that all right. But you can't. The newspapers have too many pictures in their morgues showing you with your arms around jockeys and owners and trainers—and some other guys—and they might get the wild idea that you're not quite on the level about this public-censure business. . . . I'm getting kind of fed up with you myself, and you know I don't do flip-flops very easy. And if the big leagues think the way to make baseball look better is to make racing look worse, they ought to get somebody who can make the speeches ring true."

Senator Chandler veered away from comments about horse racing after that. Joe Jordan, of the Lexington *Leader,* announced that Happy had promised his racing friends he would soft-pedal his remarks about the turf thereafter.

Then the senator announced, without consulting the magnates, that he would retain Walter Mulbry, his secretary, in the dual role of secretary-treasurer, thus creating a new post after they had voted to retain Leslie O'Connor, Judge Landis' secretary, for another year. The upshot of this was that the American League, with Colonel MacPhail conspicuously absent, met and voted to tighten the baseball commissioner's purse strings. Later, however, the magnates relented and approved of Mulbry's appointment at a joint league meeting. They didn't raise Happy's salary, however, even though Mr. Mulbry told the press that, after paying taxes, the senator would net only about $30,000 of his $50,000 salary as commissioner.

Nineteen forty-two seems to have been a fateful year for the Three Modern Musketeers. Gottlieb not only had his jaw broken but was commissioned a lieutenant colonel that year. MacPhail saw his Dodgers blow a twelve-game lead in August, but also found solace in the army's silver oak leaves. As for Senator Chandler, he had swimming-pool trouble. In July of that year, Sen. Harry S. Truman, now President of the United States, headed a Senate committee investigating national defense. One of the matters it investigated was the gift swimming pool which Happy Chandler looked in the face every time he took a plunge behind his old Kentucky home in Versailles. Happy admitted that the pool was "a gift built in the name of friendship and accepted in the same spirit."

Investigation by the Truman committee revealed that Ben Collings, a Louisville contractor whose firm, the Colonial Supply Co., received four subcontracts from the Government on military projects, had built a concrete pool, sixty feet long, lined with blue tile, in Happy's back yard at Versailles, Kentucky. Chandler's friends explained that Collings built it during the senator's absence, and you could have knocked Happy over with a diving board when he came home, looked in his back yard, and there it was! Surprise! Kentucky racing interests saw that the swimming-pool story was revived after Happy, a member of the Senate's Military Affairs Committee, was elected baseball commissioner, and it further embarrassed the magnates who had impetuously voted him Judge Landis' job.

Senator Chandler, blissfully ignoring all this chatter, announced he would represent the ballplayers and the fans as commissioner, and let the club owners represent themselves. Club Owner MacPhail, at this point, is reported to have told Chandler to pipe down.

Did this cramp Happy's style? Not so as Ernie Stewart could notice it, at any rate. Ernie was an American League umpire with a bright future until his path crossed the talkative senator's one day last July in the umpires' dressing room at Griffith Stadium, Washington. Up to then, Ernie, youngest member of the American League umpiring staff, was in good standing with Will Harridge, president of the league. An ill wind blew him into the dressing room that day, just in time to involve him in a discussion that Senator Chandler was having with Umpires Art Passarella and Hal Weafer about salaries. Stewart says Chandler told him, "If you have anything on your mind about helping the umpires, I'd like to know it."

Complying with Chandler's suggestion that he ask the other umpires what salaries they thought they were entitled to, Ernie made a canvass of his associates. Somebody reported the junior umpire's activities to the league president, and Harridge summarily dismissed Stewart, charging him with "disloyalty and spreading dissension." Surprised, but confident of exoneration, Stewart brought his case to Commissioner Chandler, the man who was going to represent the players and, presumably, the umpires. Mustering one of his toothiest smiles, the commissioner said the case was one Mr. Harridge would have to decide under the rules of baseball. Seeing Stewart thus left hanging from the end of a limb, umpires and ballplayers who had been telling their troubles to Happy, the People's Friend, thereupon shut up like minor-league ball parks during the war.

When the major-league club owners were freed from what they considered the "tyranny" of Judge Landis by his death last November,

they went out looking for someone they could handle. In Happy Chandler, they seem to have come up with more than they can handle just now. However, in spite of his politician's approach to everything and his propensity for popping off, or maybe because of them, he may fill baseball's postwar requirements perfectly. Maybe baseball needs not another Landis, but a supersalesman, in the postwar era of expansion. Should it work out that way—and already Happy has won an appropriation of $50,000 to promote the game among boys— the magnates will be happy with Happy. At any rate, they'd better be, because already he has notified them that, though they elected him for only seven years, he intends to be with them for life.

THE FOLLOWING appeared in Westbrook Pegler's column "Speaking Out On Sports" in the Chicago *Tribune* of September 21, 1931, together with this introductory note: "Baseball has always been regarded as a man's game, but in response to the growing feminine interest in the sport the following story has been prepared to describe from the woman's angle the stirring double-header in Washington in which the White Sox fought to clinch eighth place in the American League."

From the Woman's Angle

WESTBROOK PEGLER

BY EMMA O'MAGORD
Our Medium-Sized Girl Reporter per
Westbrook Pegler
WASHINGTON, D. C., Sept. 21.

IT WAS perfectly thrilling! The players were all so nimble and the shouts of the crowd of 7,000 people in their "best bib and tucker" were so exciting. Actually, I found myself pounding my escort on the arm with my tiny fist in my excitement in the fourth inning when that poor man fell down running to his goal. My escort had to smile because he said the man fell down purposely trying to slide to his goal, and, of course, I blushed my confusion because it all looked so accidental and I suppose the maternal in me cried out for the poor boy when he went down so hard.

"Oh, you women," my escort exclaimed with a joking expression.

"Oh, is that so?" I demanded with a pout. "Well, we women are learning fast and we will soon know all about baseball, too, and let me tell you, mister man, we will be better critics than you men, too, because of our feminine intuition."

But I must not go any further before I tell you about that wonderful referee who stood behind home base in the second game. My escort told me his name was Mr. Brick Owens. I think men choose the ugliest nicknames, but then I suppose that is their way of showing their masculinity. I should think they would let the women choose them for them. Then Mr. Owens would be called "honey boy" or "wonderful" or something more expressive.

Such poise, such stature. I found myself involuntarily screaming "Oh, Mr. Owens!" and it seemed to me that he did half turn around and recognize me with a wan, rather melancholy smile. My escort did not seem to like this very much, however, so I gave him a playful poke with my program and after that I had to admire in silence.

The other referee, Mr. Hildebrand, I did not like so well. He seemed a rather elderly man and all business and this made him seem rather a cross-patch at times, but as for Mr. Owens, it is a matter of natural charm which he exudes from every angle of his personality.

Between games you should have seen me eating a "hot dog" standing right up in front of the bar among the men, and I must say that although they sometimes forget themselves in the heat of the baseball match and shout in the angriest tones, they were all exceedingly polite and did not use any objectionable language at the "hot dog" bar. I am not a prude, of course, and modern business or professional women frequently find that they have to calmly ignore many things if they are to get along in the happy partnership of the give and take of life, but there is something in the feminine nature which, after all, does enjoy the little courtesies, or so I have always thought.

And there I stood, smearing yellow mustard on my "hot dog" and getting my fingers all nasty sticky and enjoying it hugely. Then I drank a soft drink right out of the bottle and my escort remarked, "They ought to have a brass rail here so you could put your foot up."

The White Sox are the Chicagos and they are in the midst of a contest to clinch eighth place in their league, so the excitement was even more unusual than is customary when the Washingtons won both games. The Washingtons won the first game, four scores to three, and the second one, six scores to four. I must confess that I am too new to the game in my first journey to the baseball grounds to thoroughly understand the intricacies of the system of scoring and particularly how the more games the White Sox lose the more they clinch eighth place in their league, but that is what my escort told me and I am afraid our sex is still dependent on the men in some things.

The Washingtons won the first game because they made the same number of hits as the Chicagos, each side making nine hits. Then the Washingtons won the second because the Chicagos made ten hits to their eight. But this is all very technical and I was only interested in the woman's angle without regard to the technical details.

The Washingtons' pitcher in the first game was a Mr. Crowder and I was certainly taken aback when I heard that he was General Crowder of the army, who ran the draft in the war, because I thought General Crowder must be a much older man. He seems very versatile to become a baseball player after serving his country. The Chicagos used two pitchers, which struck me as unfair, but I did not say anything to my escort for fear he would laugh at me and make me blush for my ignorance again. Their pitchers were Frasier and Caraway, but still Mr. Frasier pitched eight innings and only gave up his place because another man named Mr. Fonseca was anxious to bat. It shows the generosity of the game when a man will let another man bat in his turn, because I understand that the batting is the most fun of all. I am afraid that if women played baseball they would not give up so generously, but then, honestly, the men, though they sometimes get cross and use bad words, are really big and unselfish about some things.

Mr. Blue of the Chicagos was awfully cross at Mr. Hildebrand during the first game and he was still so angry in the ninth inning that he hit the ball viciously, as though he were exclaiming, "There, now you take that," knocking it for a three-baser and sending a runner over the home goal with the tying run. But the Washingtons got one run in their hits after that, so the Chicagos didn't win after all.

But dear me, I could run on and on about the excitement and my escort is waiting for me. Mustn't keep him waiting or he will joke me about women never being on time.

In August of 1952, ballplayer Jim Piersall found himself in a mental hospital outside of Boston. Shock treatments had numbed his memory, and it was afterward, in the course of his recovery, that he learned of the wild antics that caused the Boston Red Sox to farm him out to Birmingham . . . where this excerpt from Piersall's book, *Fear Strikes Out*, takes up.

From *Fear Strikes Out*

JIM PIERSALL and AL HIRSHBERG

I WAS with the Barons exactly twenty days. During that time, I had countless arguments with the umpires. I was thrown out of half a dozen ball games and suspended four different times. I baffled my teammates, infuriated my manager, insulted the umpires, squabbled with opposing ballplayers and delighted the sports writers and fans. Once I nearly got into an open fist fight. Twice, at my own expense, I flew back to Boston.

At first, the Birmingham baseball people welcomed my clowning. Eddie Glennon, the Barons' general manager, announced a few days after my arrival that I had injected new spirit into the team. "He's the greatest center fielder that I've ever seen," Glennon said. "A one hundred-and-fifty-thousand-dollar ballplayer." I added color to the Barons and made them the talk of the Southern Association—indeed, the talk of baseball. Every unconventional move I made was relayed to the nation's newspapers and splashed all over the sports pages.

But it didn't take long for everyone, including Glennon, to get sick and tired of Piersall. He was funny only as long as he added something refreshing to the ball game. But when he tried to make his antics take the place of the ball game, he was in trouble. His clowning was turning games into travesties. He did stupid little things—anything he could think of —to delay the games, and the angry umpires, anxious to hustle things up, reached a point where they had to banish him in order to get contests completed at all.

Piersall put on one of his most aggravating performances in New Orleans on July 5. Aside from going through the regular routine which had first attracted attention when he was in the majors, Piersall added a whole new bag of tricks, making them up as he went along.

When he went up to hit, he stood in the batter's box, dropped his bat and imitated the pitcher as he wound up. Naturally, the umpire had to call time, and the game would be held up while Piersall stooped to pick up his war club. He pulled the stunt two or three times each time he came up.

When Piersall wasn't imitating the pitcher, he was holding up the works while he ran either down the first- or the third-base line to give instructions in a dramatic stage whisper to one of the coaches or to a base runner. Sometimes he rushed back to the dugout to talk to Mathis, who repeatedly ordered him to get back up there and hit.

After Birmingham's turn at bat, Piersall loafed his way out to center field, stopping to talk to infielders on the way, taking his time about picking up his glove, sauntering over near the stands to exchange quips with the crowd and spending so much time reaching his position that the game had to be held up while an umpire came out to hustle him up. Once while New Orleans was at bat, Piersall suddenly ran into the Birmingham dugout from his center-field position and the game had to be stopped. Mathis, who was catching, had to leave his position to come over and tell Piersall to get back on the job.

About halfway through the game, one of the Barons hit what Mathis thought was a home run, and when the umpire called it a foul ball, Red blew his top. He rushed over to George Popp, the plate umpire, yelling and gesticulating—and Piersall rushed right behind him, imitating every move he made. Mathis got so excited that Popp finally threw him out of the game. Piersall didn't stop aping Red until he turned around to go into the locker room.

When Birmingham's half of the inning was

over, Piersall went out to the pitcher's mound, picked up the ball, and walked out to the shortstop's position. When Johnny McCall, the Barons' pitcher, came out to warm up, he yelled to Piersall to throw the ball. Piersall wound up and slammed it right at McCall. McCall had to put up his gloved hand fast to keep from getting hit in the face. Boiling mad, McCall threw the ball right back at Piersall, who fell flat on his face, then got up holding his stomach in mock hysterics after the ball had sailed to the outfield.

The crowd laughed, but neither McCall nor Popp thought it was very funny. Popp came halfway out on the diamond and called to Piersall, "Go out and get that ball in here before I throw you out of the game." The ball had stopped in dead center field. Piersall dropped his glove on the ground and kicked it as he went along. Just before he reached the ball, he crouched and crept toward it as though he were a pointer dog and it were his quarry. Then he kicked it a few feet, and kept repeating the performance until the ball and he had reached the scoreboard.

Piersall finally picked it up and threw it to the scoreboard boy, who threw it back. They began playing catch, but that game didn't last long. All of the umpires at once were screaming at Piersall to get out of the ball game. When the scoreboard boy refused to throw the ball back, Piersall walked off the field.

Then, still in uniform, he wandered over to the right-field side of the grandstand, where five hundred boys, guests of Joe L. Brown, the president of the New Orleans club, were chanting, "We want Piersall!" Piersall stood in front of them and led them in the cheers. Somehow they got the game started again on the field, but nobody was watching. Everyone was looking over at Piersall.

Finally, he went down to the Birmingham locker room and changed into street clothes. Then he went back to the stands and sat down in a box occupied by Charles Hurth, the president of the Southern Association. From there, Piersall heckled Popp, as well as Danny Murtaugh, the New Orleans manager, who had been giving him a pretty rough going-over all through the game. For that performance he was suspended.

A few days later, everyone in the league had four days off while the Southern Association all-star game was being played. I hopped a plane and flew back to Boston, wiring Mary ahead of time. I thought that the Red Sox might let me stay with them, once I was in

Boston. But when I called Cronin, he told me to go back to the Barons and stick to baseball. I left the next day.

By this time, Glennon was worried about me, too. He persuaded me to let him take me to a doctor in Birmingham, and I was given some pills to calm me down. I behaved all right for a day or so, but then I went off again worse than ever. We were starting a long home stand, and the Birmingham fans and I were enjoying each other hugely. The only trouble was, nobody else was enjoying me.

I became worse and worse. Nobody could keep me under control, including the umpires. One night I stood at the plate and screamed over a called third strike, and when the umpire thumbed me out of the game, I pulled a water pistol out of my pocket, squirted the plate with it and said, "Now maybe you can see it." I drew another suspension for that, my fourth since I had arrived in Birmingham.

It looked as if I were going to be stuck there for the season, so I decided to go back to Boston to get Mary and the children. Up to that point they hadn't moved South because we always had the hope that I'd get back to the Red Sox any day. They kept the house in Newton while I stayed with Garrett Wall in Birmingham.

Garrett had had no more luck trying to settle me down than anyone else did. He was placed in a position similar to that of Ted Lepcio when I was with the Red Sox. Like Mary, they both had to stand by and watch me crack up, doing what they could by talking to me but not daring to go much further, in the desperate hope that I might get straightened out by myself. Every morning when they got up, they were saying to themselves, "This might be the day." And every night they went to bed, thinking, "Maybe tomorrow."

I bought a ticket on a Boston plane that left Birmingham late in the afternoon of July 17. We made several stops on the way, including one at LaGuardia Airport in New York, where Bill Cunningham, the able Boston *Herald* sports columnist, and his secretary, Miss Frances Donovan, got aboard. Apparently, as soon as I saw Cunningham, I rushed over to him and began pouring my troubles into his unwilling ear. Evidently I talked all the way to Boston, where we arrived at one-thirty in the morning. Here, in part, is what he wrote in his column a day or so later:

"I chanced to be on the plane that unexpectedly brought the Red Sox problem child Jimmy Piersall into Boston at one-thirty A.M

From *Fear Strikes Out*

From approximately eleven-forty-five P.M. until the ship set down in Boston, I heard little but the machine-gun chatter of this tormented youth who so foolishly is throwing away a promising career . . .

"It's my considered opinion that the less written now the better, and if anybody's really interested in helping the young man, a complete press blackout until he can get his bearings would be the best medicine that could possibly be prescribed.

"I'm no authority on such matters, but my guess is he's heading straight for a nervous breakdown."

Cunningham was an accurate prophet. My breakdown was just around the corner. It happened within forty hours after I arrived in Boston. And, suffering more pangs than I suffered, living more horrible minutes than I lived, fighting more fights than I fought, sinking farther into depths of desperation than I sank, hoping more than I hoped, and praying more than I prayed was Mary. I went through it all under the unhealthy anesthesia of a mental blackout. Mary was fully aware of everything that went on. She carried me through every step of the way without so much as a sleeping pill—and, to this day, she remembers every dreadful minute. She told me all about it during those days when we sat quietly in our rented house and relived the past together.

The house was alive with reporters and photographers the day after I flew into town from Birmingham. All of the papers, the major press services, the radio and television stations—every conceivable dispenser of news—sent out representatives. Everyone interviewed me, and while I reveled in the prospects of so much publicity, I was reasonable and rational in my speech. I told them all the same story—that I was through with clowning, and from that moment on, was going to be no more and no less than a ballplayer. I said that I would go back to Birmingham and do the best I could to help the Barons win the Southern Association pennant, and that my one hope was to get back to the Red Sox as soon as possible. And once with them, I would forget all about these mad antics.

I parried the embarrassing questions—

"Did you spank Stephens' little boy?" . . . Of course not—I just patted him, that's all. . . . "Did you really calm down the way Boudreau told you to?" . . . Certainly. . . . "What about all those stories of your tearing through the Southern Association the way you tore through the American League?" . . . Nothing

to them—I've just been sticking to baseball. . . . "Are you really carrying on a running feud with the umpires down there?" . . . Not that I know of—the umpires and me have been getting along fine. . . . "Is it true that you mimicked your own manager behind his back while he was protesting a decision?" . . . Absolutely not—my manager is a close friend of mine. . . . "Did you squirt the plate with a water pistol?" . . . Someone dreamed that one up. . . . "And play catch with a scoreboard boy?" . . . I should say not. . . . "Why did you make two trips back to Boston in less than three weeks?" . . . To see my family. . . . "Are you going to take your wife and children back to Birmingham?" . . . As soon as I can get them packed and out of here. . . . "Do you really think McKechnie and not Boudreau is running the Red Sox?" . . . Boudreau is the manager—do you think I'd say anything like that? . . . "Well, did you say it?" . . . I was sore—I didn't know what I was talking about—Boudreau runs the team, not McKechnie. . . . "And how about Vollmer—did you say he couldn't blow his nose?" . . . A fine ballplayer and a good friend of mine—why should I say anything to hurt him? . . . "Is it true that some of the Red Sox wanted to beat you up on a train and Lepcio stopped them?" . . . I don't know—ask Lepcio. . . .

All day and all evening that sort of thing went on. Questions, questions, questions—one interviewer after another. Sometimes there would be slight variations, but in general the questions were the same. Mary hovered in and out of the living room while I held court. Every so often, she would suggest that I be excused from answering any more questions, but I wouldn't stand for it. I insisted on seeing everyone and answering everything.

Late that afternoon, the Red Sox office called. Cronin wanted to see me. He would expect me in his office at ten o'clock the next morning. I had a long talk with him, then went home and said to Mary, "I'm going to see a doctor. They want you there, too." We drove back to the ball park, where Cronin met us, and then we headed for the doctor's.

Before we sat down, the doctor called in another doctor, and then the five of us—the two doctors, Cronin, Mary and me—went into a long huddle. The conversation was pretty general, as if we were all just passing the time of day, and I took part in it. After a while, one of the doctors suggested, "I think it would be a good idea for Jimmy to go off somewhere for a rest."

267

MR. POVICH, sports editor of the Washington *Post*, doesn't specify, but it ought to be noted that Mr. Lincoln had the build of a first baseman.

From *The Washington Senators*

SHIRLEY POVICH

THE THREAT of a great civil war hung heavy over Washington, D.C., in 1859, and the people of the nation's capital moved with uncertain step, caught up in the restive spirit of the onrushing schism between North and South. Never a gay city, Washington in that year appeared to the visitor even more solemn. Crime was at a new high, uniforms were more numerous than usual in the streets, and the slavery issue was flaring in the taverns, the drawing rooms, and on Capitol Hill.

But with the wishful thinking characteristic of some people in grim times, one segment of Washingtonians was attempting to continue with the usual social activities. They went to dances at the Drover's Rest to whirl in the Virginia Reels or skip in the Boston Fancy, or to Odd Fellows Hall to laugh at the antics of one Wyman, a comedian of the times. During the summer they piled on the steamer *James Guy* for cruises down the Potomac to Piney Point.

It was during this tense period that the Game of Base Ball—thus it was called, with capital letters—first made its appearance in the parks of Washington. In the summer of '59, government clerks, fascinated by newspaper accounts of the Game of Base Ball in other cities, formed a team called the Potomacs.

The government clerk of that era was a considerable force in the social life of the city. He was an upper-bracket, middle-class worker envied for the wages and security of his job. Thus a team of government clerks could give tone to the new game. Historians of the times report that many were "thrilled" by the prospect of deserting the Willard and Ebbitt Hotel bars for the wholesome, invigorating outdoors, and the game caught on to the extent that a second team, the National Club, was organized in November of the same year.

Most of the team members came from the then-fashionable Capitol Hill section. James Morrow and J. L. Wright, both government officials, were elected president and vice president of the National Club. The secretary was Arthur Pue Gorman, scion of a noted Maryland family, who was later to be United States Senator from his state.

It was the Potomacs, though, from the "first ward" area, roughly bounded on the east by Fifteenth Street and on the west by Rock Creek Park, who were the more skilled team. In the spring of 1860 the interloping Nationals were challenged to a series of battles at Base Ball.

On the White Lot, then called the backyard of the White House and now known as the Ellipse, the first game was played. The Potomacs won, but the score is still clouded in doubt created by a lack of common understanding of the rules. It was conceded that the Potomacs scored thirty-five runs, but varied accounts of the game credit the Nationals with as few as fifteen and as many as thirty runs.

It soon developed that the Nationals could not provide the opposition the Potomacs needed, so the latter team looked curiously toward Baltimore, where a club called the Excelsiors was establishing a reputation as one of the finest teams in the East. On June 6, on the White Lot, the Excelsiors satisfied the curiosity of the Potomacs, who gained a better understanding of the game, plus a 40-to-24 defeat. In the polite reportorial language of the day, an account of the game read:

The friendly match between the Potomac Club of this city and the Excelsior Club of Baltimore came off on the grounds south of the President's Mansion yesterday afternoon. Quite a number of visitors were present and witnessed the sport and were

International News

MEANS TO AN END...

The gentleman who is making such a desperate (and successful) effort to score is Junior Gilliam of the Dodgers (top). Bob Swift of the Tigers is making the valiant but futile try (center). This is the old Pepper Martin style, and Mr. Martin did not always come in contact with earth-bound objects. Sometimes (bottom) he flew.

Wide World

United Press

HOW TO CATCH A FLY BALL...

Willie Mays illustrates his basket catch for the camera (below). But there are times—such as when Duke Snider hits the ball in a vital pennant game (top, right), or Vic Wertz belts one in the World Series (bottom, right)—when this technique must be modified.

International News

THE TWO GREAT ARTS OF BASEBALL...

Unusual photographs of each: In the first picture, Davey Williams has laid down a squeeze bunt—so expert a job that everybody was safe. The expert in the second picture is unidentified.

International News

highly pleased with the result throughout, the opposing clubs bearing their defeats with perfect equanimity. The Excelsiors came out winner at the close of the game. At night they partook of rich entertainment prepared for them by Gunther at the order of the Potomac Club. We understand the Baltimore club made 40 runs to 24 by the Washington Club.

(The city directory listed Gunther as the bartender at the Ebbitt Hotel, so the type of "rich entertainment" provided may be well imagined.)

The Potomacs disbanded with the outbreak of the Civil War, but the Nationals, despite depletions in manpower when many team members left to join the colors, culled enough players to stay in competition. Baseball didn't ask for a green light from President Abraham Lincoln, but it is assumed any such request would have gained favorable consideration. The President was a fan. One of his biographers, in a pamphlet entitled "Abraham Lincoln in the National Capital," tells of Lincoln's frequent visits to the games.

In fact, Lincoln brought a baseball background to the White House, according to the late Steve Hannegan, the high-powered publicist engaged by Baseball Commissioner Landis in 1939 to help acclaim baseball's Centennial Year. Hannegan either resurrected or invented an episode which supposedly took place in Springfield, Illinois, in 1860 and illustrated President Lincoln's affection for the game. The following appeared in the Centennial Year literature:

"Tell the gentlemen they will have to wait a few minutes until I get my next turn at bat."

The speaker was a tall, gaunt man named Abraham Lincoln. And the gentlemen he was telling to cool their heels were a side-whiskered delegation from the Republican National Committee . . . If they gasped through their facial foliage, it was quite understandable . . . because to Abe Lincoln, whom they found playing baseball on a Springfield, Illinois, stubble field, they had come bearing momentous tidings. They had come to tell him the Chicago convention had nominated him for the Presidency of the United States.

But Lincoln, engrossed in his ball game, would suffer no interruption. Not even to learn that he might become the nation's sixteenth president . . . You see, he didn't want to miss his turn at bat.

The close of the Civil War found the Nationals solidly in the esteem of Washington fans, with the club's shortstop, slight, twenty-three-year-old Arthur Pue Gorman, the darling of the spectators. Young Gorman quickly rose to stardom on the not-too-brilliant Nationals. He worked on Capitol Hill, and the fact that he later became a senator from Maryland moved many historians to associate the name of "Senators" with the Washington baseball teams.

By 1865, the nation's capital was so baseball-conscious that clerks of the government agencies were excused early to permit them to watch the Nationals play the Brooklyn Atlantics and the Philadelphia Athletics in an intercity tournament on the White Lot. By game time six thousand fans were assembled, and on that August day a President of the United States, Andrew Johnson, became the first chief executive in history to watch an intercity baseball game.

High officialdom turned out in force with army and navy bigwigs flanking President Johnson in chairs that lined the field for the two days of the series. The first game was a sad blow to the Nationals, who lost to the Athletics, 87 to 12. Although no charge of a rabbit ball was raised, it is a fact that the visitors hit eighteen home runs. On the following day the Atlantics added to the misery and disillusionment of the Nationals by winning a 34-to-19 victory, scoring twenty-two runs in the last two innings.

The tournament, if not a competitive success for the Nationals, was a social bonanza for both teams and the game of baseball. With the visiting players, the members of the Nationals called on President Johnson at the White House and later were received by Congress and banqueted at the Willard Hotel.

Not content with their local games, the Nationals bravely struck out on the first western tour in the history of baseball, a staggering undertaking for the time because it was a nine-game trip into six different cities in states as far west as Missouri. The entire journey was three thousand miles.

At whose expense? Their own, of course. They were amateurs and gentlemen, were they not? To accept pay or guarantees would be profaning the social implications of the game.

THE SUMMER of 1955 was marked by such memorable events as the summit conference at Geneva, the floods in the northeast, and the coming to television of a program called "The $64,000 Question." Two grandmothers—one an expert on the Bible, the other on baseball—won $32,000 each and quit. Here are the questions that M.C. Hal March asked septuagenarian Myrt Power. Try yourself along with the baseball grandma; the answers follow.

"The $64,000 Question"

MRS. MYRTLE POWER

QUESTIONS—

$64—What is the keystone base?

$128—What is meant when a player is "on deck"?

$256—What is meant by a "duster"?

$512—What is meant by a "Texas Leaguer"?

$1,000—A baseball manager dreams of a player who can hit safely every time he comes to bat. The record for batting safely—successive times at bat—stands at 12. Two men hold that record. Walt Dropo, who hit 12 successive times for Detroit in 1952, and one other man. For $1,000 name the other man who shares the record for successive hits since 1900.

$2,000—Bob Feller is the only pitcher to pitch three no-hitters,[1] but here are a number of pitchers who have pitched two no-hitters. Allie Reynolds is one. For $2,000 name a pitcher who pitched for Detroit and a pitcher who pitched for Cincinnati, both having two no-hitters to their credit.

$4,000—Babe Ruth leads all other batters in home runs hit during a season. His major league record is 60 homers in 1927. Two other major league batters are tied for second place,[2] having hit the same number of homers each, though in two different years. Now—for $4,000—I want three things—the names of

the two batters—and the number of homers each hit.

$8,000—The St. Louis Cardinals have won the National League pennant at least nine times. Give me the exact dates of the last four times that the Cardinals won the pennant. You can give the four dates in any order you please.

$16,000—One of baseball's all-time highlights took place in the 1934 All-Star Game when Carl Hubbell struck out five men in a row. The brilliance of this performance can be measured by averaging the hitting record of those five American League sluggers. It comes out to .332. Now, for $16,000, name the five men struck out in succession by Carl Hubbell in the 1934 All-Star Game. You may list them in any order.

$32,000—The official record books list seven players who are credited with over three thousand hits during their careers in the major leagues. Ty Cobb heads the list with 4,191 hits garnered in his 24 years of play. Name the remaining six players who have a lifetime total of three thousand or more hits.

Answers—

$64—Second base.

$128—He is the next batter up.

$256—A pitch thrown too close to the batter.

---

[1] The statement should have read "The only pitcher in modern times." After all, there were a couple of fellows named Larry Corcoran and Cy Young . . . ED.

[2] Second place, to be fussy, belonged to a player named Babe Ruth. He hit 59 home runs in 1921. . . . ED.

$512—A looping hit, too far out for the infield and too close in for the outfield.

$1,000—Frank (Pinky) Higgins for the Boston Red Sox in 1938.

$2,000—Virgil Trucks, Detroit, and Johnny Vander Meer, Cincinnati.

$4,000—Jimmy Foxx in 1932 and Hank Greenberg in 1938, 58 each.

$8,000—1946, 1944, 1943, 1942.

$16,000—Babe Ruth, Lou Gehrig, Jimmy Foxx, Al Simmons, Joe Cronin.

$32,000—Adrian (Cap) Anson, Honus Wagner, Napoleon Lajoie, Tris Speaker, Eddie Collins, Paul Waner.

JOHN GALLAGHER

Courtesy *Sport* Magazine. ©

"There's something about wearing a Yankee uniform that gets you. I think it's the wool—it itches."

"CLEAN OUT THE CELLAR—the Dodgers is coming . . ." states this account from the days of yore (1931).

Wisdom in Brooklyn

QUENTIN REYNOLDS

I SHOULD ought to have known better. I went to Ebbets Field yesterday, and the game was called off on account of the rain, and it wasn't raining violets, either. So I met a feller by the name of Mac, and he says, "Come over to the Plumbers' and Mechanics' Bridge and Whist Club, and there is a feller there who will give you a story for the paper."

"What!" I sez. "Play cards on Sunday?"

"You never seen chicken in chicken pot pie or eggs in eggplants, did you?" Mac says. "Well, you never saw a card game in the Plumbers' and Mechanics' Bridge and Whist Club."

So I went over there, and it turned out to be a place where you say "Two up" and you get two long ones and if you say "Two down" you get two short ones. Very tasty, too. So this feller introduces me to Barney, who runs the place.

"I am pleased to make your acquaintance," he says. "I think I seen you somewhere before. Your face is familiar, but I can't place the body."

Mac bursts out laughing. "Ain't he a riot? He certainly is a wit!"

"Yes," Barney says modestly. "I am a guy that is full of laughs, and sometimes when people go out of here they are almost dying laughing. They say, 'That feller certainly is a card.'

"Now lots of times on rainy days I help the newspaper boys out with stories. Like, for instance, a feller named Robinson come in here after the St. Louises had clipped the Dodgers three in a row. I tell him to just say:—'The Cards is stacked against us.' . . . How's that, hey? . . . Then once when we lost four straight I tell a feller named Kase to say:—

'Clean out the cellar, the Dodgers is coming.'

"I am always thinking of things like that, and, in fact, I should have been a sports writer, but it woulda broke my mother's heart, so I am now in the rum business, which is at least honest."

A gentleman at the end of the mahogany was making a great deal of noise singing a song called "Sweet Analine," or something like that. Barney got sore. "Stop that nerse," he growls, "or I will inject you outa the joint.

"Getting back to the Dodgers," he says, "the trouble with them is they don't live right. I hear they go to bed early and do setting up exercises every morning.

"Them Dodgers are too tense. They are all tightened up like a cop on his night off. They should unlax a bit.

"The last time they win the pennant I usta know a lot of them. After the game they would come in here and have a few. I remember one big guy who played for them. The first time he comes in here I say, 'What do you want?'

"'Three beers and a gin rickey,' he growls, and right away I knew he was a real ballplayer. He had a couple of more rounds like that, and the next day he hits five for five and gets himself a fifty-clam bonus."

Barney was frankly disgusted. "What do them Dodgers do now on their off days? They play bridge or they play Ping-pong, the big pansies. They ought to be out raising a little hell. It would do them good and they would get all that tenseness out of their systems . . . What? You gotta? . . . Well, so long and the next time you come in we will discuss the Yankees."

THE TIME is out of joint when the late Grantland Rice should be thought to merit no more than three stanzas of verse in an anthology of this kind and size. In truth, he merits more than any book can give —even his own, called *The Tumult and the Shouting,* which every fan should read. Rice was so much more than his fecklessly assigned title, "Dean of American Sports Writers," conveyed. He was a warm and joyful person, who used to observe that he was the only man in North America who could send a poem via Western Union collect. More too, he was one hell of a writer.

It is hoped that the following piece, brief though it is, will be found as memorable as any in this collection. It is the spirit of Grantland Rice in a time of sadness. The date: August 14, 1948. Babe Ruth is dead.

Game Called

GRANTLAND RICE

Game called by darkness—let the curtain fall,
No more remembered thunder sweeps the field.
No more the ancient echoes hear the call
To one who wore so well both sword and shield.
The Big Guy's left us with the night to face,
And there is no one who can take his place.

Game called—and silence settles on the plain.
Where is the crash of ash against the sphere?
Where is the mighty music, the refrain
That once brought joy to every waiting ear?
The Big Guy's left us, lonely in the dark,
Forever waiting for the flaming spark.

Game called—what more is there for one to say?
How dull and drab the field looks to the eye.
For one who ruled it in a golden day
Has waved his cap to bid us all good-by.
The Big Guy's gone—by land or sky or foam
May the Great Umpire call him "safe at home."

Do NOT CONFUSE the author of this article, who is the editor of *Real* magazine, with the boxer of the same name. Kindly also do not confuse him or anybody else with the fella he's writing about. There was only one Rube Waddell.

This piece appeared in 1955.

Hey, Rube!

RAY ROBINSON

Mr. CONNIE MACK, who is now in his ninety-third year, and presumably remembers the day when the game of baseball was invented, has celebrated most of his birthdays in recent years by confiding to the American public his secret of longevity, and also by announcing that an old left-handed employee of his, one Rube Waddell, was the greatest pitcher that ever lived.

There is no denying that Rube Waddell, a big, gawky, generous man who roamed baseball diamonds and barrooms in the late 1890s and early 1900s, was the most successful enemy of gloom ever produced in a ball park, with possible apologies to Dizzy Dean. But Mr. Mack's unequivocal yearly endorsement of the Rube is an added accolade that must be taken seriously, much more seriously, of course, than Waddell ever took baseball or Mr. Mack.

It isn't hard to understand Mr. Mack's position on Waddell. The first day that Rube was ever commissioned to pitch for Connie, in 1900, when baseball's Grand Old Man was managing Milwaukee in the newly christened American League, Rube labored through both games of a double-header with the Chicago White Sox. The first one was a rather grueling 17-inning, 3-2 affair, that Rube himself won with a triple. Waddell had no desire to go into extra innings in the second game, so he won it in regulation time, 1-0. Instead of waiting for congratulations from his teammates and Mr. Mack —which certainly were due him after his Herculean chores of the day—Waddell then repaired to his favorite fishing creek. It was always that way with the Rube. Except that he usually did his repairing to a creek, or a fire, or a saloon, or a parade, or into a lady's boudoir

before, and not after, his contracted work for Mr. Mack, or whatever manager he happened to be working for at the time.

Waddell had a simply phenomenal mound record while he toiled for Connie. He pitched for the Philadelphia Athletics, Mr. Mack's celebrated team, from 1902 through 1907. He averaged almost 22 victories in each season; struck out 343 batters in 1904, a mark that stood until Bob Feller topped it in 1946; and was the leading percentage pitcher in the American League in 1905, when he amassed a 27-10 won-and-lost record.

The cold statistics tell one story. But Waddell's brilliance and eccentricity in Mr. Mack's service are perhaps best illustrated by the manner in which he handled Messrs. Napoleon Lajoie, Elmer Flick, and William Bradley on an afternoon in 1904.

The Cleveland Indians were trailing the Athletics in the ninth inning, 1-0. Waddell's usually faultless control of his curve suddenly deserted him, and the Indians managed to load the bases with nobody out.

But the clown that dominated Waddell's personality reared its pixieish head even in such a critical situation. The Rube waved all his outfielders in, and commanded them to sit down just beyond the base line. While Mr. Mack gazed in horror, Waddell then proceeded to strike out Lajoie, Flick, and Bradley on nine pitched balls! When that season was over it was found that Lajoie had an average of .381, Flick an average of .303, and Bradley an average of .300—so Rube wasn't picking on any patsies.

Mr. Mack's "greatest pitcher ever" was born George Edward Waddell in Bradford, Pennsyl-

274

vania, in October 1876. In his teens, when he already had reached a growth of six feet, three inches, and a weight over 200 pounds, Waddell was just about the best left-handed pitcher around. They knew all about his stuff in Butler, where he worked on a farm and pitched ball, and in Oil City, where he picked up his first cash for pitching, and in Franklin, Prospect and Homestead.

Soon the young fellow with the typical long-gait stride of the farmer and the insouciance of a three-year-old came to the attention of the Louisville team of the old National League. Louisville offered Waddell $500 for the season, scarcely appreciating at the time that Rube couldn't handle his liquor any better than he could handle his women. (In ensuing years Waddell was to have a covey of wives that would have put Tommy Manville to shame; he had Manville's appetite for marriage, but never his money.)

Waddell made his introduction into the big leagues at 3:30 in the morning. Wearing a dinky country cap, general store clothes, and carrying a tiny suitcase loaded with red neckties, which always were his favorite, Rube rapped on the door of Fred Clarke, the Louisville manager, who had the misfortune of being Rube's first pilot in the big leagues.

"Open up," mumbled Clarke, after Waddell had assured Clarke it was a "friend."

The door flew open, and Waddell presented a tremendously meaty hand and an affectionate grin, neither of which Clarke was in the habit of accepting at that hour.

"Hi, Freddie," was Rube's greeting. "How are you, old man? Lend me two bucks, will you?"

Clarke squinted at the formidable figure in the half-light coming through his window, and screeched, "Who the hell are you?"

"I'm your new man—Waddell, the world's greatest pitcher," said Rube, thereby immediately justifying his appearance. "I just got in town. I haven't eaten. I'm hungry and I need two dollars."

Clarke's response to this nocturnal request has never been accurately reported in any encyclopedia. But whatever it was, it didn't discourage Waddell from waking up the entire team before the night was over, for in the morning it was discovered that Rube had collected $16, all in two-dollar contributions.

Waddell was with Clarke in Louisville, and later in Pittsburgh. He never was much help to the veteran manager, for he won only sixteen games and lost eighteen in four seasons under Clarke. The manager simply never found the formula for handling his incorrigible pitcher. It was only the gentle prodding and diplomacy of Mr. Mack, plus the talent of Pinkerton detectives, that produced the fast balls from Waddell's muscular left arm. When Waddell finally severed his relationship with Clarke in 1901, when he was traded to Chicago of the National League, the manager's sigh of relief could be heard all the way to California.

"Of all the men I ever handled," said Clarke, "no player ever gave me half the trouble that Rube did. But no matter what the guy ever did, somehow you couldn't stay mad at him for long." Obviously Fred stayed mad at him long enough to trade him off to the Windy City.

A conspicuous failure with Chicago, Rube made a post-season trip to Los Angeles, where large crowds screaming "Hey, Rube!" turned out to see him every time he was scheduled to pitch. The adulation of the fans kept Rube in line more than ever before. When he had worked under Fred Clarke he often ran out on a pitching assignment to tend bar someplace in the neighborhood, or interrupted his pitching chores to travel to a nearby fire.

Hearing of his work in California, Mr. Mack, always convinced that the comic southpaw was a wonderful performer—as a pitcher, that is—had two detectives pick up Waddell in Los Angeles and bring him to Philadelphia, where the A's had just become part of the "outlaw" American League.

The vagabond hurler became an immediate success. In his first year under Connie—1902 —Rube won 23 games, lost only 7, and fanned 210. As a matter of fact, everything worked out fine for the eccentric ballplayer. Connie even got him a roommate who shared some of his interests. Ossee Schreckengost, the catcher, who changed his name to Schreck to convenience harassed sports writers and editors, had an amazing appetite for animal crackers and alcohol. This made him a natural for Rube's company. The two shared many an antic together.

One year Rube insisted that Mr. Mack insert a clause in Schreck's contract that would prohibit Ossee from eating crackers in the bed that the two of them shared. Rube had threatened to leave the club for a career in vaudeville unless Mr. Mack enforced this prohibition on his roommate's eating habits.

Waddell's popularity was such that he was called to the stage, just like many prominent prizefighters of the day. If John L. Sullivan and Jim Corbett could be featured, so could the Rube. He appeared in a melodrama called "The Stain of Guilt." Each exaggerated swing of the stoop-shouldered athlete's arms and legs was greeted with cheers, much as he was received when he strode to the pitcher's mound. In one sequence of the play Rube was called upon to put the slug on a villain, a role that was, in some respects, precariously true to real life. He delighted in the fisticuffs to the extent that the producers had to keep him well supplied with villains. Relays of mustached culprits bit the dust, and Waddell was never happier.

Fully appreciative of Waddell's box-office value to the Athletics, Mr. Mack was willing to put up with almost everything that Rube had to offer. Once, late at night, Rube and Schreck, a battery that for sheer zaniness probably surpasses anything that baseball has ever produced, stole into Connie's room and threw a foul-smelling combination onion and limburger cheese sandwich on the manager's bed.

"What's the big idea, Rube?" Connie asked, as he groped for his nostrils.

"We heard you weren't feeling well, Mr. Mack," replied Rube. "We thought this would fix you up real fine."

Connie almost suffocated because of the combined humanity of Rube and Ossee. But the incident had no adverse effect on his health; in fact, he is still alive today, at least fifty years later.

Waddell must have been in his cups when he pulled that cheese play on Mr. Mack. He might have been drunk, too, when he dived into the icy Delaware River one day in a vain effort to "rescue" a man who had supposedly fallen off the ferry. After several futile attempts to recover the "body," Rube had to settle for the soothing cheers of the thousand people who had followed his every move from the sidelines.

A man of enormous strength, Rube also had a giant-sized portion of courage in his make-up —with or without liquor under his belt.

He was passing a store in Lynn, Massachusetts, in 1905, when he noticed flames roaring through the door and window. Rube ran inside, without a moment's hesitation, picked up the blazing oil stove, carried it outside, and threw it into a snowbank. Only the gloves and winter overcoat he was wearing prevented Rube from being scorched by the fire.

Mr. Mack never paid Rube more than $3,000 in any single season. If he figured to

curtail Waddell's drinking by granting him such a meager dividend, he was mistaken. Rube, for all his childish behavior, was a man of devilish ingenuity.

When he was broke—seemingly his perennial economic status—Rube would shuffle into a bar, introduce himself all around as "Waddell—the world's greatest pitcher," then proceed to take a baseball out of his hip pocket. "This is the one I beat Cy Young with in that twenty-inning game," Rube would say, holding up the scuffed, historic pellet for all eager eyes to see.

The bartender, vaguely cognizant of the fact that Waddell had ever pitched such a game— which he had, in reality—would then offer to stake the left-hander to a drink (or drinks) if only he could exhibit the prize in his window. During one period late in 1907, it is said that every saloon window from New York to Philadelphia was adorned with this particular baseball—at the same time.

Though his teammates developed a strong dislike for his habits, they could never really hate Rube—even when it became apparent that his feverish after-dark activity was curtailing his career and thus hurting the club. There was also an enigmatic, gentle side to Rube that would occasionally flabbergast his fellow-players.

On one hazy day in Boston, Jesse Tannehill hit Rube's teammate, Danny Hoffman, on the head with a fast ball pitch. Hoffman went down like he was killed, and the team doctor, examining the unconscious player, declared the man had to be whisked to a hospital or he would die.

Rube thereupon gently raised the stricken Hoffman over his shoulders, ran across the field, and outside the park, where he flagged down a carriage. That whole night Rube sat alongside Danny, and applied a comforting ice bag to Hoffman's heated, swollen head.

However, it was easy for Mr. Mack to weary of Rube's ways once Rube started to slip. Connie was continually embarrassed by Waddell's frequent marriages and more frequent jail terms for non-support. Finally, in 1908, Waddell was traded to St. Louis of the American League.

He had one last moment of glory as a pitcher —and it occurred against his old teammates. Arriving in Philadelphia for a series, Waddell told newspapermen that he was out to trim the men who had turned against him. He was true to his word, striking out sixteen A's in an exhibition of pitching wizardry that has since been surpassed by only the greatest fast-ball pitchers.

An old friend, Joe Cantillon, purchased Waddell for his Minneapolis team in 1910, and Rube won twenty games for the last time in 1911. Cantillon, in Mr. Mack's tradition, respected Rube's desires, and let him drink to his heart's content as long as he showed up at the ball park in time to pitch—when he was advertised in advance as the pitcher. It worked like a charm once more, and Cantillon had himself a powerful attraction at the gate and a big winner on the field.

That winter Joe took Waddell back home with him to Hickman, Kentucky. It turned out to be the most ill-fated trip the well-traveled Waddell ever took in his life.

As Robert Smith describes the incident in his book, *Baseball,* scores of people living in Hickman were marooned when the Reelfoot levee gave way to flood waters. Rube, with other husky volunteers, "stood in water up to his armpits for hours, fighting to plug the 60-foot gap the river had torn in the levee. The cold he took then never left him . . ."

* * *

Less than two years later, Waddell, the powerful Dutchman, was down to 140 pounds, a shrunken mockery of the man who once had thrown baseball's most effective fast ball. He was dying of tuberculosis. Some of his old friends came to see him in a Texas hospital.

The Rube's strength, the strength he'd always been so proud of, was gone. But not his spirit.

"I'll come over tomorrow to show you guys how to run," Rube whispered to his pals. Then, a few days later, on April Fool's Day, 1914, he left the world forever—just 37 years after he had come into it.

Thirty-two years later he was elected to Baseball's Hall of Fame. "Colorful left-handed pitcher," is how the plaque in his honor starts out up at Cooperstown. But Mr. Mack remembers him more for the games he won, for his biting curve ball, for his good humor. Not for his drinking or his hooky-playing.

RAY HELLER

"Three errors in one inning—he'd better have a good excuse."

HARRY RUBY, one-half of the song-writing team of Kalmar and Ruby whose life stories were made into the motion picture hit *Three Little Words* (one of their famous songs), is known to many as baseball's number one fan. While putting together this collection, I wrote to him and asked him to set a few of his experiences down on paper.

A Letter to the Editor

HARRY RUBY

MY INTEREST in baseball came, strangely enough, at age 26 (not as a kid, as it does to everyone else). At that tender age, I started to play, or learn to play, which was kind of late in life for an athlete. I shall always believe that had I started as a kid, I would have made the grade. Anyway, let me dream.

I cannot tell you all the things I did, silly things, in my love for baseball. I'll give you a few of them. I played hooky from a job at RKO (AWOL) to go to Washington to play one inning with the Senators against the then Baltimore Orioles. That was in 1931. I traveled 6,000 miles to play one inning and lost a good job. I also loused up a double play, which, if you remember a certain thing that Shakespeare said about the evil men do, will live long after my good deeds are forgotten. (See Al Schacht about that dark spot in my life.)

In the good old early days, while I had two hit shows on Broadway at the same time, I lived in Pelham, New York, and was a utility second-sacker for the New Rochelle Fire Department Ball Club. This was my first big moment. The next came when I went to bat against Walter Johnson in 1930 in an intersquad game in Biloxi, Mississippi. I *really* struck out on two strikes: walked away from the plate after the second pitch whizzed by me. Please remember that my first time at bat, outside of semipro ball, was against the immortal Johnson, who, they tell me, scared the greatest with his speed. You might call this experience a real psychic trauma—batting against the "Big Train," I mean.

I got to play in four official league games

on the coast . . . with Hollywood and Los Angeles a few years back. They always let me in the last inning of the last day—and the umpires turned their backs, making like they didn't see me. My being in a regular game, as you know, was not legal.

In one of those games, Hollywood vs. the Angels, I hit a real Texas Leaguer—a sure hit, if there ever was one. The Angels' second baseman, Carl Ditmar, one of the greats, came up with the most sensational catch of the season . . . so I was out. I didn't talk to Ditmar for two years after that, but we made up and still are good friends.

Mind you, I know all of this is crazy. But for those things I would never have been dubbed America's Number One Baseball Fan —in most papers and particularly in a "Looping the Loops" article done about me in the Bible of Baseball: *The Sporting News*. (By the way, this was the first time, and possibly the only time, they did one of those profiles on someone not a regular part of baseball—in some way. It was a thrill for me.)

I have had a small part, a bit, in four or five baseball movies. This is almost an unwritten law here—that I play in a baseball movie. But here is the big story. Many years back, Joe E. Brown was starring in a movie: *Elmer the Great*. I was cast as an outfielder. They made the baseball sequences here in Los Angeles at Wrigley Field. They were just about to shoot my part when they told me I was to miss a fly just hit by Brown. Infuriated, I walked off the location set and said, "I wouldn't miss a ball on purpose for ten thousand dollars." I was serious. Brown told this story to

Lou Gehrig in my presence. I blushed. Lou said it was the greatest baseball story he'd ever heard. (This was two years before his tragic end.)

In a game between Pittsburgh and Portland —a few years ago in Paso Robles, California— I hit for Lindstrom. I got hold of a fast pitch and sent it sailing into deep center field. I tore around the bases and got to third, where the great and late Honus Wagner was waiting to wave me in for an "in-the-park" home run. Imagine my feelings when I discovered that the then manager, George Gibson, had called in the outfield. There wasn't one player in the outfield. Well, this was too much of an insult, so I walked to the bench from third—and quit. (It was not Gibson who called in the outfield. It was the manager of Portland, come to think of it.)

Most of the stories are like the foregoing, so I don't think I'd better give you any more. They are all silly, but they show how I loved the game and how I wanted to play baseball (even more than I wanted to write songs).

This might be of interest: I have been to many places on this earth—Trinidad, Barbados, Cuba, Puerto Rico, Alaska, Hawaii, Panama, Venezuela, Mexico City, etc., etc. I did not get to see anything of those places. I always went right from the train or boat to a ball field. In Barbados and Trinidad, where there was no baseball, I bribed the caretaker of a cricket field and had a catch with some passengers. I always carried baseball equipment wherever I went—and still do at my age. What's my age? I'll tell you. I am 61.

I have, in other words, been to many foreign places, but, because of my zany love for baseball, I have seen nothing of these places. It is almost as if I had never been away from this country.

This might interest you: I have a wonderful collection of the greats in baseball—signed pictures of those I knew and played with. Among them are the real immortals, Cobb, Wagner, Clark Griffith, Connie Mack, etc. The following are some of the inscriptions:

TO HARRY RUBY: A ballplayer's ballplayer . . . BABE RUTH

TO HARRY RUBY: He could do anything on the ball field except go to his left and right . . . WALTER JOHNSON

TO HARRY RUBY: The best second baseman outside of baseball . . . JOE CRONIN

I do hope this helps you. If you need more, let me know. But I do believe this is enough. After all, I am only a fan. . . .

Sincerely,
HARRY RUBY

IF YOU THINK of Casey Stengel as a manager but never as a player —if you think of Damon Runyon as an author but never as a reporter—then never must you stand so spectacularly corrected as right now. Read!

1923:
New York Giants 5,
New York Yankees 4

———————— DAMON RUNYON ————————

THIS IS the way old Casey Stengel ran yesterday afternoon, running his home run home.

This is the way old Casey Stengel ran running his home run home to a Giant victory by a score of 5 to 4 in the first game of the World Series of 1923.

This is the way old Casey Stengel ran, running his home run home, when two were out in the ninth inning and the score was tied and the ball was still bounding inside the Yankee yard.

This is the way—

His mouth wide open.

His warped old legs bending beneath him at every stride.

His arms flying back and forth like those of a man swimming with a crawl stroke.

His flanks heaving, his breath whistling, his head far back.

Yankee infielders, passed by old Casey Stengel as he was running his home run home, say Casey was muttering to himself, adjuring himself to greater speed as a jockey mutters to his horse in a race, that he was saying: "Go on, Casey! Go on!"

People generally laugh when they see old Casey Stengel run, but they were not laughing while he was running his home run home yesterday afternoon. People—60,000 of 'em, men and women—were standing in the Yankee stands and bleachers up there in the Bronx

roaring sympathetically, whether they were for or against the Giants.

"Come on, Casey!"

The warped old legs, twisted and bent by many a year of baseball campaigning, just barely held out under Casey Stengel until he reached the plate, running his home run home.

Then they collapsed.

They gave out just as old Casey slid over the plate in his awkward fashion as Wally Schang made futile efforts to capture the ball which eluded him and rolled toward the dugout. Billy Evans, the American League umpire, poised over him in a set pose, arms spread to indicate that old Casey was safe.

Half a dozen Giants rushed forward to help Casey to his feet, to hammer him on the back, to bawl congratulations in his ears as he limped unsteadily, still panting furiously, to the bench where John J. McGraw, chief of the Giants, relaxed his stern features in a smile for the man who had won the game.

Casey Stengel's warped old legs, one of them broken not so long ago, wouldn't carry him out for the last half of the inning, when the Yankees made a dying effort to undo the damage done by Casey. His place in center field was taken by young Bill Cunningham, whose legs are still unwarped, and Casey sat on the bench with John J. McGraw.

No one expected much of Casey Stengel when he appeared at the plate in the Giants' side of the ninth inning, the score a tie at 4 to 4.

Ross Young and Irish Meusel, stout, dependable hitters, had been quickly disposed of by the superb pitching of Bullet Joe Bush.

No one expected Stengel to accomplish anything where they had failed. Bush, pitching as only Bush can pitch in an emergency, soon had two strikes and three balls on Casey.

He was at the plate so long that many of the fans were fidgeting nervously, wondering why he didn't hurry up and get put out, so the game could go on. Casey Stengel is not an imposing figure at bat, not an imposing figure under any circumstances. Those warped old legs have something to do with it. A man with warped legs cannot look very imposing.

People like to laugh at Casey—Casey likes to make people laugh.

A wayfarer of the big leagues—Brooklyn, Pittsburgh, Philadelphia, and finally New York —he has always been regarded by the fans as a great comedian, a funny fellow, a sort of clown.

The baseball land teems with tales of the strange didoes cut by Casey Stengel, whose parents started him out as Charles, with his sayings.

Who knows but that "Bullet Joe" may have been thinking of Casey Stengel more as a comedian than as a dangerous hitter when he delivered that final pitch yesterday afternoon? Pitchers sometimes let their wits go woolgathering.

"Bap"—Stengel's bat connected with the last pitch, connected surely, solidly. The ball sailed out over left field, moving high, moving far.

Long Bob Meusel and Whitey Witt, the Yankee outfielders, raced toward each other as they marked the probable point where the ball would alight, and in the meantime Casey Stengel was well advanced on his journey, running his home run home.

As the ball landed between Meusel and Witt it bounded as if possessed toward the left center-field fence. Everybody could see it would be a home run inside the yard, if Casey Stengel's warped old legs could carry him around the bases.

Witt got the ball about the time Stengel hit third, and about that time Stengel was laboring, "all out." Witt threw the ball in to Bob Meusel who had dropped back and let Witt go on. Meusel wheeled and fired for the plate, putting all his strength behind the throw. Few men have ever lived who can throw a baseball as

well as Bob Meusel.

Stengel was almost home when Meusel's throw was launched, and sensing the throw Casey called on all that was left in those warped old legs, called no doubt on all the baseball gods to help him—and they helped.

It is something to win a World Series with a home run, and that home run inside the yard.

John J. McGraw perhaps feels that his judgment in taking Stengel on at a time when Casey was a general big-league outcast has been vindicated.

*   *   *

If you are curious to know the origin of the nickname "Casey," it might be explained that Stengel's home town is Kansas City.

The nickname comes from "K.C." One of these many little coincidences that are always popping out in baseball is the fact that Stengel and Bullet Joe Bush are great pals. They made the baseball four to Japan last winter as roommates.

Stengel is around thirty-three, if you are seeking more information about the first hero of the World Series of 1923. They call that old in baseball. He has been with the Giants since 1921, from the Philadelphia club. He is all right, Casey Stengel is, and you can prove it by John J. McGraw.

The expected struggle of Mind vs. Matter, or Intelligence against Brute Force, with John J. McGraw representing the one, and Babe Ruth the other, did not materialize.

Both sides began batting the ball so freely that thinking was not necessary.

Ruth got a three-bagger and was cheated out of another hit through an astonishing play by Long George Kelly, perhaps one of the most sensational plays ever seen in a World Series. Kelly got a hit from Ruth's bat with one hand at a seemingly impossible angle and threw a man out at the plate.

Quite as sensational was a play by Frankie Frisch, who backed out into short right field, caught a short fly from Bob Meusel's bat, turned and threw Ruth out at the plate. This was immediately after Ruth's three-bagger. Perhaps if Casey Stengel had not run his home run, Frisch's play would be picked as the feature of the whole afternoon.

The Yanks were three runs ahead of the Giants when McGraw's men caught and passed them, hammering Waite Hoyt for all their runs except Stengel's home run. It was the first real bad inning the one-time Brooklyn schoolboy ever had in a World Series, so say the experts.

Bush took Hoyt's place and pitched marvelous ball. Poor Bush, as usual, suffered from "the breaks," from the bad luck of the game. He has been in a number of World Series, and was always what baseball calls a "tough luck pitcher" in them. He won one game for the Athletics in his first year in the big leagues. Since then he has been a consistent loser.

The Yanks drove John Watson, of Louisiana, from the game early. Then Wilfrid Ryan did the pitching for McGraw's men—and did it well. The Yanks outhit the Giants, however, twelve to eight.

It seemed to this writer that the Yanks were very stupid in some of their base running. At least one example probably cost them a run.

However, it was a great game for the spectators. A thrill a minute, finally topped off by the real big thrill of Casey Stengel, running his home run home.

*   *   *

The umpires, four solemn-looking gentlemen in dark, funeral blue uniforms with little blue caps, held a meeting at the home plate just before game time. They were Billy Evans of the American League, who can wear an umpire's uniform in such fashion that he looks trim and neat, Dick Nallin, of the same league, and Bill Hart, and Hank O'Day, a dour-looking man of the National League.

After the umpires conferred, the Yanks posed in a group at the plate, and Benny Bengough, the Yankee catcher, a young man from Buffalo, was presented with a traveling bag, presumably by his admirers.

Meanwhile, in front of the stand, Waite Hoyt and John Watson were warming up with deliberate motions, to the great surprise of some of the experts who had expected Arthur Nehf and Herb Pennock, left-handers, to start the series.

The breeze died away and the flags were hanging limply on their staffs when Miller Huggins, the little short-legged manager of the Yankees, and Davy Bancroft, captain of the Giants, held their last conference with the umpires and presented their line-ups.

Babe Ruth got the honor of making the first put-out of the game. He easily caught a fly from Beauty Bancroft. Hoyt's first pitch to Bancroft was right over the plate. Bancroft let it go by and Evans called it a strike. The next pitch was a ball, then Bancroft hit the fly to Ruth.

The bandy-legged Groh, waving his bottle-shaped bat, was at the plate but a short time. He hit the first ball thrown by Hoyt for a sharp single across second. The crowd babbled as Groh rushed to first.

Frankie Frisch, slim, graceful—called the "Fordham Flash"—was next to face Hoyt. The first pitch was called a ball, then Hoyt put over a strike. Frisch hit a bounder to Scott, who threw the ball to Ward at second, forcing out Groh.

With Ross Young, the Texan, at bat, Frisch, fastest of the National League base runners, tried to steal second. Schang whipped the ball to Aaron Ward at second, and Ward slapped the ball on Frisch's head as the "Fordham Flash" went sliding in, head foremost, as he always slides, and as few other players slide. That ended the inning.

McGraw was starting his old line of attack early. McGraw is a great believer in speed. He always sends his fast men out to run on the opposing pitcher when they have the opportunity. McGraw argues that a man may as well be thrown out stealing as to have a put-out in some other fashion.

The Yankees quickly set the stage for Babe Ruth in their side of the first inning. That was what perhaps two-thirds of the crowd was waiting for—the appearance of Ruth.

Babe came with Joe Dugan on first base, after Whitey Witt had hit a liner to Bancroft. Whitey was first of the Yankees at bat. Dugan got a base on balls from John Watson. Then "Along came Ruth."

The crowd buzzed as Ruth stood his stalwart frame alongside the plate, his legs slightly spraddled, his long bat waving menacingly at Watson. The first pitch was inside, but over the plate, and Evans motioned a strike. Babe set his feet more firmly. He swung at the next pitch and missed the ball by several inches. The crowd, always buzzing at Ruth's slightest move at bat, now murmured loudly.

The next pitch was a ball far outside the plate. On the following pitch Ruth swung. He drove the ball solidly toward third, directly at Heine Groh. The ball took one fierce bound before reaching Heine. It was going with such force that it bounced off Heine's glove. Then Groh recovered the ball and threw it to Frisch at second for a force play on Dugan.

Now came Long Bob Meusel, brother of the Giants' "Irish," batting one notch ahead of his usual place in the Yankee line-up.

The tall Californian hit the ball a solid

smack. As it sailed to center Casey Stengel raced for the spot in which he saw it would land. He got one hand on the ball as it struck the ground, then it twisted away from him elusively.

Meantime, Ruth was thundering around the bases. Stengel threw the ball in the general direction of third, but Ruth was home by that time. Meusel was at second, and the crowd was roaring.

It went as a two-base hit for Meusel. Pipp, the next man up, a tall, raw-boned Michigander, once called "the Pickler," because of his slugging ability, raised a fly to Irish Meusel, leaving brother Bob on second.

Events now began moving with great rapidity. One thrill after another swept the slopes of Islanders.

The Giants were retired without incident in their side of the second. Ward, first of the Yankees up in the last half of the inning, singled to left. Schang followed with a single. Scott bunted to Kelly who tagged him out, but necessarily permitted Ward and Schang to advance.

Hoyt struck out, but Witt banged a single past Frisch and Ward and Schang scored. The Yankees were three runs ahead, as Dugan ended the inning by grounding out to Watson.

It seemed a terrific load to the supporters of the Giants. The fans asked each other why McGraw had not taken Watson out when it was evident that the North Carolina farmer "had nothing."

They were still murmuring their discontent when George Kelly, towering first baseman of the Giants, opened the Giants' third with a single. The murmuring stopped momentarily as Lank Hank Gowdy drew a base on balls. Gowdy, lean backstop of the McGraw club, and once the greatest of heroes of a World Series, was taken out of the game immediately and Maguire, a fleet young Giant recruit, put on first base to run for him. The "Master Mind" on the Giant bench seemed to be working.

Now Watson—John Watson the Third, of North Carolina—also was out of the game. Big Jack Bentley, the left-handed pitcher from Baltimore, who looks something like Babe Ruth, was advancing to the plate to bat in place of Watson. Bentley was accounted a tremendous hitter when he was the star of Jack Dunn's Baltimore Orioles.

Hoyt worked on him with great care, knowing Bentley's reputation, having seen him hit in exhibition games between the Yankees and the Orioles. He soon had two strikes on Bentley, one of them a vicious foul bounder across first which barely missed being safe.

Bentley dropped a looping fly in center field, just outside the clutches of Whitey Witt. It was not far enough out for anyone to score, but it filled the bases.

McGraw, from the Giant bench, called Bentley in and Danny Gearin, a midget recruit pitcher, went to first to run in place of Bentley.

The bases full and no outs. Small wonder the Giant sympathizers were roaring with excitement. Beauty Bancroft drove a slow roller at Everett Scott, and the Yankee shortstop threw the ball to Ward at second, forcing out Gearin. Meantime, Kelly scored and Maguire reached third.

Now the bandy-legged Groh and his bottle-shaped bat were before Hoyt, and the Yankee rooters were squawking nervously "Take him out."

Bancroft suddenly quit first on a pitch to Groh, stealing second well ahead of Schang's throw—so far ahead, in fact, some of the Giant fans laughed derisively.

Now Groh clipped the ball across first, the drive hitting in fair territory, bouncing away past Pipp to right field. Ruth was lumbering in to meet the ball when it struck the screen in right field, and bounded away at a wicked angle. Ruth got his hands on the ball, but the carom deceived him. He could not hold it, and away it went across the grass.

While Ruth was chasing it, two Giants were scoring, the crowd was in a spasm of excitement, and Huggins was raging on the Yankee bench and motioning at Hoyt. Groh reached third before Ruth got the ball. Then Hoyt dejectedly left the field, and out of the flurry of players in front of the Yankee bench came Joe Bush another one-time hero of other World Series.

Bush pitched to Frisch, who singled past Pipp, scoring Groh. Young forced Frisch at second on an infield bounder, and Young himself was an easy out when he tried to steal second.

The Giant rooters fell back limply in their seats, completely exhausted from their vocal efforts during the inning.

Four runs—and the Giants now one run ahead. The Giant rooters felt they had earned their right to demonstration.

Wilfred Ryan—nicknamed "Rosey," for no apparent reason—went in to pitch for the Giants. Nearly all ballplayers have nicknames.

Some of them mean much. Some of them mean little, if anything. "Rosey" is one of those names.

Ryan is a Holy Cross man, and a good right-handed pitcher when he is "right," that is to say, when the ball is obeying his muscles as it should.

In the Yankee half of the fifth inning, Ruth, in his fourth trip to the plate, took a shorter grip on his bat than is his habit—"choked up," the ballplayers call it—and swatting a short, sharp smash at the first ball pitched by Ryan drove the ball to deep left. It struck the low concrete in front of the left field pavillion, and bounded away from Irish Meusel.

Ruth was rambling into third when Meusel got the ball and let fly to Groh. The big slugger of the Yankees fairly threw himself at the bag, his long feet reaching for the base as Groh got the ball and plunged at him. It was a close play. Groh thought he had the Babe. He raged for a fleeting instant when Bill Hart waved the runner safe. The scorers called it a three-base hit.

Dugan had gone out just before Ruth went to bat, and now Long Bob Meusel lifted a little fly that rose slowly over the infield and floated on back over short right field, well back of the base line between first and second.

It was a dangerous looking little fly, one of the kind called "Texas Leaguers." Young came racing up from right field and Frisch went running backward, his eye on the ball, his hands waving Young away.

Frisch was twisting and turning with the descending ball; his back was turned from the infield when he caught it. Ruth instantly left third and tore for home. Frisch turned and threw blindly in the direction of the plate, and it happened to be an accurate throw.

The ball bounded in straight and true to huge Frank Snyder, who had taken Gowdy's place behind the plate. As Snyder clasped the ball Ruth came lunging in. The big men collided with terrific force, but Snyder clung to the ball, tagged Ruth with it, and Ruth was out. It was a great play—it was a thrilling play.

Casey Stengel got the first hit off Bush since he relieved Hoyt in the seventh. It was a single. Kelly hit into a double play immediately afterwards.

Bush was given a round of applause when he went to the plate in the Yankees' seventh and Joe, as if by way of acknowledgment, singled to center, his second hit. Witt lifted an easy fly to Meusel in short left field. The Yankee rooters, briefly stirred by hope, sighed dismally and sank back in their seats only to come up shrilling an instant later when Jumping Joe Dugan, third baseman of the Yanks, smashed the ball to the right-field bleacher barrier.

It was a clean, hard drive, well out of reach of Young. Bush raced around the bases, and on across the plate, with Dugan not far behind him. Kelly's throw was right to the mark, and Snyder tagged Dugan a yard from the plate. Bob Meusel ended the inning with a fly to Young, after Ruth had almost been caught napping off first.

"The Giants are getting all the breaks," moaned Yankee sympathizers.

However, it seemed to the ordinary observer that the Yankees made some of the breaks against themselves.

THIS PIECE, done in 1955 by the veteran H. G. Salsinger of the Detroit *News* and reprinted in *Baseball Digest*, offers an interesting comparison to the article by Arthur Daley elsewhere in this book.

Brains in His Feet

H. G. SALSINGER

MEMORANDUM: *Fifty years ago the name "Cobb" appeared in a box score for the first time. It appeared in 3,032 more box scores before it vanished twenty-four years later.*

* * *

Brilliant and unorthodox, a fiery genius and the game's outstanding individualist, Ty Cobb made baseball history for more than two decades. He dominated the game.

He gained pre-eminence not because he was the fastest base runner, nor the best base stealer, nor the fleetest fielder, nor the leading hitter, but because he had the nimblest brain that baseball has known.

He had the ability to perceive a situation and take advantage of it before his opponents became aware of it. He was a keener student of the game than his contemporaries and understood the game better than they did. More than that, he understood them better than they understood themselves. He knew their mechanical faults and weaknesses but he also knew their strength.

He was baseball's greatest player because he outthought them, kept a play ahead of them. He was not the greatest fielder, since there were several better. He was not the greatest place hitter since Wee Willie Keeler was admittedly better. He was not the greatest slugger since a dozen or more players could hit the ball farther. He was not the fastest man in the game since several others were just as fast and a few probably faster. His wide edge over the field was mental. He thought quicker than any rival and he put his mechanical skill to better use than they did. Many of his hits were attributed to superior speed but the explanation does not hold since several other players were as fast but they did not cause

fielders to overhurry the way Cobb did. They did not upset infields the way Cobb did.

In running bases, Cobb's lightning brain worked faster than his legs. Branch Rickey, who managed the St. Louis Browns when Cobb was at the peak of his career, commented one day:

"He has brains in his feet."

He continually crossed up infielders. He would break unexpectedly and fail to break when they expected him to run.

Every move he made was carefully planned. Going into a base he knew what the infielder would do. He developed different slides, including the hook, the fallaway and fadeaway. He would go straight into a bag or to the outside or inside. He would purposely slide wide, past the bag, then hook the outside corner with his toe.

He was not a natural hitter when he entered organized baseball and he could not get a loud foul off a left-hander. By the time he became established as the league's top player he could hit left-handers better than right-handers.

He could not slide at the start of his career but became the most expert slider in the game.

He studied infielders, outfielders, pitchers and catchers and made mental note of their individual playing habits. Nothing escaped him.

He used no mystic powers, had no occult gifts. Some of his plays looked downright stupid but they were anything but that. He would let himself be caught flat-footed between bases. Then the rundown started. Nine out of ten times Cobb would advance. He had a simple explanation:

"All you've got to do is make them keep on throwing the ball. Sooner or later somebody will make a wild throw."

Someone generally did.

Cobb upset batteries and infields. He was responsible for more wild throws than any other man who played the game. He constantly harried pitchers, saying:

"When I'm up there at the plate I know the pitcher is under a lot more pressure than I am, especially in a close game. I've got a psychological advantage over him."

He scored from first on singles, streaked from first to third, or scored from second on sacrifice bunts and infield outs. The delayed steal was one of his favorites. He would turn first base on an outfield single, come to a stop, and when the outfielder pulled back his arm to lob the ball to the infield, Cobb was off. He knew the outfielder would have to change position to make a fast throw to second.

He was so far ahead of the field that comparisons seem odious. When he retired in 1928, after twenty-four years of big league competition, he left behind enough records to convince even the most skeptical of his rightful place at the head of the all-time ranking.

Cobb was probably the greatest competitor any sport has known, the fiercest. He was at his best when the pressure was on. He gloried in the clutch. His most brilliant plays generally came when the odds were heavily against him. He was one of the poorest losers in sport and his bitter dread of defeat made him a spectacular winner. He could endure anything but failure. There was no amount of drudgery that he would not undertake to reach his goal.

He is baseball's lonely figure sitting on the Olympian heights. There has been only one Tyrus Raymond Cobb and the game will never see his like again for the pattern of play has changed and not for the better.

WHILE first at work on this collection, I was told by several friends to look up a *Saturday Evening Post* story about a horse that played outfield for the Dodgers. I told them there could not be such a story, and I was right, of course. The horse played third base.

My Kingdom for Jones

WILBUR SCHRAMM

THE FIRST DAY Jones played third base for Brooklyn was like the day Galileo turned his telescope on the planets or Columbus sailed back to Spain. First, people said it couldn't be true; then they said things will never be the same.

Timothy McGuire, of the Brooklyn *Eagle*, told me how he felt the first time he saw Jones. He said that if a bird had stepped out of a cuckoo clock that day and asked him what time it was, he wouldn't have been surprised enough to blink an Irish eye. And still he knew that the whole future of baseball hung that day by a cotton thread.

Don't ask Judge Kenesaw Mountain Landis about this. He has never yet admitted publicly that Jones ever played for Brooklyn. He has good reason not to. But ask an old-time sports writer. Ask Tim McGuire.

It happened so long ago it was even before Mr. Roosevelt became President. It was a lazy Georgia spring afternoon, the first time McGuire and I saw Jones. There was a light-footed little breeze and just enough haze to keep the sun from burning. The air was full of fresh-cut grass and wistaria and fruit blossoms and the ping of baseballs on well-oiled mitts. Everyone in Georgia knows that the only sensible thing to do on an afternoon like that is sleep. If you can't do that, if you are a baseball writer down from New York to cover Brooklyn's spring-training camp, you can stretch out on the grass and raise yourself every hour or so on one elbow to steal a glance at fielding practice. That was what we were doing—meanwhile amusing ourselves halfheartedly with a game involving small cubes and numbers—when we first saw Jones.

The Times wasn't there. Even in those days they were keeping their sports staff at home to study for "Information Please." But four of us were down from the New York papers—the *World,* the *Herald,* Tim and I. I can even remember what we were talking about.

I was asking the World, "How do they look to you?"

"Pitchers and no punch," the World said. "No big bats. No great fielders. No Honus Wagner. No Hal Chase. No Ty Cobb."

"No Tinker to Evers to Chance," said the Herald. "Seven come to Susy," he added soothingly, blowing on his hands.

"What's your angle today?" the World asked Tim.

Tim doesn't remember exactly how he answered that. To the best of my knowledge, he merely said, "Ulk." It occurred to me that the Brooklyn *Eagle* was usually more eloquent than that, but the Southern weather must have slowed up my reaction.

The World said, "What?"

"There's a sorsh," Tim said in a weak, strangled sort of voice—"a horse . . . on third . . . base."

"Why don't they chase it off?" said the Herald impatiently. "Your dice."

"They don't . . . want to," Tim said in that funny voice.

I glanced up at Tim then. Now Tim, as you probably remember, was built from the same blueprints as a truck, with a magnificent red nose for a headlight. But when I looked at him, all the color was draining out of that nose slowly, from top to bottom, like turning off a gas mantle. I should estimate Tim was, at the moment, the whitest McGuire in four generations.

Then I looked over my shoulder to see where

Tim was staring. He was the only one of us facing the ball diamond. I looked for some time. Then I tapped the World on the back.

"Pardon me," I asked politely, "do you notice anything unusual?"

"If you refer to my luck," said the World, "it's the same pitiful kind I've had since Christmas."

"Look at the infield," I suggested.

"Hey," said the Herald, "if you don't want the dice, give them to me."

"I know this can't be true," mused the World, "but I could swear I see a horse on third base."

The Herald climbed to his feet with some effort. He was built in the days when there was no shortage of materials.

"If the only way to get you guys to put your minds on this game is to chase that horse off the field," he said testily, "I'll do it myself."

He started toward the infield, rubbed his eyes and fainted dead away.

"I had the queerest dream," he said, when we revived him. "I dreamed there was a horse playing third base. My God!" he shouted, glancing toward the diamond. "I'm still asleep!"

That is, word for word, what happened the first day Jones played third base for Brooklyn. Ask McGuire.

*   *   *

When we felt able, we hunted up the Brooklyn manager, who was a chunky, red-haired individual with a whisper like a foghorn. A foghorn with a Brooklyn accent. His name was Pop O'Donnell.

"I see you've noticed," Pop boomed defensively.

"What do you mean," the Herald said severely, "by not notifying us you had a horse playing third base?"

"I didn't guess you'd believe it," Pop said.

Pop was still a little bewildered himself. He said the horse had wandered on the field that morning during practice. Someone tried to chase it off by hitting a baseball toward it. The horse calmly opened its mouth and caught the ball. Nothing could be neater.

While they were still marveling over that, the horse galloped thirty yards and took a ball almost out of the hands of an outfielder who was poised for the catch. They said Willie Keeler couldn't have done it better. So they spent an hour hitting fungo flies—or, as some wit called them, horse flies—to the horse. Short ones, long ones, high ones, grass cutters, line

drives—it made no difference; the animal covered Dixie like the dew.

They tried the horse at second and short, but he was a little slow on the pivot when compared with men like Napoleon Lajoie. Then they tried him at third base, and knew that was the right, the inevitable place. He was a great wall of China. He was a flash of brown lightning. In fact, he covered half the shortstop's territory and two thirds of left field, and even came behind the plate to help the catcher with foul tips. The catcher got pretty sore about it. He said that anybody who was going to steal his easy put-outs would have to wear an umpire's uniform like the other thieves.

"Can he hit?" asked the World.

"See for yourself," Pop O'Donnell invited.

The Superbas—they hadn't begun calling them the Dodgers yet—were just starting batting practice. Nap Rucker was tossing them in with that beautiful smooth motion of his, and the horse was at bat. He met the first ball on the nose and smashed it into left field. He laid down a bunt that waddled like a turtle along the base line. He sizzled a liner over second like a clothesline.

"What a story!" said the World.

"I wonder—" said the Herald—"I wonder how good it is."

We stared at him.

"I wouldn't say it is quite as good as the sinking of the *Maine*, if you mean that," said Tim.

"I wonder how many people are going to believe it," said the Herald.

"I'll race you to the phone," Tim said.

Tim won. He admits he had a long start. Twenty minutes later he came back, walking slowly.

"I wish to announce," he said, "that I have been insulted by my editor and am no longer connected with the Brooklyn *Eagle*. If I can prove that I am sober tomorrow, they may hire me back," he added.

"You see what I mean," said the Herald.

We all filed telegraph stories about the horse. We swore that every word was true. We said it was a turning point in baseball. Two of us mentioned Columbus; and one, Galileo. In return, we got advice.

*   *   *

THESE TROUBLED TIMES, NEWSPAPERS NO SPACE FOR FICTION, EXPENSE ACCOUNT NO PROVISION DRUNKEN LEVITY, the *Herald's* wire read. The *World* read, ACCURACY, ACCURACY,

ACCURACY, followed by three exclamation points, and signed "Joseph Pulitzer." CHARGING YOUR TELEGRAM RE BROOKLYN HORSE TO YOUR SALARY, my wire said. THAT'S A HORSE ON YOU!

*   *   *

Have you ever thought what you would do with a purple cow if you had one? I know. You would paint it over. We had a horse that could play third base, and all we could do was sit in the middle of Georgia and cuss our editors. I blame the editors. It is their fault that for the last thirty years you have had to go to smoking rooms or Pullman cars to hear about Jones.

But I don't entirely blame them either. My first question would have been: How on earth can a horse possibly bat and throw? That's what the editors wondered. It's hard to explain. It's something you have to see to believe—like dogfish and political conventions.

And I've got to admit that the next morning we sat around and asked one another whether we really had seen a horse playing third base. Pop O'Donnell confessed that when he woke up he said to himself, *It must be shrimp that makes me dream about horses.* Then all of us went down to the park, not really knowing whether we would see a horse there or not.

We asked Pop was he going to use the horse in games.

"I don't know," he thundered musingly. "I wonder. There are many angles. I don't know," he said, pulling at his chin.

That afternoon the Cubs, the world champs, came for an exhibition game. A chap from Pennsylvania—I forget his name—played third base for Brooklyn, and the horse grazed quietly beside the dugout. Going into the eighth, the Cubs were ahead, 2-0, and Three-Finger Brown was tying Brooklyn in knots. A curve would come over, then a fast one inside, and then the drop, and the Superbas would beat the air or hit puny little rollers to the infield which Tinker or Evers would grab up and toss like a beanbag to Frank Chance. It was sickening. But in the eighth, Maloney got on base on an error, and Jordan walked. Then Lumley went down swinging, and Lewis watched three perfect ones sail past him. The horse still was grazing over by the Brooklyn dugout.

"Put in the horse!" Frank Chance yelled. The Cubs laughed themselves sick.

Pop O'Donnell looked at Chance, and then at the horse, and back at Chance, as though he had make up his mind about something. "Go in there, son, and get a hit," he said. "Watch out for the curve." "Coive," Pop said.

The horse picked up a bat and cantered out to the plate.

"Pinch-hitting for Batch," announced the umpire dreamily, "this horse." A second later he shook himself violently. "What am I saying?" he shouted.

On the Cubs' bench, every jaw had dropped somewhere around the owner's waist. Chance jumped to his feet, his face muscles worked like a coffee grinder, but nothing came out. It was the only time in baseball history, so far as I can find out, that Frank Chance was ever without words.

When he finally pulled himself together he argued, with a good deal of punctuation, that there was no rule saying you could play a horse in the big leagues. Pop roared quietly that there was no rule saying you couldn't, either. They stood there nose to nose, Pop firing methodically like a cannon, and Chance crackling like a machine gun. Chance gave up too easily. He was probably a little stunned. He said that he was used to seeing queer things in Brooklyn, anyway. Pop O'Donnell just smiled grimly.

Well, that was Jones's first game for Brooklyn. It could have been a reel out of a movie. There was that great infield—Steinfeldt, Tinker, Evers and Chance—so precise, so much a machine, that any ball hit on the ground was like an apple into a sorter. The infield was so famous that not many people remember Sheckard and Slagle and Schulte in the outfield, but the teams of that day knew them. Behind the plate was Johnny Kling, who could rifle a ball to second like an 88-mm. cannon. And on the mound stood Three-Finger Brown, whose drop faded away as though someone were pulling it back with a string.

Brown took a long time getting ready. His hand shook a little, and the first one he threw was ten feet over Kling's head into the grandstand. Maloney and Jordan advanced to second and third. Brown threw the next one in the dirt. Then he calmed down, grooved one, and whistled a curve in around the withers.

"The glue works for you, Dobbin!" yelled Chance, feeling more like himself. Pop O'Donnell was mopping his forehead.

The next pitch came in fast, over the outside corner. The horse was waiting. He leaned into it. The ball whined all the way to the fence. Ted Williams was the only player I ever saw hit one like it. When Slagle finally got to the ball, the two runners had scored and the horse was on third. Brown's next pitch got away from Kling a few yards, and the horse stole home in a cloud of dust, all four feet flying. He got up, dusted himself off, looked at Chance and gave a horselaugh.

If this sounds queer, remember that queerer things happen in Brooklyn every day.

"How do we write this one up?" asked the Herald. "We can't put just 'a horse' in the box score."

That was when the horse got his name. We named him Jones, after Jones, the caretaker who had left the gate open so he could wander onto the field. We wrote about "Horse" Jones.

Next day we all chuckled at a banner headline in one of the Metropolitan papers. It read: JONES PUTS NEW KICK IN BROOKLYN.

* * *

Look in the old box scores. Jones got two hits off Rube Waddell, of Philadelphia, and three off Cy Young, of Boston. He pounded Eddie Plank and Iron Man McGinnity and Wild Bill Donovan. He robbed Honus Wagner of a hit that would have been a double against any other third baseman in the league. On the base paths he was a bullet.

Our papers began to wire us, WHERE DOES JONES COME FROM? SEND BACKGROUND, HUMAN INTEREST, INTERVIEW. That was a harder assignment than New York knew. We decided by a gentlemen's agreement that Jones must have come from Kentucky and got his first experience in a Blue Grass league. That sounded reasonable enough. We said he was long-faced, long-legged, dark, a vegetarian and a non-smoker. That was true. We said he was a horse for work, and ate like a horse. That was self-evident. Interviewing was a little harder.

Poor Pop O'Donnell for ten years had wanted a third baseman who could hit hard enough to dent a cream puff. Now that he had one he wasn't quite sure what to do with it. Purple-cow trouble. "Poiple," Pop would have said.

One of his first worries was paying for Jones. A strapping big farmer appeared at the club-house, saying he wanted either his horse or fifty thousand dollars.

Pop excused himself, checked the team's bank balance, then came back.

"What color is your horse?" he asked.

The farmer thought a minute. "Dapple gray," he said.

"Good afternoon, my man," Pop boomed unctuously, holding open the door. "That's a

horse of another color." Jones was brown.

There were some audience incidents too. Jonathan Daniels, of Raleigh, North Carolina, told me that as a small boy that season he saw a whole row of elderly ladies bustle into their box seats, take one look toward third base, look questioningly at one another, twitter about the sun being hot, and walk out. Georgia police records show that at least five citizens, cold sober, came to the ball park and were afraid to drive their own cars home. The American medical journals of that year discovered a new psycho-neurosis which they said was doubtless caused by a feeling of insecurity resulting from the replacement of the horse by the horseless carriage. It usually took the form of hallucination —the sensation of seeing a horse sitting on a baseball players' bench. Perhaps that was the reason a famous pitcher, who shall here go nameless, came to town with his team, took one incredulous look at Brooklyn fielding practice, and went to his manager, offering to pay a fine.

But the real trouble was over whether horses should be allowed to play baseball. After the first shock, teams were generally amused at the idea of playing against a horse. But after Jones had batted their star pitchers out of the box, they said the Humane Society ought to protect the poor Brooklyn horse.

The storm that brewed in the South that spring was like nothing except the storm that gathered in 1860. Every hotel that housed baseball players housed a potential civil war. The better orators argued that the right to play country. The more practical ones said a few to vote or the responsibility of fighting for one's baseball should not be separated from the right more horses like Jones and they wouldn't have any jobs left. Still others said that this was probably just another bureaucratic trick on the part of the Administration.

Even the Brooklyn players protested. A committee of them came to see old Pop O'Donnell. They said wasn't baseball a game for human beings? Pop said he had always had doubts as to whether some major league players were human or not. They said touché, and this is all right so long as it is a one-horse business, so to speak. But if it goes on, before long won't a man have to grow two more legs and a tail before he can get in? They asked Pop how he would like to manage the Brooklyn Percherons, instead of the Brooklyn Superbas? They said, what would happen to baseball if it became a game for animals—say giraffes on one team, trained seals on a second and monkeys on a third? They pointed out that monkeys had already got a foot in the door by being used to dodge baseballs in carnivals. How would Pop like to manage a team of monkeys called the Brooklyn Dodgers, they asked.

Pop said heaven help anyone who has to manage a team called the Brooklyn Dodgers. Then he pointed out that Brooklyn hadn't lost an exhibition game, and that the horse was leading the league in batting with a solid .516. He asked whether they would rather have a World Series or a two-legged third baseman. They went on muttering.

But his chief worry was Jones himself.

"That horse hasn't got his mind on the game," he told us one night on the hotel veranda.

"Ah, Pop, it's just horseplay," said the World, winking.

"Nope, he hasn't got his heart in it," said Pop, his voice echoing lightly off the distant mountains. "He comes just in time for practice and runs the minute it's over. There's something on that horse's mind."

We laughed, but had to admit that Jones was about the saddest horse we had ever seen. His eyes were great brown pools of liquid sorrow. His ears drooped. And still he hit well over .500 and covered third base like a rug.

One day he missed the game entirely. It was the day the Giants were in town, and fifteen thousand people were there to watch Jones bat against the great Matty. Brooklyn lost the game, and Pop O'Donnell almost lost his hair at the hands of the disappointed crowd.

"Who would have thought," Pop mused, in the clubhouse after the game, "that that (here some words are omitted) horse would turn out to be a prima donna? It's all right for a major league ballplayer to act like a horse, but that horse is trying to act like a major league ballplayer."

It was almost by accident that Tim and I found out what was really bothering Jones. We followed him one day when he left the ball park. We followed him nearly two miles to a race track.

Jones stood beside the fence a long time, turning his head to watch the thoroughbreds gallop by on exercise runs and time trials. Then a little stable boy opened the gate for him.

"Po' ol' hoss," the boy said. "Yo' wants a little runnin'?"

"Happens every day," a groom explained to us. "This horse wanders up here from God knows where, and acts like he wants to run, and some boy rides him a while, bareback,

pretending he's a race horse."

Jones was like a different horse out there on the track; not drooping any more—ears up, eyes bright, tail like a plume. It was pitiful how much he wanted to look like a race horse.

"That horse," Tim asked the groom, "is he any good for racing?"

"Not here, anyway," the groom said. "Might win a county-fair race or two."

He asked us whether we had any idea who owned the horse.

"Sir," said Tim, like Edwin M. Stanton, "that horse belongs to the ages."

"Well, mister," said the groom, "the ages had better get some different shoes on that horse. Why, you could hold a baseball in those shoes he has there."

"It's very clear," I said as we walked back, "what we have here is a badly frustrated horse."

"It's clear as beer," Tim said sadly.

That afternoon Jones hit a home run and absent-mindedly trotted around the bases. As soon as the game was over, he disappeared in the direction of the race track. Tim looked at me and shook his head. Pop O'Donnell held his chin in his hands.

"I'll be boiled in oil," he said. "Berled in erl," he said.

Nothing cheered up poor Pop until someone came in with a story about the absentee owner of a big-league baseball club who had inherited the club along with the family fortune. This individual had just fired the manager of his baseball farm system, because the farms had not turned out horses like Jones. "What are farms for if they don't raise horses?" the absentee owner had asked indignantly.

   * * *

Jones was becoming a national problem second only to the Panama Canal and considerably more important than whether Mr. Taft got to be President.

There were rumors that the Highlanders—people were just beginning to call them the Yankees—would withdraw and form a new league if Jones was allowed to play. It was reported that a team of kangaroos from Australia was on its way to play a series of exhibition games in America, and President Ban Johnson, of the American League, was quoted as saying that he would never have kangaroos in the American League because they were too likely to jump their contracts. There was talk of a constitutional amendment concerning horses in baseball.

The thing that impressed me, down there in the South, was that all this was putting the cart before the horse, so to speak. Jones simply didn't want to play baseball. He wanted to be a race horse. I don't know why life is that way.

Jones made an unassisted triple play, and Ty Cobb accused Brooklyn of furnishing fire ladders to its infielders. He said that no third baseman could have caught the drive that started the play. At the end of the training season, Jones was batting .538, and fielding .997, had stolen twenty bases and hit seven home runs. He was the greatest third baseman in the history of baseball, and didn't want to be!

Joseph Pulitzer, William Randolph Hearst, Arthur Brisbane and the rest of the big shots got together and decided that if anyone didn't know by this time that Jones was a horse, the newspapers wouldn't tell him. He could find it out.

Folks seemed to find it out. People began gathering from all parts of the country to see Brooklyn open against the Giants—Matty against Jones. Even a tribe of Sioux Indians camped beside the Gowanus and had war dances on Flatbush Avenue, waiting for the park to open. And Pop O'Donnell kept his squad in the South as long as he could, laying plans to arrive in Brooklyn only on the morning of the opening game.

The wire said that night that 200,000 people had come to Brooklyn for the game, and 190,000 of them were in an ugly mood over the report that the league might not let Jones play. The governor of New York sent two regiments of the national guard. The Giants were said to be caucusing to decide whether they would play against Jones.

By game time, people were packed for six blocks, fighting to get into the park. The Sioux sent a young buck after their tomahawks, just in case. Telephone poles a quarter of a mile from the field were selling for a hundred dollars. Every baseball writer in the country was in the Brooklyn press box; the other teams played before cub reporters and society editors. Just before game time I managed to push into Pop O'Donnel's little office with the presidents of the two major leagues, the mayor of New York, a half dozen other reporters, and a delegation from the Giants.

"There's just one thing we want to know," the spokesman for the Giants was asking Pop. "Are you going to play Jones?"

"Gentlemen," said Pop in that soft-spoken,

firm way of his that rattled the window blinds, "our duty is to give the public what it wants. And the public wants Jones."

Like an echo, a chant began to rise from the bleachers, "We want Jones!"

"There is one other little thing," said Pop. "Jones has disappeared."

There were about ten seconds of the awful silence that comes when your nerves are paralyzed, but your mind keeps on thrashing.

"He got out of his boxcar somewhere between Georgia and Brooklyn," Pop said. "We don't know where. We're looking."

A Western Union boy dashed in. "Hold on!" said Pop. "This may be news!"

He tore the envelope with a shaky hand. The message was from Norfolk, Virginia. HAVE FOUND ELEPHANT THAT CAN BALANCE MEDICINE BALL ON TRUNK, it read. WILL HE DO? If Pop had said what he said then into a telephone, it would have burned out all the insulators in New York.

Down at the field, the President of the United States himself was poised to throw out the first ball. "Is this Jones?" he asked. He was a little nearsighted.

"This is the mayor of New York," Pop said patiently. "Jones is gone. Run away."

The President's biographers disagree as to whether he said at that moment, "Oh, well, who would stay in Brooklyn if he could run?" or "I sympathize with you for having to change horses in midstream."

That was the saddest game ever covered by the entire press corps of the nation. Brooklyn was all thumbs in the field, all windmills at bat. There was no Jones to whistle hits into the outfield and make sensational stops at third. By the sixth inning, when they had to call the game with the score 18-1, the field was ankle-deep in pop bottles and the Sioux were waving their tomahawks and singing the scalp song.

You know the rest of the story. Brooklyn didn't win a game until the third week of the season, and no team ever tried a horse again, except a few dark horses every season. Pittsburgh, I believe, tried trained seals in the outfield. They were deadly at catching the ball, but couldn't cover enough ground. San Francisco has an entire team of Seals, but I have never seen them play. Boston tried an octopus at second base, but had to give him up. What happened to two rookies who disappeared trying to steal second base against Boston that spring is another subject baseball doesn't talk about.

There has been considerable speculation as to what happened to Jones. Most of us believed the report that the Brooklyn players had unfastened the latch on the door of his boxcar, until Pop O'Donnell's *Confidential Memoirs* came out, admitting that he himself had taken the hinges off the door because he couldn't face the blame for making baseball a game for horses. But I have been a little confused since Tim McGuire came to me once and said he might as well confess. He couldn't stand to think of that horse standing wistfully beside the track, waiting for someone to let him pretend he was a race horse. That haunted Tim. When he went down to the boxcar he found the door unlatched and the hinges off, so he gave the door a little push outward. He judged it was the will of the majority.

And that is why baseball is played by men today instead of by horses. But don't think that the shadow of Jones doesn't still lie heavy on the game. Have you ever noticed how retiring and silent and hangdog major league ballplayers are, how they cringe before the umpire? They never know when another Jones may break away from a beer wagon or a circus or a plow, wander through an unlocked gate, and begin batting .538 to their .290. The worry is terrible. You can see it in the crowds too. That is why Brooklyn fans are so aloof and disinterested, why they never raise their voices above a whisper at Ebbets Field. They know perfectly well that this is only minor league ball they are seeing, that horses could play it twice as well if they had a chance.

That is the secret we sports writers have kept all these years; that is why we have never written about Jones. And the Brooklyn fans still try to keep it a secret, but every once in a while the sorrow eats like lye into one of them until he can hold it back no longer, and then he sobs quietly and says, "Dem bums, if dey only had a little horse sense!"

DICK CAVALLI

"Stop complaining about errors. You've still got your no-hitter, haven't you?"

Now, this is ridiculous. Mr. Schwed's piece appeared in *Harper's* in May 1953, and you will notice from the title and text that it is futuristic fantasy, and anyway, the Dodgers *won* the 1953 pennant, and . . .

Come to think of it, why *doesn't* Furillo . . . ?

What Happened to the Dodgers at the End of the 1953 Season

FRED SCHWED, JR.

Now THAT the 1954 season is under way, when the last pennant race is only an exciting memory, we can review dispassionately the influence, if any, of Mrs. Updyke of Richmond Hill, on what happened last season.

It is, of course, a rare occurrence when any of the millions of deeply interested fans can be said to influence in any real sense the performance of the professional players. Wives, and especially sweethearts, are sometimes supposed to be important factors, but in actual practice this is largely a romantic view mostly put forward by imaginative fiction writers. Mrs. Updyke, like the vast majority of us, has never even spoken to a real player in her life. The general consensus has come to be that she had not a thing, not a single, solitary thing, to do with last year's final standings. Yet one still occasionally encounters some mad mullah, nearly always a woman, who will dispute this hotly, paying no attention at all to cold logic.

It will be recalled that on that supposedly fateful day for the contending teams, the Fourth of July, 1953, the Brooklyn team, while not in first place, was not very far out of it. The single team that was ahead of them, the Chicago club, was not seriously considered as an eventual winner by any of the *cognoscenti*. In early August, when a sports page editor of the Brooklyn *Eagle* decided to print, in its entirety, an unusual type of letter from one of his readers, a Mrs. Updkye, the situation was still much the same save that Pittsburgh, of whom the experts took even a dimmer view, was now unaccountably in the van by a few games. The

sports editor in question has steadfastly refused to say in what spirit he ran the letter. There was no editorial comment at the time save the head which the editor set above the letter, if that can be construed as comment. It appeared in the following fashion and, it may be noted, was accorded a generous amount of page space which might otherwise have been used for other material, such as paid advertising linage.

LOYAL LOCAL LADY
MAKES LITTLE SUGGESTION

To the Editor

DEAR SIR:

I think I know a good deal about baseball, but I will not claim to "Know it all," since I have only studied it on TV, having never had the opportunity to see a real game in a real "park" as you call it in your paper which I read carefully every day of the season. I cannot claim to be one of these enthusiastic younger women either, for the fact is and I am proud to mention it that for the last two years I have been a grandmother. In our family marriages have usually taken place quite young. In fact, I guess it is on account of my little grandson (he is named William) that I am now a "fan." I go over to my daughter's house to help take care of him and it is she and my son-in-law who have the set. I do not mind telling you that I look forward to the day when William is old enough to watch the games with me and we can discuss together the different players and their personalities and all the interesting and complicated things that happen in baseball games.

I will admit that my son-in-law was helpful to

294

me at first. He explained the game and he answered all my questions except the last one. That is the reason I am writing to you. My son-in-law is very much against my writing to you, but he finally said that you would not print my "foolish question" anyway, so what the heck?

My question is concerned with Mr. Roy Campanella, our catcher. This fine man was once voted by you sporting writers, not just the most valuable player on the Dodgers, but the most valuable in the entire league, and that time you were *absolutely right!* It is a real pleasure to see people in important positions like yourself make the right decision sometimes. Roy is quick and graceful and cheerful and also a powerful batsman. I have seen pictures of him in your paper with his cute family. He is a credit to the great game of baseball and I think he is an inspiration to his people. He also, and this is what I am really writing to you about, although I admit it is true of most other catchers, *does more work* during a game, and especially during a double-header, than all the other eight men on the team put together, and I also include in this the manager, coaches, umpires, and so forth!

He is a wonderful athlete, but I will admit that he happens to be a little bit pudgy, or as they sometimes say, "portly." It is hard for such a man to work in August in terribly hot cities like Philadelphia and St. Louis, or even here in Brooklyn where you at least get a sea breeze. I happen to know about this because my husband happens to be fat, so I know how he suffers in August, although I assure you he is not required to do nearly as much as Mr. Campanella. My husband is associated with Abraham and Straus as a Section Manager. I will admit that pitchers work hard, too. But *when* do they work? About once every four days, *if that.* Also, pitchers are stuck-up.

Now when a grounder is hit to an infielder, which is the most frequent thing that happens in baseball games, I noticed that every time Mr. Campanella tore off his mask and rushed down to first base along with the runner. I asked my son-in-law why was that? He said Roy was required to do that in case the first baseman missed the ball, Roy would then be there to pick it up. Well, I guess I just about "boiled over" when I heard that one!

In the first place our infield is a good one and it is very rare that the ball scoots past the first baseman. So practically all those rushes of Roy's are just a childish waste of energy which is the sort of thing that men are always thinking up, like wars. I am sure it is not Roy's idea to wear himself out for no good purpose but that it is Mr. Dressen's idea. Even my son-in-law agrees with me

on this point. Another thing is that of all the men on the field Roy is the least suitably dressed for tearing about unnecessarily in the heat. They have him dressed like knights in armor in museums.

Now if it is really thought necessary to "back up first base," as my son-in-law puts it, I have a little suggestion. I am amazed that all those men could not have thought it up for themselves years and years ago. Mr. Furillo, our right fielder, is a young, spry man, suitably dressed for sprinting, whether necessary or unnecessary. Need I say more? Need we send the most valuable player in the entire league panting up and down on account of a mere theory?

Moreover, there is little chance of wearing Mr. Furillo out. In yesterday's game for instance he batted four times, was on base once, and he caught one fly ball. I kept count. That game lasted two hours and forty minutes. The rest of the time he was just watching.

You, Mr. Sports Editor, are doubtless acquainted with Mr. Dressen and the rest of the "top brass." I would be deeply grateful if you would pass on to them my little suggestion and I think that Roy Campanella would be too.

> Respectfully yours,
> (Mrs.) LEAH HANFORD UPDYKE
> Richmond Hill, New York

Whether or not the printing of the above item in the paper had the faintest influence on the pennant race is the argument. Many people claim it was not even an argument, pointing out with scorn that an argument is supposed to have two sides. However, it is also beyond dispute that certain things did actually occur that were of national and even international interest for a brief time. It is only fair to list them carefully:

—The editor was grateful but bewildered at the large influx of mail that hit his office. Nearly all of it was in favor of the suggestion and nearly all of it was from women. The few letters received from males were either facetious, outraged, or not fit to print. Indeed, one from Leo Durocher was all three.

—Branch Rickey discussed the matter at a press conference and touched on such matters as the ancient traditions of the great national pastime. His remarks were profound but that was all.

—A large number of charming but rather cynical young men bearing notebooks called on Mrs. Updyke at her modest residence in Richmond Hill. At first she was flattered and flustered but she grew weary of fame in record time and slipped away to visit a sister who lived in a remote part of Ohio.

—Dressen grinned about it when first consulted but, after the so-called "disputed game," got so peevish about the whole affair that he absolutely refused to discuss anything that had to do with Mrs. Updyke or her little suggestion.

—Campanella also grinned and said "no comment" right from the beginning, but he did, without consulting the front office or anyone else save Mrs. Campanella, send Mrs. Updyke an autographed ball. Mrs. Updyke had it gilded and put it in a little glass case.

—A weekly picture magazine published a complex diagram showing just how far both Campanella and Furillo would have to run under various circumstances. It was accompanied by pictures of Campanella, Furillo, a chest protector, a mask, two shin guards, a catcher's mitt, and a fielder's glove. The exact weight of each item was set under each, in pounds and ounces.

—Female attendance increased markedly at Ebbets Field, especially on Ladies' Days when women got in free. On such days, every time a grounder was hit, there were shrill cries of, "Stay where you are, Roy!" and, "Let Carl do it!" and a striking variety of other witticisms. The male patrons claimed that all this was mildly amusing for a time but that it soon became a silly bore.

—*Campanella continued to cover first when there was no one in immediate scoring position.* It is upon this last negative fact that the claim is almost universally made that Mrs. Updyke could not be said to have influenced the result of a single game, let alone the winning of the pennant. As luck would have it, for the first three weeks the Brooklyn catcher never once usefully retrieved a wild throw although he was always in position to do so.

Then, on the third Ladies' Day since the appearance of the letter, came the disputed game with the Phillies. This game was not disputed by the players, managers, or umpires. It was disputed mostly by women.

The play upon which this game hinged, for it was decided by a single run, was not especially bizarre as such things go. Philadelphia's Ashburn, a notoriously fast and daring runner, was on first. On a hit and run signal, the batter slashed a wicked bounder down the third base line and the Brooklyn third baseman managed to stop it with his solar plexus. He scrambled

after it while his teammates yelled, "First, first!" because the rapid Ashburn, who had taken wing before the ball was even hit was already only a few paces from second base. The sound advice to the third baseman was all but drowned out by the high-pitched advice to the catcher from the stands, "Roy Campanella, you stay right where you are!" Campanella tore off his mask and also took wing. He took it as fast as he could, which as it happens is not very fast. He realized instinctively that his services as a retriever might well be needed. Sure enough, the third baseman, heaving the ball in desperation and in abdominal pain, hit the concrete wall of Box 77, a box which for many years had been pock-marked with hasty heaves. Ashburn, hearing a certain hysterical note in the roar of the crowd, sensed that something had happened, and that it wasn't good for Brooklyn. He rounded for third without a sidewise glance.

Campanella, arriving as usual in the neighborhood of Box 77, was this time a busy man. He chased after the bouncing ball with his ungainly glove, skillfully got possession of it, and wheeled for the throw to third. But again, Ashburn was virtually at the base, so there was, as the players put it, no play there. Tragically, there was no play at home plate either. The Dodger pitcher, a recent recruit with a very fast ball and very little experience, had failed to take Campanella's place at the plate, as he was, of course, supposed to. He was still standing on the mound, watching his catcher's breathless efforts with fascinated interest. Ashburn scored the winning run without the necessity of soiling his pants.

All over the nation, starting at half-past four, there ensued long discussions or disputes. The pith of them was approximately this:

HE: But it was simply the pitcher's fault, I'm telling you. That sort of thing has happened many a time before. If he had known enough to cover home plate the run would never have scored.

SHE: It still seems to me that if Roy had stayed where he was there would have been no trouble.

HE (*with intense sarcasm*): You think somehow he should have got hold of the ball and then thrown it to himself where he was still standing at the plate?

SHE: *Carl* should have got hold of it.

What Happened to the Dodgers at the End of the 1953 Season

HE: *Oh, for the . . . ! Oh, well . . .*

SHE: I'll kindly thank you not to use that tone of voice to *me.*

If a fiction writer had dreamed up this account he would contrive the story so that Brooklyn lost the pennant by a single game. This would give a spurious significance to a single incident that had a spurious significance in the first place, as all we men comprehend easily enough. The actuality is attested to in the files of a thousand newspapers just beginning to turn yellow. Campanella for the rest of the season continued to run down the first base line. Brooklyn played better than five hundred ball during this period but unfortunately could not match the efforts of Philadelphia which won the National League Championship by two games. Not a few of the sports writers have pointed out that the Phillies played inspired ball at the end of the 1953 season.

However, Philadelphia lost the World Series to Yogi Berra and his companions. Catcher Berra, a squat man with a short neck, of course raced religiously away on what some people still insist on calling bootless errands.

B. TOBEY

THE TOUGHEST ASSIGNMENT a baseball reporter has is the annual major league All-Star game, because of its many added dimensions. Not only what happens on the field, but the players' team affiliations, and past All-Star records or lack of same, plus ever-changing lineup and position switches, plus the unique characteristics of the game itself—all these must be handled swiftly, completely, briefly, colorfully if possible, and with some semblance of putting first things first. When the game is an extra-inning, many-faceted one, such as the 1955 All-Star game where the American League led 5 to 0 and lost in twelve innings 6 to 5, a piece such as Howard Sigmand wrote in separated bulletin paragraphs is a shining model.

The 1955 All-Star Game

HOWARD SIGMAND

STAN MUSIAL, the dream player of modern-day baseball and king of the All-Stars, smashed a tremendous home run into the right-field bleachers in the twelfth inning today to give the National League a 6 to 5 victory over the American League in the twenty-second All-Star game.

Dramatically, and emphatically, Musial broke up the ball game when he slammed Frank Sullivan's first pitch out of sight ending three hours and seventeen minutes of a struggle that had everything and maybe more than any dream games preceding it.

The sensational St. Louis Cardinal veteran, appearing in his twelfth All-Star Game—a record-shattering performance in itself—received a royal ovation from the 45,643 fans at Milwaukee's County Stadium as he ran out his game-deciding wallop.

His happy National League teammates crowded around home plate and also gave Mr. Ballplayer a king-sized reception.

Perhaps fitting into the weird pattern that marked this exciting overtime battle of the stars was the fact that Musial's efforts prior to his four-bagger consisted of a strikeout and double-play bouncer to the pitcher and a walk.

This was the second extra-inning game in All-Star history. The first one took place in Chicago in 1950. That one went fourteen innings and the N. L. won it, coincidentally, when Musial's teammate, Red Schoendienst, socked a homer.

This time "The Man" did it in twelve, in a hectic contest that featured some stout hitting, some stellar pitching, a nifty catch; and some shoddy defense by the American League which helped the Nationals overcome a 5-0 deficit in the late innings to tie the score.

There was Mickey Mantle's tremendous three-run homer in the first inning which capped a four-run splurge against N. L. starter Robin Roberts and made it appear for a long while that the A. L. was headed for its second straight Name Game triumph and fourteenth in the series.

To add strength to this belief was the brilliant first-line hurling of southpaw Billy Pierce and right-hander Early Wynn.

Pierce, 28-year-old lefty ace of the Chicago White Sox, limited the Nationals to only a single in the three innings he worked. Wynn, whose notable contribution was three scoreless innings while allowing three hits, also boasted another achievement. The 35-year-old Cleveland Indian star was the culprit who whiffed Musial and got "The Man" to hit into a double play.

Almost fittingly, the winning pitcher was "native son" Gene Conley, the skyscraping, six-foot-eight right-hander who works for the Braves during the regular season.

Conley was accorded the second biggest ovation of the occasion when he came in to pitch in the top of the twelfth and calmly struck out the three men he faced—Al Kaline, Mickey Vernon and Al Rosen.

Sullivan was tagged with the loss, but the elongated Boston Red Sox right-hander distinguished himself by doing some stylist hurling of his own before Musial ruined him.

There was also a stouthearted relief chore by the National League's unheralded southpaw Joe Nuxhall in this chock-full-of-thrills affair.

The National League, dormant for the first seven innings as their rivals went five runs to the good by scoring four runs off Roberts before the strong-armed righty could get a man out in the first inning and a run off Lefty Harvey Haddix in the sixth, suddenly came wide awake in their half of the seventh against Whitey Ford.

The spark at this point in the struggle was to be Willie Mays, the "Say Hey" kid who plays center field for the world champion Giants. And helping the N. L.'s cause was a collapse in what was supposed to have been a stellar defense.

First off, Mays brought the crowd to a roar of appreciation when he raced to the right center field wall to make a spectacular leaping catch on a drive that robbed none other than magnificent Ted Williams of what looked like a seventh-inning home run.

Then Willie singled off Ford to start a two-run rally in the seventh and his single with two out in the eighth also ignited his team's three-run splurge in that frame.

With two out and Mays on first in the seventh, Ford walked Henry Aaron. The home folks made with a collective lusty cheer when Johnny Logan of the Braves also singled to drive in the first run for the Nationals. Chico Carrasquel, usually sure-gloved shortstop for the Chicago White Sox, became his team's first of two fielding delinquents on the next play, first bobbling and then throwing badly to second baseman Bobby Avila as he attempted to convert Stan Lopata's grounder into an inning-ending force-out on Logan.

Aaron raced home with the second run and the Nationals were in business, but still three runs shy. This was taken care of in their next turn at bat. Successive singles by Mays, Ted Kluszewski and Randy Jackson made it 5-3.

Al Lopez, who failed to get the World Series revenge he was seeking at the expense of National League pilot Leo Durocher, gave the bull-pen call for Sullivan.

Aaron greeted the big boy with a single to right field, scoring the mountainous Kluszew-

ski. Jackson legged it for third on the blow and right fielder Kaline zoomed a throw in the direction of the hot corner.

It apparently was too hot for third baseman Rosen, and last season's batting star for the Americans allowed the ball to get through his legs for an error. Jackson came home to score the tying run.

Sullivan hurled shutout ball until his twelfth-inning delivery, a fast ball right down the middle.

Nuxhall, Cincinnati Redleg lefty who was also making his first All-Star game appearance, proved the pleasant surprise that supplied the brakes to the offensive hopes of the A. L. in the late stages.

The southpaw's most distinguished accomplishment up to today's game was the fact that at the ripe young age of fifteen he made his major league debut for Cincinnati. In 1944 he became the youngest player ever to appear in a major league game. On July 12, 1955, he became a pitching man.

With the bases loaded and two out in the eighth inning Nuxhall took over from Sam Jones. The southpaw, whose record for the season is 8-6, then held the A. L. in check through the eleventh, striking out the side in the tenth and stoutheartedly stopping threats in both the ninth and eleventh.

Mantle, with his homer and single in six trips, was the big gun for the Americans in their thirteen hits off the seven pitchers used by Durocher.

The Yankee center fielder could have been the game's hero, but the late show beat out the early show.

Roberts, making a record-equaling fifth All-Star game start, almost said good-by before he said hello.

Harvey Kuenn and Nellie Fox greeted him with singles, and with the mighty Williams at the plate, Roberts wild-pitched the game's first run across. He then walked Thumping Theodore.

Up stepped Mantle and the New York Yankee strongboy blasted one 425 feet over the center field wall into an area in the stadium known as "Perini's Woods." This spot is so called in honor of Braves' owner Lou Perini, who has trees planted there to provide better background for the batters.

Nobody else hit one into this target for the rest of the afternoon. But neither did anyone but Musial find the range of the treeless right center field bleachers.

Refer to the letter D on page 248 and you will agree that no further introduction to the following piece is needed.

Ol' Diz

AL SILVERMAN

Mr. Silverman gratefully acknowledges his reliance on material in a book written by J. Roy Stockton, sports editor of the St. Louis *Post-Dispatch*, entitled *The Gashouse Gang*, from which many of the anecdotes repeated in "Ol' Diz" have been taken.

It was Paul Richards, the empire builder of the Baltimore Orioles, who once remarked of Dizzy Dean, "If Diz ever gets smart, he's through."

Dean himself had the answer for Richards, as he has always had an answer for everyone, and he gave it to him, appropriately enough, on the August day in 1953 when he was being enrolled in baseball's Hall of Fame. "I want to thank the good Lord," Dizzy said, "for giving me a good right arm, a strong back and a weak mind."

Without a doubt, Dean had a good arm, quite possibly one of the very best that ever propelled a baseball from the right side of the pitcher's mound. No one can doubt that he had a strong back, either; picking cotton from the time he was old enough to walk until he was sixteen and had escaped into the army (to the relative comfort of manure-shoveling), he developed certain strategic muscles. About his weak mind, though, there is doubt.

Perhaps it was television panelist Dorothy Kilgallen who best summed up the mental paradox of Dizzy Dean. One night a couple of years ago Dizzy appeared on *What's My Line*, a program dedicated to the unearthing of rare and wonderful occupations. Dizzy was the guest celebrity that night and the panelists had to operate from behind blindfolds to make the guessing interesting. Well, when it came to Miss Kilgallen's turn, she asked a couple of routine questions and then said blandly, "You talk something like Dizzy Dean. Only you couldn't be Dean. You sound much too intelligent."

She apologized to Diz after the show, but she really didn't have to. She was merely perpetuating a myth that has helped make Dizzy Dean today one of the great and legendary personalities of American life. If that myth were ever in any way to be broken down, he would be finished.

Let it be stated here and now that Dizzy Dean does *not* have a weak mind. He might best be called a suave hillbilly. He does everything in his power to have the public picture him as a country boy, a homespun backwoodsman full of fatback and hominy grits and all the good, rural, slow-moving things in life. But he is far from slow-moving. His mind, if anything, is in a constant state of turmoil, working overtime in behalf of Ol' Diz himself.

One day in 1931, to get down to cases, Dizzy lost a fight; he lost that fight solely because the Dean mind was working overtime. The story is best told in Diz's own words:

"A fella named Al Todd gets a hit off me and that makes me mad. The next time he comes to bat, I knock him down with one at the head. He picks hisself up and gives me a dirty look and says if I do that again he'll give me a punch in the nose. So I lets him have it again and down he goes. He drops his bat and comes towards the mound. I walk in towards him. But before I can say a word he floors me. Now, every fight I was ever in, there's been a lot of talkin'. I had a small wisecrack ready for him, but there wasn't no talkin'. He just ups and gives it to me on the jaw and I see more stars than there is in Florida on a clear night. I figured the talkin' was comin' then, sure, but when I get up he knocks me down again. And he never did go

OLD-TIME MOVIE...

(Top) The Baltimore Orioles, pre-1900. Front row: Robinson, Kelley, Kitson, McGann, Jennings, Clark. Back row: McGraw, Keeler, Nops, Demontreville, Hughes.

(Bottom) And here's one by Civil War photographer Matthew Brady. Subject: The original Cincinnati Red Stockings.

International News

CAN YOU TOP THIS?

Johnny VanderMeer (above) pitched two no-hit games in succession; Charley
(Kid) Nichols (below), with Branch Rickey at the time of his induction into the
Hall of Fame, once pitched three victories in three successive days.

No, thanks . . . You hit against Robin Roberts.

300C

Bob Feller, only modern-day pitcher to hurl three no-hit games . . .

GLORY FOR CLEVELAND!

. . . and Tris Speaker, scoring the final and winning run of the 1920 World Series—at the climax of his career as Indians' player-manager.

to talkin' and I never did get so tired of being knocked down in all my life."

Dizzy faced a similar crisis many years later, as a baseball announcer, but this time he rose to the occasion with considerably more skill. A group of St. Louis schoolteachers had got together and declared that Dean was ruining the schoolchildren of Missouri with his atrocious mangling of the English language and his improper use of grammar and syntax. "Sin tax?" Diz shot back. "Are them jokers in Washington puttin' a tax on that, too?" Then, after he had had his little joke, he got serious. "Maybe I am butcherin' up the English language a little," he declared, "but all I gotta say is that when me and Paul were pickin' cotton in Arkansas, we didn't have no chance to go to school much. But I'm glad the kids are gettin' that chance today."

Nothing else was needed. With that simple bit of eloquence, St. George had slain the dragon. Everyone lined up on Diz's side. Even such a highbrow magazine as the *Saturday Review of Literature* editorially denounced the misguided schoolteachers. Dean's alleged misuse of our language, the magazine said, was merely a wonderful folk manifestation of American democracy at work. "Weak-minded" Dizzy Dean had carried the day.

Today, Jay Hanna Dean ("I was named after some big shot on Wall Street, or he was named after me, I don't know which.") is still on the air, still throwing out his memorable prose and still delighting baseball fans all over the country. He works with Buddy Blattner on CBS's television game of the week, earning some $25,000 for helping describe one game every Saturday for the Falstaff Brewing Company, which was his original radio sponsor way back in 1941. Every Saturday the game of the week is televised from a different major-league city. Dizzy hops a plane from his home town of Dallas, Texas, on the day before the broadcast and rushes back to Dallas immediately after his chores are over. It is easy work and it leaves him plenty of time for his favorite recreations—golf, poker, hunting and fishing, and home-style loafing. It also gives him the opportunity to pick up some additional loose change (every buck is a found one for Diz) with personal appearances and talks before various civic groups. Ol' Diz is quite a public speaker. He once lectured an English class at Southern Methodist University. The title of his address was, "Radio Announcing I Have Did."

Dizzy is a large-jawed, handsome, jolly-look-

ing man who would make a perfect department-store Santa Claus. His only concessions to his 44 years are a profusion of silver hair and a six-foot-two frame that no longer quite compensates for the weight it packs. His usual working dress is a white Texas sombrero, a bright yellow sports shirt, green gabardine slacks and slick, shiny cowboy boots. In recent years Dean has broadened his horizons a bit. He made a record of "Wabash Cannonball," the song he used to croon during lulls in a ball game (once he engaged in a duet on "Cannonball" with opera singer Jessica Dragonette). Now he would be happy to accept a few night-club bookings, to tide him over the slack season.

Back home in Dallas, Dean lives the life of a country squire, or, better still, a retired oil millionaire. He has a $45,000 ranch-style home in the Preston Hollow suburb of Dallas. He has a farm in nearby Kaufman County. He owns a number of other farms, an office building in Lancaster, Texas, and various other properties. He and his brother Paul—the famous if misnamed Daffy Dean of baseball—both bought real estate when it was low and sold it when it was high. "Paul done even better than me, though," Dizzy says. "He got three times his money back from most of the things he bought. I usually only got twice my money."

One thing Dizzy has no worries about is money. Thanks to the good offices of his wife, Patricia, who took charge of the purse strings way back in 1931 when she married him, Dean is a monument of financial stability. He earned $200,000 in his playing days (most of it coming not from salaries but personal appearances, testimonials and the like). He got another $100,000 for the movie rights to his life story, *The Spirit of St. Louis,* which, like most Hollywood movie biographies, did a grave artistic injustice to his life. (Speaking of spirit, Dean once accused a ball team of not havng enough "spart." Pressed for an explanation he said, "Spart is pretty much the same as fight or pep or gumption. Like the Spart of St. Louis, that plane Lindbergh flowed to Europe in.") As a radio and television personality his cumulative earnings have come to a conservative $300,000. Tack on his real-estate deals and various other enterprises and it can be seen that Diz is no wallflower in Texas, where even the caddies at the golf clubs keep their tips in safe-deposit boxes.

A couple of years ago he could have made even more money by acting as a disc jockey on a classical music program. But he turned it down. "I just couldn't stand listenin' to myself trying to pronounce them Rooshian and Kraut names. I can't even pronounce everybody's name in the Cleveland Indians' infield."

What has come to be known as the Dizzy Dean legend is compounded of three specific elements, each of them bound to the others. They are:

1. *Dean the Pitcher.* Time has been kind to Dizzy. There has been more and more talk in recent years to the effect that he was one of the two greatest right-handed pitchers the game has ever known, the other one being, of course, Walter Johnson. Such conjecture would probably have been an unquestioned fact if Dean had enjoyed a full major-league career. But he lasted only six full seasons before being cut down by a cruel turn of fate, and his total record of 150 games won and 83 lost makes him low man for pitchers in the Hall of Fame. But in five of those six years he achieved everything any other pitcher ever had, and a little more. In those five seasons he chalked up 120 of his 150 victories, an average of 24 games per season. In each one of those years he struck out over 100 men. His lifetime earned-run average was 3.03 per game.

Dizzy Dean's 1934 season was as magnificent a single season as any pitcher has enjoyed in the modern era of baseball. That year Dizzy won 30 games and lost only 7. No other pitcher has won 30 games in a single season since. At the beginning of the year Dean had boasted that "me and Paul will win 40 or 45 games for the Cards." Paul won 19, giving the Dean brothers a total of 49 and putting Dizzy for once on the side of modesty. Both Deans won two games apiece in the World Series against the Tigers, one of the most riotous affairs in the history of the game.

Grantland Rice, the late dean of American sports writers, liked to tell how Dizzy came up to him before the '34 series and asked if Granny could fix it up with Frankie Frisch for Diz to pitch the entire series. "You can't possibly win four straight games," Rice told Dean. "I know I can't," Diz replied. "But I can win four out of five."

2. *Dizzy the Eccentric.* Being a ballplayer wasn't enough. Dizzy would never have evolved into the public figure he is today if it hadn't been for his personality. He was an authentic character and as a result he became the greatest drawing card since Babe Ruth. There probably will never be another one like him in baseball. The game simply does not breed such figures any more.

Dizzy labored earnestly to build his reputation. One day in 1933, during a game played in 100-degree weather, he built himself a bonfire in front of the dugout, covered himself with blankets and squatted down to warm his hands. One time, during a game in Cincinnati, he put a cake of ice on home plate to cool off his fast ball. Another time, at a rodeo, Dizzy engaged in a calf-roping contest. The horse wasn't fast enough for Diz so he leaped to his feet and wrestled with it.

Dizzy always claimed "me and Paul" were the best pitchers in baseball, but he denied he was a braggart. "The way I see it," Dizzy always said, "braggin' is when you do a lot of poppin' off and ain't got nothing to back it up."

3. *Dean the Voice.* When Dizzy went to work for Falstaff beer in 1941, broadcasting the St. Louis Browns' home games, the American public had no idea of what was about to happen to them. But they soon found out. One day in that first year, Dizzy took a gulp of the sponsor's beer and then murmured to an unprepared audience, "Excuse me folks, I jest had a nice cold drink of beer and liketa belched right into the dern thing." When he was admonished for using ungentlemanly language, he replied, "I belched, but I apologized, didn't I? What else can you do when you belch but apologize?"

Once during a re-created broadcast of a Cardinal road game, he became so disgusted he said, "Folks, we ain't gettin' the stuff the way we're handin' it out to you. They send a few words from the ball park and we have to make up the rest. It's a lotta bunk."

Since switching to television, Dizzy has evolved his own unique TV philosophy. "I'm just as calm and confidential in front of these cameras as any place else. The only difference between television and radio is that there ain't much to talk about in television. If a batter is takin' his stanch at the plate, all you got to do is name him. They ain't no point in sayin' he is taking his stanch at the plate.

"Say that Roo-zoo-toe (Phil Rizzuto, Yankee shortstop) had got forked out while tryin' to steal second. If you got your eyes on your set you seen him tagged out or seen the empire's signal. So they ain't no use for me to say much except commertate maybe why Roo-zoo-toe has taken such a chance and tried to steal second."

Diz wasn't always so reticent. His pet exclamation during a scoreless game was, "Folks, the score's nothin'-to-nothin', and nobody's winnin'."

Into the lexicon of broadcasting, Dizzy has introduced a number of pet expressions that, for better or worse, are likely to last forever. "The runner just slud into third base safely, but he was almost throwed out . . . Look how calmly and confidentially the batter is standing up down there next to the plate . . . The side is out and the runners is left at their respectable bases . . . He looks mighty hitterish to me . . . Don't fail to miss tomorrow's game."

Of course he knows now that such terms are not exactly grammatical, but he still repeats them whenever he has the opportunity. He knows what the listener wants, Dizzy does, and he knows that what's good for the listener is doubly good for Ol' Diz. When people ask him why he speaks the way he does, Dizzy quotes his favorite American, Will Rogers. "A lot of people who don't say ain't—ain't eatin'. I'm gonna keep on sayin' ain't and keep on eatin'."

There are certain aspects of the Dean career that have nothing to do with the elements previously mentioned—pitching skill, eccentric behavior and flavorful announcing. These other factors were founded on a very nebulous thing called luck. Who can say, for instance, how far the Dean legend would have got if he hadn't been nicknamed Dizzy? But the nickname was pinned on him, not because of any quirk of character. It was born simply and purely and basically because of his natural-born artistry with a baseball. The fact is that in 1930, when Dean was a rawboned twenty-year-old pitcher with the Houston club of the Texas League, he wasn't even known as Jay Hanna Dean. His first two names then were Jerome Herman. "It was this way," Dizzy says. "When I was a kid in the cotton fields, I was very popular with the neighbors and especially with a man who had a little boy about my age—six or seven, I guess. I often wondered whether the man thought more of me or his little boy. Then all of a sudden the boy took sick and died. We sure did feel sorry for his dad. He just moped around and didn't care for nothin' no more. So I went to him and told him I thought so much of him that I was going to take the name of Jerome Herman, which I did."

So it was as Jerome Herman Dean that the young fireballing right-hander strode out to the mound to meet the Chicago White Sox in the spring of 1930. He struck out eighteen major-leaguers that day. The third-base coach for the White Sox, Lena Blackburne, was steaming

mad. "What's going on here?" Blackburne would yell. "You're supposed to be major-leaguers! You're lettin' that dizzy kid make a fool outta you. Are you gonna take that from this dizzy kid?"

They had to take it. There wasn't a thing they could do about it that afternoon. And after that it was always Dizzy Dean, and Dizzy became the prop which sent the untutored country boy swooshing to fame.

Just exactly where in the country Dizzy was born became a dark and mysterious question for some time after he first emerged as a national figure. A *Saturday Evening Post* article in 1935 had Dizzy born in three different places on three different dates: Lucas, Arkansas; Holderville, Oklahoma; Bond, Mississippi; on January 16, August 22 and February 22, 1911. It seems that one day in New York, when he was visited by three different sports writers, Dean, out of the goodness of his heart, decided he would treat each one to a scoop by giving each one a different birthplace and date. "I got lots of friends at all three places," he explained later. "My wife comes from Bond, Mississippi, and it makes her feel good for me to say Bond. Maybe I'll add Bradenton, Florida, before long, especially if they change the name to Deanville like they said."

Well, Bradenton is still Bradenton and it has since been pretty thoroughly established that Diz's one and only place of birth was Lucas, Arkansas, on January 16, 1911. One thing is certain. Diz was born without the proverbial silver spoon in his mouth. He came into the world the third son of a destitute cotton-picking sharecropper, born in a rickety wooden bed in a clapboard shack that stood on worked-over cotton soil. Mrs. Albert Monroe Dean bore five children. Diz's oldest sister, Sara May, died when she was four months old. His oldest brother, Charles, died when he was nine. Diz's mother died of tuberculosis when Dizzy was three. Albert Dean, who had played minor-league baseball when he was a youngster, was a migratory worker who moved his family from one patch of land to another, from one state to another, following the crop.

Dizzy spent a total of two years in grade school. "If I'd'a went to third grade," he once joked, "I'd of passed up my old man. I didn't want to show Paw up." Later, when he was twelve years old, though he had long since given up a formal education, he pitched for Spaulding High near Holderville as a ringer. His brother Paul, whose schooling was as extensive as Dizzy's, played second base for Spaulding High. Dizzy once shut out the Oklahoma City Teachers College with two hits and fourteen strikeouts. On occasion Dizzy liked to picture himself as a college man. Bob Hope once asked him which school he attended and he replied, "Me and Maxie Rosenbloom, we went to Harvard together."

It wasn't precisely true that Dizzy never had a pair of shoes until he joined the army, although that is a piece of legend firmly attached to the Dean story, "Me, Paul and Elmer had one pair of shoes each," Dizzy says. "They was our winter shoes, and we took 'em off in the summer to save the leather."

Elmer, incidentally, was the eldest Dean brother. Dizzy believes he would have made a fine ballplayer if he had had the opportunity. "Why, that boy was a great catcher and infielder. He could whip that ball around like any other Dean. He just had to work too hard and he never got no chance to show what he could do." In 1934, when Dizzy and Paul were pitching the Cardinals to a pennant, brother Elmer showed what he could do as a peanut vendor at Sportsmans Park. He earned quite a reputation for the accuracy and distance of his throws to the customers.

Father Dean started preparing his boys for a baseball career as soon as they were able to toddle. He would chuck hickory nuts and stones at them and the boys soon learned to catch them and pitch them back to Paw. From hickory nuts they advanced to baseballs, which Albert would fashion from twine, an old shoe tongue, a hunk of inner tube, the thread from a stocking.

But there was never enough time for baseball. Dizzy worked in the cotton fields doing hard manual labor at fifty cents a day. "When I was ten years old," he says, "I could do a man's work. I could pick me four to five hundred pounds of cotton a day. I'd get up at five in the morning, set to milkin', eat me some sowbelly and black-eyed peas and go into the field."

When he was sixteen, Dizzy enlisted in the army. He said he was eighteen and nobody bothered to check on it. His first and only job in the service, at Fort Sam Houston, was to shovel horse manure from the horse corral. "I was the worst soldier in God's living world," Dean says. "I played my first formal baseball game when the Third Wagon Company met the 12th Field Artillery. Top Sergeant Johnny Brought of the 12th liked the way I done in

the game. He said if I'd transfer to the 12th I could play ball more and shovel manure less. I was in trouble anyhow with an officer. This here officer had called me up and asked me when I was going to haul over some manure to put on the flower bed at his quarters. And I answered, 'Right soon, sir. You are number two on my manure list.' He figured I was gettin' smart with him, and my chances of gettin' promoted to PFC in the Third Wagon Company wasn't so good. So I said to Sarge Brought that I'd like to come over to the 12th. Well, all the lieutenants and colonels and captains got together and talked it over, and had me transferred into the 12th."

After almost three years of pitching baseballs and manure, Dizzy bought himself out of the army, a standard practice in those easygoing days between wars. In Dizzy's case, it cost him $120. He took a job in San Antonio, Texas, working as an assistant to a man who read the gas meters. "I used to follow that fellow around just to keep him company and carry his tools. But I guess my main job was to pitch ball for the Public Service Company team."

In 1929, when he was eighteen, Dizzy was signed to a St. Louis Cardinals' contract by a Cardinal scout, Don Curtis. Already, Diz had a tremendous fast ball, a fine curve and a tantalizing change of pace. All he needed was actual experience against the professionals. He reported to Houston that spring but was almost immediately shipped to St. Joseph, Missouri, in the Western Association. He won his first game in organized baseball, 4-3, and he did it in typical Dizzy Dean fashion. He introduced himself to the opposing players and courteously requested what pitch each preferred; then he served it up with lightning speed. To top it all off he started a triple play, the first that was ever made in the Western Association.

He also quickly established himself as a brash hayseed and something of a problem child. When he joined St. Joe he had the clothes he was wearing, none to carry and no suitcase. When he needed a change he bought a shirt, changed in a hotel room and stuffed his soiled clothing in a bureau drawer. Once that year he borrowed an automobile and raced the chief of police through traffic until he was crowded to the curb and finally deposited in the pokey. But Dizzy forgave the police chief for his intemperate action and also talked himself out of a fine.

He won seventeen games for St. Joe and

then transferred to Houston where he made his debut under the lights, winning, 12-1. The next morning he was in the front office telling the president, Fred Ankenman, that he didn't have his fast ball working right. "I'm awfully sorry about what happened last night, Mr. Ankenman," he said, "I promise if you give me another chance it will never happen again. Can you imagine them bums gettin' a run off me?"

A few days later, Diz wandered into his hotel at two in the morning and found the club president in the lobby. "Well, I guess you and me will get the devil for this, Mr. Ankenman," Dizzy said. "But I won't say nothin' about it if you don't."

* * *

Diz had a brilliant season for Houston in 1930 and was called up to the Cardinals late in the year. But the Cards were in the middle of a tight pennant race and manager Gabby Street didn't want to take a chance on Diz. He finally pitched him on the last day of the season and Dizzy won a three-hitter against the Pirates.

Dizzy should have made the Cardinals in 1931, but he didn't, and he had no one to blame but himself. He loafed his way through spring training and made an enemy of Gabby Street, who was known as the "Sergeant" because of his World War I background and also because of the way he ran the ball club. Street became exasperated with Dean a thousand times that spring and once ordered Dizzy to turn in his uniform.

Whenever he was allowed to pitch that spring, he was a sensation. Once, in a game against the Athletics, with Cardinal president Sam Breadon and general manager Branch Rickey in the audience, Diz deliberately loaded the bases, then struck out three power hitters —Al Simmons, Mickey Cochrane and Jimmy Foxx—on ten pitched balls. He made his first appearance as a relief pitcher when the Cardinals held a 5-4 lead. "Don't worry none, Gab," he told Street, "those guys couldn't get a hit off me with a handful of birdshot." Then the first man doubled. Diz struck out the next three batters. The next inning he filled the bases and then fanned the next two men and got the third on a pop-up to win the game.

But his peculiar behavior was too much for the Cardinal brass, and he was sent down to Houston again. There he not only had another tremendous season, winning 26 games, but he also found himself a wife. The former Patricia

Nash was a salesgirl in a five-and-ten-cent store when Diz chanced upon her one day. They hit it off from the very beginning. Dizzy, in his inimitable fashion, would have liked the wedding ceremony performed at home plate, but the lady put her foot down and they were married respectably in church. Before his marriage, Dizzy had a reputation as a free spender. In fact, during his spring fiasco with the Cardinals, he was put on a dollar-a-day allowance because of the sums he was running up in meals, slot machines and other recreational incidentals. But after their marriage, Patricia took over Dizzy's finances and ran them with an iron hand. "Somebody in the family had to have practical sense," she says. "Dizzy had it in a ball game and it was up to me to have it for both of us off the field." It was Mrs. Dean who negotiated the lush contract Hollywood handed out for the Dizzy Dean movie. She could have taken the $100,000 in a lump sum, but for income-tax purposes the shrewd Mrs. Dean got the film company to make the payments to Dizzy over the five-year period in which the company had the rights to the story.

As it was she had to go to Dizzy for help in getting brother Paul in line. Originally, he refused to sign away his rights to the movie. "I ain't signin' no Hollywood fellas the right to make a fool outta me," he said.

"They ain't aimin' to make no fool outta you," Dizzy argued. "You ought to be proud they want to make a picture story about a couple of sockwads like me and you." Paul signed.

In 1932, Dizzy became a full-fledged member of the famous Gas House Gang. He signed a contract that called for him to receive $3,000, terrible money in terms of today but an adequate starting salary in those days. Diz earned his money, all right; he won eighteen games and lost fifteen. In 1933, still not earning much more than $3,500, he won twenty games and lost eighteen. His most notable feat that season was in setting a new National League strikeout record by fanning seventeen Chicago Cubs in a single game. That record still stands in the league today, although Bob Feller holds the major-league record with eighteen.

It was the 1934 season which did more to establish Dizzy than all the other years of his life put together. Unquestionably, it was his greatest year in baseball. It was the year he and Paul wrought untold miracles. It was also the year that the Gas House Gang came to full power.

Whom did the Cardinals have in 1934? Well, they had Frankie Frisch as manager, a regular fire-eater who was closing out a magnificent career at second base. They had peppery Leo Durocher at shortstop, the irrepressible Pepper Martin at third base, Ducky Medwick in the outfield—and Paul Dean up from Columbus. Paul was the complete antithesis of his brother, and the sports writer who labeled him "Daffy" did him an injustice. He was quiet to the point of diffidence, and he was hard-working (which Dizzy was not, except on occasions). His only fellowship with the Gas House Gang, that high-living bunch of roisterers, was that he was Dizzy Dean's brother. He idolized Dizzy, and anything Dizzy did and told Paul to do, Paul also did.

The only time in their joint baseball career that Paul ever blew up at Dizzy occurred in 1934 in a game at Sportsmans Park. Paul was pitching and having his troubles, and by the fifth inning Dizzy was riding him harshly. "I hollered to him," Dizzy remembers, " 'Hey boy, you better tie yourself to that rubber!' Paul got mad as hell and he comes in to me and he plunks the ball in my hand and he says, 'Diz, if you kin do better, get out there and do it.' Well, there was nothin' for me to do but go out there and pitch. We won that one together, Paul and me."

The guts of the Gas House Gang that year were Diz and Pepper Martin, who had a soul as droll as the Lucas lunatic. They made a dashing pair. One night at the midget auto races, a group of men pushed a midget auto around the track until only a pair of pushers remained—Martin and Dean. During exhibition games (which Dean attended only infrequently) he and Pepper would take over the public-address system and entertain the spectators with a wisecracking account of the game, calling from time to time for members of the Cards' troupe to take a bow. Once, before a double-header with the Dodgers, with Dizzy scheduled to pitch the first game, the question of Martin's and Dean's wrestling ability arose and they grappled on the concrete floor for half an hour. When they got through, Martin had scraped his nose and Dizzy had hurt his arm. But he went out and pitched anyway, and won, sore arm and all.

By mid-August of that year, the Cardinals were floundering badly in second place, well off the pace being set by the New York Giants. Then came a rebellion of the Dean brothers.

Dizzy and Paul pitched and lost a double-header with the Cubs on August 12, and that night, when Frisch counted noses, not a Dean was in sight. They had decided to stage one of their numerous wildcat walkouts. Frisch got boiling mad and fined Dizzy $100 and Paul $50. When the Deans heard about the fine, after rejoining the team two days later, they refused to go out on the field. Frisch promptly suspended them and Dean tore up two uniforms in the clubhouse, one for the benefit of the photographers. But this time the brothers were not to have their way. The Cardinals promptly went on a rampage, winning seven out of their next eight games. Dizzy and Paul were called before the austere Commissioner of Baseball, Kenesaw Mountain Landis, and he lashed into them for their willfulness. Thoroughly chastised, the Deans rejoined the team and the pennant drive was on. By Labor Day the Cardinals were still six games behind the Giants. They clinched the flag on the last day of the season.

One of the turning points of those last few weeks was a double-header on September 21 against the Brooklyn Dodgers. The Dean brothers were listed to pitch, Dizzy the first game and Paul the second. Before the game there was the usual clubhouse meeting, with manager Frisch going over the Dodger batters, mostly for the benefit of the pitchers.

"Dizzy," Frisch said, "I want you to keep the ball high and outside on Leslie. He'll hit it over the fence if you get it inside."

"That ain't how I pitch to him," Diz said. "I give him nothin' but low and inside stuff and he ain't got a hit off me yet."

Frisch ignored Dizzy and passed to Tony Cuccinello. "Nothing but curves for Tony," he warned.

"That's funny," Diz said, "I never have bothered to dish him up a curve yet and he's still tryin' for his first loud foul off Ol' Diz."

Frisch went on down the list, checking off how to pitch to Joe Stripp and Johnny Frederick, Len Koenecke and Al Lopez, and for each, Diz protested he pitched exactly the opposite way. It was obvious to everyone in the clubhouse but Frisch that Dean was just having a little fun with the manager. Finally, as Frisch got redder and redder, Dizzy applied the frosting. "This is a silly business, Frank. I've won 26 games already this season and it don't look exactly right for an infielder like you to be tellin' a star like me how I should pitch."

Frisch stuttered and fumed and told Dean to go to hell, that he didn't care if he went out and had his royal ears royally pinned back.

"They ain't pinnin' Ol' Diz' ears back now. I doubt if them Dodgers get a hit off either me or Paul today."

Dizzy was almost 100 per cent correct. He had a no-hitter until two were out in the eighth, and he wound up with a brilliant two-hit shutout. But Paul went him one better. He pitched the no-hitter in the second game! When the team was in the clubhouse after the double-header and everyone was congratulating Paul, Dizzy came up to him and said in a very hurt tone, "Whyn't you tell Ol' Diz you were gonna pitch a no-hitter? If I'd'a knowed that, I'd of pitched one, too."

Meanwhile, Frankie Frisch took his troubles to Casey Stengel, the Dodger manager. "Case," Frankie said, "I don't know what to do about them boys, they're driving me nuts."

"How many games they win this year?" Stengel asked.

"Forty-two."

"You think you got trouble?" Casey shot back. "I got two pitchers who *lost* 42 games between them."

The 1934 World Series was the pinnacle for the Dean brothers. It gave them a fitting stage to display their dramatics and they made the most of it. It was an absolute triumph for Dizzy and Paul.

Dizzy won a sedate opener, 8-3, pitching a relaxed eight-hitter, and things looked better for the Cardinals, who had been installed as underdogs. But the Tigers bounced back and won the second game 3-2, with nary a Dean seeing action. Paul took over in the third game and beat Tommy Bridges in a tight pitching duel. The Cardinals won it, 4-1. The fourth game was a rout and it was the Cards who were routed, 10-4. Dizzy got into that one as a pinch-runner and, as usual, livened things up immediately. Shortstop Billy Rogell of the Tigers sent a fast throw to third and the ball bounced off Dizzy's head. He was carried groggy and unconscious into the clubhouse where it was thought that he was through for the rest of the Series. But he was in there pitching the next day. He may still have been a little woozy because he lost the game, 3-1, although he pitched creditable seven-hit ball. With the Tigers needing only one more victory in the next two games, they went away empty-handed—thanks to the brothers. Paul Dean

pitched the sixth game and beat Schoolboy Rowe on a seven-hitter, 4-3; and he won the game for the Cardinals with a run-scoring base hit. In the clubhouse, after the game, Dizzy took credit for the strategy. "You know, that lick on the head sort of set me to thinking, and I thought to myself, I know what I'm going to do; I'm going to send my little brother after those rascals. And he brought 'em home with him, too, didn't he?"

Dizzy brought 'em home with him personally in the seventh and deciding game, the maddest of the lot. He held the Tigers to six hits and no runs as his teammates pounded out a 10-0 victory. That was the game in which Ducky Medwick was pelted by lettuce, tomatoes, bottles and other solid objects from Tiger bleacher fans. He barely escaped into the dugout with his life.

Although his contract only called for an $8,500 salary, Dizzy actually earned over $40,000 in 1934. He collected a $1,000 bonus and a World Series check for $5,000. He and Paul divided $24,000 for exhibition games, a vaudeville tour and a movie short. Dizzy made weekly appearances on the radio back home, which netted him another $3,000. He endorsed sweaters, shirts, caps, hats, gloves, shoes, toothpaste, pocket watches and harmonicas. And a New York advertising agency gave him $15,000 for the right to use his name for a year on a comic strip pushing a food product. Dizzy also won the National League's Most Valuable Player Award. Jay Hanna Dean had truly arrived.

In 1935, Dizzy won 28 games, lost 12 and was booed in every ball park in which he showed his face. Aside from his actual pitching record, which was superb, as usual, it was not a good year for Diz. A little bit of his phenomenal '34 success had gone to his head and he was cranky toward the fans, irritable toward his fellow players and a nuisance to the Cardinal front office.

At Forbes Field, Pittsburgh, one afternoon, he enraged the crowd by his antics on the mound. In an early inning he thought he had a batter struck out, but the umpire called the pitch a ball and the batter walked. A couple of base hits followed and the Pirates led by three runs. In a rage, Dizzy threw all his skill into the discard. He lobbed the ball over the plate and Pirate hits rattled off the fences. The customers booed and hissed and many of them left the park. There was tension in the dugout.

too, when Dizzy made sarcastic remarks about the team. One of the players suggested that if Dean so much as walked in his direction, he'd get a baseball bat across the skull. He was finally taken out of the box.

Then he engaged in a tussle with his catcher, Virgil Davis, that had wide repercussions. The feud with Davis started in Cincinnati when Dizzy accused Virgil of failing to try hard enough for a foul ball. Diz lost the game, 3-2. A few days later, when he was scheduled to pitch again, he announced in the clubhouse that he was not going to throw to Davis. Trainer Pop Haines brought the news to Frisch. The manager threw his hands in the air. "What is that boy trying to do? You go back and tell him he's got to pitch!"

Dizzy refused. "You tell Ol' Frankie that Diz will pitch to anybody's mother-in-law, but he ain't a-goin' to pitch to Davis." Frisch finally put Bill Delancey behind the plate, and ironically enough it was Delancey who won a 1-0 game for Dizzy with a home run.

Behind almost all of Dizzy's sullen behavior was his quarrel with the Cardinal front office. He had been raised to $18,000 but he felt he was being underpaid. He berated the front office publicly, and specifically he accused Breadon and Rickey of being callous cheapskates.

At the end of the season Dean had slipped so much in popularity that his extracurricular earnings, which had amounted to so much in 1934, were down practically to nothing. And Branch Rickey applied the squeeze, too, threatening not to permit Dizzy to play at all in 1936 if he didn't get in line. It was an economic blockade and it finally awoke Dean to his responsibilities. Before the beginning of spring training in 1936, he wrote this letter to Rickey:

"All I've got to say give me a ball and a glove and put Davis behind the plate and I'll show you whether I'll pitch to Davis or not. We're out to win the pennant."

Rickey rewarded this display of spirit with a contract calling for a salary of $25,005, making Dean $5 richer than Lefty Gomez of the Yankees and the highest-paid pitcher in the game. And Diz went out and had himself a time, with a 24-13 season. He was a model of decorum. He was on the best terms with players and fans. He signed autographs willingly, he pitched out of turn, he worked in the bull pen, he even kept his peace with the umpires—well, almost. Once the gentlemanly Mr. Dean disputed a pitch with umpire George Barr and got no answer from Barr. "Why don't you answer my question, Mr. Barr?" Dizzy asked politely.

"I did," replied Barr. "I shook my head."

"That's funny," Diz cracked, unable to resist the temptation. "I didn't hear nothin' rattle."

On July 7, 1937, the whole wonderful show came to an untimely and abrupt ending. The setting, at least, was appropriate. Dizzy was on the mound for the National League in the annual All-Star game between the two major leagues, being held that year in Washington. At the plate was Earl Averill, Cleveland's fine outfielder. Dean cranked and sent his wonderfully fluid overhand motion toward the plate and Averill got hold of the ball and lined it right back to Diz. The ball hit Dean squarely on his big left toe. Down he went, and he was carried out of the game. The injury was later diagnosed as a broken toe.

Now, ordinarily a broken toe is not the most damaging injury in the world. But it was in Dean's case. At Branch Rickey's request—he wanted to keep up Cardinal morale, so he said, though it is more likely he wanted to keep the customers coming—Dizzy stayed with the team. And he was sent back into action too soon. Dizzy remembers sitting in the clubhouse one afternoon soon after his injury and Frisch coming up to him. "First thing Frisch asks me is if I could pitch. The toe was stickin' outta my shoe with a splint on it, but when somebody asks me will I pitch, I can never say no."

With his toe paining him on every pitch, he developed an unnatural jerky delivery without a full follow-through. The jerk brought a kink to his arm and it never quite left him. Before All-Star time he had won twelve games. From July to the end of the season, he pitched in seven games and won only one. His final record that dismal season of '37 was 13-10.

That winter, Diz tried all kinds of treatment. He went to a dentist and had some teeth pulled. He went to Johns Hopkins Hospital where they unearthed an assortment of ills—an inflammatory condition of a deltoid muscle, a stretched and inflamed muscle near the back, a bursitis in the shoulder aggravated by a spreading sinus infection. Finally they told him the bad news. He would never again be able to throw a ball effectively with his natural overhand motion. In April of 1938, knowing full well the extent of his injuries, owner Phil Wrigley of the Chicago Cubs bought Dizzy for $185,000, an outfielder and two pitchers.

Wrigley defended his trading judgment. "We got Dizzy's spirit, courage and enthusiasm—in addition to his arm." He also got baseball's biggest gate attraction, sore arm or not.

That year the Cubs won the National League pennant, but Dizzy's contributions were limited. He won seven games and lost one, mostly on sheer guts. In appreciation for his courage, they let Dizzy pitch a World Series game against the Yankees. Ol' Diz did a magnificent job with what he had left. For eight innings, his fast ball merely a shadow of what it used to be, Dean held the Yankees down. Then, with two away in the eighth, a man on first, and the Cubs leading, 3-2, Frank Crosetti came to the plate.

"That was the lowest moment in my life," Diz remembers. "I knowed my arm was gone. I couldn't break a pane of glass. But Crosetti never was a powerful hitter, so I figured I had a chance."

Frankie hit Dean's first pitch over the right-field fence, breaking up the game.

At 27, when he should have been in the very prime of his career, Dizzy was through.

He stayed with the Cubs in '39 and compiled a 6-4 record, but in 1940 the Chicago management told him he would have to be farmed out. Dizzy asked to be sent to Tulsa in the Texas League where he could develop a sidearm delivery and take advantage of the warm Texas sun. This was poor reasoning because Tulsa played most of its games at night. But Tulsa was close to home for Diz and the Texas League was where he had got his start. Possibly a miracle could happen. Wrigley even sent along a special tutor to give Dean some pointers on sidearm pitching. But no miracle developed. Diz won eight games and lost eight and then quit the game for good.

One career had ended, but another one was beginning, and without so much as a waste of breath.

Early in 1941, the president of the Falstaff Brewing Company met with the board of directors to discuss the possibility of having someone broadcast the St. Louis Browns' home games. The president's son, who had met Dizzy in 1935 at a barbecue and had become friendly with him, suggested they try Dean as a broadcaster. The suggestion was accepted, and Ol' Diz became an instantaneous success. He started "commertatin'" the Browns' games for $25,000. Year after year he won the national award for the announcer with the worst diction. In those early years, Dizzy could hardly refrain from interjecting himself in the ball game. Once he leaned out of his radio booth to warn a player that the hit-and-run was on. The umpire behind the plate had to shoo him back behind the microphone.

In 1950 he said he was fed up with the straight diet of "them sloggish Browns" and he signed with the New York Yankees at $40,000 as a television announcer. He soon had sophisticated New Yorkers eating out of his hand. One day when things were dull at Yankee Stadium, Dean pointed to a flock of pigeons going over the park and said, "Swing up the camera, Mr. Cameraman, and let everybody see them pigeons. Wish my old Texas meat dog, Suds, was here. Bird-huntingest dog I ever owned."

Soon he was in demand for all kinds of television appearances. Once he appeared on a news-type panel show with the distinguished commentator, H. V. Kaltenborn. Diz referred to Kaltenborn during the show as Cottonbalm, Kattenborn and Cattlebaum. A little irritated at these distortions, Kaltenborn decided to trip Dean up. He asked him his opinion on how to handle Russia.

"I'd get me a bunch of bats and balls," Dizzy said, "and sneak me a couple of empires and learn them kids behind the Iron Curtain how to tote a bat and play baseball instead of totin' a rifle. And if Joe Stallion knowed how much money they was in the concessions at a ball park, he'd get outta politics and get in an honest business."

This, then, is Jay Hanna Dean, one of the greatest pitchers the game has ever known, one of the most exuberant characters who ever lived, one old soldier who would be constitutionally unable to fade away. The best way to wrap it all up might be to liken Dizzy to one of his own pet phrases, the one in which he refers to a lazy, high fly ball to the outfield as "a tall can o' corn." Dizzy Dean *is* that tall can o' corn—with brains.

I'm old John King . . . men walk around me like I was a swamp. . . ."

The Man Who Hated Southpaws

COLLIE SMALL

BACK IN BASEBALL'S Pleistocene period, a triangular era bounded on the hypotenuse by John McGraw and on the other sides by Speaker and Cobb, a strange and wondrous outfielder roamed the minor leagues. A giant Texan of prodigious strength and temper, his name was John King, and he raged through a dozen leagues in his time, leaving in his wake a monumental legend of violence and destruction.

Yet, for all his greatness, he never got a tryout in the majors, and you can go a long way without ever finding his name in the newspapers of the period. Old ballplayers and umpires in their dotage tell of John King with an easy and disarming familiarity. But if they would only confess it, many of them are often assailed privately with serious doubts that he ever existed.

More is the pity, for John King, at this very moment, lives in semi-retirement with his wife and son on a ranch near Lubbock, Texas. What is more, he is only about a furlong away from his first $1,000,000, according to the informal estimates of his neighbors, who may or may not be close. In any event, they found oil on his property a few years ago, and he certainly is not wanting.

A heavy-shouldered man with hands like huge bunches of bananas, King moved with an uncommon grace, and no minor leaguer of the day could match his powerful throwing arm. His speed was the talk of baseball—as well as anyone remembers now, he led every league he ever played in in stolen bases. The fame of John King was truly a wonderful thing.

It is therefore painful to relate that John King had a melancholy weakness. He could not, for all his Herculean efforts, hit left-handed pitching. Ultimately, this defection reduced him to a crying impotency, and in time he became so enraged at the mere thought of a left-hander that no portsider could be said to be safe even in the general vicinity. This was the tragedy of John King.

Thus it was, on a sunny afternoon more than thirty years ago, that John King was playing center field for Selma, Alabama, in the Southeastern League, against Pensacola, Florida. Selma was leading, 3-1, in the last half of the ninth inning, but Pensacola had filled the bases with two out, and the count on the batter had gone to three balls and two strikes.

In these historic circumstances, the batter, a left-handed hitter, lofted a lazy fly out to King. King stood patiently, waiting with outstretched glove to make the last put-out.

"Float on down here, little ball," he said. "Old John King is waiting to catch you. Come on down, now."

This the ball did. But to the astonishment of one and all, it popped out of his glove and fell to the ground. The Pensacola runners were already moving. Savagely, King pounced on the ball while his teammates shouted for him to throw it to the plate. Instead, in his consummate rage, he took the ball in his teeth, trying to tear it apart as he would a juicy apple, and the game was lost while John King tried to eat the baseball.

Neither money nor the passing of the years has lessened John King's burning hatred of left-handers. There are some who will tell you that he might have been the greatest ballplayer of all time if it had not been for the southpaws, and though this is an exaggeration, it is true that left-handers wielded a mysterious power over him that robbed him of his great strength when he needed it most and finally reduced him to the stature of ordinary mortals. Now fifty-six and long out of baseball,

John King has neither forgotten nor forgiven.

The vast word-of-mouth literature that makes up the legend of John King frequently violates all the laws of credibility. On the other hand, many of the stories, improbably enough, are true. No one can now be found who actually saw John King sitting on the steps of the dugout, malevolently sharpening his spikes with a long file, though this is part of the legend. Yet it is true that he ran the bases as though the devil himself were after him, and many an old ballplayer in the Southwest still carries the mark of John King's spikes.

If the play was close and he was called out, he was infuriated. "Damn it, man!" he would bellow to the umpire. "Old John King *refuses* to be out!"

Once, with Lubbock, in the West Texas League, he was called out at second base on an attempted steal. The injustice of it all outraged him.

Spreading wide his arms, he appealed to the blue sky and cried in an aggrieved voice, "May God strike me dead if I was out!"

Everyone in the park waited tensely for the bolt to strike. When nothing happened, King relaxed. Triumphantly, he turned to the umpire. "See," he said, "he didn't!"

When he was with Cisco, in the same league, he encountered a Fancy-Dan shortstop named Bobby Stow in an exhibition game, and Stow, who had a flair for throwing runners out in the last step, treated the mighty John King with an irreverence that, for one game, threatened his very sanity.

His first time at bat, he hit a sharp bounder down to Stow, who held the throw for a split second and then threw him out by half a step. Disgusted, King returned to the bench, muttering darkly. The next time up, he hit a high hopper over the pitcher's head. With a tremendous burst of speed, Stow crossed over and again nipped King by half a step.

Enraged, King kicked furiously at first base until he had knocked it loose from its buckles. Then he carried it out to right field and hurled it over the fence. Slowly he walked back in and went over to the surprised shortstop.

"Now let's see you throw old John King out," he said.

When with Ardmore, in the Western Association, King taunted a young left-handed pitcher so successfully that the young man imprudently charged our man. It was a one-blow affair. King threw a bucket of water in the pitcher's face, and the latter warily opened his eyes.

"What happened?" he asked.

"Why, son, you just got hit by old John King," King explained kindly.

In another game the same pitcher had two strikes on King when King suddenly stepped out of the batter's box and pointed a finger at him.

"I'm old John King," he announced, somewhat unnecessarily, "and men walk around me like I was a swamp. I'm going to hit your next pitch and drive it into the next state. As I go around the bases, I'm going to undress all the infielders with my spikes. Then, if you're not already running, I'm going to chase you out of the park."

So saying, John King spat in the dust and stepped back into the batter's box. Having no choice, the frightened young southpaw wound up, threw and ducked. And old John King, bless him, struck out, swinging.

All that night he raged at his misfortune to be cast with left-handers. The next morning he was still trumpeting his disgust from the porch of the ramshackle hotel where the team was staying when a string was lowered silently from the manager's third-story window with a piece of paper on the end of it. It was John King's release.

Sadly he went to Fort Smith, Arkansas, the curse of left-handers still weighing heavily on him. Against right-handers he was his usual devastating self. Against southpaws he was more defenseless than ever, and his fury increased. One afternoon in Fort Smith, a whimsical fan brought a beribboned pet pig to the ball game. Poor John was having all sorts of trouble trying to cope with the opposing southpaw, when, late in the game, he popped up for the fourth successive time. Unfortunately, the pig picked that precise moment to run out on the field. With one mighty swipe of his bat, John King killed him.

A few weeks later he was walking down the street with another player when they passed a blind beggar with a violin. King reached into his pocket, drew out a quarter and dropped it into the beggar's cap. In his gratitude, the beggar began to play. Suddenly King wheeled. The blind man was fiddling left-handed. Indignantly, King snatched his quarter out of the cap.

"Damn it," he said to the other player, "I can't seem to get away from 'em."

Even players on his own team steered a careful course around King, particularly left-handers. Once he was playing the sun field when a hitter drove a low line drive at him. Unable to see, he threw up his hands and, by the merest chance, the ball caromed off his glove and rolled insolently to the wall, while the batter galloped happily around the bases for an inside-the-park homer. Considerably chagrined, King retrieved the ball finally and threw it in to the pitcher. Humorlessly, the pitcher, in an ill-considered gesture of contempt, flung it back at him. John King stalked in to the mound, threw one punch and flattened his own pitcher.

It got so that even spectators were in jeopardy. John King did not enjoy being heckled, and there is a story that, in Dallas, where he was the prime target of grandstand jockeys, he once appeared dramatically at the ball park with an armload of dripping meat and bones, which he hurled at the spectators, crying the while, "Here, you wolves, catch this!"

It was, however, the fan in Oklahoma City who asked for it and really got it—with a bottle. It was this particular citizen's dodge to seat himself on a three-legged stool outside the park and yell at King through a knothole. For days the voice tormented King with abuse. Finally, one afternoon while the outfielders were shagging fly balls in a pre-game warm-up, King heard the familiar voice nagging him. "Yah-yah-yah!" it went. "Yah-yah-yah!"

The hairs on the back of John King's neck stood up and a dangerous glint came into his eyes. Quietly he eased away from the other players and stole out of the park. Slipping along the outside of the fence, he came to a corner. There were voices on the other side. Stealthily, King stooped over and picked up an empty bottle. Then he peered around the corner. There, with friends, was his antagonist.

Suddenly the man noticed that King was not on the field with the other players. "I wonder," he mused aloud, "where that no-good King went."

King bellowed like an enraged bull. "Here I am!" he yelled. And with that he let fly.

The bottle, betimes, caught the voice from the knothole squarely between the eyes and tumbled him off his stool while his friends scattered wildly. Hearing the commotion, a policeman rushed up.

"What happened here?" he demanded.

King pointed to the limp figure on the ground. "He attacked me," he said simply.

John King played his first baseball at Polytechnic College in Fort Worth, Texas, circa 1912, doubling in the fall as fullback on the football team. In 1913 he made his debut in the Texas League with Fort Worth as a pinch hitter, but after twelve games in which he was confronted by what seemed like an entire league full of nothing but left-handers, he slipped quietly into the limbo of the lower leagues, happy to find an occasional right-hander on whom to wreak his vengeance.

The Texas League, where he reappeared briefly on several subsequent occasions, represented the pinnacle of his success. Each time the routine was the same. Word would come from the Central League or the Cotton States League that a brawling young giant named John King was burning up the circuit. Back he would come to the Texas League, only to fail against left-handers again. There was a war, too, and a ruptured appendix, and even John King could not win over it all.

Once it looked as though he might make it. In an exhibition game with the New York Giants, when he was with Oklahoma City, he threw a runner out at the plate with a rifle-like shot from deep left field that made John McGraw's eyes bug. When King trotted in at the end of the inning, McGraw patted him on the shoulder.

"You've got something there," he said. "Keep playing ball like that and you'll be in the major leagues before you know it."

Then McGraw and the Giants found out about John King and left-handers.

It was always the same. The Boston Braves hinted once that they were interested in King. Several years later he was released by Galveston, in the Texas League, and he decided to advise the Boston club of his availability.

"Am loose and going good," he wired hopefully.

The Braves were unimpressed. "Stay loose and keep going," they answered.

So John King sank even lower into the minors, his greatness wasting. Men still marveled at his great strength, his speed, his throwing arm and his batting prowess against right-handers. But there was also his temper and the mysterious spell cast over him by left-handers. More and more he railed against his plight.

One afternoon a small boy whistled to him in the outfield for help in scaling the fence. King obliged and the youngster clambered over and skipped away toward the bleachers.

Unfortunately, he made one fatal mistake. He stopped suddenly, playfully scooped up a pebble from the grass and threw it—with his left hand. John King whirled on him angrily, grabbed him and threw him back over the fence.

"What do you mean," he roared at the shrinking figure, "trying to sneak into this ball game?"

When the war came, John King went to Europe with the army and stayed for part of the occupation. Finally he came home and looked around to see what had changed. Almost immediately he protested.

"Fifty thousand left-handed soldiers went to France," he said, "and all fifty thousand of them came back without a scratch. There is no justice."

Because of the humiliation inflicted on him by southpaws, King began punishing himself for his failures against them. When he was with Longview, in the East Texas League, for example, he struck out one afternoon at a most inopportune moment on a sweeping curve thrown by an enemy portsider. In disgust he broke his bat over the dugout steps and then went to the water pail and drew a dipper of ice water. Holding the dipper high, in the manner of a man proposing a toast, he shouted so that all in the park could hear, "John King, you'd like a drink of water, wouldn't you? Your jaws are dry and there's cotton on your tongue and your taste buds need sprinkling! But, dang your worthless hide, you're not going to get any water! You're not going to drink one swallow until you've got yourself a hit off that cunnythumbed varmint of a pitcher out there!"

With that, he hurled the dipper in the direction of the pitcher, kicked over the water bucket and sat down in the dugout. Fortunately, late in the game, he did indeed scratch one puny infield single off the pitcher, and did therefore permit himself one lovely swallow of ice-cold water.

Fact and legend demonstrate John King was such a man. But, curiously enough, the most widely circulated John King story never happened at all.

Even though it never happened, there is scarcely an old-time Texas ballplayer now alive who does not insist he remembers a singular afternoon at Abilene, Texas, when John King was engaged in a particularly bitter duel with a rookie left-hander. King used all his tricks, but the young pitcher refused to blow up.

Finally King laid down a bunt and rocketed down to first base before the pitcher could field the ball.

Puffing mightily, he asked for time out and retired to the dugout, where he filled his mouth with water. Play was duly resumed on his return to first base, and the next hitter responded by driving the ball into center field for a long single. King was off like a shot.

Unfortunately, the umpire was stationed behind the pitcher's mound, according to the vogue of the day, and he was obliged to turn his back to observe the flight of the ball. King thereupon dashed straight across the diamond behind the umpire's back and squirted water in the startled pitcher's face as he raced past. Then, in a great cloud of dust and clods, he slid into third base, got to his feet, and squirted water in the third baseman's face.

The umpire, discovering King on third base, naturally assumed he had arrived there via second base, and was disposed to call him safe when the crowd started to descend menacingly onto the field. Hurriedly he changed his decision, and John King, who might have changed the whole conception of baseball, was ingloriously out.

Since John King denies that the incident ever happened, it is obvious that someone has been tampering with the legend. However, he does concede that he often spit in left-handed pitchers' faces, though never in Abilene.

Actually, it was his custom to fill his mouth with water at third base, and, while the pitcher was winding up, dash out to the mound, squirt the water into his face, and then run back to third base while the pitcher, helpless to stop his windup without committing a balk, pitched the ball and suffered in silence.

"I spit in an awful lot of left-handers' faces that way," King says happily.

It was only a moral victory, however. In 1930 John King had run out his string as a player. Reluctantly he hung up his spikes. The left-handers had triumphed. John King had never reached the major leagues.

Then he did an astonishing thing. He became an umpire. John King umpired in the Texas League for a year before he found out that he had oil on his property. As an ump he was almost as tempestuous as he had been as a player. He once spent most of an afternoon in Galveston arguing with a fan behind first base when he was supposed to be umpiring the bases. The fan was so infuriated that he hunted down King in the umpires' dressing room after the game. King was changing his clothes when the irate spectator, mayhem bent, opened the door. Old John King did not even look up. He simply picked up a broken bat that was standing in the corner, fondled it affectionately in his huge hands, and said quietly, "Stick your head in here and you'll draw back a neck." The fan quickly withdrew.

Ziggy Sears, the erstwhile National League umpire and a graduate of the Texas League, indicated recently that, as he remembered it, King chased the fan clear out of the ball park and into an adjoining parking lot with a .45 in one hand and a gleaming bowie knife in the other. King, who actually did carry a gun frequently, insists, however, that his only weapon on this occasion was a baseball bat and that he wouldn't run that far to catch any fan.

J. Alvin Gardner, president of the Texas League, says that King was an outstanding umpire, but it is doubtful that he was very interested in becoming a great umpire. Most of his pleasure in that capacity came from watching batters knock the ears off left-handed pitchers. It was a soul-satisfying experience to stand behind the plate and watch southpaws suffer.

Toward the end of his one season as an umpire he worked a game in Houston. Shortly before starting time, one of the pitchers, a left-hander, approached him.

"I know you don't like left-handers, Mr. King," he said, "but will you give me a break?"

King looked at him stonily. "Do the best you can," he said. "That's what I'm going to do."

A few minutes later, the other pitcher, also a southpaw, came to him. "Just because I'm a left-handed pitcher doesn't mean you're going to make it tough for me, does it?"

Again King said icily, "Do the best you can. That's what I'm going to do." Then he went behind the plate.

From the outset, both pitchers were in dire straits at the hands of the hitters. Old John King danced in delight as base hits whistled past their ears. Finally he could contain himself no longer. Leaning over the catcher, he asked confidentially, "Did you ever see a left-handed pitcher skipping rope?"

The catcher opined that he had not.

"Well, take a look," John King said happily, as the batter bounced a fast ball through the pitcher's legs. "There is a left-handed pitcher skipping rope."

In 1931 they discovered John King's oil, and he retired from baseball forever. From the proceeds of his holdings, he built a house exactly like Tara in *Gone With the Wind*. Then he and Mrs. King settled down to a life of comparative ease in their mansion on the plains of West Texas.

Still, John is not completely happy. The old bitterness toward left-handers still rankles. When his only son was born, he lived in genuine dread that he would turn out to be a "cunnythumb." At the very beginning, he was shocked speechless when the baby reached for a rattle with his left hand. Frightened, John King called on heaven to witness the cruel injustice. Then, desperately, he stuffed the tiny left hand into a tobacco sack and tied the drawstring around the baby's wrist. There his son's hand stayed until John King was satisfied he was going to be right-handed after all.

During the recent difficulty between the countries he was even under the impression that Hitler was a portsider. "I bought a hundred thousand dollars' worth of War Bonds before I found out he was right-handed," he said solemnly.

A few months ago John King was still endeavoring to explain the mystifying curse of left-handers. "All I know is that I've studied those birds and there is something funny about 'em," he said. "Look around, find a left-hander, watch him. Sooner or later, he'll do one little thing a normal person won't do."

John King shook his head sadly.

"You'll find out," he said. "Just like I did."

THE CONTENTS of this anthology are 99 44/100% baseball, of course. The other 56/100% is right here . . . out of *Life in a Putty-Knife Factory*. Burn-ball, the man says.

Burn-Ball and Other Matters

H. ALLEN SMITH

IN A LAND where major emphasis is placed on sports, it seems I have always missed out completely or got going in the wrong direction. In the parochial schools I attended I can recall but four athletic pursuits: fist fighting, throwing rocks at telephone poles, running around the block and burn-ball.

The game of burn-ball was a variation of baseball. It was played with a hollow rubber ball slightly smaller than a tennis ball. The pitcher delivered with an underhand swing and the batter used his fist, knuckles forward, for striking. It was permissible to pull the sleeve of the shirt or sweater down over the fist, or wrap a handkerchief around it, to take out the sting. After the batter hit the ball, he pursued the usual course toward first base, though it wasn't necessary for the fielders to throw to the first baseman. All they had to do was hit the runner with the ball. I hurt all over just thinking about it. Nobody ever *tossed* the ball at the runner. It was thrown always with full force, and the most capable fielders were those who could hit a runner in the face. Getting hit in the cheek, or even on the arm or leg, was as painful as an earache on an elephant. If you were ever stung on the cheek by a wasp, or hit in the leg by a shotgun blast, you have some idea of what it meant to be put out in burn-ball.

Once or twice a week Father John, our parish priest, was accustomed to play burn-ball with us. He was a man in his forties, a stern, frightening figure to most of us. Though we didn't know the word tyrant, we considered him to be one, and he knew that we did. I know now that he was a good man and a reasonable one. He proved it by forgetting old scores and coming out regularly to join in that brutal pastime of ours.

He made a little game out of getting into the game. He'd come out of his house and wander into the schoolyard, reading his office, pretending he wasn't aware of the burn-ball game. After a while he'd close his book and stand and watch us a bit. Then he'd ask if he could get in, and we would joyfully welcome him into the contest. He'd shuck himself down to his shirt, even removing his collar, and he'd play until he could no longer stand the punishment.

How we gave it to him! At all other times Father John was in the driver's seat, but in burn-ball we had him where we wanted him. Meaning no disrespect, I am impelled to say that Father John was sensitive where he sat. He was inclined toward pudginess in that direction and his black britches had no slack at the hips. It was a glorious experience to get a square shot at that bottom, and an ignominious thing to miss it. Father John rarely hit the ball out of the infield and the fielder who got it almost always ran forward so he could get a good bead on Father's sensitive spot. We rarely missed, and I can see him now, scampering toward first base and, on coming within a few feet of it, hunching his shoulders a little against the awful stab that he knew was coming. He was well aware of our sadistic intentions but he never complained, and I don't think he ever padded himself against those painful assaults. Nonetheless, he couldn't stand up under them for more than four or five direct hits, at which point he'd make his excuses, pick up his clothes, and head for the house, never giving us the satisfaction of rubbing the sore places while in our view. It was great sport to have him in the game for a while, but it was a relief when he departed because we could never take the name of the Lord while he was around. There was only one proper remark for a boy to make when, running the bases, he was stung with a full-bodied hit. That was "Jee-zusss Kay-ryst!" Father John's presence placed us under severe restraints.

My athletic background was meager, then, when I left school and went to work on the Huntington *Press*. After a time they put me to work covering basketball games and, a little later, somebody on the paper got the notion of making a sports editor out of me. This project failed because of a sort of stubborn iconoclasm on my part. The fellow who had been serving as sports writer was going away somewhere and he was told to break me in for the job.

We had a semipro baseball team in Huntington and a nice enough ball park for a town of its size. I knew the fundamental rules of baseball but the job was to learn score-keeping. The retiring sports editor took me to the park one Sunday afternoon and set me to work scoring a regular game. It was simple enough until we came to the first strike-out. He told me to put down a *K*.

"Why?" I wanted to know. "Why a *K*?"

"Because," he said, "a *K* stands for a strike-out."

To this day I don't understand what caused me to rebel. I told him that *K* didn't stand for strike-out to me and didn't make sense to me. He argued that baseball scorers from the time of Abner Doubleday had been using a *K* as the strike-out symbol, and that I would have to use a *K* whether it appealed to me or not. I said the hell I would. I said I would use *SO* for struck-out, or *FA* for fanned, or *WH* for whiffed, but I was not going to fly in the face of all logic and use a *K* when the *K* didn't even suggest a strike-out. He explained to me that the scorebook beneath my hand was the team's official scorebook and for that, if for no other reason, I'd use *K* and like it. I lost my temper and he lost his and we ended up with his taking the scorebook away from me and finishing off the job without further conversation. Back at the office he went to the boss and told him that I'd never, never, so long as I lived, make a sports writer because I had no respect for tradition. So they hired another fellow as sports writer and left me to get in trouble in other directions.

Since the ancient incident of the scorebook and the *K*, my interest in baseball has been casual, almost academic. Yet, during the last couple of years I managed to work myself into a mild lather over a baseball controversy, to wit: Is there such a thing as a curve ball?

As I recall it, the argument started with a piece in *The New Yorker* magazine. An old baseball scout let loose "the secret." He said that there was no such thing as a curve and that everybody in baseball knew it. He added that the secret had been guarded because the fans would lose interest if word got out that Cooper and Feller and Hubbell and Higbe were incapable of throwing anything but a straight ball.

Newspapers took up the argument and I remember hearing Waite Hoyt broadcast a vigorous denunciation of the no-curve theory. Hoyt is called "Hurt" in Brooklyn. Once when he was struck by a pitched ball, a fan cried, "Holy Jeez! Hurt's Hoyt!" Well, Hoyt was bitter about the curve-ball argument, but don't forget he was once a big-league pitcher, and a pitcher would be the last person on earth to admit a pitcher can't throw a curve.

Life magazine assigned a high-speed photographer to investigate the dispute. He came away with a series of pictures showing the flight of baseballs pitched by Carl Hubbell and Cy Blanton. All these photographs failed to show the existence of a curve.

It soon developed that the curve question was an old one and that various tests had been made in the past. Baseballs had been thrown through a series of hoops covered with thin paper, to show that they curved. Tall stakes had been driven along base lines and pitchers had thrown balls that curved out and in and in and out. Yet, to my knowledge, the argument was never clearly settled to the satisfaction of all concerned. Personally, being a skeptic, I'm on the no-curve side.

My specific interest in having a decision made is minor. In my files I have a notation concerning "the first deliberate curve ever pitched in baseball." This historic event occurred, according to the memorandum, back in 1866 and in Brooklyn. The pitcher was a gentleman named Arthur Cummings, who played with the Brooklyn Excelsiors.

Mr. Cummings' performance that day back in 1866 has interested me for a long time. It gives me something to speculate on when I have nothing else to occupy my mind. I've often tried to reconstruct the scene where Mr. Cummings pitched the first deliberate curve in all history.

How did he happen to make up his mind to do it?

Let's visualize Mr. Cummings out there on the mound. Let's assume the Excelsiors were trailing. Mr. Cummings, as the saying goes, was in the clutch. What did he do?

"Well," he may have said to himself, "I reckon I'll have to try something new on these bums. Lemme see, now. Mebby if I threw a ball down there and made it sorta curve on the way, then they couldn't hit it. Yep. That's what I'll do. Wonder how a feller oughta fix his fingers to make a ball curve. This way—this oughta do 'er. Okay. Here we go. Look out, you big bum, here comes the first deliberate curve ever pitched in history."

After that, what? Did the batter know it was a curve? Did the catcher know it was a curve? Did the spectators know it?

I think it's improbable that any of these people knew Arthur Cummings had deliberately thrown a curve. I believe he was the only person present who knew it. Having thrown the ball, I can picture him swaggering down to the plate, chuckling to himself as he approached the batter.

"Hey," I can hear him saying, "Hey, dopey. Know why you wasn't able to hit that last'n?"

"Sure," says the batter, "I got dust in my eyes and my hind foot slipped and your catcher jabbed me in the side with his glove and I got a bad head cold."

"Like hell," says Arthur Cummings. "You didn't hit it because it curved. I throwed a curve. Deliberate."

"No kid," says the batter.

"Swearta God I throwed a curve," says Arthur Cummings. "And listen. Soon as you're out, run up an' tell th' boys in th' press box about it, will ya? I don't wanna do it myself. Wouldn't look good."

Maybe that's the way it happened but, so far as I can learn, the actual details are lost in time. I do think, however, that it would be a lovely thing, after all these years, to learn that cocksure Arthur Cummings outsmarted himself —that his first deliberate curve in all history was as straight as a hoe handle.

JOHN GALLAGHER

Courtesy *True, The Man's Magazine.* ©

It would date too rapidly the contents of this book to go into the membership in the Hall of Fame, which grows larger every year. But there is more to the Hall than a mere reciting of its immortal roster. Ken Smith has devoted an entire book, *Baseball's Hall of Fame*, to the subject, and here, in excerpt form, is the story of baseball's birthplace—and a man named Doubleday.

Cooperstown

KEN SMITH

From a standpoint of participation, baseball is essentially a small-town game. Big-city attendance enables the sport to operate as a big business, but a preponderance of the players first see the light of day in country villages. . . . The tourist from the big city, viewing Cooperstown for the first time, regards the village as quaint, neat and different. But to the majority of baseball players making the pilgrimage to the shrine for the first time, it is merely a nostalgic duplication of earlier surroundings. A pasture or an open lot means baseball to the American boy in all forty-eight states. Here is a big-league player's-eye view of Cooperstown as he reported to his teammates in the dugout:

"Everything was green up there—so many lawns, parks, lots of lake shore—trees and growth come right down to the water's edge. Pretty good bass and perch in that lake. There was room—plenty of space and lush trees, with green everywhere, and most of us got a little homesick.

"Main Street's nice and wide and paved, too. You can find most anything you want in the stores, especially if you farm it. I saw coulters, spare discs, lots of lawn mowers, which they sure need in the summer for all that grass. The town's surrounded by farms, big ones and modern. Plenty of dairy cattle, purebred herds, too. Barns looked in good repair, and that's always a sign of a well-fixed farmer who hustles.

"The Hall of Fame is practically in the center of the town, and the ball park is just down the street from the museum. The heavy growth of trees beyond the outfield fence makes a swell background for hitting. Fences aren't too near the plate, but you can reach 'em. I saw Stan Hack and Ted Williams, both lefties, clear the left-field fence. Swish Nicholson cleared right field, and Joe Kuhel put one over right-center.

"Best of all about the whole business, though, is the people. They give you a good welcome. They don't treat ballplayers like inmates of a zoo. We got a good reception, and they seemed glad to have us around. Every player should go up whenever he can. He'll never forget the experience, especially when he walks through that museum and sees uniforms, gloves, and shoes of the great players he used to dream about as a kid."

Baseball's birthplace is now an incorporated village of 3,000, situated in the east-central part of New York state, about two hundred miles northwest of New York City. It lies on a line between Albany and Buffalo, though barely sixty miles due west of the state capital. Nestling at the south end of Lake Otsego, it marks the beginning of the Susquehanna River, launched by a waterfall on its long journey through southern New York, Pennsylvania and over to Chesapeake Bay.

Wild game, bears, panthers, deer and Indians, the only early inhabitants of Cooperstown, little knew that someday people would be naming baseball nines after them. Council Rock still stands where the Iroquois Indians turned the territory into a meeting place, later occasionally setting up trading posts. The name Lake Otsego means "Place of the Meeting."

General James Clinton camped in the neighborhood in 1779 with his Revolutionary Army and dammed the lake, later blasting it in order that his soldiers might float down the swollen waters of the Susquehanna River to join General Sullivan at Tioga Point to engage in border warfare. George Washington, investigating inland water routes, looked over Otsego Lake in 1783.

Judge William Cooper, father of James Fenimore Cooper, acquired large tracts of land and saw his Otsego Lake holdings for the first time in 1785. No one lived there at that time, but he sold forty thousand acres to immigrants and within three years a village sprang up named Cooperstown. He moved in permanently with his family in 1786. James Fenimore Cooper, who was born in Burlington, New Jersey, was one year old when his father brought him to Cooperstown to live. He grew up, according to William Cullen Bryant:

". . . the vast forest around him stretching up to the mountains that overlook the Lake and far beyond; in a region where the Indian yet roamed, and the white hunter, half Indian in dress and mode of life, sought his game—a region in which the bear and the wolf yet hunted, and the panther, more formidable than either, lurked in the thicket . . ."

But the Cooperstown man who touched most lives—in fact, exerted more influence indirectly on the folklore of our country and others than perhaps any other one American—was, of course, Abner Doubleday. About a half-century after Judge William Cooper founded the community, Cooperstown boys, like lads 'most everywhere in a free country, romped in the fields, playing one o'cat with a padded ball built of wound twine. Ball playing, in some form or other, goes back to the shaggy-haired young stalwarts of the Stone Age. The object of one o'cat was to take your turn with the stick, club, paddle, wheel spoke or wagon tongue, hit and run to a base. You were out when struck with a ball thrown by your opponent, and went to the end of the line in the field.

From a simple recreation for two, three or four, the fun grew into a scramble of thirty or more boys from all over town. They called it Town Ball. There was no limit to the number of players on a side. The side remained at bat until everybody was out on a fly, a catch on first bounce or being "soaked" with a thrown ball while running bases. In some interpretations, whenever a side made three home runs, the entire side was allowed to bat around again until everybody was out. The distance between bases was not always the same.

Abner Doubleday, who was born in Ballston Spa, Saratoga County, on June 26, 1819, the son of Ulysses Freeman and Hester Doubleday, was a student at Otsego Classical and Military Academy in Cooperstown, studying to enter West Point. He was a Town Ball player and a young man with a sense of order, later borne out by his engineering career and success at military maneuvers in the Civil War. He felt that Town Ball would be a more interesting after-school pastime if simplified and organized, instead of remaining a wild frolic that no doubt often broke up in confusion and horseplay as the sides grew larger and the boys got to pelting each other with the ball as in a snowball battle or pillow fight.

To replace the carelessly staked out base paths, he devised a diamond with bases equidistant, limited the sides to eleven players and reduced the amount of wild throwing of the ball at the runner. He ruled that put-outs could be made by throwing to a fielder covering the base, or by tagging the runner.

These radical and pioneering changes, made in 1839, constituted the birth of baseball: 1. Diagramed bases. 2. Limited number of players. 3. Put-outs by touching a base.

The establishment of equidistant base lines, first at 60 feet apart, was an engineering calculation that has never ceased to draw the interest of mathematicians, a study that comes directly before the eyes of everyday Americans. The whole game is based on the relationship of the race to first base between a batter and the ball fielded and thrown by the infielder. Changes in the resilience of the ball, due to improved manufacturing methods, and skill in hurrying throws increased to favor the fielder. But better bats, spikes, improved baseline tracks and generally increased speed kept the batter in step. Eventually the 90-foot distance, evolved by Alexander Cartwright, proved to be the fairest contest. This universally adopted distance hastened the nationalizing of the sport.

After laying out the first diamond on Farmer Phinney's lot and, supposedly, starting the ball rolling, young Doubleday, twenty years old, explained his game of baseball in other parts of town and at schools. He was not only the inventor, but a crusader. Like many influential inventions, the game was not an overnight hit. Rather, it apparently made a gradual development away from Town Ball. Doubleday is known to have played the game considerably before he was graduated from West Point at the age of twenty-three. He had been graduated from the military school and was a West Point plebe when his baseball invention was perfected.

His connection with the sport was dropped along the grim wayside of his advance through the ranks of the army. He fought in the Mexican War when he was twenty-seven and in several engagements of Indian warfare. As an artillery captain, he fired the first gun on the Union side in the Civil War, defending Fort Sumter on April 12, 1861. He commanded a division of the Army of the Potomac and was such a distinguished major general in the Battle of Gettysburg that, when he died in 1893, his body lay in state in City Hall in New York City, viewed by thousands. But, though the war separated Doubleday from his baseball brain child which was to play such a part in the folklore of his country, it did help nationalize the sport. It became a favorite time-passer for war prisoners in Southern concentrations where young men from all sections of the country played the game with their captors watching from the sidelines. Sometimes in the excitement of close games, baseball must have blended enemies into one mind rooting for a batter to beat the throw home.

In New York City they were playing a form of ball around Doubleday's time and with his fundamental theory. Soon the core of the game's growth became a lot at Twenty-seventh Street and Madison Avenue, a favorite spot for the city boys in 1842.

Alexander Cartwright, one of these New York "sports" organized the Knickerbocker Baseball and Social Club on September 23, 1845, the first such team to issue a challenge to the baseball world. Victory went to the team first making twenty-one runs in those days, but the rules were rapidly shaped into modern status, the most important one being Cartwright's ninety-foot baseline clause.

Putting a runner out by throwing the ball at him was dropped from the rules. Cartwright went West in the Gold Rush of 1849, spreading the game across the Mississippi to the Pacific and later to Hawaii. By 1850 the ballplayers were sporting natty uniforms. The game was on. Admission was charged for a game between New York and Brooklyn clubs in 1858, and that year the National Association of Baseball Players was formed, all classed as amateurs. The Excelsiors of Brooklyn took the first baseball trip in 1860 to upstate New York and as far south as Baltimore. The first western trip was dared by the Washington Nationals in 1867. A professional nine, the Cincinnati Red Stockings, was organized in 1869, and the next season the Rockford, Illinois, club, with A. G. Spalding, made the first eastern invasion. By 1871 there was a ten-club professional league.

Visitors to Cooperstown who don't know a blessed thing about the game stop at Doubleday Field just to look at the ground, as deeply hallowed to baseball as Kitty Hawk, North Carolina, is to aviation. Passing through the imposing stone gateway, past a circular memorial of white pillars, with trees on all sides, visitors proceed into a modern stadium seating 8,000 with grandstand and bleachers encircling the entire arena. They see a verdant infield and outfield laid out with the advice and supervision of the late groundkeeper of the Polo Grounds, the justly famous Harry Fabian.

Those who know now think back to an old settler from Connecticut named Elihu Phinney, who hauled a printing press to Cooperstown with oxen and sled and set up the *Otsego Journal* or *Western Advertiser,* the second newspaper west of the Hudson. The journal lasted twenty-seven years. The Phinney family became publishers of textbooks and Bibles, distributing their goods via the Erie Canal. A Phinney Bible is now a collector's item, and the Phinney Almanac became celebrated the country over after, through a typographical error, it predicted snow on July fourth, and by some cruel quirk of nature the frigid and prophetic error came true.

The first game of baseball was played on old man Phinney's farm, but if, in his Almanac, some garbled type had come out to read that on his cow pasture thousands of people would some day gather to see a group of boys romp with a ball, while a million others as far west as California would sit in their parlors and follow every play out of the very air, why the issue would have been scrapped as the most nonsensical balderdash ever to find its way into type.

HERE is a column by Red Smith, whose greatness as a sports writer may be traced in part to the fact that he does not indulge in exaggerated phraseology. He was not exaggerating when he entitled this column, "Miracle of Coogan's Bluff." We kid you not.

1951:
New York Giants 5,
Brooklyn Dodgers 4

RED SMITH

NOW IT IS DONE. Now the story ends. And there is no way to tell it. The art of fiction is dead. Reality has strangled invention. Only the utterly impossible, the inexpressibly fantastic, can ever be plausible again.

Down on the green and white and earth-brown geometry of the playing field, a drunk tries to break through the ranks of ushers marshaled along the foul lines to keep profane feet off the diamond. The ushers thrust him back and he lunges at them, struggling in the clutch of two or three men. He breaks free, and four or five tackle him. He shakes them off, bursts through the line, runs head-on into a special park cop, who brings him down with a flying tackle.

Here comes a whole platoon of ushers. They lift the man and haul him, twisting and kicking, back across the first-base line. Again he shakes loose and crashes the line. He is through. He is away, weaving out toward center field, where cheering thousands are jammed beneath the windows of the Giants' clubhouse.

At heart, our man is a Giant, too. He never gave up.

From center field comes burst upon burst of cheering. Pennants are waving, uplifted fists are brandished, hats are flying. Again and again the dark clubhouse windows blaze with the light of photographers' flash bulbs. Here comes that same drunk out of the mob, back across the green turf to the infield. Coattails

flying, he runs the bases, slides into third. Nobody bothers him now.

And the story remains to be told, the story of how the Giants won the 1951 pennant in the National League. The tale of their barreling run through August and September and into October. . . . Of the final day of the season, when they won the championship and started home with it from Boston, to hear on the train how the dead, defeated Dodgers had risen from the ashes in the Philadelphia twilight. . . . Of the three-game play-off in which they won, and lost, and were losing again with one out in the ninth inning yesterday when—Oh, why bother?

Maybe this is the way to tell it: Bobby Thomson, a young Scot from Staten Island, delivered a timely hit yesterday in the ninth inning of an enjoyable game of baseball before 34,320 witnesses in the Polo Grounds. . . . Or perhaps this is better:

"Well!" said Whitey Lockman, standing on second base in the second inning of yesterday's play-off game between the Giants and Dodgers.

"Ah, there," said Bobby Thomson, pulling into the same station after hitting a ball to left field. "How've you been?"

"Fancy," Lockman said, "meeting you here!"

"Ooops!" Thomson said. "Sorry."

And the Giants' first chance for a big inning against Don Newcombe disappeared as they tagged Thomson out. Up in the press section, the voice of Willie Goodrich came over the amplifiers announcing a macabre statistic: "Thomson has now hit safely in fifteen consecutive games." Just then the floodlights were turned on, enabling the Giants to see and count their runners on each base.

It wasn't funny, though, because it seemed for so long that the Giants weren't going to get another chance like the one Thomson squandered by trying to take second base with a playmate already there. They couldn't hit Newcombe, and the Dodgers couldn't do anything wrong. Sal Maglie's most splendrous pitching would avail nothing unless New York could match the run Brooklyn had scored in the first inning.

The story was winding up, and it wasn't the happy ending that such a tale demands. Poetic justice was a phrase without meaning.

Now it was the seventh inning and Thomson was up, with runners on first and third base, none out. Pitching a shutout in Philadelphia last Saturday night, pitching again in Philadelphia on Sunday, holding the Giants scoreless this far, Newcombe had now gone twenty-one innings without allowing a run.

He threw four strikes to Thomson. Two were fouled off out of play. Then he threw a fifth. Thomson's fly scored Monte Irvin. The score was tied. It was a new ball game.

Wait a minute, though. Here's Pee Wee Reese hitting safely in the eighth. Here's Duke Snider singling Reese to third. Here's Maglie wild-pitching a run home. Here's Andy Pafko slashing a hit through Thomson for another score. Here's Billy Cox batting still another home. Where does his hit go? Where else? Through Thomson at third.

So it was the Dodgers' ball game, 4 to 1, and the Dodgers' pennant. So all right. Better get started and beat the crowd home. That stuff in the ninth inning? That didn't mean anything.

A single by Al Dark. A single by Don Mueller. Irvin's pop-up, Lockman's one-run double. Now the corniest possible sort of Hollywood schmaltz—stretcher-bearers plodding away with an injured Mueller between them, symbolic of the Giants themselves.

There went Newcombe and here came Ralph Branca. Who's at bat? Thomson again? He beat Branca with a home run the other day. Would Charley Dressen order him walked, putting the winning run on base, to pitch to the dead-end kids at the bottom of the batting order? No, Branca's first pitch was a called strike.

The second pitch—well, when Thomson reached first base he turned and looked toward the left-field stands. Then he started jumping straight up in the air, again and again. Then he trotted around the bases, taking his time.

Ralph Branca turned and started for the clubhouse. The number on his uniform looked huge. Thirteen.

IF YOU BELIEVE that anything that took place in baseball before 1900 is dry, dull, ancient history, then you had better not read this chapter from Robert Smith's wonderful book *Baseball*. It might change your mind.

The Wild Irishman and the Gentle Indian

ROBERT SMITH

THERE WERE great infielders abroad in the 1890's, and good pitchers, too—men like Amos Rusie, whose curve ball was just a fast ball "with a tail on it"; or like Cy Young, who lasted so long in the major leagues that it seemed they'd have to shoot him, on Judgment Day, with his baseball shoes still on; or like Ted Breitenstein, who was given up for lost because of his taste for liquor, then swore off and kept pitching until he was past fifty. The truly great men of that day, however, were the hitters, one or two of whom have never been outdone. Some, like old Pop Anson, were coasting home after leading the league in the eighties. Others were just starting on careers that would make small boys in the early twentieth century learn to whisper their names with reverence.

There was Big Ned Williamson, of Chicago, the home-run king who loved to pull line drives down inside the left-field foul line. He had a teammate named Fred Pfeffer, whose batting average was even fiercer than his piratical mustache, which was by itself almost enough to frighten a pitcher. Jesse Burkett of Cleveland, called "the Crab" because he used to trade insults with spectators who tried to heckle him, was getting two hits about every five times at bat. Keeler and Kelly of Baltimore practiced punching hits "where they ain't"—that is, into the holes which were left when the fielders took their normal positions. Hugh Duffy, the Boston outfielder, attained the highest batting average ever entered on the books—.438. Billy Hamilton (who once stole 115 bases in a season), Fred Tenney, Fred Clarke, John McGraw, and Hughey Jennings were all piling up base hits in this decade.

But the most spectacular batsmen of the time, from a ball crank's point of view, were a wild Irishman and a gentle Indian.

The wild Irishman was Big Ed Delahanty, whose like has seldom been seen. Del was a "bad-ball" hitter, a man with such a quick eye that he could pick a ball right out of the dirt, time after time, with the end of his bat, and hit it squarely enough to send it over the fence. Pat Tebeau, manager of the Cleveland Spiders, who was Delahanty's boss for a time, said that the worst thing to throw at the big fellow was a wild pitch, for Ed loved to hit wild pitches out of the park. He would stand on tiptoe, hold his bat apparently by the utmost inch of its handle, and clout an out-of-reach ball so far the fielders would lose it.

Delahanty was over six feet tall and weighed a generous 190 pounds. Men who met him had to admit he was a handsome fellow, though there was an air about him that indicated he was a roughneck at heart and no man to tamper with. He had that wide-eyed, half-smiling, ready-for-anything look that is characteristic of a certain type of Irishman. He had a towering impatience, too; and a taste for liquor and excitement. He created plenty of excitement, for opponents and spectators, when he laid his tremendous bat against a pitch. One day he broke a third baseman's ankle with a drive that barely skimmed the turf. Another time he split a ball right in two, just as everyone said he would, someday, if he wasn't careful.

In a game in Chicago in 1896 Delahanty got five hits in five times at bat. The manner in which he slashed these hits—four of them home runs—into various parts of the field was typical of his prodigious ability. In his first time at bat, Del sent one of pitcher Terry's straight balls into the left-field bleachers. The second hit went to right field, far out into the grass, for another home run. On his third time at bat, Del smashed a line drive chest-high across the infield. Bullhead Dahlen, the Chicago shortstop, leaped in front of the ball and went down as if he had been struck by a cannon shot. With Dahlen sitting on the infield turf, the ball caromed into fair territory and Del reached first base safely.

On his fourth time at bat, Del met a pitch squarely and drove it straight out into center field, into territory that few fielders ever trod. He made the circuit of the bases without trouble. When he came to bat the fifth time even the hostile spectators were excited.

"Another one, Del!" they shouted. "Another home run!"

Bill Terry, the pitcher, had taken his stance, with what trepidation in his heart it is not hard to guess, when Bill Lange, the Chicago center fielder, called to him.

"Hold it up a minute!" he yelled.

Then Lange set out for the distant reaches of center field, where the groundkeeper did not bother to keep the grass in trim. The clubhouses were out there, in the no man's land where no ball ever fell and no play was ever made. Lange, while the laughter in the stands grew and grew, kept trotting farther out toward the clubhouses, until at last he was right between them, a ridiculously small figure in the distance. Even Delahanty had to grin now; and the stands, from left field around to first base, were in an uproar. Because he was too far off to be heard, Lange waved both hands above his head to signal that play could begin. Terry wound up and slammed a fast ball toward Delahanty. Del swung at the first pitch and the bat made a sound like a rifle shot. The ball, amid a crescendo of screams, carried on a line out to right center, hit the roof of one clubhouse, bounded over to the roof of the other, and rattled away out of the reach of Bill Lange. Delahanty was on his way from third to home before Bill had even recovered the ball. And when Lange did get the ball, he did not throw it in but hid it under the floor of the home team's clubhouse, so that he might have a souvenir of the day.

Ed was a swift and clever fielder as well as a hitter. He played shortstop, second base, and left field; and he had even been a catcher. He stole a great many bases while he was with Philadelphia; but one of his teammates was the Billy Hamilton who had 115 stolen bases

to his credit, so Del earned no particular notice for his speed.

Delahanty was one of the most consistent hitters in baseball history, almost miraculous for his time, still listed among the leaders, and especially notable because the ball he hit was no juiced-up, cork-centered job manufactured to sail over fences, but the old dead ball, the pitcher's delight, often pounded out of shape, usually rough and darkened, frequently doctored by being scraped against a pitcher's spikes or belt buckle.

Del was not getting rich with the Philadelphia Nationals, even though people were crowding the parks to see him. When a man named Ban Johnson appeared with a new league and urged men to free themselves from the unjust and onerous chains of the reserve rule, Del happily accepted the invitation and jumped to the Washington team of the new American League, where he continued to powder the ball as thunderously as ever, leading the league in batting in 1902.

At the end of that season Delahanty accepted a fat offer from John McGraw, now manager of the New York Giants. Del felt now as if all his dreams had come true. Like most ballplayers of his day, Del wanted more than anything else to play in New York, where a man could really make a name for himself and stood a chance of finding some real money at last. But the sauce which Ban Johnson had so liberally doused upon the goose was apparently never meant to flavor the gander. The American League made peace with the National League, agreed to respect the reserve rule, and carefully sorted out all the players, returning the most recent contract jumpers to the teams they had played for in 1902.

Del was disappointed down to the very soles of his shoes; and he let loose curse words enough to keep a ball park supplied for a season. He had taken a $4,500 advance from McGraw and had had a tough season at the race tracks, anticipating the big money that lay ahead. He swore he'd never play for Washington again and made as if to report to New York, along with George Davis, another recalcitrant, who had jumped from Comiskey's American League White Sox. When the leadership of both leagues refused him any relief he wired the "outlaw" California State League for terms. Eventually, however, he went back to Washington, with the understanding, some said, that he would be traded to New York before the season was very old. He did have to pay back the $4500, however, and he was hard put to dig it up.

Delahanty started the 1903 season glumly, half wishing he had told the league to go to hell and had taken his chances in California. He began to find more and more comfort in the bottle; and over the bottle he brooded on his wrongs and on what his wife might be doing while he was on the road with the team. In Cleveland, after he had been consistently drunk for several days, he was suspended by Manager Loftus. Then he began to devote his full time to drinking. He accompanied the team to Detroit on July 3, left the ball park before the game was over and—when he was wearing as merry a jag as a man could buy—wired his wife to meet him in Washington, and bought a ticket on the first train for New York. He had no time to pack all his belongings; and he left a number of articles, including his uniform, in the hotel room while he raced to catch the 4:25 P.M. Michigan Central train for the East.

On the train the dining-car attendants saw fit to sell Big Ed five more drinks; and they were sufficient to put him further over the edge than he had ever been in his life before. Whereupon he set out to make merry, or at least to make noise, to shout his troubles to the world, and to find people who would stand and listen. By this time most of the people on the train were abed, so Del undertook to drag a few of them out where he could see them. The conductor remonstrated with him and found that Del was in no mood to be thwarted. There was a hell of a row; and when the train stopped at Fort Erie, Ontario, at the Canadian end of the International Bridge, Conductor Cole and a handful of mussed-up trainmen tossed Del out, to work off the railroad company's liquor on somebody else's—anybody else's—domain.

There was no one at the station to make even a pretense of restraining the half-crazed man. In a weeping rage Delahanty set out after the train, determined perhaps to show that crowd that he could still lick the lot of them if they'd stand still.

It was tricky going on the ties. It was far, far down to the rushing water; and the night was black dark. As Del approached the middle of the bridge an old man with a lantern appeared, flashed the lantern in his face, and told him to get the hell back, for the draw was open.

Delahanty tried to shove by the old man, a watchman named Kingston, and the two of them grappled there on the uneasy footing. They tugged and pushed and grunted and swore, then Kingston tore loose for a moment and, as men will, fumbled around for the hat that had been knocked off his head. He found the hat on the ties, jammed it down on his head, and turned to see the big fellow stumble away from him and suddenly drop out of sight in the dark.

Kingston's heart turned cold. There did not seem to be any noise at all, except the water and the far-off train. Then from far below someone called for help, again and again and again. Kingston recovered his lantern and picked his way on wobbling knees back to the station.

Big Ed Delahanty may perhaps have lost consciousness there, in the quick eddying water, or he may have held his head above the stream and kept calling into the dark, until at last a straight swift current held him and swept him down into the dreadful thunder of the Niagara Horseshoe Falls.

There was no one to know who the man was who had gone off the bridge in the night. Kingston gulped out his story when he found a man to talk to, then discovered that the hat he had jammed on his head was not his at all but the hat of the big man he had fought with.

In Washington Ed Delahanty's wife went nearly out of her mind while she tried to locate him by wiring friends in Detroit, New York, and Cleveland, where his boyhood home was. She had almost no money—Ed had been paying back his advance—and she had a small daughter to keep. Some of Ed's teammates laughed and said the big fellow would show up at the New York race tracks, don't worry. But Manager Loftus did worry; and he, too, sent wires to everyone Ed might have gone to see.

A week later Ed Delahanty's mangled body was found against a wharf twenty miles below the bridge, and identified by the teeth and the injured fingers. By that time the railroad had got around to identifying his luggage and connecting the stories of the conductor and the bridge tender. Delahanty, they said, had been scaring folks with an open razor. But Ed, his family knew, had used a safety razor all his life.

*　　*　　*

The gentle Indian was Louis Sockalexis, a Penobscot from Maine, whose amazing feats with a baseball were said to have inspired Gilbert Patten, another Maine man, to create the fiction character of Frank Merriwell. Sockalexis was no Frank Merriwell. He was just a ballplayer who might have been great.

Sockalexis played professional baseball in the Knox County League in Maine and soon received an invitation to attend Holy Cross, where baseball had sunk to a very low estate. Inasmuch as Louis had never been graduated from high school, he and many of his teammates—all recent recruits from the professional ranks—were put in a "special class" together. Within a year most of them were sufficiently educated to take up freshman subjects at the college; and many of them stayed at Holy Cross for a number of years, slowly gathering a very good education and helping make the ball team invincible. A few became successful lawyers and doctors after graduation.

But Sockalexis played just one season at Holy Cross, where he had a batting average of .444. He was expelled for drinking, went to Notre Dame, where he played one season, then accepted an invitation to join the Cleveland Spiders, who were soon renamed the Indians in his honor. He created a wild stir wherever he appeared that first season. Every time he came to bat, spectators would greet him with imitation Indian war whoops.

Sockalexis made a noble appearance. He had a fine gentle face and luxuriant hair. He was nearly as big as Delahanty, and he could run even faster. He did a hundred yards in ten seconds, with his baseball uniform on, which was about as fast as any man in the world could run in those days. There has never been a stronger throwing arm in the professional leagues than Louis Sockalexis owned. While he was touring with the Holy Cross team he used to give throwing exhibitions before each game.

He would stand in deep center field and hurl the ball in to the catcher, straight and fast as if he had pitched it from the mound, and high enough and true enough to be called a strike.

When Sockalexis first came to New York the newspapers featured his appearance as if it were to be a personal duel between him and Amos Rusie, who was then acknowledged by most sports writers to be the best pitcher in the National League. Sockalexis stepped up to the plate with the usual wild whoops ringing all around him. His face was perfectly impassive, yet mild and boyish; and he faced the great man as if he were just another college pitcher. When Rusie's famous blazing curve came down toward him, Sockalexis hammered it far into center field and sped around the bases for a home run before the New York team could even make a play on him.

In sixty-six games with Cleveland that first year, Sockalexis hit for .331, which was fairly good; and he began to drink whisky steadily, which was the end of him. He made sixteen outfield errors that year, faded at the bat his second year, and then trickled down into the minors. He played for a short time with Hartford and with Lowell, but soon stopped pretending he was a ballplayer. He became a street beggar, shuffling along the Hartford sidewalks, with the toes out of his shoes, and his hand extended for the few cents he needed to get a mouthful of whisky.

Eventually Sockalexis found his way back to Maine, where he died of heart trouble before he was forty. He left no records to prove his greatness, nothing but the wondering admiration of a few old men who had never seen a cleaner, more accurate swing or a better-muscled body, or ever known a ball to be hit so far as when Sockalexis hit it.

IF THIS ANTHOLOGY were limited to discussing only one game, I swan but what this might be the one. Here's everybody: Smoky Joe Wood and Christy Mathewson; Fred Snodgrass making his immortal muff of a fly ball and Fred Merkle nearly being charged with a boner as deathless as his failure to touch second against the Cubs in 1908; here are Buck Herzog and Red Murray, and Larry Doyle, Chief Meyers and Josh Devore; here is probably the greatest outfield of all time —Duffy Lewis, Harry Hooper and Tris Speaker. Speaker calls this his greatest day in baseball. I think he'd be right on batting orders alone.

1912:
Boston Red Sox 3,
New York Giants 2

——— **TRIS SPEAKER** ———
as told to FRANCIS J. POWERS

I'LL ALWAYS THINK of the 1912 season as one of the greatest in major league history. That's natural, for it was in 1912 that I first played with a pennant winner and world's championship team, and there are no greater thrills for a young player. Our Boston Red Sox, managed by Jake Stahl, a former University of Illinois star, won the American League pennant while the New York Giants were the winners on the National League side.

There were a couple of great teams. The Red Sox won 105 games that season for a league record that stood till the Yankees won 110 in 1926. And the Giants came home with 103 victories, and no other National League winner since touched that total till the Cardinals won 106 in 1942. Joe Wood won 34 games for us, almost one-third of our total, and 10 of them were shutouts.

Many a time I have heard Smoke say in our clubhouse meetings, "Get me two runs today and we'll win this one." Woody won sixteen in a row and beat Walter Johnson after the Big Train had won a similar string and no one has beaten those marks although they have been tied. We had Duffy Lewis and Harry Hooper in the outfield and there never were any better, Larry Gardner at third, Heinie Wagner at short and Buck O'Brien and Hugh Bedient on the pitching staff, just to mention some of our stars.

While Wood (and Johnson) made pitching history in the American League that summer Rube Marquard was writing an unequaled chapter in the National. The gangling, wry-necked left-hander won nineteen straight and no one has come along to wipe out that performance. Those Giants were a hard-hitting, fast-running team with the likes of Josh Devore, Red Murray, Buck Herzog, Chief Meyers and Fred Merkle and had great pitchers in Christy Mathewson, Marquard, Jeff Tesreau and Red Ames.

In the opening game of the World Series Woody beat Tesreau, 4 to 3. I guess maybe John McGraw figured Smoke would beat any of his pitchers, so he held Marquard and Mathewson back; although Tesreau was a great pitcher. The second game went eleven innings to a six-all tie with Matty pitching for the Giants and Bedient, Ray Collins and Charlie Hall, who died recently, working for Boston.

In the third game the Giants made it all even with Marquard getting a 2-1 decision over O'Brien. Then Wood and Bedient beat Tesreau and Mathewson in terrific 3-1 and 2-1 duels and we were ahead three games to one and it looked as if the series was about finished.

But the Giants weren't through by any means. In the sixth game, Marquard beat O'Brien and Collins and in the seventh, the Giants took a toe-hold and pounded Wood out of the box and kept on hammering O'Brien and Collins to win 11-4. So the series went into its eighth game on October 16 and that's where I had my biggest day.

McGraw called on Christy Mathewson with the chips down and that was natural for Matty still was in his prime; his fadeaway was tough to hit and he knew every angle of the pitching business. Since Wood already had worked three games, and had been beaten the day before, Stahl couldn't send him back, so he started Bedient.

The game quickly took the form of a magnificent pitchers' battle and I don't think Matty ever was much better than that autumn afternoon. He turned us back with machine-like precision for six innings and by that time the one run the Giants had scored in the third began to look awful big. I got a double into right field in the first inning but through six innings that was about our only scoring chance. The Giants got their run when Devore walked, advanced on two outs and scored when Red Murray hit a long double. That the Giants weren't another run to the good in the fifth was due to one of the greatest catches I ever saw. Larry Doyle hit a terrific drive to right that appeared headed for a home run but Harry Hooper cut it off with a running, leaping catch that was easily the outstanding play of the series.

Boston tied the score in the seventh due to confusion among the Giants. Stahl hit a Texas Leaguer toward left and it fell safe when Murray, Fred Snodgrass and Art Fletcher couldn't agree on who was to make the catch. Wagner walked and then Stahl sent Olaf Hendrickson up to bat for Bedient. Now Hendrickson was one of the greatest pinch-hitters ever in the game—like Moose McCormick of the Giants. He was one of those rare fellows who could go up cold and hit any sort of pitching. Matty worked hard on Hendrickson but the Swede belted a long double that scored Stahl. Then Joe Wood came in to pitch for us.

The score still was one-one going into the tenth and the Giants tried their best to put the game away in their half. Murray doubled again and he was the tough man for us all through the series and raced home on Merkle's single. So there we were behind again with the last chance coming up.

Once more the breaks and big breaks went our way. Clyde Engle batted for Woody and reached second when Snodgrass muffed his fly in center field. Hooper flied out and Yerkes worked Matty for a pass. And I was the next batter.

It looked as if I was out when I cut one of Matty's fadeaways and lifted a high foul between the plate and first base. The ball was drifting toward first and would have been an easy catch for Merkle. I was going to yell for Meyers to make the catch for I didn't think he could, but before I could open my mouth I heard Matty calling: "Meyers, Meyers."

Meyers chased the ball but it was going away from him and finally Merkle charged in but he was too late and couldn't hold the ball. Fred was blamed for not making the catch and the term "bonehead" was thrown at him again, recalling his failure to touch second base in 1908. I never thought Merkle deserved any blame at all. It was Matty who made the blunder in calling for Meyers to try for the catch.

That gave me a reprieve and I didn't miss the second chance. I got a good hold of a pitch for a single to right that scored Engle and the game was tied again. Then Matty walked Lewis, purposely, for Duffy always was a money hitter, filling the bases. With Gardner at bat the Giant infield played in close on the chance of cutting Yerkes off at the plate. But Gardner was another who did his best when the chips were on the table and crashed a long fly that sent Yerkes home with the deciding run.

I was in other World Series, but outside of the game between Cleveland and Brooklyn in 1920, when Bill Wambsganss made his unassisted triple play, I can't recall any when there was more drama and when there were more unusual incidents. It was a great thrill for me to manage the Cleveland Indians to the 1920 world's championship, with my mother looking on; but from strictly a playing angle, that single off Matty was my biggest moment.

SAFEST way to handle Mr. Arbuthnot is get him in here with everybody else.

The Cliché Expert Testifies on Baseball

FRANK SULLIVAN

Q—Mr. Arbuthnot, you state that your grandmother has passed away and you would like to have the afternoon off to go to her funeral.

A—That is correct.

Q—You are an expert in the clichés of baseball—right?

A—I pride myself on being well versed in the stereotypes of our national pastime.

Q—Well, we'll test you. Who plays baseball?

A—Big-league baseball is customarily played by brilliant outfielders, veteran hurlers, powerful sluggers, knuckle-ball artists, towering first basemen, key moundsmen, fleet base runners, ace southpaws, scrappy little shortstops, sensational war vets, ex-college stars, relief artists, rifle-armed twirlers, dependable mainstays, doughty right-handers, streamlined backstops, power-hitting batsmen, redoubtable infielders, erstwhile Dodgers, veteran sparkplugs, sterling moundsmen, aging twirlers, and rookie sensations.

Q—What other names are rookie sensations known by?

A—They are also known as aspiring rookies, sensational newcomers, promising freshmen, ex-sandlotters, highly touted striplings, and youngsters who will bear watching.

Q—What's the manager of a baseball team called?

A—A veteran pilot. Or youthful pilot. But he doesn't manage the team.

Q—No? What does he do?

A—He guides its destinies.

Q—How?

A—By the use of managerial strategy.

Q—Mr. Arbuthnot, please describe the average major-league-baseball athlete.

A—Well, he comes in three sizes, or types. The first type is tall, slim, lean, towering, rangy, huge, husky, big, strapping, sturdy, handsome, powerful, lanky, rawboned, and rugged.

Q—Quite a hunk of athlete.

A—Well, those are the adjectives usage requires for the description of the Type One, or Ted Williams, ballplayer.

Q—What is Type Two like?

A—He is chunky or stocky—that is to say, Yogi Berra.

Q—And the Third?

A—The third type is elongated and does not walk. He is Ol' Satchmo, or Satchel Paige.

Q—What do you mean Satchmo doesn't walk?

A—Not in the sports pages, he doesn't. He ambles.

Q—You mentioned a hurler, Mr. Arbuthnot. What is a hurler?

A—A hurler is a twirler.

Q—Well, what is a twirler?

A—A twirler is a flinger, a tosser. He's a moundsman.

Q—Moundsman?

A—Yes. He officiates on the mound. When the veteran pilot tells a hurler he is to twirl on a given day, that is a mound assignment, and the hurler who has been told to twirl is the mound nominee for that game.

Q—You mean he pitches?

A—That is right. You have cut the Gordian knot.

Q—What's the pitcher for the other team called?

A—He is the mound adversary, or mound opponent, of the mound nominee. That makes them rival hurlers, or twirlers. They face each other and have a mound duel, or pitchers' battle.

Q—Who wins?

A—The mound victor wins, and as a result he is a mound ace, or ace moundsman. He excels on the mound, or stars on it. He and the other moundsmen on his team are the mound corps.

Q—What happens to the mound nominee who loses the mound duel?

329

A—He is driven off the mound.

Q—What do you mean by that?

A—He's yanked. He's knocked out of the box.

Q—What's the box?

A—The box is the mound.

Q—I see. Why does the losing moundsman lose?

A—Because he issues, grants, yields, allows, or permits too many hits or walks, or both.

Q—A bit on the freehanded side, eh? Where does the mound victor go if he pitches the entire game?

A—He goes all the way.

Q—And how does the mound adversary who has been knocked out of the box explain his being driven off the mound?

A—He says, "I had trouble with my control," or "My curve wasn't working," or "I just didn't have anything today."

Q—What happens if a mound ace issues, grants, yields, allows, or permits too many hits and walks?

A—In that case, sooner or later, rumors are rife. Either that or they are rampant.

Q—Rife where?

A—In the front office.

Q—What's that?

A—That's the place where baseball's biggies—also known as baseball moguls—do their asking.

Q—What do they ask for?

A—Waivers on erratic southpaw.

Q—What are these baseball biggies further known as?

A—They are known as the Shrewd Mahatma or as Horace Stoneham, but if they wear their shirt open at the neck, they are known as Bill Veeck.

Q—What do baseball biggies do when they are not asking for waivers?

A—They count the gate receipts, buy promising rookies, sell aging twirlers, and stand loyally by Manager Durocher.

Q—And what does Manager Durocher do?

A—He guides the destinies of the Giants and precipitates arguments with the men in blue.

Q—What men in blue?

A—The umpires, or arbiters.

Q—What kind of arguments does Durocher precipitate?

A—Heated arguments.

Q—And the men in blue do what to him and other players who precipitate heated arguments?

A—They send, relegate, banish, or thumb them to the showers.

Q—Mr. Arbuthnot, how do you, as a cliché expert, refer to first base?

A—First base is the initial sack.

Q—And second base?

A—The keystone sack.

Q—What's third base called?

A—The hot corner. The first inning is the initial frame, and an inning without runs is a scoreless stanza.

Q—What is one run known as?

A—A lone run, but four runs are known as a quartet of tallies.

Q—What is a baseball?

A—The pill, the horsehide, the old apple, or the sphere.

Q—And what's a bat?

A—The bat is the willow, or the wagon tongue, or the piece of lumber. In the hands of a mighty batsman, it is the mighty bludgeon.

Q—What does a mighty batsman do?

A—He amasses runs. He connects with the old apple. He raps 'em out and he pounds 'em out. He belts 'em and he clouts 'em.

Q—Clouts what?

A—Circuit clouts.

Q—What are they?

A—Home runs. Know what the mighty batsman does to the mighty bludgeon?

Q—No. What?

A—He wields it. Know what kind of orgies he fancies?

Q—What kind?

A—Batting orgies. Slugfests. That's why his team pins.

Q—Pins what?

A—All its hopes on him.

Q—Mr. Arbuthnot, what is a runner guilty of when he steals home?

A—A plate theft.

Q—And how many kinds of baseball games are there?

A—Five main classifications: scheduled tussels, crucial contests, pivotal games, drab frays, and arc-light tussles.

Q—And what does the team that wins—

A—Sir, a baseball team never wins. It scores a victory, or gains one, or chalks one up. Or it snatches.

Q—Snatches what?

A—Victory from the jaws of defeat.

Q—How?

A—By a ninth-inning rally.

Q—I see. Well, what do the teams that chalk up victories do to the teams that lose?

A—They nip, top, wallop, trounce, rout, down, subdue, smash, drub, paste, trip, crush, curb, whitewash, erase, bop, slam, batter, check, hammer, pop, wham, clout, and blank the visitors. Or they zero them.

Q—Gracious sakes! Now I know why ballplayers are old at thirty-five.

A—Oh, that isn't the half of it. They do other things to the visitors.

Q—Is it possible?

A—Certainly. They jolt them, or deal them a jolt. They also halt, sock, thump, larrup, vanquish, flatten, scalp, shellac, blast, slaughter, K.O., mow down, topple, whack, pound, rap, sink, baffle, thwart, foil, maul, and nick.

Q—Do the losers do anything at all to the victors?

A—Yes. They bow to the victors. And they taste.

Q—Taste what?

A—Defeat. They trail. They take a drubbing, pasting, or shellacking. They are in the cellar.

Q—What about the victors?

A—They loom as flag contenders. They're in the first division.

* * *

Q—Mr. Arbuthnot, what is the first sign of spring?

A—Well, a robin, of course.

Q—Yes, but I'm thinking of our subject here. How about when the ballplayers go south for spring training?

A—Ballplayers don't go south for spring training.

Q—Why, they do!

A—They do *not*. They wend their way southward.

Q—Oh, I see. Well, do all ballplayers wend their way southward?

A—No. One remains at home.

Q—Who is he?

A—The lone holdout.

Q—Why does the lone holdout remain at home?

A—He refuses to ink pact.

Q—What do you mean by that?

A—He won't affix his Hancock to his contract.

Q—Why not?

A—He demands a pay hike, or salary boost.

Q—From whom?

A—From baseball's biggies.

Q—And what do baseball's biggies do to the lone holdout?

A—They attempt to lure him back into the fold.

Q—How?

A—By offering him new contract.

Q—What does lone holdout do then?

A—He weighs offer. If he doesn't like it, he balks at terms. If he does like it, he inks pact and gets pay hike.

Q—How much pay hike?

A—An undisclosed amount in excess of.

Q—That makes him what?

A—One of the highest-paid baseball stars in the annals of the game, barring Ruth.

Q—What if baseball's biggies won't give lone holdout pay hike?

A—In that case, lone holdout takes pay cut, old salary, or job in filling station in home town.

Q—Now, when baseball players reach the spring training camp and put on their uniforms—

A—May I correct you again, sir? Baseball players do not put on uniforms. They don them.

Q—I see. What for?

A—For a practice session or strenuous workout.

Q—And why must they have a strenuous workout?

A—Because they must shed the winter's accumulation of excess avoirdupois.

Q—You mean they must lose weight?

A—You put it in a nutshell. They must be streamlined, so they plunge.

Q—Plunge into what?

A—Into serious training.

Q—Can't get into serious training except by plunging, eh?

A—No. Protocol requires that they plunge. Training season gets under way in Grapefruit and Citrus Leagues. Casey Stengel bars night life.

Q—Mr. Arbuthnot, what is the opening game of the season called?

A—Let me see-e-e. It's on the tip of my tongue. Isn't that aggravating? Ah, I have it— the opener! At the opener, fifty-two thousand two hundred and ninety-three fans watch Giants bow to Dodgers.

Q—What do those fifty-two thousand two hundred and ninety-three fans constitute?

A—They constitute fandom.

Q—And how do they get into the ballpark?

A—They click through the turnstiles.

Q—Now, then, Mr. Arbuthnot, the climax of the baseball season is the World Series, is it not?

A—That's right.

Q—And what is the World Series called?

A—It's the fall classic, or crucial contest,

also known as the fray, the epic struggle, and the Homeric struggle. It is part of the American scene, like ham and eggs or pumpkin pie. It's a colorful event.

Q—What is it packed with?

A—Thrills. Drama.

Q—What kind of drama?

A—Sheer or tense.

Q—Why does it have to be packed with thrills and drama?

A—Because if it isn't, it becomes drab fray.

Q—Where does the fall classic take place?

A—In a vast municipal stadium or huge ball park.

Q—And the city in which the fall classic is held is what?

A—The city is baseball mad.

Q—And the hotels?

A—The hotels are jammed. Rooms are at a premium.

Q—Tickets, also, I presume.

A—Tickets? If you mean the cards of admission to the fall classic, they are referred to as elusive series ducats, and they *are* at a premium, though I would prefer to say that they are scarcer than the proverbial hen's teeth.

Q—Who attends the series?

A—A milling throng, or great outpouring of fans.

Q—What does the great outpouring of fans do?

A—It storms the portals and, of course, clicks through the turnstiles.

Q—Causing what?

A—Causing attendance records to go by the board. Stands fill early.

Q—What else does the crowd do?

A—It yells itself hoarse. Pent-up emotions are released. It rides the men in blue.

Q—What makes a baseball biggie unhappy on the morning of a series tussle?

A—Leaden skies.

Q—Who is to blame for leaden skies?

A—A character known to the scribes as Jupiter Pluvius, or Jupe.

Q—What does rain dampen?

A—The ardor of the fans.

Q—If the weather clears, who gets credit for that?

A—Another character, known as Old Sol.

Q—Now, the team that wins the series—

A—Again, I'm sorry to correct you, sir. A team does not win a series. It wraps it up. It clinches it.

Q—Well, then what?

A—Then the newly crowned champions re-

pair to their locker room.

Q—What reigns in that locker room?

A—Pandemonium, bedlam, and joy.

Q—Expressed how?

A—By lifting youthful pilot, or his equivalent, to the shoulders of his teammates.

Q—In the locker room of the losers, what is as thick as a day in—I mean so thick you could cut it with a knife?

A—Gloom. The losers are devoid.

Q—Devoid of what?

A—Animation.

Q—Why?

A—Because they came apart at the seams in the pivotal tussle.

Q—What happens to the newly crowned champions later?

A—They are hailed, acclaimed, and fêted. They receive mighty ovations, boisterous demonstrations, and thunderous welcomes.

Q—And when those are over?

A—They split the series purse and go hunting.

Q—Mr. Arbuthnot, if a powerful slugger or mighty batsman wields a mighty bludgeon to such effect that he piles up a record number of circuit clouts, what does that make him?

A—That is very apt to make him most valuable player of the year.

Q—And that?

A—That makes the kids of America look up to him as their hero.

Q—If most valuable player of the year continues the batting orgies that make the kids of America worship him, what then?

A—Then he becomes one of Baseball's Immortals. He is enshrined in Baseball's Hall of Fame.

Q—And after that?

A—Someday he retires and becomes veteran scout, or veteran coach, or veteran pilot. Or sports broadcaster.

Q—And then?

A—Well, eventually a memorial plaque is unveiled to him at the opener.

Q—Thank you, Mr. Arbuthnot. You have been most helpful. I won't detain you any longer, and I hope your grandmother's funeral this afternoon is a tense drama packed with thrills.

A—Thanks a lot. Good-by now.

Q—Hold on a moment, Mr. Arbuthnot. Just for my own curiosity—couldn't you have said "thanks" and "good-by" and let it go at that, without adding that "lot" and "now" malarkey?

A—I could have, but it would have cost me my title as a cliché expert.

(Top) At the Little League World Series.
(Bottom) Who knows? Just be glad *you* aren't in it.

United Press

Sport **Magazine**

SMALL FRY

SANDLOT BASEBALL

Waiting for the signal

Fancy Dan

Slugger

Circus catch

"Here it is. Take a good look at it."

Three easy outs

Rookie

Relief pitcher warming up

Butterfingers

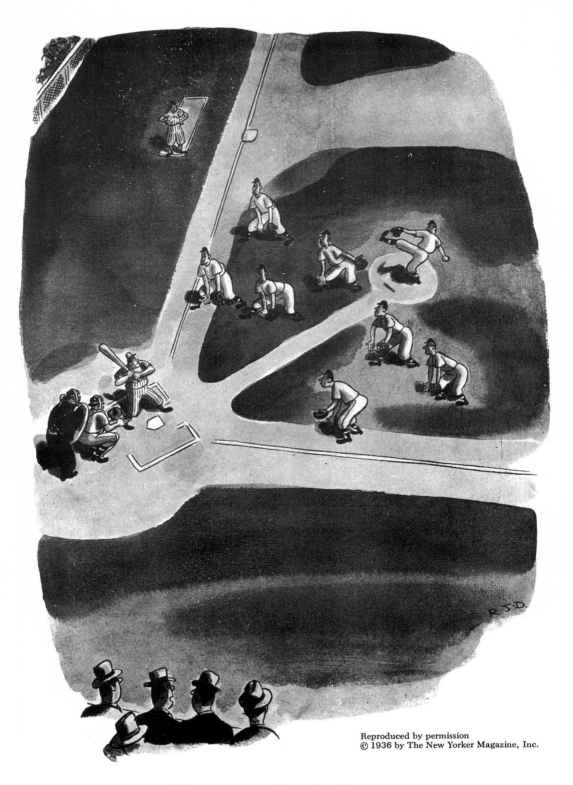

"They must expect him to bunt."

THE Reverend Billy Sunday was a renowned ballplayer in his time—you will find a passing but admiring reference to his speed on the bases in the Frank Menke piece elsewhere in this collection—and his heart was always with the game ("The greatest of all sports—baseball!"). The following article appeared in *Collier's* in 1908. Perhaps James Farrell's Danny O'Neill missed it.

All-American Baseball Team

REV. W. A. (BILLY) SUNDAY

Now I have named my men, and as I finish the task I feel the old baseball fever churning in my veins. It is the best of all games—this baseball—and I am twenty years younger today as I think my way back into days of old; the valiant deeds of the gladiators of the diamond of those days are forever enshrined in my heart. No lapse of time can ever efface them. I am not an old-timer today—I am young in heart, for time is measured by heartbeats, not by gray hairs and a bald spot. I am back on the diamond! Mike Kelly on the coaching line, yelling like a Comanche Indian! Anson at bat! Everybody breathless! "Whang!" The ball sails out over the fielders, the winning run crosses the plate, the shouts of triumph ring out, and we gather up our bats and go to the clubhouse. But I have not backslid; my interest and love for the old game have ever been intense, warm, and true. I believe baseball to be the cleanest sport in America, and I never miss an opportunity to go on record as its uncompromising friend. Gamblers have never been able to creep in and spoil the game. Men in control, both magnates and players, have always been united in the effort to keep the game clean. All this talk about baseball being crooked, the game being decided before it is played, is all bosh. Such a charge is an unmitigated lie. This is my conviction, and I would back up my statement with my reputation and all I have. I love baseball. I know the game is clean and will not allow to go unchallenged any false statements. Then, too, the game is not only clean but democratic—no favorites here. On the bleachers and in the grandstand all meet on a common level.

The old-time fan may have a Wall Street broker, a college president, and a few others gather about him or sit close, in order to get pointers and listen to his "dope," but that's not favoritism! It is this democratic spirit and this cleanness that have given baseball such a grip on the American people.

There has never been witnessed such a magnificent contest as has been fought this year. No wonder the strain proved too much for my friend Frank De Hass Robinson. I do not believe the individual players of today are superior in ability to those of twenty years ago. Who can surpass such giants of the diamond as Ewing, Kelly, Conner, Keefe, Bennett, Anson, Pfeiffer, Dunlap, Brouthers, Galvin, Clarkson, Radbourne, O'Rourke, Comiskey, Browning, Nash, Gore, and old Sam Thompson? However, the game has become more scientific; in fact, baseball, or at least the teamwork, is now a perfect science, while formerly it was a "batting fest."

Now, in conclusion, I want to say a word to the boys of the diamond, those who are now in their prime. You will not take this as a "preachment"—you will take the advice of an old-timer in the spirit in which it is given, for I am deeply interested in you. Ballplayers, as a rule, are the best class of hale-fellows-well-met that can be found on the face of God's dirt. I would not have you be "grouchers" and "tightwads." No; if you were such, I could not be proud of the men of my old profession, but sometimes a man is a "good fellow" to his own hurt, and to the hurt of his loved ones.

Fellows, listen to me! You will not always be in the spotlight. Your eye will grow dim

—you will get a glass arm or a Charley horse —down will come the "is" and up will go the "was" and you are all in, and pork and beans for yours. You work hard for your money. Get all you can and can all you get! Pass up the booze like a pay car does a tramp, or a WCTU Convention passes up a brewery wagon.

Now a clip from history and I'll break my quill, for I am not a scribe anyway. It was just twenty-two years ago that I walked down State Street, Chicago, in company with some ballplayers whose names were world-renowned. We dropped into a booze joint, tanked up, and sauntered down to the corner of State and Van Buren Streets, where we sat on the curbstone to listen to some men and women who stood on the street corner singing gospel hymns—songs that I had heard my dear old mother sing in the old log cabin out in Iowa. A feeling irresistible shot through me and I bowed my head to hide the tears. Then I said "Good-by, boys, I am done with this way of living." And, saying this, I dropped into the Pacific Garden Mission, at 100 East Van Buren Street, and yielded myself to God. But the battle came later, when I joined the church and the newspapers printed columns of comment. I dreaded to go to the grounds to practice for fear of the horselaugh the boys would give me; but, imagine my surprise, when I walked in the first man to meet me was Mike Kelly. Mike had a heart in him as big as a woman's heart. He said: "Bill, I ain't long on religion, but if old Kell can help you, let me know." Up came Cap. Anson, Pfeiffer, Williamson, Gore—in fact, every man gave me the glad hand. That day we played Detroit, and in that game I prayed my first prayer. Clarkson was pitching, Kelly catching. John could sail them over so fast the thermometer would drop two degrees as the ball whizzed past the batter. We had them beat last half ninth, two were on bases, two out, Charley Bennett at bat. Charley could not touch a high-and-in ball, but could kill a low one. John shot one over and it went low—Charley caught it on the nose and out to right center she came. It was up to me. I turned and ran with all my might, and I said: "O God! If ever you helped mortal man in your life, help me get that ball, and you haven't much time to decide." I looked over my shoulder and saw the ball near—I shot out my left hand, the ball struck and stuck. You can't convince me God did not help me that day, because I tried to "trot square."

And now, here is my heart! And here is my hand and best wishes to the boys and the greatest of all sports—baseball!

THE TEAM
Donlin, cf.

Clarke, lf.   Cobb, rf.
Lajoie, 2b.
Wagner, ss.
Bradley, 3b.   Chance, 1b.
Mathewson, p. Brown, p. Walsh, p.
Joss, p. Johnson, p. Waddell, p.
Kling, c. Bresnahan, c. Sullivan, c.
Hofman and Isbell,   Stone, outfield
utility infield

FIRST BASE and CAPTAIN—Chance. He has proved by past and present work that he is a great player, fast on the bases, a reliable batter, a great first-sacker, and a magnificent leader. Chase is a more finished player and very fast; and Tenney, if a few years younger, would make them all hustle. Jordan is also a great player.

SECOND BASE—Lajoie. He works as noiselessly as a Corliss engine, makes hard plays easy, is great in a pinch, and never gets cold feet. Evers is coming at a furious clip—thinks quickly and acts like a steel trap; he is second choice.

SHORTSTOP—Wagner. He is in a class alone. "Hats off to Hans!" I fail to find a flaw. He is always there with the goods, express charges prepaid. Wallace is next choice.

THIRD BASE—This is difficult to decide, but, all considered, I will give it to Bradley, although Steinfeldt and Devlin are princes in their positions. Bradley is great on bunts, and as good a batter as the others—is fast on bases and a good thrower—big, angular, just the build for a third-baser, a run-getter, and runs win. Devlin is second choice.

RIGHT FIELD—Cobb. I think most players in both leagues, without protest, will give the palm to Ty. He is as fast as the Twentieth Century Limited, and a heady player. Magee of the Phillies suits me too.

CENTER FIELD—Donlin. Mike is a ballplayer, every inch, works all the time. Some players are no good after they reach second; they have made their base hit, stolen second, and are satisfied, and they might as well cross the diamond to the bench; but Mike goes for all there is in him for the home plate, and you must touch the rubber to count. Stone of St. Louis is second choice.

LEFT FIELD—Clarke of Pittsburgh looks

good to me. He is the game all the way. Jones of the Sox has all the earmarks, but after wrestling with the problem for three hours, it's Clarke.

PITCHERS—And now I am up against it good and hard for pitchers. There are a multitude of headliners. Rhoades, McQuillen, Powell, Cy Young, White, Donovan, Smith, Willis, Overall, Reulbach, Wiltse, and half a dozen others, but I would choose Mathewson, Brown, Walsh, Joss, Johnson, and Waddell, assuming that Rube's eccentricities are not overemphasized. For consistent work, under all conditions, and to meet all clubs and make good, week in and week out, and go all the way, I pick the above. I choose Johnson because he is young and has shown himself a wonder, and I believe him destined to be a great pitcher.

CATCHERS—Kling, Bresnahan, Sullivan. Kling is a general, runs the team when behind the bat—the pitchers bank on his judgment. Bresnahan is more aggressive, but a clean fighter. Sullivan is as reliable as Texas for a Democratic majority.

UTILITY MEN—Stone for outfield, Hofman and Isbell for infield. I regard Hofman and Issy as the best utility men in the business—you can assign them any position and they are there with the "cap and bells."

JOHN GALLAGHER

Courtesy *Sport* Magazine. ©

"Hey! You guys are supposed to be in Chicago!"

WHEN the following stanzas first appeared, in the San Francisco *Examiner* of June 3, 1888, they bore the author's own subtitle "A Ballad of the Republic." Remarkable prophecy! Remarkable ballad!

Casey at the Bat

ERNEST L. THAYER

The outlook wasn't brilliant for the Mudville nine that day;
The score stood four to two with but one inning more to play;
And then, when Cooney died at first, and Barrows did the same,
A sickly silence fell upon the patrons of the game.

A struggling few got up to go, in deep despair. The rest
Clung to that hope which "springs eternal in the human breast";
They thought, If only Casey could but get a whack at that,
We'd put up even money now, with Casey at the bat.

But Flynn preceded Casey, as did also Jimmy Blake,
And the former was a lulu and the latter was a cake;
So, upon that stricken multitude grim melancholy sat,
For there seemed but little chance of Casey's getting to the bat.

But Flynn let drive a single, to the wonderment of all,
And Blake, the much despised, tore the cover off the ball,
And when the dust had lifted and men saw what had occurred,
There was Jimmy safe at second, and Flynn a-huggin' third.

Then from five thousand throats and more there rose a lusty yell,
It rumbled through the valley; it rattled in the dell;
It knocked upon the mountain and recoiled upon the flat,
For Casey, mighty Casey, was advancing to the bat.

There was ease in Casey's manner as he stepped into his place;
There was pride in Casey's bearing and a smile on Casey's face,
And when, responding to the cheers, he lightly doffed his hat,
No stranger in the crowd could doubt 'twas Casey at the bat.

Ten thousand eyes were on him as he rubbed his hands with dirt;
Five thousand tongues applauded when he wiped them on his
    shirt.
Then, while the writhing pitcher ground the ball into his hip,
Defiance gleamed in Casey's eye, a sneer curled Casey's lip.

And now the leather-covered sphere came hurtling through the
    air,
And Casey stood a-watching it in haughty grandeur there,
Close by the sturdy batsman the ball unheeded sped—
"That ain't my style," said Casey. "Strike one," the umpire said.

From the benches, black with people, there went up a muffled
  roar,
Like the beating of the storm-waves on a stern and distant shore.
"Kill him; kill the umpire!" shouted someone from the stand;—
And it's likely they'd have killed him had not Casey raised his
  hand.

With a smile of Christian charity great Casey's visage shone;
He stilled the rising tumult; he bade the game go on;
He signaled to the pitcher, and once more the spheroid flew;
But Casey still ignored it, and the umpire said, "Strike two."

"Fraud," cried the maddened thousands, and echo answered
  "Fraud,"
But one scornful look from Casey, and the multitude was awed.
They saw his face grow stern and cold; they saw his muscles
  strain,
And they knew that Casey wouldn't let that that ball go by again.

The sneer is gone from Casey's lip; his teeth are clenched in hate;
He pounds with cruel violence his bat upon the plate.
And now the pitcher holds the ball, and now he lets it go,
And now the air is shattered by the force of Casey's blow.

Oh! somewhere in this favored land the sun is shining bright;
The band is playing somewhere, and somewhere hearts are light.
And somewhere men are laughing, and somewhere children
  shout;
But there is no joy in Mudville—mighty Casey has Struck Out.

ALBERT G. SPALDING, a star pitcher of the 1860s and recognized in the Hall of Fame as "organizational genius of baseball's pioneer days," issued in 1911 a remarkably complete baseball almanac, called *America's National Game*. From that book comes this letter, which to me is absolute delight, not only for its contents but for the sheer musicality of the line "Thatcher was the catcher," and the fact that the wording bears striking resemblance to a Sherlock Holmes adventure.

A Letter to A. G. Spalding

FRED W. THAYER

116 FEDERAL STREET
BOSTON, MAY 18, 1911

MY DEAR MR. SPALDING:

I am in receipt of your favor of the 9th instant. You shall have the facts in regard to the catcher's mask, and I think you can feel assured that the data are all correct.

In order to give you the whole story I shall have to ask you to go back to the year '76 that you may know what the conditions were in Harvard Base Ball matters.

Thatcher was the catcher in the season of '76. He left college at the end of the year.

You will recall the fact that college nines especially had rarely more than one, possibly two, substitutes, and these were "general utility" men.

Tyng was the best all-around natural ballplayer of my time. He had played third base, center field, and helped out in other positions, including catcher, in the season of '76. In one or two games in which he caught behind the bat he had been hit by foul tips and had become more or less timid.

He was, by all odds, the most available man as catcher for the season of '77, and it was up to me to find some way to bring back his confidence.

The fencing mask naturally gave me the hint as to the protection for the face, and then it was up to me to devise some means of having the impact of the blow kept from driving the mask onto the face. The forehead and chin rest accomplished this and also made it possible for me to secure a patent, which I did in the winter of 1878.

Tyng practiced catching with the mask, behind the bat, in the gymnasium during the winter of '77, and became so thoroughly proficient that foul tips had no further terrors for him.

The first match game in which the mask was used was on Fast Day, in Lynn, against the Live Oaks, in April 1877. Thereafter the Harvard catcher used it in all games.

I hope this will give you the data which you wish. At all events it gives you the real facts in regard to the Base Ball mask.

Yours faithfully,
(signed) FRED W. THAYER.

FACT frequently inspires fiction, but the only case I know of where the reverse applied in baseball is here—Mr. Thurber's hilarious story, which, ten years later, as a picture elsewhere in this volume shows, came startlingly true.

You Could Look It Up

JAMES THURBER

IT ALL BEGUN when we dropped down to C'lumbus, Ohio, from Pittsburgh to play a exhibition game on our way out to St. Louis. It was gettin' on into September, and though we'd been leadin' the league by six, seven games most of the season, we was now in first place by a margin you could 'a' got it into the eye of a thimble, bein' only a half a game ahead of St. Louis. Our slump had given the boys the leapin' jumps, and they was like a bunch a old ladies at a lawn fete with a thunderstorm comin' up, runnin' around snarlin' at each other, eatin' bad and sleepin' worse, and battin' for a team average of maybe .186. Half the time nobody'd speak to nobody else, without it was to bawl 'em out.

Squawks Magrew was managin' the boys at the time, and he was darn near crazy. They called him "Squawks" 'cause when things was goin' bad he lost his voice, or perty near lost it, and squealed at you like a little girl you stepped on her doll or somethin'. He yelled at everybody and wouldn't listen to nobody, without maybe it was me. I'd been trainin' the boys for ten year, and he'd take more lip from me than from anybody else. He knowed I was smarter'n him, anyways, like you're goin' to hear.

This was thirty, thirty-one year ago; you could look it up, 'cause it was the same year C'lumbus decided to call itself the Arch City, on account of a lot of iron arches with electric-light bulbs into 'em which stretched acrost High Street. Thomas Albert Edison sent 'em a telegram, and they was speeches and maybe even President Taft opened the celebration by pushin' a button. It was a great week for the Buckeye capital, which was why they got us out there for this exhibition game.

Well, we just lose a double-header to Pittsburgh, 11 to 5 and 7 to 3, so we snarled all the way to C'lumbus, where we put up at the Chittaden Hotel, still snarlin'. Everybody was tetchy, and when Billy Klinger took a sock at Whitey Cott at breakfast, Whitey threwed marmalade all over his face.

"Blind each other, whatta I care?" says Magrew. "You can't see nothin' anyways."

C'lumbus win the exhibition game, 3 to 2, whilst Magrew set in the dugout, mutterin' and cursin' like a fourteen-year-old Scotty. He bad-mouthed everybody on the ball club and he bad-mouthed everybody offa the ball club, includin' the Wright brothers, who, he claimed, had yet to build a airship big enough for any of our boys to hit it with a ball bat.

"I wisht I was dead," he says to me. "I wisht I was in heaven with the angels."

I told him to pull hisself together, 'cause he was drivin' the boys crazy, the way he was goin' on, sulkin' and bad-mouthin' and whinin'. I was older'n he was and smarter'n he was, and he knowed it. I was ten times smarter'n he was about this Pearl du Monville, first time I ever laid eyes on the little guy, which was one of the saddest days of my life.

Now, most people name of Pearl is girls, but this Pearl du Monville was a man, if you could call a fella a man who was only thirty-four, thirty-five inches high. Pearl du Monville was a midget. He was part French and part Hungarian, and maybe even part Bulgarian or somethin'. I can see him now, a sneer on his little pushed-in pan, swingin' a bamboo cane and smokin' a big cigar. He had a gray suit with a big black check into it, and he had a gray felt hat with one of them rainbow-colored hatbands onto it, like the young fellas wore in them days. He talked like he was talkin' into a tin can, but he didn't have no foreign accent. He might 'a' been fifteen or he might 'a' been a hundred, you couldn't tell. Pearl du Monville.

After the game with C'lumbus, Magrew headed straight for the Chittaden bar—the train for St. Louis wasn't goin' for three, four hours—and there he set, drinkin' rye and talkin' to this bartender.

"How I pity me, brother," Magrew was tellin' this bartender. "How I pity me." That was alwuz his favorite tune. So he was settin' there, tellin' this bartender how heartbreakin' it was to be manager of a bunch a blindfolded circus clowns, when up pops this Pearl du Monville outa nowheres.

It give Magrew the leapin' jumps. He thought at first maybe the D.T.'s had come back on him; he claimed he'd had 'em once, and little guys had popped up all around him, wearin' red, white and blue hats.

"Go on, now!" Magrew yells. "Get away from me!"

But the midget clumb up on a chair acrost the table from Magrew and says, "I seen that game today, Junior, and you ain't got no ball club. What you got there, Junior," he says, "is a side show."

"Whatta ya mean, 'Junior'?" says Magrew, touchin' the little guy to satisfy hisself he was real.

"Don't pay him no attention, mister," says the bartender. "Pearl calls everybody 'Junior,' 'cause it alwuz turns out he's a year older'n anybody else."

"Yeh?" says Magrew. "How old is he?"

"How old are you, Junior?" says the midget.

"Who, me? I'm fifty-three," says Magrew.

"Well, I'm fifty-four," says the midget.

Magrew grins and asts him what he'll have, and that was the beginnin' of their beautiful friendship, if you don't care what you say.

Pearl du Monville stood up on his chair and waved his cane around and pretended like he was ballyhooin' for a circus. "Right this way, folks!" he yells. "Come on in and see the greatest collection of freaks in the world! See the armless pitchers, see the eyeless batters, see the infielders with five thumbs!" and on and on like that, feedin' Magrew gall and handin' him a laugh at the same time, you might say.

You could hear him and Pearl du Monville hootin' and hollerin' and singin' way up to the fourth floor of the Chittaden, where the boys was packin' up. When it come time to go to the station, you can imagine how disgusted we was when we crowded into the doorway of that bar and seen them two singin' and goin' on.

"Well, well, well," says Magrew, lookin' up and spottin' us. "Look who's here. . . . Clowns, this is Pearl du Monville, a monseer of the old, old school. . . . Don't shake hands with 'em, Pearl, 'cause their fingers is made of chalk and would bust right off in your paws," he says, and he starts guffawin' and Pearl starts titterin' and we stand there givin' 'em the iron eye, it bein' the lowest ebb a ball-club manager'd got hisself down to since the national pastime was started.

Then the midget begun givin' us the ballyhoo. "Come on in!" he says, wavin' his cane. "See the legless base runners, see the outfielders with the butter fingers, see the southpaw with the arm of a little chee-ild!"

Then him and Magrew begun to hoop and holler and nudge each other till you'd of thought this little guy was the funniest guy than even Charlie Chaplin. The fellas filed outa the bar without a word and went on up to the Union Depot, leavin' me to handle Magrew and his new-found crony.

Well, I got 'em outa there finely. I had to take the little guy along, 'cause Magrew had a holt onto him like a vise and I couldn't pry him loose.

"He's comin' along as masket," says Magrew, holdin' the midget in the crouch of his arm like a football. And come along he did, hollerin' and protestin' and beatin' at Magrew with his little fists.

"Cut it out, will ya, Junior?" the little guy kept whinin'. "Come on, leave a man loose, will ya, Junior?"

But Junior kept a holt onto him and begun yellin', "See the guys with the glass arm, see the guys with the cast-iron brains, see the fielders with the feet on their wrists!"

So it goes, right through the whole Union Depot, with people starin' and catcallin', and he don't put the midget down till he gets him through the gates.

"How'm I goin' to go along without no toothbrush?" the midget asts. "What'm I goin' to do without no other suit?" he says.

"Doc here," says Magrew, meanin' me—"doc here will look after you like you was his own son, won't you, doc?"

I give him the iron eye, and he finely got on the train and prob'ly went to sleep with his clothes on.

This left me alone with the midget. "Lookit," I says to him. "Why don't you go on home now? Come mornin', Magrew'll forget all about you. He'll prob'ly think you was some- thin' he seen in a nightmare maybe. And he ain't goin' to laugh so easy in the mornin', neither," I says. "So why don't you go on home?"

"Nix," he says to me. "Skiddoo," he says, "twenty-three for you," and he tosses his cane up into the vestibule of the coach and clam'ers on up after it like a cat. So that's the way Pearl du Monville come to go to St. Louis with the ball club.

I seen 'em first at breakfast the next day, settin' opposite each other; the midget playin' "Turkey in the Straw" on a harmonium and Magrew starin' at his eggs and bacon like they was a uncooked bird with its feathers still on.

"Remember where you found this?" I says, jerkin' my thumb at the midget. "Or maybe you think they come with breakfast on these trains," I says, bein' a good hand at turnin' a sharp remark in them days.

The midget puts down the harmonium and turns on me. "Sneeze," he says; "your brains is dusty." Then he snaps a couple drops of water at me from a tumbler. "Drown," he says, tryin' to make his voice deep.

Now, both them cracks is Civil War cracks, but you'd of thought they was brand-new and the funniest than any crack Magrew'd ever heard in his whole life. He started hoopin' and hollerin', and the midget started hoopin' and hollerin', so I walked on away and set down with Bugs Courtney and Hank Metters, payin' no attention to this weak-minded Damon and Phidias acrost the aisle.

Well, sir, the first game with St. Louis was rained out, and there we was facin' a double- header next day. Like maybe I told you, we lose the last three double-headers we play, makin' maybe twenty-five errors in the six games, which is all right for the intimates of a school for the blind, but is disgraceful for the world's champions. It was too wet to go to the zoo, and Magrew wouldn't let us go to the movies, 'cause they flickered so bad in them days. So we just set around, stewin' and frettin'.

One of the newspaper boys come over to take a pitture of Billy Klinger and Whitey Cott shakin' hands—this reporter'd heard about the fight—and whilst they was standin' there, toe to toe, shakin' hands, Billy give a back lunge and a jerk, and throwed Whitey over his shoulder into a corner of the room, like a sack a salt. Whitey come back at him with a chair, and Bethlehem broke loose in that there room.

The camera was tromped to pieces like a berry basket. When we finely got 'em pulled apart, I heard a laugh, and there was Magrew and the midget standin' in the door and givin' us the iron eye.

"Wrasslers," says Magrew, cold-like, "that's what I got for a ball club, Mr. du Monville, wrasslers—and not very good wrasslers at that, you ast me."

"A man can't be good at everythin'," says Pearl, "but he oughta be good at somethin'."

This sets Magrew guffawin' again, and away they go, the midget taggin' along by his side like a hound dog and handin' him a fast line of so-called comic cracks.

When we went out to face that battlin' St. Louis club in a double-header the next after- noon, the boys was jumpy as tin toys with keys in their back. We lose the first game, 7 to 2, and are trailin', 4 to 0, when the second game ain't but ten minutes old. Magrew set there like a stone statue, speakin' to nobody. Then, in their half a the fourth, somebody singled to center and knocked in two more runs for St. Louis.

That made Magrew squawk. "I wisht one thing," he says. "I wisht I was manager of a old ladies' sewin' circus 'stead of a ball club."

"You are, Junior, you are," says a familyer and disagreeable voice.

It was that Pearl du Monville again, poppin' up outa nowheres, swingin' his bamboo cane and smokin' a cigar that's three sizes too big for his face. By this time we'd finely got the other side out, and Hank Metters slithered a bat acrost the ground, and the midget had to jump to keep both his ankles from bein' broke.

I thought Magrew'd bust a blood vessel. "You hurt Pearl and I'll break your neck!" he yelled.

Hank muttered somethin' and went on up to the plate and struck out.

We managed to get a couple runs acrost in our half a the sixth, but they come back with three more in their half a the seventh, and this was too much for Magrew.

"Come on, Pearl," he says. "We're gettin' outa here."

"Where you think you're goin'?" I ast him.

"To the lawyer's again," he says cryptly.

"I didn't know you'd been to the lawyer's once, yet," I says.

"Which that goes to show how much you don't know," he says.

With that, they was gone, and I didn't see

'em the rest of the day, nor know what they was up to, which was a God's blessin'. We lose the nightcap, 9 to 3, and that puts us into second place plenty, and as low in our mind as a ball club can get.

The next day was a horrible day, like anybody that lived through it can tell you. Practice was just over and the St. Louis club was takin' the field, when I hears this strange sound from the stands. It sounds like the nervous whickerin' a horse gives when he smells somethin' funny on the wind. It was the fans ketchin' sight of Pearl du Monville, like you have prob'ly guessed. The midget had popped up onto the field all dressed up in a minacher club uniform, sox, cap, little letters sewed onto his chest, and all. He was swingin' a kid's bat and the only thing kept him from lookin' like a real ballplayer seen through the wrong end of a microscope was this cigar he was smokin'.

Bugs Courtney reached over and jerked it outa his mouth and throwed it away. "You're wearin' that suit on the playin' field," he says to him, severe as a judge. "You go insultin' it and I'll take you out to the zoo and feed you to the bears."

Pearl just blowed some smoke at him which he still has in his mouth.

Whilst Whitey was foulin' off four or five prior to strikin' out, I went on over to Magrew. "If I was as comic as you," I says, "I'd laugh myself to death," I says. "Is that any way to treat the uniform, makin' a mockery out of it?"

"It might surprise you to know I ain't makin' no mockery outa the uniform," says Magrew. "Pearl du Monville here has been made a bone-of-fida member of this so-called ball club. I fixed it up with the front office by long-distance phone."

"Yeh?" I says. "I can just hear Mr. Dillworth or Bart Jenkins agreein' to hire a midget for the ball club. I can just hear 'em." Mr. Dillworth was the owner of the club and Bart Jenkins was the secretary, and they never stood for no monkey business. "May I be so bold as to inquire," I says, "just what you told 'em?"

"I told 'em," he says, "I wanted to sign up a guy they ain't no pitcher in the league can strike him out."

"Uh-huh," I says, "and did you tell 'em what size of a man he is?"

"Never mind about that," he says. "I got papers on me, made out legal and proper, constitutin' one Pearl du Monville a bone-of-fida member of this former ball club. Maybe that'll shame them big babies into gettin' in

there and swingin', knowin' I can replace any one of 'em with a midget, if I have a mind to. A St. Louis lawyer I seen twice tells me it's all legal and proper."

"A St. Louis lawyer would," I says, "seein' nothin' could make him happier than havin' you makin' a mockery outa this one-time baseball outfit," I says.

Well, sir, it'll all be there in the papers of thirty, thirty-one year ago, and you could look it up. The game went along without no scorin' for seven innings, and since they ain't nothin' much to watch but guys poppin' up or strikin' out, the fans pay most of their attention to the goin's-on of Pearl du Monville. He's out there in front a the dugout, turnin' handsprings, balancin' his bat on his chin, walkin' a imaginary line, and so on. The fans clapped and laughed at him, and he ate it up.

So it went up to the last a the eighth, nothin' to nothin', not more'n seven, eight hits all told, and no errors on neither side. Our pitcher gets the first two men out easy in the eighth. Then up come a fella name of Porter or Billings, or some such name, and he lammed one up against the tobacco sign for three bases. The next guy up slapped the first ball out into left for a base hit, and in come the fella from third for the only run of the ball game so far. The crowd yelled, the look a death come onto Magrew's face again, and even the midget quit his tomfoolin'. Their next man fouled out back a third, and we come up for our last bats like a bunch a schoolgirls steppin' into a pool of cold water. I was lower in my mind than I'd been since the day in nineteen-four when Chesbro throwed the wild pitch in the ninth inning with a man on third and lost the pennant for the Highlanders. I knowed somethin' just as bad was goin' to happen, which shows I'm a clairvoyun, or was then.

When Gordy Mills hit out to second, I just closed my eyes. I opened 'em up again to see Dutch Muller standin' on second, dustin' off his pants, him havin' got his first hit in maybe twenty times to the plate. Next up was Harry Loesing, battin' for our pitcher, and he got a base on balls, walkin' on a fourth one you could 'a' combed your hair with.

Then up come Whitey Cott, our lead-off man. He crotches down in what was prob'ly the most fearsome stanch in organized ball, but all he can do is pop out to short. That brung up Billy Klinger, with two down and a man on first and second. Billy took a cut at one you could 'a' knocked a plug hat offa this here

Carnera with it, but then he gets sense enough to wait 'em out, and finely he walks, too, fillin' the bases.

Yes, sir, there you are; the tyin' run on third and the winnin' run on second, first a the ninth, two men down, and Hank Metters comin' to the bat. Hank was built like a Pope-Hartford and he couldn't run no faster'n President Taft, but he had five home runs to his credit for the season, and that wasn't bad in them days. Hank was still hittin' better'n anybody else on the ball club, and it was mighty heartenin', seein' him stridin' up towards the plate. But he never got there.

"Wait a minute!" yells Magrew, jumpin' to his feet. "I'm sendin' in a pinch hitter!" he yells.

You could 'a' heard a bomb drop. When a ball-club manager says he's sendin' in a pinch hitter for the best batter on the club, you know and I know and everybody knows he's lost his holt.

"They're goin' to be sendin' the funny wagon for you, if you don't watch out," I says, grabbin' a holt of his arm.

But he pulled away and ran out towards the plate, yellin', "Du Monville battin' for Metters!"

All the fellas begun squawlin' at once, except Hank, and he just stood there starin' at Magrew like he'd gone crazy and was claimin' to be Ty Cobb's grandma or somethin'. Their pitcher stood out there with his hands on his hips and a disagreeable look on his face, and the plate umpire told Magrew to go on and get a batter up. Magrew told him again Du Monville was battin' for Metters, and the St. Louis manager finely got the idea. It brung him outa his dugout, howlin' and bawlin' like he'd lost a female dog and her seven pups.

Magrew pushed the midget towards the plate and he says to him, he says, "Just stand up there and hold that bat on your shoulder. They ain't a man in the world can throw three strikes in there 'fore he throws four balls!" he says.

"I get it, Junior!" says the midget. "He'll walk me and force in the tyin' run!" And he starts on up to the plate as cocky as if he was Willie Keeler.

"I don't need to tell you Bethlehem broke loose on that there ball field. The fans got onto their hind legs, yellin' and whistlin', and everybody on the field begun wavin' their arms and hollerin' and shovin'. The plate umpire stalked over to Magrew like a traffic cop, waggin' his

jaw and pointin' his finger, and the St. Louis manager kept yellin' like his house was on fire. When Pearl got up to the plate and stood there, the pitcher slammed his glove down onto the ground and started stompin' on it, and they ain't nobody can blame him. He's just walked two normal-sized human bein's, and now here's a guy up to the plate they ain't more'n twenty inches between his knees and his shoulders.

The plate umpire called in the field umpire, and they talked a while, like a couple doctors seein' the bucolic plague or somethin' for the first time. Then the plate umpire come over to Magrew with his arms folded acrost his chest, and he told him to go on and get a batter up, or he'd forfeit the game to St. Louis. He pulled out his watch, but somebody batted it outa his hand in the scufflin', and I thought there'd be a free-for-all, with everybody yellin' and shovin' except Pearl du Monville, who stood up at the plate with his little bat on his shoulder, not movin' a muscle.

Then Magrew played his ace. I seen him pull some papers outa his pocket and show 'em to the plate umpire. The umpire begun lookin' at 'em like they was bills for somethin' he not only never bought it, he never even heard of it. The other umpire studied 'em like they was a death warren, and all this time the St. Louis manager and the fans and the players is yellin' and hollerin'.

Well, sir, they fought about him bein' a midget, and they fought about him usin' a kid's bat, and they fought about where'd he been all season. They was eight or nine rule books brung out and everybody was thumbin' through 'em, tryin' to find out what it says about midgets, but it don't say nothin' about midgets, 'cause this was somethin' never'd come up in the history of the game before, and nobody'd ever dreamed about it, even when they has nightmares. Maybe you can't send no midgets in to bat nowadays, 'cause the old game's changed a lot, mostly for the worst, but you could then, it turned out.

The plate umpire finely decided the con-track papers was all legal and proper, like Magrew said, so he waved the St. Louis players back to their places and he pointed his finger at their manager and told him to quit hollerin' and get on back in the dugout. The manager says the game is percedin' under protest, and the umpire bawls, "Play ball!" over 'n' above the yellin' and booin', him havin' a voice like a hog-caller.

The St. Louis pitcher picked up his glove and beat at it with his fist six or eight times, and then got set on the mound and studied the situation. The fans realized he was really goin' to pitch to the midget, and they went crazy, hoopin' and hollerin' louder'n ever, and throwin' pop bottles and hats and cushions down onto the field. It took five, ten minutes to get the fans quieted down again, whilst our fellas that was on base set down on the bags and waited. And Pearl du Monville kept standin' up there with the bat on his shoulder, like he'd been told to.

So the pitcher starts studyin' the setup again, and you got to admit it was the strangest setup in a ball game since the players cut off their beards and begun wearin' gloves. I wisht I could call the pitcher's name—it wasn't old Barney Pelty nor Nig Jack Powell nor Harry Howell. He was a big right-hander, but I can't call his name. You could look it up. Even in a crotchin' position, the ketcher towers over the midget like the Washington Monument.

The plate umpire tries standin' on his tip-toes, then he tries crotchin' down, and he finely gets hisself into a stanch nobody'd ever seen on a ball field before, kinda squattin' down on his hanches.

Well, the pitcher is sore as a old buggy horse in fly time. He slams in the first pitch, hard and wild, and maybe two foot higher 'n the midget's head.

"Ball one!" hollers the umpire over 'n' above the racket, 'cause everybody is yellin' worsten ever.

The ketcher goes on out towards the mound and talks to the pitcher and hands him the ball. This time the big right-hander tries a under-shoot, and it comes in a little closer, maybe no higher'n a foot, foot and a half above Pearl's head. It would 'a' been a strike with a human bein' in there, but the umpire's got to call it, and he does.

"Ball two!" he bellers.

The ketcher walks on out to the mound again, and the whole infield comes over and gives advice to the pitcher about what they'd do in a case like this, with two balls and no strikes on a batter that oughta be in a bottle of alcohol 'stead of up there at the plate in a big-league game between the teams that is fightin' for first place.

For the third pitch, the pitcher stands there flat-footed and tosses up the ball like he's playin' ketch with a little girl.

Pearl stands there motionless as a hitchin' post, and the ball comes in big and slow and high—high for Pearl, that is, it bein' about on a level with his eyes, or a little higher'n a grown man's knees.

They ain't nothin' else for the umpire to do, so he calls, "Ball three!"

Everybody is onto their feet, hoopin' and hollerin', as the pitcher sets to throw ball four. The St. Louis manager is makin' signs and faces like he was a contorturer, and the infield is givin' the pitcher some more advice about what to do this time. Our boys who was on base stick right onto the bag, runnin' no risk of bein' nipped for the last out.

Well, the pitcher decides to give him a toss again, seein' he come closer with that than with a fast ball. They ain't nobody ever seen a slower ball throwed. It come in big as a balloon and slower'n any ball ever throwed before in the major leagues. It come right in over the plate in front of Pearl's chest, lookin' prob'ly big as a full moon to Pearl. They ain't never been a minute like the minute that followed since the United States was founded by the Pilgrim grandfathers.

Pearl du Monville took a cut at that ball, and he hit it! Magrew give a groan like a poleaxed steer as the ball rolls out in front a the plate into fair territory.

"Fair ball!" yells the umpire, and the midget starts runnin' for first, still carryin' that little bat, and makin' maybe ninety foot an hour. Bethlehem breaks loose on that ball field and in them stands. They ain't never been nothin' like it since creation was begun.

The ball's rollin' slow, on down towards third, goin' maybe eight, ten foot. The infield comes in fast and our boys break from their bases like hares in a brush fire. Everybody is standin' up, yellin' and hollerin', and Magrew is tearin' his hair outa his head, and the midget is scamperin' for first with all the speed of one of them little dasshounds carryin' a satchel in his mouth.

The ketcher gets to the ball first, but he boots it on out past the pitcher's box, the pitcher fallin' on his face tryin' to stop it, the shortstop sprawlin' after it full length and zaggin' it on over towards the second baseman, whilst Muller is scorin' with the tyin' run and Loesing is roundin' third with the winnin' run. Ty Cobb could 'a' made a three-bagger outa that bunt, with everybody fallin' over theirself tryin' to pick the ball up. But Pearl is still maybe fifteen, twenty feet from the bag, tod-dlin' like a baby and yeepin' like a trapped rabbit, when the second baseman finely gets a holt of that ball and slams it over to first. The first baseman ketches it and stomps on the bag, the base umpire waves Pearl out, and there goes your old ball game, the craziest ball game ever played in the history of the organized world.

Their players start runnin' in, and then I see Magrew. He starts after Pearl, runnin' faster'n any man ever run before. Pearl sees him comin' and runs behind the base umpire's legs and gets a holt onto 'em. Magrew comes up, pantin' and roarin', and him and the midget plays ring-around-a-rosy with the umpire, who keeps shovin' at Magrew with one hand and tryin' to slap the midget loose from his legs with the other.

Finely Magrew ketches the midget, who is still yeepin' like a stuck sheep. He gets holt of that little guy by both his ankles and starts whirlin' him round and round his head like Magrew was a hammer thrower and Pearl was the hammer. Nobody can stop him without gettin' their head knocked off, so everybody just stands there and yells. Then Magrew lets the midget fly. He flies on out towards second, high and fast, like a human home run, headed for the soap sign in center field.

Their shortstop tries to get to him, but he can't make it, and I knowed the little fella was goin' to bust to pieces like a dollar watch on a asphalt street when he hit the ground. But it so happens their center fielder is just crossin' second, and he starts runnin' back, tryin' to get under the midget, who had took to spiralin' like a football 'stead of turnin' head over foot, which give him more speed and more distance.

I know you never seen a midget ketched, and you prob'ly never even seen one throwed. To ketch a midget that's been throwed by a heavy-muscled man and is flyin' through the air, you got to run under him and with him and pull your hands and arms back and down when you ketch him, to break the compact of his body, or you'll bust him in two like a matchstick. I seen Bill Lange and Willie Keeler and Tris Speaker make some wonderful ketches in my day, but I never seen nothin' like that center fielder. He goes back and back and still further back and he pulls that midget down outa the air like he was liftin' a sleepin' baby from a cradle. They wasn't a bruise onto him, only his face was the color of cat's meat and he ain't got no air in his chest. In his excitement, the base umpire, who was runnin' back with the center fielder when he ketched Pearl,

yells, "Out!" and that give hysteries to the Bethlehem which was ragin' like Niagry on that ball field.

Everybody was hoopin' and hollerin' and yellin' and runnin', with the fans swarmin' onto the field, and the cops tryin' to keep order, and some guys laughin' and some of the women fans cryin', and six or eight of us holdin' onto Magrew to keep him from gettin' at that midget and finishin' him off. Some of the fans picks up the St. Louis pitcher and the center fielder, and starts carryin' 'em around on their shoulders, and they was the craziest goin's-on knowed to the history of organized ball on this side of the 'Lantic Ocean.

I seen Pearl du Monville strugglin' in the arms of a lady fan with a ample bosom, who was laughin' and cryin' at the same time, and him beatin' at her with his little fists and bawlin' and yellin'. He clawed his way loose finely and disappeared in the forest of legs which made that ball field look like it was Coney Island on a hot summer's day.

That was the last I ever seen of Pearl du Monville. I never seen hide nor hair of him from that day to this, and neither did nobody else. He just vanished into the thin of the air, as the fella says. He was ketched for the final out of the ball game and that was the end of him, just like it was the end of the ball game, you might say, and also the end of our losin' streak, like I'm goin' to tell you.

That night we piled onto a train for Chicago, but we wasn't snarlin' and snappin' any more. No, sir, the ice was finely broke and a new spirit come into that ball club. The old zip come back with the disappearance of Pearl du Monville out back a second base. We got to laughin' and talkin' and kiddin' together, and 'fore long Magrew was laughin' with us. He got a human look onto his pan again, and he quit whinin' and complainin' and wishtin' he was in heaven with the angels.

Well, sir, we wiped up that Chicago series, winnin' all four games, and makin' seventeen hits in one of 'em. Funny thing was, St. Louis was so shook up by that last game with us, they never did hit their stride again. Their center fielder took to misjudgin' everything that come his way, and the rest a the fellas followed suit, the way a club'll do when one guy blows up.

'Fore we left Chicago, I and some of the fellas went out and bought a pair of them little baby shoes, which we had 'em golded over and give 'em to Magrew for a souvenir, and he took it all in good spirit. Whitey Cott and Billy Klinger made up and was fast friends again, and we hit our home lot like a ton of dynamite and they was nothin' could stop us from then on.

I don't recollect things as clear as I did thirty, forty year ago. I can't read no fine print no more, and the only person I got to check with on the golden days of the national pastime, as the fella says, is my friend, old Milt Kline, over in Springfield, and his mind ain't

as strong as it once was.

He gets Rube Waddell mixed up with Rube Marquard, for one thing, and anybody does that oughta be put away where he won't bother nobody. So I can't tell you the exact margin we win the pennant by. Maybe it was two and a half games, or maybe it was three and a half. But it'll all be there in the newspapers and record books of thirty, thirty-one year ago and, like I was sayin', you could look it up.

CHON DAY

PRIOR TO October 8, 1956, the closest anybody ever came to pitching a World Series no-hitter was Bill Bevens (see page 389). As for the incredibility of a *perfect* no-hitter, with no enemy runner even reaching base—well, the way to tell about Don Larsen of the Yanks in the fifth game of the '56 Series is just to tell it play-by-play, first batter to the last.

1956:

New York Yankees 2,
Brooklyn Dodgers 0

UNITED PRESS

YANKEE STADIUM, Oct. 8.

Dodger First—Larsen's first pitch to Gilliam was wide of the plate. Gilliam ran the count to 2-2 and then looked at the third strike. Reese fouled off the first pitch and then was called out on strikes on a 3-2 pitch. Swinging at a 2-1 offering, Snider flied to Bauer.

Yank First—Bauer missed on a bunt attempt for a strike. Maglie's next pitch was over Bauer's head. The next was wide and on the following pitch Bauer swung and missed. Bauer then popped to Reese. Collins, with a 2-0 count bunted and Robinson threw him out. Mantle lifted a short fly to Amoros.

Dodger Second—With one strike on him, Robinson sent a hot grounder which caromed off Carey's hands to McDougald, who threw him out. Hodges struck out. Amoros took a called strike, fouled off the next pitch. The next two were wide and then Amoros popped to Martin.

Yank Second—With a strike on him, Berra popped to Reese in short left. Slaughter, with a 1-2 count, lifted a fly to Amoros. Martin took a called strike and fouled off the next pitch. Then he swung and missed for the third strike.

Dodger Third—With a strike on him, Furillo flied to Bauer. Campanella looked at an outside curve for the third strike. Maglie flied to Mantle on Larsen's first pitch.

Yank Third—McDougald out, Robinson to Hodges. Carey fouled to Campanella. So did Larsen.

Dodger Fourth—Gilliam rolled to Martin. Reese out, Martin to Collins. Snider was called out on strikes.

Yank Fourth—Robinson threw out Bauer. Collins looked at the third strike. Mantle, with a 2-2 count, hit into the lower right field stand for his third homer of the Series. Mickey's blow was the first hit of the game. Snider made a running one-hand grab of Berra's drive just above the grass. ONE RUN.

Dodger Fifth—Bauer took Robinson's fly. Hodges sent a drive to left center which Mantle grabbed in his gloved hand after a long run. Amoros, after driving a foul into the lower right field stands, grounded to Martin.

Yank Fifth—Slaughter walked on five pitches for the first pass of the game. Martin forced Slaughter, Maglie to Reese, who had to reach for Sal's high throw. McDougald lined to Reese, whose throw to Hodges doubled Martin.

Dodger Sixth—Larsen, who had retired 15 batters in a row, got Furillo on a pop fly to Martin. Campanella also popped to Martin. Maglie struck for Larsen's sixth strike-out.

Yank Sixth—Carey singled to center on the first pitch. Larsen sacrificed, Campanella to Gilliam. Bauer singled to left, scoring Carey. Collins singled to right center, Bauer going to third. Mantle grounded to Hodges and, after the out, Bauer, trapped between third and home, was doubled, Hodges to Campanella to Robinson to Campanella to Robinson. ONE RUN.

Dodger Seventh—Gilliam out, McDougald to Collins. Reese sent an easy fly to Mantle. Snider lifted to Slaughter and Larsen had retired 21 batters in succession.

Yank Seventh—Paid attendance 64,519. Berra lifted a foul to Robinson. Amoros ran back for Slaughter's fly. Martin singled to left.

McDougald walked on four pitches. Carey forced McDougald, Reese to Gilliam.

Dodger Eighth—Robinson, with a 0-2 count, was out, Larsen to Collins. Hodges lined to Carey. Amoros flied to Mantle and Larsen had retired 24 Dodgers in a row.

Yank Eighth—Larsen struck out. Bauer also fanned. Collins struck for Maglie's fifth victim.

Dodger Ninth—Furillo up. Foul, strike one. Foul, strike two. Ball one. Foul. Foul. Furillo flied to Bauer. Campanella up. Foul, strike one. Martin threw out Campanella. Mitchell batted for Maglie. Ball one. Strike one, called. Strike two, swinging. Foul. Strike three, called.

DODGERS	AB	R	H	2B	3B	HR	RBI	TB	SB	SO	BB	PO	A	E
Gilliam, 2b	3	0	0	0	0	0	0	0	0	1	0	2	0	0
Reese, ss	3	0	0	0	0	0	0	0	0	1	0	4	2	0
Snider, cf	3	0	0	0	0	0	0	0	0	1	0	1	0	0
Robinson, 3b	3	0	0	0	0	0	0	0	0	0	0	2	4	0
Hodges, 1b	3	0	0	0	0	0	0	0	0	1	0	5	1	0
Amoros, lf	3	0	0	0	0	0	0	0	0	0	0	3	0	0
Furillo, rf	3	0	0	0	0	0	0	0	0	0	0	0	0	0
Campanella, c	3	0	0	0	0	0	0	0	0	1	0	7	2	0
Maglie, p	2	0	0	0	0	0	0	0	0	1	0	0	1	0
aMitchell	1	0	0	0	0	0	0	0	0	1	0	0	0	0
TOTALS	27	0	0	0	0	0	0	0	0	7	0	24	10	0

YANKEES	AB	R	H	2B	3B	HR	RBI	TB	SB	SO	BB	PO	A	E
Bauer, rf	4	0	1	0	0	0	1	1	0	1	0	4	0	0
Collins, 1b	4	0	1	0	0	0	0	1	0	2	0	7	0	0
Mantle, cf	3	1	1	0	0	1	1	4	0	0	0	4	0	0
Berra, c	3	0	0	0	0	0	0	0	0	0	0	7	0	0
Slaughter, lf	2	0	0	0	0	0	0	0	0	0	1	1	0	0
Martin, 2b	3	0	1	0	0	0	0	1	0	1	0	3	4	0
McDougald, ss	2	0	0	0	0	0	0	0	0	0	1	0	2	0
Carey, 3b	3	1	1	0	0	0	0	1	0	0	0	1	1	0
Larsen, p	2	0	0	0	0	0	0	0	0	1	0	0	1	0
TOTALS	26	2	5	0	0	1	2	8	0	5	2	27	8	0

a Struck out for Maglie in 9th.

DODGERS	0	0	0	0	0	0	0	0	0 —0
YANKEES	0	0	0	1	0	1	0	0	x —2

EARNED RUNS—Yankees, 2. SACRIFICE—Larsen, 6th. DOUBLE PLAYS—Dodgers, 2 (Reese and Hodges, 5th; Hodges, Campanella, Robinson, Campanella and Robinson, 6th). LEFT ON BASES—Dodgers, 0; Yankees, 3. BASES ON BALLS—Off Maglie 2 (Slaughter, 5th; McDougald, 7th). STRUCK OUT—By Larsen 7 (Gilliam, 1st; Reese, 1st; Hodges, 2nd; Campanella, 3rd; Snider, 4th; Maglie, 6th; Mitchell, 9th); Maglie 5 (Martin, 2nd; Collins, 4th and 8th; Larsen, 8th; Bauer, 8th). HITS—Off Larsen, 0 in 9 innings; Maglie, 5 in 8. RUNS & EARNED RUNS—Larsen, 0-0; Maglie, 2-2. WINNING PITCHER—Larsen. LOSING PITCHER—Maglie. UMPIRES—Pinelli (N.L.), plate; Soar (A.L.), 1b; Boggess (N.L.), 2b; Napp (A.L.), 3b; Gorman (N.L.), lf; Runge (A.L.), rf. TIME OF GAME—2:06. ATTENDANCE—64,519.

"UNKNOWN" differs from "Anonymous," as far as I can see, in that the latter assumes the piece was written but doesn't know who did it. The former doesn't even know if the piece was originally written, or, instead, done by word of mouth, like the *Iliad* or that great burlesque routine, *Floogle Street*. I have never seen "Who's on First?" in print, and I have been unable to learn if it exists in that form, with the possible exception of some latter-day script version. Old-timers have told me that nobody in history did it better than Bud Abbott and Lou Costello. I have never heard anybody do it except Abbott and Costello. I have heard them many times; in fact, I literally wore out their record of the routine some seven years ago. It is a routine that is three times funnier heard than read. I include it here in abbreviated textual form because it's funny even in cold print, but also because of a conversation I had some years ago with an old football coach who had been appointed athletic director of his college and was planning an alumni banquet. "You know the kind of entertainment they like," he said. "They want to hear the fellas do 'Who's on First?.'" I agreed that it was a wonderful routine. "I guess it is," he said. "I've never heard it." Have you? In the following, Abbott and Costello are given the speaking parts.

Who's on First?

UNKNOWN

COSTELLO: Hey, Abbott, tell me the names of the players on our baseball team so I can say hello to them.

ABBOTT: Sure, Now, Who's on first, What's on second, I-Don't-Know on third . . .

COSTELLO: Wait a minute.

ABBOTT: What's the matter?

COSTELLO: I want to know the names of the players.

ABBOTT: I'm telling you. Who's on first, What's on second, I-Don't-Know on third . . .

COSTELLO: Now, wait. What's the name of the first baseman?

ABBOTT: No, What's the name of the second baseman.

COSTELLO: I don't know.

ABBOTT: He's the third baseman.

COSTELLO: Let's start over.

ABBOTT: Okay. Who's on first . . .

COSTELLO: I'm asking *you* what's the name of the first baseman.

ABBOTT: What's the name of the second baseman.

COSTELLO: I don't know.

ABBOTT: He's on third.

COSTELLO: All I'm trying to find out is the name of the first baseman.

ABBOTT: I keep telling you. Who's on first.

COSTELLO: I'm asking YOU what's the name of the first baseman.

ABBOTT (*Rapidly*): What's the name of the second baseman.

COSTELLO (*More rapidly*): I don't know.

BOTH (*Most rapidly*): Third base!!

COSTELLO: All right. Okay. You won't tell what's the name of the first baseman.

ABBOTT: I've *been* telling you. What's the name of the second baseman.

COSTELLO: I'm asking *you* who's on second.

ABBOTT: *Who's* on *first*.

COSTELLO: I don't know.

ABBOTT: He's on third.

COSTELLO: Let's do it this way. You pay the players on this team?

ABBOTT: Absolutely.

COSTELLO: All right. Now, when you give the first baseman his paycheck, who gets the money?

ABBOTT: Every penny of it.

COSTELLO: *Who?*

ABBOTT: Naturally.

COSTELLO: *Naturally?*

ABBOTT: Of course.

COSTELLO: All right. Then Naturally's on first . . .

ABBOTT: No. Who's on first.

COSTELLO: *I'm asking you!* What's the name of the first baseman?

ABBOTT: And I'm telling you! What's the name of the second baseman.

COSTELLO: You say third base, I'll . . . (*Pause*) Wait a minute. You got a pitcher on this team?

ABBOTT: Did you ever hear of a team without a pitcher?

COSTELLO: All right. Tell me the pitcher's name.

ABBOTT: Tomorrow.

COSTELLO: You don't want to tell me now?

ABBOTT: I said I'd tell you. Tomorrow.

COSTELLO: What's wrong with today?

ABBOTT: Nothing. He's a pretty good catcher.

COSTELLO: Who's the catcher?

ABBOTT: No, Who's the first baseman.

COSTELLO: All right, tell me that. What's the first baseman's name?

ABBOTT: No, What's the second baseman's name.

COSTELLO: I-don't-know-third-base.

ABBOTT: Look, it's very simple.

COSTELLO: I know it's simple. You got a pitcher. Tomorrow. He throws the ball to Today. Today throws the ball to Who, he throws the ball to What, What throws the ball to I-Don't-Know, *he's* on third . . . and what's more, I-Don't-Give-A-Darn!

ABBOTT: What's that?

COSTELLO: I said, I-Don't-Give-A-Darn.

ABBOTT: Oh, he's our shortstop.

JOHN GALLAGHER

"I've been traded to the Elm Street Eagles for a cracked bat."

CHARLES VAN LOAN was, Grantland Rice once wrote flatly, "sport's greatest fiction writer." Here is an excerpt from a story in Van Loan's book of baseball fiction pieces, *Score by Innings,* which was published in 1919.

From *Chivalry in Carbon County*

CHARLES E. VAN LOAN

SAY," demanded Bud, "did you ever see a female baseball club?"

I said that I understood there were such organizations, but that I had never seen one. Bud drew out a sack of tobacco and a packet of brown papers.

"You're lucky!" he said. "Wisht I never had!"

And then, with the spell of the sagebrush upon him and a two-thousand-miles-away look in his eyes, my New Jersey roughrider opened his heart.

"Speaking of baseball," said he, by way of preface, "that team we had in Saratoga wasn't the softest in the state by no means. We whaled the everlasting daylights out of everything between Green River and Laramie. Of course, the Rawlins bunch put one over on us when they hired five professionals from Cheyenne. They beat us three to two in eleven innings, and if it hadn't been for the 'ringers' they wouldn't have stood a show in the world.

"One day last June I met Baldy Sisson on the street. He was waving an envelope, kind of excited-like. Baldy used to run the team—him and Comstock.

" 'Say, Buddy,' says Baldy, 'I've got a game for next Saturday!' and then he opens up the letter. Right across the top of the page it says, in big, blue print: 'Baltimore Bloomer Girls' Baseball Club.' Just like that. Well, of course, I'd heard about female ball clubs traveling through the country, and giving a kind of a burlesque on the game, but none of 'em ever came our way.

" 'You ain't a-going to stack us up against anything as soft as that, are you?' I asks.

" 'How do you know they're soft?" says Baldy. 'They beat a lot of teams in Colorado. And they ought to be a good attraction.'

"Well, that part of it sounded reasonable. But there's a lot of difference between a good attraction and a good show. Ever think of that?

" 'I'm going to telegraph that manager to come running,' says Baldy.

"You'd be surprised to know what an excitement was kicked up in that town when word got around that a she-male ball team was coming. In a day or so Baldy got a big roll of advertising posters in the mail. All colors. On the top was a picture—made from a photograph it was—of a girl in a baseball uniform. Well, not a *regular* uniform exactly. Part of it sort of looked like a skirt to me. Loose and bunched up at the knee. Under the picture it said:

MISS PANSY DE MARR,
The Peerless Shortstop of the Baltimore
Bloomer Girls B.B.C.

"You know how a fellow's mind will get to running on photographs and things. The minute I saw Pansy's picture I was glad Baldy had made the date for us. She was a bird, Pansy was, young, and considerable of a looker. You can't fake up an old girl so that she looks like sweet sixteen; it shows through somehow, even in a photograph. Yes, Pansy was young, and as cute as a little sage rabbit. I wasn't the only one in town that took a shine to her. Curt' Mahafey stole one of the posters and took it home with him.

"Well, there was other things on the poster, too. 'A genuine scientific exhibition of inside baseball,' was what it said, 'as played by the leading female exponents of the national game.' There was a lot of that kind of hogwash, and then came a string of newspaper write-ups, and not a knock amongst 'em.

Down at the bottom was a string of scores. According to the posters, the girls had cleaned up mostly all of Kansas, and by awful one-sided figures at that. It got us to thinking.

" 'You don't suppose this is on the level, do you?' says Henry Kamphefner, our first baseman. 'Did they beat all these clubs or is this just an advertising fake? And them newspaper accounts! Did they pay for them, or how?'

"Well, we talked it all over, and made up our minds that we couldn't afford to have a lot of bloomer ladies traveling through Wyoming, advertising that they had licked the Saratoga Antelopes. That sort of thing would set the town back ten years and make us the laughing-stock of the state.

" 'Here's how we'll do it,' says Jeff Blood-good, our catcher. 'We'll *play* these girls, all right enough, and we won't be any rougher with 'em than we have to be. We'll hand them a nice, polite, gentlemanly trimming—say about twenty-five to nothing—and if they paste up any lies about us we'll sue for libel and defalcation of character. Anyhow, we'll *tell* 'em we'll sue, and that'll scare 'em. None of these fly-by-night shows like to get mixed up with the courts.'

" 'Yes,' says Fred Gilroy, the shortstop. 'We can do that 'r take a poke at their manager. He's a man, ain't he?'

"But we decided that wouldn't answer. Jeff's idea was the best.

"Well, Saturday morning came, and most of us were down at the depot to see the bloomer troupe come in. I didn't hardly think they'd wear 'em in the streets, but Jeff Bloodgood did. He said they'd do it for the advertising.

"As soon as the train came in sight, we spotted an extra coach—a Pullman sleeper it was.

" 'Humph!' says Billy French, one of our boys. 'They put on plenty of dog, don't they? Private car! You lose, Dan!'

"Dan McLaurin, our second baseman, was pretty much peeved about that private car, and I don't blame him. Dan runs the hotel, and he'd been figuring on some transients. Had the whole place cleaned up on purpose, and went out at daylight to catch a mess of trout for dinner. I'd have been sore, too.

"Well, we stood around and watched 'em switch the Pullman onto the siding by the depot. That car was a regular rolling hotel, with a cook house and everything complete, and when Dan saw the smoke coming out of the roof he said he didn't care *how* bad we'd

beat 'em, but he hoped it wouldn't be less than fifty to nothing.

"I got a peek at one of the bloomer ladies. She was setting by a window, combing her hair and fixing up a lot of yellow puffs and things, and her mouth was full of hairpins. I knew right away that *she* wouldn't answer to the name of Pansy. No, there wasn't nothing delicate about that lady. Or young, either. Some folks like these big preferential blondes; some don't. Me, I'd just as lief their hair and eyebrows would be the same color.

"While we were sort of standing around, waiting for something to happen, the yellow-headed lady looked out and saw us. You might have thought it would embarrass her some to be caught doing her hair in public that way, but this lady certainly wasn't the embarrassing kind. She was the sort that can look straight at a fellow until he begins to wonder what there is about him that's so peculiar.

"She opened the window and stuck her head out. I took off my hat because I'm always polite, but she didn't seem to pay any attention to good manners.

" 'What's the matter with you yaps?' says she, and her voice was like her face—hard. Kind of shrill, too, like a parrot. 'What are you staring at, little boys?' she goes on. 'Ain't you ever seen a lady before? Or haven't you got the price to see the game? This ain't no free show, so beat it while your shoes are on your feet! Git!'

"Some more of the bloomer ladies showed up at the windows and passed out quite a line of conversation. I didn't see Pansy among 'em, so I came away. Jeff Bloodgood said afterward that he stuck around and jollied 'em back. Jeff always was a liar. He couldn't *think* fast enough to hold up his end in a kidding match with those ladies. Yes, sir, they seemed to know exactly what to say that would be the hardest to answer right off the reel.

"Well, we went up to Dan's place and talked some more. We decided that a real licking might take some of the freshness out of the bloomer people. Then in came Baldy Sisson with a big whale of a man that had a kind of a wry neck. Baldy introduced him as the manager of the girl team.

"Of course, him being a man, we could talk to him, and we started in. I don't know yet who made the first break, but all at once out comes a big roll of bills, and the wryneck said he'd take the short end of any two-to-one betting that might be flying around. He was mighty near mobbed, and I suppose, all told, we dug up close to two hundred dollars. Dan locked the money up in the safe until after the game.

"I guess everybody in Saratoga that could walk turned out that afternoon. People came from away down by Tilton's ranch and over on Jack Creek. It was the biggest bunch I ever saw at a ball game in the town.

"We were practicing, along about two o'clock, when all at once the crowd began to cheer and yell, and here came the bloomer ladies, walking two by two, the big blonde out in front. There was a lot of laughing mixed up with the applause that I didn't quite understand at first, but I mighty soon tumbled. There, at the tail end of the line, was two of the biggest old battle-axes I ever saw in my life, one of 'em with a wind-pad, a catcher's mitt, and a mask; and the other one with an armful of bats. I began to laugh, too, until I noticed that the one with the bats had a wry neck; then I got up closer. Both of 'em had on bloomers and about forty dollars' worth of store hair, and they were painted and powdered and fussed up to beat the band, but a blind man could have seen that those two battle-axes were *men* dressed up in women's clothes!

"Well, there we were, up against it. For a minute we didn't know whether to make a kick or not. Henry Kamphefner was our team captain, and he had bet forty bucks on the game.

" 'Look at them ringers!' says Henry. 'Maybe we ought to call the bets off.'

" 'Call off nothing!' says Dan McLaurin. Dan hadn't put up any two to one, you understand. 'We'd be joshed to death about it. Let 'em have their gentlemen friends for a battery if they want 'em. The *rest* of 'em are women, and if we can't beat seven women and two men, we'd ought to be arrested.'

"That was reasonable again. I took a look, and there wasn't any question about the rest of the bloomer outfit. Most of 'em had been women so long that there wouldn't have been any excuse for mistaking 'em for anything else. Some of those bloomer ladies must have been playing baseball ever since the war.

"They knew their business all right enough. First thing they did was to scatter through the crowd and take up a collection. There wasn't any fence around the ball grounds, but if any of the folks in the crowd thought they were going to see that game for nothing, they had another think coming.

"I was warming up with Jeff Bloodgood when I caught sight of Pansy, and forgot about everything else. She was a little late getting on the field. The posters hadn't flattered her a little bit; they hadn't even given her all that was coming. She was just about the neatest, modestest little trick a man ever treated his eyesight to, and nothing like the others. They looked kind of loud in that foolish baseball uniform, but Pansy—why, to look at her, you'd say she never ought to wear any other kind of clothes! Slim and neat and graceful as a cat. The others looked big and clumsy beside her.

"The bloomer ladies went through that crowd, joshing everybody right and left, and bawling out the cheap ones something scandalous, but Pansy, she didn't have a word to say. I know, because I went over and borrowed a dollar from George Bainbridge, and when she came my way I dropped it into her cap. She looked up at me kind of surprised-like, and then she smiled. Gee! It gave me a warm chill all over! I remember thinking at the time that it was a privilege to give money to any lady as pretty as Pansy was. Did I tell you she had brown eyes?

"Well, the bloomer ladies didn't take much preliminary practice, but the wryneck, he got out and heaved a few to the other fat-he-male, and then him and Henry Kamphefner tossed a coin. The wryneck called the turn, and sent us to bat first.

"Pansy went skipping down to short, the rest of the bloomer ladies took their places, and the big, fat catcher buzzed a couple down to second a mile a minute. Pansy came across to the bag like a big leaguer, took the throws as pretty as you would want to see, and chucked 'em back just like a boy. My, how the crowd cheered her! Pansy was the hit of the show, right from the start.

"Martin Carey umpired, and Fred Gilroy, our shortstop, led off for us. The wryneck sort of uncoiled himself, and broke a fast one across Fred's letters, and all the bloomer ladies began to chirp.

" '*That's* pitchin!' they yelled. 'You've got everything to-day, Pearl! He couldn't hit you with an ironing board, girlie!'

"Pearl and girlie! What do you think of that for gall?

"Well, of course, that first strike and all the joshing he got from the bloomer ladies made Fred mad, and he took an awful wallop at the next one. It broke toward him this time, and he missed it a foot. That rattled him so that he stood still and let Carey call the third one on him, and what the bloomer people did to Fred when he walked away from the plate was certainly plenty. I've seen some pretty fair single-handed joshers in my time, but the bloomer ladies had it figured down to scientific teamwork.

"'Ain't he the cute thing?' chirps the big blonde over on first base. 'I'll bet his best girl saw him stand up there like a cigar-store Indian and let 'em call a third strike on him!'

"'Mother's darling boy!'" squawks the old lady over on third. 'Don't let Hazel make you angry, Clarence!'

"There was plenty more of the same kind, and the crowd laughed fit to bust. It was as good as a show for them.

"Pete Townes, our third baseman, batted next. Pete chopped at the first one, and poked a little foul over back of first. The big blonde ran right into the crowd, and made a nice one-handed stab. All the bloomer ladies yelled, 'Nice work, Hazel!' Then they whirled in on Pete, and told him a few things about himself.

"I'd been watching the wryneck, and beginning to see that we wasn't up against any tapioca. That old fat boy was *there!* He had swell curves, a dandy fast ball with a nice hop to it, and a change of pace, and when you come right down to it, that's all the *best* of 'em have got—that and control, and the wryneck didn't have no trouble putting 'em where he wanted 'em to go.

"While I was studying him, he pulled a stunt on Charlie Kennedy, our center fielder, and the best hitter we had, that made me respect the wryneck more than ever. He had a strike on Charlie to begin with, and he put another one right in the same place. Charlie took a good toe-hold, and lammed that ball over third base pretty near a mile on a line. It struck foul, though, and that made two strikes. The wryneck saw that he couldn't afford to let Charlie hit any more as hard as that, and what do you think he did? He'd been pitching right-handed, but he faced the other way in the box and *lobbed up the third strike with his left!* When you're all set for right-handed pitching, and looking for a wide outcurve, it balls you up something awful to have the next one break from two feet outside the plate and come in toward you. Charlie was so paralyzed that he stood still, and never even offered at the ball. I'd heard of pitchers who could do that stunt, but I never saw one before. Amphibious pitchers are scarce in any man's country!

"I saw then that I was going to have to do some pitching myself, and when I walked out into the box I sort of timed myself to meet Pansy on the way. She gave me another smile. I'd noticed particular that when all the other bloomer people were yelling that Pansy kept her mouth shut and attended to business. That made her stronger with me than ever. I like the quiet ones myself.

"Well, of course, I was out there to show those bottle blondes that they didn't have the only pitcher on earth. Up came the old third baselady. 'Maudie,' they called her. Two of the women were in the coachers' boxes, and as soon as I got my toe on the slab they started after me. I usually stand that sort of thing pretty good—from men. But what can you think of to say to a lady that wears bloomers? They opened up on me for fair. They talked about my face and my feet and the way my clothes fit me. It was fierce. I know my foot is *long*, but I take a narrow last.

"'Come on, Maudie!' they squalled. 'Here's Oswald, with the big feet! He's out there on the hill, and he ain't got a thing in the world but a chew of tobacco and a prayer!'

"Now, that's a fine way for ladies to talk, ain't it?

"I didn't fool much with Maudie. She wanted to bunt, but I kept 'em too high for her, and she never even got a foul. Then came Hazel, the big blonde. I owed her something for what she said down at the depot, and I put the first one so close to her nose that she could have smelled it when it went by. She was hugging the plate, anyway, and I wanted to drive her back. Hazel didn't scare worth a cent. She shook her bat at me, and danced up and down, and said if I 'beaned' her she'd bust it over my head. What's more, I think she meant it.

"I fed her the old McKinstry special, the wide outdrop, and she missed two of 'em. Hazel was no piker. She'd swing at anything she could reach. I figured she'd be looking for a third one, so I banged the ball straight over, she shut her eyes, and popped a fluky little 'Texas Leaguer' back of first base. Pure luck. Hazel wasn't built for speed, but any fat lady could have made first on that hit. I was mad enough to fight until I looked up and saw Pansy at the plate—Pansy and her cute little bat.

"'Come on, girlie!' squalled the coachers. 'Here's where we put the rollers under Oswald! Get a hit, girlie, get a hit!'

"I hated to do it, but I slipped Pansy one over the inside corner that nearly took Jeff off his feet. I was going to show *her* that I was a pitcher if I didn't do anything else. I tried it again; Pansy swung with all her might, and the ball came back at me like it was shot out of a gun. I just had time to get my glove up in front of my face when bam! the ball hit right in the middle of it and stuck there. I chucked it over to Henry Kamphefner on first, and we doubled Hazel by forty feet, but somehow I felt kind of rotten about robbing Pansy of that hit.

" 'Take the horseshoes out of your pockets, Oswald!' squalls Hazel when she finally got it through her head that we'd stopped 'em with a double play. 'Pretty lucky! Pretty lucky!'

"I ran into Pansy again as we changed sides, and this time she grinned when she saw me coming.

" 'Pretty tough, little one,' I says. 'A foot on either side, and that ball would be going yet.' She never said a word; just trotted out and picked up her glove.

"Well, that's the way it started. Skipping the details, the wryneck pitched swell, elegant baseball, and when he got in a hole, he'd switch and roll a few down the alley with his left. He had us all swinging like a farmyard gate, and when you've got a team doing *that,* you've got the boys guessing. We put some men on the bases here and there, but we didn't seem to be able to hit 'em around, and there wasn't much nourishment in trying to steal— not with Pansy covering the bag and handling the throw. The wryneck hit me an awful soak in the ribs in the third inning, and I did my level darndest to steal second, because I wanted to be where I could talk to Pansy. I'm supposed to be a pretty fast little fellow on my feet, and I was up and gone with the wryneck's wing, but that fat catcher slammed the ball down like a white streak, and when I arrived, feet first, Pansy had the ball waiting for me.

"Along about the sixth we slipped a run across. Pete Townes drew a base on balls, Charlie Kennedy pushed him along with a sacrifice bunt, and Billy French brought him home with a single to center. You bet that one run looked mighty good to us. We'd forgotten all about beating those bloomer ladies forty to nothing, and considering the way the wryneck was going, we were thankful for that ace. It looked big enough to win with, but in the eighth we had another guess. Old double-barrel tied the score on us.

"I hadn't been worrying so much about the wryneck being a hitter, because he'd been swinging at anything, but he came up first in the eighth and tied into one good and plenty. It would have been a home run if he hadn't been so fat. Of course, he blamed it on the altitude. He got as far as third base, and then he sat down on the bag with his tongue hanging out a foot. His bloomer friends certainly knew the fine points of the game. Hazel broke a shoelace, and took five minutes to fix it, and then Pansy had to stop to do up her hair, and Maudie's belt got twisted, and between 'em all they gave the old rascal a fine breathing spell. At that I'd have left him marooned on third base if Fred Gilroy hadn't played Ping-pong with a ball that Myrtle hit straight at him. Fred made a high peg to the plate, Jeff had to jump for it, and he came down square on top of the wryneck. I've never seen a hippopotamus slide to the plate, but I don't need to. I saw the wryneck, and there we was with the score tied up and the ninth inning coming.

"By this time we was pretty much worked up about them two-to-one bets, and the bloomer ladies were chirping like a lot of canaries. That one run put a lot of life into 'em.

"We didn't do any good in our half of the ninth, and then here was Maudie again, leading off for the ladies. Maudie was tolerable soft for me. She was afraid of a fast ball, and I didn't give her anything else. Three strikes for Maudie. The bloomer ladies rooted hard for Hazel, but I got her in a hole and made her swing at a curve, and *she* went back.

"Pansy waltzed up to the plate. She had a bigger bat this time. Pansy hadn't hit a ball out of the diamond all the afternoon, and Henry Kamphefner, who'd been reading the magazines, and thought he knew all about inside baseball, wigwagged to the outfielders to get in close.

"When I saw that big bat I had to laugh. It was 'most as big as Pansy was.

" 'Hey, little one,' I sings out, 'what are you going to do with that telegraph pole?'

"Pansy laughed back at me, waved her hand, and then I hope I may choke if she didn't throw me a kiss! Honest Injun, that's just what she did! You could have knocked me down with a lead pencil.

"Next thing I knew there was a terrible racket over back of first base. Hazel and Maudie and Myrtle and Jennie and all the rest of the bloomer ladies were yelling at Martin Carey:

" 'Mister Umpire! *Oh,* Mister Umpire!'

" 'Well, what's wrong now?' says Martin. The crowd hushed up to listen to their kick. Hazel cut loose with a howl that you could have heard half a mile away.

" 'You make that pitcher stop flirting with Pansy!' she bawls. 'He's been making goo-goo eyes at her all through the game! You make him quit it!'

"Well, she got the crowd a-going, and I suppose that's what she wanted. Laugh? They laughed their heads off. First thing I knew my ears were burning up, and I didn't hardly know what end I was on. I'll bet if I'd took off my shoes and dropped my glove I'd have gone straight up in the air like a balloon.

" 'Come on there!' yells Hazel. 'Quit stalling and pitch! Call time on him, Mister Umpire!'

"I must have been pretty badly rattled. Wasn't that bawl-out enough to rattle anybody? I set myself to pitch, but I was so plum' full of other ideas and things that I midlaid the plate entirely, and before I knew it there was Hazel and Maudie and the rest of those squaws doing a ghost dance along the side lines, and the crowd roaring like a menagerie at dinner time.

" 'What's the count, Martin?' I says. You can tell how upset I must have been to ask a question like that.

" 'Three balls and no strikes,' says Martin. 'For the love of Heaven, Bud, take a brace! Don't let those old battle-axes scare you. Steady down and *get 'em over!'*

"Well, I knew I had to do it. I aimed the next one straight down the groove, and there wasn't a thing on that ball but the cover—not a thing. With three and nothing, I figured that Pansy would wait me out for a base on balls, and I heaved that one up there as straight as I knew how, looking to cut the plate where it was biggest.

"Pansy saw that it was a groover, and back went that big bat, and then bing! she landed on it as hard as she could swing! I got one flash at the ball as it went out over my head. It was another one of those low line drives. I whirled around, and there was Charlie Kennedy and Billy French and George Perkins, all hitting the high spots in the direction of the river. Kamphefner had pulled 'em in close, and Pansy had crossed us by lamming it out over their heads.

"The next thing I noticed was Pansy rounding second base, and *run?* She could have

given a coyote a head start and run him breathless around them bags! She was straightened out for third before Charlie caught up with the ball at all. Dan McLaurin had the best wing in the infield, and he ran back to handle the relay. Charlie let fly just as Pansy rounded third base, and Dan made a chain-lightning peg to the plate, but little Pansy hit the dirt like an avalanche, and Jeff never did find her in the dust she kicked up.

" '*Safe!*' yells Martin Carey, and there went our old ball game, two to one, and licked by the bloomer ladies! Jeff Bloodgood heaved the ball away, he was so mad. I don't blame him."

Bud paused and rolled another cigarette, whistling between his teeth as he did so. I offered some consolatory remarks, but Bud held up a restraining hand.

"Wait!" he said. "The worst is yet to come. I wouldn't have left home for a little thing like that."

He lighted his cigarette, blew a few clouds from deep down in his lungs, and resumed his narrative:

"After the game the wryneck took off his wig, and so did the catcher, and they went up to the hotel with our bunch. The girls beat it back to the private car. Dan got the money out of the safe, and turned it over to the wryneck. I got to say for him that he acted like a true sport, and did the right thing by the gang. Then Dan said we'd all have one on the house and we did; and then some more of the boys had a stroke of enlargement of the heart, and then the wryneck started it all over again. It got to be quite a party after a while. The wryneck, he said we'd given him the toughest battle of the season so far, but then I guess he was just salving us a little. Goodness knows he could afford to.

"Other folks dropped in, and finally there must have been fifty or sixty of us. Then someone—no, it wasn't me—suggested that it would be a right cute little idea to go down to the depot and give three cheers for the bloomer girls, just to show 'em that we were true sports, and knew how to lose like gentlemen. Everybody thought well of the scheme, and then Luke Fosdick got up on a table, and said if we were going to do anything of that sort we might just as well do it *right.*

" 'We'll get the band boys together, and go down there and give 'em a serenade!' says Luke. Luke played the E-flat cornet, and thought he was quite a bunch on that solo business.

"Well, that wasn't any trouble, because most of the band boys were with the gang. They rustled out their instruments, and away we went across the bridge and over toward the depot, the band taking an awful fall out of that 'Hot Time in the Old Town' piece. We marched up alongside of that private car, and opened the celebration with three cheers. Then the band played some more—rotten, it was— and the wryneck went into the car and brought out some of the bloomer ladies and introduced 'em. They didn't look any better to me in their regular clothes.

"I rubbered and I rubbered, but I didn't see anything of Pansy, so after a while I edged over to Hazel, who had borrowed the bass drum and was leading the band, and I asked her about it.

" 'Where's the little shortstop?' I says. 'Why don't you trot her out? This is her party, and she oughtn't to run out on it this way.'

"Hazel threw back her head, and began to laugh, and she laughed so long and so loud that all the gang gathered around to find out what was so funny.

" 'Oh, Joe!' says Hazel to the wryneck. 'Pansy has another mash! Oswald says he'd like to meet her.'

"Of course, the boys had the laugh on me, but shucks! they just as anxious as I was to see her. They began to yell:

" 'Pansy! Oh, Pansy! We want Pansy!' and things like that.

" 'All right, boys,' says the wryneck. 'I'll go in and coax her to come out. Pansy ain't very strong for the rough stuff, but I guess I can persuade her.' And he climbed into the car.

"He was gone quite some time. We bunched up around the car steps and waited, and while we were waiting we made it up among ourselves to give her three regular ring-tail peelers and a tiger the minute she poked her nose outdoors.

"Finally the door opened, and there was the wryneck.

" 'Gentlemen,' says he, 'the young lady was dressing, or she wouldn't have kept you waiting. Allow me to present to you Miss Pansy de Marr, the greatest lady shortstop in the world!'

"He made a flourish with his arm like a ringmaster in a circus, and there was Pansy, standing in the vestibule and looking down at us. She had on what looked like a long robe of some sort, all embroidery and lace, and she smiled when we gave her a real Wyoming send-off with a tiger that started the dogs to barking for miles and miles.

" 'Speech! Speech!' yells Charlie Patterson, and we all took it up like a lot of parrots.

"Pansy looked over at the wryneck and he nodded at her. She put one hand up to her hair, and the other one went for her throat. I could see that she was fumbling with the catch to that robe, and just as I was beginning to wonder what was coming off next two things came off at once—Pansy's head of hair and her dressing gown! She kicked the robe backward, and hopped down on the car steps—*as pretty looking a boy as ever you saw in your life!*

"Maybe you've heard the sound that goes through a crowd at a prize fight, when one lad slips over a fluke knockout, and takes everybody by surprise, including himself? A sort of a cross between a grunt and a sigh. I'll bet there wasn't enough wind left in the whole lot of us to fetch out one decent, healthy cuss word! Flabbergasted? That ain't no *name* for it. And before we could get breath enough to say anything, Pansy made the speech we'd been asking for—made it in the kind of a voice that goes with pants.

" 'Where's that rube pitcher?' says he. 'I want to give him a kiss!' "

There was a long silence, while Bud traced patterns in the gravel with his boot heels.

"At that," he remarked defiantly, "I wasn't fooled any worse'n the rest of 'em. That kid could have fooled anybody. Why, he used to be on the *stage*. One of those female impersonators. But you know how it is in a small town. Once they get anything on you, they never let go. They just keep riding you and riding you, and I got sick of it. Baldy Sisson had everybody in Carbon County calling me 'Pansy.' I couldn't stand that, so I ducked, but if you've got a heart at all you won't tip it off to Baldy what I'm doing now."

Bud rose, stretched himself, and looked at his dollar watch.

"I feel quite some better!" he said. "Come on, let's go down to that fish place, and see those Wyoming trout. Somebody must have fooled them, too, or they wouldn't be here!"

FROM *My Biggest Baseball Day*—the game's greatest pitching duel —told—not too happily—by the man who lost it.

1917:
Cincinnati Reds 1,
Chicago Cubs 0

———————————— JIM VAUGHN ————————————
as told to HAL TOTTEN

I DON'T BELIEVE there has been another game in the history of baseball like the one I'm going to talk about. It was between the Cubs and the Cincinnati Reds at Weeghman Park on May 2, 1917—it wasn't until two years later that it became known as Wrigley Field.

The attendance that day was only about 3,500, but since then at least 10,000 people and maybe more have told me they saw that game. In fact, a couple of years ago a young lad rushed up and told me about it—said he was there. I asked him how old he was, and he said 23. Now—that game had been played 22 years before, so I said:

"How did you go, in your mother's arms?"

"Naw," he said, "my dad took me, but—" and he grinned a bit sheepishly—"I was pretty young."

Well—to get back to that game—it was the one where neither Fred Toney nor I allowed a hit for nine innings, but I lost out in the tenth. There didn't seem to be very much unusual about the game as it went along. I was just taking care of each batter as he came up there, that was all. And I didn't even notice what Toney was doing.

As a matter of fact, I never even spoke to Toney in the entire game—but I'll have to go back a little to explain that. When I broke into the big leagues with the Yankees in 1908, it was with such hard-boiled old-timers as Willie Keeler, Jack Chesbro, Al Orth, Jack Newton—a bunch of old heads. I learned my baseball from them.

We never spoke to a player on another team on the field—there was none of this glad-handing and hello business. Why, if anyone on the other club ever spoke pleasantly to me, I thought he was framing on me. I didn't want 'em to speak to me at all.

I'd always given Toney's team, Cincinnati, a fit, so this day they laid for me. One feature that seldom has been mentioned is the fact that there wasn't a left-handed hitter in the Reds' line-up that day. They even took Ed Rousch out of there to give 'em another right-handed hitter and an all-right-handed line up.

Another feature is this—after I'd got the first two men out in the first inning, Greasy Neale came up and hit a little looping fly just back of second base. The second baseman could have gotten it easy, but Cy Williams came in from center and made the catch. That was the only ball hit out of the infield off me until the tenth inning.

Well, while we were having our "outs" in the eighth inning, I was sitting on the bench. Remember how that old dugout was—with a partition in the middle cutting the bench in two? I was sitting on the end nearest the clubhouse. One of the fellows at the other end said, "Come on, let's get a run off this guy." Another one chimed in, "Run, hell; we haven't even got a hit off 'im!" "Well," another chap chimed in, "they haven't got a hit off Vaughn, either."

Well, I figured, "If this is a no-hitter and only one more inning to go, I'm going to give it everything I've got to get through that inning." And with the last three men in the batting order coming up, I really intended to get past them. I got Cueto on a line fly to Charley Deal at third and I got a third strike past Kuhn. Then that big Toney came to bat.

Remember how he used to hit—with that powerful, stiff-armed swing? Well, I gave him everything I had on that first pitch—and was careful to keep it inside. He took that big swing and missed. It looked like he might have hit it a mile, but he missed it with the handle of his bat.

He missed the second one. And I made up my mind to give him everything I had on the next one. I pitched—he missed—and I'll never forget the great cheer that went up. But Toney went out and set us down too, and we went into the tenth inning. I knew I was tired, but I felt that I still had my stuff.

Getz, the first man up, hit a pop fly which our catcher, Art Wilson, got in front of the plate. Then came the first hit of the game. Larry Kopf hit one into right center for a single. But Neale hit an easy fly to Williams in center and Hal Chase also hit a fly out that way. It was a hard hit ball, but not a line drive, and it was right at Williams. He got both hands on it—and dropped it. Any outfielder ordinarily would catch it easy. It was just a plain muff. Kopf got to third on that one, and Chase stole second.

There's been a lot of discussion about the play that came up next—the one that lost the ball game. Indian Jim Thorpe, the famous old football player who was trying to make good in baseball, was at bat and he sent a swinging bunt toward third. I knew the minute it was hit that I couldn't get Thorpe at first. He was fast as a race horse. So I went over to the line, fielded the ball, and scooped it toward the plate. Kopf, running in, was right behind me and he stopped when he saw me make the play to the plate. I didn't see him, or I could have just turned around and tagged him out.

Now, some of the writers said that Wilson didn't expect the play. The truth is that Art just went paralyzed—just stood there with his hands at his sides staring at me. The ball hit him square on the chest protector—I'll never forget—it seemed to roll around there for a moment—and then dropped to the ground. The instant Kopf saw it drop, he streaked for the plate. But Wilson still stood there, paralyzed. I looked over my shoulder and saw Chase round third and start in, too. So I said to Art:

"Are you going to let him score, too?"

He woke up, grabbed the ball and tagged Chase out easily. But it was too late, the one big deciding run was in. Wilson cried like a baby after the game. He grabbed my hand and said, "I just went out on you, Jim—I just went tight."

In the clubhouse afterward everybody was pretty sore. Charley Weeghman, the boss, stuck his head in the door and yelled: "You're all a bunch of ———s."

But I wasn't sore. I'd just lost another ball game, that's all.

I do remember this about it, though. After the game I told Fred Toney, "You've got to pitch the kind of ball you did against me today to beat me from now on, Old Man." He shook hands, but he looked at me kind of funny when I said that. He must have taken it as a bad omen. Anyway, he never did pitch that well against me again—and I don't believe he ever beat me again. We met a lot of times, and most of the games were close, but he'd licked me for the last time.

THE LATE, great Honus Wagner, shortstop extraordinary, remembers a time when enemy rooters hired three bands to keep the Pirates from getting any sleep . . .

1909:
Pittsburgh 8,
Detroit 0

—————— **HONUS WAGNER** ——————
as told to CHET SMITH

WHEN A FELLOW has played 2,785 games over a span of 21 years it's not the easiest thing in the world to pick out a single contest and say it was his best or that it gave him his biggest thrill. But I was never sharper than in the last game of the World Series our Pirates played with the Detroit Tigers of 1909, and I never walked off any field feeling happier.

It was the afternoon of October 16 and not only a big day for me but for all the sport fans, for on that same afternoon Big Jack Johnson, heavyweight prize-fight champion, knocked out Stanley Ketchel in the twelfth round of their battle in San Francisco to retain his crown.

I regard that final game with the Bengals as tops because it meant the end of a grand fight against a bunch of real fighters. I'm still willing to testify that the club of Hughie Jennings and Ty Cobb, of Wahoo Sam Crawford and Donie Bush, of Davey Jones and George Moriarity, was a holy terror. And it tickles my vanity to think the Pirates outbattled and defeated them.

Cobb stole two bases in the series, but I was lucky and got six. Cobb made six hits, I made eight.

Ask Ty what happened the day he stood on first and yelled at me, "Hey, Kraut Head, I'm comin' down on the next pitch." I told him to come ahead, and by golly, he did. But George

Gibson, our catcher, laid the ball perfect, right in my glove and I stuck it on Ty as he came in. I guess I wasn't too easy about it, 'cause it took three stitches to sew up his lip. That was the kind of a series it was from start to finish. Fred Clarke, our manager, told us we'd better sharpen our spikes since the Tigers would be sure to, and we took him at his word. We were sorta rough, too, I guess.

Cobb surprised the Pirates by playing an unusually clean series, but some of the others weren't so careful.

The trouble started in the first game. Both sides had their jockeys warmed up. The Tigers let us have it and we gave it back to 'em with interest. There was a jawing match on nearly every pitch, and it was a good thing we had two of the greatest umpires who ever worked —Bill Klem and Silk O'Loughlin. They were young fellows then, but they knew their business and kept us in line. At least there weren't any riots.

In that first game, Fred Clarke hit a home run off big George Mullin, who was Detroit's best pitcher that year. I followed Clarke at the plate, and I could see that Mullin was boiling, and anxious to get back at us. I always stood pretty far away from the plate, but this time took every inch I could, figuring Mullin would throw at me. I wasn't wrong. He laid his fast ball right in my ribs. Of course, you can't say a thing like that is deliberate, but our boys reckoned it was, and from that minute the rough-housing was on.

We came into the final game tied up at three apiece. It was played in Detroit, and the night before, the Tiger rooters hired two or three bands to play in front of our hotel and keep us awake, but Clarke fooled 'em by taking us all out to a tavern along the lake shore.

We knew our pitcher was going to be Babe Adams, the kid who had won two of our three victories. Babe was hardly old enough to shave, but Clarke had a hunch on him all along. I'll never forget the look on Adams' face when I told him Clarke wanted him to pitch the opener. He asked me if I wasn't fooling and I told him I wasn't and he hadn't better fool, either, when he got to the mound. What a job he did for us.

I guess I don't have to tell you what the feeling was that last day. Wild Bill Donovan, who started for the Tigers, lived up to his name and we got two runs off him in the second. Mullin came in to pitch in the fourth and couldn't find the plate, either. There were two walks and two singles, giving us two more. In the sixth I got my only hit, but it was a three-bagger that drove in Clarke and Tommy Leach, and I kept coming and crossed the plate when Davey Jones made a bad throw from the outfield. We certainly didn't need the run we picked up in the seventh, but it made us eight, and with Adams pitching perfect ball that was the score, 8 to o. But it's far from being the whole story.

On my hit Jones kicked the ball into the overflow crowd, trying to hold it to a double under the ground rules, but O'Loughlin saw him and wouldn't allow it. Another time there was a close play at first and the Tiger runner hit Bill Abstein, our first baseman, in the stomach with his fist. Abstein folded up and Ham Hyatt had to take his place. Another Tiger slid into second and cut Jack Miller on the head and leg. Bobby Byrne, our third baseman, banged into Moriarity so hard that Bobby had to leave the field with a broken ankle, and George, who concealed his injury until the next inning, went to the doctor to have eleven stitches put in his knee. Talk about "bean balls"—they were flying around everybody's head all afternoon.

THE REMARKS in this book prefacing Howard Sigmand's story of the 1955 All-Star game apply equally to this account, written for the same news agency, of the 1946 game, except that Sigmand's piece is reprinted in its entirety whereas the following story is used as it appeared after a newspaper, the Los Angeles *Examiner*, had finished shortening it for space requirements. It's exciting to see how beautifully the story withstood cutting, but not surprising, for its author, Davis J. Walsh, has been, dating back to the Golden Age of the twenties, the greatest of them all under the gun. You may be interested in learning that it was Mr. Walsh who originated the phrase, "You don't have to be crazy, but it helps." He was covering the Indianapolis Speedway at the time.

Is 1946 too recent for nostalgia to set in? Lookee here: Batting star —Williams; winning pitcher—Feller.

The 1946 All-Star Game

DAVIS J. WALSH

AMERICAN LEAGUE power erupted with almost sadistic violence today, and with Ted Williams and Charlie Keller hitting home runs of prodigious proportions, left the National League humiliated, bedraggled and all but comatose under a 12-0 defeat in baseball's first All-Star game of the postwar period.

Williams, baseball's prize hitting exhibit, put on a historic show for the delighted hometown crowd of 34,906—which furnished a record gross of $111,338.75. The gangling Ted hit two home runs, the first a boisterous fourth-inning wallop of 420 feet off Brooklyn's Kirby Higbe, dead on a line into the distant center-field stands.

Ted's second was, if anything, even more ostentatious. It was hit off Rip Sewell's "blooper" pitch, which travels almost perpendicularly, and came in the midst of a four-run splurge in the eighth inning, just after Vern Stephens had pushed the "blooper" just out of first baseman Cavaretta's reach.

With Jack Kramer on second and Stephens on first, the stage was dramatically set for Williams' farewell gesture of the greatest one-man exhibition yet vouchsafed in an All-Star game.

The first "blooper" was wide and well off

the plate. The second was what the auto trade would call a special body-job.

The pitch settled down slightly inside at the height of Williams' remarkably fluent wrists.

Ted shifted his feet to give this one the "Sunday," and away it roared over Slaughter's agitated dome in deep right field, finally clearing the low fence in front of the bleachers.

It also was Ted's fourth hit which with a first-inning walk, gave him a perfect day at four-for-four. He drove in five runs. Barring this, he was practically helpless.

It was the worst defeat for either league in the 13-year history of the event and left the American League holding a strong advantage in victories at 9 to the Nationals' 4.

The latter today were like Jess Willard before Jack Dempsey. They never got their hands up, if indeed those were hands the National Leaguers were using during a puny three-hit attack against the combined pitching of Cleveland's Bob Feller, Detroit's Hal Newhouser and St. Louis' Kramer.

Feller, the fire-god of the profession, and Newhouser, its two-year bellwether, were in there with less than 48 hours' rest. Both had turned in nine-inning chores for their respective clubs on Sunday. But if they were tired, the National League would pay good money now for the privilege of seeing somebody on the verge of exhaustion.

Feller's first three innings saw him fan three, allow two scratch hits and, until Johnny Hopp flied to Dom DiMaggio to end the third, no ball had been hit beyond the limits of the inner defense.

Newhouser came on in the fourth and was,

if possible, even better. He retired the first eight men in order and Peanuts Lowrey's sharp single in the sixth was the only hit off Hal, who fanned four in three innings.

For the final three, Kramer walked one man, Gustine, in the eighth. The rest went out in order and he fanned three of them to bring the American League strike-out total to ten for the afternoon.

JIMMY HATLO

THEY'LL DO IT EVERY TIME

LETTERS FROM A "BUSHER" appeared in *Sport* under the by-line of John C. Steadman, of the Baltimore *News-Post*, who conceived the idea of having Tex Warfield, a young friend breaking into the minor leagues, report his progress by mail. Steadman then organized the letters into publishable form, pruning where necessary but without altering fact or flavor. Do not mistake this in any way for Ring Lardner's "You Know Me, Al." That was fiction. This isn't.

Letters from a "Busher"

TEX WARFIELD *to* JOHN C. STEADMAN

TARBORO, NORTH CAROLINA
APRIL 27, 1949

DEAR JOHN,

Well, we lost again tonite, 3 to 1. We need a couple of infielders, which are due in tomorrow. Then we are going to have a hell of a club. We have played five games now, won one and lost four. But that's okay. In five games I'm hitting over .400. Nothing to get happy about since it's only five games—but it's a good start. Last year I never was that high in the beginning.

You know, John, that full year really did wonders for me and I never realized it until now. I'm so much smarter. Take tonite (by the way John, I'm taking this game now as a business, *no* more clowning around. Oh, I'm a little bit of a showboat but now I'm bearing down, playing this game like it should be played, smart, heads up). Well, anyway, I tried the bunt tonite for the first time. It was the first inning, man on first. A left-hander was throwing. Now don't get me wrong; I can hit those dopes. But now I'm playing percentages. Smart baseball keeps them guessing. I never did that before. It was always swinging from the heels, clowning around. Well, anyway, I said to myself if I catch the third baseman playing back, I'll drop it. If he isn't, I'll go for the long one. 'Cause John, as you know, I can really hit that fast one and that could take me to the big show. And just the short time I've been in this league I can see these guys 22 and 23 and up who either hit it upstairs or down, and that's why they're down here. If

they have great power downstairs and are pretty good in the other departments, it's okay. BUT THEY'RE NOT! Well, anyway, the third baseman was back and I dropped a honey down the line. I was across first base before the third baseman had the ball! You know, John, things come so easy to me in baseball. Hell, I've got the bunt down perfect now. I don't know why I didn't do it last year. I guess I was just too lazy or just didn't care. But that's all over now.

The next time I came up I went for the long one. I tripled to the right-center-field fence (370 feet). Didn't score, though. I was first man up. Next time up we were behind, 3 to 1. (I'm a better team man this year, John. You have to be unless you're a Williams and even Williams is starting to hustle.) Well, anyway, I started using my brain. I'm leading off so I wanted to get on there somehow because next man up is a power hitter and he might hit the long one and tie it up. If I hit one out we would still be one run behind and he would be more careful to the next batter in order to guard that one-run lead (all this is going through my mind as I'm walking up to hit). So I make up my mind I'm going to bunt. The third baseman is probably playing me on the grass, so I fake my bunt to third, pull the third baseman in, have the pitcher moving to third and, hell, the first baseman is day-dreaming or counting his hits, so I drag it along with me. (Mind you, John, I place my bunts.) Well, anyway, the pitcher made a hell of a play getting over there after he started towards third. I beat the throw but mind you they gave the pitcher an error because he lost it for a second after getting way over there. Well, hell, I'm on first. That's where I wanted to be.

Well, I was left right there. Then I came up in the eighth with a man on first, so here's the spot to go for the fence. He threw me a high fast ball. I got good wood on it but it wasn't good enough. I drove it right up against the fence, the right fielder catching it. That was the ball game, John.

You know, John, I believe this manager of mine thinks he can make me a great ballplayer. I can tell from just the way he looks at me. That's no kidding. And he's handling me a lot different than the other manager did. He makes me feel important, as if I have to carry the club. He always passes remarks around to the sports writers or radio men about me. Like the other day he was on the radio here and we were at the hotel listening to it. The guy was asking him questions about the ball club and Joe said, "Well, I need a couple of men but I'm counting on our first baseman Warfield to carry a lot of the load." (They go for baseball in big-league ways down here.) "I'm really building my club around him," he said. "He had a little trouble with other managers but that's because he was just a kid. He's okay now."

Here's another thing he said, John! It was opening night; he was giving the batting order. He said, "Warfield, second," and then he stops and said, "I'm putting Warfield second instead of third, fourth or fifth because he can run!"

Can you beat that, John! And tonite after the game in the shower he said to me, "You played a hell of a game, left-hander. You're using your brain and I knew you could."

I remember one day after the season opened, we were eating lunch in the hotel. It was myself, Joe and a kid pitcher. We were talking baseball and it got around to temperamental players. Joe smiled and said, "I've got only one on this ball club—that's Warfield. But I think his temperamental days are over. Warfield, you show me a good year and I'll see to it you go to Savannah or Lincoln next year. You can have that year if you give yourself a chance. And if you do, don't worry, you won't go back to B. I'll send you right through B into A."

Well, John, I hope so. You never know, though. I guess that's it for now.

TEX

TARBORO, NORTH CAROLINA
JUNE 14, 1949

DEAR JOHN,

Well kids, old Warfield has done it again. Yes, John, I'm on the hot seat again. But it's not as dark as it seems.

To make a long story short, here's what happened. This ump isn't giving us anything all night. I'm up. He calls one down around my ankles a strike. I said get the damn ball up. He takes off his mask and says, "You're out, Warfield." Mind you, no warning at all. Well! I blew sky high. I said something, then he said something. I pushed him. By that time I was boiling. I went after him again.

By that time, Joe Antolik and the players were out there holding me off. If it hadn't been for Joe, I'd be out of baseball now 'cause I know I'd have hit him.

That was Saturday night. Sunday I played (went four for six), Monday a telegram came from the league saying, "Suspend Warfield indefinitely until further investigation." Well, there are a few big shots in Tarboro who put Ray Goodman in as president. They called him and told him that the umpire didn't give Warfield any warning. Well, that was a big thing in my favor. In fact it saved me, I guess. But as Dr. Green said (he's a Doc in Tarboro and a close friend of Goodman's), Warfield shouldn't have pushed him but he was in such a state because of the ump's fast thumbing. The ump has to warn a player. Ray Goodman agreed.

So, to make a long story short, he is going halfway—a fine or ten days suspension for me —I'm not sure yet. I'll know tomorrow.

Well, that's it, Johnny. Never a dull moment when I'm around. But I'm sure going to hate sitting out those ten days. Say hello to everyone.

Your friend,
TEX

RED SPRINGS, NORTH CAROLINA
AUGUST 23, 1949

DEAR JOHN,

Well we got rained out, so I thought I'd drop you a line. There are a couple of things I have to get off my chest. You know, John, I had a nice long talk tonight with the catcher. He was at Savannah this year until he came down here. Last year he was at Lincoln, second-string catcher. He really is a swell guy. He tried to help me because I have major league written all over me. I mean—like I'll say on the bench—"Well, that gives me 100 RBI's" or "That will pull my average up."

That doesn't go with the other players and he said up in A you will be playing with some ex-major-leaguers and that stuff doesn't go. I know it, John, in a way. But if there ever was anyone like Ruth it's me. Of course I mean color. 'Course that stuff I'll stop. But clowning —never. That's my nature. John, there is one thing I have to lick and that's my temper. And the only way is to be a clown.

I've tried everything and clowning is the only way out. My temper has hurt me now for the first time. I really realize it. I thought I could get by with my temper but I see I can't. That was the first thing Ehlers (*Editor's note: Art Ehlers, then the A's farm director*) asked about yesterday when he called from Philadelphia. Red—he's the manager—said, "Hell, I haven't seen any such temper." Ehlers couldn't get over it. Ehlers said, "I bet he's hitting .400." Red said, "Yah, that's right. How did you know?" Ehlers said, "Because, Red, I know Warfield. When that kid isn't fighting himself, he is one hell of a ballplayer." There is no doubt about it, John, I'll go to 'A' next year and 1951 I'll be in the big show. I mean that, John.

Well, I guess that's it.   Your pal, TEXAS

RED SPRINGS, NORTH CAROLINA
SEPTEMBER 7, 1949
DEAR JOHN,
Well the season is over. Now the play-offs. They start tomorrow. Well, here is my record. I finished up hitting .340 for Red Springs. That's what you wanted, didn't you? You told me to hit .300 for you at Red Springs. My season's average was .281. That's not bad when you figure I drove in 116 runs. And I hit my 20 homers, too.

I hit my 19th on Friday, came back and hit my 20th on Saturday. Red said if I had played in the Carolina League, I would have hit anywhere from 30 to 40 homers. Reason? Mountain air in Martinsville and Danville and short fences throughout most of the Carolina League. Mountain air which is thin air makes the ball travel farther. Danville's right-field fence is 290. Martinsville is 300.

You should get a look at the fences in this league. For that matter, even the Coastal Plain League fences! I tried like hell to hit .300 for the year, John, but the strain of playing double-headers the last seven days was too much. I

lost my strength and also eight pounds. Last Wednesday I had it up to .293, but then I fell.

Now, here is the good news. They are sending me to A next year. I don't know yet whether it is Savannah or Lincoln. Red told me this last week. Ehlers is going to be down here for some of the play-offs. *Just think, John, A in 1950 and I'm not 21 yet!* Oh! And let me tell you this. I could still be drafted by a AA or AAA club. I'll tell you how that works when I get home, if you don't already know. And a few scouts are watching me closely.

TEX

SUNBURY, PENNSYLVANIA
MAY 9, 1950
DEAR JOHN,
Well this is the "old pro" talking. We are losing like hell. We have a good club but just can't seem to win. We have two wins and nine losses. Lost six games by one run. I hit my first homer Sunday in the first half of a double-header. We have played 12 games. One game was a tie. Everything counts except that we must play it over.

Well, John, we are in York on Saturday, Sunday and Monday. Are you coming up Sunday? I think the game starts 2 P.M. I'm going home after the game, so I'll be home for Mother's Day. Then I can thumb a ride back to York on Monday afternoon.

You and Arky could leave after church and make the game easy. I'm hitting close to .300. About ten points off. Two hits tomorrow and I'll be over .300. I'll hit. And the reason I'll hit is because I can murder a fast one high or low. Not too many can do that. Well, I guess that's it. Don't mind the writing because I'm lying in bed.

TEX

HOPEWELL, VIRGINIA
JUNE 22, 1950
DEAR JOHN,
Well, I just got out of the hospital. I had an infected toe. I was in there four days.

Well, John, it happened. Suffolk has pulled a Williams shift on me. They really respect me. Now, John, I'm playing the outfield every day. And I'm looking better all the time. I'm starting to get that long, overhand throw down pat. Now I can say good-by to first base. Yessir, Baltimore must really want to make me an outfielder when they call and ask why I'm not playing it. They get me back at the end of the season for a 100 dollars. I always wanted to belong to Balts. Now I am and I'm content.

'Member you once said it was smarter to sign with a AAA club. You're right! And to prove your point, look at Taylor, the pitcher for Balts. Never had a winning year in the low minors but they keep moving him up!

Boy, John, I'm a lot thinner now and a lot looser. I was too fat in Sunbury and it was too cold! This is the last year for me, John. Next year I either stay with Balts or I'm through.

The other night I was on first, a hit went into left field. The left fielder threw to second to hold the runner on first. I kept right on going and beat the second baseman's throw to the plate. That brought a roar from the crowd.

I was going to write Sleater, but what does he want to hear from a D ballplayer! I see in the Sporting News he has two wins. That's swell. Walt Fiala is going great guns. I bet he will be the next Bums second baseman. He jumped from D to AA to AAA!

Well, John, this is two days later. I'm in a little slump but I'll come out of it. I've been fooling with my stance again. Now I've learned my lesson. I'll sink or swim with my old stance. Too bad I haven't you down here with me. They would never get me out then.

Well, that's it for now.

TEX

HOPEWELL, VIRGINIA
JULY 26, 1950

DEAR JOHN,

Well, kiddo, this is the last year for me. There's no use kidding myself. I haven't got it. There's something missing. I was hitting .300. Now I'm hitting .272 and, get this, I was hitting .300 with not a bloop hit or infield hit!

In other words some nights I'd get 2-for-4 or 2-for-5 and at least two times they would get me out on line drives. That was okay. With luck I could have been hitting .340 but around .300 was okay. Now in the last week I have been knocking line smashes right at someone. And that's the truth. Joan can tell you the same thing.

And there's one reason for it. I'm stuck in a damn big park and it hurts a long ball hitter. If I had played in Suffolk like I should have I'd have about 15 homers right now instead of eight and I'd be hitting .350 instead of .272. And Suffolk really is sorry. But not as sorry as I am.

See, John, fate just seems to go against me.

Take Sunbury. I had the park to hit in and couldn't show Staller the power he likes. Now I come down here and play half my games in the biggest park in the league. I don't know why parks in D are so big. Maybe because they don't want to lose balls. I don't know. Oh, I've hit two out of this park but most of my drives have been caught. I try to make up for it on the road and what happens—someone is always there to catch it. The other night on the road I lined out twice, doubled and popped out. The next time I come up in the ninth with no outs and a man on second and they walked me intentionally. Does that makes sense? Hell, they don't even give me half a chance any more. And I'm the only power hitter on the club and that's bad, too, John. I'm telling you, you should see me. That ball really jumps when I hit it.

Tonight, I played and went 0-for-4. I popped up, flied out, hit a hot smash off the first baseman's legs only to be out on a close play.

Next time up, I drove a line drive up against the center-field fence for a big can of corn. I'm not kidding you, John, I'm giving you the straight dope. It's just that this game isn't for me. I should never be in D this year and you know it as much as I. Went up and saw Bill the other night and he said the same thing. And who do you think is playing first base? Bob Reid, the guy I beat out for the All-Star team in Panama. He couldn't carry my glove and he is playing for Richmond and I'm playing D ball. And what do you think I'd do in that park with the fences 315 down the lines. Also the ball carries well.

Just like Dabek said, with my power and swing I could hit in AAA and he is catching for Mobile and should know. No, John, I'm just kidding myself and after this year I'm through. The club isn't going anywhere and we're just the door mat.

Fate says, "No, get out, you sucker," and that's just what I am going to do. It could have given me a break and let me play at Suffolk with those short fences. It could have given me a break and let me do a lot of things. It could have given me at least an even break. I had to laugh when I read about Bobby Morgan's supposedly tough breaks. If he ever read mine he would think he had a picnic! There's something wrong with me, John. Maybe it's just that I don't have the luck.

They call me Stan the Man and Ted the Kid. I guess it's because I hit something like them. I don't hit like I did when you saw me. My arms were out then. Now they are in close and I spring into the ball when I hit it and I am as loose as a goose. And now I hit the hell out of that low curve ball.

Now you are going to say hang in there and all that but it's no use. I lack something. Maybe it's this D ball all the time that has got me. You have to get the breaks, John. I don't get them and it's ruining me. I look in the *Sporting News* and see where guys I know are playing in the high minors and here's me in D ball. I see guys in this league hitting .330 and they are a bunch of bloop hitters. It disgusts me.

I got a letter from Lou Sleater. I wrote him and I got a quick reply. He is a swell guy and I hope he goes to the big leagues. Then I can sit in the stands and say I know that guy Sleater. I'm not feeling sorry for myself, John. I'm just smarting up to the fact that I'm through! You have to have that record and it looks like I'm not going to have that record. Well, the hell with it, is all I can say.

I've got a car, John, a 1948 Fleetline Chevvy.

Lou's letter really was interesting. When he gets home in September I guess he will have something interesting to tell. And me? Well I guess the guys get tired of hearing about D ballplayers.

I can hardly wait to get the hell out of here. Well, take it easy and write again soon.

Your pal,
The "D" ballplayer!

ELIZABETH CITY, TENNESSEE
AUGUST 5, 1951

DEAR JOHN,

Well, I got in trouble again, but this time it wasn't my fault. Course, a lot of people I know won't believe me. Well, here is the story.

We have a game in Franklin, first inning, yours truly is up. Ump misses a couple on me, puts me in a hole. I give him a couple of dirty looks but say nothing. Next pitch, I top one down the first-base line. I think I've got it beat. Ump calls me out. I give him a look and went back to bench. I run behind the ump who was behind the plate and say, "Boy, you two guys are two of a kind." Now is that enough to get thrown out, I ask you?

I got thrown out for that. I came back and asked him what's the story. Paul, the manager, comes running out and asked the same question. Ump, who has a few in him, tells Paul

to get back to the bench. Paul tells him that he is the manager and he has a right to know why I was thrown out, so he throws out Paul. Paul, of course, being part Indian, goes into a rage. We all are standing around home plate. Course, not any of us see the chief of police coming except Paul, and he turns and starts walking for the clubhouse right away.

I'm still at home plate. He grabs me by my belt and starts pushing and just about throwing me at the clubhouse. I'm still trying to hold my temper. I said a few things to him like, boy, a small-town cop trying to make an ———— out of himself, and a couple of other things. But he had no right putting his hands on me, and besides, John, he could have asked me nicely to leave the field.

Well, anyway, we came from behind to win the game. So we leave the clubhouse and walk right into the whole police force—*five cops.* I'm under arrest, so down we go to the police station. I'm put under $250 bond. Case comes up in a week. Now, is that one for the book! Hell, those crazy people might put me on the road! Come to think about it, maybe they will.

I guess McQuillen, their manager, wouldn't mind that. I've just about ruined his pitching staff. When I take batting practice, McQuillen stands by the cage and watches my swing. I'm the only left-hander who has a homer in the Franklin park, and I hit two. It's over 400 feet to right center and I blasted both my homers in right center. Yessir, when I swing that bat someone might get killed by a line drive. I don't really know what I'm so happy about when I may be swinging a pick instead of a bat. Oh well, why worry, 'cause you need a brain to worry and I don't think I have any brains. Well, that's what the scouts say! But I can sure hit that baseball.

Well, I'll write again when I have some more to say, and I'll probably have plenty to say next week. Take it easy, John.

Your pal,
TEX

DURHAM, NORTH CAROLINA
APRIL 1, 1952

DEAR JOHN,

Well, I've been in Durham ten days now and things are going along fine. Ace Parker seems like a nice fellow. He is still just as famous as ever. That's all you hear about in Durham, Ace Parker, the one-man football team. And there's always the story of who was the better football player, Justice or Ace. They're some heroes.

Well, enough of that. I'm starting to find the wall here in Durham. It's a real high wall, about as high as your house. Saturday I hit six or seven out in batting practice. We take infield practice every day and, of course, there is no one who can beat me with the glove. I look as great as ever around the bag, and, of course, I've heard them say so, through the grapevine, of course.

We play Duke Saturday and that will be my first look at Dick Groat. They say Rickey has him headed for Pittsburgh, and he probably will get 40 thousand dollars or better. Never played pro, so he is worth that kind of money —what a joke! You know, if that's the case, Williams and that bunch, who have already proved themselves, should be worth ten times that.

Baseball is nothing but breaks. Mr. Perry, general manager, sent my wife a schedule. She wrote and asked him if he would be kind enough to send one. So, to her surprise, he sent a note along with it, saying I hope Don likes Durham and that he has his best season this year. He also said if he did, they would send him to AAA, that they wouldn't hold him down.

Yes, like I said over the phone, John, they've been swell to me, and it means a lot. Johnny Allen, the great Cleveland Indians pitcher, is umpire-and-chief in this league. I'll make sure I know which one is Allen. That way I won't get thrown out of any ball games. Now there's a man with a temper.

This league is built for left-handed power. I could hit a lot of homers. It would be funny if I was in Detroit in September—it could happen. They need a first baseman, that's for sure. A lot of players have made the jump from B to the big leagues. You know the way some people who said I was nuts and never would go anywhere, would probably be the first to say I knew he could do it. That's usually the way. Don't you think I'm right?

Well, I guess that's all I have to say for now, John. I'll write again soon.

Your friend,

Tex

JOHN GALLAGHER

Courtesy *Sport* Magazine. ©

THE DEPRESSION. Philadelphia, October 6, 1931.
As an aftermath to this piece, President Hoover told Mr. Williams
he left the game before it ended because of two urgent telegrams delivered to him in his box during the seventh inning.

Boos for the President

JOE WILLIAMS

IT IS the third game of the World Series between the Athletics and the St. Louis Cardinals. A bright, flinty sun beats down on the
thousands in the stands. The two rival pitchers,
Grove and Grimes, are sharpening their control. From the high, swaying press box they
look dwarfish. The illusion grows they are
throwing cotton balls. You are so far removed
from the ground all sound is blotted out.

The minutes tick by and presently a squad
of bluecoats assembles in front of the Athletics'
dugout. You know what this means. The story
was in the morning newspapers. The President of the United States is about to arrive.

There is a break in the crowd to the left of
the Athletics' dugout and the President's party,
headed by two uniformed army men, comes
on the field. It is easy to identify Mr. Herbert
Hoover, his squat, square figure being so familiar. A gray-haired woman walks by his
side, his wife. She is in a burgundy ensemble;
gay orchids nod from her tailored coat.

The crowd back of the dugout recognizes
the President and there is a pattering of
palms and Mr. Hoover waves a gray, soft hat at
mechanical intervals, and smiles his greetings.
An official box has been set aside for the visitors from Washington. Grove and Grimes, who
have paused in deference to the President's
entrance, go back to their mysteriously silent
labors.

And then something happens. Someone boos.
Or it may be a whole section which surrenders
to this spontaneous, angry impulse. In any
event, the boos rise from the stands and break
with unmistakable vehemence around your
ears. They grow in volume and pretty soon it
seems almost everybody in the park is booing.
Booing what? It doesn't take long to get the
answer. They are booing the President of the
United States.

By now the boos have changed to a chant.
From thousands of voices come the cry: "We
want beer. We want beer." It has the swing
and resonance of a college cheer at a football
game. It is a shocking manifestation of bad
manners and lack of respect. Many in the
stands sense this and begin to applaud, but
the applause is light and the ugly overtones
drown it out.

All the while you keep your eyes on Mr.
Hoover. If he is surprised and resentful he
gives no sign. He sits in his box with his hands
folded across his stomach and looks straight
out on the field where the umpires are beginning to group together at the plate. Mrs.
Hoover seems to be studying a scorecard.

Once the game is started the rabble of the
crowd fades and everybody in the park, including the Hoovers, presumably, concentrates on
the vitally American issue of the respective
strength of the American and National Leagues.
But somehow, sitting up in the press box, it is
hard to get your mind on the game.

This must be the first time a President ever
has been booed in public, and at a ball game,
of all places. There is something about a ball
game that is supposed to make everybody kin
and it's a high honor to sit in on a ball game
where the President becomes a fan, just as
you and I. Why, then, this brutal reception?

Well, these are dark days, you tell yourself.
Unemployment is vast, yet not so bitter and
pressing that these thousands can't find money

enough to buy World Series tickets, many of which must have been bought at scalpers' prices. "We want beer!" That cry is, at least, understandable, even if the moment and place are not fitting. Prohibition has proved an evil, vicious thing and Mr. Hoover is lined up on the side of the drys.

You go on thinking out loud. Mr. Hoover is our leader and if the country has fallen on hard times perhaps it's only natural that the citizenry should single him out as a target. But the demonstration is so extraordinary, and you like to believe it is so un-American, you feel shaky and a little frightened. What if this mob mood should be translated into realistic action?

Your sympathies, meanwhile, mount for the Hoovers and you find yourself abstractedly following the game. The Cardinals get to Grove for two runs in the second and two more in the fourth. It is evident the Athletics' fireballer hasn't his customary swift ball and you get the impression he looks tired and is pitching with an effort. On the other hand, the burly, surly, unshaven Grimes is pitching shutout ball, enjoying one of his superlative afternoons on the mound.

The eighth inning is over and the National League champions are out in front, 4-0, when a voice crackles sharply through the amplifiers. . . . "Silence. Silence, please." The President and his party are leaving the park. The voice asks for courtesy. Everybody is to remain seated, too.

But the voice is ignored. As the President, holding the arm of Mrs. Hoover, walks slowly past the Athletics' dugout and through the entrance which will lead him to his special train, the booing breaks out anew and rocks the stands and when the booing does stop it gives way to the chant, "We want beer. We want beer."

We can only imagine how Mr. Hoover, a real sportsman, who had taken a day off to relax at a ball game, a privilege at the command of even the most obscure citizen, must have felt as the train sped him back to his awesome duties in a troubled and distressed Washington.

THIS is a splendid Wodehouse story, and I would love to see a box score with "Van Puyster, p" in it. But its best line, undimmed by the nearly fifty years that have passed since the story was written, has naught to do with baseball. "Hush!" the girl says, "we must be quiet. Daddy and Grandpa are busy in there cornering wheat."

The Pitcher and the Plutocrat

P. G. WODEHOUSE

THE MAIN DIFFICULTY in writing a story is to convey to the reader clearly yet tersely the natures and dispositions of one's leading characters. Brevity, brevity—that is the cry. Perhaps, after all, the playbill style is the best. In this drama of love, baseball, frenzied finance, and tainted millions, then, the principals are as follows, in their order of entry:

Isabel Rackstraw (a peach).

Clarence Van Puyster (a Greek god).

Old Man Van Puyster (a proud old aristocrat).

Old Man Rackstraw (a tainted millionaire).

More about Clarence later. For the moment let him go as a Greek God. There were other sides, too, to Old Man Rackstraw's character; but for the moment let him go as a Tainted Millionaire. Not that it is satisfactory. It is too mild. He was *the* Tainted Millionaire. The Tainted Millions of other Tainted Millionaires were as attar of roses compared with the Tainted Millions of Tainted Millionaire Rackstraw. He preferred his millions tainted. His attitude toward an untainted million was that of the sportsman toward the sitting bird. These things are purely a matter of taste. Some people like Limburger cheese.

It was at a charity bazaar that Isabel and Clarence first met. Isabel was presiding over the Billiken, Teddy Bear, and Fancy Goods stall. There she stood, that slim, radiant girl, buncoing the Younger Set out of its father's hard-earned with a smile that alone was nearly worth the money, when she observed, approaching, the handsomest man she had ever seen. It was—this is not one of those mystery stories—it was Clarence Van Puyster. Over the heads of the bevy of gilded youths who clus-

tered round the stall their eyes met. A thrill ran through Isabel. She dropped her eyes. The next moment Clarence had bucked center; the Younger Set had shredded away like a mist; and he was leaning toward her, opening negotiations for the purchase of a yellow Teddy Bear at sixteen times its face value.

He returned at intervals during the afternoon. Over the second Teddy Bear they became friendly; over the third, intimate. He proposed as she was wrapping up the fourth Golliwog, and she gave him her heart and the parcel simultaneously. At six o'clock, carrying four Teddy Bears, seven photograph frames, five Golliwogs, and a Billiken, Clarence went home to tell the news to his father.

Clarence, when not at college, lived with his only surviving parent in an old red-brick house at the north end of Washington Square. The original Van Puyster had come over in Governor Stuyvesant's time in one of the then fashionable ninety-four-day boats. Those were the stirring days when they were giving away chunks of Manhattan Island in exchange for trading-stamps; for the bright brain which conceived the idea that the city might possibly at some remote date extend above Liberty Street had not come into existence. The original Van Puyster had acquired a square mile or so in the heart of things for ten dollars cash and a quarter interest in a peddler's outfit. The *Columbus Echo and Vespucci Intelligencer* gave him a column and a half under the heading: "Reckless Speculator. Prominent Citizen's Gamble in Land." On the proceeds of that deal his descendants had led quiet, peaceful lives ever since. If any of them ever did a day's work, the family records are silent on the point.

Blood was their long suit, not Energy. They were plain, homely folk, with a refined distaste for wealth and vulgar hustle. They lived simply, without envy of their richer fellow citizens, on their three hundred thousand dollars a year. They asked no more. It enabled them to entertain on a modest scale; the boys could go to college, the girls buy an occasional new frock. They were satisfied.

Having dressed for dinner, Clarence proceeded to the library, where he found his father slowly pacing the room. Silver-haired old Vansuyther Van Puyster seemed wrapped in thought. And this was unusual, for he was not given to thinking. To be absolutely frank, the old man had just about enough brain to make a jay-bird fly crooked, and no more.

"Ah, my boy," he said, looking up as Clarence entered. "Let us go in to dinner. I have been awaiting you for some little time now. I was about to inquire as to your whereabouts. Let us be going."

Mr. Van Puyster always spoke like that. This was due to Blood.

Until the servants had left them to their coffee and cigarettes, the conversation was desultory and commonplace. But when the door had closed, Mr. Van Puyster leaned forward.

"My boy," he said quietly, "we are ruined."

Clarence looked at him inquiringly.

"Ruined much?" he asked.

"Paupers," said his father. "I doubt if when all is over, I shall have much more than a bare fifty or sixty thousand dollars a year."

A lesser man would have betrayed agitation, but Clarence was a Van Puyster. He lit a cigarette.

"Ah," he said calmly. "How's that?"

Mr. Van Puyster toyed with his coffee-spoon.

"I was induced to speculate—rashly, I fear—on the advice of a man I chanced to meet at a public dinner, in the shares of a certain mine. I did not thoroughly understand the matter, but my acquaintance appeared to be well versed in such operations, so I allowed him to—and, well, in fact, to cut a long story short, I am ruined."

"Who was the fellow?"

"A man of the name of Rackstraw. Daniel Rackstraw."

"Daniel Rackstraw!"

Not even Clarence's training and traditions could prevent a slight start as he heard the name.

"Daniel Rackstraw," repeated his father. "A man, I fear, not entirely honest. In fact, it seems that he has made a very large fortune by similar transactions. Friends of mine, acquainted with these matters, tell me his behavior toward me amounted practically to theft. However, for myself I care little. We can rough it, we of the old Van Puyster stock. If there is but fifty thousand a year left, well—I must make it serve. It is for your sake that I am troubled, my poor boy. I shall be compelled to stop your allowance. I fear you will be obliged to adopt some profession." He hesitated for a moment. "In fact, work," he added.

Clarence drew at his cigarette.

"Work?" he echoed thoughtfully. "Well, of course, mind you, fellows *do* work. I met a man at the club only yesterday who knew a fellow who had met a man whose cousin worked."

He reflected for a while.

"I shall pitch," he said suddenly.

"Pitch, my boy?"

"Sign on as a professional ballplayer."

His father's fine old eyebrows rose a little.

"But, my boy, er— The—ah—family name. Our—shall I say *noblesse oblige*? Can a Van Puyster pitch and not be defiled?"

"I shall take a new name," said Clarence. "I will call myself Brown." He lit another cigarette. "I can get signed on in a minute. McGraw will jump at me."

This was no idle boast. Clarence had had a good college education, and was now an exceedingly fine pitcher. It was a pleasing sight to see him, poised on one foot in the attitude of a Salome dancer, with one eye on the batter, the other gazing coldly at the man who was trying to steal third, uncurl abruptly like the mainspring of a watch and sneak over a swift one. Under Clarence's guidance a ball could do practically everything except talk. It could fly like a shot from a gun, hesitate, take the first turning to the left, go up two blocks, take the second to the right, bound in mid-air like a jack rabbit, and end by dropping as the gentle dew from heaven upon the plate beneath. Briefly, there was class to Clarence. He was the goods.

Scarcely had he uttered these momentous words when the butler entered with the announcement that he was wanted by a lady at the telephone.

It was Isabel.

Isabel was disturbed.

"Oh, Clarence," she cried, "my precious angel wonder-child, I don't know how to begin."

"Begin just like that," said Clarence approvingly. "It's fine. You can't beat it."

"Clarence, a terrible thing has happened. I told Papa of our engagement, and he wouldn't hear of it. He was furious. He c-called you a b-b-b—"

"A what?"

"A p-p-p—"

"That's a new one on me," said Clarence, wondering.

"A b-beggarly p-pauper. I knew you weren't well off, but I thought you had two or three millions. I told him so. But he said no, your father had lost all his money."

"It is too true, dearest," said Clarence. "I am a pauper. But I'm going to work. Something tells me I shall be rather good at work. I am going to work with all the accumulated energy of generations of ancestors who have never done a hand's turn. And some day when I—"

"Good-by," said Isabel hastily, "I hear Papa coming."

The season during which Clarence Van Puyster pitched for the Giants is destined to live long in the memory of followers of baseball. Probably never in the history of the game has there been such persistent and widespread mortality among the more distant relatives of office-boys and junior clerks. Statisticians have estimated that if all the grandmothers alone who perished between the months of April and October that year could have been placed end to end they would have reached considerably further than Minneapolis. And it was Clarence who was responsible for this holocaust. Previous to the opening of the season skeptics had shaken their heads over the Giants' chances for the pennant. It had been assumed that as little new blood would be forthcoming as in other years, and that the fate of Our City would rest, as usual, on the shoulders of the white-haired veterans who were boys with Lafayette.

And then, like a meteor, Clarence Van Puyster had flashed upon the world of fans, bugs, chewing gum, and nuts (pea and human). In the opening game he had done horrid things to nine men from Boston; and from then onward, except for an occasional check, the Giants had never looked back.

Among the spectators who thronged the bleachers to watch Clarence perform there appeared week after week a little, gray, dried-up man, insignificant except for a certain happy choice of language in moments of emotion and an enthusiasm far surpassing that of the ordinary spectator. To the trained eye there is a subtle but well marked difference between the fan, the bug, and—the last phase—the nut of the baseball world. This man was an undoubted nut. It was writ clear across his brow.

Fate had made Daniel Rackstraw—for it was he—a Tainted Millionaire, but at heart he was a baseball spectator. He never missed a game. His library of baseball literature was the finest in the country. His baseball museum had but one equal, that of Mr. Jacob Dodson of Detroit. Between them the two had cornered, at enormous expense, the curio market of the game. It was Rackstraw who had secured the glove worn by Neal Ball, the Cleveland shortstop, when he made the only unassisted triple play in the history of the game; but it was Dodson who possessed the bat which Hans Wagner used as a boy. The two men were friends, as far as rival connoisseurs can be friends; and Mr. Dodson, when at leisure, would frequently pay a visit to Mr. Rackstraw's country home, where he would spend hours gazing wistfully at the Neal Ball glove buoyed up only by the thought of the Wagner bat at home.

Isabel saw little of Clarence during the summer months, except from a distance. She contented herself with clipping photographs of him from the evening papers. Each was a little more unlike him than the last, and this lent variety to the collection. Her father marked her new-born enthusiasm for the national game with approval. It had been secretly a great grief to the old buccaneer that his only child did not know the difference between a bunt and a swat, and, more, did not seem to care to know. He felt himself drawn closer to her. An understanding, as pleasant as it was new and strange, began to spring up between parent and child.

As for Clarence, how easy it would be to cut loose to practically an unlimited extent on the subject of his emotions at this time. One can figure him, after the game is over and the gay throng has dispersed, creeping moodily—but what's the use? Brevity. That is the cry. Brevity. Let us on.

The months sped by. August came and went, and September; and soon it was plain to even the casual follower of the game that, unless something untoward should happen, the Giants must secure the National League pennant. Those were delirious days for Daniel Rackstraw. Long before the beginning of October his voice had dwindled to a husky whisper. Deep lines appeared on his forehead; for it is an awful thing for a baseball nut to be compelled to root, in the very crisis of the season, purely by means of facial expression. In this time of affliction he found Isabel an ever-increasing comfort to him. Side by side they would sit at the Polo Grounds, and the old man's face would lose its drawn look, and light up, as her clear young soprano pealed out above the din, urging this player to slide for second, that to knock the stitching off the ball; or describing the umpire in no uncertain voice as a reincarnation of the late Mr. Jesse James.

Meanwhile, in the American League, Detroit had been heading the list with equal pertinacity; and in far-off Michigan Mr. Jacob Dodson's enthusiasm had been every whit as great as Mr. Rackstraw's in New York. It was universally admitted that when the championship series came to be played, there would certainly be something doing.

But, alas! How truly does Epictetus observe: "We know not what awaiteth us around the corner, and the hand that counteth its chickens ere they be hatched ofttimes graspeth but a lemon." The prophets who anticipated a struggle closer than any on record were destined to be proved false.

It was not that their judgment of form was at fault. By every law of averages the Giants and the Tigers should have been the two most evenly matched nines in the history of the game. In fielding there was nothing to choose between them. At hitting the Tigers held a slight superiority; but this was balanced by the inspired pitching of Clarence Van Puyster. Even the keenest supporters of either side were not confident. They argued at length, figuring out the odds with the aid of stubs of pencils and the backs of envelopes, but they were not confident. Out of all those frenzied millions two men alone had no doubts. Mr. Daniel Rackstraw said that he did not desire to be unfair to Detroit. He wished it to be clearly understood that in their own class the Tigers might quite possibly show to considerable advantage. In some rural league down South, for instance, he did not deny that they might sweep all before them. But when it came to competing with the Giants—here words failed Mr. Rackstraw, and he had to rush to Wall Street and collect several tainted millions before he could recover his composure.

Mr. Jacob Dodson, interviewed by the Detroit *Weekly Rooter*, stated that his decision, arrived at after a close and careful study of the work of both teams, was that the Giants had rather less chance in the forthcoming tourney than a lone gumdrop at an Eskimo tea-party. It was his carefully considered opinion that in a contest with the Avenue B Juniors the Giants might, with an effort, scrape home. But when it was a question of meeting a live team like Detroit—here Mr. Dodson, shrugging his shoulders despairingly, sank back in his chair, and watchful secretaries brought him round with oxygen.

Throughout the whole country nothing but the approaching series was discussed. Wherever civilization reigned, and in Jersey City, one question alone was on every lip: Who would win? Octogenarians mumbled it. Infants lisped it. Tired businessmen, trampled underfoot in the rush for the West Farms express, asked it of the ambulance attendants who carried them to hospital.

And then, one bright, clear morning, when all Nature seemed to smile, Clarence Van Puyster developed mumps.

New York was in a ferment. I could have wished to go into details, to describe in crisp, burning sentences the panic that swept like a tornado through a million homes. A little encouragement, the slightest softening of the editorial austerity, and the thing would have been done. But no. Brevity. That was the cry. Brevity. Let us on.

The Tigers met the Giants at the Polo Grounds, and for five days the sweat of agony trickled unceasingly down the corrugated foreheads of the patriots who sat on the bleachers. The men from Detroit, freed from the fear of Clarence, smiled grim smiles and proceeded to knock holes through the fence. It was in vain that the home fielders skimmed like swallows around the diamond. They could not keep the score down. From start to finish the Giants were a beaten side.

Broadway during that black week was a desert. Gloom gripped Lobster Square. In distant Harlem red-eyed wives faced silently scowling husbands at the evening meal, and the children were sent early to bed. Newsboys called the extras in a whisper.

Few took the tragedy more nearly to heart than Daniel Rackstraw. Each afternoon found him more deeply plunged in sorrow. On the last day, leaving the ground with the air of a father mourning over some prodigal son, he encountered Mr. Jacob Dodson of Detroit.

Now, Mr. Dodson was perhaps the slightest bit shy on the finer feelings. He should have respected the grief of a fallen foe. He should have abstained from exulting. But he was in too exhilarated a condition to be magnanimous. Sighting Mr. Rackstraw, he addressed himself joyously to the task of rubbing the thing in. Mr. Rackstraw listened in silent anguish.

"If we had had Brown——" he said at length.

"That's what they all say," whooped Mr. Dodson. "Brown! Who's Brown?"

"If we had had Brown, we should have——" He paused. An idea had flashed upon his overwrought mind. "Dodson," he said, "listen here. Wait till Brown is well again, and let us play this thing off again for anything you like a side in my private park."

Mr. Dodson reflected.

"You're on," he said. "What side bet? A million? Two million? Three?"

Mr. Rackstraw shook his head scornfully.

"A million? Who wants a million? I'll put up my Neal Ball glove against your Hans Wagner bat. The best of three games. Does that go?"

"I should say it did," said Mr. Dodson joyfully. "I've been wanting that glove for years. It's like finding it in one's Christmas stocking."

"Very well," said Mr. Rackstraw. "Then let's get it fixed up."

Honestly, it is but a dog's life, that of the short-story writer. I particularly wished at this point to introduce a description of Mr. Rackstraw's country home and estate, featuring the private ball park with its fringe of noble trees. It would have served a double purpose, not only charming the lover of nature, but acting as a fine stimulus to the youth of the country, showing them the sort of home they would be able to buy some day if they worked hard and saved their money. But no. You shall have three guesses as to what was the cry. You give it up? It was "Brevity! Brevity!" Let us on.

The two teams arrived at the Rackstraw house in time for lunch. Clarence, his features once more reduced to their customary finely chiseled proportions, alighted from the automobile with a swelling heart. He could see nothing of Isabel, but that did not disturb him. Letters had passed between the two. Clarence had warned her not to embrace him in public, as McGraw would not like it; and Isabel accordingly had arranged a tryst among the noble trees which fringed the ball park.

I will pass lightly over the meeting of the two lovers. I will not describe the dewy softness of their eyes, the catching of their breath,

their murmured endearments. I could, mind you. It is at just such descriptions that I am particularly happy. But I have grown discouraged. My spirit is broken. It is enough to say that Clarence had reached a level of emotional eloquence rarely met with among pitchers of the National League, when Isabel broke from him with a startled exclamation, and vanished behind a tree; and, looking over his shoulder, Clarence observed Mr. Daniel Rackstraw moving toward him.

It was evident from the millionaire's demeanor that he had seen nothing. The look on his face was anxious, but not wrathful. He sighted Clarence, and hurried up to him.

"Say, Brown," he said, "I've been looking for you. I want a word with you."

"A thousand, if you wish it," said Clarence courteously.

"Now, see here," said Mr. Rackstraw. "I want to explain to you just what this ball game means to me. Don't run away with the idea I've had you fellows down to play an exhibition game just to keep me merry and bright. If the Giants win today, it means that I shall be able to hold up my head again and look my fellow man in the face, instead of crawling around on my stomach and feeling like thirty cents. Do you get that?"

"I am hep," replied Clarence with simple dignity.

"And not only that," went on the millionaire. "There's more to it. I have put up my Neal Ball glove against Mr. Dodson's Wagner bat as a side bet. You understand what that means? It means that either you win or my life is soured for keeps. See?"

"I have got you," said Clarence.

"Good. Then what I wanted to say was this. Today is your day for pitching as you've never pitched before. Everything depends on whether you make good or not. With you pitching like mother used to make it, the Giants are some nine. Otherwise they are Nature's citrons. It's one thing or the other. It's all up to you. Win, and there's twenty thousand dollars waiting for you above what you share with the others."

Clarence waved his hand deprecatingly.

"Mr. Rackstraw," he said, "keep your dough. I care nothing for money."

"You don't?" cried the millionaire. "Then you ought to exhibit yourself in a dime museum."

"All I ask of you," proceeded Clarence, "is your consent to my engagement to your daughter."

Mr. Rackstraw looked sharply at him.

"Repeat that," he said. "I don't think I quite got it."

"All I ask is your consent to my engagement to your daughter."

"Young man," said Mr. Rackstraw, not without a touch of admiration, "you have gall."

"My friends have sometimes said so," said Clarence.

"And I admire gall. But there is a limit. That limit you have passed so far that you'd need to look for it with a telescope."

"You refuse your consent."

"I never said you weren't a clever guesser."

"Why?"

Mr. Rackstraw laughed. One of those nasty, sharp, metallic laughs that hit you like a bullet.

"How would you support my daughter?"

"I was thinking that you would help to some extent."

"You were, were you?"

"I was."

"Oh?"

Mr. Rackstraw emitted another of those laughs.

"Well," he said, "it's off. You can take that as coming from an authoritative source. No wedding bells for you."

Clarence drew himself up, fire flashing from his eyes and a bitter smile curving his expressive lips.

"And no Wagner bat for you!" he cried.

Mr. Rackstraw started as if some strong hand had plunged an auger into him.

"What!" he shouted.

Clarence shrugged his superbly modeled shoulders in silence.

"Say," said Mr. Rackstraw, "you wouldn't let a little private difference like that influence you any in a really important thing like this ball game, would you?"

"I would."

"You would hold up the father of the girl you love?"

"Every time."

"Her white-haired old father?"

"The color of his hair would not affect me."

"Nothing would move you?"

"Nothing."

"Then, by George, you're just the son-in-law I want. You shall marry Isabel; and I'll take you into partnership this very day. I've been looking for a good, husky bandit like you for years. You make Dick Turpin look like a preliminary three-round bout. My boy, we'll be the greatest team, you and I, that ever hit Wall Street."

"Papa!" cried Isabel, bounding happily from behind her tree.

Mr. Rackstraw joined their hands, deeply moved, and spoke in low, vibrant tones:

"Play ball!"

Little remains to be said, but I am going to say it, if it snows. I am at my best in these tender scenes of idyllic domesticity.

Four years have passed. Once more we are in the Rackstraw home. A lady is coming down the stairs, leading by the hand her little son. It is Isabel. The years have dealt lightly with her. She is still the same stately, beautiful creature whom I would have described in detail long ago if I had been given half a chance. At the foot of the stairs the child stops and points at a small, wooden object in a glass case.

"Wah?" he says.

"That?" says Isabel. "That is the bat Mr. Wagner used to use when he was a little boy."

She looks at a door on the left of the hall, and puts a finger to her lip.

"Hush!" she says. "We must be quiet. Daddy and Grandpa are busy in there cornering wheat."

And softly mother and child go out into the sunlit garden.

LEE ALLEN has written, "It is said that when Thomas Wolfe died, a ticket to the Baseball Writers' dinner in New York was found in the suit he was wearing. One of Wolfe's greatest characters, Nebraska Crane, was a big-league player, although a completely fictional one. It is thought that he represented Wolfe's childish ambition to become a player."

From *You Can't Go Home Again*

THOMAS WOLFE

A T THE FAR END of the car a man stood up and started back down the aisle toward the washroom. He walked with a slight limp and leaned upon a cane, and with his free hand he held onto the backs of the seats to brace himself against the lurching of the train. As he came abreast of George, who sat there gazing out the window, the man stopped abruptly. A strong, good-natured voice, warm, easy, bantering, unafraid, unchanged—exactly as it was when it was fourteen years of age—broke like a flood of living light upon his consciousness:

"Well I'll be dogged! Hi, there, Monkus! Where you goin'?"

At the sound of the old jesting nickname George looked up quickly. It was Nebraska Crane. The square, freckled, sunburned visage had the same humorous friendliness it had always had, and the tar-black Cherokee eyes looked out with the same straight, deadly fearlessness. The big brown paw came out and they clasped each other firmly. And, instantly, it was like coming home to a strong and friendly place. In another moment they were seated together, talking with the familiarity of people whom no gulf of years and distance could alter or separate.

George had seen Nebraska Crane only once in all the years since he himself had first left Libya Hill and gone away to college. But he had not lost sight of him. Nobody had lost sight of Nebraska Crane. That wiry, fearless little figure of the Cherokee boy who used to come down the hill on Locust Street with the bat slung over his shoulder and the well-oiled fielder's mitt protruding from his hip pocket had been prophetic of a greater destiny, for Nebraska had become a professional base-

ball player, he had crashed into the big leagues, and his name had been emblazoned in the papers every day.

The newspapers had had a lot to do with his seeing Nebraska that other time. It was in August 1925, just after George had returned to New York from his first trip abroad. That very night, in fact, a little before midnight, as he was seated in a Childs Restaurant with smoking wheatcakes, coffee, and an ink-fresh copy of next morning's *Herald-Tribune* before him, the headline jumped out at him: "Crane Slams Another Homer." He read the account of the game eagerly, and felt a strong desire to see Nebraska again and to get back in his blood once more the honest tang of America. Acting on a sudden impulse, he decided to call him up. Sure enough, his name was in the book, with an address way up in the Bronx. He gave the number and waited. A man's voice answered the phone, but at first he didn't recognize it.

"Hello! . . . Hello! . . . Is Mr. Crane there? . . . Is that you, Bras?"

"Hello." Nebraska's voice was hesitant, slow, a little hostile, touched with the caution and suspicion of mountain people when speaking to a stranger. "Who is that? . . . Who? . . . Is that *you*, Monk?"—suddenly and quickly, as he recognized who it was. "Well I'll be dogged!" he cried. His tone was delighted, astounded, warm with friendly greeting now, and had the somewhat high and faintly howling quality that mountain people's voices often have when they are talking to someone over the telephone: the tone was full, sonorous, countrified, and a little puzzled, as if he were yelling to someone on an adjoining mountain peak on a gusty day in autumn when the wind was thrashing through the trees. "Where'd you come from? How the hell are you, boy?" he yelled before George could answer. "Where you been all this time, anyway?"

"I've been in Europe. I just got back this morning."

"Well I'll be dogged!"—still astounded, delighted, full of howling friendliness. "When am I gonna see you? How about comin' to the game tomorrow? I'll fix you up. And say," he went on rapidly, "if you can stick aroun' after the game, I'll take you home to meet the wife and kid. How about it?"

So it was agreed. George went to the game and saw Nebraska knock another home run, but he remembered best what happened afterwards. When the player had had his shower and had dressed, the two friends left the ball park, and as they went out a crowd of young boys who had been waiting at the gate rushed upon them. They were those dark-faced, dark-eyed, dark-haired little urchins who spring up like dragon seed from the grim pavements of New York, but in whose tough little faces and raucous voices there still remains, curiously, the innocence and faith of children everywhere.

"It's Bras!" the children cried. "Hi, Bras! Hey, Bras!" In a moment they were pressing round him in a swarming horde, deafening the ears with their shrill cries, begging, shouting, tugging at his sleeves, doing everything they could to attract his attention, holding dirty little scraps of paper toward him, stubs of pencils, battered little notebooks, asking him to sign his autograph.

He behaved with the spontaneous warmth and kindliness of his character. He scrawled his name out rapidly on a dozen grimy bits of paper, skillfully working his way along through the yelling, pushing, jumping group, and all the time keeping up a rapid fire of banter, badinage, and good-natured reproof:

"All right—give it here, then! . . . Why don't you fellahs pick on somebody else once in a while? . . . Say, boy!" he said suddenly, turning to look down at one unfortunate child, and pointing an accusing finger at him—"what you doin' aroun' here again today? I signed my name fer you at least a dozen times!"

"No, sir, Misteh Crane!" the urchin earnestly replied. "Honest—not me!"

"Ain't that right?" Nebraska said, appealing to the other children. "Don't this boy keep comin' back here every day?"

They grinned, delighted at the chagrin of their fellow petitioner. "Dat's right, Misteh Crane! Dat guy's got a whole book wit' nuttin' but yoeh name in it!"

"Ah-h!" the victim cried, and turned upon his betrayers bitterly. "What youse guys tryin' to do—get wise or somep'n? Honest, Misteh Crane!—" he looked up earnestly again at Nebraska—"Don't believe 'em! I jest want yoeh ottygraph! Please, Misteh Crane, it'll only take a minute!"

For a moment more Nebraska stood looking down at the child with an expression of mock sternness; at last he took the outstretched notebook, rapidly scratched his name across a page, and handed it back. And as he did so, he put his big paw on the urchin's head and gave it a clumsy pat; then, gently and playfully, he shoved it from him and walked off down the street.

The apartment where Nebraska lived was like a hundred thousand others in the Bronx. The ugly yellow brick building had a false front, with meaningless little turrets at the corners of the roof, and a general air of spurious luxury about it. The rooms were rather small and cramped, and were made even more so by the heavy, overstuffed Grand Rapids furniture. The walls of the living room, painted a mottled, rusty cream, were bare except for a couple of sentimental colored prints, while the place of honor over the mantel was reserved for an enlarged and garishly tinted photograph of Nebraska's little son at the age of two, looking straight and solemnly out at all comers from a gilded oval frame.

Myrtle, Nebraska's wife, was small and plump, and pretty in a doll-like way. Her corn-silk hair was frizzled in a halo about her face, and her chubby features were heavily accented by rouge and lipstick. But she was simple and natural in her talk and bearing, and George liked her at once. She welcomed him with a warm and friendly smile and said she had heard a lot about him.

They all sat down. The child, who was three or four years old by this time, and who had been shy, holding onto his mother's dress and peeping out from behind her, now ran across the room to his father and began climbing all over him. Nebraska and Myrtle asked George a lot of questions about himself, what he had been doing, where he had been, and especially what countries he had visited in Europe. They seemed to think of Europe as a place so far away that anyone who had actually been there was touched with an unbelievable aura of strangeness and romance.

"Whereall did you go over there, anyway?" asked Nebraska.

"Oh, everywhere, Bras," George said—"France, England, Holland, Germany, Denmark, Sweden, Italy—all over the place."

"Well I'll be dogged!"—in frank astonishment. "You sure do git aroun', don't you?"

"Not the way *you* do, Bras. You're traveling most of the time."

"Who—*me?* Oh, hell, I don't get anywhere —just the same ole places. Chicago, St. Looie, Philly—I seen 'em all so often I could find my way blindfolded!" He waved them aside with a gesture of his hand. Then, suddenly, he looked at George as though he were just seeing him for the first time, and he reached over and slapped him on the knee and exclaimed: "Well I'll be dogged! How you doin', anyway, Monkus?"

"Oh, can't complain. How about you? But I don't need to ask that. I've been reading all about you in the papers."

"Yes, Monkus," he said. "I been havin' a good year. But, boy!—" he shook his head suddenly and grinned—"do the ole dogs feel it!"

He was silent a moment, then he went on quietly:

"I been up here since 1919—that's seven years, and it's a long time in this game. Not many of 'em stay much longer. When you been shaggin' flies as long as that you may lose count, but you don't need to count—your legs'll tell you."

"But, good Lord, Bras, *you're* all right! Why, the way you got around out there today you looked like a colt!"

"Yeah," Nebraska said, "maybe I *looked* like a colt, but I felt like a plow horse." He fell silent again, then he tapped his friend gently on the knee with his brown hand and said abruptly, "No, Monkus. When you been in this business as long as I have, you know it."

"Oh, come on, Bras, quit your kidding!" said George, remembering that the player was only two years older than himself. "You're still a young man. Why, you're only twenty-seven!"

"Sure, sure," Nebraska answered quietly. "But it's like I say. You cain't stay in this business much longer than I have. Of course, Cobb an' Speaker an' a few like that—they was up here a long time. But eight years is about the average, an' I been here seven already. So if I can hang on a few years more, I won't have no kick to make. . . . Hell!" he said in a moment, with the old hearty ring in his voice, "I ain't got no kick to make, no way. If I got my release tomorrow, I'd still feel I done all right . . . Ain't that so, Buzz?" he cried genially to the child, who had settled down on his knee, at the same time seizing the boy and cradling him comfortably in his strong arm. "Ole Bras has done all right, ain't he?"

"That's the way me an' Bras feel about it," remarked Myrtle, who during this conversation had been rocking back and forth, placidly ruminating on a wad of gum. "Along there last year it looked once or twice as if Bras might git traded. He said to me one day before the game, 'Well, ole lady, if I don't get some hits today somethin' tells me you an' me is goin' to take a trip.' So I says, 'Trip where?' An' he says, 'I don't know, but they're goin' to sell me down the river if I don't git goin', an' somethin' tells me it's now or never!' So I just looks at him," continued Myrtle placidly, "an' I says, 'Well, what do you want me to do? Do you want me to come today or not?' You know, gener'ly, Bras won't let me come when he ain't hittin'—he says it's bad luck. But he just looks at me a minute, an' I can see him sort of studyin' it over, an' all of a sudden he makes up his mind an' says, 'Yes, come on if you want to; I couldn't have no more bad luck than I been havin', noway, an' maybe it's come time fer things to change, so you come on.' Well, I went—an' I don't know whether I brought him luck or not, but somethin' did," said Myrtle, rocking in her chair complacently.

"Dogged if she didn't!" Nebraska chuckled. "I got three hits out of four times up that day, an' two of 'em was home runs!"

"Yeah," Myrtle agreed, "an' that Philadelphia fast-ball thrower was throwin' 'em, too."

"He sure was!" said Nebraska.

"I know," went on Myrtle, chewing placidly, "because I heard some of the boys say later that it was like he was throwin' 'em up there from out of the bleachers, with all them men in shirt-sleeves right behind him, an' the boys said half the time they couldn't even see the ball. But Bras must of saw it—or been lucky—because he hit two home runs off of him, an' that pitcher didn't like it, either. The second one Bras got, he went stompin' an' tearin' around out there like a wild bull. He sure did look mad," said Myrtle in her customary placid tone.

"Maddest man I ever seen!" Nebraska cried delightedly. "I thought he was goin' to dig a hole plumb through to China. . . . But that's the way it was. She's right about it. That was the day I got goin'. I know one of the boys said to me later, 'Bras,' he says, 'we all thought you was goin' to take a ride, but you sure dug in, didn't you?' That's the way it is in this game. I seen Babe Ruth go fer weeks when he couldn't hit a balloon, an' all of a sudden he lams into it. Seems like he just cain't miss from then on."

* * *

All this had happened four years ago. Now the two friends had met again, and were seated side by side in the speeding train, talking and catching up on one another. When George explained the reason for his going home, Nebraska turned to him with open-mouthed astonishment, genuine concern written in the frown upon his brown and homely face.

"Well, what d'you know about that!" he said. "I sure am sorry, Monk." He was silent while he thought about it, and embarrassed, not knowing what to say. Then, after a moment: "Gee!—" he shook his head—"your aunt was one swell cook! I never will fergit it! Remember how she used to feed us kids—every danged one of us in the whole neighborhood?" He paused, then grinned up shyly at his friend: "I sure wish I had a fistful of them good ole cookies of hers right this minute!"

Nebraska's right ankle was taped and bandaged; a heavy cane rested between his knees. George asked him what had happened.

"I pulled a tendon," Nebraska said, "an' got laid off. So I thought I might as well run down an' see the folks. Myrtle, she couldn't come—the kid's got to git ready for school."

"How are they?" George asked.

"Oh, fine, fine. All wool an' a yard wide, both of 'em!" He was silent for a moment, then he looked at his friend with a tolerant Cherokee grin and said, "But I'm crackin' up, Monkus. Guess I cain't stan' the gaff much more."

Nebraska was only thirty-one now, and George was incredulous. Nebraska smiled good-naturedly again.

"That's an ole man in baseball, Monk. I went up when I was twenty-one. I been aroun' a long time."

The quiet resignation of the player touched his friend with sadness. It was hard and painful for him to face the fact that this strong and fearless creature, who had stood in his life always for courage and for victory, should now be speaking with such ready acceptance of defeat.

"But, Bras," he protested, "you've been hitting just as well this season as you ever did! I've read about you in the papers, and the reporters have all said the same thing."

"Oh, I can still hit 'em," Nebraska quietly agreed. "It ain't the hittin' that bothers me. That's the last thing you lose, anyway. Leastways, it's goin' to be that way with me, an' I talked to other fellahs who said it was that way with them." After a pause he went on in a low tone: "If this ole leg heals up in time, I'll go on back an' git in the game again an' finish out the season. An' if I'm lucky, maybe they'll keep me on a couple more years, because they know I can still hit. But, hell," he added quietly, "they know I'm through. They already got me all tied up with string."

As Nebraska talked, George saw that the Cherokee in him was the same now as it had been when he was a boy. His cheerful fatalism had always been the source of his great strength and courage. That was why he had never been afraid of anything, not even death. But, seeing the look of regret on George's face, Nebraska smiled again and went on lightly:

"That's the way it is, Monk. You're good up there as long as you're good. After that they sell you down the river. Hell, I ain't kickin'. I been lucky. I had ten years of it already, an' that's more than most. An' I been in three World's Serious. If I can hold on fer another year or two—if they don't let me go or trade me—I think maybe we'll be in again. Me an' Myrtle has figgered it all out. I had to help her people some, an' I bought a farm fer Mama an' the Ole Man—that's where they always wanted to be. An' I got three hundred acres of my own in Zebulon—all paid fer, too!—an' if I git a good price this year fer my tobacco, I stan' to clear two thousand dollars. So if I can git two years more in the League an' one more good World's Serious, why—" he turned his square face toward his friend and grinned his brown and freckled grin, just as he used to as a boy—"we'll be all set."

"And—you mean you'll be satisfied?"

"Huh? Satisfied?" Nebraska turned to him with a puzzled look. "How do you mean?"

"I mean after all you've seen and done, Bras—the big cities and the crowds, and all the people shouting—and the newspapers, and the headlines, and the World Series—and—and—the first of March, and St. Petersburg, and meeting all the fellows again, and spring training—"

Nebraska groaned.

"Why, what's the matter?"

"Spring trainin'."

"You mean you don't like it?"

"Like it! Them first three weeks is just plain hell. It ain't bad when you're a kid. You don't put on much weight durin' the winter, an' when you come down in the spring it only takes a few days to loosen up an' git the kinks out. In two weeks' time you're loose as ashes. But wait till you been aroun' as long as I have!" He laughed loudly and shook his head. "Boy! The first time you go after a grounder you can hear your joints creak. After a while you begin to limber up—you work into it an' git the soreness out of your muscles. By the time the season starts, along in April, you feel pretty good. By May you're goin' like a house afire, an' you tell yourself you're good as you ever was. You're still goin' strong along in June. An' then you hit July, an' you get them double-headers in St. Looie! Boy, oh, boy!" Again he shook his head and laughed, baring big square teeth. "Monkus," he said quietly, turning to his companion, and now his face was serious and he had his black Indian look— "you ever been in St. Looie in July?"

"No."

"All right, then," he said very softly and scornfully. "An' you ain't played *ball* there in July. You come up to bat with sweat bustin' from your ears. You step up an' look out there to where the pitcher ought to be, an' you see four of him. The crowd in the bleachers is out there roastin' in their shirt-sleeves, an' when the pitcher throws the ball it just comes from nowheres—it comes right out of all them shirtsleeves in the bleachers. It's on top of you before you know it. Well, anyway, you dig in an' git a toe-hold, take your cut, an' maybe you connect. You straighten out a fast one. It's good fer two bases if you hustle. In the old days you could've made it standin' up. But now—boy!" He shook his head slowly. "You cain't tell me nothin' about that ball park in St. Looie in July! They got it all growed out in grass in April, but after July first—" he gave a short laugh—"hell!—it's paved with concrete! An' when you git to first, them dogs is sayin', 'Boy, let's stay here!' But you gotta keep on goin'—you know the manager is watchin' you— you're gonna ketch hell if you don't take that extra base, it may mean the game. An' the boys up in the press box, they got their eyes glued on you, too—they've begun to say old Crane is playin' on a dime—an' you're thinkin' about next year an' maybe gittin' in another Serious

—an' you hope to God you don't git traded to St. Looie. So you take it on the lam, you slide into second like the Twentieth Century comin' into the Chicago yards—an' when you git up an' feel yourself all over to see if any of your parts is missin', you gotta listen to one of that second baseman's wisecracks: 'What's the hurry, Bras? Afraid you'll be late fer the Veterans' Reunion?'"

"I begin to see what you mean, all right," said George.

"See what I mean? Why, say! One day this season I ast one of the boys what month it was, an' when he told me it was just the middle of July, I says to him: 'July, hell! If it ain't September I'll eat your hat!' 'Go ahead, then,' he says, 'an' eat it, because it ain't September, Bras—it's July.' 'Well,' I says, 'they must be havin' sixty days a month this year— it's the longest damn July I ever felt!' An' lemme tell you, I didn't miss it fer, either— I'll be dogged if I did! When you git old in this business, it may be only July, but you think it's September." He was silent for a moment. "But they'll keep you in there, gener'ly, as long as you can hit. If you can smack that ole apple, they'll send you out there if they've got to use glue to keep you from fallin' apart. So maybe I'll git in another year or two if I'm lucky. So long's I can hit 'em, maybe they'll keep sendin' me out there till all the other players has to grunt every time ole Bras goes after a ground ball!" He laughed. "I ain't that bad yet, but soon's I am, I'm through."

"You won't mind it, then, when you have to quit?"

He didn't answer at once. He sat there looking out the window at the factory-blighted landscape of New Jersey. Then he laughed a little wearily:

"Boy, this may be a ride on the train to you, but to *me*—say!—I covered this stretch so often that I can tell you what telephone post we're passin' without even lookin' out the window. Why, hell yes!—" he laughed loudly now, in the old infectious way—"I used to have 'em numbered—now I got 'em *named!*"

"And you think you can get used to spending all your time out on the farm in Zebulon?"

"Git used to it?" In Nebraska's voice there was now the same note of scornful protest that it had when he was a boy, and for a moment he turned and looked at his friend with an expression of astonished disgust. "Why, what are you talkin' about? That's the greatest life in the world!"

1955:
New York Yankees 11,
Tokyo Giants 0

YOMIURI MORNING PRESS

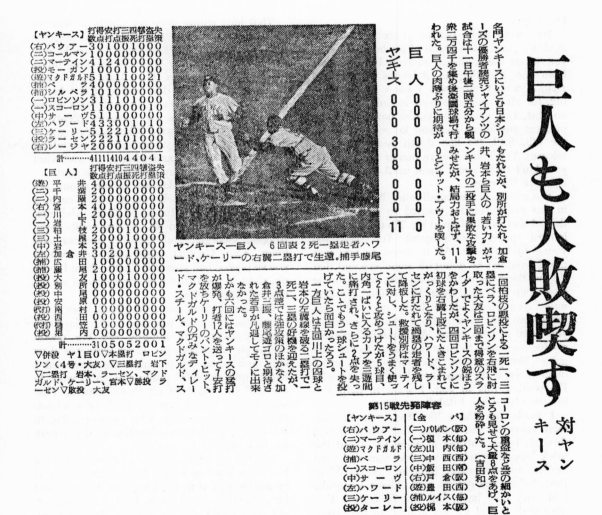

巨人も大敗喫す 対ヤンキース

【ヤンキース】打得安打三四犠盗失
数点打点振打死塁策
(右)バウアー　3 0 1 0 0 1 0 0 0 0
(二)コールマン　1 0 0 0 0 0 0 0 0 0
(二)マーテイン　4 1 2 4 0 0 0 0 0 0
(投)モーガン　1 0 0 0 0 1 0 0 0 0
(遊)マクドガルド　5 1 1 1 1 0 0 2 1
(捕)ベ　ラ　4 0 0 0 0 0 0 0 0 0
(捕)シル ベ ラ　1 0 1 0 0 1 0 0 0 0
(一)ロビンソン　3 1 1 1 1 0 1 0 1 0
(一)スコーロン　1 0 0 0 0 0 0 0 1 0
(中)サ ー ヴ　5 1 1 1 1 0 0 0 0 0
(左)ハワード　4 3 3 0 0 0 1 0 1 0
(投)ケ ー リ ー　5 2 2 1 0 1 0 0 0 0
(右)ラ ー ジ ャ　2 0 0 0 0 1 0 0 0 0
　　計　41 11 14 10 4 4 0 4 1

【巨人】打得安打三四犠盗失
数点打点振打死塁策
(遊)平　井　4 0 0 0 0 0 0 0 0 0
(二)内　藤　4 2 0 0 0 0 0 0 0 0
(右)宮　本　2 0 0 0 0 0 0 0 0 0
(中)川　上　2 0 1 0 0 0 0 0 0 0
(三)岩　本　2 1 0 1 0 0 0 0 0 0
(三)土　屋　1 0 0 0 0 0 0 0 0 0
(一)岩　下　2 2 2 1 0 0 0 0 0 0
(左)加　藤　3 0 1 0 0 0 0 0 0 0
(捕)広　田　1 0 0 0 0 0 0 0 0 0
(捕)藤　尾　3 0 2 0 0 0 0 0 0 0
(投)別　所　1 0 0 0 0 0 0 0 0 0
(投)中　村　1 0 0 0 0 0 0 0 0 0
(投)安　西　0 0 0 0 0 0 0 0 0 0
(投)西　村　0 0 0 0 0 0 0 0 0 0
(投)樋　笠　0 0 0 0 0 0 0 0 0 0
(代)倉　内　1 0 0 0 0 0 0 0 0 0
　　計　31 0 5 0 5 2 0 0 1

▽併殺　ヤ1巨0 ▽本塁打　ロビンソン（4号・大友）▽三塁打　岩下
▽二塁打　岩本、ラーセン、マクドガルド、ケーリー、宮本 ▽勝投　ラーセン ▽敗投　大友

巨人　000 000 000　0
ヤンキース　000 308 000　11

ヤンキース―巨人　6回表2死一塁走者ハワード、ケーリーの右翼二塁打で生還。捕手藤尾

名門ヤンキースにいどむ日本シリーズの優勝者読売ジャイアンツの一戦、岩本ら巨人の“若い力”がヤンキースの二投手に果敢な攻撃をみせたが、結局力およばず、11―0とシャット・アウトを喫した。試合は十一日午後二時五分から観衆二万四千を集めた後楽園球場で行われた。巨人の肉薄ぶりに期待がもたれたが、別所が打たれ、加倉塁にベラ、ロビンソンを右飛に討取った大友は三回まで得意のスライダーでよくヤンキースの鋭ほうをかわしたが、四回ロビンソンに初球を右翼上段にたたきこまれがっくりとなり、ハワード、ラーセンに打たれて尚塁の走者を残して降板した。救援別所はマーティンに対し、シュートをうまく使って2―2と攻めつけたが5球目、内角一ぱいに入るカーブを三遊間に痛打され、さらに2点を失った。こんでもう一球シュートを投げていたら面白かっただろう。

一方巨人は五回川上の四球と岩本の左翼線を破る二塁打で一死二、三塁の好機を迎えたが、3点差では強攻策のほかなく加倉井三振、藤尾遊ゴロと期待された若手が凡退してモノに出来なかった。

しかも六回にはヤンキースの猛打が爆発、打者12人を送って7安打を放ちケーリーの巧みなバント・ヒット、マクドガルドの巧みなディレード・スチール、マクドガルド、

一回柏枝の悪投による一死一、三塁にベラ、ロビンソンを右飛に討取った大友は三回まで得意のスライダーでよくヤンキースの鋭ほうをかわしたが、四回ロビンソンに初球を右翼上段にたたきこまれ……

コーロンの塁盗など芸の細かいところも見せて大量8点をあげ、巨人を粉砕した。（吉田和）

第15戦先発陣容
【ヤンキース】
(右)バ ウアー
(二)マーテイン
(遊)マクドガルド
(捕)ベ　ラ
(一)スコーロン
(中)サ ー ヴ
(左)ハワード
(三)ケ ー リ ー
(投)タ ー レ

【全　パ】
(二)バルボン（阪）
(一)榎 本（毎）
(左)山 内（西）
(三)中 西（西）
(中)飯 田（南）
(右)戸 倉（阪）
(遊)豊 田（西）
(捕)ルイス（毎）
(投)梶 本（阪）

"A LETTER TO MY SON" appeared in *Sport* magazine, the result of a series of interviews which Furman Bisher, sports editor of the Atlanta *Constitution* and a fine baseball writer, held with Rudy York. The letter was addressed to York's teen-age son, who wanted to become a professional ballplayer.

A Letter to My Son

RUDY YORK
as told to FURMAN BISHER

DEAR SON:

You were only twelve years old and it couldn't have made much of an impression on you when the mailman delivered my release from the Philadelphia Athletics in January 1949. I wasn't surprised. I knew it was coming, for after you've played in only 31 games and hit .157, you know you're not scaring the pitchers any more and you know you're over the hill. Still, it's like death and taxes, and releases. You know they're bound to come, but you don't think about them until they hit you between the eyes.

The release was unconditional. No other club in the major leagues wanted to sign me. So there I was, washed up at 35. Then I began the longest spring I ever spent. You were too young to realize it. All it meant to you was that I wouldn't be going off anywhere and that I'd be there at night when you came home from school. Nobody can know what it's like, unless you're one of the lucky guys who has been going off to a training camp ever since you were in your teens. And baseball players are lucky—lucky to have the ability to play the game, like you have. And lucky in a lot of other ways, if they use their heads. That's why I'm writing this to you. I want to help you use your head like I didn't use mine.

I made something like $250,000 in thirteen years in the majors, but when I was through I had nothing to show for it but the brick bungalow where we live, you and your mother, and your sister, Blanche Fay, and Mary Jane, before she got married. That's a mistake you can't take back, but there's a story that goes with it and I'll get around to that later.

That long spring gave me plenty of time to think, and I've been thinking ever since, for me and for you. The first thing I thought was that I hadn't used my head for anything but a place to hang my cap. Then I got to thinking about what I'd have done different if I had a chance to do it all over again, and that's where you come in. I made my mistakes, plenty of them, but I didn't have what you've got. I didn't have anybody going ahead for me telling me what it was like, and what to do and what not to do. I was on my own from the start.

You never have known much about my young days, so I'll tell you. I was born in a little mountain mill town, Ragland, Alabama, and then we moved to another mill town, Aragon, Georgia, and then to another mill town, Atco, Georgia, right over here where you've played ball yourself. That's where I grew up, right in the shadow of the mill here on the edge of Cartersville.

Our family was poor. We lived from hand to mouth, and from pay day to pay day, and the pay days were nothing like the major-league pay days later on. There were five of us kids, and when my parents were separated I had to quit the third grade and go to work in the mill to help feed all those mouths. That was the last time I saw the inside of a schoolroom. At the same age when you're going to school and getting an education, I was sweating in a mill.

I'm not going to say that you should have had it as hard as I did. I wouldn't wish that on anybody. But in the long run, it turned out just as well for me, I guess. I was thirteen years old and I could play baseball for the mill team.

From that time on, all I ever knew was baseball, and I'm thankful for it, for baseball was my ticket out of the mill. I pitched, played the outfield or infield, and caught—anywhere they put me, just like you've been doing in high school and on the American Legion team. We're a lot alike in some ways. I just wanted to play, and so do you, and I could give the ball a long ride, and so can you. Somebody told Colonel Bob Allen in Knoxville about me. Knoxville was in the Southern Association in those days, and Allen asked me to meet the club in Atlanta for a tryout. That's how I got my start.

Knoxville signed me and kept me on the bench for about a month. Now, you'll run into all sorts of people in baseball, and you'll find them all, even the smart ones, making mistakes now and then. This Colonel Allen made one, and he was known as a smart baseball man. I could spit over the left-field fence in Knoxville. It was built for a right-handed power hitter like me. In fact, five years later Hank Greenberg and I hit eight over it in two days when Detroit stopped there on an exhibition tour.

But Colonel Allen made a mistake. He released me. If he had held onto me another year, he could have sold me for $50,000 or more.

I was playing semipro ball down in southern Georgia when Eddie Goosetree came through and signed me for Detroit later that year. That was the best break I ever got, because there never have been better people to play baseball for than the Briggs family.

There I was, just a kid nineteen years old, on my way to the big leagues. It sounds easy, but, son, that's where the hard knocks begin to set in, and you've got to find out if you can take it or not. There's a lot more to it than just stepping up to bat and knocking your way into the majors. You've got to remember to be patient. I went through enough to discourage most any kid, but baseball was all I knew and I stayed with it.

Here's what I mean. At Knoxville I was an outfielder. At Shreveport, where they sent me after Goosetree signed me, I was a second baseman. At Beaumont I was a catcher, pitcher, first baseman, third baseman and outfielder. At Fort Worth I was a catcher and outfielder. At Detroit I was a catcher, outfielder and third baseman before they finally put me on first base to stay.

I didn't ask any questions. I played where they told me and did the best I could. But I think the best thing for a young fellow like you is to find his position as soon as he can and stick to it. You've been playing all over, third base, outfield, first base and pitching. You're still young, but it's getting about time we figured out what is your best position.

You've got good footwork. That's awfully important in playing third, good foot action. If you're a good judge of a fly ball, maybe you ought to settle in the outfield, because you've got a good arm and you can hit. Anybody that hits around .500 for the Legion team, like you did a couple of years ago, hits enough to play the outfield, and hitting does come first out there. Your arm is good enough for pitching, too. We'll just have to see how that works out this year. There's no rush about it yet, but pretty soon it will be time to settle down to one position, before you start into pro ball, anyway.

It was a long time coming for me, but finally, in 1940, Del Baker, who managed the Tigers then, sent Greenberg to the outfield and me to first base. A lot of these big-league sports writers would try to make you believe I wasn't much of a fielder. I guess you've read that famous line in my scrapbooks that described me as "part Indian, part first baseman." Well, I can read you another line that said I was the best first baseman the Red Sox had during the Tom Yawkey regime, and there was a guy by the name of Jimmy Foxx there before me. The fielding averages show that your old man was a pretty good first baseman. I never was under .980 in the majors, and in 1947 I led the American League with .995. Because of the pivot he's got to make, it's difficult for a right handed first baseman to make the double play at second. Still, in 1943 I set a league record for assists by a first baseman, and the next year I set a major-league record for double plays by a first baseman.

But don't pay too much attention to averages of any kind. I'll confess that fielding averages don't always tell the whole truth. There was 1939, for instance, when I led the American League catchers in fielding. I'd be the last man in the world to claim that I was a good catcher. I threw sinkers to second; I was so big I had trouble shifting behind the plate—and that's mighty important—and I never was a bear on pop fouls. I never was a good outfielder, either. I always did insist they should have let me wear the mask out there. But just to show you how deceiving those averages are —in 1947, when I was traded from the Red

Sox to the White Sox, my batting average was only .233, but I hit 21 homers and drove in 91 runs.

I never was much of a hitter for an average, but a fellow who winds up with .275, 277 homers, drives in 1,152 runs and plays in three World Series and five All-Star games in the majors shouldn't feel too badly about his career. My best season was 1943, when I led the league in total bases, home runs and runs batted in.

When you do settle down to that one position, son, work at it, slave at it, if necessary. I guess I didn't do as well at all the positions as I did at first base because I didn't work as hard at them. There was one stretch, though, when I gave third base everything I had. Mickey Cochrane was managing the Tigers in 1936 and he decided I was a third baseman. For a month during spring training, I and Del Baker—he was a coach then—and twenty baseballs played third base. Del wore out the fungo bat hitting ground balls to me before and after exhibition games. During the games I played first base, for Greenberg was holding out, and Marv Owen, a pretty fair country ballplayer, was at third. But they were going to make a third baseman out of me and put me in the infield with Billy Rogell at short, Charley Gehringer at second and Greenberg at first.

When Greenberg signed, though, they decided I wasn't a third baseman, either. They sent me to Milwaukee, and when the American Association opened, I was a first baseman again. I had my greatest season, was voted the most valuable player, and went back to Detroit to stay. But I was still a man without a position.

This had been going on since the time I reported to Beaumont, Texas, in 1934. Beaumont had two fine catchers, Mike Tresh and Dutch Lorbeer, but Jack Zeller, the Detroit farm director, said I was a catcher. I worked five weeks taking lessons in catching, and on opening day Zeller called me in.

"Did you ever play first base?" he asked me.

"I've fooled around with it some," I told him.

"Well, you're our first baseman," he said. Just like that.

I didn't even have a first baseman's mitt, and George Archie, who had been playing first, wouldn't let me use his. I played the bag with a finger glove until Greenberg sent me a mitt from Detroit. That was the first thing he ever did for me, but he's done a lot for me since, especially in the last few years when I've needed help. He's the best friend a guy ever had.

When I got to Detroit, it was more of the same. I reported on my birthday, August 17, 1934, and that No. 24 that I put on my back was the first major-league uniform I ever saw. First thing when I arrived, Mickey Cochrane said to me: "You're a catcher, aren't you?"

I told him I had caught some, so they gave me a mitt and sent me to the bull pen.

As I said, that sort of thing went on for years. The newspapermen always wrote that they couldn't find a position for me. They had the position, but Hank Greenberg was playing it. Nobody was moving Greenberg off first—not until they saw that I had to play there or no place at all. That's why I say, find your position and stick to it and work at it every minute. Become so good at it that nobody can move you.

It's a good business, too, in these days of the bonus. I'm not one of these fellows, son, who thinks "bonus" is a nasty word. If a boy is worth it, I think he should collect when he signs. There are always stories about bonuses ruining young ballplayers. I don't believe it—that money can ruin a boy who's got the ability and the character. If he's got it, he's going to make it. A bonus won't hinder the right kind of kid. I hope you're going to be good enough to get a bonus when you sign, because it's nice to have a bank account to start out with. A lot of lucky things have happened to ballplayers since I was a kid. Once you get to the big leagues you'll get in on this pension plan, a great thing for the player. I'm looking forward to becoming eligible for my pension. It's almost ten years away, but when I reach fifty I start drawing $100 a month. That's an advantage you've got to build on, and it's another reason you should put everything you've got into reaching the big leagues.

Since hitting runs in the family, I guess it comes natural with you. I like to think you're a chip off the old block, a hitting fool. But don't go power crazy. Use good judgment as you go along. You're just seventeen and you shouldn't be using a heavy bat just because it has a star's name on it. Get a bat you can master, about 28 or 30 ounces now, and increase the weight as you go. As the season goes on and the days get hotter you'll find the bat getting heavier and heavier, anyway.

Still, the best hitting streak I ever had was in August, the hottest month of them all. That was in 1937, when I hit eighteen homers in one month and broke Babe Ruth's record of seventeen. Incidentally, that happened while I was catching. Mickey Cochrane had been beaned and I took his place. I went into the last day of the month needing two homers for the record. I honestly never gave it much thought. You just don't think about things like that; they either happen or they don't. We played Washington and I got my two, both off Pete Appleton. It's a strange thing, but August always was my month. I could hit anything they threw at me, golf ball, tennis ball or Ping-pong ball.

Son, there are some things about my baseball career I'm proud of, and some I'm not so proud of. They gave me a reputation for boozing, but you can take any story about ballplayers and drinking with several grains of salt. Sure, I had my drink when I wanted it. So did a lot of other fellows. But remember this—I'm an Indian, so that means you're part Indian, too. All an Indian's got to do is be seen drinking a beer and he's drunk. Any time an Indian puts on a baseball uniform he becomes about six times as much of a character as any other player.

We're Cherokee and I'm proud of it. I've run into some pretty good Indian ballplayers in my time, like Bob and Roy Johnson, Ben Tincup, Chief Bender and Elon Hogsett, who was my roommate at Detroit for a while. I'd like to add the name of Joe Wilburn York to that list.

You've noticed that scar on my left cheek. I got it when I was nine years old. I ran into an axe my brother was swinging while he chopped wood. It makes me look tough, I guess, so I didn't have to do much to be called a bad boy.

But son, leave that liquor alone. I can tell you it never helped anybody, and if I had to do it over again that's one thing I'd use a lot less. I'd have had a couple more years of baseball left in me if I'd stayed away from it.

I guess you've read in the scrapbooks that I led the major leagues in arson. I've gone to sleep with a cigarette in my hand and smoked up a hotel room a little, but by the time the stories went the rounds, I was supposed to have set fire to every hotel in the country. When I was with the White Sox in '47, I was two blocks down the street buying a shirt when fire engines pulled up at the Stevens Hotel, where I lived. When I got to the lobby I heard there was a fire on my floor, and on my floor I heard it was in my room. But a cigar started that one, and I never did smoke cigars.

What all this means is that ballplayers have to be twice as careful of their behavior away from their work as anybody else. On the field I never had any trouble, and I hope you get along with umpires as well as I did. I never "got on" them because I figured they had a job to do, too, and that they were going to make some mistakes, same as me. I have no raps against umpires and I think they have none against me.

Don't be a clubhouse lawyer, either. That has ruined as many good ballplayers as booze has. Go about your job and keep your mouth shut, except to kid with the fellows. Leave the lawyering to somebody else. The only time I ever really raised my voice in the clubhouse was in 1946, when I was with the Red Sox and we were battling for the pennant. It was a close race and one day it seemed to some of us that Ted Williams was slow playing a hit out in left field. A run scored on it and we lost the game. When we got to the clubhouse I had a few things to say to him. "We're about to win this pennant," I told him, "and everybody's in it together. All we got to do is play our best and we've got it in the bag. Anybody who loafs on this ball club has got to answer to me. I'm about washed up and you've got a long way to go. I'm not aiming to let a pennant slip away from me now, and I'm not aiming to see you let it slip away, either."

Williams was a good friend of mine and he took it in the right spirit. I always did say he's the greatest hitter I ever saw step in the box. He's one of those rare fellows with so much natural talent that he didn't have to work at it much.

Be sure not to forget the folks back home. Make friends here in Cartersville, for this is where you're going to live. I don't think I left an enemy behind in baseball, and I can't think of a man I played with or against that I don't like. That's a pretty good record, when you consider the jealousies and the competition in the game. I never was much for emotion; it isn't part of my nature. But I always tried to be friendly. Newspapermen were nice to me, too, in spite of some of the things they wrote about me. I've even got a lot of respect for Dave Egan, a Boston writer that most of the guys hated. I've got to give him credit for being smart. But I never did put much into making friends back home. I don't think it was all my fault, though, even if I was a little stand-offish. I never was one for standing on the street corner or in the drugstore shooting the breeze. I like to hunt, and you know yourself how much time we've spent together out with the bird dogs.

Not many folks around Cartersville paid me much attention, except when I was in trouble. I can understand some of it now, though, for to them I was an Indian from the mill village. They were glad to claim me and brag about me when I was hitting home runs, but when the shouting was over they weren't breaking their backs to socialize with me.

I said I wasn't much of a hitter for an average. The reason I wasn't was I learned to hit just one way—overpower the ball. I want you to learn how to hit with the pitch. In other words, if it's an outside pitch, punch it into right field. If that ball was outside to me, I was willing to take a strike. Those pitchers will have more respect for you if you're able to meet the ball where it is instead of trying to pull everything. Del Baker was one reason I hit as well as I did. The guy is the greatest sign-stealer who ever lived, and he used to call the pitches for me. When I knew what was coming I could usually hit it a mile.

You'll find that players have funny hitting habits, anyway, as you go along. Charley Gehringer was the best second baseman who ever lived, and Charley had a habit of taking the first pitch. We roomed together some when I was with the Tigers and I asked him once why he did it.

"So the pitcher can start off even with me," he said.

That Charley was a card. He didn't say much, but when he did, he was a card. I hope you're lucky enough to have some good friends like him and Greenberg.

I said earlier there's a story that explains why I'm broke and fighting fires for the Georgia Forestry Commission for $150 a month. Like I wrote, I made a lot of money, around $250,000, maybe more. But I never saved any. When I started making money it burned a hole in my pocket. I'd never had anything when I was a kid, and I wanted to spend it for things I'd always wanted, and for you and Viola and the rest of the family. You can imagine what happens to a poor mill-town boy who makes $40,000 a year, which I did in '41. I bought new cars every year. I'd take long hunting trips, like that time when I packed all of us off to South Dakota. I bought everything in sight. But the best buy I ever made

was our house. I'd be in bad shape if I didn't have it now.

When you start making money, son, get an adviser, somebody to help you invest it. I never did know who I could trust, and the only place I ever put mine was in a checking account, and that made it too easy to get at. Get your money to work for you, because I don't want you to finish up with nothing to show for it but your clippings. You never think it's going to end while you're riding high. I lived from game to game and for each time I went to bat. I was always happy with a bat in my hand.

Don't be shortsighted. Remember there's a future after you're through playing ball. If you make a good name and a good reputation for yourself, you can always stay in baseball. There'll always be a good job as a manager, or a coach, or in some end of the game, for a fellow who conducts himself wisely while he's a player. If I do say so myself, you're smart, you've got a good head on your shoulders, and I want to see you use it. Go ahead and play your football and basketball now, but when you get out of high school, put everything else away but baseball.

I had it pretty rough trying to stay with baseball after the Athletics released me. Me and the minor leagues didn't get along too well. In June 1949, I got a call to manage Griffin, Georgia, in the Georgia-Alabama League, Class D.

"We've got a team," the man told me over the telephone. "All we need is a manager."

Buck Etchison, who played some first base for the Braves, had been the manager, and when I got there I could see why he had left. They had two ballplayers. The rest were a bunch of kids who couldn't tie their shoelaces. They were in last place when I got there and they finished last. That's where they belonged. You remember when I came back home and Greenberg called me to finish out the season managing Union City, Tennessee, in the Kitty League.

Then, in 1951, Greenberg came for me again, to play for Youngstown, Ohio, in the Middle Atlantic League. Now, there was an experience. By June 1, we had drawn 1,912 attendance, believe it or not. They moved the franchise to Oil City, Pennsylvania, and after Mike Garbark, the old Yankee catcher, quit as manager, I took over. I had a great season as a player, hit 34 homers, drove in 107 runs and had an average of .291. But we won just 24 games before the club disbanded in August.

That was the end of my playing days. Now it's either managing or scouting or coaching for me, or I'm out of baseball, and I hate to think of having to give it up. After all, it's the only life I ever knew, and it was good to me. That's why I'm warning you not to abuse your opportunity and to profit by the mistakes your old man made.

I saw sights I'd never seen before, rode in Pullman cars, stayed in fancy hotels and ate high-priced food. I'll never forget the first time I saw Yankee Stadium. "They don't play baseball here, do they?" I asked Gehringer. "It's too big."

You can imagine what it was like the first time I saw a subway in New York. I was afraid they'd run so fast they'd never come out from under the ground. Everything was pretty exciting in those days.

I've had my picture on breakfast cereal signs as big as the side of a house. I've had kids mob me for my autograph. I've heard thousands cheer for me, like the time when I hit the home run that beat the Cardinals in the first game of the 1946 World Series. I've been

rich. It was a great life and I miss it.

That's the reason I'm writing this to you. I want to save you the heartaches I've had. I want to tell you about the mistakes you might make before you make them. I want you to have everything I had, plus the advantage of an assured future after you're through playing. There's nothing that would make me happier than to see you play in the major leagues, and some day you'll get there. When you do, make the most of it. Live a little, but plan a lot. Look around you. You can learn something every day. Listen. There's always somebody willing to give you a helping hand, if you'll take it. And when you're through, there'll be somebody there with a job for you. You won't have to give it up and come back home to fight fires for $150 a month.

I made enough mistakes for both of us. Let it stay that way. Sure, I lived, but I'd be living a lot better now. I want to be sure that you do when it comes time for you to put your glove and bat away. I don't want you to have to write a letter to your son about the mistakes you've made.

Your Dad,
RUDY YORK

COVERING BASEBALL, as opposed to other sports, is often easier from the pressure standpoint, because the more that happens, the more time you have to work with in the press box—a big rally will lead to the changing of pitchers, which takes time, and so forth. The exception is the last-minute stroke that changes everything—Thomson's home run, for example, and certainly this game, which had the most unforgettable ending in the history of the World Series. Dick Young of the New York *Daily News,* with a deadline and a totally unforeseen climax thrown in his lap, wrote an unforgettable story.

1947:

Brooklyn Dodgers 3,
New York Yankees 2

DICK YOUNG

OUT OF THE MOCKERY and ridicule of "the worst World Series in history," the greatest baseball game ever played was born yesterday. They'll talk about it forever, those 33,443 fans who saw it. They'll say: "I was there. I saw Bill Bevens come within one out of the only series no-hitter; I saw the winning run purposely put on base by the Yankees; I saw Cookie Lavagetto send that winning run across a moment later with a pinch-hit double off the right-field wall—the only hit, but big enough to give the Brooks the 3-2 victory that put them even-up at two games apiece."

And maybe they'll talk about the mad minute that followed—the most frenzied scene ever erupted in this legendary spot called Ebbets Field: How some of the Faithful hugged each other in the stands; how others ran out to the center of the diamond and buried Lavagetto in their caresses; how Cookie's mates pushed the public off because they themselves wanted the right to swarm all over him; how Cookie, the man who had to plead for his job this spring, finally fought his way down the dugout steps—laughing and crying at the same time in the first stages of joyous hysteria.

Elsewhere in the park, another man was so emotionally shaken he sought solitude. That was Branch Rickey, the supposedly cold, calloused businessman, the man who has seen thousands and thousands of ball games and should therefore be expected to take anything in stride. But Rickey had to be alone. He left his family, sat down in a quiet little room just off the press box, and posted a guard outside the door.

After ten minutes of nerve-soothing ceiling-staring, Rickey was asked if he'd see a writer. He would. Now he was calm and wanted to talk. He wanted to talk about the ninth-inning finish—but he started a little earlier than that.

He flashed back to the top half of the frame, when Hughie Casey had come in with the bases loaded and one out, and got Tommy Henrich to hit a DP ball right back at him on the first serve. "Just one pitch, and he's the winning pitcher of a World Series game," Branch chuckled. "That's wonderful."

Rickey then turned to his favorite subject. "It was speed that won it," he said. This tickled Rickey because it had been the speed of Al Gionfriddo which saved the game. They had laughed at Gionfriddo when he came to the Brooks back in June in that $300,000 deal with the Pirates. They had said: "What did Rickey get that little squirt for; to carry the money in a satchel from Pittsburgh?" And they had added, "He'll be in Montreal in a couple of weeks."

But, here it was World Series time, and "little Gi" was still around. Suddenly he was useful. Furillo was on first with two out. Carl had got there just as eight Brooks before him had—by walking. For a prospective no-hit pitcher, Bevens had been under constant pressure because of control trouble. A couple of these passes had led to the Brooks' run in the fifth, and had cut New York's lead down to 2-1.

That's the way it still was when Gionfriddo went in to run for Furillo, and Pete Reiser was sent up to swing for Casey. Only now Bevens was just one out away from having his bronze image placed among the all-time greats in Cooperstown. Already, at the conclusion of the eighth frame, the chubby Yank righty had pitched the longest string of no-hit ball in series history—topping Red Ruffing's 7⅔ innings against the Cards in '42.

Now Bill was out for the jackpot. He got the first out in the ninth on a gasp provoker, a long drive by Edwards which forced Lindell up against the left wall for the stretching grab. Furillo walked and Jorgensen fouled meekly to McQuinn, who was white as a sheet as he made the catch.

One out to go—and then came the first of several switches that were destined to make a genius of Burt Shotton and an eternal second-guess target of Bucky Harris.

"Reiser batting for Casey," boomed the loud-speaker, "and Gionfriddo running for Furillo."

Soon the count was 2-1 on Pete. Down came the next pitch—and up went a feverish screech. Gionfriddo had broken for second. Berra's peg flew down to second—high, just high enough to enable Gi to slide head first under Rizzuto's descending tag. For the briefest moment, all mouths snapped shut and all eyes stared at umpire Babe Pinelli. Down went the umpire's palms, signaling that the Brooks had stolen base No. 7 on the weak-winged Yankee backstop corps.

The pitch on which Gionfriddo went down had been high, making the count on Reiser 3-and-1. Then came the maneuver that makes Bucky Harris the most second-guessed man in baseball. The Yankee pilot signaled Berra to step out and take an intentional fourth ball from Bevens.

The cardinal principle of baseball had been disdained by Harris. The "winning run" had

been put on—and Miksis replaced the sore-ankled Reiser on first.

It was possible for Reiser to hurt more than Stanky in such a situation—and the Brooks had run out of lefty pinch hitters. But a good right-side swinger, a clutch money player like Lavagetto, who batted for Muggsy, didn't get to be a fourteen-year man by being able to hit only one kind of chucking.

On the first pitch, Harris' guess still looked like a good one. Cookie swung at a fast ball and missed. Then another fast one, slightly high and toward the outside. Again Lavagetto swung. The ball soared toward the right corner —a territory seldom patronized by Cookie.

Because of that, Tommy Henrich had been swung over toward right-center. Frantically, Tommy took off after the drive, racing toward the line. He got there and leaped, but it was a hopeless leap. The ball flew some six feet over his glove and banged against the wooden wall. Gionfriddo was tearing around third and over with the tying run.

The ball caromed under Henrich's legs as Tommy struggled to put the brakes on his dash. On the second grab, Henrich clutched it and, still off balance, hurried a peg to McQuinn at the edge of the infield. The first-sacker whirled desperately and heaved home—but even as he loosed the ball, speedy young Miksis was plowing over the plate with a sitting slide. A big grin on his puss, Eddie, just turned 21 last week, sat right on home plate like an elated kid. He was home with the winning run, and he didn't want to get up. For what seemed like much more than the actual three or four seconds, Miksis just sat there, looked up at his mates gathered around the plate and laughed insanely.

That's when God's Little Green Acre became a bedlam. The clock read 3:51, Brooklyn Standard Time—the most emotional minute in the lives of thousands of Faithful. There was Lavagetto being mobbed—and off to the side, there was Bevens, head bowed low, walking dejectedly through the swarming crowd, and completely ignored by it. Just a few seconds earlier, he was the one everybody was planning to pat on the back. He was the one who would have been carried off the field—the only pitcher ever to toss a no-hitter in a series.

Now he was just another loser. It didn't matter that his one-hitter had matched the other classic performances of two Cub pitchers —Ed Reulbach against the Chisox in '06 and Passeau against Detroit in '45. The third one-hitter in serres annals—but Bevens was still nothing more than a loser.

Bev felt bluer than Harry Taylor had at the start of this memorable struggle. In the first five minutes, Taylor had been a momentous failure. Unable to get his sore-elbowed arm to do what his mind demanded of it, the rookie righty had thrown his team into a seemingly hopeless hole before a Yankee had been retired.

Stirnweiss had singled. So had Henrich. And then Reese had dropped Robinson's peg of Berra's bouncer, loading the bases. Then Harry walked DiMaggio on four straight serves, forcing in a run. Still nobody out, still bases full. Taylor was through; he had been a losing gamble. In one inning, the Yanks were about to blow the game wide open and clamp a 3-1 lock on the series.

But, just as has happened so often this year, the shabby Brook pitching staff delivered a clutch performer. This time it was Hal Gregg, who had looked so mediocre in relief against the Yanks two days before. Gregg got McQuinn to pop up and then made Johnson bang a DP ball right at Reese.

Only one run out of all that mess. The Faithful regained hope. This optimism grew as DiMag was cut down at the plate attempting to score from first when Edwards threw McQuinn's dumpy third-frame single into short right. But, in the next stanza, as the Yanks did their only real teeing off on Gregg, the Brook hopes drooped. Johnson poled a tremendous triple to the center-field gate and Lindell followed with a booming two-bagger high off the scoreboard in right.

There was some hope, based on Bevens' own wildness. The Brooks couldn't buy a hit, but they had men aboard in almost every inning, sometime two. Altogether, Bev was to go on to issue ten passes, just topping the undesirable series record set by Jack Coombs of the A's in the 1910 grapple with the Cubs.

Finally, in the fifth, Bill's wildness cost him a run. He walked Jorgensen and Gregg to open the stanza. Stanky bunted them along, and Jorgy scored while Gregg was being nailed at third on Reese's grounder to Rizzuto. Pee Wee then stole second for his third swipe of the series, and continued on to third as Berra's peg flew into center. But Robinson left him there with a whiff.

Thus, before they had a hit, the Brooks had a run. And right about now, the crowd was starting to grow no-hit conscious. A fine catch by DiMaggio, on which Joe twisted his left ankle slightly, had deprived Hermanski of a long hit in the fourth, and Henrich's leaping stab of another Hermanski clout in front of the scoreboard for the final out in the eighth again saved Bill's blossoming epic.

Then the Yanks threatened to sew up the decision in the ninth. Behrman had taken over the chucking an inning earlier as a result of Gregg's being lifted for a pinch swinger and Hank got into a bases-bulging jam that wasn't exactly his responsibility. Lindell's lead-off hit through the left side was legit enough, but after Rizzuto forced Johnny, Bevens' bunt was heaved tardily to second by Bruce Edwards. Stirnweiss then looped a fist-hit into right center. Hugh Casey was rushed in.

Hugh threw one pitch, his million-dollar serve which had forced DiMag to hit into a key DP the day before. This time the low-and-away curve was jammed into the dirt by Henrich. Casey's glove flew out for a quick stab . . . the throw home . . . the relay to first . . . and Hughie was set up to become the first pitcher credited with World Series victories on successive days.

Tough luck cost Hughie two series defeats against these same Yanks in '41. Things are evened up a bit now.

Index of People

Index of People

Index of People

About the Editor

CHARLES EINSTEIN, *first as baseball editor of International News Service and later as a free-lance writer, has written some three or four million words about the game in the postwar era. His output has included articles and short stories in some forty different magazines, and a number of books, among which were a novel,* The Only Game in Town, *and a collaboration with Willie Mays on the latter's autobiography,* Born to Play Ball. *All this has combined to make him not only a ranking expert, particularly well fitted to have put together this collection of outstanding baseball literature, but, by inference, a Giant fan as well.*

Born in Boston, and a graduate of the University of Chicago, he nonetheless has spent most of his life to date as a resident of the New York area. Recently, however, he and his wife and four children moved from Ardsley, New York (an easy half hour's drive to the Polo Grounds, where the Giants then played), to a desert mountain home in Scottsdale, Arizona (an easy half hour's drive to Phoenix, where the Giants train).

THE GAME IS OVER... Two DiMaggios.